Albania in Transition

NATIONS OF THE MODERN WORLD: EUROPE
edited by W. Rand Smith and Robin Remington

This series examines the nations of Europe as they adjust to the changing world order and move into the twenty-first century. Each volume is a detailed analytical country case study of the political, economic, and social dynamics of a European state facing the challenges of the post–Cold War era. These challenges include changing values and rising expectations, the search for new political identities and avenues of participation, and growing opportunities for economic and political cooperation in the new Europe. Emerging policy issues such as the environment, immigration, refugees, and reordered national security priorities are evolving in contexts still strongly influenced by history, geography, and culture.

The former East European nations must cope with the legacies of communism as they attempt to make the transition to multiparty democracy and market economies amid intensifying national, ethnic, religious, and class divisions. West European nations confront the challenge of pursuing economic and political integration within the European Union while contending with problems of economic insecurity, budgetary stress, and voter alienation.

How European nations respond to these challenges individually and collectively will shape domestic and international politics in Europe for generations to come. By considering such common themes as political institutions, public policy, political movements, political economy, and domestic-foreign policy linkages, we believe the books in this series contribute to our understanding of the threads that bind this vital and rapidly evolving region.

BOOKS IN THIS SERIES

Albania in Transition: The Rocky Road to Democracy, Elez Biberaj

The Czech and Slovak Republics: Nation Versus State, Carol Skalnik Leff

The Politics of Belgium, John Fitzmaurice

Great Britain: Decline or Renewal? Donley Studlar

Spain: Democracy Regained, Second Edition, E. Ramón Arango

Denmark: A Troubled Welfare State, Kenneth E. Miller

Portugal: From Monarchy to Pluralist Democracy, Walter C. Opello, Jr.

Albania in Transition

The Rocky Road
to Democracy

Elez Biberaj

Westview Press
A Member of the Perseus Books Group

Nations of the Modern World: Europe

Copyright © 1999 by Westview Press, A Member of the Perseus Books Group

Published in 1998 in the United States of America by Westview Press, 5500 Central Avenue, Boulder, Colorado 80301-2877, and in the United Kingdom by Westview Press, 12 Hid's Copse Road, Cumnor Hill, Oxford OX2 9JJ

A CIP catalog record for this book is available from the Library of Congress.
ISBN 0-8133-3502-7 (hc.)   ISBN 0-8133-3688-0 (pbk.)

The paper used in this publication meets the requirements of the American National Standard for Permanence of Paper for Printed Library Materials Z39.48-1984.

10   9   8   7   6   5   4   3   2   1

Contents

Tables

Acknowledgments

This book is based on years of research on Albanian domestic and foreign policy. The Voice of America has given me a unique and invaluable opportunity to closely follow events and maintain regular contacts with the main players in Albania. I have attempted to keep the analysis as objective and as detached as possible from my personal values. Needless to say, all statements of fact and expressions of opinion contained in this book are the sole responsibility of the author and should not be ascribed to the Voice of America or the U.S. government. I am very grateful to former Senator Dennis DeConcini for the opportunity to accompany U.S. Helsinki Commission delegations that monitored Albania's 1991 and 1992 elections. I also had the privilege and honor to serve as Secretary of State James Baker's interpreter during his historic June 1991 visit to Tiranë.

Many people have contributed to this book. Since my first visit in March 1991, I have traveled to Albania extensively, conducting interviews with key participants in these momentous events and with people from all walks of life. I am grateful to the many Albanian politicians, policymakers, journalists, academics, and diplomats who gave their time and shared their views with me.

I would like to thank Professor Robin Alison Remington for her advice and consistent encouragement. Professor Remington read the manuscript at several stages of writing and provided many useful comments, suggestions, and discussions on the broad theme of this book. I am greatly indebted to Professor Nicholas C. Pano, friend and colleague, for his support over the years. I am grateful to Robert Hand and Constantine P. Danopoulos, who provided expert critique of the draft of this book. I also owe a debt to a number of other persons who provided useful ideas, data, and thoughtful critiques on one or more drafts. My gratitude extends to my many friends and colleagues in the United States, Albania, Kosova, and Macedonia.

I want to express my deep appreciation to my parents, Hysen and Ajshe, my brothers, Hasan, Mus, and Selim, my sisters, Zoja, Sabrije, Bute, and Zade, and my sister-in-law, Shkendije, for their moral and material support. They always stood by me in the best tradition of an Albanian family. I also want to thank my nieces Teuta, Drita, Lirie, and Linda, and my nephews Agim, Albert, Arben, and Besnik for general inspiration. Finally, I want to acknowledge the assistance of my wife, Kadire, to whom this book is dedicated, and of our children, Cen, Adem,

Diana, and Adriana for their encouragement, patience, and forbearance during the many hours I spent researching and writing this volume.

Elez Biberaj
Fairfax Station, VA

Foreword

Albania is a state slightly larger than Maryland with a strategic importance the size of China. For notwithstanding the focus of international security planners and media on the dangers of greater Serbia for consolidating the 1995 Dayton agreed upon multiethnic Bosnia, the unanswered Albanian Question is at least as important in determining whether the emerging post-Cold War European security architecture stands or falls. Population figures are disputed. Elez Biberaj estimates 3.3 million Albanians in Albania, roughly two million in Serbian controlled Kosova (Serbian language, Kosovo) and about half a million in Macedonia. However, regardless of exact numbers, the high birth rate of Albanians is seen as a threat by their Slavic neighbors in Serbia and Macedonia alike.

Among Albanians as among Serbs and Macedonians, there is a spectrum of political moderates, militants, and extremists. There also are competing mass-elite agendas. In Albania, the Democratic Party was voted out of office largely due to mismanagement of the 1997 political-economic crisis set off by pyramid schemes that destroyed the economic security of an estimated one quarter of the country's population. Albanian Socialists—winners in the internationally demanded June 1997 elections—want to consolidate their power, restore government control throughout the country, and rebuild international confidence. Meanwhile, the Democratic Party suffers from the identity trauma of having become an opposition party after five years of governmental power. It must regroup and decide whether to rally around or scapegoat former President Dr. Sali Berisha. Much depends on whether these parties continue the sectarian maneuvering that Biberaj documents or abandon political gridlock in favor of a shared goal to get democratization back on track.

Yet whatever the outcome of the internal political game in Albania, Kosovar Albanians and Albanians living in Macedonia can not count on meaningful economic aid or substantial political support from an Albania struggling to pull itself back from the brink of anarchy. The Kosovar Albanian leadership itself is split between moderates who would settle for significant autonomy within Serbia, separatists who want independence via a diplomatic settlement, and extremists who believe that terrorism is the only answer to Serbian occupation. These attacks provoke more heavy handed Serbian repression and likely more support for Serbian Radical Party Vojislav Šešelj's ultranationalist challenge to Yugoslav President Slobodan Milošević.

Meanwhile, there is reason to fear that unless preventive diplomacy is given higher priority, Macedonia is another Bosnia in the making. Televised police brutality during the July 1997 crisis over demands to fly the Albanian flag in front of municipal buildings reinforced simmering resentment centering on government refusal to recognize the Albanian University in Tetovo and what the Albanians consider unequal distribution of public jobs. Conversely, there is rising Macedonian backlash against what many see as danger to the very survival of an independent Macedonia which feeds into a cycle of reactive nationalism. As both sides become radicalized, talk of withdrawing UN troops from Macedonia when its current mandate expires makes less and less sense.

These developments are particularly worrying in light of the virtual disappearance of Albania from Western media following the June 1997 elections and August departure of the multinational troops sent in to protect humanitarian aid. If the West is seen as unwilling to help repair the road to democracy in Albania while insisting that Kosovar Albanians settle for what many Albanians see as sham autonomy within Serbia, the nonviolent path advocated by Dr. Ibrahim Rugova looks more and more like a dead-end. Indeed, there are unconfirmed reports that money from the Albanian diaspora in the U.S. and Europe that has funded his Kosova Democratic League is already shifting into the pockets of the self proclaimed Kosova Liberation Army. True or not, violent attacks on symbols of Serbian power in Kosova are on the rise.

As I write, CNN, President Clinton and the Washington security establishment are preoccupied by the danger of biological warfare from Iraq; the White House, IMF and economic pundits with the looming economic crisis of former Asian tigers and most especially South Korea. For those who remember, this mirrors the role that the 1990 Gulf War and 1991 prospects for a European Monetary System played in deflecting international attention from the Yugoslav crisis while there was still time to prevent the tragedies of Sarajevo, Mostar and some two million refugees from Bosnia and Herzegovina.

The 8 December *New York Times* coverage of the November 1997 Bosnian Serb parliamentary elections and as yet inconclusive December presidential elections in Serbia ignored potential security repercussions for Kosova. Yet without Serbian Renewal candidate Vuk Drašković to split the nationalist-extremist vote, there is no guarantee that Socialist Party candidate Milan Milutinović can hold his lead or that 50 per cent of the eligible voters will stay home. If Šešelj wins, further militarization of the Kosova problem could backfire into civil war in Serbia, pull in Macedonia, and still armed Albanian rebels if not the official Albanian army; thereby setting the stage for the nightmare of a wider Balkan war involving Bulgaria, Greece, and Turkey. It is cold comfort to wake up to a National Public Radio report that the best hope for avoiding this worse case scenario is Serbian godfather Slobodan Milošević's experience in rigging election results.

Elez Biberaj's indepth study of Albania's rocky road to democracy is the story of a country that set about the transition to democracy from a position of weakness. It is the story of opposition leader Dr. Sali Berisha, hero of a democratic fairy tale and lightening rod of dashed hopes. This story explores the limits of external powers to foster democratic change. One does not have to agree with Jane Perlez's 29 March 1997 *New York Times* article that the U.S. and Western Europe virtually colonized Albania to conclude that in their enthusiasm to showcase Albanian democracy strengthened presidential power at the expense of the Albanian parliament. In short, Berisha's Western advisers sent him confusing and perhaps conflicting signals.

These stories are entangled with that of the Albanian people granted independence as the Balkan Wars of 1912-1913 ended at the price of becoming a divided nation. Kosova and Kosovar Albanians became part of Serbia, then interwar Yugoslavia. This solution undoubtedly made perfect sense to the power brokers of the European balance of power security system at the time. However, the result has become much more problematical for Albanians in Kosova and Macedonia on the threshold of the twenty-first century. How to explain to a generation of young Albanians living under virtual martial law in Kosova or those who feel like second class citizens in Macedonia why the right of self- determination that led to a united Germany and justified the destruction of the former Yugoslavia does not apply to them?

Unlike most studies of contemporary Albania, Biberaj's book attempts to place the Albanian transition process within a broader social science literature on democratic transition and consolidation. He cautiously characterizes the June 1997 elections as a first step toward Larry Diamond's minimalist definition of democracy. Although, it is far too soon to tell when or whether the next steps will follow, hopefully this is also the first step in a more balanced academic dialogue on the transition process underway in East Central Europe.

Notwithstanding the higher level of violence, the outcome of Albanian anarchy is a pattern not that different from the political development of the three Central European Countries invited in 1997 to apply for membership in NATO and the European Union. In Poland and Hungary opposition leaders were followed by socialist, former communist coalition governments. In the much-lauded Czech Republic, Prime Minister Vaclav Klaus resigned at the end of November 1997 under charges of corruption and economic mismanagement.

There is a need to separate political reality from academic stereotypes. For example, Michael G. Roskin's 1997 third edition of his introductory text, *The Rebirth of Eastern Europe*, describes the dangers of the lustration laws in East Germany and the Czech Republic saying that in the Czech Republic, "Things did not go as far; President Havel was against recrimination and in favor of a new beginning" (p.186). When he then refers to the Berisha government's 1995 ban on senior members of the former Communist government from running for office until 2002 as a genocide law, the reader could logically assume that this was something quite different from the Czech law. This is because Roskin neglected to mention that in 1995 the Czech Parliament overrode President Havel's veto and extended the ban on leading former communists from holding political office until the year 2000.

In short, Elez Biberaj's book is important not just for what he writes but for what other authors in this area have not written. His study is a valuable, detailed reference for scholars trying to sort out the relationship of party institutionalization to electoral systems during democratic transitions. He captures the flavor of Albanian political culture in the power struggles between individuals and factions as well as parties. But in my view, his book's most significant contribution remains its author's systematic attempt to untangle the complex domestic-foreign policy linkages that are at the heart of the Albanian Question. In this regard Biberaj's book fills an information gap essential for policymakers as well as scholars of American and European foreign policy.

For example, it might have helped the French Foreign Ministry spokesman who stated that it is not clear why the Serbs walked out of the 10 December 1997 conference on Bosnia in Bonn in protest over references to Kosova in the final declaration. Even in the unlikely case that the Serbian delegation agreed with his view that the final text is not directed against Belgrade but is rather aimed at helping it overcome its isolation, signing on the eve of the fourth round of Serbian presidential elections could have been political suicide for the governing Socialist Party's already shaky candidate.

Robin Alison Remington

To my wife, Kadire

Albania in Transition

Introduction

Albania, like other postcommunist East Central European countries, has been undergoing a multiple transition: a political transition from one party to many, an economic transition from command to market economy, and a national security transition in an unpredictable, post-Cold War international security regime. For nearly half a century one of the most repressive communist dictatorships in the world, economically impoverished, and lacking a democratic political culture, Albania was considered one of the least likely countries in the region to complete the transition to a stable and prosperous democracy. Since the March 1992 elections, when the Albanian Democratic Party defeated the former Communists, Albania has undergone profound political, economic, and social transformations. The Communist-era constitution has been thoroughly revised, a new institutional architecture is largely in place, and the relationship between the state and the citizen has undergone fundamental change. Nonetheless, more recent developments have uncovered political-economic land mines on the Albanian road to democracy. The May 1996 parliamentary elections were marred by serious irregularities and opposition boycotts, which undermined faith in the country's democratization process.

Albanian democracy suffered a further setback in early 1997, when the collapse of fraudulent pyramid schemes sparked violent unrest and armed revolt, plunging the country into its worst political and economic crisis since the downfall of communism. By March, the ruling Democratic Party was forced to form a coalition government with the opposition and to agree to early parliamentary elections. Meanwhile, the international community dispatched a multinational protection force of 6,000 under a U.N. mandate to contain new mass emigration by desperate Albanians, which would further destabilize Albania and might set off a dangerous ripple effect across the entire Balkan region. The June 1997 elections resulted in a landslide victory for the opposition Socialist Party. The balloting represented a significant affirmation of democracy, as the country's main political actors in both major parties showed a renewed commitment to democratic norms and procedures. Nonetheless, having experienced a comprehensive breakdown of state authority and a serious political disorder, Albania still faces enormous obstacles in its attempts to establish and consolidate an indigenous form of democracy.

The traditional literature on democratic transition and consolidation has focused on the important prerequisites for democracy: experience with pluralism, the degree of Western sociopolitical influence, ethnic homogeneity, broad-based economic development, social modernization, respect for human rights, and a civil society.[1] More recently, students of democratic transitions have cautioned against political, cultural, and economic determinism, maintaining that some factors are as much the outcome as the cause of democracy. Studies of transitional countries in what Samuel P. Huntington has called the "third wave"[2] of democratization have emphasized the crucial importance of political leadership, institutional arrangements, and international commitment to the promotion and development of democracy.[3] Prior to the 1990s, countries such as Albania and other East European states lacked key institutions deemed indispensable for democracy, including a free media, an independent judiciary, and autonomous civic organizations. However, the findings of these studies indicate that such countries may still be able to establish and consolidate democratic regimes. Although scholars recognize the important correlation between the level of economic development and the sustainability of democracy, the particular configuration of institutions that has emerged in Western democracies is no longer viewed as an essential prerequisite. As Ghia Nodia wrote, "If, for one reason or another, the idea of democracy becomes powerful enough on the elite level, a democratic transition may proceed with reasonable prospects of success whatever the 'objective' conditions of the country."[4]

In assessing the degree of progress made in recasting Albanian political order and political culture along more democratic lines, it is useful to define the concepts of "democracy" and "consolidation." Scholars distinguish between formal, procedural democracy and substantive, liberal democracy. Huntington asserts that a political system is democratic "to the extent that its most powerful collective decision makers are selected through fair, honest, and periodic elections in which candidates freely compete for votes and in which virtually all the adult population is eligible to vote."[5] According to this minimalist definition, which Larry Diamond calls "electoral democracy,"[6] democracy involves "a set of rules by which representatives are elected, policies are chosen, and laws are made and enforced."[7] But Diamond recognizes that merely institutionalizing the selection of rulers or policies is insufficient to classify a political system as a genuine democracy, arguing that liberal democracy must meet minimal conditions of civil freedom in order to achieve meaningful competition and participation.[8]

> In addition to regular, free, and fair electoral competition and universal suffrage, [liberal democracy] requires the absence of "reserved domains" of power for the military or other social and political forces that are not either directly or indirectly accountable to the electorate. Second, in addition to the "vertical" accountability of rulers to the ruled (which is secured most reliably through

regular, free, and fair elections), it requires "horizontal" accountability of officeholders to one another; this constrains executive power and so helps protect constitutionalism, the rule of law, and the deliberative process. Third, it encompasses extensive provisions for political and civic pluralism, as well as for individual and group freedoms.[9]

In their article on democratization in East Central Europe, Mary Kaldor and Ivan Vejvoda have defined substantive democracy as "a process that has to be continually reproduced, a way of regulating power relations in such a way as to maximize the opportunities for individuals to influence the conditions in which they live, to participate in and influence debates about the key decisions which affect society."[10]

A third type of regime, which does not meet the minimal conditions for either procedural or substantive democracy but which is distinct from authoritarian regimes, is most often encountered in the study of transitions in East Central Europe. George Schöpflin has emphasized that despite their efforts to build postcommunist polities, the East Europeans' idealized vision of West European democracy thus far has eluded them.[11] What is emerging in the region are "protodemocracies," in other words, systems that meet certain procedural democratic criteria but that are only partially developed substantive democracies. According to Daniel Nelson protodemocracies are " political systems in which one sees parliaments, parties and elections, and the rudiments of representative governance such as free and fair elections, due process in the judicial procedure, openness in public discourse via independent media, and other tenets of democracy. Yet, these are simultaneously systems in which neither public attitudes nor the making of public policy mirror the norms of equal opportunity, tolerance, or public accountability that citizenry within democracies have come to expect."[12]

The concept of democratic "consolidation" refers to the broad and deep legitimation of the political system. As Larry Diamond put it, "Consolidation is the process of achieving broad and deep legitimation, such that all significant political actors, at both the elite and mass levels, believe that the democratic regime is better for their society than any other realistic alternative they can imagine."[13] A similar definition was provided by Adam Przeworski, who wrote that a democracy if considered institutionalized "when it becomes self-enforcing, that is, when all the relevant political forces find it best to continue to submit their interests and values to the uncertain interplay of institutions."[14] Juan J. Linz and Alfred Stepan emphasize that consolidated democracy requires "a political regime in which democracy as a complex system of institutions, rules, and patterned incentives and disincentives has become, in a phrase, 'the only game in town.'" These authors' definition of consolidation combines behavioral, attitudinal, and constitutional dimensions:

> Behaviorally, democracy becomes the only game in town when no significant political group seriously attempts to overthrow the democratic regime or to promote domestic or international violence in order to secede from the state. ...

> Attitudinally, democracy becomes the only game in town when, even in the face of severe political and economic crises, the overwhelming majority of the people believe that any further political change must emerge from within the parameters of democratic procedures. Constitutionally, democracy becomes the only game in town when all of the actors in the polity become habituated to the fact that political conflict within the state will be resolved according to established norms, and that violations of these norms are likely to be both ineffective and costly.[15]

While in many cases transitions from authoritarianism to democracy have been rapid, nonviolent, and definitive, there is general agreement that the consolidation of democracy in East Central Europe is likely to be "lengthy, conflictual and inconclusive."[16]

After being virtually ignored by the West for the previous half century, Albania began to attract considerable attention in the early 1990s, primarily in connection with international attempts to contain the Yugoslav wars of secession. Several books have been published on Albania in recent years,[17] but few deal with the transition and the complex processes of change currently under way. This book therefore focuses on the trials and tribulations of Albania's efforts to create a democratic political order. It assesses the degree and significance of changes since the early 1990s, providing a detailed account of the transition from Communist Party rule to multiparty competition and exploring Albania's prospects for democracy and a market economy after forty-seven years of highly centralized rule. This study examines Albania within the context of regional and global changes, with particular attention to the challenges presented to its decisionmakers by the erosion of the boundary between domestic politics and foreign policy. As a corollary, it places Albania in the context of the proliferating literature on postcommunist democratization.[18]

I have approached this task with a few key assumptions. First, Albanians are experiencing democracy for the first time in their history; therefore, the transition and process of democratic consolidation are likely to be exceptionally difficult. Albania's political tradition and social and economic conditions have not been conducive to a democratic order: Because the country is small, weak, and economically unviable, its overriding objective historically has been to preserve its independence and territorial integrity from its more powerful neighbors. Prolonged and ruthless foreign occupation; suppression of Albanian cultural and national identity; the loss of compact, Albanian-inhabited territories to neighboring countries; economic and social backwardness; and regional, tribal, and religious differences all obstructed Albania's political development. While the majority of its neighbors established a parliamentary system at one time or another, Albania never developed a genuine democracy; its experiment with a multiparty system in the early 1920s was short-lived.

Second, no other European country in the post-1945 period bore the extreme isolation from the West and the utter subjection experienced by Albania. Under the totalitarian rule of Enver Hoxha (1944-1985), Albania became known as one of the most repressive communist countries in the world. After aligning and then dealigning his country in turn with Yugoslavia, the Soviet Union, and finally China, Hoxha embarked on a policy of self-reliance, almost totally cutting Albania off from the outside world. While other communist East European countries experienced short periods of policy "thaw" or relaxation, experimented with limited economic and political reforms, and expanded political participation by tolerating the existence of nonofficial groups and organizations, Albania remained bound to a Stalinist system that had been denounced long before even by the Soviet Union. The Albanian regime under Hoxha and his successor, Ramiz Alia, prohibited any organized activity outside the Communist Party's control. No other ruling communist party in Europe, including the Romanian Communist Party under the leadership of Nicolae Ceauşescu, exercised as tight a grip on society for as long a time as did the Party of Labor in Albania.

Third, given the inauspicious conditions under which Albanian democratization began, the task of successfully making the transition is likely to be far more daunting and torturous in Albania than in any other former communist country. Albania embarked on its transition at a time when it still lacked an independent judiciary, free media, and autonomous civic groups and associations. After a prolonged period of political turmoil, the Communist authorities had lost effective control over the country, resulting in a serious breakdown in law and order. Between 1990 and 1992, several hundred thousand Albanians, evidently including some of the country's best and brightest, had fled abroad. The economy had all but collapsed. Albania had become Europe's orphan, dependent on foreign humanitarian assistance to feed its people. In short, in 1992, the Democratic Party inherited a country in a state of apocalyptic societal breakdown.

Fourth, during the initial phase of its transition, Albania remained vulnerable to dangerous currents of instability originating outside its borders. Like other former communist countries, Albania was confronted with the simultaneous challenges of instituting a new democratic order and creating a market economy. But unlike most East European nations, Albania, adjacent to a hot spot, had to operate in a regional context that was particularly unfavorable to its democratic transition. In spite of fundamental post-Cold War changes, the external threat from Serbia remained unchanged. Indeed, Albanian leaders found themselves guiding the transition to democracy under the ever-present threat of their country's becoming entangled in the Yugoslav war, as Serbia continued to pursue a highly repressive policy toward the two million ethnic Albanians in Kosova (Kosovo, in Serbian).

The history of Albania since it first achieved independence in 1912 has encouraged gloomy prognostication. In view of Albania's implosion in early 1997, serious questions have been raised about its ability to face up to the many challenges of establishing a democracy. Given the volatile situation in Albania, it is impossible to forecast with any degree of certainty how its new system will develop. Thus, this book should be viewed as a preliminary assessment of Albania's democratization.

Why should the outcome of the transition in Albania matter to the outside world? First, the Albanians deserve a better fate than they have experienced thus far. For too long, the international community forgot Albania, giving its Communist leaders a free hand in committing horrendous human rights violations that bordered on crimes against humanity. Leaving aside the moral obligation to assist a country that has been ravaged by one of the most repressive communist regimes the world has ever seen, it is in the interest of Western nations to help Albania consolidate its democracy and thus to contribute to stability and peace in the southern Balkans. Albania has enormous geostrategic importance in the region. As Nicholas C. Pano, a longtime observer of the Albanian scene, has pointed out, the smallest and least developed Balkan state has traditionally played a role disproportionate to its size and power.[19] Developments in Albania are likely to resonate far beyond its borders, particularly in neighboring rump Yugoslavia (Serbia and Montenegro) and Macedonia, where sizeable Albanian communities live. Given political instability in the Balkans, the considerable risk of further regional conflict, and Albania's importance to regional stability and peace, Tiranë should receive continued international attention and increased political, economic, and military assistance. Although since 1992 Albania has enjoyed increased stature in world affairs, the international attempt to showcase Albanian democracy did not include helping the Albanian government cope with the threats and pressures that led to the 1997 collapse into anarchy.

Unfortunately, insufficient international attention has been devoted to the unresolved issue of ethnic Albanians in Yugoslavia and Macedonia, a potential tinder box that could ignite the entire Balkan region. The unification of Germany and the Yugoslav wars of secession have strengthened the hand of those seeking self-determination at the expense of long-standing international borders. There are now an estimated six million Albanians living in the region, only 3.3 million of whom live in Albania. Almost as many reside in neighboring countries. The majority—about two million—live in Kosova, which since the early 1980s has been under virtual military occupation by Serbia. At least half a million live in Macedonia. This newly independent former Yugoslav republic is officially defined as a state of the Macedonian nation, thus automatically relegating the ethnic Albanians there, who represent about a quarter of the population, to the status of second-class citizens. With the continued Serbian military crackdown, political and economic marginalization of Kosovar Albanians, and growing friction between ethnic Albanians and Slav Macedonians, Albanians remain highly vulnerable to nationalistic rhetoric, despite a necessary preoccupation with recovery from their own economic devastation. The overwhelming majority consider current borders, which were imposed by the Great Powers in 1913 without consideration for ethnolinguistic divisions, unjust. Although many see unification as part of their integration into Europe, with the disintegration of Yugoslavia, a vocal but increasing minority see a chance to set right what they consider a great historical injustice. Nationalists argue that if other Balkan nations can redefine borders along ethnic lines, then Albanians should have the same right.

A basic assumption of this book is that Albania and the Albanians are not peripheral to the West; rather, strategic interests are involved. The Albanian national question could present a greater, longer term threat to peace and stability in the Balkans than Bosnia. The outbreak of ethnic hostilities in Kosova or Macedonia might spill over into a wider Balkan war, which would be disastrous for the entire region and perhaps even beyond. This geostrategic reality creates an urgent need for the United States and its West European allies to focus on and attempt to manage the Albanian problem. Stability and peace in the region will to a large degree depend on how the emerging Albanian question is resolved.

Although it was primarily domestic developments that led to the disintegration of the Albanian Communists' support base, other nations played a decisive role both in inducing the Communists to accept pluralism and in facilitating peaceful regime change. External pressures exerted on the Albanian government in 1990 and 1991, particularly by the administration of U.S. President George Bush and by U.S. congressional leaders such as the former Chairman of the Commission on Security and Cooperation in Europe, Senator Dennis DeConcini, reinforced domestic democratic tendencies, making the Communists' position untenable. Economic assistance, membership in international organizations, and the expansion of bilateral ties were conditioned on the implementation of democratic reforms. This fact, combined with internal pressure, forced the Communist regime to accept political pluralism. Since 1992, the international dimension has been crucial in Albania's transition, and it will continue to have a profound impact on the country's further democratization. While it is up to the Albanians to stem the decline of their democracy and bring about its recovery, the role of the international community remains critical. Without continued foreign political and economic support, Albania's fledgling democracy could sink beneath the weight of economic difficulties and social tensions.

In writing this book, I have relied on primary Albanian sources, Western publications on Albanian developments, and my own interviews and conversations with numerous Albanian officials, politicians, intellectuals, and journalists. For reasons of practicality, the titles of articles published in Albanian newspapers and journals are given in English. Throughout the book I have used the indefinite forms of place- names used in Albania, e.g., Tiranë, Shkodër, Gjirokastër, and so on.

The book begins by providing a historical background and reviewing the main aspects of Communist Party rule. The next three chapters deal with the decomposition of the Communist regime, the rise of opposition political parties, the first phase of transition from communism to pluralism, and the Democratic Party's victory in 1992. Chapters 5 and 6 provide a comprehensive overview and analysis of the major political, economic, and social events, processes, and trends that occurred from 1992 to 1996. Foreign policy and the national question are treated in Chapter 7. The next chapter deals with Albania's volatile party system and the controversial 1996 parliamentary elections. Chapter 9 explores the political, economic, and social strains that forced Albania away from communism and toward democracy, then into armed anarchy, and analyzes the June 1997 elections. I hope it will contribute to a wider appreciation of Albania's struggle to return to the path of democracy and to aid the establishment of peace and democratic rule in the Balkan region.

Notes

1. See Samuel P. Huntington, *The Third Wave: Democratization in the Late Twentieth Century* (Norman, OK: University of Oklahoma Press, 1991), pp. 38-39.

2. Ibid.

3. See Larry Diamond and Marc F. Plattner, eds., *The Global Resurgence of Democracy* (Baltimore: Johns Hopkins University Press, 1996), Second Edition; Geoffrey Pridham, Eric Herring, and George Sanford, eds., *Building Democracy? The International Dimension of Democratisation in Eastern Europe* (New York: St. Martin's Press, 1994); Stephen White, Judy Batt, and Paul G. Lewis, eds., *Developments in East European Politics* (Durham, NC: Duke University Press, 1993); Raymond Taras, *Consolidating Democracy in Poland* (Boulder: Westview, 1995); and Mary Ellen Fischer, ed., *Establishing Democracies* (Boulder: Westview, 1996).

4. Ghia Nodia, "How Different Are Postcommunist Transitions?" *Journal of Democracy* 7, no. 4 (October 1996), p. 20.

5. Huntington, *The Third Wave*, p. 7.

6. Larry Diamond, "Is the Third Wave Over?" *Journal of Democracy* 7, no. 3 (July 1996), p. 21.

7. Mary Ellen Fischer, "Introduction," in Mary Ellen Fischer, ed., *Establishing Democracies* (Boulder: Westview, 1996), p. 3.

8. Diamond agrees with Robert Dahl that a democracy must ensure substantial levels of freedom and pluralism, and that government must be accountable to the citizens who elect it. See Robert Dahl, *Polyarchy: Participation and Opposition* (New Haven: Yale University Press, 1971), p. 3.

9. Diamond, "Is the Third Wave Over?" p. 23.

10. May Kaldor and Ivan Vejvoda, "Democratization in Central and East European Countries," *International Affairs* 73, no. 1 (1997), p. 62.

11. George Schöpflin, "The Problems of Democratic Construction," *Daedalus* 123, no. 3 (Summer 1994), p. 140.

12. Daniel Nelson, "The Comparative Politics of Eastern Europe," in Stephen White, Judy Batt, and Paul G. Lewis, eds., *Developments in East European Politics* (Durham, NC: Duke University Press, 1993), p. 255. See also Diamond, "Is the Third Wave Over?" p. 25.

13. Diamond, "Is the Third Wave Over?" p. 33.

14. Adam Przeworski, *Democracy and the Market: Political and Economic Reforms in Eastern Europe and Latin America* (Cambridge: Cambridge University Press, 1991), p. 26.

15. Juan J. Linz and Alfred Stepan, *Problems of Democratic Transition and Consolidation: Southern Europe, South America, and Post-Communist Europe* (Baltimore: The Johns Hopkins University Press, 1996), p. 5. See also Guillermo O'Donnell, "Illusions About Consolidation," *Journal of Democracy* 7, no. 2 (April 1996), pp. 34-51.

16. Philippe C. Schmitter with Terry Lynn Karl, "The Conceptual Travels of Transitologists and Consolidologists: How Far to the East Should They Attempt to Go?" *Slavic Review* 53, no. 1 (Spring 1994), p. 185.

17. Derek Hall, *Albania and the Albanians* (London: Pinter Reference, 1994); Raymond Zickel and Walter R. Iwaskiw, eds., *Albania: A Country Study* (Washington, DC: Federal Research Division, Library of Congress, 1994); Miranda Vickers, *The Albanians: A Modern History* (London: I.B. Tauris, 1995); Edwin E. Jacques, *The Albanians: An Ethnic History from Prehistoric Times to the Present* (Jefferson, NC: McFarland and Company, 1995); Miranda Vickers and James Pettifer, *Albania: From Anarchy to a Balkan Identity* (New York: New York University Press, 1997); and Nicholas J. Costa, *Albania: A European Enigma* (Boulder: East European Monographs, distributed by Columbia University Press, 1995). See also Gazmen Xhudo, *Diplomacy and Crisis Management in the Balkans: A U.S. Foreign Policy Perspective* (New York: St. Martin's Press, 1996).

18. For background on the transition in other East European countries, see Fischer, ed., *Establishing Democracies;* Taras, *Consolidating Democracy in Poland;* White, Batt, and Lewis, eds., *Developments in East European Politics;* Karen Dawisha, and Bruce Parrott, eds., *The Consolidation of Democracy in East-Central Europe* (New York: Cambridge University Press, 1997); Ivo Banac, ed., *Eastern Europe in Revolution* (Ithaca: Cornell University Press, 1992); J. F. Brown, *Hopes and Shadows: Eastern Europe After Communism* (Durham, NC: Duke University Press, 1994); Janusz Bugajski, *Nations in Turmoil: Conflict and Cooperation in Eastern Europe* (Boulder: Westview, 1993); Robert Weiner, *Change in Eastern Europe* (Westport, CT: Praeger, 1994); Sabrina Petra Ramet, ed., *Adaptation and Transformation in Communist and Post-Communist Systems* (Boulder: Westview, 1992); Constantine C. Menges, ed., *Transition from Communism in Russia and Eastern Europe* (Lanham, MD: University Press of America, 1993); Gale Stokes, *The Walls Came Tumbling Down: The Collapse of Communism in Eastern Europe* (New York: Oxford University Press, 1993); John S. Micgiel, ed., *Perspectives on Political and Economic Transitions after Communism* (New York: Columbia University, Institute on East Central Europe, 1997); and Carol Skalnik Leff, *The Czech and Slovak Republics: Nation vs. State* (Boulder: Westview, 1997).

19. Nicholas C. Pano, "Albania," in Joseph Held, ed., *The Columbia History of Eastern Europe in the Twentieth Century* (New York: Columbia University Press, 1992), p. 17.

1

Albania in Geographical
and Historical Context

Albania occupies a highly strategic position at the southern entrance to the Adriatic and it has been a tempting prize for any Great Power interested in dominating or exerting an influence in the Balkans. The country's strategic location has greatly influenced its history and development and has been the source of many vicissitudes. A battleground between Eastern and Western influences, Albania has witnessed successive invasions and conquests by Celts, Romans, Goths, Slavs, and Turks. Yet, despite centuries of foreign occupation, the rugged remoteness of Albanian territories and the sheer willpower of Albanians to resist assimilation made the preservation of a separate Albanian identity and language possible. Although Albanians at various times have occupied a much wider territory, foreign invasions drove them into the areas in which they now live.

Physical and Human Geography

Albania is bounded to the north by Yugoslavia, to the east by Macedonia, and to the south and east by Greece. The 529-kilometer border with Yugoslavia and Macedonia runs northward from Lake Prespë to the Adriatic Sea, west of Shkodër. The border with Greece is 271 kilometers long, running southwest from Lake Prespë to the Ionian Sea. To the west and southwest, Albania is bordered by the Adriatic and Ionian Seas. Its immediate western neighbor, Italy, lies less than 100 kilometers away.

The smallest of the Balkan countries, Albania encompasses an area of 28,748 square kilometers, with a maximum length from north to south of about 340 kilometers and a maximum width of about 150 kilometers. It is predominantly a mountainous country with rugged terrain, which hindered internal communication as well as the growth of a national consciousness. The greater part of its territory, 76.6 percent, consists of mountains and hills more than 200 meters above sea level; the remainder, 23.4 percent, consists of plains and valleys. The Alps of Albania, part of the Dinaric mountain system, extend over the northern portion of the country, with elevations of close to 2,700 meters. The region has limited arable land and is sparsely populated. Forestry and animal husbandry form the main economic activities. The central mountain region, extending from the valley of the Drin river in the north to the central Devoll and the lower Osum valleys in the south, has a less rugged terrain and is more densely populated than the Alps region. It is characterized by substantial deposits of such minerals as chromium, ferronickel, and copper. Forestry, animal husbandry, mining, and to an extent, agriculture are the main economic activities in this region. South of the central mountain region is a series of mountain ranges, with elevations of up to 2,500 meters, and valleys. Although the Alps and the mountains of the central region are covered with dense forests, the mountains of the southern region are mostly bare and serve essentially as pasture for livestock. In contrast to the three mountain regions, western Albania, stretching along the Adriatic coast, consists of low-lying, fertile plains. The most densely populated region in the country, this area extends over a distance of nearly 200 kilometers into the interior of the country. This is Albania's agricultural and industrial heartland. The 740-kilometer-long Albanian littoral on the Adriatic is well known for its splendid beaches and the beauty of the surrounding landscape.

Endowed with considerable mineral resources, Albania can be divided into two distinct geological regions. The southwestern part of the country is rich in hydrocarbons and fuels, including oil and natural gas. With its reserves of oil and gas, Albania should be in a position to meet its domestic needs. In recent decades, however, oil production has declined steadily, primarily due to the lack of modern technology for exploration and recovery. After a peak in 1974 at 2.25 million tons, oil production in 1994 was reported at less than 535,345 tons. Natural gas production has suffered a similarly drastic decline, from a peak of 940 million cubic meters in 1982 to 52,118 cubic meters in 1994.[1] The northeastern region has substantial reserves of chromite, copper, lignite, iron, and nickel. Before it experienced a drastic contraction in economic activity in 1990-1992, Albania was the world's third largest chromium producer, after the former Soviet Union and South Africa. Its chromium reserves are estimated at 37 million tons. Albania also has huge amounts of copper, with reserves amounting to some 50 million tons.[2]

Demographic Trends

Albania has one of the highest birth rates in Europe. Between 1945 and 1990, its population increased at an annual rate four to five times higher than the average in other European countries. Since 1990, however, population growth

TABLE 1.1 Albanian Vital Population Statistics (Per 1,000 of the population)

	1950	1960	1980	1990	1992	1994
Births	38.5	43.3	26.5	25.2	23.7	22.46
Deaths	14.0	10.4	6.4	5.6	—	5.32
Natural increase	24.5	32.9	20.1	19.6	—	1.19
Infant mortality	—	33.3	26.5	28.3	32.0	30.00
Life expectancy (in years)	53.5	64.9	69.5	72.20	—	73.4

Sources: Vladimir Misja, Ylli Vejsiu, and Arqile Bërxholli, *Popullsia e Shqipërisë* [The Population of Albania] (Tiranë, 1987), pp. 22, 102, and 351; Directory of Statistics, *Statistical Yearbook of Albania 1991* (Tiranë, 1991), pp. 36, 41, and 71; the Institute of Statistics, *Statistika* (Tiranë), no. 1 (May 1993), p. 1.

rates have declined. In 1994, Albania registered a birth rate of 22.46 per thousand, down from 25.2 in 1990 (see Table 1.1). The highest rates of live births per thousand in 1990 were registered in the districts of Kukës (35.1), Dibër (32.7), Pukë (30.6), Mat (29.2), Librazhd (28.9) and Tropojë (28.0), and the lowest in Tiranë (21.1), Korçë (21.1), Sarandë (22.1), Permet (22.8), and Kolonjë (22.9).

Family planning was introduced in 1992. Nevertheless, according to the Health Ministry's Family Planning Center, only an estimated 32,000 women used contraceptives in 1993. Although Albania registered 82,177 newborns in 1990, the number in 1993 was down to 67,766. Maternal mortality declined from 49 per 100,000 live births in 1989 to 31 in 1992.[3] During Communist rule, abortions were illegal. Nevertheless, unsafe abortions took place outside the health-care system and were a major cause of death among women of childbearing age. Abortions were legalized in June 1991. Since then, the number of registered abortions has increased significantly, averaging about 30,000 per year.[4] The introduction of family planning and the legalization of abortion have been controversial.[5] In late 1995, the parliament passed a law aimed at strictly regulating abortion.[6]

During the early 1990s, the population increased yearly by about 60,000, but the total population showed only a slight increase, rising from 3,182,417 in 1989 to 3,256,000 in mid-1995.[7] These numbers reflect the mass exodus from Albania during the upheaval that accompanied the demise of the Communist regime. Since late 1990, close to half a million Albanians have fled the country in search of jobs and a better life, making this one of the most massive outward migrations of Albanians since the fifteenth century. While increased emigration has served as a safety valve, high birth rates will continue to strain the country's resources.

Albania has the youngest population in Europe: The average age in the mid-1990s was twenty-six years, and more than a third of the total population was under fifteen. By 1995, life expectancy had reached seventy-three years. But despite significant improvements in health care during recent decades, Albania has continued to have a high mortality rate (5.32 per thousand, in 1994). The infant mortality rate also has remained disturbingly high, at 30 per 1,000 live births in 1994. The highest infant mortality rates for 1990 were registered in the northeastern districts of Kukës (38.9 for every 1,000 live births), Dibër (36.6), Pukë (36.4), and Tropojë (35.0).[8] These districts are also Albania's poorest in economic terms.

Albania has one of the most ethnically homogeneous populations in the world, with Albanians accounting for 98 percent of the total population. The other two percent is made up of ethnic Greeks, Slavs, Vlachs, and Roma. According to official statistics, in 1989 there were 58,758 ethnic Greeks, concentrated mainly in the Gjirokastër and Sarandë districts. The postcommunist government has estimated the number of ethnic Greeks at between 70,000 and 90,000.[9] Greek sources, however, have given contradictory statistics, depending on the state of Albanian-Greek bilateral ties. The most often heard Greek figures indicate that there are between 100,000 to 400,000 ethnic Greeks live in Albania. Albanians respond by insisting that Athens considers all Albanian citizens of the Orthodox faith ethnic Greeks. Whatever the exact number, the size of the ethnic Greek community has declined since 1991, due to a continuous outmigration to Greece.[10]

Until 1992, Albania was divided into twenty-six administrative districts *(rrethe)*. In 1992, the number of *rrethe* was increased to thirty-six. The largest and economically most important are Tiranë, Durrës, Shkodër, Elbasan, Vlorë, Korçë, and Fier. The capital, Tiranë, the country's main industrial and cultural center, in 1992 had a population of some 260,000. Other large cities include: Durrës (about 125,000), Shkodër (85,000), Elbasan (101,000), Vlorë (85,000), and Korçë (73,000).[11] Under Communism, population movement was strictly controlled and migration from the countryside into the cities was discouraged. Although the Communist policy of rapid industrialization resulted in the gradual increase of urban population, the population remained unevenly distributed between rural and urban areas: In 1992, the majority, 63.5 percent, lived in the countryside, and 36.5 percent in the cities.[12] The end of Communism, however, brought significant changes in the country's urban and regional population distribution. By mid-1997, the rural population had dropped to about 55 percent as a result of migrations, primarily from the impoverished northeastern regions, into the cities. Tiranë's population was estimated to have increased to more than 400,000.

Albanians Outside Albania

Ironically, more Albanians live outside than inside Albania. Along almost all its borders with Yugoslavia and Macedonia are Albanian-speaking regions, which in the opinion of most Albanians, should have been incorporated within the Albanian state when the Great Powers delimited its borders in 1913.

The number of Albanians outside Albania is uncertain. Ethnic Albanians have questioned official Yugoslav censuses, insisting that the authorities deliberately underreported their number for political reasons. They boycotted the last census held by former Yugoslavia, in 1991. Belgrade estimated the number of Albanians in Kosova in 1991 at 1.6 million; but the Albanians put their number at about 2 million. While there are disagreements regarding the size of the Albanian community, there is widespread agreement that the Albanians account for over 90 percent of Kosova's population. Ethnic Serbs constitute a majority in only four Kosova communes: Zveçan (79 percent), Subin Potok (53 percent), Leposavić (87.7 percent), and Stroc (66.3 percent).[13] Some 100,000 Albanians live in Serbia proper, 80,000 of them in three southern communes on the border with Kosova: Presheva, Bujanovc, and Medvegja.

According to the 1994 census, the Albanians in Macedonia number about 442,000, or about 23 percent of the total population.[14] The Albanians dispute these figures, claiming that they represent between 30 and 40 percent of the total population. They maintain that several hundred thousand Albanians were not counted in the census because the law on citizenship, approved by the Macedonian parliament in 1992, established a fifteen-year residency requirement for citizenship. Albanian residents who did not have appropriate documents or who had lived for extended periods in other parts of former Yugoslavia were not counted.

Montenegro also has a sizeable Albanian population. According to the 1991 census, there were 40,880 Albanians there, representing more than 6 percent of the total population. Albanians are concentrated in the east, in Plavë (Plav) and Guci (Gusinje), and on the coast, around Ulqin, where they represent more than 70 percent of the population of Ulqin.[15]

Although Albania, Kosova, and Albanian-inhabited areas of Macedonia and Montenegro have developed independently of each other since their forced partition in 1912, Albanians on both sides of the border view themselves as members of the same nation and use the same standard literary language. Demographic developments among the Albanians in Serbia, Montenegro, and Macedonia closely resemble those among their counterparts across the border. Population growth in Kosova is estimated at about thirty per thousand, making it among the highest in the world. About 67 percent of the population live in rural areas. Sixty percent of Kosova's total population is under twenty-seven years old. Infant mortality, however, is very high. In 1994, it was reported at 33.6 per 1,000 live births.[16] The Albanians in Macedonia, inhabiting compact territories in the western part of the country adjacent to Albania and Kosova, have a very high birth rate. More than half of them (52.6 percent) are under the age of nineteen. Since 1981, the Albanian population in Macedonia has witnessed an average annual increase of about 35,000, while the more numerous Macedonians have increased by about 45,000.[17] With their lower birth rates, the Macedonians fear that the Albanians eventually will outnumber them.

Large Albanian communities also reside in Greece, Italy, and Turkey. Greece does not recognize the existence of an indigenous Albanian ethnic group and the number of indigenous Albanians there is not known. At the end of World War II, the Greeks expelled some 30,000 Albanians (Çams) from Çamëria in northern Greece, accusing them of having collaborated with Nazi invaders. The Çams have become a contentious issue in relations between Albanian and Greece, with Albania insisting that they be permitted to return to Greece and receive compensation for their confiscated properties. Greece has rejected Albania's demands. Since 1991, some 300,000 Albanians have fled to Greece, most of them illegally. The future of these Albanians remains uncertain, as Greece has on numerous occasions sent thousands of them back to Albania.

It has been estimated that some 150,000 Albanians migrated to Italy during the early 1990s. In addition to recent arrivals, Italy has a large Albanian community in Calabria and Sicily—descendants of immigrants who settled there in the fifteenth century after the Turkish occupation of Albania. The number of Albanians in Turkey is estimated at more than a million; but most of them have been assimilated, and only since the collapse of communism in Albania have they reestablished contacts with Tiranë. In addition, there is an ever growing Albanian population in the United States. Estimated at about 250,000 and concentrated in the northeastern part of the country, Albanian Americans have been politically active in lobbying the U.S. Congress and administration on Albanian-related issues.

Gegs and Tosks

The Albanians are divided into two subgroups, the Gegs and the Tosks, the Shkumbin River serving as a natural border between them. Almost all the Albanians in Kosova, Macedonia, and Montenegro are Gegs. Differences in dialects used by the two groups as well as in their outlooks and ways of life were pronounced until the Communist regime sought to integrate the two, and the terms Geg and Tosk disappeared from the political vocabulary. Before 1945, the more numerous Gegs traditionally had dominated Albanian politics. Well known for their independent spirit and fighting abilities, the Gegs enjoyed a great degree of independence and generally resisted the authority of foreign invaders, and subsequently, that of the Albanian government.

Before the Communist takeover, the Geg society was organized according to tribal groups, with the clan chieftain, *bajraktar,* playing an important political and social role. Social behavior among the Gegs was regulated by customary laws, the most important of which was the *Kanun* (Canon). The laws and customs included in the *Kanun* were framed in the fifteenth century by Lekë Dukagjini, and were transmitted orally from generation to generation. Father Shtjefën Gjeçovi, a prominent Franciscan scholar, codified the canon in the beginning of the twentieth century.[18] While the clan system and the traditional Geg way of life had largely disappeared in Albania by the beginning of the 1990s, the precepts of the *Kanun* continue to play a role in some areas of northern Albania and Kosova.

The Tosks live in southern Albania and parts of northern Greece. Because their territories were easily accessible, the Tosks developed substantial contacts with the outside world, and as a result, foreign influences were more pronounced among them than among the Gegs. Before World War II, the south was characterized by a semifeudal society. The peasantry, which made up the majority of the population, was exploited by a small group of landowners who controlled about two-thirds of the arable land.

The two subgroups have alternated in dominating Albanian politics—the Gegs during King Zog's reign (1925-1939) and the Tosks under communism (1945-1992). While there have never been open Geg-Tosk conflicts, latent feuds have existed and may have been further fueled by the Communist regime's ruthless attempts to homogenize the two. The Communist movement was largely based in the south, and before Hoxha's death in 1985, most influential Party and government posts were generally held by Tosks. Hoxha pursued a heavy-handed policy against the Gegs (especially against Roman Catholics who had forcefully resisted the imposition of Communist rule), neglected their economic and cultural development, and imposed on them what was ostensibly a common standard language but in reality was heavily dominated by the Tosk dialect.[19] Communist policies widened the gap in the educational and economic levels between north and south. Many Gegs resented what they saw as political, economic, and cultural domination by the more prosperous southerners.

Historical Influences

Its relative weakness in comparison with more powerful and larger neighbors has made Albania vulnerable to external pressures, and as a result, it has had a constant preoccupation with ensuring its survival as an independent entity. While it has had periods of glory and greatness, Albania also has endured scores of invasions throughout its tumultuous history. In more recent times, it has had to rely on outside powers to keep its neighbors' territorial ambitions in check.

Most scholars believe that the Albanians are descendants of the Illyrians, who settled the western part of the Balkan Peninsula at the end of the Bronze Age (about 1000 B.C.) or shortly thereafter. Albanian archaeologists have conducted extensive research to corroborate the thesis of Albania's ancient civilization and document the continuity between the Illyrians and the Albanians. The Albanians refer to themselves as *shqiptarë* and to their country as *Shqipëri*. *Albania*, the term used by foreigners to refer to the country, derived from *Albanoi*, the name of an Illyrian tribe, which was said to have inhabited present-day central Albania.

The Illyrians established their own states during the fifth and the third centuries B.C. The Adrians kingdom, founded in the third century B.C., was the most prominent. It extended from the Dalmatian coast to the coastal regions of present-day Albania and reached the peak of its power during King Agron's reign (250-231 B.C.). The Adrians kingdom was a major naval power, preying on Roman ships and thus endangering the Roman republic's trade. In 168 B.C., Rome conquered the entire Illyrian kingdom and thereafter ruled it for more than five centuries. In the beginning of the Roman occupation, Albania became an important center, connecting Rome with Byzantium by its Via Egnatia. The Illyrian people also played a significant role in the Roman Empire: Several emperors were of Illyrian origin, including Claudius II, Aurelian, Diocletian, and Probus in the third century A.D., Constantine the Great in the fourth century, and Justinian in the sixth century.

With the division of the Roman Empire in A.D. 395, Albania became part of the Eastern Empire. Albanian ports became important trade centers, and during this period Durrës (Durrachium) and some other cities reached the height of their prosperity. As the Roman Empire declined, the Illyrian provinces were invaded by migrating tribes vying for control of the western Balkans. The Goths and Huns invaded in the fourth century, and the Bulgars in the fifth. During the sixth and seventh centuries, large numbers of Slavs also began to penetrate Illyrian territories. Faced with the danger of assimilation, the Albanians, who by this time had converted to Christianity, moved southward, concentrating mainly in the rugged mountain regions, where they remained nominally under the rule of the East Roman, or Byzantine, Empire.

During the eleventh and twelfth centuries, Albania was overrun by the Normans. But in 1190, during a period of Byzantine weakness, the Albanian prince Progon established an independent state. This lasted until the middle of the thirteenth century, after which the country relapsed into disunity, subsequently being conquered by the Serbs. With the collapse of Stephan Dušan's Serbian Empire in 1355, Albania fell under the domination of local feudal lords. The Topias and the Dukagjinis ruled in the north, the Muzakas and the Shpatas in the south.

Ottoman Turks invaded Albania at the end of the fourteenth century. Under the leadership of Gjergj Kastrioti Skënderbeu (Skanderbeg), the Albanians waged a successful twenty-five-year struggle against the Turkish occupiers. In 1448 and in 1466, Skanderbeg repulsed large Turkish expeditions; but after his death in 1468, Albania became part of the Ottoman Empire. Many Albanians emigrated to Italy, and the majority of the population converted to Islam. During the nearly five centuries of Turkish occupation, many Albanians rose to high positions in the empire. Nevertheless, given Albania's rugged topography and its people's determination to preserve their autonomy, the Turks were never able to establish total control over the country. During the later part of the eighteenth century, several native princes rose to prominence. From 1775 to 1796, the Bushatis ruled the Shkodër duchy, extending their authority over northern and central Albania. From 1790 to 1822, Ali Pasha ruled the duchy of Janina, which extended from Vlorë and Berat to Çamëria and Thessaly.

The Albanians lacked ethnic or religious affinity with any of the Great Powers. Unlike the Greeks and the Serbs, the Albanians could not rely on a big brother's assistance against Turkey. Thus, they were the last Balkan people to gain independence from the Turks. The first signs of an organized Albanian nationalist movement appeared in the late 1800s. In June 1878, representatives from all over Albania met at Prizren, Kosova, and established the Albanian League, also known as the Prizren League. The league's primary objectives were to prevent the cession of Albanian-inhabited regions to Montenegro and Serbia and to obtain administrative autonomy from Turkey. It succeeded in frustrating most but not all Great Power plans to hand over Albanian territories to its neighbors, and it failed to gain administrative and cultural autonomy from Turkey and to unite Albanian lands into one *vilajet* (province).The Turks crushed the league in 1881 and imprisoned or killed its leaders. Yet the movement had a lasting impact and would inspire later nationalist activity, especially in northwest and northeast regions such as Kosova, which continued to face the threat of occupation by Serbia and Montenegro.

On 28 November 1912, after a series of revolts originating in Kosova and after the Balkan states had declared war on Turkey, Albanian patriots led by Ismail Qemal proclaimed the country's independence. Their dream of incorporating all predominantly Albanian-inhabited territories into one state was shattered, however, as Serbia, Montenegro, and Greece occupied large parts of Albania. At the London Conference in December 1912, the Great Powers recognized Albania's independence. However, the 1913 frontier demarcation by a special commission appointed by the Great Powers excluded from Albania more than half of its territory, including Kosova and Çamëria, and about 40 percent of the ethnic Albanian population.

The Great Powers selected the German prince Wilhelm zu Wied as Albania's ruler. He arrived in Durrës in March 1914, but because of local opposition and the outbreak of World War I, fled the country six months later. Although its independence was recognized and guaranteed by the Great Powers, Albania's existence as an independent entity was not readily accepted by its more powerful neighbors. During World War I, the country was occupied by a dozen foreign armies, and at the end of the war, Serbia, Greece, and Italy made efforts to further partition it. Albania's independence was preserved largely thanks to U.S. President Woodrow Wilson's support at the Paris Peace Conference and due to the inability of neighboring states to agree on how to divide the tiny Balkan state.

Faced with an extremely hostile external environment, the political groups, forces, and parties that emerged during Albania's period of independence were oriented toward ensuring the nation's sovereignty and independence and recovering lost territories. They had less clear programs on the internal organization of the Albanian polity. Western political ideas were slow to penetrate the country, as few Albanians had been educated in the West. Albania lacked a well-developed middle class imbued with democratic ideals and most of the emerging political, cultural, and military elites had been educated in Turkey, a country that also lacked a democratic political tradition. The semifeudal Albanian society was characterized by widespread authoritarian tendencies, and apparently there were strong sentiments for the selection of a strong leader in the mold of Skanderbeg.

The first Albanian political parties in the Western sense of the word, appeared in the early 1920s. The two most important political groups were the People's Party, led by Fan S. Noli,[20] a Harvard-educated, Orthodox clergyman who served briefly as prime minister in 1924, and the Progressive Party, led by Ahmet Zogu, a chieftain from Mati. But Albania's experiment with political pluralism was short-lived: The main political parties engaged in endless feuding, the parliament was ineffective, and the country was plagued by political instability. Order was restored following Zogu's accession to power in December 1924. Three years later, he proclaimed himself king of the Albanians. Although the king proceeded to establish an authoritarian monarchy, Albania under his rule was a much freer society than under the subsequent Communist rule of Enver Hoxha. King Zog succeeded in laying the foundations of a modern state and carried out significant cultural and economic reforms.[21]

One of the first European victim of the Axis powers, Albania was annexed by Italy in April 1939, as King Zog fled the country. The Albanians were slow to organize a resistance movement, partly because of the Italian and German decision to attach Kosova and other Albanian-inhabited areas in Yugoslavia to Albania in 1941. For the first time since 1912, most Albanians were living in a single, unified state. Moreover, after Italy capitulated and the Germans moved into Albania, the latter granted the country a substantial degree of independence.

Albania's highly turbulent historical experience had given rise to a defensive nationalism. The experience of long foreign domination and the loss of contiguous, compact Albanian territories had psychologically scarred the Albanian nation, fostering xenophobia and a siege mentality among many of Albania's people and leaders. Albanians attributed their inability to achieve their main national aspirations to the hostile policies of their neighbors, supported by the Great Powers. They came to view themselves as the great underdogs of history, surrounded on all sides by enemies bent on destroying their state or preventing their national union. These perceptions have largely influenced the way Albanians have related to their neighbors and the outside world in general.

Communist Rule

Predominantly a backward agrarian society with no tradition of a working class, Albania was less suited for Communism than any other nation in Eastern Europe. While small communist groups began to appear in the major cities in the 1920s and the 1930s, the Albanian Communist Party (ACP) was established only in 1941, with the direct assistance of the Yugoslav Communists. It soon became the best organized and most influential of all the parties created during the war. With material assistance from the West and guidance from the Yugoslav Communist Party, the Albanian Communists organized a resistance movement. Under the guise of fighting for the national liberation of their country, the Communists attracted significant popular support. They emphasized the national liberation character of their movement and deliberately downplayed their ideological commitment to the creation of a communist society. On the eve of the liberation of the country, the ACP launched a civil war against its opponents. Within a short period, the well-armed Communists overpowered their weaker and poorly organized opponents grouped around the Legality Movement (Legaliteti), which advocated King Zog's return, and the National Front (Balli Kombëtar), which favored the establishment of a democratic republic.

In contrast to the experience of other East European countries, Communism in Albania was homegrown: The ACP was not installed in power by an outside force, but won on its own, admittedly with some assistance from the Yugoslav Communists and the Allies. Thus, Albanian Communists enjoyed a higher degree of legitimacy than their colleagues in other East European states, who, except for those in former Yugoslavia, were installed in power by the Soviets. This factor made it possible for Hoxha, the ACP's lifelong leader, to impose upon his people one of the most repressive regimes the world has known.[22]

The Communists inherited a war-ravaged country. Some 28,000 Albanians lost their lives in the war against Italian and German occupiers and in the subsequent civil war between the communists and the nationalists. Italy, which had announced plans to settle some two million Italian farmers in Albania, had fully integrated the Albanian economy with its own war economy. It also had intensified the exploitation of Albania's substantial reserves of strategic assets, particularly oil, chrome, and copper. The Germans had pursued a similar policy during their occupation of the country (1943-1944). Before the war, more than 80 percent of the population had been engaged in agriculture. In the lowlands, a small landowning class owned large estates worked by tenants, while in the hilly and mountainous regions, independent, small farmers engaged in primitive farming and livestock raising. With the exception of oil and chromium production, Albania had no other significant industry. Although the Italians had upgraded Albania's communications network, improved port facilities, and constructed new roads linking mining regions with the ports, these were insufficient to stimulate significant economic activity.

After forming a provisional government in November 1944, the Communists moved swiftly to extend and consolidate their control throughout the country, and proceeded to establish a one-party state in the Soviet mold. In December 1945, elections were held for a Constituent Assembly, which a month later proclaimed Albania a "people's republic," clearly signaling the determination of the new leaders to forge a close alliance with the emerging Eastern bloc. The assembly promulgated a new constitution, closely modeled after Yugoslavia's communist constitution. Although the document made no reference to the "special role" of the Communist Party, a phrase that was included in the constitutions of other East European countries allied with the Soviet Union, the Albanian Communists excluded the possibility of a coalition with other parties and groups. Hoxha, who in addition to serving as Party general secretary also simultaneously held the posts of prime minister, foreign minister, and commander in chief of the armed forces, launched a series of political, economic, and military policies designed to consolidate the new order.

In an unprecedented campaign of terror, the pre-war political elites were decimated by purges and war-crimes trials; leaders of the opposition groups who survived were forced to flee abroad. By the end of 1946, the regime had succeeded in eliminating all organized opposition, with the notable exception of small groups in northern Albania, which continued their armed struggle until the late 1940s. The government also adopted economic and social measures intended to destroy the support base of the country's pre-war elite and to lay the foundations for a command economy. The property of exiled or imprisoned political opponents was seized, and foreign-owned assets were confiscated. The Communist state took over all industrial and commercial enterprises, asserting a monopoly in both domestic and foreign trade. In accordance with the Stalinist economic model, Albania's economic plans emphasized the rapid development of heavy industry over agriculture and light industry. The government announced an agrarian reform, nationalizing all forests and pasturelands, confiscating large estates, and distributing land to landless peasants. Although farmers were urged to join collective farms, collectivization of agriculture gained momentum only in the mid-1950s and was not completed until the following decade.[23]

The constitution adopted in 1946 guaranteed freedom of religion. However, the Communists from the outset left no doubt about their eventual objective of destroying all organized religion. The three main religious communities—Muslim, Catholic, and Orthodox—became the object of a well coordinated government campaign aimed at discrediting them and terrorizing them into submission. Most of the property belonging to religious organizations was confiscated without compensation. By the early 1950s, most prominent religious leaders had been executed or imprisoned or had fled the country. The antireligious campaign intensified in the 1950s and the 1960s, climaxing with the government's decision in 1967 to outlaw religion altogether and to close all houses of worship.

The new elite was young and highly inexperienced in governing. With the intensification of the East-West conflict, Hoxha's regime closely allied itself with the Soviet bloc, to the detriment of relations with the West, including such neighboring countries as Greece and Italy. It blindly copied Yugoslavia's domestic and foreign policies. Thus, between 1944 and 1948, Albania had to all practical purposes become a Yugoslav colony.

Break with Belgrade and Moscow

From its inception, the ACP was characterized by factional struggles. Hoxha, who was a compromise choice for Party leader during the war, was challenged by members of the top leadership who questioned his leadership abilities and feared his dictatorial tendencies. A series of purges during and immediately after the war led to high turnover in the leading organs of the party. During 1947-1948, Hoxha appeared to be losing the struggle for power, as the Yugoslavs threw their weight behind the Party organizational secretary and secret police chief Koçi Xoxe. The pro-Yugoslav faction became the dominant faction, and Albania was about to be swallowed by Yugoslavia when Tito broke with Stalin in 1948. Dissatisfaction with Tiranë's alliance with Belgrade had become widespread, which was not surprising given the long enmity between Albanians and Serbs and the fact that at the end of the war Kosova again became part of Yugoslavia. The Yugoslav-Soviet break provided the Albanian governing elite with the opportunity to break with Belgrade and ally itself with Moscow.

In the wake of the break with Belgrade, Hoxha moved swiftly to consolidate his power, emerging as undisputed leader in Albanian politics. Through a series of show trials, Hoxha eliminated real and potential opponents within and outside the Communist Party, which at its first congress in 1948 changed its name to the Albanian Party of Labor (APL). Although before 1948 Stalin had practically given Yugoslavia a free hand in Albania, the Soviets now offered Tiranë substantial economic and military assistance as Albania came to play a critical role in Stalin's strategy of exerting pressure on Yugoslavia. With Soviet and East European assistance, the Albanian government launched an ambitious program of economic development with the aim of transforming the country into what the official propaganda termed an agrarian-industrial state. Albania adopted the Soviet system of centralized economic planning, emphasizing the rapid development of heavy industry. Its external interactions were almost totally restricted to the Soviet bloc, and political and economic relations with the West remained frozen. Albania also joined the Council of Mutual Economic Assistance (CMEA) and became a founding member of the Warsaw Treaty Organization. However, the Soviet Union never signed a defense treaty with Albania.

By the mid-1950s, Hoxha's government had earned a reputation as the most Stalinist regime in Eastern Europe. It was not surprising, therefore, that Albanian

Communist leaders would oppose Soviet leader Nikita S. Khrushchev's de-Stalinization campaign. Hoxha's opposition to Khrushchev was conditioned primarily by his well-founded fears that de-Stalinization would result in his replacement as party and state leader. Moscow's rapprochement with Belgrade in 1955 also played a role, as Albania feared renewed Yugoslav domination. In 1956, Hoxha faced the most serious challenge to his leadership since 1948, when senior members of the Politburo demanded a reassessment of the Party's policy after the break with Yugoslavia. He was able to weather the crisis partly because his opponents were poorly organized and partly because Moscow had loosened its grip on its allies. Hoxha purged his opponents and took advantage of the 1956 unrest in Hungary and Poland to reassert his Stalinist policies.

While Stalin was denounced throughout the region, Albania avoided the de-Stalinization process. Tiranë's failure to toe the Soviet line had an adverse impact on Albanian-Soviet relations. Khrushchev's visit to Albania in 1959 served only to drive the wedge in farther between the two allies. Meanwhile, the Albanians had begun to forge an alliance with the Chinese Communists, who also objected to Khrushchev's domestic and foreign policies. Hoxha made what was perhaps the most significant decision of his political career in 1960, when he openly challenged the Soviet leader, thus precipitating a break with Moscow, which would have dire consequences for his country's future. The Soviet Union responded to Albania's defiance by breaking diplomatic relations with Tiranë—an unprecedented development in ties between two socialist countries. Moreover, Moscow canceled all grants and credits, cut off all trade, expelled Albanians studying in the Soviet Union, withdrew its many advisors, and excluded Albania from the CMEA trading bloc and the Warsaw Treaty Organization.[24]

The Chinese Connection

Some observers had predicted that Albania would follow Yugoslavia's example in 1948 and move toward a rapprochement with the West. Hoxha, however, embarked upon a policy of total reliance on distant Communist China, thus missing an excellent opportunity to open up his country. Given the general state of East-West relations at the time, Western countries would have welcomed Albania wholeheartedly and would have invested substantial resources to shore up an Albania independent of the Warsaw Pact.

Albania's break with the Soviet Union and Eastern Europe and its alliance with China were monumental developments in its post-World War II history. Albania entered a long period of political and cultural isolation from the outside world. The alliance with Beijing resulted in the severance of even the limited cultural ties that had been reestablished with selected Western countries in the 1950s. While Soviet bloc members improved political and economic ties with the West, relaxed Communist Party control over their societies, and experimented with limited economic reforms, Albania moved in the opposite direction, becoming almost totally isolated, developing relations only with China and selected Third World countries.

Domestically, Hoxha increased the repression and attempted to extend Party control over all aspects of life. Tiranë went even further than Beijing in totally abolishing the private sector and fully collectivizing agriculture. In 1966, Hoxha launched his own version of China's Cultural Revolution, with the objective of eliminating any center of potential power that could threaten the APL's primacy. This and other Chinese-inspired policies brought misery and havoc to the whole nation. Under the guise of attacking deeply rooted traditions of social conservatism that ostensibly were incompatible with communist ideas, the regime initiated coordinated campaigns against traditional customs, religious beliefs, and what was officially termed alien foreign influences. In 1967, all religious institutions were closed down, and Albania became the world's first official atheist state. Many mosques and churches, some dating back centuries, were destroyed. Imams and priests were imprisoned or executed. The intelligentsia, long regarded by Hoxha as unreliable, came under severe attack. Prominent writers were chastised for ideological deformations and were ordered to go and live for extended periods in the countryside. Through harsh administrative measures, the regime succeeded in suppressing all dissent among the intelligentsia. For the next two decades, writers and intellectuals faithfully carried out the APL's policies of socialist realism, propagandizing the party's role among the masses. The Albanian intelligentsia never fully recovered from the onslaught it experienced during its country's cultural revolution and the subsequent purges.

China considered Albania an important ally, its only true ally in the 1960s. It therefore devoted considerable resources to ensuring Albania's continued economic development. Between 1962 and 1978, Beijing provided several billion dollars in economic and military aid to Albania. Thus, the Albanian government was able to pursue its ambitious policies of rapid industrialization, achieving particularly impressive results in extending the country's hydropower network, constructing oil refineries and ore processing plants. From a predominantly agrarian society at the end of World War II, by the beginning of the 1980s Albania had forged a significant working class.

This latter goal was achieved only at great cost: Hoxha waged an all-out, violent assault on the peasantry, pushing it into a state of extreme impoverishment after the full collectivization of agriculture in 1967. Even in the most remote, mountainous areas, land was taken away from peasants and they were prohibited from raising livestock outside collective cooperatives. At the same time, the Communists created an elaborate social welfare system, that guaranteed Albanian citizens job security, price stability, and free education and medical care. Moreover, through a concerted policy of reducing wage differentials, the Communists ensured that the social and economic differentiation was kept at a low level.

Clearly, without substantial assistance from China, Albania would have been forced to reconsider its anti-Western and anti-Soviet foreign policy orientations. For its part, Albania proved an important political ally, serving as China's mouthpiece in the United Nations and other international fora. Relations between the two countries expanded rapidly after China's own break with the Soviet Union in 1963, reaching their climax during the cultural revolution (1966-1969). While there were evidently differences between the two countries even in the 1960s, numerous Chinese delegations, including top leaders, visited Tiranë, expressing strong support for Hoxha's leadership at a time of international isolation. Albania became totally dependent on China for its economic survival. While the Chinese provided considerable help, Albania paid an extremely heavy price for its defiance of the Soviet Union. Distant and underdeveloped China was in no position to offer the assistance, both in terms of the amount and quality, that the Soviet bloc was providing its allies. The technology used in some of the projects Albania built with Chinese assistance was from the 1930s and the 1940s. The result was that Albania's overall economic development stagnated, resulting in a widening gap between it and its immediate neighbors.

Albania's alliance with China lasted seventeen years.[25] The first signs of problems emerged in 1971, when China took steps to normalize ties with the United States. The Albanians publicly criticized the Chinese for departing from their previously stated policy of having no dealings with the two superpowers. The Chinese responded by gradually reducing their economic and military assistance to Albania. However, Hoxha could not follow his Chinese allies in improving ties with the West, because he feared the possible repercussions such a development would have on Albania's domestic policies. Indeed, despite increased centralization and repression, with the deepening crisis in relations with China and the obvious costs of international isolation, Hoxha's policies were encountering considerable domestic opposition from young technocrats who questioned the course the party was pursuing both internally and externally. Hoxha responded by carrying out a series of purges between 1973 and 1975 that resulted in the downfall of several senior officials, including APL Central Committee members and prominent advocates of cultural liberalization Fadil Paçrami, Todi Lubonja, and Agim Mero; Politburo member and Minister of Defense Beqir Balluku, as well as Chief of Staff Petrit Dume and the head of the army's Political Directorate, Hito Çako; Chairman of the State Planning Commission Abdyl Këllezi; Minister of Industry Koço Theodhosi; and Minister of Trade Kiço Ngjela. Invariably, Hoxha accused the purged officials of plotting to overthrow his regime. Balluku and Këllezi were executed and the others were sentenced to long prison terms.

It subsequently became clear that the victims of the purges of the 1970s had not engaged in antiregime activity, nor were they plotting to overthrow Hoxha.[26] The dictator's motives appear to have been to eliminate potential opponents and bring in younger officials who owed their rise to power personally to him rather than to a broader political base. Moreover, Hoxha had begun to prepare the ground for his own succession. Concerned that his unique policies might not continue when he was gone, he tried to institutionalize them with the adoption in 1976 of a new constitution, that embodied his views on major policy issues. The document sanctioned the one-party system, abolished private property, prohibited the government from seeking foreign credits or forming joint enterprises with foreign companies or countries, and reaffirmed the regime's 1967 decision to abolish institutionalized religion.

With Mao Zedong's death in 1976 and the accession to power in Beijing of what Tiranë viewed as a "revisionist" leadership bent on pursuing capitalist policies, Albanian-Chinese relations reached a low ebb. The breakup of the alliance two years later removed Albania's last and only source of foreign assistance and placed it in a precarious position. Rather than opening the country to the West or to Albania's former Soviet bloc allies, Hoxha's regime turned ever farther inward, self-reliance becoming the main element in Albania's economic development. Within a few years, the disastrous consequences of Hoxha's policies were evident, as the economy entered a phase of rapid decline. Nevertheless, the regime stayed its course.

Albania in the 1980s: Still the "Odd Man Out"

Hoxha had begun to prepare the ground for his own succession as early as the mid-1970s. Not until the end of 1981, however, did it become clear that Ramiz Alia, one of the youngest members of the Communist elite that had emerged from the partisan war, would inherit Hoxha's mantle. Alia became Hoxha's successor almost by default: Other candidates either had been eliminated by the dictator himself or had died. Mehmet Shehu, reputedly the second most powerful person in Albania, and prime minister for more than three decades, reportedly committed suicide in December 1981. He had developed a reputation as a brutal leader and was widely blamed for the regime's reign of terror. Although the two of them had worked together closely since the war days, Hoxha apparently did not believe Shehu was the right man to succeed him. The younger Alia, on the other hand, was more acceptable. He had become Hoxha's closest confidant, faithfully promoting his mentor's foreign and domestic policies without ever expressing independent views. In 1982, Hoxha charged that Shehu had all along been a foreign spy, linking him with the senior officials purged from 1973 to 1975. It appears, however, that Shehu was pushed to suicide by disagreements with Hoxha; there is no evidence that the prime minister was a foreign spy or had plotted against Hoxha.[27] Shehu's demise was followed by yet another extensive purge.[28]

Hoxha's death in April 1985 raised hopes that Albania would finally follow the example of other communist countries, end its international isolation, and initiate much-needed political, economic, and social reforms. From the very beginning of his reign, Alia came under pressure from both the conservative and the more liberal elements of the Party. The old guard was suspicious of Alia, who had close links with senior officials purged in 1973 on charges of cultural liberalization. The more liberal wing of the Party, particularly the intellectuals who had begun to show signs of increasing restiveness, had great hopes in Alia and saw him as Albania's Gorbachev. But whereas Alia appeared to recognize the growing political, economic, and social crises facing his country, he shied away from radical reforms, instead stressing continuity with Hoxha's policies.

For more than four decades, the regime had attempted to live up to an unwritten social contract that had kept the population politically quiescent: It had boosted living standards and maintained an elaborate social welfare system in return for unquestioning political obedience. With substantial foreign assistance, first from the Soviet bloc and later from China, Albania had in fact achieved significant economic progress. Although the country's isolation and its all-powerful official propaganda had made comparisons with the outside world difficult, Albania's gains paled compared to the progress its neighbors made during the same period.

By the mid-1980s, Albania was confronted with serious problems. The cut in Chinese assistance in 1978, the regime's refusal to seek alternate sources of foreign aid, the strict implementation of Hoxha's self-reliance policy prohibiting foreign credits and investments, and the overly centralized economic system had taken a heavy toll. The seriousness of the crisis was reflected by a sharp economic decline, low productivity, pervasive shortages of basic foodstuffs, an ailing infrastructure, and huge subsidies.[29] Most Albanians saw their standards of living, already the lowest in Europe, plummet further. Social mobility had declined dramatically, social malaise had become pervasive, and adverse social trends had reached critical proportions, reflecting the waning hold of the regime's communist ideology. The crisis was compounded by increased unemployment, which was not acknowledged officially, and ever shrinking resources to deal with social issues. Albania's high birth rates and the regime's policy of strict control of population movement further compounded the economic crisis, especially in rural areas. With about two-thirds of the population living in the countryside, arable land per capita continued to decline, seriously threatening the livelihood of the already impoverished peasantry. Economic problems were further complicated by a severe drought, which lasted throughout the second half of the 1980s. By 1990, national income had decreased by 12 percent compared to a decade earlier. During the same period, labor productivity in industry had declined by 15 percent.[30] Agriculture was especially hard hit, as farmers were not producing enough to feed themselves, let alone supply the cities. Shortages reportedly had become so pervasive that many people were suffering from malnourishment; infant mortality rates rose dramatically, and many babies were being born deformed.[31] These economic hardships were causing widespread disaffection.

Alia's public pronouncements reflected a keen understanding of the acute problems facing his country. His responses, however, fell far short of the decisive steps that were required to solve the nation's problems. Between 1985 and the end of 1989, he tinkered with changes in the highly centralized economic system, loosened the party's grip in the cultural sector, and gradually expanded Albania's relations with other countries. Alia's measures clearly were aimed at improving the functioning of the Communist system rather than at changing it. He tried to hold the populace's discontent in check by rallying Albanians to defend their country and reminding them of the economic and social gains that Albania had achieved under Communist rule. But for most Albanians, these gains were tarnished by the regime's brutal repression and denial of basic human rights, the rampant corruption of Communist officials, and the growing gap between Albania and its neighbors.

The APL remained largely insensitive to popular demands. Moreover, leadership opinion was divided on the seriousness of the economic downturn and the nature and extent of the measures needed to reverse it. Alia did not accept suggestions that would have permitted competition between economic units and the development of markets. He was equally adamant in opposing the legalization of private property, insisting that the APL would make no concession on such a capital issue.[32]

Exercising a tight grip over society at a time when Communist parties in other East European countries were relaxing their control, the APL desperately attempted to discourage the population from coveting the democratic reforms under way in the Soviet bloc. It linked Eastern Europe's internal problems with what it termed "revisionist" policies and betrayal of socialism. In a speech to the Eighth Plenum of the APL Central Committee in September 1989, Alia called for greater vigilance against the dangers of revisionism and the restoration of capitalism in Albania, and added:

> We have not opened up. We do not open up or close up. Nor do we make changes under anyone else's influence. ... [W]e will never retreat, no matter what the circumstances may be, in certain directions. We will never permit the weakening of the common socialist property. We will never permit that the way be opened to the return to private property and capitalist exploitation. We will never permit the weakening of the people's authority, the weakening of the dictatorship of the proletariat, in the same way that we have never and will never share power with any antipopular force. *We will never relinquish and will never permit the weakening of the leadership role of our Marxist-Leninist party for the sake of the so-called pluralism dished out by the bourgeoisie.*[33]

The official media insisted that the Communists in Albania enjoyed legitimacy, because they had come to power on their own, in contrast to the Communists in the Warsaw Pact countries, who were installed in power by the Soviet Red Army. Vangjel Moisiu, in an article deploring the demise of Communism in

Eastern Europe, argued that political pluralism and socialism were incompatible, adding that the sanctioning of opposition parties would contradict "the basic principles of socialism and Marxist-Leninist theory."[34]

Alia not only rejected the notion of giving up the APL's constitutionally guaranteed monopoly on power but also failed to change the most damaging aspects of Hoxha's policy, which were leading the country into deep political and economic turmoil. He did not reject the self-reliance policy, insisting that, "the principle of self-reliance has been and remains the foundation of our entire development."[35] The honoring of constitutional prohibitions on accepting foreign aid and investments had a disastrous effect on economic performance. The economy continued to be plagued by overcentralization, persistent interference from the center, tremendous waste of resources, distorted prices, inefficient enterprises, widespread corruption, and rampant shortages of basic goods. Similarly, there was no appreciable improvement in the negative human rights situation, which had given the country a bad image abroad. The regime continued to insulate the population from "alien" influences through severe restrictions on travel abroad by Albanians as well as by limiting the number of foreigners allowed to visit Albania. Political and economic interactions with most other countries were kept at a minimum, although a slight expansion of ties with East European countries and the West was evident.

Anemic Pressure

The deepening crisis was associated with the gradual defection of significant sectors of society. The youth were perhaps most restive, showing signs of growing alienation with the regime's strict norms. Officials complained that the youth had become dangerously susceptible to "alien" influences. Growing access to foreign radio and television broadcasts and increased contacts with foreign tourists were blamed as many youths fell victim to "subversive foreign propaganda," violating "socialist" norms of conduct.[36] Young Albanians expressed a preference for Western life styles, art, literature, music and fashion. Increasing numbers of college graduates refused to accept assignments in the countryside.[37] Moreover, there were increased manifestations of pacifism, religious belief, hooliganism, theft, and crime.

Albanian authorities displayed a lack of imagination and foresight in addressing the concerns of the youth. To the consternation of many young people, party ideologues relied on strict administrative measures and called for an intensification of the struggle against what it called bourgeois-revisionist ideology and foreign ideological aggression directed against socialist Albania.[38] But other senior officials acknowledged that the Union of Working Youth, one of the most important Communist front organizations, had become largely irrelevant, as its members could not freely express their views. Discussions of important political issues and international developments continued to be considered "almost sacrilegious."[39] Nevertheless, the authorities continued with their strict approach. Students were publicly denounced for wearing jeans, listening to rock music, and having long hair.[40] In an article published in June 1990, the newly appointed leader of the youth organization, Lisen Bashkurti, wrote that one of the main objectives of the youth organization was to convince its members of the superiority of socialism over other systems:

> Today, the task of consolidating convictions about our social order is more closely tied than ever to developments and situations in the world around us, which have led the anger of the bourgeoisie and reaction against socialism to assume unprecedented proportions. For this reason, we must oppose the anti-socialist fury that rages in the world and that cannot fail to be felt and reflected in forms of pressure against our country and its people with work to consolidate enduring convictions about the effectiveness of the socialist order in the history of our people.[41]

By the late 1980s, the authorities were confronted with widespread dissatisfaction among the workers. The abolishment of private property, lack of material incentives, and poor working conditions had destroyed morale, which was reflected most dramatically by a drastic decline in labor productivity and widespread absenteeism. While labor strikes were illegal, workers expressed their dissatisfaction by engaging in massive thefts and misappropriation of state property. By 1990, the so-called "workers' state" was obviously unable to meet the most basic needs of the working class in whose name the Communists claimed to rule. Economic decline was rapidly eroding the authority of the once all-powerful APL.

Equally ominous for the APL was the creeping defection of the intellectuals, who for decades had been in the forefront of the Party propaganda campaign. By autumn 1989, there were signs that some intellectuals were metamorphosing from loyal subjects of the party into semi-independent thinkers. This gradual but unmistakable transformation was reflected in subtle resistance to party controls, propaganda, and campaigns. Taking advantage of the easing of Communist political controls over cultural and intellectual life in the wake of Hoxha's death, some intellectuals began to engage in lively debates and to advocate greater freedom of expression. Ismail Kadare, the country's best-known writer and the only one with an international reputation, played an important role in galvanizing support for democratic changes.

A very talented writer, Kadare had an ambivalent relationship with the Communist regime.[42] His works, translated into more than thirty languages, evinced both praise and criticism of Hoxha's dictatorship. Although Kadare had problems with the regime and some of his writings were banned, he was the only Albanian writer permitted to travel abroad regularly. Taking advantage of his popularity at home and his international reputation, Kadare spoke out on the necessity of immediate changes in the fields of human rights and cultural affairs, but was careful not to call for political reforms. He skillfully exploited the publication of a book by Neshat Tozaj to denounce the flagrant violation of human rights by the secret police, the Sigurimi.

A member of the APL, Tozaj had worked for many years for the Sigurimi, gaining firsthand knowledge of the secret police's brutality and absolute power. In 1981, he reportedly wrote a letter to Hoxha informing the dictator of "antiparty" activities in the Ministry of Internal Affairs. In his novel *Thikat* (Knives), Tozaj tells the story of how police agents falsified evidence and arrested and imprisoned innocent people.[43] The novel could not be considered a dissident book, since it did not contain even veiled criticism against the APL. Indeed, it portrayed the party, which eventually uncovered the secret police's misdeeds, as savior. Moreover, there were striking similarities between *Thikat* and Hoxha's book *The Titoists*, in which the dictator credited the Party for unmasking the hideous crimes committed by Prime Minister Mehmet Shehu and the former ministers of internal affairs.[44] Nevertheless, the publication of Tozaj's novel, which received considerable publicity in the West, was undoubtedly a significant event. The fact alone that human rights violations, although ostensibly committed by "the enemies of the Party," were publicly being denounced was remarkable given the state of affairs in Albania at the time.[45]

Kadare praised Tozaj's book, saying that only by admitting and correcting past mistakes would Albania be able to forge ahead. Throwing his weight behind Tozaj in case the latter came under attack from Party hard-liners, Kadare deplored the fact that Albanian writers in the past had paid little attention to violations of law and human rights.[46] At a literary conference in November 1989, Kadare went even further, this time publicly criticizing the government's interference in literature. In a statement that must have earned him the wrath of powerful *apparatchiks*, Kadare said that no government had the power to grant or deny the writer his freedom to create. He was careful, however, to avoid criticizing Alia and to leave the impression that he was a strong supporter of the president's efforts to carry out reforms.[47] Although the dictatorial nature of the regime prevented the creation of an organized opposition, Kadare's increasingly vocal statements against the entrenched cultural bureaucracy and human rights violations appear to have encouraged the growing independence of thought among intellectuals.

The intellectuals also seem to have been influenced by developments in Kosova. There, ethnic Albanian intellectuals were leading the struggle to preserve Kosova's autonomy and to establish a pluralist democracy. With the accession to power of Serbia's strongman Slobodan Milošević in 1986, ethnic Albanians gradually lost their political autonomy and became the object of an unprecedentedly repressive policy. Belgrade's policy reduced the Albanian majority in Kosova to a position of subordination, and during 1988-1990 there were violent demonstrations in the province. Under such inauspicious conditions, Kosova witnessed the emergence of several noncommunist political parties, which in addition to advocating full autonomy and republic status for Kosova, demanded the establishment of a multiparty system and a market economy—both anathema to Alia's regime. The fact that the ethnic Albanians in Kosova, under Serbian military occupation, were demanding political pluralism could not but encourage similar demands by their brethren in Tiranë.

Albania and the East European Revolution

The Albanians had followed with great concern economic and political changes in the Soviet Union and Eastern Europe in the wake of Mikhail Gorbachev's rise to power, which coincided with Alia's own accession to power. Gorbachev and Alia had inherited similar problems: a political system insensitive to the population's needs and demands, and a declining economy. The Albanian leader, however, turned out to be less daring than his Soviet counterpart in efforts to reinvigorate his society. Although many hoped he would become Albania's Gorbachev, Alia did not act as a decisive and determined leader.

Despite Albania's near total lack of contact with the Soviet Union, the Albanian ruling elite perceived Gorbachev's reforms as potentially destabilizing to their own regime. Albanian officials, including Alia, and state-controlled media described Gorbachev as a disciple of former Soviet leader Nikita S. Khrushchev, and his *perestroika* as a revisionist policy that would lead to the total restoration of capitalism in the Soviet Union. But perhaps of more concern to the Albanian regime was Gorbachev's *glasnost'* policy, which coincided with increasing internal demands in Albania for an end to taboos and for a more objective media treatment of both domestic and foreign developments. In March 1989, the Institute for Marxist-Leninist Studies, headed by Hoxha's widow, Nexhmije, sponsored a conference devoted to Soviet reforms. Foto Çami, reputedly the most liberal member of the APL Politburo, accused Gorbachev of having launched a general onslaught against socialism. He argued that Soviet revisionist reforms were adversely affecting the implementation of reforms in Albania by strengthening conservative forces who insisted that change would eventually lead to the decline of the APL's leading role in society.[48] A party theoretician, Ismail Lleshi, denounced the emerging political pluralism in the Soviet Union, claiming that the toleration of pluralist ideas was incompatible with socialist ideology.[49]

The 1989 revolution in Eastern Europe did not take the Albanian regime or population by surprise. Despite the country's isolation, Albanians were well informed about developments in the region. The APL's ability to control information was seriously undermined as many Albanians followed developments in Eastern Europe by tuning in to foreign radio broadcasts, particularly the Voice of America's Albanian language programs, and to Italian and Yugoslav television.

Alia explained the collapse of Communism in Eastern Europe in 1989 as a result of the ruling elites having deviated from Marxism-Leninism. Insisting that the Communist regime enjoyed widespread popular support, Alia urged Albanians to draw lessons from the dangers of following the example of the Soviet bloc and allowing the restoration of capitalism.[50] As late as his speech to the Communist-controlled Trade Unions Council on 11 December 1989, on the eve of the violent overthrow and execution of Romania's dictator Nicolae Ceauşescu, Alia confidently declared: "There are people abroad who ask: Will processes like those taking place in Eastern Europe also occur in Albania? We answer firmly and categorically: No, they will not occur in Albania." He insisted that Albania was not confronted by problems similar to those facing the other East European states: "The crisis that is sweeping the countries in the East is the crisis of a definite community, the crisis of what used to be called the socialist community, but not the crisis of socialism as a theory and practice. Consequently, the events taking place there have nothing to do with us."[51]

The overthrow of Ceauşescu's regime, however, sent shock waves throughout the Albanian ruling elite. The symbolism of the execution of Ceauşescu, whose brutal methods of rule paled in comparison with those used by Hoxha, could not escape either the Albanian *nomenklatura* or the population at large. Only a month before his demise, Ceauşescu had ruled out the possibility that Romania might follow the example of other East European countries, insisting that "the country under the leadership of the [Communist] party is determined to continue down the revolutionary path we have taken."[52] In contrast to its negative stand on previous developments in Poland, Hungary, East Germany, Czechoslovakia, and Bulgaria, the Albanian leadership was quick to distance itself from any identification with Ceauşescu. Moreover, to downplay the striking similarities between Europe's two most dictatorial regimes, Albania was among the first countries to recognize the post-Ceauşescu government and to denounce the late Romanian dictator. In a speech to the People's Assembly, Çami condemned Ceauşescu's "personal and dictatorial rule" and his "antipopular and antisocialist policies." Çami maintained an uncompromising position, however, insisting that developments in Eastern Europe would have no direct bearing on Albania.[53] Albanian ideologues continued to explain the events in Eastern Europe as results of the Communist Parties' having deviated from Marxism-Leninism.[54] In a nationwide New Year's address on 1 January 1990, Alia reminded his fellow citizens of the victories achieved under Communist rule and added that Albania would not deviate from its socialist path: "The events that have occurred recently in East Europe have inspired certain known anti-Albanian forces to resume the campaign of slander against our country. But as our people say, they cannot succeed in doing us harm. We Albanians are used to forging ahead through struggle and efforts, we are used to being on the watch so as not to be caught unaware. The Albanian has never submitted to any enemy, however big, cunning, or perfidious it might be. We have never allowed and will never allow anybody to dictate his laws and norms."[55]

However, following events in Romania, the Albanian government came under increased foreign and domestic pressures to initiate systemic changes long overdue. In early January 1990, an American human rights organization, the Minnesota Lawyers International Human Rights Committee, published a report documenting widespread human rights violations by the Albanian Communist regime. In the foreword to this widely publicized report, former U.S. Vice President Walter F. Mondale described Albania as "a bastion of international repression and self-imposed isolation." Emphasizing the human rights organization's objective of focusing the world's attention on Albania, Mondale wrote that "the Albanian people, too, deserve the human rights and fundamental freedoms guaranteed by international law."[56] Albanian émigrés, who throughout the 1980s had concentrated their activities against Yugoslavia and had toned down their campaign against Tiranë, organized demonstrations in several Western capitals to focus attention on Alia's regime. Leka Zogu, the pretender to the Albanian throne, called upon the Albanian people and the armed forces to overthrow the Communists.[57] Meanwhile, foreign media reported incidents of antigovernment demonstrations inside Albania.[58]

The Albanian authorities reacted in typical communist fashion, initiating a propaganda campaign aimed at convincing the domestic and foreign public that the reports of unrest were false. In an unprecedented move, senior Communist officials appeared on national television, charging that a conspiracy was afoot against "socialist Albania." Çami termed foreign press reports "anti-Albanian slander," claiming that they were orchestrated by the Yugoslav government to deflect attention away from demonstrations in Kosova.[59] Deputy Foreign Minister Muhamet Kapllani echoed Çami's statements. In an interview, Kapllani insisted that Albania "is a special case and has no connection whatsoever with events in East Europe." He said that foreign forces who wished to see similar changes in Albania had "made a serious mistake" and were "dreaming."[60] Meanwhile, the Albanian ambassador in Rome, Dashnor Dervishi, claiming that the situation in Albania was "normal," suggested that George Bush and Mikhail Gorbachev had agreed at their 1989 Malta summit meeting to destabilize Albania.[61] On 14 January 1990, antigovern-ment demonstrators in Shkodër tried to topple a statue of Stalin.[62] Predictably, the government took drastic measures against the anti-communist demonstrators, re-lying heavily on its traditional instruments of control—the secret police and the military. On 28 January, students organized a large, silent protest in the center of Tiranë, raising their hands in a victory sign.[63] Some observers predicted that Alia and his regime would meet the same fate as had their counterparts in Romania.[64]

Falling back on a tactic the Communists had often used in the past when the regime was under attack, the officially controlled media carried daily professions of support for Alia and the APL. Prominent personalities published letters and telegrams proclaiming their continuing faith in the Party. A letter written by historian Arben Puto was indicative of the type of material churned out by the official propaganda machine in an attempt to project an image of the APL as enjoying the unswerving support of the people. Denouncing the persistent foreign media reports of unrest in Shkodër as "anti-Albanian slander" and "flagrant interference in the affairs of a sovereign state," Puto wrote: "We ourselves have chosen our path, socialism. How correct has this choice been is shown by the unprecedented victories we have achieved, which have changed the face of the entire country. Therefore, we are determined to continue on this path."[65] The media published similar letters from and interviews with other prominent intellectuals, including Stefanaq Pollo, director of the Institute of History; Hasan Banja, director of the Institute of Economic Studies; and Hekuran Mara, vicepresident of the Academy of Sciences. They excoriated the foreign media for allegedly false reporting and claimed that foreign powers were interested in destabilizing Albania's Communist regime.[66]

The government also attempted, with little success, to mobilize its supporters in the Albanian diaspora. In an unprecedented move that reflected the regime's increased nervousness, Albania's mission to the United Nations in New York had its supporters place an advertisement in *The New York Times*. It contained excerpts from Alia's recent speeches denouncing the foreign media's "campaign of slanders and fabrications" against Albania. Alia was quoted as saying: "The people of Albania are masters of their own destiny, determined to march forward on the socialist road, to preserve their freedom and independence. ... Let the enemies of Albania bark as much as they can—the Albanian caravan will always continue to march forward. The anti-Albanian campaign that is being blown up by reactionary forces and some Western journalistic circles will end like a soap bubble, because it is based on lies and falsehoods."[67]

Incipient Moves Toward Reform

Although chilled by the winds of democratic change in other Communist countries and by increasing domestic opposition, at first the APL's old guard dug in its heels and refused to loosen its monopoly on political power. It was only after the fall of the Romanian regime that Alia began to contemplate initiating significant reforms; but by then, it was too late. Opposition to Com-munist rule had become widespread, and it was only a matter of time before the APL's monopoly on power would be openly challenged.

At a hastily convened Central Committee meeting in January 1990, Alia said Albania had to draw lessons from the demise of Communism in Eastern Europe. He argued that yielding to demands for radical economic reforms and allowing the establishment of other political parties would exacerbate economic and political problems and could even lead to the collapse of Albania's socialist system. Denying reports of growing anticommunist opposition and countering external criticism of Albania's human rights record, he said, "The calls that are being made abroad for changes in our country, for departure from the path that we are following, do not find support in our country and are not in tune with the opinion and will of the broad strata of the working people." Claiming that the domestic situation was "solid," he specifically linked his opposition to the creation of other political parties to a broad concern that a multiparty system would undermine Albania's independence and stability. In an attempt to enhance his regime's legitimacy and ensure political stability, Alia resorted to the old Communist tactic of putting heightened emphasis on nationalist themes and linking the APL and socialism with the preservation of the country's independence.

Simultaneously, however, Alia launched what he termed a democratization process, a cautious program of political and economic reforms.[68] The Central Committee plenum decided that henceforth Party organizations at the lower levels would hold open meetings, workers would play a greater role in the selection of managers, competition would be introduced in the election of cadres, and terms of elected officials would be limited. In the economic field, the plenum approved decentralization of decisionmaking, giving local authorities and enterprises greater autonomy. To stimulate agricultural production and deal with growing shortages in the cities, cooperatives would be allowed to sell their surplus products freely. For the first time since the Communist takeover in 1944, the authorities were acknowledging the important role that market forces played in regulating production.[69]

In April 1990, at the Tenth Plenum of the Central Committee, Alia announced further changes, formally approved by the People's Assembly in May, which were aimed at bettering Albania's abysmal human rights record. He pledged that the government would take steps to bring its human rights practices to the level of international standards. Albanians were guaranteed the right to travel abroad, the ban on "religious propaganda" was lifted, and the death penalty for defectors was abolished. The Ministry of Justice, which had been eliminated in the 1960s, during the cultural revolution, was reinstituted, and the government committed itself to the rule of law. Moreover, in a break with Hoxha's ideological legacy, Alia reversed the government's long-standing policy on several other major issues. He indicated that new laws would be promulgated to allow the government to accept foreign investments. Although only two months earlier Foreign Minister Reis Malile had reiterated Tiranë's opposition to the restoration of ties with the two superpowers and acceptance of foreign credits and investments,[70] Alia expressed his country's desire to normalize ties with Washington and Moscow. Albania also requested admission to the Conference on Security and Cooperation in Europe (CSCE), which it had shunned for fifteen years.[71] This was a clear departure from Hoxha's foreign policy, the pillar of which was rejection of all contacts with the two superpowers and with multilateral institutions. In early May, U.N. Secretary-General Javier Perez de Cuellar visited Tiranë, the first senior foreign dignitary to do so since China's Premier Zhou Enlai in 1967. De Cuellar criticized Albania's one-party system when speaking to reporters before meeting with Alia. The Albanian leader insisted that Tiranë would not allow the establishment of opposition parties, but reportedly promised that all political prisoners would be released and religious believers permitted to open churches and mosques.[72]

APL Relaxes Control Over Media

Anxious to give as much publicity as possible to de Cuellar's visit, the Albanian authorities had granted visas to many Western journalists, including, surprisingly, a Voice of America reporter, Laura Silber.[73] Alia became the first Albanian leader ever to give a live news conference. Officials from various ministries, journalists, economists, and writers were mobilized to explain Alia's policies to Western correspondents. In interviews with the Voice of America, Shaban Murati, a *Zëri i Popullit* correspondent, insisted that "the Party and the people" were united,[74] while Remzi Lani, the chief editor of the youth newspaper *Zëri i Rinisë*, argued that Albania had developed its own brand of socialism, adding, "We will not allow the implementation of Yugoslav or East European models in Albania."[75] The director of Radio Tiranë's International Service, Napoleon Roshi, offered unqualified support for Alia.[76] Gramoz Pashko, professor of economics at Tiranë University and a member of a commission advising the leadership on economic matters, said Alia was implementing significant economic reforms, but ruled out the possibility of the legalization of private property.[77] In a subsequent telephone interview with the Voice of America, Pashko said that it was an exaggeration to say that Albania was facing an economic crisis. But he added that the announced measures had to be followed by other, more significant reforms.[78] Fatos Nano, then an economist with the influential Institute of Marxist-Leninist Studies, made a similar argument, but did not, as he subsequently claimed, call for the introduction of a market economy.[79]

In addition to interviewing officials and experts who portrayed Alia's policies in the best possible light, foreign journalists for the first time were able to talk to opponents of the regime, who confirmed reports of antigovernment demonstrations. Through Voice of America broadcasts, the Albanians were able for the first time to hear public expressions of dissent against the regime from within the country. The Voice of America broadcast a series of interviews with workers, economists, and youths, who in contrast to Murati, Lani, Roshi, and Pashko, dismissed Alia's latest moves as cosmetic changes aimed at impressing the outside world and called for the legalization of political opposition parties. The response of a twenty-six-year-old worker was typical of government opponents: "Life in Albania is very difficult. All human rights are violated. People are not free to say what they believe. The standard of living has declined significantly and now is at the lowest level, especially in the village." Significantly, all were critical of the intellectuals, seeing them as regime apologists. An economist chastised the intellectuals for their failure to articulate demands for political pluralism, saying that they were products of "the ruling clique." He added: "In my opinion, the

Albanian economy cannot go even one step further, but will continue to decline, reaching the lowest possible level, if economic policy continues to be decided by a single party, as has been the case until now. In my opinion, [other] political parties must be created in Albania. Political pluralism ... will make economic development possible."[80] Although these persons had requested they not be identified for fear of retribution, they had agreed that the interviews would be aired in their own voices.

The regime's ability to control information was further undercut by Albania's decision in spring 1990 to establish telephone links with the outside world, including the United States. Taking advantage of their new-found freedom to have contact with foreign journalists, and skillfully exploiting Alia's proreform rhetoric, many intellectuals appeared eager to grant telephone interviews to foreign media, particularly to the Voice of America's Albanian Service.

Concomitantly, the domestic media came to play an important role in criticizing official malfeasance and incompetence and in developing an awareness of the need for reforms. Some newspapers, including the APL's organ, *Zëri i Popullit*, began a remarkable airing of views and concerns on different issues. In the forefront of this campaign were some of the nation's most prominent intellectuals, including Kadare.[81] They publicly advocated greater openness and emerged as the strongest proponents of Alia's so-called democratization process. *Zëri i Popullit* published an article by Ylli Popa, a prominent cardiologist who had been Hoxha's personal doctor. Arguing that Albania had already wasted precious time, Popa lauded Alia's reforms but warned that genuine democratization could not be carried out through partial measures and "old thinking." He said that the measures taken recently would succeed only if people could freely speak their minds.[82]

Writing in the same newspaper, Hamit Beqja, Albania's leading sociologist and an advocate of a more lenient approach toward youth than that adopted by the regime, emphasized that because of their past political experience the Albanians had only a rudimentary understanding of democracy. Recognizing the need to cultivate what he termed the democracy of thinking and free debate, Beqja complained that citizens lacked civil and individual courage to freely air their views. He sharply criticized the media for failing to provide timely and comprehensive information, adding that true democracy "cannot be attained without a sufficient and satisfactory degree of information on all matters, domestic and international, [and] without broad and comprehensive publicity." Beqja concluded his article by suggesting that in the absence of an environment conducive to a free and constructive dialogue, Albania could not "break the conservative and bureaucratic shackles."[83]

In a long interview with the literary weekly *Drita* in May 1990, Sali Berisha, also a prominent cardiologist who seven months later would establish Albania's first opposition party since World War II, said that the prevention of the expression of diverse opinions and the lack of contact with the outside world had caused serious damage to Albania's development. Intellectuals, he said, were still reluctant to engage in a free debate because of the personal risks involved. In a veiled attack against Alia's chief foreign policy advisor, Sofokli Lazri, head of the Institute of International Affairs and reportedly an opponent of the expansion of ties with the West, Berisha stressed that continued isolation would only protect the privileges that certain people in power enjoyed, while it would have serious repercussions for the country as a whole. He deplored the fact that unqualified people occupied leading positions in many sectors of society. Such people, he said, "are not interested in encouraging a free and lively debate, but in extinguishing it." In a clear attack on the officially held view, Berisha urged the authorities to tolerate the expression of diverse opinions.[84]

Although still inhibited by the ignominious legacy of the Communist literary inquisitions, established intellectuals were beginning to see a chance to influence the APL leadership toward more tolerance of independent thinking. Arguably, such articles and interviews, which were careful to avoid challenging Alia, did not directly endanger the regime. Nonetheless, their publication corroded political authority and fostered social attitudes that ultimately undermined Communist legitimacy and eroded the APL's capacity to govern the country. While the leadership expressed concern regarding the growing dissipation of the APL's ideological control, it failed to take drastic measures to increase state and Party control over the media.

Alia's Survival Strategy

By taking measures to redress some of the government's most severe transgressions and expanding foreign relations, Alia evidently hoped to ensure the population's acquiescence to continued Communist rule as well as to improve his regime's image abroad, thus paving the way for Albania's reintegration into the international community. Apparently, he believed he could initiate a well coordinated process of gradual change, one that would not only arrest the declining authority of the ruling APL but would result in the Party's retaining power. In view of developments in other East European countries, Alia's new policies did not go far enough and indeed amounted to little more than a mild relaxation of the authoritarian regime. But in the context of Albania, with its long self-imposed isolation and no conspicuous signs of active or organized opposition, these were significant changes. Indeed, the announced measures were enthusiastically welcomed by the Albanian people, and Alia's popularity soared. In spring 1990, anticommunist demonstrators in Kavajë,[85] Shkodër, and other cities reportedly chanted pro-Alia slogans, reflecting the widespread perception that he was genuinely interested in carrying out reforms but that hard-liners, including Hoxha's widow, Nexhmije, were preventing him. Foreign journalists who visited Albania at the time reported that Alia was enjoying considerable popular support because he had toned down the APL's harsh ideological rhetoric, raising widespread hopes that finally Albania was on the way to rejoining Europe.[86]

But Alia botched the chance to take a dramatic leap toward instituting genuine democratic reforms and adopting the radical economic measures that Albania's truly untenable situation required. The regime's contradictory behavior caused many people to suspect that the recent measures were intended solely to impress foreigners. It also undermined Albania's efforts to win acceptance as a full member of the international community. The Communist bureaucracy remained very strong. There were thousands of bureaucrats, at all levels of society, who had no interest in reforms and strongly resisted them. While encouraging greater freedom of expression, the authorities were willing to tolerate the discussion of issues only so long as the debate took place in the Communist-controlled media—and therefore under party supervision—and did not question the APL's supremacy. Measures allowing travel abroad were implemented slowly and on a selective basis. Notwithstanding the government pledge to respect human rights and issue passports to all Albanians wanting to travel abroad, citizens trying to flee the country were shot and killed by border guards or severely punished. Such actions embarrassed Tiranë and added ammunition to those in the West who argued for increased pressure on the only remaining bastion of Stalinism in Europe.

Foreign Pressures

Alia's new realism in foreign policy met with a lukewarm international reception. His contention that Albania was different from other East European countries and that Albanian Communists enjoyed full popular support did not sound convincing to most Westerners. Moreover, the downfall of Communism in Eastern Europe and the end of the Cold War had resulted in the decline of Western strategic interests in Albania. Socialist Albania had missed its window of opportunity by rejecting diplomatic overtures from the West in the 1970s and the early 1980s and by being the one and only European state to boycott the "Helsinki process" of ongoing multilateral debate on Europe's future, which began with the singing of the Helsinki Final Act in 1975. Although the Western alliance had been willing to bail out Albania economically during the Cold War, in 1990 it was unwilling to contribute to the survival of Europe's most corrupt and repressive Communist regime, whose policies were having disastrous effects on the Albanian nation. Therefore, while the West welcomed Albania's steps to improve the state of human rights, and as an incentive, granted it observer status at the Copenhagen meeting of the CSCE in June 1990, the Albanian government was told in unequivocal terms that it had a long way to go before Albania could become a full member of the international community. Western governments' determination to maintain a tough stand on political pluralism and human rights was a watershed event and a very important contributing factor to the eventual fall of Albania's Communist regime.

The United States responded to Alia's overtures by expressing willingness to open a dialogue, but noted that it continued to regard Albania as a repressive regime.[87] In testimony before the Senate Foreign Relations Committee, Secretary of State James Baker said that the United States would link the restoration of ties to Albania's acceptance of political pluralism and movement toward a market economy. The U.S. Commission on Security and Cooperation in Europe, also known as the Helsinki Commission, bluntly laid out the conditions that Albania had to meet if it wanted to join the community of nations. In a statement in May 1990, Senator Dennis DeConcini and Representative Steny H. Hoyer, Chairman and Co-Chairman of the U.S. Helsinki Commission, said:

> As a participant in the Helsinki process, Albania will have to commit itself to respect the rights of its citizens to freedom of expression, association, and assembly, as well as freedom of movement. It will undertake specific commitments regarding the protection of the rights of members of national or ethnic minorities, as well as regarding freedom of religion, conscience or belief. It will agree to facilitate human contacts, including the reunification of divided families, as well as to encourage a free flow of information. *It will accept the concepts of political pluralism and the rule of law, and to that end move toward free elections and undertake necessary legal reforms.*[88]

Alia received a similar, direct message from Congressman Tom Lantos, who in May 1990 became the first U.S. official to visit Albania in more than four decades. In an interview with the Voice of America after his visit to Tiranë, Rep. Lantos said:

> We expect Albania to implement the same reforms as other Eastern European countries and permit the development of political opposition. It is not credible to claim, as Albanian officials do, that there is no political opposition in their country. Of course opposition exists, but it is afraid to come out openly. A multiparty system should be created in Albania, the press should be free, and the Albanians should enjoy freedom of speech, religion, and assembly, and freedom to travel abroad. *These are necessary changes if Albania wants to be included in the Helsinki process.*[89]

Other Western countries also predicated an improvement in their relations with Albania on its progress toward political pluralism, full respect for human rights, and the implementation of reforms that would eventually lead to the creation of a market economy.

Tiranë's ideological commitment, however, left little room for pragmatism or compromise. At the Copenhagen CSCE meeting in June 1990, Albanian Ambassador Petrit Bushati could not hide his anxiety that the West had made the strengthening of ties dependent on major changes in the regime's policies.

Echoing Alia's stand on opposition parties, Bushati said that Albania had no intention of permitting the creation of opposition parties.[90] A member of the Albanian delegation, Sazan Bejo, told journalists that a multiparty system in Albania was unnecessary since "everyone in Albania supports the government and there is no opposition."[91] Bejo added: "If there is full approval by the people for the government, there is no need to artificially create opposition to government."[92] The authorities also launched a media campaign to convince domestic opinion to reject political pluralism.[93]

But by this time, it was becoming increasingly clear that despite its prolonged and almost total isolation from the rest of Europe, Albania could not escape the process that had precipitated the decay of communism in other East European countries. The disastrous failure of the ruling party's political and economic policies, combined with increased international pressure and the emergence of noncommunist political parties in the Serb military-occupied Kosova, was encouraging the defection of significant sectors of the populace.

Notes

1. *Rilindja Demokratike*, 18 September 1993, p. 2. See also Mario I. Blejer, Mauro Mecagni, Ratna Sahay, Richard Hides, Barry Johnston, Piroska Nagy, and Roy Pepper, *Albania: From Isolation Toward Reform* (Washington, DC: The International Monetary Fund, 1992), p. 20; and the Institute of Statistics, *Statistika* (Tiranë), no. 8 (March 1995), p. 14.

2. Blejer et al., *Albania*, p 19.

3. *Lajmi i Ditës*, 26 February 1994, p. 8.

4. United Nations Development Program, *Human Development Report: Albania 1995.* (Tiranë, 1995), p. 28.

5. See Edvin Morava, "What Legal Name Should We Give to Dramatic Abortions?" *Sindikalisti*, 14 November 1993, p. 1. In a highly polemical article, writer Aurel Plasari called abortion a crime against the nation. He accused the industrialized countries, particularly the United States, of linking foreign assistance to control of population growth. He also accused the International Monetary Fund of attempting to control Albania's population growth. Aurel Plasari, "How Can Crime Against the Nation Begin in Albania?" *Republika*, 26 May 1994, p. 3. For a critique of Plasari's stand, see articles by Fjodor Kallajxhiu and Sami Milloshi in, respectively, *Republika*, 19 June 1994, p. 3 and *Rilindja Demokratike*, 26 June 1994, p. 3.

6. *Rilindja Demokratike*, 8 December 1995, p. 2.

7. *Koha Jonë*, 18 October 1995, p. 5.

8. Directory of Statistics, *Statistical Yearbook of Albania 1991* (Tiranë, 1991), p. 71.

9. See interview with President Berisha in *NRC Handelsblad* (Rotterdam), 7 August 1993, p. 7, translated in Foreign Broadcasting Information Service, *Daily Report: East Europe* (hereafter FBIS-EEU) 93-155, 13 August 1993, p. 5.

10. Aleksandër Milo, "The Greek Minority in Albania: Facts and Figures," *Lajmi i Ditës*, 4 October 1994, p. 1; and Arqile Bërxholli, Sejfi Protopapa, and Kristaq Prifti, "The Greek Minority in the Albanian Republic: A Demographic Study," *Nationalities Papers* 22, no. 2 (1994), pp. 427-434.

11. *Statistika*, no. 1 (May 1993), pp. 2-3.

12. Ibid., p. 2.

13. *Borba* (Belgrade), 27 January 1992, p. 8.

14. *Nova Makedonija* (Skopje), 11 January 1995, p. 2, translated in FBIS-EEU 95-011, 18 January 1995, pp. 55-56.

15. Nail Draga, *Shqiptarët në Mal të Zi* [Albanians in Montenegro] (Ulqin, Montenegro: Art Club, 1994), p. 16.

16. Kosova Information Center, *Informatori ditor* (Prishtinë), no. 789, 19 July 1994, p. 4.

17. Tefik Basha, "Some Demographic Characteristics of the Albanians in Macedonia," *Flaka e Vëllazërimit* (Skopje), 30 September 1994, p. 12.

18. Shtjefën Gjeçovi, *The Code of Lekë Dukagjini* (New York: Gjonlekaj Publishing Company, 1989), translated from Albanian by Leonard Fox. See also Margaret Hasluck, *The Unwritten Law in Albania* (Cambridge: Cambridge University Press, 1954).

19. See Arshi Pipa, *The Politics of Language in Socialist Albania* (Boulder: East European Monographs, distributed by Columbia University Press, 1989).

20. On Noli's political career, see Bernd J. Fischer, "Fan Noli and the Albanian Revolutions of 1924," *East European Quarterly* 22, no. 2 (June 1988), pp. 147-158; Robert Austin, "Fan Noli, Albania and the Soviet Union," *East European Quarterly* 30, no. 2 (Summer 1996), pp. 153-169; and Nikolaos A. Stavrou, "Albanian Communism and the 'Red Bishop,'" *Mediterranean Quarterly* 7, no. 2 (Spring 1996), pp. 32-59.

21. See Stavro Skendi, *The Political Evolution of Albania 1912-1944* (New York: Mid-European Studies Center, 1954); Arben Puto, *Demokracia e rrethuar* [The Besieged Democracy] (Tiranë: "8 Nëntori," 1990); and Bernd Jürgen Fischer, *King Zog and the Struggle for Stability in Albania* (Boulder: East European Monographs, distributed by Columbia University Press, 1984).

22. For background information, see Nicholas C. Pano, *The People's Republic of Albania* (Baltimore: Johns Hopkins University Press, 1968); Anton Logoreci, *The Albanians: Europe's Forgotten Survivors* (London: Victor Gollancz, 1977); Peter R. Prifti, *Socialist Albania Since 1944: Domestic and Foreign Developments* (Cambridge, MA: MIT Press, 1978); and Arshi Pipa, *Albanian Stalinism: Ideo-Political Aspects* (Boulder and New York: East European Monographs, distributed by Columbia University Press, 1990).

23. Pano, *The People's Republic of Albania*, pp. 58-62; and Prifti, *Socialist Albania Since 1944*, pp. 52-55.

24. William E. Griffith, *Albania and the Sino-Soviet Rift* (Cambridge, MA: MIT Press, 1963); and Harry Hamm, *Albania: China's Beachhead in Europe* (New York: Praeger, 1963).

25. Elez Biberaj, *Albania and China: A Study of an Unequal Alliance* (Boulder: Westview, 1986).

26. See Todi Lubonja, *Nën peshën e dhunës* [Under the Weight of Violence] (Tiranë: Progresi, 1993). A member of the Central Committee and Director of Radio and TV, Lubonja was among the first victims of the 1970s purges. Together with Fadil Paçrami, he was accused of advocating cultural liberalization. They were sentenced to long prison terms and their families were sent into internal exile.

27. There was widespread speculation disputing the official version that Shehu had committed suicide. Some, including his personal guards, have alleged that Hoxha had Shehu killed. Shehu's sons, however, insisted that Shehu in fact was driven by Hoxha to

commit suicide. See Bashkim Shehu, *Vjeshta e Ankthit* [The Nightmare Autumn] (Tiranë: Albinform, 1993).

28. Elez Biberaj, *Albania: A Socialist Maverick* (Boulder: Westview, 1990), pp. 33-38.

29. Per Sandström and Örjan Sjöberg, "Albanian Economic Performance: Stagnation in the 1980s," *Soviet Studies* 43, no. 5 (1991), pp. 931-947.

30. *Republika*, 5 December 1993, p. 2.

31. Ismail Kadare, *Nga një dhjetor në tjetrin* [From One December to Another] (Paris: Fayard, 1991), p. 35.

32. Ramiz Alia, *Fjalime e biseda* [Speeches and Conversations], vol. 4 (Tiranë: "8 Nëntori," 1988), p. 377.

33. *Zëri i Popullit*, 29 September 1989, p. 2. Emphasis added.

34. Vangjel Moisiu, "What Is This Pluralism Offered by the Bourgeoisie?" *Zëri i Popullit*, 4 October 1989, pp. 3-4. Commenting on events in Poland and Hungary, Agim Popa, an official in the APL Central Committee apparatus, argued that the sanctioning of political pluralism in those countries marked the defeat of revisionism and not of socialism. "The Albanian Party of Labor has made it quite clear, not only now, but ever since the events that followed the infamous Twentieth CPSU Congress, that the anti-Marxist course adopted by the modern revisionists could not fail to lead to the restoration of capitalism and that this capitalist course would result in crises, disillusionment, and severe failures. The whole world is now a witness to this." Agim Popa, "The Logical End of the Revisionist Course," *Zëri i Popullit*, 26 August 1989, p. 4. See also Arben Karapici, "Fruit of the Ideology of Counterrevolutionary Reformism," *Zëri i Popullit,* 11 October 1989, p. 4; Shaban Murati, "It Is Not Communism, but a Distortion of It, That Has Failed in Eastern Countries," *Zëri i Popullit*, 28 October 1989, pp. 3-4; and Adem Mezini, "Revisionist Treachery Cannot Sap the Strength of the Ideas of the October Revolution," *Zëri i Popullit*, 7 November 1989, p. 4.

35. *Zëri i Popullit*, 29 September 1989, p. 1.

36. Hamit Beqja, "Current Problems of Manners in Society," *Rruga e Partisë* 36, no. 11 (November 1989), pp. 27-36.

37. Halil Lalaj, "A Decision on the Way to Resolution: How to Work with Cadres Returning from and Assigned to the Northeast Zones," *Zëri i Popullit*, 4 January 1989, p. 4.

38. Lisen Bashkurti, "Raising the Standards of Conduct and of Young People's Behavior in Society: the Focus of the Youth Organization's Attention," *Rruga e Partisë* 35, no. 9 (September 1988), pp. 57-63.

39. See the speech by Mehmet Elezi, then first secretary of the Albanian Union of Working Youth, in *Zëri i Rinisë*, 28 May 1988, pp. 1 and 3-4. See also Elezi's article "Educational Work with the Youth Cannot Be Developed Based on Some Empirical Findings, It Requires Arguments and Creativity," *Rruga e Partisë* 36, no. 10 (October 1989), pp. 39-47; and Lisen Bashkurti, "The Improvement of Educational Work with the Youth Demands the Further Increase of the Organization's Initiative and Activity," *Rruga e Partisë* 37, no. 2 (February 1990), pp. 48-57. Elezi was succeeded by Bashkurti as leader of the youth organization.

40. Rrapo Zguri, "Someone Asks: 'How Should We Dress, How Should We Dance, How Should We Sing...'?!" *Rruga e Partisë* 37, no. 6 (June 1990), pp. 85-89.

41. Lisen Bashkurti, "A Movement Matching Young People's Tasks to the Demands of the Times," *Zëri i Popullit*, 2 June 1990, pp. 1-2.

42. For a critical review of Kadare's works and relationship with the Hoxha regime see Noel Malcolm, "In the Palace of Nightmares," *New York Review of Books,* XLIV, no. 14 (6 November 1997), pp. 21-24.

43. Neshat Tozaj, *Thikat* [Knives] (Tiranë: "Naim Frashëri," 1989).

44. Enver Hoxha, *The Titoists* (Tiranë: "8 Nëntori," 1982). An advisor to Alia has described Tozaj as "an exemplary Sigurimi worker and a very vigilant individual." See Sofokli Lazri, "The Bitter Fruits of Megalomania," *Zëri i Popullit,* 19 February 1991, p. 3.

45. For Tozaj's version of developments before pluralism, see his book *Pse flas...* [Why Do I Speak Out...] (Tiranë: The Publishing House of the Writers' League, 1993). Tozaj is among the very few former Communists who have publicly apologized for their past actions. He has confessed his role in trials of persons accused of antigovernment activities. After the sanctioning of political pluralism in December 1990, Tozaj played an important role in denouncing the abuses of the Communist regime. His critics claim that he was acting on orders from Alia, who wanted to infiltrate his own people into the emerging opposition parties. The writer's brother, Sihat Tozaj, held the influential post of secretary of the presidium of the People's Assembly before the 31 March 1991 elections. Democratic Party leaders, however, held Tozaj at arm's length, and after assuming power did not offer him a government position. Soon after the March 1992 elections, he went on the offensive, becoming an outspoken critic of the government's domestic and foreign policies. By 1994, Tozaj had come full circle, supporting the former Communists and regularly publishing articles in *Zëri i Popullit.*

46. Ismail Kadare, "'Knives': An Important Novel in the Albanian Literature," *Drita,* 15 October 1989, p. 11.

47. Ismail Kadare, "Literature and Today's Society," *Drita,* 19 November 1989, pp. 5-6.

48. *Zëri i Popullit,* 17 March 1989, pp. 1-3.

49. Ismail Lleshi, *"Glasnost',* Ideological Pluralism: The Further Degeneration of State Life in the Soviet Union," *Studime Politiko Shoqërore* 16, no. 1 (1989), p. 44.

50. Alia's analysis of the East European revolution was in line with Tiranë's evaluation of earlier developments in the region, including unrest among workers in Poland in early 1981, and in China after Mao's death. See Paskal Milo, "Comrade Enver Hoxha: The Founder of the Foreign Policy of Our Party and of Our Socialist State," *Studime Historike* 22, no. 3 (1985), pp. 39-56; Spiro Dede, *The Counter-Revolution Within the Counter-Revolution* (Tiranë: "8 Nëntori," 1983); Vangjel Moisiu, *Thellimi i kursit revizionist në BS* [The Deepening of the Revisionist Line in the S.U.] (Tiranë: "8 Nëntori," 1988); Raqi Madhi, *Shtrembërimi i teorisë marksiste-leniniste për socializmin nga PK e Kinës* [The Distortion of the Marxist-Leninist Theory on Socialism by the C.P. of China] (Tiranë: "8 Nëntori," 1983); Fatos Nano, *Politika ekonomike e Kinës për t'u bërë superfuqi* [China's Economic Policy to Become a Superpower] (Tiranë: "8 Nëntori," 1984); and Petro Ciruna, *Partitë revizioniste, parti borgjeze* [Revisionist Parties, Bourgeois Parties] (Tiranë: "8 Nëntori," 1981).

51. Tiranë Domestic Service in Albanian, 1430 GMT, 12 December 1989, translated in FBIS-EEU 89-239, 14 December 1989, pp. 1-4.

52. Ceauşescu had made these comments at the Fourteenth Congress of the Romanian Communist Party. See U.S. Commission on Security and Cooperation in Europe, *Human Rights and Democratization in Romania* (Washington, DC) June 1994, p. 3; and Vladimir Tismaneanu, *Reinventing Politics: Eastern Europe from Stalin to Havel* (New York: The

Free Press, 1992), pp. 230-231.

53. ATA in English, 0916 GMT, 29 December 1989, in FBIS-EEU 90-003, 4 January 1990, pp. 4-5.

54. See Genc Kondi, "The Inexorable Pace of the East," *Bashkimi*, 16 December 1989, pp. 3-4; and Sokol Gjoka, "The Year's Reformist Wave," *Zëri i Popullit*, 31 December 1989, p. 6.

55. ATA in English, 0730 GMT, 1 January 1990, in FBIS-EEU 90-002, 3 January 1990, p. 1.

56. Minnesota Lawyers International Human Rights Committee, *Human Rights in the People's Socialist Republic of Albania* (Minneapolis, Minnesota, January 1990). In an apparent response to the report, Minister of Internal Affairs Simon Stefani dismissed reports of large numbers of political prisoners. Stefani said only 83 people were serving prison terms for seeking to overthrow the government by force. See *Zëri i Popullit*, 22 February 1990, p. 1.

57. *Wall Street Journal*, 5 January 1990, p. A4; Simon Haydon, "Ousted Albanian King Ready to Lead Revolt," *Washington Times*, 24 January 1990, p. A7; and Peter Honey, "Half-century from Home: Leka I Cherishes Hope of Return to Albania," *Sun* (Baltimore), 1 February 1990, p. 13.

58. Tim Witcher, "Unrest, Stiff Repression Detected Inside Albania," *Washington Times*, 29 December 1989, p. A6; and "Albania's Communists Feel Pressure of Change," *Chicago Tribune*, 9 January 1990, p. 4.

59. See ATA in English, 0935 GMT, 13 January 1990, in FBIS-EEU 90-011, 17 January 1990, p. 2.

60. Tiranë Domestic Service in Albanian 1900 GMT, 17 January 1990, translated in FBIS-EEU 89-230, 18 January 1990, pp. 3-4. Other senior Communist officials made similar statements. First secretary of the Albanian Union of Working Youth, Lisen Bashkurti, said "...our youth is extremely indignant at the campaign of slander and lies prepared and dished out by the Great-Serbian kitchens in Belgrade and Athens, as well as those of ex-monarchs and traffickers who have been overthrown once and for all time by the Albanian people." Tiranë Domestic Service in Albanian, 1430 GMT, 16 January 1990, translated in FBIS-EEU 90-012, 18 January 1990, p. 4.

61. ANSA (Rome) in English, 0950 GMT, 15 January 1990, in FBIS-EEU 90-011, 17 January 1990, p. 2.

62. Within days of the 14 January 1990 demonstration in Shkodër, the authorities took down the monument. For an eyewitness report of the first anticommunist demonstrations in Shkodër, see Pëllumb Sulo, "January 1990-April 1991: Shkodër As I Witnessed It," *Bashkimi*, 24 July 1991, p. 1.

63. Reports of the silent protest in Tiranë were confirmed only in May 1990, when a group of foreign reporters was granted visas to cover the U.N. Secretary General's visit. See Laura Silber, "Protests and Strikes Reported in Albania," *Financial Times*, 17 May 1990, p. 3. The organizers' hopes of attracting greater attention were dashed when leading intellectuals, including Kadare, refused to join them. See Kadare, *Nga një dhjetor në tjetrin*, pp. 19-21.

64. See Robin Wright and Doyle McManus, "Albania, Last of Stalinist States, May Fall Next," *Los Angles Times*, 10 January 1990, pp. A1, A8; and editorial "The Last Domino," *New York Times*, 26 January 1990, p. A30.

65. Arben Puto, "We Chose Socialism, We'll Build and Protect it Ourselves," *Bashkimi*, 17 January 1990, p. 2.

66. Tiranë Domestic Service in Albanian, 1430 GMT, 18 January 1990, and ATA in English, 0730 GMT, 18 January 1990, in FBIS-EEU 90-013, 19 January 1990, pp. 3-4. See also Skendër Buçpapaj and Rudolf Marku, "Poor [Yugoslav] Chauvinists, This Is How They End the Twentieth Century and Start the Twenty-first!" *Drita*, 21 January 1990, pp. 1-2; and Napoleon Roshi, "After the Noise About Pluralism and Press Freedom," *Zëri i Rinisë*, 21 February 1990, pp. 3-4.

67. The ad was signed by "The Albanian American Community" and "American Friends of Albania." *New York Times*, 9 February 1990, p. A31.

68. Ramiz Alia, *Për thellimin e revolucionarizimit të jetës së partisë dhe të vendit* [For the Further Revolutionization of the Life of the Party and the Country] (Tiranë: "8 Nëntori," 1990).

69. *Zëri i Popullit*, 4 February 1990, pp. 1-2.

70. Helsinki International Service in Finnish, 1600 GMT, 9 February 1990, translated in FBIS-EEU 90-030, 13 February 1990, pp. 1-2. Earlier, in an interview with a Japanese newspaper, Deputy Foreign Minister Muhamet Kapllani was quoted as saying: "We have no intention of restoring relations with [the superpowers]. Of late, the United States has offered to establish diplomatic relations with our nation. However, the United States has not recognized the democratic revolution by the late General Secretary Hoxha in the postwar years. Even if the United States wants to establish relations with Albania, I want to tell them that this cannot be determined by the will of a superpower alone." See *Yomiuri Shimbun* (Tokyo), 5 February 1990, p. 5, translated in FBIS-EEU 92-027, 8 February 1990, pp. 1-2.

71. Even at this late stage, Alia sounded an optimistic note on support for the APL and warned that "anyone, whether the external enemies or the internal enemies, the dregs of our society, who dares to lay a finger on the freedom of the homeland, on the people's state power and socialism will find himself confronting a people united firmly around the Party of Labor, a people determined to defend the victories achieved even with their life." Ramiz Alia, *Democratization of Socio-Economic Life Strengthens the Thinking and Action of the People* (Tiranë: "8 Nëntori," 1990), p. 33.

72. David Binder, "Albanian Leader Says the Country Will Be Democratized but Will Retain Socialism," *New York Times,* 14 May 1990, p. 6.

73. The Voice of America's Albanian-language broadcasts were closely monitored. Special bulletins with transcripts of Albania-related reports broadcast by the Voice of America were compiled by the directorate of Radio Tiranë's International Service and the Albanian Telegraphic Agency. They were distributed to Politburo and Central Committee members, senior government officials, regional party secretaries, and editors and journalists. Bulletins containing reports highly critical of the government were reportedly leaked and circulated among a wide number of readers. See Mary Battiata, "Refugees Say Western Radio Pierced Albania's Armor of Isolation," *Washington Post,* 12 July 1990, p. A25.

74. For Murati's interview, see the Directorate of Radio Tiranë's International Service, *Buletini i radiove të huaja në gjuhën shqipe* [The Bulletin of Albanian-Language Foreign Radios], no. 242, 9 May 1990. In 1994, Murati became Albania's first ambassador to Macedonia.

75. *Buletini i radiove të huaja në gjuhën shqipe*, no. 247, 11 May 1994.

76. Ibid., no. 262, 18 May 1990.

77. Ibid., no. 264, 21 May 1990.

78. Ibid., no. 320, 29 June 1990.

79. Nano's interview with the Voice of America appeared in the Albanian Telegraphic Agency [ATA], *Buletini i radiove të huaja në gjuhën shqipe*, no. 405, 3 August 1990, pp. 1-7.

80. *Buletini i radiove të huaja në gjuhën shqipe*, no. 265, 22 May 1990.

81. In February 1990, Kadare had a meeting with Alia in which he reportedly urged the president to put an end to human rights violations, implement democratic reforms, take immediate measures to improve the precarious economic situation, and open up the country to the outside world. Disappointed with Alia's slow reaction, Kadare publicly raised some of these issues in an interview with the youth newspaper. See *Zëri i Rinisë*, 21 March 1990, pp. 3-4; and Kadare, *Nga një dhjetor në tjetrin*, pp. 29-41.

82. Ylli Popa, "In Search of Lost Time," *Zëri i Popullit*, 28 and 29 April 1990, p. 3.

83. Hamit Beqja, "On the Deepening of a Free and Constructive Dialogue," *Zëri i Popullit*, 20 May 1990, pp. 3-4.

84. *Drita*, 20 May 1990, pp. 5-6.

85. On 26 March 1990, several hundred people demonstrated in Kavajë, shouting such slogans as "Down With Dictatorship," and "Freedom, Democracy." Dozens reportedly were arrested. Some demonstrators were said to have been tortured in the presence of Minister of Internal Affairs Simon Stefani and district APL secretary Muho Asllani. Unrest in Kavajë also broke out on 10 July. Units of special forces known as Sampist, were used to restore order. See *Rilindja Demokratike*, 16 March 1991, p. 5, and 25 March 1994, p. 3.

86. See David Binder's reports in *New York Times*, 14, 15, 25, and 27 May 1990; and *Times* (London), 30 April 1990.

87. Norman Kempster, "Ready to Resume Albania Relations, U.S. Says," *Los Angeles Times*, 25 April 1990, p. A7. See also David Binder, "Hard-Line Albanians Signal Desire to Resume Ties," *New York Times*, 20 April 1990, p. A7.

88. U.S. Commission on Security and Cooperation in Europe, *CSCE News Release* (Washington, D.C.) 10 May 1990. Emphasis added.

89. *Buletini i radiove të huaja në gjuhën shqipe*, no. 304, 16 June 1990. Emphasis added.

90. "Albania Ready to Adopt Helsinki Accords," *Financial Times*, 7 June 1990, p. 16.

91. "Albania On Its Own," *Financial Times*, 7 June 1990, p. 14.

92. "Albania Ready to Adopt Helsinki Accords," *The Financial Times*, 7 June 1990, p. 16.

93. Servet Pëllumbi, "'Political Pluralism' in Theory and Practice," *Rruga e Partisë* 37, no. 5 (May 1990), pp. 87-96. See also Ismail Lleshi, "Freedom, Independence, and Socialism: An Indivisible Whole," *Zëri i Popullit*, 29 May 1990, pp. 3-4.

2

The Demise of Communism

For decades a bastion of Stalinism in Europe, Albania was the last East European Communist domino to fall. As long as Hoxha was alive, few if any observers believed that radical reforms were possible. Ramiz Alia's accession to power following the dictator's death in April 1985 raised hopes that Albania, too, would embark on much-needed political and economic changes. Although Alia tried to foster the impression that he was modernizing Albania's socialist system, he ruled out an overhaul of the system that by the end of the 1980s had brought the country to a hideous quandary. He insisted that Albania was immune to the forces that during the 1970s and the 1980s had opened the way for credible political alternatives to Communist regimes in other East European countries.

Although Alia was willing to tinker with reforms in order to improve prospects for better ties with the West and for foreign investments, he refused to bow to the new political reality, rejecting changes that might threaten the APL's political monopoly. He argued that the country was not ready for democracy, leaving no doubt that his intention was to maintain one-party rule and centralized economic planning.[1] He hoped to bolster his regime's popular support and neutralize growing dissatisfaction by asserting that the changes represented a commitment to the democratization and modernization of party and government structures. But Alia's failure to press ahead with major reforms only worsened economic conditions, causing widespread disenchantment. If in May 1990 Alia was seen as a reformer, by July, popular support for him had eroded because of his adamant opposition to political pluralism and radical economic reforms. Many people dismissed Alia's rhetoric about the democratic nature of his new policies and criticized the duplicitous nature of his policies. For example, in June 1990, the government decreed that all citizens would be issued passports to travel abroad. While the new measures guaranteed freedom of movement, the authorities were slow and highly selective in issuing passports. Moreover, they took measures to tighten border control, as many Albanians attempted to flee the country.[2] While the official propaganda machine spoke of democratization, the regime continued to pursue an uncompromising policy against its opponents and critics. The secret police, the Sigurimi, remained as powerful as ever.

Embassy Crisis

The APL's supremacy, however, was increasingly being challenged. Many disgruntled party members and intellectuals who in the past had faithfully served the party concluded that to survive the system had to undergo fundamental changes. Faced with growing antigovernment opposition and labor unrest, the APL showed signs of declining control over the domestic political scene. By early July 1990, this was most dramatically reflected in the boldest display of antiregime sentiment since the 1940s, when thousands of Albanians stormed foreign embassies in Tiranë in an attempt to flee the country. Tensions had been building for several months as an increasing number of Albanians sought to gain freedom by scaling fences and entering Western embassies. Although Albanian police entered foreign missions to seize asylum seekers, on one occasion even manhandling the French ambassador and his wife,[3] in two instances, involving the Greek and the Turkish embassies, the authorities granted those seeking asylum safe passage out of the country. These concessions, in addition to the resolution on 16 May 1990 of the case of six elderly Albanians who had spent five years awaiting asylum in the Italian embassy in Tiranë, apparently set off the mass attempt. In December 1985, only eight months after Hoxha's death, the Popaj family, two brothers and four sisters, entered the Italian embassy in Tiranë. Albanian authorities demanded the unconditional surrender of the six, but Italy insisted that they be allowed to leave the country. The case attracted worldwide attention and contributed to an almost total freeze in Albanian-Italian relations. In an effort to create a favorable international image, days after U.N. Secretary-General Javier Perez de Cuellar's visit in May 1990, Albanian authorities gave in and the Popajs departed for Italy on 16 May. The decision had a profound impact. After the Popajs' departure, there were more incidents of Albanian citizens seeking asylum at foreign embassies.

The storming began on 2 July, when between 100 and 150 Albanians entered the Italian, French, and German embassies. The situation rapidly got out of control. Within days, six thousand Albanians, some coming from the farthest parts of the country, entered foreign embassies.[4] Ten thousand Albanians reportedly staged a public demonstration in the capital in support of the refugees.[5] For the first time, Albania dominated world headlines, which put tremendous pressure on the government. Alia was faced with the most severe crisis he had thus far encountered. After several days of confusion and hesitation, the authorities finally agreed to allow the refugees to emigrate. On 7 July, Alia issued a decree assuring those who had entered the embassies that they would not be persecuted, while those who chose to leave the country would be issued passports. Thousands of angry citizens from all parts of the country converged on Durrës in the largest out-pouring of popular sentiment that Communist Albania had ever seen. Altogether, 4,794 Albanians left the country, most going to Germany. The overwhelming majority (3,405, or 70 percent) were workers. There were only 155 white-collar workers. Ironically, there were no prominent intellectuals among the group, a fact that was used by the authorities in their attempt to portray the refugees as "hooligans and vagabonds."[6]

Intellectuals Versus Refugees

This massive outmigration, which plunged the Albanian regime into a crisis of legitimacy, highlighted the untenable position of reform-minded intellectuals. While in the wake of de Cuellar's visit intellectuals had competed with each other in giving interviews to foreign correspondents, during the refugee crisis they suddenly were no longer accessible. Whether or not their sympathies were with the asylum seekers, none had the courage to publicly support them or to criticize the government. Indeed, some issued statements characterizing the refugees as degenerates from the poorer fringes of society, portraying them as too base to have political ideas. Dritëro Agolli, the chairman of the Union of Writers and Artists, said: "Foreign reaction attempts to spread the infectious epidemic among our people, to turn them against socialism which has been present in our country for fifty years. We the writers, who are the conscience of history, resent these actions which are directed against our Fatherland and socialism. With our voices, we should denounce the wrongdoers and explain things to the naive ones. Our aim is Socialist Albania."[7]

For their part, the refugees were harshly critical of the intellectuals. In interviews broadcast by the Voice of America, many refugees expressed deep disappointment with the failure of intellectuals to articulate clear political demands, suggesting that they were collaborators with Alia. Surprisingly, the brunt of their criticism was directed personally at writer Ismail Kadare. Many Albanians and some Western observers had hoped that Kadare, who had criticized past regime abuses, could do for Albania what Vaclav Havel and Aleksandr Solzhenitsyn had done for Czechoslovakia and Russia, respectively. But Kadare was badly tainted by his close association with the regime and lacked the moral rectitude of a Havel or Solzhenitsyn, both of whom had paid a heavy personal price for publicly denouncing the horrors of Communist rule in their native lands.

Although criticism from recent émigrés evidently did have some impact on intellectuals, it did not jolt them into undertaking any concerted action. In an interview with the Voice of America on 23 September, Kadare angrily rejected criticism that he and other prominent intellectuals were not doing enough for the democratization of their country. Kadare said Albanian intellectuals had often spoken out against government abuses, but their views were not reflected in the

Communist-controlled media. He said the democratization of Albania would take a long time. Drawing an analogy with ethnic Albanian intellectuals in Kosova, who by the end of 1989 had emerged as leaders of noncommunist parties and were leading the resistance against Serbian repression, Kadare implied the day would come when intellectuals in Albania, too, would play a leading role in the reinvigoration of their country.[8]

The Party Strikes Back

The embassy episode, which marshaled unprecedented international public opinion against the Albanian regime, reflected a serious lack of trust in the government and represented a dramatic indication of the wide gulf separating the *nomenklatura* from the masses. It not only represented a major setback for the APL, from which the Party never recovered, but it served as a clear indication that the regime, despite its highly repressive nature, was not invincible. Alia's relatively mild response suggested that the government did not want to risk the popular alienation or international opprobrium that a massive display of force would have provoked. As a result, the breakdown in the perceived ability to control or punish openly hostile behavior seriously undermined the regime.

Alia's response to the crisis was halfhearted and contradictory. He skirted the issue of the regime's faltering control and attempted to counter any perception that the refugees' anticommunist attitudes were shared by the general population. In a speech at a special Central Committee plenum on 6 July, he called the refugees hooligans and misguided individuals who were being manipulated by foreign forces interested in the overthrow of Albania's Communist regime. He said there was no room "for indifference or generosity or any underestimation of the situation." He called for a new class struggle against "reactionary domestic forces." At the same time as he said important changes were forthcoming, he remained steadfast in his demand that reforms be gradual.[9] The following day, in his concluding speech to the plenum, Alia announced additional measures to arrest the decline of the economy and placate the alienated populace. Termed the new economic mechanism and modeled after Hungary's economic reforms of the 1960s and the 1970s, Alia's new initiatives granted enterprises greater autonomy. The regime legalized small-scale private activity in the service sector, although this was a radical departure from previous policy. Alia tried to assure members of the Central Committee that "a limited and controlled private sector does not run counter to our moral and ideological principles. There is no danger of creating a class of proprietors or exploiters."[10] In order to stem the spread of labor unrest, on 9 July, the Council of Ministers issued two decrees: The first guaranteed that workers would receive 80 percent of their wages if their work was interrupted through no fault of their own; and the second called for workers to be paid according to their job categories.[11]

The plenum also dismissed several hard-line senior officials, including Minister of Internal Affairs Simon Stefani. But the importance of these measures was mitigated by the fact that the newly appointed member of the Politburo, the arch-conservative Xhelil Gjoni, immediately emerged as the number-two man in the Albanian hierarchy. A highly unpopular figure, Gjoni overshadowed the more reformist members of the Politburo, including Foto Çami, who had been blamed by the conservatives for the decline of the party's control over the media. Under Gjoni's direct supervision, a fierce campaign was launched against families and relatives of refugees, many of whom were expelled from the party and fired from their jobs.

The embassy incident caught Alia off guard and left him scrambling to recover his political balance. Reflecting heightened leadership concern over the security situation, the APL held a massive rally on 13 July. It was reported that 100,000 people gathered in Skanderbeg Square, where they heard Gjoni denounce the refugees in very harsh terms: "[W]e say with one voice to our enemies that Albania and its people's power are unshaken by degenerate people who abandon their homeland, or by anybody else." Other speakers, including First Secretary of the Tiranë District Party Committee Pirro Kondi, leader of the youth organization Lisen Bashkurti, and writer Kiço Blushi, echoed Gjoni's statement.[12]

Nevertheless, in the wake of the embassy incident, the security situation continued to deteriorate and the country's pressing problems only grew worse. Conservatives within the leadership pressed for tough measures to curtail political activities that undermined the regime's control. In an attempt to make a comeback, conservatives intensified their criticism of the youth and intellectuals. Bashkurti denounced young people who had fallen victim to foreign influences and called for an intensification of the campaign to instill proper socialist values in the youth.[13] Kadare came under attack for suggesting the rehabilitation of pre-Communist writers such as publicist and diplomat Faik Konica (1876-1942), poet Gjergj Fishta (1871-1940), and writer Ernest Koliqi (1900-1975). Their writings had been banned because of their "antinational activities in the political field." Konica had served as ambassador to the United States during King Zog's rule, Fishta was one of Albania's most prominent clerics and poets of the inter-war period, and Koliqi had served as Minister of Education under the Italian occupation. Kadare had called for the rehabilitation of these writers in an interview with *Zëri i Rinisë* in March 1990.[14] Ironically, some fifteen years earlier, in the wake of the purge of senior officials responsible for cultural affairs, Kadare had engaged in one of the harshest criticisms of Fishta:

Let us recall some facts from the history of our literature. Who has been the greatest conservative in Albanian letters, and not letters alone, but also our entire culture? The answer is clear to all: This conservative was Gjergj Fishta. Rabid fanatic, idealizer of everything patriarchal, apologist for religion and medieval institutions, hymnist of primitivism, fierce enemy of all progress—such is the portrait of this writer-priest. But, on the other hand, if we ask who was the greatest liberal in our literature, the answer is again the same: Gjergj Fishta, irrepressible Italophile, agent of the Vatican, emissary of the Fascist government, partisan of denationalization and Romanization of our culture; hence, on the one hand, a fanatical arch-conservative, and on the other, an arch-liberal—a rabid chauvinist and at the same time a rabid cosmopolite. Where new social ideas, progress, and revolution were concerned, he was the most fanatic conservative. Where the fate of the Fatherland, freedom, and boundaries were concerned, he was the biggest liberal.[15]

Echoing Alia's statement that "no concession must be made to bourgeois ideology in any field,"[16] literary critic Koço Bihiku warned against "concessions to alien methodological viewpoints" attempting to reappraise the past. He insisted that in studying the country's literary heritage, Albanian scholars should "rigorously observe the Leninist principle of the two cultures within a national culture that are an expression of opposing trends of historical development. If we do not adhere to this principle, we are at risk of falling into bourgeois objectivism or subjective and one-sided attitudes, which means a concession to alien methodological viewpoints."[17] Notwithstanding this Marxist jargon, as the leadership struggled unsuccessfully to dispel the crisis atmosphere, expressions of anxiety and criticism of the APL increased.

Alia's Strategy of Cooptation

Alia's attitude toward the intellectuals was ambivalent. While he considered their support vital for the success of his policies, he recognized that their agenda differed radically from his own. Because he allowed them a degree of freedom of expression, the Albanian leader expected the intellectuals to defend the APL's policies, especially in interviews and other contact with foreigners. Indeed, the overwhelming majority of intellectuals did continue to express public support for the regime far longer than was the case elsewhere in East Europe. The Albanian intelligentsia had been terrorized during Hoxha's reign and was slow to recover from the purges of its ranks. Nevertheless, some intellectuals expressed views that until then had been anathematized by the Party. Although many reform-minded intellectuals shared similar views on the most critical issues facing the nation, they did not coalesce into an organized group. Neither did they have a recognized leader. The APL continued to exercise such tight control over society and the tentacles of the Sigurimi were so pervasive, that it appeared virtually impossible for an organized opposition to emerge. Hence, instances of public defiance of the authorities were more or less spontaneous.

In August, Alia convened a meeting with the country's most prominent intellectuals, ostensibly to acquaint himself with their views. However, it soon became clear that this was not the actual agenda. Alia set the tone of the meeting in his opening remarks by ruling out the idea of a multiparty system. With Gjoni standing by his side, Alia asserted that the foreign enemy had found support "among people who favor another, nonsocialist alternative, individuals who are against the government, against the Party, against socialism."[18] Insisting that there were no divisions within the leadership or between him and Mrs. Hoxha, Alia said all the changes being implemented were aimed at strengthening socialism.[19] He signaled concern over shrinking support and criticized the media and the intelligentsia for being insufficiently supportive of the regime. Alia not only offered no hint that the APL leadership was willing to moderate its stance on political reform, he also reminded the intellectuals of their responsibility to support the APL in the face of growing Western media attacks. He expressed particular displeasure with the Voice of America, at the time the only major Western radio station broadcasting in Albanian. At the center of the Voice of America's "propaganda," he insisted, were demands for political pluralism, human rights, and the establishment of a market economy. He said "the greatest danger is that there are people who believe in what the Voice of America says. ..."[20] Alia then invited participants to speak their minds "without any reservations."

Although the meeting was held in a tense atmosphere, the intellectuals expressed concern with the slow pace of reforms and raised such subjects as violations of human rights, excesses by the Sigurimi, lack of freedom of press, privileges of the *nomenklatura*, and the issue of Stalin. There were heated discussions and individual confrontations with Alia, who demanded that the intellectuals help the party counter foreign demands for the establishment of a multiparty system. Dr. Sali Berisha, who two years later would succeed Alia as president, challenged the limits on reform set by the government and questioned the APL's constitutionally guaranteed monopoly on power. He accused the media of serving as a Communist mouthpiece, denying the population vital informatic on domestic and foreign developments. Berisha said that many Albanians were tuning in to foreign radios because they did not trust the domestic media. While being careful not to question the validity of the Communist system, he confronted Alia with the demand for political pluralism. Alia rejected Berisha's demands, insisting: "There are no alternatives. This should be clear to us."[21] Berisha, the only hero of the meeting, was abandoned, with no participant having the courage to support him.

Kadare later maintained that he and economist Gramoz Pashko had agreed to voice a demand for political pluralism, but at the meeting they changed their minds.[22] Kadare said the participants were concerned that the meeting was called to provoke the intellectuals and then take action against them. He quoted a colleague as wondering whether they would leave the meeting alive.[23] Such insecurity and fear were understandable in view of the past treatment of opponents, but it is highly unlikely that the regime, at such a late hour and on the eve of a fact-finding visit by a U.S. Congressional delegation, would have launched a major crackdown against the intellectuals. Faced with increased isolation and a collapsing economy, Alia was not likely to take any drastic action that would have caused an international outcry over human-rights violations and dimmed whatever hope Albania had of being admitted as a full member of the CSCE.

The meeting was a serious blow to the credibility of reform-minded intellectuals. While it is highly questionable, as some have argued, that Alia would have agreed to demands for the creation of independent political parties had he been faced with a tougher stand,[24] the intellectuals' failure to clearly endorse political pluralism handed the regime a badly needed, albeit a temporary, propaganda victory: Communist officials could now claim that the intelligentsia had rejected the idea of a multiparty system. Alia's position had been seriously undermined in the wake of the July events. He now was confronted with challenges on all fronts: a rapidly deteriorating domestic situation, increased international pressure, and criticism over his stewardship of the Party and the state. But the nation's leading intellectuals, most of whom evidently supported the establishment of opposition parties, were too divided to confront the APL leader with a common stand. While many workers and students openly defied the Communists, the intellectuals, who had lived in terror under Hoxha, were still reluctant to challenge the system because of fear of government retribution and the resultant loss of their social position.

Although party officials largely viewed the meeting as positive, it had negative repercussions. Instead of gaining support, Alia had widened the gulf between himself and the intellectuals, many of whom had supported him in the past but who now concluded that he was an obstacle to the democratization of the country. Meanwhile, the international pressure on Albania intensified. In the wake of the July incident, most Western countries closed down their embassies in Tiranë, for all practical purposes freezing ties with Albania. An official U.S. Congressional delegation, led by Senator Dennis DeConcini, chairman of the Helsinki Commission, paid a three-day visit to Albania on 19-21 August. In a statement released after the visit, the Helsinki Commission praised Albania's government for its reform efforts but expressed concern over gross violations of human rights, the large number of political prisoners, severe restrictions on religious practices, total Communist control of the media, and the ruling party's refusal to allow the formation of independent organizations. Responding to Albania's request for full membership in the CSCE, the Helsinki Commission asserted that given Tiranë's level of performance in the area of human rights and political pluralism, as a full CSCE member "Albania would be glaringly out of step with the rapidly developing process of democratization, political pluralism, the rule of law and free market economies that is taking place throughout Europe."[25]

The End of the One-Party System

Pressured by growing international demands to permit political pluralism, Alia introduced the notion of "pluralism of ideas," which meant Albanians would be allowed to express their ideas but not to form other political parties. In an attempt to improve the image of his regime and to make a personal plea for Albania's admittance as a full member of the CSCE, in September Alia attended the U.N. General Assembly session. In his speech, he said Albania was committed to implement the Helsinki Accords, but rejected what he called outside attempts to force his country to change its system.[26] Despite Tiranë's best efforts to portray Alia's visit as a success, it was a failure.[27] The Albanian media's accounts of Alia's visit put the best face on what were insignificant official meetings. More importantly, in New York Alia was met by Albanian American protesters. Not surprisingly, he had made no effort to contact representatives of the large anti-Communist Albanian American community, meeting only with supporters of the Communist regime. Anthony Athanas, a well- known Albanian American restauranteur in Boston, organized a dinner reception for Alia. Participants were mostly members of the Boston-based, procommunist Free Albania Organization. In his speech, Alia denounced asylum seekers who had stormed foreign embassies in Tiranë in July 1990. Acknowledging that Albania was faced with serious problems, Alia said: "There are difficulties, just as there are no forests without wild boars, or immature people like those who entered the embassies. They are not Albania, however, and are not the people."[28]

Intellectuals Find Their Voice

After the initial shock caused by the embassy crisis, prominent Albanian intellectuals began publicly to voice views at odds with those of the Party leadership. Sali Berisha became the first to publicly make a case for political pluralism. In an article published in September in *Bashkimi*, the organ of the Demo-cratic Front, the country's largest mass organization, he launched a broadside at hard-liners' resistance to reforms and their divisive approach to ideological issues. Berisha gave short shrift to conservative ideological themes, referring only in passing to Alia and not mentioning the APL's standard ideological bromides. He wrote that the country was in the throes of an acute crisis and time was running out. Berisha called on the intellectuals to mobilize their forces and energies in support of democratization, saying the process was also supported by Albanians in Yugoslavia and in the West. In the most direct challenge to prevailing views on political pluralism, Berisha launched a sweeping attack against what he termed "antidemocratic and conservative elements" that were opposing the democrat-ization of Albania:

Although the broad masses and the overwhelming majority of working people among us see the democratization of our society as a decisive process for the country's present and future, there are antidemocratic and conservative elements that take an opposite view. These are, in fact, neither few in number nor impotent in respect of the power they exert. ... It is first of all bureaucratized cadres and employees who have created and allowed themselves unfair privileges who are conservatives and antidemocrats. Now that the time has come for them to surrender these things, these people, like those unfortunate persons who concoct a lie and end up believing it themselves, think that these privileges are fair—even that these privileges are their birthright. ... All fanatical and intolerant people, and those who instead of pluralism of thought prefer monism (and probably their own monism) are doubtless antidemocrats. There can, however, be no democracy without democrats. Uniformity of thought is fraught with dire social consequences. It makes thinking uniform, and like all uniforms (in the health service, in the army, etc.), it hides more than it reveals. ... A monist meeting hall, auditorium, assembly, or society is a pure illusion.

In a biting rebuttal to official statements that pluralism would divide the nation, Berisha stressed that the Albanians had a long tradition of pluralism. He suggested that only in a pluralist system could leaders make wise decisions. In a direct challenge to Alia and the Sigurimi, which had launched a disinformation campaign alleging that the intellectuals had told the Albanian leader they did not favor political pluralism, Berisha accused Party officials of deliberately distorting the nature of demands being put forward at meetings with senior officials. He complained that intellectuals could not freely express their opinions because of fear of reprisals and prevalent conformist attitudes.[29]

Berisha's article was the most courageous public defiance displayed by an Albanian intellectual at that time. He was reportedly about to be transferred from Tiranë to a provincial town because of his demand for political pluralism at the August meeting with Alia. But with the publication of his article in *Bashkimi*, Berisha became an instant celebrity. Since by this time he also had attracted foreign attention, the authorities apparently concluded that his transfer could backfire.

While opposition to the regime was growing and the media were becoming more daring, intellectuals still failed to articulate and publicly present alternative political programs, evidently fearing that the sanctioning of political pluralism was premature. Even reform-minded intellectuals did not advocate replacing the Communist regime. In this regard, they were clearly far behind popular demands for the overthrow of Communist rule.

Kadare Votes with His Feet

In October 1990, Tiranë hosted the Balkan Foreign Ministers' Conference, the highest-level meeting of regional Communist officials ever held in Albania. The government had made elaborate preparations and built up the meeting as a major event marking the beginning of a new phase in its foreign policy. Albania hoped to enlist its neighbors' support for its full membership in the CSCE, which would have represented a major step toward the country's eventual integration into Europe after decades of self-imposed isolation. The conference came less than four months after the July refugee crisis had thrust Albania into the limelight and focused international attention on human rights violations and lack of democracy. With the Tiranë conference, Alia hoped to improve his regime's tarnished image and portray Albania as a politically stable country poised for democratic reforms. To this end more than ninety foreign correspondents were invited to cover the meeting. To Alia's chagrin, the conference failed to support Tiranë's request for full membership in the CSCE because of continued human rights problems.

On 25 October, at the close of the two-day meeting, Ismail Kadare announced in Paris that he had asked French authorities for political asylum. Although Kadare claimed that the announcement of his decision was not deliberately set to coincide with the Tiranë meeting, the news of his defection overshadowed the conference. He had been considered by many a supporter of Alia's policies, and at the time of his defection was vice president of the Democratic Front, the country's largest Communist-controlled mass organization. From 1970 to 1982, he had been a member of the People's Assembly. Kadare expressed disappointment with the slow pace of political reforms. He said he had met with Alia in spring 1990, and after that, he had been hopeful that genuine reforms would be implemented; but in the wake of the refugee crisis in July, he said Alia bounced back to traditional Communist hard-line policies. In an interview with *Le Monde,* Kadare said he had written a letter to Alia complaining about the slow pace of reforms, and the president's reply convinced him that "the promises of democratization were dead." He said he had "lost all hope of contributing, from the inside, to any softening of the regime." He warned that unless radical measures were taken, Albania could face a more tragic confrontation than did Romania when Ceauşescu was overthrown. He added that a multiparty system in Albania was possible and that despite more than four decades of dictatorship, communism "has not really penetrated into the depth of Albanian society."[30] In a statement addressed to his nation and broadcast by the Voice of America's Albanian Service, Kadare said that Albania was going through one of the most difficult periods in its history, and added, "Having no other way to express my position, since there is no possibility of legal opposition in Albania, I have therefore chosen this route that I never would have wished to take and that I would not recommend to anyone."[31]

Kadare's defection caused such a shock that Albanian officials initially dismissed foreign reports of the event as lies and provocations. It took the government more than twenty-four hours to confirm the news. In a terse statement, the authorities accused the writer of having "placed himself in the service of the enemies of Albania and the Albanian people."[32] The Union of Writers and Artists issued a similar statement: "Through this shameful act [Kadare] has offended especially the Albanian intelligentsia, the creators and the national consciousness of the people, putting himself on the same line with those who do not love Albania and its progress. His fleeing the country is not justified either from the social positions or from the literary ones."[33]

Reaction in nonofficial circles was mixed. Some reacted angrily, expressing concern that Kadare's dramatic action might do more harm than good to the reformist cause. There were also those who dismissed Kadare's stated reasons, suggesting instead that he wanted to distance himself from the regime at a time when Communist authority was on the decline. But in an unprecedented challenge to the regime, some intellectuals publicly defended Kadare. Gramoz Pashko, characterizing the writer as a "genius," seconded Kadare's calls for rapid change and the establishment of a multiparty system. "Something has to be done quickly," Pashko warned. "Anything could trigger more unrest, and the most important thing is for Albania to avoid bloodshed." Such defiance of the Party line would have been unthinkable only a few months earlier.

In neighboring Yugoslavia, Albanian intellectuals expressed overwhelming support for Kadare. Although well aware of Communist repression in Albania, Kosovar Albanians both at home and abroad had almost never publicly criticized Tiranë's regime. By overwhelmingly supporting Kadare, they sent a message Tiranë could not ignore: Unless there was real movement toward democracy, Alia could no longer take for granted the Kosovars' allegiance. This message was perhaps best reflected in a statement by Rexhep Qosja, Kosova's most eminent intellectual. Echoing Kadare's warning about the possibility of a violent confrontation, Qosja called for a rapid democratization of Albania. In an emotional appeal to Alia, whom he called "the prophet of Albanian democracy," the Kosovar scholar said Albania must move toward a multiparty system for the sake of its own future and also for Kosova. "Only a democratic Albania can help Kosova," Qosja said.[34] But Kosovar opinion was not uniform in support of Kadare. Adem Demaçi, who had spent close to thirty years in Yugoslav jails for nationalistic activities and was widely referred to as Yugoslavia's Mandela, sharply criticized Kadare, accusing him of abandoning Albania for life in "luxurious" Paris. Demaçi said that Kadare should not have defected even if he had known that he would be "crucified."[35]

The government did not launch a public campaign against the writer, nor were his books banned, which suggests that leaders were concerned that Kadare's defection might cause violent protests and wished to placate popular resentment. Rather, in well coordinated efforts at damage control, official spokesmen and intellectuals with close ties to the government claimed that no writer had enjoyed more privileges than Kadare, that he was free to travel and publish abroad, and that he had every opportunity to freely express his views. Deputy Foreign Minister Muhamet Kapllani characterized Kadare as "a spoiled child."[36]

In reality, like other writers, Kadare had been forced to operate in an environment in which intellectuals were considered mere servants of the Party. He had supported the Party line, going so far as to participate in regime-orchestrated campaigns against writers who had fallen out of favor with the APL.[37] As recently as autumn 1989, Kadare had defended socialist realism, writing that the "remarkable" period of socialist rule wis "the greatest emancipation that the Albanian people have ever witnessed."[38] In an autobiographical work published only a month before his defection, Kadare gave glimpses into his difficult encounters with the regime, the pressures he had to endure, and the persecution and harassment by hard-line bureaucrats charged with keeping intellectuals in line. He also wrote about the trauma he had experienced in the late 1960s, during Albania's cultural revolution. During this period, he claimed, he came close to giving up writing altogether. He was forced to pay lip service to the Party, exercise self-censorship, and engage in self-criticism.[39] But despite his occasional difficulties with the authorities, Kadare was an honored artist of Communist Albania and was among the most privileged people in the country. Most observers have dismissed his allegations that before his defection he was in danger of being arrested. Even Alia acknowledged that Kadare's domestic and international reputation had made him untouchable.[40]

Whatever his motives, Kadare's dramatic warning of the rapidly deteriorating situation galvanized reformist forces and helped put an end to fear of the Communist dictatorship, a fear that for decades had silenced everyone, including prominent intellectuals with considerable moral courage and integrity. Expressions of public support for Kadare's defection indicated that the Communists' control over the country was much less certain than it outwardly appeared. Although many Albanians continued to publicly profess support for the APL, many of them evidently believed the Party was in decline.

Alia's Survival Strategy: Act II

Meanwhile, Alia chafed under the burden of the disastrous failure of Albanian communism, but evidently feared that an acknowledgment of the devastation that the APL's policies had brought to the Albanian people would imperil the regime's survival. Instead, he intensified his efforts to restructure the Communist system. In a major speech to the 12th Plenum of the Central Committee, held on 6-7 November, Alia announced measures to strengthen the rule of law and separate the Party from the state. He declared that the constitution, which was promulgated in 1976, would be revised to guarantee human rights and religious practices and to permit foreign investments and foreign credits. He also said the APL would give up its constitutionally guaranteed monopoly of power but would not sanction political pluralism. Mass organizations such as the Democratic Front, the veterans' organization, the trade unions, the writers association, and the youth organization, which had served as transmission belts for the Party line, were declared independent from the APL and granted the right to put their own candidates forward in elections to the People's Assembly.[41] Although ostensibly designed to institute a more pluralistic political system, the measure in reality ensured the APL's supremacy, since the principles of all mass organizations had to be consistent with those of the ruling party. In addition, senior Communist officials headed the mass organizations. The new election law, approved by parliament on 13 November 1990, also permitted independent candidates if they could obtain the endorsement of 300 registered voters.

Even at this eleventh hour, Alia hoped his regime could successfully ride out the crisis. However, Albania's failure to win acceptance as a full member of the CSCE at the Paris summit meeting in November, was a serious blow to Alia. The implication of this event was that Albania needed to carry out fundamental reforms in order to be accepted as a full-fledged member of the international community. The West, which throughout the 1960s and 1970s had pursued a policy of benign neglect toward Albania, conditioned the strengthening of ties on a major change in Alia's domestic policy. But as late as the 12th Central Committee Plenum, Alia was clearly signaling his determination to combat political liberalization. He continued to gloss over contentious issues and avoided confrontations that could severely strain party unity. He resisted efforts to push reform beyond the boundaries of traditional APL ideological assumptions. His reluctance to carry out radical reforms that might have addressed the country's serious economic and social problems suggested he still believed the Communist regime would survive.

But events were moving at a pace that was far outdistancing the regime's ability to keep up. Even members of the establishment, reflected the gloomy atmosphere that was pervasive among the political elite, betrayed a loss of confidence in the system and expressed heightened concern that a failure to reverse the economic decline would lead to serious political and social unrest that could unravel the regime. Still, Alia continued to be less alarmist, claiming that the Party was capable of rectifying the situation. But his cosmetic changes had no discernible effect, and it became increasingly clear that the regime would not be able to stem the growth of dissent. Popular dissatisfaction was fueled by a drastic decline in production and exports, dramatic increases in unemployment and infla-tion, a disintegrating social order, rampant corruption, and the desperate desire of many people, especially the youth, to leave the country.

As 1990 approached its end, many Albanians, particularly in urban areas, appeared to be in an unusually rebellious mood. They expressed their diminishing confidence in the effectiveness of the Alia regime, apparently convinced that the measures he had introduced were aimed at placating international criticism of the regime rather than democratizing the country's political and economic system. With the economy in a shambles, the APL's inability to deal with the situation, and the dwindling legitimacy of existing political institutions, reform-minded intellectuals, radical students, and rebellious workers pushed for an overhaul of the political system. In an interview with the Voice of America, economist Gramoz Pashko launched a devastating attack on Alia's policies, warning that unless urgent measures were taken Albania could face violent social unrest and remain outside the process of European integration. He added that the economy could not be revived in the absence of political reforms aimed at creating a genuine democracy.[42] In another extraordinary example of criticism of official policy, *Zëri i Popullit* published in mid-November excerpts of a debate among several intellectuals. Sali Berisha argued that the notion of a pluralism of ideas, the main aspect of Alia's so-called democratization process, was meaningless in the absence of new, alternative organizations. Berisha called for political pluralism.[43] Meanwhile, the recently approved election law was sharply criticized by historian Mentar Belegu, who suggested that Albania's experiment with a multiparty system in the 1920s could serve as a model for Albania in the 1990s. He criticized the parliament for having refused demands of some deputies to discuss the introduction of a multiparty system.[44] Writer Besnik Mustafaj, in an article in *Drita*, argued that intellectuals were extremely concerned about the situation in the country, but that despite Alia's calls for an open debate, they were encountering difficulties in publicizing their views. Denouncing what he termed conservative and dogmatic forces, Mustafaj asserted that only through the free exchange and debate of ideas would Albania find the best solution to the challenges confronting it.[45]

Kadare had been considered as most likely to lead an eventual opposition movement to the Communist regime. But his defection had changed Albania's political landscape, boosting the reputation of other, hitherto less prominent personalities who chose to stay behind and fight for democracy. The APL's continued intransigence inspired a coalescence of opposition centered around such people as Sali Berisha and Gramoz Pashko, both APL members. But the two emerging opposition leaders made no effort to combine forces and did not engage in any organized activity, apparently relying only on a small circle of intimate friends. With his increased political activity, Berisha risked losing everything because he had no political base or friends in higher places who could protect him. Pashko, on the other hand, was in a better position and less likely than Berisha to experience the full brunt of the regime's brutality in case of a crackdown on potential opponents because his family had close ties to Hoxha's clan.

Student Protesters

Even as late as the beginning of December 1990, the intellectuals, totally dependent on APL-controlled jobs, were still unwilling to openly confront the regime or to take part in overt antigovernment activities. Berisha and Pashko, as well as other reform-minded intellectuals, apparently believed that an organized opposition and the appearance of an alternate reform program were distant possibilities. Thus, the only stratum that appeared ready for an open confrontation with the government was the youth.

Anti-government activity was centered increasingly among restless students at Tiranë University, which at the time was the country's only university. Although the overwhelming majority of students were from Communist families, they were more favorably disposed toward open antigovernment action than adult intellectuals and the populace in general. Student activity eventually demolished the conventional wisdom of the invincibility of the regime and propelled Berisha, Pashko, and other intellectuals to the forefront of the antiregime movement.

Sporadic incidents of government defiance were reported during November and December at the University of Tiranë, which drew students from all parts of Albania. In the early days of December, Prime Minister Adil Çarçani met with a group of students who had complained about poor conditions at the dormitories. The government, however, failed to take immediate steps to improve the situation, and on 8 December, several hundred students, infuriated by a power failure, organized a demonstration. Recognizing the potential of a wider protest, Çarçani went to the campus. But the talks collapsed, reportedly because of the prime minister's confrontational approach. The authorities then send a delegation composed of Tiranë district Party secretary Pirro Kondi, Minister of Education Skendër Gjinushi, and the leader of the youth organization, Lisen Bashkurti. They, too, failed to convince the students to end their protest. Kondi was considered a hard-liner while Gjinushi and Bashkurti were unpopular with the students because they had stood side by side with Xhelil Gjoni at a rally organized by the APL in July to denounce the storming of foreign embassies. In the early hours of Sunday morning, 9 December, Alia received a delegation of four-teen students, led by Azem Hajdari, a twenty-eight-year-old philosophy major. The results of the meeting, however, were inconclusive. After the delegation returned to the campus, Minister of Internal Affairs Hekuran Isai ordered the police to intervene. The demonstrators, including Hajdari, were beaten up, and several were arrested. Later that day, there was another clash between the security forces and student protesters attempting to march from the campus toward the city center, in a desperate effort to gain support from Tiranë's inhabitants. Although news of the demonstrations had spread, the number of participants in the momentous events of 9 December was relatively small. Most of Tiranë's citizens remained passive or even apathetic and few intellectuals openly embraced the protesters' cause. Just as it began to seem that the demonstration might collapse, Hajdari, displaying extraordinary courage and leadership abilities, regrouped the demoralized protesters and salvaged the situation.

Berisha, who on the evening of 8 December had returned from a trip abroad, became the first prominent intellectual to join the demonstrators. Although he had become popular because of his confrontation with Alia back in August and his articles advocating political pluralism, initially the protesters did not trust Berisha and shouted him down when he attempted to address them. Regional ties seem to have been instrumental in his efforts to win the students' confidence. Although Berisha was not previously acquainted with Hajdari, both came from the northeastern district of Tropojë. Other student leaders also were overwhelmingly from the anticommunist north. Thus, after a brief hesitation, the protesters accepted Berisha. Because several student leaders were from Berisha's home district,[46] Alia assumed Berisha was behind the demonstrations. The president summoned Berisha and urged him to exercise his influence to convince the students to end their boycott of classes and their public demonstrations.[47] Serving as an intermediary between the demonstrators and Alia, Berisha secured the release of students arrested the day before. But more importantly, he was able to skillfully exploit the situation, urging the students to continue their peaceful demonstrations and convincing them to include in their petition demands for political pluralism. The students were poorly organized and initially did not seem to have a clear idea about their demands beyond improved conditions at the dormitories.[48] On 10 December, the protesters issued a list of demands. The petition expressed support for what it termed "the democratic reforms initiated by President Alia" and called for the sanctioning of "political pluralism as the highest degree of today's democracy." The petition specifically demanded that the authorities allow the creation of an independent organization of students and young intellectuals. The protesters also demanded the publication of United Nations documents on human rights and on freedom of press and speech. They reiterated their original demand for a meeting with Alia and called on "all those who love Albania to support student demands and unite with them."[49]

On the third day of demonstrations, support for the protesters grew. People from Tiranë and other districts began to assemble at the university. Alia was faced with a daunting choice: Either use the armed forces to suppress the demonstrations, or accept their demands for political pluralism. He apparently feared that a military crackdown would result in mass civil disorders and bloodshed. He convened an extraordinary meeting of the Central Committee to discuss the rapidly deteriorating situation. Reformists in the Central Committee prevailed, and the use of force was rejected. Thus, after months of insisting that he would not allow the formation of other parties, On 11 December, in a meeting with student representatives, Alia accepted demands for political pluralism. The next day, the Democratic Party—the country's first opposition party since 1945 —was formed. With Alia's momentous reversal of his position, the last Communist regime in Europe had lost its political monopoly.

The Rise of Opposition Parties

Alia's grudging acceptance of political pluralism reflected an ambivalence between his desire to avoid bloodshed and his desperate attempts to cling to power. On 17 December, the People's Assembly issued a decree on the creation of political parties. It reflected the Communists' determination to prevent the creation of parties of the far right and the revival of two nationalist parties of the World War II period, the National Front and Legality. It specifically prohibited the establishment of "fascist, racist, warmongering, [and] antinational" political organizations and associations. Political parties were prohibited from receiving direct or indirect financial assistance from foreign sources.[50] This provision was directed at preventing the emerging opposition parties from accepting financial assistance from the largely anticommunist Albanian diaspora. The National Front and Legality were revived only after a new law was adopted, in summer 1991.

The Democratic Party

The first opposition party, the center-right Democratic Party, was formed on 12 December 1990, five days before the People's Assembly formally sanctioned the creation of opposition parties. The founders of the party, consisting of inexperienced student leaders and a small group of intellectuals, did not have adequate time to prepare for the creation of the party. Their hastily drafted initial program nevertheless reflected the aspirations of the majority of Albania's population for democracy. It called for the establishment of a pluralistic democracy based on the rule of law, full respect for human rights, and a market economy. The document did not refer to the decommunization of the country; the preamble instead referred to "the democratic reforms initiated" by Alia.[51] Addressing a crowd of more than 100,000 people in Tiranë on 12 December, Sali Berisha, who subsequently would emerge as the party's dominant leader, spoke of a new beginning for Albania. He said the Democratic Party would struggle to establish a Western-style democracy. Berisha also touched on a very sensitive issue that had been almost totally ignored by Communist politicians—the question of ethnic Albanians in Yugoslavia. Denouncing the Serbian repression in Kosova, Berisha declared: "The Democratic Party of Albania cannot accept the division of the Albanian nation as eternal; therefore, it will struggle by peaceful means and within the context of the processes of integration in Europe to realize their rights for progress and national unity."[52]

The Democratic Party had an ill-defined ideology other than to support democracy by its very existence, and took the trappings of a mass movement involving groups and individuals who would under more normal conditions not be in political alliance with each other. Initially, it was led by a seventeen-member steering committee headed by the flamboyant student leader Azem Hajdari. From the very beginning it was evident that the intellectuals would dominate the party leadership—a fact that elicited protests from some student activists that the intellectuals had "stolen the revolution." Only six members of the steering committee were students: Hajdari, Blendi Gonxhe, Shinasi Rama, Arben Lika, Arben Sula, and Alma Bendo. In addition to Berisha, the steering committee included other intellectuals, among them Gramoz Pashko, Aleksandër Meksi, Arben Imami, Eduard Selami, Genc Ruli, and Preç Zogaj.[53] Composed of people of different political persuasions, the steering committee was plagued by factionalism and backbiting. While the students, particularly Hajdari, expressed radical views, the intellectuals, most of whom were former APL members, did not advocate overtly anticommunist policies or revolutionary strategies. With his leadership position increasingly threatened by the more astute Berisha and Pashko, Hajdari resorted more often to appeals to the population's anticommunist sentiments. While publicly Hajdari praised the two,[54] his supporters complained that Berisha's and Pashko's links with the old regime were tarnishing the democratic leadership. Popular suspicion against the Communists-turned-Democrats was widespread. In his first interview with a domestic Albanian newspaper since his defection in October, Ismail Kadare came to the defense of former Communists, saying that the criticism against them was misplaced:

> It must not be forgotten that there were hundreds of Communists, as many as if not more than others who strove for democracy in Albania and who suffered and were sentenced for it. ... To exclude Communists from the process of democratization means to consciously hinder this process and to consciously add to the numbers of the enemies of democracy. Whom will such a Stalinist approach help? One also hears harsh criticism of the fact that these activists have expressed gratitude to President Ramiz Alia after the approval of the law on party pluralism. Again, I think that this criticism does not hold water. It is human to show gratitude for an act of justice, and this has nothing to do with conformism or patronage.[55]

Berisha was born in 1944 in the northeastern district of Tropojë, on the border with Kosova. A graduate of Tiranë University, he worked for many years in the main hospital of the capital. He rose to become a prominent cardiologist, entrusted with the treatment of top Communist leaders. In 1986, Berisha, who had published several articles abroad, became a member of the Copenhagen-based European Medical Research Science Committee.[56] Although a member of the APL, a necessary precondition for anyone aspiring to higher education in Hoxha's Albania, he had an otherwise unblemished past. The region he hailed from had been under brutal repression by the Communists throughout the postwar period and remained the most underdeveloped area in the country. His background and professional service had given him unique insight into the dreary life of ordinary Albanians, especially those living in the countryside, in contrast to the privileged life of leaders in the Communist Party and government.

Pashko, reputedly the number-two man in the Democratic Party leadership, was a professor of economics at Tiranë University. Although he had become an outspoken critic of the Communist regime, many questioned his democratic credentials because he was a member of a prominent Communist family with close ties to Hoxha's clan. Both his parents had held senior government positions. His father, Josip Pashko, a founding member of the Albanian Communist Party and a member of its Central Committee, had served as deputy general prosecutor, deputy minister of internal affairs, and minister of construction. Although the elder Pashko had died in 1963, most Albanians still remembered his vicious prosecution of regime opponents in the show trials of the turbulent 1940s. A beneficiary of the many privileges reserved for the Communist *nomenklatura*, Gramoz Pashko was among the very few Albanians who had studied and traveled abroad. He joined the APL in April 1990, as the foundations of the Communist regime began to crumble. He has said that he joined the APL because he believed he could make a greater contribution to democracy by working within the system; however, when he joined the APL, he did not believe that an anticommunist opposition could be organized.[57] Pashko was among a small group of experts that Alia selected in spring 1990 to explain government policies to foreign journalists and visitors. A fluent English speaker, he developed close contacts with foreign journalists, which he later skillfully exploited while gradually distancing himself from the regime. Although Pashko's public criticism of the government in the wake of Kadare's defection had attracted widespread attention, his close ties to the *nomenklatura* raised doubts in the minds of many people as to whether he was sincere or just a Communist "agent."

Gradually, three factions, centered around Berisha, Pashko, and Hajdari, began to compete for the Democratic Party leadership. Some members of the steering committee, concerned that increased rivalry in the highest echelons would destroy the party, offered a compromise. A meeting held on 8-9 February 1991 resulted in Aleksandër Meksi's election as temporary chairman of the steering committee. But Meksi apparently was unacceptable both to Berisha's and to Pashko's supporters. On 13 February, a nineteen-member managing committee was elected and charged with the responsibility of running the party until a national conference could be held. Three new members—Blerim Çela, Neritan Ceka, and Rexhep Uka—were evidently Berisha supporters. By secret vote, Berisha was elected chairman and Eduard Selami secretary of the managing committee.[58]

Initially, the Democratic Party's main support base was among students, intellectuals, and workers in Tiranë. The fledgling party lacked organizational experience and had no resources; but in spite of these inauspicious circumstances, it moved to attract and retain a significant spectrum of pro-reform forces, rapidly emerging as the most important opposition group. The Democratic Party organized rallies throughout the country, at which it denounced the failings of the Communist system, evoking a passionate outpouring of pent-up emotion against more than four decades of Communist rule. The Democrats demanded that parliamentary elections, scheduled for 10 February 1991, be postponed to give the opposition time to prepare for them.[59] They also called for significant changes in the election law, that had been approved by the People's Assembly in November 1990—before the legalization of opposition parties.[60] The Democratic Party insisted on the full depoliticization of all state institutions, particularly the ministries of defense, internal affairs, and justice. It demanded the immediate elimination of Communist Party cells in government institutions and the abolishment of political commissars in the armed forces. An editorial in the Democratic Party newspaper argued that the rule of law could not be established without the genuine depoliticization of ministries and government power throughout the country.[61] In a wide-ranging interview with the Voice of America, Berisha explained his party's objectives: "Our strategy aims at building a democratic Albania fully integrated into the European processes, with a stable market economy, free citizens, and free movement of people, goods, and ideas; an Albania finally detached from its tragic six-hundred-year-old links with the East. Our strategy is aimed at realizing our nation's aspirations for progress and national union. But this will be achieved only in the framework of European processes and through dialogue with all interested parties."[62]

As the first opposition party, the Democratic Party enjoyed an unquestionable advantage. Resembling an umbrella organization more than a traditional party, it rapidly attracted a massive membership with diverse political interests. Its membership included former APL members, individuals who had been politically inactive until then, remnants of the National Front and Legality, and former political prisoners. Almost from the beginning, the Democratic Party was viewed as the most viable alternative to the APL. But despite the presence among its members of many die-hard anticommunists and former political prisoners, who took a more conservative stand on many issues than former APL members, the Democratic Party rapidly rallied around the common objectives of establishing a genuine multiparty system and a civil society. However, the most radical members of the party, eager to see a speedy dismantling of the Communist structures that permeated all levels of Albanian society, were soon disappointed with the leadership's leisurely assault on the Communist regime.

The Democratic Party's reluctance to launch a frontal attack on the regime was reflected in an interview that Berisha granted to the Voice of America's Albanian Service in early January 1991. Asked about Hoxha, Berisha gave an ambivalent response, characterizing the former Communist leader as a "complex figure." He said: "Under [Hoxha's] leadership, Albania witnessed undeniable progress in many fields. But he built a dictatorial regime and was a dictator."[63] In a subsequent interview with the Voice of America, writer and recently released political prisoner Kasëm Trebeshina chastised the opposition for not directly challenging Hoxha's cult, insisting that opposition leaders were not truly anti-communist.[64] But Democratic leaders, recognizing their party's weaknesses and concerned about the danger of a backlash by conservative Communist forces which would likely lead to a popular revolt or even civil war, emphasized reliance on peaceful means. They tried to reassure the Communists that they had nothing to fear from the establishment of a multiparty system.

Other Opposition Parties

Arguably the second most important opposition group, the Republican Party operated largely in the shadow of its sister Democratic Party. From its inception, it was plagued by factional infighting. Republican Party leaders were alleged to have had close ties with senior APL officials. Republican Party Chairman Sabri Godo, a prominent writer, was accused of being a Sigurimi agent, a charge he vehemently denied. Godo's rivals insisted that Alia was instrumental in Godo's election as party chairman.[65] In his public pronouncements, Godo expressed support for the Communist leader, saying that Alia was the only person who could ensure the nation's stability.[66] The Republican Party also opposed public rallies organized by the Democratic Party, insisting that they would destabilize the country.[67]

In addition to the Democratic and Republican parties, other parties were formed, including the Ecological, Agrarian, and National Unity Parties and the organization Omonia, representing the country's ethnic Greek community. It was widely believed that APL and secret police agents had infiltrated the leadership of the new parties, including the Democratic Party. Moreover, it was rumored that Alia had engineered the creation of the Ecological, Agrarian, and National Unity Parties in order to mitigate the rapid rise of the Democratic Party. In the disputes between the APL and the opposition, these parties tended to side with the Communists. Because they had less clearly defined goals and objectives than other opposition groupings, these parties failed to attract significant support.

In December 1990, a group of prominent lawyers, historians and writers established the Forum for the Protection of Basic Human Rights and Liberties. Tiranë University professor Arben Puto, who had very close ties with the Communist *nomenklatura* and had served on the commission that drafted the 1976 constitution, became chairman of the organization. Abdi Baleta, former Albanian representative to the United Nations, became secretary of the forum. With the exception of the well-known translator Jusuf Vrioni, none of the members of the forum could claim persecution under the Communist regime or distinction as anti-communist fighters.[68]

Legacies of Communism

Notwithstanding Alia's agreement to permit the establishment of opposition parties, the Albanian road to democracy was strewn with land mines in the form of the cumulative political, economic, and social legacies of Hoxha's Communist dictatorship, which made genuine democratization seem almost impossible. For close to half a century, Albania had been isolated from the outside world and from democratic values and principles. This isolation, combined with a lack of democratic traditions, had inculcated and reinforced a set of values and behavior not particularly hospitable to the development of democracy.

Hoxha's regime had engaged in gross violations of human and political rights, causing great trauma and incalculable psychological damage to the population. Tens of thousands of Albanians vanished in prisons and labor camps; another 700,000 were subjected to other forms of government repression.[69] Relying on the military, the secret police, and mass organizations, the APL ensured the population's obedience through its unchallenged monopoly over political power. The ruling party prohibited the creation of any group or organization outside its control, ensured that political behavior was overtly conformist, and left no avenues for public participation in decisionmaking. Elections were a facade, their only purpose being to legitimize the ruling party. The authorities almost always claimed unanimous popular support. In the last election for the People's Assembly or parliament before the legalization of opposition, the Central Election Commission announced a voter turnout of 100 percent. It said all had voted for the official candidates, with only one ballot in the entire country found to be void.[70] No other regime could claim such "widespread" support.

The People's Assembly played a minor role in Albanian politics. It met only twice a year, to approve decisions already made by the Party leadership. Members of the parliament had no opportunity to express independent views or to criticize government policy. Communists controlled all leading positions and members of the Politburo usually held the senior government posts—especially the chairmanships of the Council of Ministers (Prime Minister) and of ministries dealing with defense and economic matters.

The rule of law was alien to Communist Albania. During the cultural revolution of the 1960s, the government went so far as to abolish the Ministry of Justice and to prohibit the practice of law. The APL's supremacy was enshrined in the constitution. Even when ruling Communist parties in other East European countries experimented with limited political reforms, expanded the possibilities for political participation, and tolerated the creation of dissident groups and organizations, the APL did not stray from its Stalinist policy of totally suppressing the opposition. In contrast to other East European countries, where in the late 1970s and 1980s dissident communities had emerged, the development of a democratic elite in Albania and the emergence of an Albanian Havel were impossible. The noncommunist elite had long ago been obliterated, while prominent intellectuals, including Ismail Kadare, were too closely identified with the regime. Thus, the lack of a well-developed liberal elite was both the most significant political legacy of Albanian communism and the greatest obstacle to the creation of viable democratic institutions. With very few exceptions, leaders of the emerging political parties, most of them former APL members, displayed only a nascent understanding of democracy; and the population at large, at last free of Communist shackles, showed a remarkable ignorance of the responsibilities of democracy and a limited tolerance for diverse points of view. Because of Communist repression, the government and the people were separated by a deep gulf. Many Albanians continued to display little trust in the government and saw their society as divided between "us" and "them." There was a widespread percep-tion that all government officials were corrupt, interested only in looking after their selfish interests and those of their families and clans. Many displayed a lack of personal responsibility and accountability and a deeply rooted perception that others would step in and solve Albania's problems. According to a U.S. Information Agency public opinion survey conducted in 1991, while the over-whelming majority of Albanians (90 percent) favored a market economy, only a third believed that individuals should take more responsibility for themselves. More than half of the respondents expressed the view that the state should take more responsibility for providing for everyone.[71]

The APL had carried out perhaps the greatest social experimentation in Eastern Europe, imposing its total control over all aspects of life with the aim of perpetuating its rule. No room was left for any sort of activity outside Party control, including the intimate details of family life. Through an extensive spy network, supported by the all-encompassing police and military establishment, the ruling party had kept popular demands for greater freedom under control, thus ensuring the population's continued conformity with its policies. The objective of the police state was to prevent the rise of alternative power centers that might threaten or undermine APL control over Albanian society. The Communist regime not only prevented the development of a liberal elite but also left a legacy of popular conformism and apathy, thus seriously complicating the development of a civil society. In the wake of the end of one-party rule, Albanians wrestled with the question of why they had tolerated Hoxha's dictatorship for such a long time. Some suggested that unless the Albanians acknowledged their collective responsibility for the Communist devastation of their country, they would not be able to build a new and better society. Writer and former member of parliament Teodor Keko, deploring the fact that Albanians had resigned themselves to Communist rule and had not organized a single revolt against Hoxha's dictatorship, urged his fellow citizens to "ask Albania's forgiveness." Keko thus echoed the pangs of conscience troubling many Albanians: "We preserved our lives but gave up Albania's life."[72]

Hoxha's Albania went further than any other East European country in its attempts to copy the Stalinist model of economic development.[73] The model "represented an extreme form of centralism and autarky and perpetuated a stagnant economy caught in a low-level productivity trap."[74] Its main aspects included the adaptation of a highly centralized planning system, the complete abolition of private property and activity, and heavy industrialization. All decisions regarding investments and allocation of resources were made at the highest level. The self-reliance policy pursued after the break with China had devastating consequences for the country's development. With its heavy emphasis on the rapid industrialization of the country, the Communist regime pursued a policy that neglected other sectors of the economy. But perhaps more importantly, the highly rigid system had destroyed the small class of private entrepreneurs that existed when the Communists took power and had prevented the emergence of a managerial class. It left no room for initiative and destroyed the work ethic. Moreover, because of the lack of accountability on the part of decisionmakers, the system was characterized by massive waste and mismanagement of national resources. Enterprises, heavily subsidized by the state, had no incentive to improve their efficiency.

The Albanians emerged from communism illprepared for the painful transition to a market economy. The abrupt dismantling of the Communist social welfare system, combined with the soaring rate of unemployment, left many citizens in a precarious position. The state, practically bankrupt, possessed few resources with which to alleviate the social burden of new reforms. Moreover, the population in general, as well as the emerging political and economic elites, were unfamiliar with the workings of a market economy.

Through brute force and an extensive system of privileges, Hoxha had succeeded in creating a loyal *nomenklatura* class. While the majority of the population lived at the level of mere subsistence, senior Party officials enjoyed enormous wealth, luxurious living quarters for themselves and their families, villas in resort areas, fancy cars, travel and medical treatment in the West, study abroad, special stores, and unlimited access to imported goods. The highest-ranking members of the leadership lived in special housing compounds commonly referred to as *the block*, in complete isolation from the citizenry. In the late 1980s, Politburo members possessed at least 131 luxurious villas. They spent millions of dollars for personal purposes. Special stores and even factories were set up to meet the needs of the country's elite.[75] The Hoxhas lived in a house with 25 refrigerators, 28 color televisions, and 19 telephone lines.[76] Hoxha's house and those of other top leaders were connected to a network of underground tunnels.[77] According to official statistics released in 1991, the hard currency spent on clothes and cosmetics for the family of one Politburo member alone was equal to the wages of an average worker for twelve years.[78] There were also persistent reports that Communist leaders had deposited large amounts of cash in foreign banks. Responding to an article in an Italian magazine contending that the Hoxhas were among the 300 richest families in the world, Hoxha's son Sokol in 1991 apologized to the Albanian people for the privileges his family had enjoyed in the past, but denied reports that it had money or investments abroad. Speaking also on behalf of his brother and sister, Sokol Hoxha said: "I sincerely admit that we lived with such privileges, growing up, that we did not realize the gulf that separated us from ordinary people."[79]

One of the greatest challenges facing Albania at the end of 1990 was a pervasive moral and spiritual crisis, a direct legacy of the Communist regime. Large segments of the population appeared to have lost confidence in themselves, in their country, and in their government and institutions. Many saw no future in Albania. Between 1990 and 1996, close to half a million Albanians, most of them young, fled their country. Among those who emigrated were many members of the technical intelligentsia. This exodus will have a devastating long-term impact on Albania.

Many Albanian analysts have asserted that communism's most serious damage to Albania is not economic, but rather, moral and cultural: the destruction of Albanians' national traits and dignity. They have expressed less concern for the possible rise of nationalism than for what they call a lack of "Albanianism."[80] There appears to have been a widespread decline of national pride and civic morale. Some Albanians went so far as to adopt foreign names and even change their religion in an attempt to gain permission to settle in other countries.[81]

No doubt the most observable inheritance of Hoxha's rule is the country's physical landscape.[82] Hundreds of thousands of bunkers—a testimony to the Communist leadership's siege mentality—are scattered across Albania. These ugly structures can be found on the plains, at the coast, in the mountains, in school backyards, and even in urban areas. Not only are these bunkers of no value for national defense; they are a monument to the immense waste of resources under Communist rule. The average cost of one bunker was equal to that of a two-room apartment. The bunkers also occupy significant spaces of arable land and the costs of removing them are prohibitive. Had Communist authorities invested the enormous resources and labor used to build the bunkers in the civilian housing sector, Albania would have solved its critical housing shortage long ago.

With its policies of uneven economic development and its emphasis on heavy industry, the Communist regime neglected the development of infrastructure, which will seriously complicate the country's economic recovery. The road system is insufficient for Albania's rapidly growing needs. Until 1991, private vehicles were banned, and in the entire country there were no more than several hundred cars, all belonging to Party and government officials. With the introduction of market reforms, the number of private vehicles has steadily increased, and the current road network is not designed to handle the heavy traffic.

Another legacy of Communist rule is the underdevelopment of communications. Hoxha was obsessed with exercising total control over the population and preventing unauthorized contacts between the population and foreigners. There were only a limited number of telephones, reserved for the privileged members of the *nomenklatura*. Direct links with other countries were established as recently as spring 1990. The lack of a modern, well-developed communications network has discouraged foreigners from conducting business in Albania.

In their attempt to rapidly industrialize the country, the Communists pursued policies that did tremendous damage to the environment. The government constructed large steel, coal, and petrochemical projects with the aim of ensuring the country's economic independence. The emphasis was on large-scale production, with no thought for even minimal maintenance, safety standards, or protection of the environment. Albania's rivers, lakes, and coast, and the air in its major industrial centers, were heavily polluted by the antiquated machinery and technology used in mining, metallurgical industry, light industry, and thermal energy production. The emission of highly toxic gases and dust into the atmosphere had become a serious problem. A case in point was the gigantic steel mill in the industrial city of Elbasan, built in the mid-1970s with Chinese assistance. Described by Albanian leaders at the time as "the second liberation of Albania," the steel combine was built with outdated machinery and technology, without the installation of adequate equipment to control or minimize air pollution. The plant emitted a range of poisonous substances, presenting a serious health hazard for the population in Elbasan and surrounding areas. Although the steel mill apparently operated for years with an annual loss of up to $100 million, its complete shutdown was politically unacceptable; in the late 1980s, the complex employed over 10,000 people. In most industrial areas, the burning of fuel oil and coal without any measures to protect the environment caused serious air pollution. Crude oil floats freely from some oil fields into rivers and lakes as a result of lack of appropriate equipment to adequately separate oil from water.

The government campaign in the 1960s to open up virgin lands and the accompanying massive deforestation caused significant damage to the fauna. According to a joint World Bank-European Community study, overexploitation of forests, especially overcutting for fuelwood, the main source of heating, is endangering natural regeneration and is leading to further degradation. The report also suggested the government close or rebuild the worst polluting mills.[83] Inappropriate agricultural practices also were implicated as a source of serious environmental degradation. Albanians will be paying a heavy price for past errors and environmentally unsound policies far into the twenty-first century.

Albania has had the misfortune of being ruled by one of the most repressive Communist regimes in the world and for a longer period than any other East European state. As the authors of a study by the U.S. Commission on Security and Cooperation in Europe put it, "The degree of brutality and inhumanity which existed in the policies and practices of the Hoxha and Alia regimes is almost impossible to comprehend."[84] The characteristics of Hoxha's Communist regime, more totalitarian than any other in the region, made the move toward democracy in Albania monumentally more difficult than elsewhere. De-Stalinization and subsequent reformist trends, which changed the face of communism in other countries, had bypassed Tiranë. Albania's Stalinist political system and its entrenched state-run economy remained essentially unchanged for decades. While other East European states witnessed the emergence of a nascent civil society long before the collapse of their Communist regimes, the concept was alien to Albania. The influence of Western democratic ideas was limited to a small group of intellectuals, members of the establishment. Thus, from the outset, the odds against the emerging Albanian opposition were probably far greater than anywhere else in Eastern Europe.

Notes

1. Ramiz Alia, ...*Shpresa dhe zhgenjime* [...Hopes and Disappointments] (Tiranë: Dituria, 1993), p. 18.

2. Between 1989 and 1990, at least eighty people were killed by border guards. The bodies of some of these victims were paraded through villages and cities in order to terrorize and discourage others from attempting to flee the country. See Pëllumb Sulo, "They Killed and Crucified Them, and Hid Their Graves," *Lajmi i Ditës*, 17 May 1994, p. 1. See also *Gazeta Shqiptare*, 7 January 1994, p. 1.

3. AFP in English, 1916 GMT, 10 June 1990, p. 1 in FBIS-EEU 90-112, 11 June 1990, p. 1.

4. For an eyewitness account of the storming of foreign embassies and missions in Tiranë, see Ilir Demalia, *Drejt Perëndimit: E Verteta e Korrikut 1990* [Toward the West: The Truth About July 1990] (Tiranë: Dhoma e Tregtisë, 1995).

5. *New York Times*, 7 July 1990, p. 6; and *Washington Post*, 7 July 1990, p. A13

6. Hasan Muçostepa, *Në kërkim të parajsës* [In Search of Paradise] (Tiranë: Dituria, 1993), pp. 71-72.

7. "Side by Side with the Party in Every Situation: Our Intellectuals Speak Out," *Zëri i Popullit*, 8 July 1990, p. 2.

8. The interview, broadcast by the Voice of America, appeared in *Buletini i radiove të huaja në gjuhën shqipe*, no. 513, 24 September 1990. It was also published in *Koha* [Prishtinë], 10 October 1990, pp. 32-33.

9. *Zëri i Popullit*, 7 July 1990, pp. 1-2.

10. Ibid., 8 July 1990, pp. 1-2.

11. ATA in English, 1549 GMT and 1551 GMT, 9 July 1990, in FBIS-EEU 90-132, 10 July 1990, p. 2.

12. *Zëri i Popullit*, 14 July 1990, p. 1.

13. Lisen Bashkurti, "A Generation of Dedicated Patriots and Revolutionaries," *Zëri i Popullit*, 31 July 1990, pp. 3-4.

14. *Zëri i Rinisë*, 21 March 1990, pp. 3-4.

15. Ismail Kadare, "Socialist Realism: The Great Art of the Revolution," *Zëri i Popullit*, 13 January 1974, p. 3.

16. Alia had made this statement at the 8th Plenum of the APL Central Committee, in September 1989: "No concession to bourgeois ideology must be made in any field, either in politics, art and culture, or in economic relations. There must be no concession to religious ideology in any of its various forms. We take this stand as convinced atheists, but also in order to protect our unity as a people who during the centuries suffered from rifts and divisions inspired by churches and mosques. There must be no concession to alien phenomena that conflict with our socialist morality and the customs that are our national

traits." See *Zëri i Popullit*, 29 September 1989, pp. 1-3.

17. Koço Bihiku, "Let Us View the Literary Heritage of the Past with Scientific Objectivity," *Drita*, 5 August 1990, p. 5. In a note published in the same issue of the newspaper, *Drita*'s editorial board said the issue of Konica, Fishta, and other writers whose works had been prohibited should be treated "with scientific objectivity and civil responsibility." The editorial board said that in reassessing the past, the views of scholars from Kosova, where works of Konica, Fishta, and Koliqi had been published, should be taken into consideration. At a meeting with intellectuals on 10 August 1990, Alia criticized *Drita*'s editors for asking for "assistance" from the Kosovars. Under orders from above, the newspaper was forced to discontinue the debate on the rehabilitation of banned writers. See Ramiz Alia, *Demokratizim në rrugën e partisë* [Democratization on the Party's Road] (Tiranë: The Central Committee of the APL, 1990), p. 65. The publication was stamped *secret*.

18. Alia, *Demokratizim në rrugën e partisë*, p. 13.

19. Ibid., p. 26.

20. Ibid., pp. 10, 36.

21. Alia, *Demokratizim në rrugën e partisë*, p. 95. The discussion between Alia and the intellectuals was not made public, it was confidentially circulated to Party committees. According to participants, the transcript of the exchange between Alia and Berisha was altered to omit Berisha's demand for a multiparty system. In a book published after his resignation as president, Alia argues that he was convinced that his country was not ready for a multiparty system because the Albanians lacked "the necessary democratic culture and tolerance." Blerim Shala, Llukman Halili, and Hazir Reka, eds., *Unë, Ramiz Alia dëshmoj për historinë* [I, Ramiz Alia, Testify for History] (Prishtinë: Graçanica, 1992), pp. 160-162.

22. During an exchange with Alia, Kadare reportedly said he was not sure of the meaning of pluralism, to which the President responded: "No one will believe you if you say you do not know what pluralism is. If someone else said it, that's fine, but you do not know the meaning of [pluralism]?! You know what it means, you know." Alia, *Demokratizim në rrugën e partisë*, p. 88.

23. Kadare, *Nga një dhjetor në tjetrin*, p. 253.

24. Uk Zenel Buçpapa, "Six Months of Pluralism," *Bashkimi*, 20 June 1991, p. 3.

25. U.S. Commission on Security and Cooperation in Europe, "Helsinki Commission Delegation Visits Albania, Establishes Dialogue on Human Rights" (Washington, D.C.), 22 August 1990, p. 2.

26. ATA in English, 0800 GMT, 29 September 1990, in FBIS-EEU 90-190, 1 October 1990, pp. 1-5.

27. In an interview, Sofokli Lazri, who accompanied the President on his visit, left the erroneous impression that Alia had held official talks with such heads of state as U.S. President George Bush and Britain's Prime Minister Margaret Thatcher. Lazri went so far as to say, "Everything Comrade Ramiz Alia uttered and forwarded at the U.N. General Assembly, the talks and meetings he had, were a heavy blow also to the ill-willing comments of the foreign propaganda regarding the events in the embassies in Tiranë [in July 1990]." ATA in English, 0931 GMT, 9 October 1990, in FBIS-EEU-90-196, 10 October 1990, p. 4. The media went out of their way to make the case that intellectuals fully supported Alia's speech at the United Nations General Assembly. The literary journal *Drita*, in its 30 September 1990 issue, carried statements praising Alia's speech by Preç Zogaj, Feim Ibrahimi, Zija Çela, Sulejman Krasniqi, and Çesk Zadeja.

28. *Bashkimi*, 3 October 1990, p. 1.

29. Sali Berisha, "Democracy and Humanism—An Inseparable Pair," *Bashkimi*, 17 September 1990, pp. 2-3. Berisha had submitted the article for publication to the APL's organ, *Zëri i Popullit*, but it was rejected. Qemal Sakajeva, the chief editor of *Bashkimi*, was chastised for publishing the article. He said Lazri particularly objected to Berisha's statement that the democratization of Albania would also help ethnic Albanians in Kosova. Lazri reportedly said that Berisha was demanding the change of Albania's socialist system under the guise of supporting the Albanian national cause. See Qemal Sakajeva, "The Destruction of Speech Bunkers," *Zëri i Rinisë*, 18 July 1992, p. 3.

30. *Le Monde*, 26 October 1990, pp. 1, 15, translated in FBIS-EEU 90-223, 19 November 1990, pp. 3-5.

31. The full text of Kadare's statement was also published by the Kosovar weekly *Zëri i Rinisë* (Prishtinë), 2 November 1990, p. 3. The entire issue of the magazine was devoted to Kadare.

32. *Zëri i Popullit*, 27 October 1990, p. 1.

33. ATA in English, 0957 GMT, 28 October 1990, in FBIS-EEU 90-209, 29 October 1990, p. 8.

34. For the full text of Qosja's statement, broadcast by the Voice of America, see *Zëri i Rinisë* (Prishtinë), 2 November 1990, p. 14.

35. Adem Demaçi, "The Cage Is Not for Eagles," *Zëri i Rinisë* (Prishtinë), 10 November 1990, pp. 20-21.

36. Richard Bassett, "Tardy Albanian Reform Fuels Fears of Romanian Solution," *Times* (London), 29 October 1990.

37. See article by dissident writer Kasëm Trebeshina in *Zëri i Rinisë*, 29 October 1993, p. 2.

38. Ismail Kadare, "Today's Literature and Today's Times," *Studime Filologjike* 26, no. 4 (1989), p. 11.

39. Ismail Kadare, *Ftesë në studio* [Invitation to the Studio] (Tiranë: Naim Frashëri, 1990).

40. See Alia's interview in *24 Orë*, no. 19 (April 1992), p. 3. In 1996, former Sigurimi chief Zylyftar Ramizi accused Kadare of having been an agent of the secret police and having spied on his fellow writers. *Koha Jonë*, 25 May 1996, p. 5. Kadare denied the charge. See *Albania*, 26 May 1996, p. 2.

41. ATA in English, 0900 GMT, 8 November 1990, in FBIS-EEU 90-217, 8 November 1990, pp. 1-9.

42. *Buletini i radiove të huaja në gjuhën shqipe*, no. 578, 1 November 1990.

43. *Zëri i Popullit*, 18 November 1990, p. 3.

44. Mentar Belegu, "Democracy, Pluralism, [and the Role of A] Deputy," *Drita*, 18 November 1990, pp. 2-3.

45. Besnik Mustafaj, "Dealing with the Question: Where Is the Voice of the Intelligentsia?" *Drita*, 18 November 1990, p. 5. For a critical reaction to Mustafaj's article, see Hasan Hoxha, "The Intelligentsia Speaks Out: In Connection With the Article 'Dealing With the Question: Where Is the Voice of the Intelligentsia?'" *Drita*, 25 November 1990, p. 13. In an interview with the Voice of America, Mustafaj said ethnic Albanians under Serbian occupation in Kosova were better prepared to meet the challenges that lay ahead than those in Albania. He lamented what he termed a dangerous decline in Albanians' patriotic awareness and the catastrophic economic situation. *Buletini i radiove të huaja*

në gjuhën shqipe, no. 618, 29 November 1990.

46. At least eight students among the organizers were from the district of Tropojë. These included Azem Hajdari, Bardhyl Ukcama, Gjin Progni, Arbër Ahmetaj, Afrim Krasniqi, Flamur Buçpapaj, Ismet Pali, and Bislim Ahmetaj. See *Shkelzeni* (Bajram Curri), no. 17, July 1992, p. 3.

47. See Alia's interview in *24 Orë*, no. 19, April 1992, p. 3.

48. According to a highly reliable source and an eyewitness, a bewildered student leader asked Berisha: "What is political pluralism?" An intellectual who had joined the demonstrators with Berisha reportedly had to give the students a crash course on political pluralism before they would agree to include in their petition a demand to legalize opposition parties.

49. I am grateful to Professor Nicholas C. Pano of Western Illinois University for providing me with a copy of the original petition. Professor Pano was in Albania when the demonstrations took place. The petition was not published at the time, but it subsequently appeared in *Shkelzeni*, no. 17, July 1992, p. 3.

50. *Zëri i Popullit*, 19 December 1990, p. 1.

51. The initial program of the Democratic Party was not published by the Albanian media but was broadcast by the Voice of America. The Directorate of Radio Tiranë's International Service, *Buletini i radiove të huaja në gjuhën shqipe* (Tiranë), no. 666, 19 December 1990. Reference to Alia was deleted in the expanded version of the program submitted to the authorities on 17 December 1990. See *Rilindja Demokratike*, 5 January 1991, pp. 3-4.

52. *Rilindja Demokratike*, 5 January 1991, p. 5.

53. Blendi Fevziu, *Piedestale pa Statuja* [Pedestals Without Statues] (Tiranë: Albinform, 1993), pp. 60-61.

54. Hajdari interview with the Voice of America, *Buletini i radiove të huaja në gjuhën shqipe*, no. 71, 8 February 1991. Hajdari described Berisha as "the standard-bearer of political pluralism in Albania," and Pashko as "the first person [in Albania] who had [publicly] embraced the idea of a free market economy."

55. *Zëri i Rinisë*, 20 February 1991, pp. 2-3.

56. *The Democratic Party of Albania* (Tiranë, 1992), p. 27.

57. See Pashko's interview in *Zëri i Rinisë*, 14 September 1991, p. 4.

58. Members of the Managing Committee were: Arben Demeti, Arben Imami, Azem Hajdari, Aleksandër Meksi, Eduard Selami, Gramoz Pashko, Genc Ruli, Merita Zaloshnja, Mitro Çela, Preç Zogaj, Sali Berisha, Tefalin Malshyti, Shahin Kadare, Lili Dhame, Ilir Myftari, Edmond Trake, Blerim Çela, Neritan Ceka, and Rexhep Uka. *Rilindja Demokratike*, 16 February 1991, p. 1. There were reportedly four contenders for party chairman: Berisha, Pashko, Meksi, and Hajdari. On the first round, Berisha received 9 votes, Pashko 5, Meksi 4, and Hajdari 1. In the second round, Berisha was elected unanimously. See Fevziu, *Piedestale pa Statuja*, pp. 160-164; Afrim Krasniqi, "Mr. Hajdari's Negligence or Illusion?" *Rilindja Demokratike*, 29 July 1993, p. 3; and Preç Zogaj, "How Was Berisha Elected Chairman of the PD [Democratic Party]?" *Aleanca*, 8 December 1994, p. 7.

59. The Democratic Party acknowledged that it faced an uphill battle with the APL. Spokesman Genc Pollo told the *New York Times:* "There has been so much indoctrination and political intimidation, the Stalinist legacy is so strong, that we do not think there is enough time for us before the elections to develop an alternative frame of mind among the majority of the electorate. We are therefore avoiding being excessively optimistic that we

can win." However, Shkelqim Beqari, a *Zëri i Popullit* correspondent, confidently supported the official position that the sanctioning of political pluralism would not result in the demise of Communist rule as it had in other East European countries. Beqari said: "We cannot be compared directly to the other Communist countries of Eastern Europe. We certainly have problems, and the time has come for change. But we are not like the other Communist governments. They were totally dependent on Moscow. Albania has always been independent, and in this case, too, will develop independently along its own course." See Paul Anastasi, "New Albania Barely Conceals a Stalinist Bedrock," *New York Times*, 20 January 1991.

60. Editorial "Why Is the Postponement of the Elections Being Demanded," *Rilindja Demokratike*, 12 January 1991, p. 1.

61. *Rilindja Demokratike*, 26 January 1991, p. 6.

62. *Buletini i radiove të huaja në gjuhën shqipe*, no. 28, 13 January 1991.

63. Ibid., no. 28, 13 January 1991.

64. Ibid., no. 41, 21 January 1991. Kasëm Trebeshina is widely recognized as the only dissident writer in Hoxha's Albania. In the 1950s, he had written a letter to Hoxha, denouncing his policies. He spent 17 years in prison.

65. Gafur Muço and Shpëtim Spahiu, "The Truth About the Creation of the Republican Party," *Bashkimi*, 22 July 1991, p. 2.

66. *Republika*, 10 February 1991, p. 2. On the eve of the 31 March 1991 election, Godo, in a surprising move that was widely interpreted as fatal for his own party, urged the electorate in Tiranë to vote for Alia. Viron Koka, "Political Ball with Masks," *Zëri i Rinisë*, 24 June 1992, p. 2. Koka was a member of the Republican Party's top leadership.

67. Sabri Godo interview with the Voice of America, *Buletini i radiove të huaja në gjuhën shqipe*, no. 44, 23 January 1991.

68. Other members of the human rights organization were movie director Kujtim Çashku; judges Manol Konomi and Rustem Gjata; Dr. Ylli Popa; the editor of the youth newspaper *Zëri i Rinisë*, Remzi Lani; writers Besnik Mustafaj, Elsa Ballauri, Neshat Tozaj, and Zana Shuteriqi; and historian Kristo Frashëri. See The Forum for the Protection of Basic Human Rights and Liberties, *Buletin* [Bulletin], no. 1 (March 1991), p. 3.

69. See Amnesty International, *Albania: Political Imprisonment and the Law* (London, 1984); the Minnesota Lawyers International Human Rights Committee, *Human Rights in the People's Socialist Republic of Albania* (Minneapolis, 1990); and Puebla Institute, *Albania: Religion in a Fortress State* (Washington, D.C., 1989). See also Uran Butka, *Ringjallje* [Reawakening] (Tiranë: Phoenix, 1995); and Pjetër Pepa, *Dosja e Diktaturës* [Dossier of a Dictatorship] (Tiranë, 1995).

70. *Zëri i Popullit*, 3 February 1987, p. 1.

71. United States Information Agency, *Albanians Speak Out on Political Issues* (Washington, D.C.), Report M-99-91, 15 July 1991.

72. Teodor Keko, "Our Salvation: Intelligence, Realism, and Sincerity," *Rilindja Demokratike*, 7 March 1992, p. 2.

73. For background, see Adi Schnytzer, *Stalinist Economic Strategy in Practice: The Case of Albania* (New York: Oxford University Press, 1982).

74. The World Bank and the European Community, *An Agricultural Strategy for Albania* (Washington, D.C.: The World Bank, 1992), p. 2.

75. *Gazeta Shqiptare*, 10 December 1993, p. 1.

76. *Bashkimi*, 31 July 1991, p. 1.   *Zëri i Popullit* reported that the Hoxhas' annual telephone bill alone amounted to "hundreds of thousands of dollars."   See *Zëri i Popullit*, 5 July 1991, p. 3.

77. Josif Zegali, "The Fortification of the Leaders' Compound," *Rilindja Demokratike*, 30 July 1992, p. 3.

78. *Bashkimi*, 21 June 1991, p. 2.

79. Ibid., 21 July 1991, p. 1.

80. Fatos Arapi, "This Is Golgotha," *Zëri i Rinisë*, 16 September 1992, p. 3.

81. An estimated 50,000 Albanians have adopted Greek names in the hopes of gaining legal residence in Greece. ATA in English, 1104 GMT, 27 February 1996 in FBIS-EEU 96-044-A, 5 March 1996, p. 5.

82. See Dean S. Rugg, "Communist Legacies in the Albanian Landscape," *Geographical Review* 84, no. 1 (January 1994), pp. 59-73.

83. *An Agricultural Strategy for Albania*, pp. 143-150.

84. U.S. Commission on Security and Cooperation in Europe, *Human Rights and Democratization in Albania* (Washington, D.C., January 1994), p. 10.

3

The Transition Begins:
The Communists Cling to Power

The student demonstrations in December 1990 propelled Albania into a new era that held out the promise of democracy and prosperity; but Ramiz Alia's desperate attempts to orchestrate the process of change and prolong Communist control of the government as long as possible, caused a great deal of instability, massive economic destruction, and widespread anarchy. As a result, the move toward democracy turned out to be monumentally more difficult in Albania than anywhere else in the region.

The APL's Two Steps Back: Too Little, Too Late

The decision to permit the establishment of other political parties created an entirely new environment for the Albanian Party of Labor. The extent of anti-Communist feelings became evident with the outbreak of violent demonstrations in Shkodër, Kavajë, Durrës, and Elbasan only days after Alia had accepted student demands to institute political pluralism. Demonstrators attacked and burned party and government headquarters, stormed libraries, burned Enver Hoxha's books, and caused enormous material damage. Security forces and the army needed several days to restore order. The government dealt very harshly with the demonstrators. In speedy trials, some demonstrators were sentenced up to 20 years in prison. Opposition sources claimed that many demonstrators were tortured by the police.[1] Because of heightened political tensions and a pervasive sense of insecurity, during late December 1990 and early January 1991, more than ten thousand Albanians sought refuge in Greece alone. Others fled to Yugoslavia and some to Italy.[2]

The emergence of opposition parties and their popular reception became stimuli for significant changes in APL behavior. Concerned about being politically outflanked by the emerging opposition and losing control, the APL moved to regain the initiative. The official media launched a campaign, claiming that the APL and Alia personally had initiated the reforms that eventually led to the sanctioning of political pluralism. Meanwhile, the Sigurimi worked assiduously to spread rumors that opposition leaders were Alia's people. At the December 1990 Central Committee meeting that approved political pluralism, Alia had announced the expulsion of four Politburo members—Muho Asllani, Simon Stefani, Lenka Çuko, and Foto Çami—and two candidate members—Qirjako Mihali and Pirro Kondi. In an attempt to shed their rigid Stalinist image, the authorities removed the last statue of Stalin from central Tiranë, and the Council of Ministers issued a decree removing the name of the Soviet dictator from all institutions.[3] Hoxha's widow, Nexhmije, long considered the leader of the conservative camp that was blocking changes, was replaced as chairperson of the Democratic Front by Prime Minister Adil Çarçani.[4] Ironically, Çarçani's nomination to this post ran counter to Alia's insistence that the mass organizations were no longer transmission belts for the APL.

In late December 1990, the APL held a national conference and adopted a reformist election program, breaking with many traditional Marxist-Leninist principles. After having rejected for years any movement in the direction of capitalism, the APL now endorsed a pluralistic political system, protection of human rights, and freedom of religion, and committed itself to implementing reforms that would lead to the emergence of a market economy.[5] While apparently many APL members were eager to denounce Hoxha and his policies, Alia stopped short of repudiating his mentor's legacy. He acknowledged that various mistakes had been made, but Hoxha alone could not be blamed: "We all, the entire Party, bear responsibility for everything."[6] The APL's new program, the acknowledgment of past mistakes, and the dramatically different treatment of Stalin were parts of a coordinated effort to arrest the precipitous decline in the Party's already dwindling political prestige, signaling Alia's willingness to pay a significant symbolic price to keep his job. This suggested that the president would not be overly bound to the party's past propaganda lines on critical issues. However, Alia's belated measures failed to improve the APL's image. His failure to make a clean break with the past despite mounting popular pressures to do so caused a significant defection from the APL. Moreover, the depth of revulsion against the regime was reflected by increasingly violent anticommunist activities across the country. Burdened by close to fifty years of Stalinist ideological baggage, the APL had become so discredited that its last-ditch attempt at renovation could not reverse its decline. While ostensibly seeking a dialogue, Alia clearly regarded the opposition as a threat to the APL's political future.

Although Alia was forced to allow the formation of opposition parties, he was not prepared to relinquish the APL's reins of power. Initially, the Communists rejected demands for the postponement of the elections, scheduled for 10 February 1991, arguing that the date was set by the now disbanded parliament. They also resisted calls for the release of all political prisoners. Evidently concerned that political prisoners once released would join opposition parties and advocate retaliation against the Communists, the regime engaged in a gradual release of prisoners, at each stage insisting that they were the last prisoners. After a meeting between Alia and a U.S. Congressional delegation at the end of March, at which the Albanian leader was urged to free all the prisoners, Tiranë released 277 prisoners. The group included participants in the violent anticommunist demonstrations held in mid-December 1990.[7] But contrary to official statements, the last prisoners were not released until July 1991.[8]

Although its influence had waned, the APL continued to control the main levers of power, including the military and the secret police. During decades of Communist rule, Albanian society had been subjected to a greater degree of militarization than any society in Eastern Europe. A powerful institution that had grown from the victorious partisan forces in World War II, the armed forces, together with the much dreaded Sigurimi, had been considered the bastion of Albanian communism and the main pillars of Hoxha's dictatorship. A cardinal rule of Hoxha's regime was the total control of the military and internal security forces by the Communist Party. Probably in no other East European country did a ruling communist party exercise such continuous and pervasive control over the military, or intermesh party and state as closely with the military as did the APL. The constitution promulgated in 1976 had designated the First Secretary of the APL as commander in chief of the armed forces. Throughout 1989 and 1990, the military hierarchy had maintained a high profile and strongly supported Alia's refusal to relinquish the APL's monopoly of power. In mid-December 1990, Alia ordered army troops, backed by armored vehicles, to put down anticommunist demonstrations in Shkodër, Elbasan, Kavajë, and Durrës. As tensions mounted in January and February 1991, Alia relied increasingly on military and security forces to maintain order and intimidate the opposition.

Recognizing that the army and Sigurimi were thoroughly penetrated by the Communists and likely to carry out APL leadership orders, opposition leaders were careful not to provoke a backlash from conservative forces. Democratic Party Chairman Sali Berisha adopted a conciliatory attitude toward the armed forces in the hope of convincing military leaders to stay aloof from the political changes. While the Democratic Party insisted on the complete depoliticization of the armed forces, opposition leaders made every effort to see to it that the army remained on the sidelines.

Although an arm of the regime, the military was not entirely unsympathetic to democratization. In the wake of the purge of Defense Minister Beqir Balluku in 1974, the armed forces had been subjected to devastating purges. Nevertheless, rumblings of discontent had become evident within the ranks of the officer corps, which still harbored individuals with decidedly undemocratic values. In an interview with the Voice of America on 7 February 1991, Berisha said there were increasing signs that Minister of Defense Kiço Mustaqi was preparing a *coup d'etat.* He said that army units had been redeployed around the main cities, the focus of opposition support, and that reserve forces had been mobilized. Berisha appealed to the patriotic sentiments of the armed forces, adding that "the Democratic Party has full trust that you will never, under any circumstance, rise against your own children, against the vital interests of your fatherland."[9] Mustaqi denied Berisha's allegations,[10] but an editorial in the APL newspaper warned the opposition not to press for swift changes affecting the role of the armed forces. It said that the army should be fully prepared to defend "the country's freedom and independence and the victories achieved by the people with so many sacrifices." The editorial added that "to demand reorganization, disorganization, structural changes, and new structures in the Army at such a time is the same as to demand a weakening of the homeland's defenses."[11]

The introduction of political pluralism had an immediate and significant impact on the formulation and implementation of foreign and security policies. Under the Communist regime, foreign policy had been the prerogative of the First Party Secretary and the Politburo, and it was not a subject for public debate. The democratization of the country's life saw the emergence of several, at times competing, foreign policy actors: the president and the executive branch agencies, opposition political parties, and interest groups.

One of the first actions of the emerging democratic opposition was to challenge the APL's monopoly over foreign policy formulation and to demand Albania's "return to Europe," including integration in West European political, economic, and security institutions. For the first time since the end of World War II, foreign policy came under close public scrutiny as the Democratic Party and other opposition forces pushed for the depoliticization of the foreign affairs establishment. While in the past domestic public opinion had played no role in formulating and implementing foreign policy, the emergence of a multiparty system heightened national feelings. Issues long considered taboo, such as the question of ethnic Albanians in the former Yugoslavia and in Greece, became subjects of heated public debate.

In early 1991, under the leadership of the Democratic Party, the emerging opposition advocated a reorientation of Albania's policy toward Western Europe and the United States. The Democratic Party leveled sharp criticism against Foreign Minister Reiz Malile and President Alia's chief foreign policy adviser Sofokli Lazri, who reportedly had exercised a restraining influence on Albania's expansion of ties with the West. Lazri, who apparently played a critical role in formulating foreign policy, was blamed for the poor state of relations with West Germany and the deterioration of ties with Italy. The establishment of diplomatic relations with Bonn in 1987 had raised hopes that the Germans would assist in Albania's economic development. The much hoped-for cooperation with West Germany never materialized because of the Albanian government's intransigence on questions of human rights and its rejection of foreign credits and investments. Tiranë's refusal to permit an Albanian family that had entered the Italian embassy in 1985 to leave the country until May 1990 had brought relations with Rome virtually to a standstill. Because of opposition criticism, Malile was replaced in early 1991 and Lazri was forced to resign.

In the wake of the legalization of the opposition, the authorities announced significant changes affecting the media. The Council of Ministers appointed a state commission to draft a media law. In the meantime, state radio and television as well as the official news agency, the Albanian Telegraphic Agency, were placed under the supervision of the Presidium of the People's Assembly. The newly formed political parties, organizations, and societies were given the right to publish their own newspapers and magazines. With the publication of opposition newspapers, especially *Rilindja Demokratike* [Democratic Reawakening] and *Republika*, the respective organs of the Democratic and Republican Parties, the media experienced significant changes, and the APL's monopoly over the press eroded.

Journalists, who for more than four decades had been totally subservient to the APL and played the role of propagandists, now began to play the roles of government critics and social advocates. They lost no time in exposing the lies and hypocrisy of the Communist system and puncturing its myths. Journalists also demanded constitutional guarantees of a free press. *Bashkimi*, the organ of the Democratic Front, took an increasingly independent position, and *Zëri i Rinisë*, although still carrying the Communist youth organization's label, published articles that conflicted with the APL's views. Meanwhile, the newspaper of the Union of Writers and Artists, *Drita*, became a strong supporter of the democratic opposition. Still, the APL continued to exercise tight control of official radio and television.

Despite its small circulation compared to the Communist newspaper *Zëri i Popullit*, *Rilindja Demokratike* emerged as the most important publication of the opposition press and a forum for prominent personalities. Writers began to disclose the full extent of the horrors of Hoxha's rule: the massive prison labor camps where thousands died, and the physical and psychological tortures that bred a sense of fear and betrayal in generations of Albanians. The paper published embarrassing exposés of APL leaders' misdeeds. But the opposition newspapers had to operate under severe constraints. The state continued to control their distribution and the supply of newsprint. Opposition complaints over the unfair advantages the Communist press enjoyed went unheeded.

Communist forces, especially at the local level and mainly in the countryside, spared no means to impede opposition activities. Significantly, the Communists chose the locale of Bajram Curri—Berisha's and student leader Azem Hajdari's hometown—to stage the first of what became known as "antirallies" against the Democratic Party. Reportedly acting on direct instructions from Alia, local Communists used force to disrupt a rally being addressed by Berisha. Berisha had just finished telling participants at the rally that "political pluralism marks the end of the savage class struggle waged by Enver Hoxha's regime for almost half a century," when Communist activist Sadri Metaliaj, accompanied by two other individuals, walked to the podium, took the microphone away from the Democratic Party leader, and began shouting "Long live the Albanian Party of Labor and Comrade Ramiz Alia." Radio Tiranë's local correspondent Ilir Buçpapaj reported that thousands of APL supporters staged their own rally, "shouting slogans calling for progress on the road of democratization under the leadership of the APL."[12] The Communists evidently hoped to humiliate Berisha and Hajdari, implying that if the two Democratic Party leaders did not enjoy the support of their hometown how could they be supported by others? The official media described the incident as a spontaneous reaction by the APL's supporters and published a telegram the people of Tropojë allegedly sent Alia, reiterating their *besa* (pledge of support) for the party.[13] The Bajram Curri incident ushered in a period of increasingly violent confrontations between Democratic Party and APL supporters.

Conservative Communists' Last Stand

Meanwhile, Alia came under increasing attack from two sides within his own party. The reformists increasingly castigated him for failing to make a clean break with the past. They expressed concern that Alia was moving too slow in renovating the Party. *Zëri i Popullit* journalist Sami Milloshi, who was closely allied with the reformists, publicly criticized the party leadership for refusing to put an end to the many privileges enjoyed by the *nomenklatura*, at a time when poverty in the country had reached unprecedented levels.[14] Party conservatives, on the other hand, accused Alia of leading the country to anarchy and warned of impending civil war. Alia had to tread with great caution, but he displayed significant political skill in manipulating both sides. While refusing to repudiate Hoxha, he pledged to proceed with the full democratization of the country's political and economic life. But as in the past, he continued to vacillate, relying on halfmeasures.

Despite the increasing nastiness of their confrontation and intimidation of the opposition, the Communists continued to lose ground, as the newly organized Union of Independent Trade Unions brought crushing pressures on the regime. Faced with a miners' strike in Valias near Tiranë, labor unrest in several other cities in early January, the exodus of thousands of citizens to Greece, and increasing foreign criticism, Alia gave in to opposition demands and agreed to postpone parliamentary elections until 31 March. Although the opposition parties demanded a delay until May 1991, insisting that they needed more time to organize, they now pledged to end labor unrest.[15] Alia appealed to the patriotism of Albanians, urging them to avoid paralyzing strikes and help rescue the country's stagnant economy. However, his agreement with the opposition was short-lived.

Alia's actions during this period suggested that his main objective was to ensure his selection as president by the new People's Assembly. This was part of his effort to distance himself from the APL, which he had apparently come to believe was a spent force. The draft constitution prepared by a special commission appointed by Alia in November 1990 provided extensive powers to the president. For their part, the official media began to portray Alia as a true national figure, above party affiliations. But Alia's ambiguous stand satisfied neither the reformers nor the conservatives. He responded to demands for the denunciation of Hoxha and increased attacks on Hoxha's monuments by issuing a decree for the protection of monuments dedicated to Albanian national figures such as "the leader of the National Liberation War and founder of the new Albanian state, Enver Hoxha."[16] The opposition was quick to denounce the decree as evidence of Alia's duplicity.

At the same time, Berisha and his associates came under increasing pressure from more radical elements, particularly students and workers, who were unwilling to accept any outcome short of the total overthrow of the Communist system. Edi Rama, a young artist who had organized antigovernment activities at the prestigious Institute of Fine Arts, argued that Democratic Party leaders, who were former APL members, could not lead the anticommunist struggle. He said that the "official" opposition was more interested in reaching an accommodation with the regime than in attacking the Communist legacy. In an interview with the Voice of America, Rama urged opposition parties to boycott the elections.[17] However, the leadership rejected maximalist demands from the rank and file and worked to transform the Democratic Party into a moderate party.

Meanwhile, the political situation continued to deteriorate, with the outbreak of politically motivated violence in many parts of the country. In early February, some ten thousand Albanians, having heard rumors that ferries would take them to Italy, clashed with the police in the port of Durrës. In Tiranë, furious crowds raided bookstores, burned books by Hoxha, and attacked the APL headquarters. Students in Tiranë went on strike, demanding the removal of Hoxha's name from the university.[18] In a meeting with student representatives, Aleks Luarasi, general secretary of the Council of Ministers, expressed the government's willingness to accept their demands regarding curricular changes and improved conditions at the university. But with regard to the demand that the name of the university be changed the government was uncompromising: "Tiranë University is a national institution, and as such, belongs to the entire nation. Its name, therefore, cannot be changed on the basis of the demands of a section of its students, and still less when they do not represent the entire student population. This issue involves the feelings and wishes of the entire people."[19] The youth organization, which a short time earlier had declared its independence from the APL, distanced itself from the student strike. Lisen Bashkurti, the first secretary of the Central Committee of the Union of Working Youth, said his organization could not support the strikers' political demands because the students were being used "as party political instruments."[20] The Democratic Party initially appeared less than enthusiastic in its support of the student strike. Pashko reportedly urged the students to end the strike, saying the Democratic Party had reached an agreement with Alia to this effect.[21] Democratic leaders were apparently concerned not to move precipitously, lest they cause a backlash and lose control.

But events took on a life of their own. With the government maintaining an uncompromising position, more than seven hundred students and faculty members went on a hunger strike. The students, led by Blendi Gonxhe, Ridvan Peshkëpia, and Arben Lika, refused to compromise, insisting that the future of democracy in Albania hinged on the government's acceptance of student demands. The regime's efforts to restrict media coverage of the event were unsuccessful, as the Voice of America broadcast daily reports and interviews with hunger strikers and their supporters. The Council of Ministers rejected student demands, a position also endorsed by the APL Central Committee on 19 February. The Democratic Party responded by throwing its full weight behind the students.[22] Berisha declared, "It would be tragic if the cult of Enver Hoxha were to become the cause for a great national drama, which history could never justify."[23]

The dangerous political polarization also raised the concerns of ethnic Albanians in Kosova, then in the throes of an upheaval against Yugoslav military occupation. Mark Krasniqi, chairman of the Forum of Kosova's Intellectuals, appealed to the students to end their strike, saying Albania's stability and sovereignty were at stake: "We want democratic Albania to march toward Europe. Hence we are calling on you to return to your studies, work, and production. Kosova is calling on you not to forget this: Do not allow Albania to be destroyed by chaos and anarchy. Democracy is not anarchy; return to unity and tolerance, which are in the interest of the country."[24]

The former leader of the Communist League of Kosova, Mahmut Bakalli, who had been dismissed in 1981 following ethnic Albanian demonstrations demanding republic status for Kosova, also called on the students to end their strike.[25] Messages by Krasniqi and Bakalli, widely disseminated by the Albanian official media, were harshly criticized by students and the opposition in Albania. The director of Radio Tiranë's International Service, Napoleon Roshi, accused Alia's government of manipulating the Kosovar public opinion.[26] Meanwhile, in contrast to Krasniqi and Bakalli, academician Rexhep Qosja, no doubt at the time the most popular Kosovar in Albania, urged Alia to meet student demands. In an interview with the Voice of America, Qosja said: "One cannot live off the fame of a dead man, especially one who has died in two ways—as a man and as a symbol. ... From every vantage point—political, moral, and state—it is unacceptable that even a drop of blood be shed in the Skanderbeg Square for a dead name.[27] And at the peak of the crisis, Ibrahim Rugova, leader of the Democratic League of Kosova, arrived for a visit in Tiranë, providing much-needed moral support to the opposition. In an interview, Rugova advised Albania's leaders: "to act with cool heads, to not slacken the pace of the democratic process. To avoid events like those of recent days, the ruling Albanian Party of Labor and the other political parties should be calm and moderate, putting aside feuds and hostilities. They must understand that pluralism is a factor of unity and is to Albania's benefit. ... Everyone must realize that there must be tolerance and open discussion among the parties, and things must not be considered matters of life or death for one party or another."[28]

The contradictory messages coming from Kosova reflected the deep divisions that developments in Albania had caused in the ranks of ethnic Albanians. But more significantly, for the first time in the memory of most Albanians on both sides of the border, Kosovar Albanians were publicly taking a stand on an issue of vital importance for internal developments in Albania. The implication of this event was clear: The Kosovars, considering themselves an integral part of the larger Albanian nation, were asserting their right to have a say in the affairs of their mother country. This was seen by the Communists as unacceptable interference in Albania's internal affairs.

Although the effect of the student strike was not immediately apparent, in the long run it galvanized the anticommunist movement. On 20 February, more than 100,000 people gathered in Tiranë's central square and tore down Hoxha's statue. The statue was loaded onto a truck and sent to the campus of Tiranë University, where it was broken up into small pieces and handed out to the crowd as mementoes. To the horror of conservative Communists, the demonstrators cut off the head of Hoxha's statue, placed it back on the truck and paraded it through the city. The most important remaining symbol of communism in Albania had fallen.[29] While these dramatic events were unfolding in Skanderbeg Square, the APL Central Committee was holding an urgent meeting. Hoxha's widow, Nexhmije, who walked out of the Central Committee meeting crying after the announcement of the downing of Hoxha's monument, chastised the leadership for not using force to prevent it, adding that "at least one person should have been killed that day for Enver." Mrs. Hoxha claimed that "it was all a plot prepared by the state organs and people within the Interior Ministry. The monument's screws had been loosened the night before. The truck [that carried the monument around Tiranë] belonged to the Interior Ministry."[30]

Only hours after the toppling of Hoxha's monument, the authorities dramatically reversed their position. The government negotiator, Minister of Education Skendër Gjinushi, informed the students that the dictator's name would be removed from Tiranë University.[31] The official media carried a terse decree, signed by Prime Minister Çarçani: "Because Tiranë University will be reorganized, it will no longer carry Enver Hoxha's name. This decree goes into effect immediately."[32]

The events of 20 February led to a rapid and dangerous radicalization of the political scene. Democratic supporters toppled Hoxha's statues in many cities around the country, attacked the APL leadership's compound in Tiranë, and set fire to a bookstore selling Hoxha's works. Conservative Communists, taking advantage of the controversy surrounding Hoxha's name, had already mobilized their forces, launching a nationwide campaign against the opposition. Despite cadre changes carried out during the previous year, the APL leadership still contained many holdovers from the World War II period.

The old guard sanctioned the formation of an organization called the Enver Hoxha Voluntary Activists' Union. The organization, founded in Berat on 12 February 1991, was led by Hysni Milloshi, a relatively unknown writer. Although a member of the APL, Milloshi had not held any influential position. It was subsequently disclosed that Milloshi founded the organization on the specific instructions of Politburo member Xhelil Gjoni and Minister of Defense Mustaqi, who was alleged to have been preparing a *coup d'etat*. District and local APL committees and military divisions were ordered to assist Milloshi.[33] Military vehicles were used to transport Hoxha supporters to different rallies. There were also reports that the military was arming the Enverists, as members of the group were called.[34] The organization recruited its members mainly in the countryside, primarily in the south, the bastion of Communist conservatism. In a message to Alia, dated 12 February but published belatedly on 19 February, leaders of the organization accused opposition forces of destabilizing the country and vowed to defend Hoxha's name and legacy. In an apparent move aimed at discrediting Gramoz Pashko, the message listed his father Josip Pashko as an honorary member of the organization.[35]

The publication of the message at a time of heightened tensions indicated that the Enverists enjoyed the support of powerful members of the Politburo. In the wake of the downing of Hoxha's statue in Tiranë, the group organized pro-Hoxha rallies all over the country, intimidated and beat up opposition supporters, demanded that the Democratic Party be outlawed, and restored Hoxha's statues in many places. At these rallies, Hoxha supporters also shouted slogans against Kosova, blaming ethnic Albanians in Yugoslavia for having exported political pluralism to Albania.[36] Members of the organization threatened to march on the capital and restore the dictator's monument, and to declare the city of Vlorë, where Albanian patriots proclaimed the country's independence in 1912, the new capital. In a subsequent interview, Milloshi claimed that tens of thousands of people had volunteered to join the organization. He claimed that in Sarandë alone, 10,400 volunteers were registered, and in Has, 9,500.[37]

This period saw a dangerous escalation of terrorist violence against Democratic Party members and supporters. Several prominent opposition activists were killed in Tiranë, Elbasan, Fier, and Korçë. Security forces hunted down the most outspoken activists, arresting and torturing hundreds of them. Pro-Hoxha demonstrators tied up Democratic Party members and paraded them before restored statues of the former dictator.[38] The deepening political crisis caused another mass exodus: Some twenty thousand Albanians, most of them potential supporters of the Democratic Party, fled to Italy. Albania appeared perilously close to a civil war.

Alia responded by assuming personal control over the country and announcing a new government, replacing Prime Minister Çarçani with thirty-nine-year-old economist Fatos Nano. He appointed a nine-member presidential council, which with the exception of Nano, was made up of well-known hard-liners. They included former Chairman of the Presidium of the People's Assembly (titular head of state) Haxhi Lleshi, President of the Supreme Court Kleanth Koçi, writer Kiço Blushi, Tiranë University professors Lufter Xhuveli and Rexhep Meidani, journalist Minella Dalani, and military officer Xhenet Muço. The Presidential Council issued a statement urging support for the new government. It warned that if law and order were not restored, a state of emergency would be declared.[39] Alia's decision to assume personal control over the country's affairs and form a presidential council was in direct violation of the country's constitution. Sabri Godo, the leader of the Republican Party, had publicly suggested that Alia take these two measures, thus adding credence to accusations by his rivals that he was playing Alia's game.[40] Godo also had suggested suspending all activities relating to Hoxha's name and deciding the issue through a national referendum after the elections.[41]

Soldiers in Multiparty Politics

Meanwhile, disgruntled officers at the Enver Hoxha military academy in Tiranë had announced the creation of an Initiating Commission of the Movement for the Defense of the Interests of the People and the Homeland. An ultimatum addressed "to the President, political parties, and the entire Albanian people" demanded an immediate national referendum on Hoxha; the implementation of laws on the protection of economic, social, cultural, and historical objects (for example, Hoxha's monuments); a meeting with Alia, representatives of political parties and defense and internal affairs ministries, and reporters; and the placement of radio and television under the supervision of the Presidential Council.[42]

In a meeting held on 22 February 1991, there were rancorous exchanges between officers and representatives of political parties. Agim Bajraktari, chairman of the Initiating Commission, described the toppling of Hoxha's statue as "a barbaric act." He said the Commission had the duty "of defending the victories achieved by our people, and to guard democracy from vandals and dark forces that seek to destabilize the situation and create savage confrontations."[43] Radio Tiranë did not report on the officers' sharp criticism of Alia. According to the minutes of the meeting, published for the first time in December 1995, Bajraktari accused the president of being indecisive. He said the officers were determined to defend Hoxha, whom he described as Albania's "greatest historical figure" after Skanderbeg. Other officers said Alia had failed to carry out his responsibilities as commander in chief. They blamed the president for the breakdown of law and order. Abdi Baleta, professor of law at Tiranë University and member of the Forum for the Protection of Basic Human Rights and Liberties, said the officers' action was unconstitutional and tantamount to a *coup d'etat*. Both Baleta and Neritan Ceka, the Democratic Party representative, insisted that the officers respect the constitution and obey Alia, their commander in chief. Ceka left no doubt that on this issue his party was fully behind Alia, emphasizing that "the Democratic Party will consider any attempt to act in contravention of the constitution and against Ramiz Alia a military putsch."[44]

While the meeting was still under way, amid rumors of a potential military coup, opposition supporters gathered in front of the military school. The word had spread that military officers were planning to take Hoxha's bust from the academy and place it in the center of Tiranë. Clashes broke out between cadets, officers, police, and opposition supporters. Four people, including a policeman, were killed and dozens injured.[45]

Alia was summoned by disgruntled military and security officials to the headquarters of the Ministry of Internal Affairs to explain why he had failed to take measures to prevent the removal of Hoxha's statue in Tiranë. Alia reportedly responded that he had ordered the police and security forces to open fire on the demonstrators but that his order was ignored. Later, Hekuran Isai, then minister of internal affairs, would claim that he did not carry out Alia's order because he feared a major massacre.[46] In the meeting with Alia, the officers demanded that Mustaqi continue to serve as minister of defense, that a state of emergency be declared, the ultimatum be broadcast by the official media, Hoxha's family be provided full security, and the Democratic Party be outlawed. Alia reportedly said that the armed forces were not prepared to take over if a state of emergency was declared. He also said that the Democratic Party could not be outlawed because of adverse international reaction. Alia, however, accepted the other three demands, reversing his decision to name a new defense minister—Manxhar Binaj, former district party secretary in Gjirokastër.[47]

The Democratic Party, warning of the possibility of a military dictatorship,[48] swiftly mobilized its supporters. A spokesman for the Ministry of Defense, rebutting Democratic Party accusations, assured the nation that the armed forces "will carry out the orders and instructions issued by Comrade Ramiz Alia, our commander in chief."[49] Supporting elements of the coup attempt failed to materialize.

The incident at the military academy remained shrouded in mystery. No immediate action was taken against its organizers, an indication that senior officials were behind the affair. It appeared that the coup attempt had been in the works for weeks and stemmed from a broad-based plot by hard-liners, headed by Mustaqi, to stifle growing anticommunist activities by the opposition.[50] Abdi Baleta suggested that Alia himself was behind the incident.[51] In July 1996, a court in Tiranë sentenced Mustaqi to five years in prison, the Director of the academy Arseni Stroka to three years, and the Commissar of the Academy Ksenofon Çoni to four years. The three, who fled Albania in 1992, were sentenced in absentia on charges of inciting cadets at the military academy.[52]

In an address to the nation on 23 February, Alia tried to reassure conservatives of his continued loyalty to Hoxha: "I wish to stress once again that Enver Hoxha is a historical personality with strong roots in the people, and that history does not judge with the mentality of manipulated crowds. Statues may be removed, but the figure of Enver Hoxha cannot be toppled, because he personifies the biography of the people and the history of new Albania. The APL and the entire Albanian people are proud to have had a leader like Comrade Enver."[53] For days, Alia, with such die-hard Communists as Çarçani, Nexhmije Hoxha, Haxhi Lleshi, Xhelil Gjoni, and World War II veteran Shefqet Peçi at his side, met with Hoxha supporters and tried to reassure them. He took no action against the Enver Hoxha Voluntary Activists Union, which had terrorized the nation for weeks. He said that the contentious issue of Hoxha's monuments would be decided by the newly elected People's Assembly or by a national referendum after the elections. At the same time, he reached an agreement with opposition parties according to which they promised to suspend all activities relating to Hoxha's name and monuments during the election campaign.[54]

Meanwhile, Nano announced his cabinet, retaining only four ministers from the previous government, including most significantly Defense Minister Mustaqi. Foreign Minister Reiz Malile was dropped and replaced by his deputy Muhamet Kapllani. Some of the newcomers, such as Deputy Prime Minister Shkelqim Cani, Chairman of the State Planning Commission Leontiev Çuçi, and Minister of Food and Light Industry Ylli Bufi, were considered moderates. Minister of Internal Affairs Gramoz Ruçi and Minister of Education Kastriot Islami were hard-liners and would play a destructive role in subsequent developments.[55]

The events surrounding the toppling of Hoxha's monument strengthened Alia's position, albeit temporarily. He skillfully played off the conservative and reformist camps against each other. Many people, echoing the official media, emphasized Alia's indispensability as the only person able to guide Albania through the difficult transition period. Mehmet Elezi, former member of the APL Central Committee and former leader of the youth organization, called on Albanians to rally around Alia, adding that he was the only leader acceptable to all sides.[56]

In an article in his party's newspaper, Berisha said that despite Communist attempts to terrorize and intimidate opposition activists, the Democratic Party would continue its peaceful struggle for the democratization of the country.[57] And despite the tense political atmosphere,[58] the Democratic Party regained the initiative and beat back the Communist backlash. Conservative Communist forces had made their last stand and had failed to derail the democratization process.

The 1991 Elections: The Communists' Pyrrhic Victory

The election campaign got under way amid a highly charged political atmosphere. In the wake of the Communist backlash after the toppling of Hoxha's statue, some 20,000 Albanians, commandeering a variety of vessels, had fled to Italy.[59]

From the beginning of the campaign, opposition leaders warned that the elections would not be free and fair,[60] since the Communists had refused to make the provisions necessary for fair electoral competition, such as allowing equal access to state media. Elections were to be held less than four months after the regime had permitted the formation of opposition parties. Although the November 1990 election law marked a significant break from the previous law, it was adopted while Albania was still a one-party state and therefore was clearly designed to ensure the Communists' electoral success. The authorities, however, refused to recognize election law flaws and resisted opposition demands for changes.

The opposition viewed the electoral system as biased in favor of the ruling party. The two largest opposition forces, the Democratic and Republican Parties, unsuccessfully advocated changes in the election law and the adoption of a proportional, rather than a majority, system.[61] The ruling party also enjoyed a clear advantage over opposition parties in that it possessed a strong nationwide organization and enormous resources. After the removal of Hoxha's statue in Tiranë, the APL reimposed its traditional censorship on radio and television, appointing a new general director—Fatmir Kumbaro, member of the APL Central Committee. The opposition, on the other hand, had at its disposal few resources and insufficient time to build a viable national organization.[62] Moreover, the opposition conducted its campaign in an atmosphere of tension and intimidation.[63] In a letter to the Presidential Council only weeks before the elections, Eduard Selami complained about attacks against Democratic Party supporters in Tiranë, Elbasan, Korçë, Fier, and Skrapar. Recognizing the power of television to shape the voters' opinions, the Democratic Party leader expressed particular concern over biased television coverage of the campaign. He also said voter registries were flawed and delayed, causing increased suspicions regarding possible phantom voters.[64] The complete list of candidates was published on 21 March, only ten days before the elections.[65]

Competing Party Platforms and Campaign Tactics

The APL campaigned on a platform of security and continuity. While admitting that mistakes had been made in the past, it promised improvements.[66] The APL said it would take steps to transform the highly centralized economy into a market economy, but that this would be done gradually in order to preserve stability. While promising that some sectors of the economy would be privatized, the APL insisted that the state would continue to play a major economic role.[67] In the area of foreign policy, the Communists promised to open up the country. But evidently recognizing that the opposition's election program was much more appealing than their own, the Communists waged an essentially negative campaign, using every means at their disposal to discredit the opposition.

The authorities had pledged to provide all contesting parties with free and equal access to radio and television.[68] However, state radio and television, under Fatmir Kumbaro's supervision, slanted their coverage of the election campaign to mirror the Communists' hard-line attitude toward the opposition. In addition, the APL controlled Tiranë's two dailies, Zëri i Popullit and Bashkimi,[69] as well as newspapers in the country's twenty-six administrative districts. In contrast, there were only two main opposition papers, Rilindja Demokratike and Republika, published twice weekly with an average circulation of sixty thousand copies. In the cities, the Democratic and Republican Parties did not encounter serious difficulties in publicizing their election platforms. In the countryside, however, where some 65 percent of the population lived, they were unable to spread their message. Thus, in the urban centers, the APL monopoly had been broken, while in the rural areas, APL committees remained very powerful and intimidated opposition supporters. Moreover, there was a massive discrepancy in the size of voting districts. While in the urban areas a voting district could have as many as thirteen thousand registered voters, in the rural areas some districts had only five thousand.

Having apparently written off most urban areas, where the Democratic Party enjoyed overwhelming support, the APL concentrated its campaign among the peasants. The opposition recognized the difficulty of securing the support of the countryside. Hysen Çobani, then deputy chairman of the Republican Party, described the countryside as "the last stronghold" of communism. He said the peasantry was largely ignorant because of lack of information. He complained that the peasantry was unfamiliar with the opposition's stand because the Democratic and Republican Parties had been unable to spread their message among that sector of the population.[70]

Moreover, the Communists waged a nasty campaign aimed at frightening peasants with stories of what the opposition would do if it came to power. At the beginning of the election campaign, Gramoz Pashko had called for the full privatization of land. But perhaps more important, he said legislation should be passed to permit foreigners to buy land in Albania. The APL ideologues focused their attacks particularly on these two aspects of the Democratic Party's agrarian policy. Because of the negative reaction to his proposals, Pashko reversed his position in an article published on 16 March, saying that land would not be sold to foreigners but would be divided among peasants based on their family size.[71] Nevertheless, Communist propaganda continued its fierce attacks on Pashko's program.[72] The Communists were quite successful in their efforts to frighten the peasantry, which had been brutalized and isolated for decades and was ill disposed toward change. Ignoring Pashko's policy shift, an article by an agronomist claimed that if the Democratic Party's agrarian program were implemented, the peasantry would simply starve and the country be sold to foreigners.[73] Moreover, on the eve of the elections, the government tried to manipulate the rural electorate with the announcement of several highly publicized decisions. The regime permitted enlarged private plots, and peasants were allowed unlimited ownership of livestock.

The ruling party also attempted to score points by releasing hundreds of political prisoners and permitting the opening of mosques and churches, that had been closed by Hoxha in 1967. In addition, interviews with foreign officials and journalists were selectively reported, distorted, or even invented to reflect support for Alia and the APL. German reporter Victor Meir was quoted as saying that Alia had distinguished himself during the difficult transition period and that he was "a seasoned politician who thinks for the present and future of Albania, and who acts in conformity with the aspirations of the Albanian people."[74] A reporter with a German television station allegedly said that no party or state leader had ever impressed him as much as Alia.[75] In their attempt to make Alia look good, the official media did not spare even senior Western officials. The state television distorted the statements of Senator Dennis DeConcini, head of a U.S. Helsinki Commission delegation that visited Albania to observe the elections. In a meeting with Alia, the U.S. lawmaker was alleged to have told the president: "You are making correct decisions in every field. ... You are the country's true reformer and are doing everything good in the service of your people."[76] The day after the broadcast, bewildered opposition leaders and ordinary Albanians approached members of the U.S. delegation, inquiring whether Senator DeConcini had indeed made those statements. Although the Senator held a news conference in Tiranë denying he had made remarks supportive of the Communist regime, Albanian television and the Communist-controlled newspapers failed to carry his denial.[77] The state television showed foreign dignitaries, including Senator DeConcini, Senator Claiborne Pell, chairman of the U.S. Senate Foreign Relations Committee, and West European parliamentarians arriving at the presidential palace to pay their respects to Alia. Their meetings with Berisha and other opposition leaders were not broadcast.[78]

The Communists also skillfully benefited from blunders by senior opposition leaders. At the invitation of the U.S. State Department, Berisha and Pashko had visited Washington to participate in the signing ceremony on the occasion on the restoration of U.S.-Albanian relations on 15 March. Upon his return from Washington, Pashko was quoted as telling a rally in Berat that if the Democratic Party won the elections, it would receive a "blank check" from the United States.[79] He repeated the same statement to a Western news agency, saying that State Department officials had told him "Just win the elections, and you'll have it."[80] The Communists used Pashko's statement to score propaganda points, suggesting that

Democratic leaders were U.S. spies and in the event they came to power, they would establish a "client" government.[81] While Pashko had indeed made a serious gaffe in claiming he had been promised a blank check, he and Berisha had been told that Albania could count on U.S. economic assistance if the Communists were thrown out of power in the upcoming election. In a meeting with opposition representatives in Tiranë on 20 March, David Swartz, the head of the State Department delegation sent to reopen the U.S. embassy in Tiranë, said that the United States would provide Albania with desperately needed humanitarian assistance but that economic aid would be granted only if democratic forces came to power.[82]

As election day approached, the campaign against opposition candidates reached a hysterical pitch. The Democratic Party continued to denounce the APL's relentless use of state media to promote its own candidates and widespread efforts to intimidate leading anticommunist candidates. Predictably, the Communist media portrayed Democratic Party candidates in an especially negative light. Top officials of the Democratic Party, among them Berisha, Pashko, Azem Hajdari, and Neritan Ceka, became the targets of a vicious character assassination campaign. The Communist press republished poems glorifying the APL, Hoxha, and Karl Marx, written before 1990 by Democratic Party candidates Besnik Mustafaj, Rudolf Marku, Koçi Petriti, Teodor Keko, and Natasha Lako.[83] *Zëri i Popullit* published an open letter sent to Pashko by a group of veterans from Tepelenë, in which they accused him of betraying his own father, who had fought with them in World War II.[84] A day before the elections, the APL organ carried what it claimed was a medical report certifying that Hajdari had been discharged from the military for medical reasons. The report, which was widely distributed in Hajdari's election district in Shkodër, termed the Democratic Party leader a "psychopath."[85] The Communists also attempted to manipulate the Albanian American community. The official media published statements by procommunist individuals, claiming to speak on behalf of the Albanians in the United States.[86]

The Democratic Party's election motto was "We want Albania to be like Europe." In its platform, the largest opposition party called for a radical transformation of the political, economic, and social systems. Berisha assembled an impressive group of young intellectuals who put together a credible alternative program to that of the APL. Democratic Party leaders outlined specific proposals for radical reforms, which called for the creation of a Western-style political system based on the rule of law and respect for human rights. They demanded dismantling APL control of the media, a thoroughgoing privatization, and an infusion of foreign aid. Insisting that only radical reforms would lead to the reinvigoration of Albania, the Democrats demanded a sharp division between state and party, including the total depoliticization of the military, security forces, and foreign policy. Blaming Hoxha for the gross misallocation of resources, which had led to destructive industrial and disastrous agricultural policies, the Democrats issued a comprehensive and far-reaching program of policies designed to transform Albania's centrally planned economy into a functioning market system. Pashko, the author of the party's economic shock therapy program, insisted it was imperative that Albania move rapidly toward a market economy through a total overhaul of the economic structure and a radical revision of existing legislation, to attract foreign capital and technology and to develop the country's abundant mineral resources.[87] In what at the time appeared a radical stand, the Democratic Party called for the elimination of collective and state farms, the full privatization of agriculture and the return of land to farmers, the elimination of state subsidies, and an end to the state monopoly over foreign trade.[88]

There were few differences between the election programs of the Democratic Party and the Republican Party. The Republicans also called for the establishment of a state based on the rule of law, full protection of human rights and liberties, and restructuring of the economy. But in contrast to the Democratic Party's radical approach to economic reform, the Republican Party advocated a middle-of-the road approach. It said that the future of cooperatives should be decided by farmers and land should be given to those who work it. The Republican Party maintained that the farmers should not be allowed to sell, buy, or rent the land.[89]

Final Tally

Altogether, eleven political parties and associations fielded 1,074 candidates for the 250 seats of the unicameral People's Assembly. Of these, only two were truly in opposition and posing a credible challenge to the Communists—the Democratic and the Republican Parties. Omonia was mainly interested in advancing the interests of the ethnic Greek community, and fielded candidates only in the southern districts of Gjirokastër and Sarandë. The Agrarian and Ecological Parties, nominally independent, were essentially Communist creations.[90] The Agrarian Party focused on rural issues and fielded more than thirty candidates in Fier, Lushnje, and Tepelenë. The Ecological Party, whose platform advocated immediate measures to protect the environment, fielded only two candidates, in the industrial centers of Elbasan and Lushnje. The others—the youth organization, women's organization, trade unions, the Democratic Front, and the National Veterans Committee—were Communist-controlled mass organizations.[91]

The Democratic Party fielded candidates in all 250 election districts; the APL, in 243; the Republican Party, in 165; and the Democratic Front, in 122. There were also seventeen independent candidates.[92] Ironically, the chairman of the Electoral Commission, Rexhep Meidani, was also a candidate.

Overall, the March 1991 election results confirmed a trend evident in the other Balkan countries—Romania, Bulgaria, and Yugoslavia's Serbian and Montenegrin republics—in which voters failed to make a clean break with the Communist past.[93] The APL won 169 (67.6 percent) of 250 seats in the People's Assembly. It achieved an overwhelming victory in the countryside, which was a function of the strict control exercised by the Party over the peasantry. Nonetheless, in a highly significant development, prominent APL candidates, including Alia, Foreign Minister Muhamet Kapllani, and Party Secretary Spiro Dede, suffered humiliating defeats. Prime Minister Nano was forced into a runoff. Alia's loss was especially significant because he was defeated by a little known Democratic Party candidate. President Alia had refused proposals to run in Librazhd, Elbasan, Pogradec, Skrapar, or Dibër, where his victory would have been almost certain. In a letter to supporters in mid-March 1991, Alia, who was the youth organization's candidate, said he would run in an election district in Tiranë, which included the neighborhood where the APL was founded in 1941.[94]

By contrast, the Democratic Party won seventy-five seats (30 percent), sweeping the major cities but doing poorly in the countryside. Other winners were Omonia, with five seats (2 percent), and the National Veterans' Committee, with one seat (0.4 percent). The Republican Party failed to win any seats. Voter turnout was very high, at 98.92 percent; 56.17 percent voted for APL candidates, while 38.71 percent voted for the Democratic Party.[95] One day after the elections, Xhelil Gjoni, one of the most conservative members of the APL Politburo, told a news conference that the election results showed that Albanians still had faith in Marxism-Leninism.[96] But while the opposition failed to deny the Communists the two-thirds majority necessary to pass major legislation, the Democratic and Republican Parties together carried about 40 percent of the popular vote. Indeed, had the Communists agreed to opposition demands for a proportional electoral system, the APL would have won 141 seats instead of 169; the Democratic Party, 97; the Republican Party, 4; the Democratic Front and Omonia, 2 each; and the other four Communist-controlled mass organizations, 1 each.[97] Nevertheless, the results represented a significant victory for an opposition that was less than four months old, had limited resources, could not get its message to the countryside, and had been denied equal access to the state-controlled radio and television.

Altogether, nineteen international groups monitored the elections. Most, however, gave rave reviews, ignoring opposition complaints of many irregularities. However, the U.S. State Department, the U.S. Helsinki Commission, the National Republican Institute for International Affairs, and the National Democratic Institute for International Affairs, which had sent monitors to Albania, expressed concern that the elections had not been entirely free and fair.[98]

Opposition leaders were disappointed with the election results but tried to put the best light on them. In an article in *Rilindja Demokratike*, Berisha said that while the elections were not free and fair, his party accepted the results and would continue its efforts to achieve its objectives by working within the system.[99] The Republican Party hailed the elections as a victory for democracy and an end to the one-party system.[100]

Although the APL scored a big win, it was a Pyrrhic victory. The elections further polarized society between the cities, which were overwhelmingly anticommunist, and the impoverished countryside. Following the elections, developments in Albania unfolded very rapidly and the situation in the country became truly precarious. On 2 April 1991, security forces in Shkodër killed four Democratic Party activists—Arben Broci, Nazmi Kryeziu, Bujar Bishanaku, and Besnik Ceka—and wounded fifty-eight others during a public demonstration of Democratic Party supporters who were protesting alleged vote fraud by the APL.[101] The Democratic Party boycotted the opening session of the new parliament to protest the killings in Shkoder. Meanwhile, leading economic indicators plummeted. There was a huge leap in unemployment and continuing labor unrest.

As expected, Alia was elected president. With the Democratic Party deputies abstaining, Alia received 172 votes. His only challenger, Namik Dokle, chief editor of *Zëri i Popullit*, received 2 votes. In conformity with recent changes in the constitution, Alia resigned all Party posts. He then named Nano to form a new government. But although Nano submitted a reformist program of economic and social change, within weeks it became evident that the Communists could not govern the country without the acquiescence of the opposition. The Independent Trade Unions, with the blessing of the Democratic Party, launched a general strike on 15 May, demanding wage increases of 50 percent, and better working conditions. In addition, the unions insisted that the government arrest and put on trial the security officials responsible for the shooting deaths on 2 April of four Democratic Party activists in Shkodër. Nano declared that the government was practically bankrupt and could not meet the demands for wage increases. The strike spread, eventually involving as many as 350,000 workers, and paralyzed the country. Miners at Valias, near Tiranë, staged a hunger strike, which led to demands for the resignation of the government. The strike also received international support. Lane Kirkland, president of the AFL-CIO, issued a statement, in which he said:

> Free trade unionists in Albania are joining their brothers and sisters in the other nations of Eastern and Central Europe in taking a leading role in the struggle for freedom and democracy. ... [T]heir courage, their solidarity, and their commitment to securing a democratic future are an inspiration to trade unionists in the United States. The AFL-CIO extends its best wishes and support to the members of the Albanian Independent Trade Unions at this critical time in Albania's history. We also urge the government of Albania to recognize the legitimate needs and aspirations of Albanian workers and to safeguard their right to engage in peaceful protest.[102]

Alia, who throughout the three-week crisis had maintained a low profile, withdrew his support of Nano. After less than two months in office, the government was forced to resign on 4 June. In his resignation speech, Nano told members of parliament, "You have no idea how bad the situation is."[103]

Constitutional Changes

One of the first items on the parliament's agenda was the debate on a new constitution. In December 1990, the APL had published a draft constitution.[104] Although the draft did not mark a clean break with the Communist system and represented a continuation of the old legal order, it was considerably different from Hoxha's 1976 constitution.[105] The document emphasized "the great socioeconomic transformations" that Albania had experienced under the rule of the APL, referred to the country as the "People's Socialist Republic," retained the flag and the emblem with the Communist five-pointed red star, and stipulated that the state "protects the victories of the people's revolution." However, it eliminated the constitutionally privileged role of the APL. The 1976 document had referred to the APL as "the sole leading political force of the state," proclaimed Marxism-Leninism the official and sole ruling ideology, and referred to Albania as "a state of the dictatorship of the proletariat." In addition to reiterating the human rights provisions included in the 1976 document, which it had never respected, such as freedom of speech, press, organization, association, assembly, and public demonstration, the 1990 draft recognized freedom of religion. Although it referred to the country's "socialist economic system," the draft recognized private property and omitted any reference to Hoxha's self-reliance policy or the prohibition against foreign aid and joint ventures with foreigners. The President of the Republic was granted substantial powers, including chairing meetings of the Council of Ministers . In a marked departure from Hoxha's constitution, the 1990 draft designated the President, rather that the APL's First Secretary, commander in chief of the armed forces and chairman of the Defense Council. The People's Assembly was defined as "the supreme body of state power and the sole legislative body." The draft also contained a separate chapter on the judiciary, which was proclaimed independent.

Nonetheless, the 1990 document was overtaken by developments following the sanctioning of political pluralism and the rise of opposition parties. After the March 1991 elections, the victorious Communists pushed to adopt the constitution as soon as possible, in the hope of preserving as much as possible of the old order. The Democratic Party, however, insisted on a modern, democratic constitution which would replace the rule of the APL with the rule of law, provide for a clear-cut separation of powers, checks and balances, and safeguards for fundamental human rights. Although the Communists enjoyed the necessary two-thirds majority in parliament, they did not wish to antagonize the democratic opposition and therefore agreed to significant revisions of the December 1990 draft.[106] Nonetheless, the Democrats, with the support of some reformist Communist deputies, rejected the new draft, arguing for a more powerful parliament and a weaker president. The drafting of a new document would require substantial work and the assistance of foreign constitutional experts, but the country urgently needed an interim solution. In one of the first and most important agreements between the Communists and the Democrats about the fundamental values and procedural norms of the new system, the parliament passed a provisional constitution on 29 April 1991.

The document, entitled the Law on the Main Constitutional Provisions, was intended to be in force for a limited period of time, until a new, complete constitution could be drafted and ratified. It merely sketched the framework of the new system, leaving other major issues to be regulated by separate laws. While it did not present a clear-cut break with the Communist legal system and in fact contained some provisions from the December 1990 draft, the new document no longer referred to Albania as a "socialist republic." The document endorsed political pluralism and a multiparty system, while guaranteeing human rights and equality of all forms of property ownership—state, collective, and private. It limited the powers of the President, to be elected by the legislature for a five-year term. The People's Assembly was given substantial authority in defining "the main directions of the internal and foreign policy of the state." The parliament also was given control over the activity of radio, television, and the Albanian Telegraphic Agency. Meeting a major opposition demand, the Law on the Main Constitutional Provisions prohibited all party activity in the Ministries of Defense, Internal Affairs, Justice, and Foreign Affairs.[107]

The APL's Tenth Congress: The Party on Its Deathbed

Alia's resignation as Party first secretary and his failure to designate a successor precipitated a frantic struggle for power within the APL. The March elections appeared to have strengthened the conservative wing of the Party. Xhelil Gjoni, who was elevated to full membership in the Politburo in the wake of the embassy incident in July 1990 and emerged as Alia's right-hand man, appeared poised to become the next Party leader. On the sixth anniversary of Hoxha's death, the Party daily *Zëri i Popullit*, reflecting the strong influence of the hard-liners, published an editorial hailing the former dictator as a "great leader." Ignoring the disastrous consequences of Hoxha's policies, the editorial bluntly asserted that there was no need for the APL to apologize to the Albanian people, because it owed them "neither a material nor a moral debt."[108] Alia joined Nexhmije Hoxha, Adil Çarçani, Gjoni, and other hard-liners in laying a wreath at the former Party leader's grave.[109] The president's actions distressed APL reformers, who were calling for a reappraisal of the party's past. In a clear affront to the hard-liners, reformist Party secretary Spiro Dede said in an interview that the party must take full blame for the crises facing the country. He deplored the excesses of the past, adding that "it would be to the Party's good if it were to criticize itself and seek public forgiveness for all cases of injustice, excesses, unjustified and undeserved punishments, and so on." Dede, who had been elevated to the Party's Secretariat in December 1990, echoed opposition calls that measures be taken against all officials who had abused their positions[110]—a direct threat to all members of the Politburo.

The APL convened its 10th Congress on 10 June 1991. Traditionally, the keynote address was delivered by the Party first secretary. Since Alia had resigned this post, the task fell to Xhelil Gjoni, reinforcing speculation that he would become the Party's leader. Although he tempered his criticism of Hoxha by saying that the late dictator had many merits, Gjoni surprisingly criticized the main aspects of Hoxha's domestic and foreign policies, including the emphasis on class struggle, full collectivization of agriculture, the country's self-reliance policy, and the isolation of Albania from the outside world. In addition, Gjoni criticized members of the Politburo for abusing their official positions. He attacked Alia, saying he had been too slow in initiating reforms and had tolerated corruption and abuses by Politburo members.[111] The arch-conservative was speaking from a moderate reformist position. It is very likely that Gjoni's speech represented a tactical move on the part of the hard-liners, who were willing to accept a mild rebuke in return for having Gjoni, a relative newcomer to the Politburo who could not be blamed for past leadership policies, elected Party leader.

In his address to the Congress, Alia acknowledged his own personal mistakes and said the APL was responsible for the crisis Albania was now facing. But he stopped short of denouncing Hoxha.[112] Meanwhile, Nexhmije Hoxha defended her husband, expressing regret that the APL leadership had not responded to increasing domestic and foreign criticism of the former dictator. She dismissed Gjoni's report, saying it reflected "the desire to please all sides" in the Party.[113]

The Congress reached a high point with Dritëro Agolli's venomous condemnation of Hoxha's dictatorship. After Ismail Kadare, Agolli was Albania's best-known writer. Since the early 1970s, when he was appointed president of the Union of Writers and Artists, Agolli had been responsible for ensuring that the Party line was reflected in the country's literature. Indeed, he had been involved in the inquisition of writers who fell out of favor with the regime and ended up in prison.[114] Because he was considered an important member of the establishment, his speech at the congress was unexpected.

The writer denounced what he called "the triple cult of Enver, the Party, and the secret police," which led to the destruction of the personality of man and the humanism of Albanian society: "Man became a collective with the personality of a crowd, without individuality and an identity. ... People became afraid of one another, and they saw a spy in everyone. They became afraid of everyone around them, even their family. This fear existed also between husband and wife." Agolli went on to say that the Communist class struggle "was in fact the most devastating biological war known in the history of the Albanian people." He described the destruction of religious institutions as "the culmination of the insanity of the class struggle," which aimed at eliminating all cults except those of Hoxha and the APL. He accused the Communists of having pursued a deliberate policy of impoverishing Albania's peasantry, which "for centuries had served as the base for Albanian patriotism." Agolli also sharply criticized Alia for having pursued policies that stressed continuity with those of Hoxha. Then, in an unprecedented and courageous move, Agolli accepted responsibility for his own personal actions during the long period of Communist rule: "As have all prominent Albanian writers, from Ismail Kadare and down, I have sung about the ideals and dreams of this party, few of which were realized. I have sung about Enver Hoxha, as I imagined him. I have sung about socialism, which I truly believed would transform the world and would enrich man spiritually and materially. But for a long time I have realized my mistake, and now, disappointed, I say we must abandon once and for all this mistaken path, a path that has caused misery to the Albanians, lowering their dignity and national pride."[115] Agolli's speech caused an uproar in the hall of congresses with hundreds of delegates rising, stamping their feet, clapping in unison, and echoing the traditional APL Congress chant: "Party, Enver, we are always ready." Unable to finish his speech, Agolli stomped off stage, but not before telling delegates "these acts are the reflection of a party on its deathbed."[116]

Although the conservatives had appeared to have a majority of delegates, in a surprise development they suffered a humiliating defeat. Fatos Nano, who only days earlier had been forced to resign as prime minister, was elected chairman of the Party. Former members of the Politburo were condemned by the Congress, and nine of them were even expelled from the party. Seeking to polish the Communists' tarnished image, the 10th Congress changed the name of the APL to the Albanian Socialist Party and replaced the Politburo with a eighteen-member Presidency and the Central Committee with an eighty-one-member Steering Committee.

On 3 July, the Party published its new program. Jettisoning the APL's fifty years of Stalinism, it rejected Marxism-Leninism and abandoned the goal of creating a Communist society. Reflecting the Party's loss of confidence in Communist ideals, the Socialist Party identified itself with the principles advocated by European social democratic parties. The restructured Party also expressed support for the creation of a market economy but maintained that reforms had to be introduced gradually. While advocating privatization, the Socialist Party favored preservation of the agricultural cooperatives and retention of vital industrial sectors under state control.[117] The new Party leadership went out of its way to emphasize that the Socialist Party was qualitatively different from the APL. But although they stressed the concept of socialism and repudiated the Marxist-Leninist nature of the old Party organization and ideology, Socialist Party leaders were unwilling to give up the substantial wealth and property they had inherited from the APL. The value of the buildings, publishing houses, and other assets the Party owned was not known, but opposition sources estimated that it amounted to hundreds of millions of dollars. In July, the Communist-dominated parliament rejected a bill introduced by the opposition to confiscate the Party's property.

Rank-and-file reaction to changes approved by the 10th Congress was mixed. Some complained that the Congress had not gone far enough. Dali Bilali, a Party veteran of thirty-eight years, described the changes as "half measures." He said former senior Party officials, whose policies had done irreparable damage to the country, should be dealt with in the same way that Hoxha dealt with regime opponents in the 1940s.[118] Faik Kerpaçi expressed regret that the Party did not distance itself from the Enver Hoxha Voluntary Activists' Union. He urged the party to expel all Enverists, and Party officials to publicly acknowledge the mistakes they had committed. He said that only by taking such measures could the Party regain "the trust of the masses and the intelligentsia."[119] Others, however, opposed the new policy. H. Hasko, Party first secretary in Vlorë district, said, "There is no reason for our party to engage in self-criticism, because it has not made any mistakes."[120] Opponents of the new line formed a rump Communist Party.

In the wake of the 10th APL Congress, President Alia's position was significantly undermined.[121] His closest former Politburo colleagues were disgraced and faced trial on charges of embezzlement, abuse of power, and corruption. Alia eventually would be charged with the same offenses. He had served in the Politburo since 1956 and had been a member of Hoxha's circle of close advisers. With Hoxha having been publicly repudiated by his own party, now Alia's role in the many bloody purges, the cultural revolution in the 1960s, Albania's isolation, and other event was subjected to increasing scrutiny by the opposition. In the final analysis, he could not escape responsibility for the exacerbation of the crisis since his accession to power in 1985. Reports that he had ordered the police to open fire against the demonstrators who toppled Hoxha's monument in Tiranë in February, and allegations of his implication in the Shkodër events of 2 April, led to increasing demands for his resignation.[122]

In contrast to his dominant role in Albanian politics before the 31 March elections, Alia came to play only a passive postelection role. The Law on the Main Constitutional Provisions had nibbled away his responsibilities and authority, leaving him exposed to constant speculation about his job security, his clout, and his effectiveness. In July, Arben Imami, a leading Democratic Party activist, publicly called for his resignation. Alia convened a meeting with representatives of the Socialist Party and the opposition parties and asked whether they in fact wanted him to resign. He was reportedly told that press articles demanding his resignation reflected individual opinions and not those of political parties.[123] Clearly, Alia was more acceptable to the opposition parties than a new, "reformed" Communist president. Alia more or less acquiesced in being cast as an ineffective leader, a leader whose time had passed. Only months after his party won a landslide victory and the parliament elected him president for a five-year term, Alia went along with a situation where his ineffectiveness was placed on glaring display.

Ramiz Alia had developed the reputation of a skillful politician with an unusual survival instinct. During his long career he had weathered many crises, surviving many bloody purges. Burdened by close to fifty years of Stalinist ideological baggage, he had delayed the implementation of radical economic and political reforms. Like Soviet leader Mikhail Gorbachev, he had attempted to orchestrate the process of reform, prolonging as long as possible the APL's monopoly of power; but his failure to act as a decisive and determined leader only deepened the crisis, and with the exception of Hoxha, no one was more responsible for Albania's deplorable state of affairs.

Some observers speculated that Alia had favored swift changes but was blocked by conservative forces within the Politburo and by Mrs. Hoxha, who was seen as being at loggerheads with the president. However, there is no evidence to support this view. Indeed, Alia strongly opposed rapid change and subordinated the nation's overall interest to ensuring continued Communist control. His legitimacy was based on Hoxha's legacy, and his political authority derived from the discredited APL and not from a popular mandate. He was willing to carry out gradual changes, but only under party control. While there is no question that he mitigated the regime's harsh dictatorship, to the end Alia remained firmly committed to the basic tenets of communism. He embraced democracy and made concessions only under pressure and when the alternative—the use of force—was politically too risky and therefore unacceptable. In his writings and public pronouncements after leaving office in April 1992, Alia attempted to carve out a place of honor for himself in Albania's history as a distinguished leader who had avoided civil war. It is true that, when his political demise seemed certain, he did not make one, last, desperate stand against the introduction of pluralism. The unwillingness of opposition leaders to be provoked and the patience of the Albanian people, however, deserve greater credit for a transition that was less violent than it could have been. Alia will go down in Albanian history not as a distinguished leader but, like other Communist politicians in his position, as a leader incapable of embracing democratic government.

Notes

1. Vienna Domestic Service in German 1100 GMT, 20 December 1990, translated in FBIS-EEU 90-245, 20 December 1990, p. 6; and Tiranë Domestic Service in Albanian 2100 GMT, 19 December 1990, translated in FBIS-EEU 90-245, 20 December 1990, p. 7.

2. For coverage on the exodus to Greece, see *New York Times*, 2-15 January 1991.

3. *Zëri i Popullit*, 22 December 1990, p. 1.

4. Ibid., 21 December 1990, p. 1.

5. Ibid., 3 January 1991, p. 1.

6. Tiranë Domestic Service in Albanian, 1900 GMT, 26 December 1990, translated in FBIS-EEU 90-250, 28 December 1990, pp. 1-9.

7. AFP in English, 1508 GMT, 30 March 1991, in FBIS-EEU 91-062, 1 April 1991, p. 14. Only two weeks earlier, the government claimed that all political prisoners had been released. See *Zëri i Popullit*, 13 March 1991, p. 1.

8. *Zëri i Popullit*, 3 July 1991, p. 1.

9. Berisha's interview with the Voice of America was also carried by *Buletini i radiove të huaja në gjuhën shqipe*, no. 70, 8 February 1991.

10. *Zëri i Popullit*, 19 February 1991, p. 1.

11. "Strengthening the Country's Defense—A Basic Task for Every Patriot," *Zëri i Popullit*, 10 February 1991, p. 1.

12. Tiranë Domestic Service in Albanian, 1900 GMT, 11 January 1991, translated in FBIS-EEU 91-009, 14 January 1991, p. 4. See also *Rilindja Demokratike*, 12 January 1991, p. 1. A year later, local democratic forces would take revenge by disrupting a Communist-organized rally and forcing Fatos Nano, leader of the renamed Socialist Party, to flee Bajram Curri.

13. Halil Buçpapaj, "We Are With You As Long As We Live," *Zëri i Popullit*, 11 January 1991, p. 1.

14. Sami Milloshi, "The Dialectics of Renewal," *Zëri i Popullit*, 1 February 1991, p. 1.

15. *Zëri i Popullit*, 18 January 1991, p. 1.

16. Ibid., 23 January 1991, p. 1.

17. *Buletini i radiove të huaja në gjuhën shqipe*, no. 84, 15 February 1991. Democratic Party officials referred to Rama and his colleagues as Sigurimi "provocateurs." See also Ardian Klosi and Edi Rama, *Refleksione* [Reflections] (Tiranë: Albania, 1991).

18. *New York Times*, 8 February 1991, p. A6; and *Rilindja Demokratike*, 9 February 1991, p. 1.

19. Tiranë Domestic Service in Albanian, 1900 GMT, 11 February 1991, translated in FBIS-EEU 91-029, 12 February 1991, P. 3.

20. Tiranë Domestic Service in Albanian, 1900 GMT, 11 February 1991, translated in FBIS-EEU 91-029, 12 February 1991, p. 4.

21. See Myftar Gjana, "Why I Do Not Believe You, Gramoz Pashko," *Kosova*, 15 December 1991, p. 5. Gjana was one of the strike organizers.

22. Tiranë Domestic Service in Albanian, 2100 GMT, 19 February 1991, translated in FBIS-EEU 91-034, 20 February 1991, p. 7.

23. Berisha interview with the Voice of America in *Buletini i radiove të huaja në gjuhën shqipe*, no. 88, 19 February 1991.

24. Belgrade Tanjug Domestic Service in Serbo-Croatian, 1610 GMT, 19 February 1991, translated in FBIS-EEU 91-034, 20 February 1991, p. 5.

25. Ibid.

26. Interview with the Voice of America, *Buletini i radiove të huaja në gjuhën shqipe*, no. 88, 19 February 1991.

27. *Buletini i radiove të huaja në gjuhën shqipe*, no. 90, 20 February 1991.

28. *Bashkimi*, 25 February 1991, pp. 1-2.

29. For coverage of the toppling of Hoxha's statue, see *Bashkimi*, 21 February 1991, pp. 1-2, and *Rilindja Demokratike*, 23 February 1991, pp. 1-2.

30. See Mrs. Hoxha's interview in *Fjala* (Prishtinë), no. 38, October 1991, pp. 8-9.

31. ATA in English, 0913 GMT, 21 February 1991, in FBIS-EEU 91-035, 21 February 1991, p. 4. See also Skendër Gjinushi, "From the Hunger Strike to the Downing of the Monument," *Koha Jonë*, 20 February 1994, p. 4.

32. Tiranë Domestic Service in Albanian, 1900 GMT, 20 February 1991, translated in FBIS-EEU 91-035, 21 February 1991, p. 4.

33. Aranit Tomorri, "The Chronicle of a Military Coup: An Appeal for Justice," *Rilindja Demokratike*, 21 February 1993, pp. 2, 4.

34. See Albert Shala, "On 'The Society of Enver's Volunteers,'" *Zëri i Popullit*, 30 June 1991, p. 2.

35. *Zëri i Popullit*, 19 February 1991, p. 1.

36. Shala, "On 'The Society of Enver's Volunteers,'" p. 2. Shala harshly criticized the APL leadership for having tolerated the destructive activities of the Enverists and for failing to distance itself from the group at the 10th Party Congress, held in early June 1991.

37. Interview with Hysni Milloshi, *Zëri i Rinisë*, 10 July 1991, p. 2.

38. Sali Berisha, "Democracy Under Dangerous Attack," *Rilindja Demokratike*, 27 February 1991, pp. 1-2.

39. *Zëri i Popullit*, 23 February 1991, p. 1. Alia claims that the presidential council was simply a consultative body, with no decisionmaking functions. See Blerim Shala, Llukman Halili, and Hazir Reka, eds., *Unë, Ramiz Alia dëshmoj për historinë* [I, Ramiz Alia, Testify for History] (Prishtinë: Graçanica, 1992), p. 203. For a similar view, see interview with Kiço Blushi in *24 Orë*, 7 December 1994, p. 2.

40. *Republika*, 10 February 1991, p. 2.

41. Sabri Godo, "Let Us Prevent a Catastrophe," *Republika*, 24 February 1991, p. 1.

42. *Zëri i Popullit*, 23 February 1991, pp. 1-2.

43. Tiranë Domestic Service in Albanian, 2220 GMT, 22 February 1991, translated in FBIS-EEU 91-037, 25 February 1991, p. 7.

44. The transcript was published in *Aleanca*, 29 December 1995, p. 9, and 5 January 1996, pp. 8-9.

45. *Zëri i Popullit*, 23 February 1991, p. 1; *Rilindja Demokratike*, 2 March 1991, p. 2.

46. *Rilindja Demokratike*, 19 June 1991, p. 3.

47. Aranit Tomorri, "The Chronicle of a Military Coup: An Appeal for Justice," *Rilindja Demokratike*, 21 February 1993, pp. 2, 4.

48. Tiranë Domestic Service in Albanian, 2100 GMT, 23 February 1991, translated in FBIS-EEU 91-037, 25 February 1991, p. 11.

49. Tiranë Domestic Service in Albanian. 1700 GMT, 24 February 1991, translated in FBIS-EEU 91-037, 25 February 1991, p. 11.

50. *Tribuna Demokratike*, 6 September 1993, pp. 2, 7.

51. See Baleta's article in *Rilindja Demokratike*, 4 September 1991, p. 4.

52. *Koha Jonë*, 20 July 1996, p. 2.

53. *Zëri i Popullit*, 24 February 1991, p. 1.

54. Ibid., 5 March 1991, p. 1.

55. Ibid., 23 February 1991, p. 1.

56. Mehmet Elezi, "Who Threatens Our Unity, or Overdoing It in Behalf of One's Right," *Zëri i Popullit*, 28 February 1991, p. 2.

57. Sali Berisha, "Democracy Under Dangerous Attack," *Rilindja Demokratike*, 27 February 1991, pp. 1-2.

58. Louis Zanga, "Albania: A Crisis of Confidence," *RFE/RL Report on Eastern Europe* 2, no. 16 (19 April 1991), pp. 1-4.

59. *New York Times*, 7-11 March 1991.

60. Azem Hajdari interview with the Voice of America, reprinted in *Rilindja Demokratike*, 9 February 1991, pp. 1, 5.

61. Joint statement by the Democratic and Republican Parties in *Republika*, 14 February 1991, p. 1. See also Veli Budo, "A Majority or a Proportional System?" *Republika*, 10 February 1991, p. 4. Aleksandër Meksi, acknowledging that the opposition preferred the proportional system as opposed to the ruling party's preference for the majority system, offered a compromise: a combination of the two systems. Aleksandër Meksi, "How Will We Go to the Elections? With a Proportional, Majority [System] Or...," *Rilindja Demokratike*, 23 February 1991, p. 3.

62. Hysen Çobani, "Let's Not Forget 31 March," *Republika*, 28 February 1991, p. 1.

63. Representatives of the Washington-based National Democratic Institute for International Affairs, which monitored the elections, were given a threatening letter that an opposition party supporter in Burrel received from supporters of the APL. The letter said "It is in your personal and family interest that you vote" for the APL. "If you don't, we cannot guarantee your life. The problem is not only for your life, for you have lived most of it, but it is also for the lives of your children and family." Quoted in Blaine Harden, "Albanian Communists Win Despite Losing Urban Vote," *Washington Post*, 2 April 1991, p. A14.

64. *Rilindja Demokratike*, 20 March 1991, p. 1.

65. *Zëri i Popullit*, 21 March 1991, p. 1.

66. See Alia's speech to the APL national aktiv in *Zëri i Popullit*, 24 March 1991, pp. 1-2.

67. See speech by Prime Minister Nano at a rally in Durrës, in Tiranë Domestic Service in Albanian, 1900 GMT, 21 March 1991, translated in FBIS-EEU 91-056, 22 March 1991, pp. 1-2.

68. *Zëri i Popullit*, 27 February 1991, p. 4.

69. Although *Bashkimi* had began to show greater independence from the APL, it was only in May 1991 that it announced its independence. The editorial board pledged that *Bashkimi* would henceforth "be free of all state and party influence; its aim will be for its journalists to be answerable only to the nation, the law, and their professional conscience." See editorial: "What Will *Bashkimi* Be Like From Now On?" *Bashkimi*, 3 May 1991, p. 1.

70. Hysen Çobani, "The Peasantry Will Decide the Fate of Democracy in Albania," *Republika*, 24 March 1991, pp. 1, 2.

71. Gramoz Pashko, "The Privatization of the Land and the Restructuring of Agriculture," *Rilindja Demokratike*, 16 March 1991, p. 5.

72. Musa Ulqini, "Peasant Dreams," *Zëri i Popullit*, 24 March 1991, p. 3.

73. Nexhmedin Dumani, "Let's Sell the Land, Let's Sell Albania?!" *Zëri i Popullit*, 19 March 1991, p. 2.

74. *Zëri i Popullit*, 24 March 1991, p. 4.

75. Ibid., 27 March 1991, p. 4.

76. Ibid., 28 March 1991, p. 1.

77. See Senator DeConcini's letter to the editor, *Washington Post*, 14 April 1991, p. B6.

78. Nicholas Bethell, "No Platform for Democracy," *Daily Telegraph*, 4 April 1991. Lord Bethell visited Albania as a member of a European Parliament delegation to observe the elections.

79. Afrim Buza, "The Blank Check," *Zëri i Popullit*, 23 March 1991, p. 3.

80. AFP in English 0804 GMT, 25 March 1991 in FBIS-EEU 91-058, 26 March 1991, p. 6.

81. Florian Birka, "Now That He Has Received His Blank Check, Where Does Gramoz Pashko Include Himself?" *Zëri i Popullit*, 27 March 1991, p. 3.

82. *Rilindja Demokratike*, 23 March 1991, pp. 1, 4. In March 1991, David Swartz became the first U.S. diplomat to set foot in Albania since 1946. Other members of the delegation included foreign service officer Richard T. Muller; Albania desk officer at the State Department, Susan Sutton; and Voice of America official Frank Shkreli. See also David Binder, "U.S. Diplomats Prepare for Return to Albania," *New York Times*, 29 March 1991, p. A3.

83. *Zëri i Popullit*, 24 March 1991, p. 3.

84. Ibid., 29 March 1991, p. 1.

85. Ibid., 30 March 1991, p. 4.

86. A message signed "the Albanian Patriotic Community in the United States" denounced the toppling of Hoxha's monument and blasted Pashko as "a bad politician, sick careerist, bureaucrat, and hypocrite, with questionable morals." *Zëri i Popullit*, 22 March 1991, p. 3.

87. *Rilindja Demokratike*, 5 January 1991, pp. 3-5, 16 January 1991, pp. 5-6, and 16 March 1991, p. 5.

88. *Rilindja Demokratike*, 2 February 1991, pp. 1-2.

89. See the Republican Party's election program in *Republika*, 17 February 1991, p. 1. See also the brochure *Partia Republikane Shqiptare* [The Albanian Republican Party] (Tiranë, January 1991).

90. A group of students reportedly submitted the first request to the authorities to form the Ecological Party. The Ministry of Justice gave the documentation to Ecological Party Chairman Alban Rabo. But then Namik Hoti, with assistance from senior APL officials, is said to have usurped the leadership of the party. See Alban Rabo, Arenc Kongoli, Kejdi Kote, Genta Popa, and Anila Mehmeti, "The Truth About the Ecological Party and Namik Hoti," *Tribuna Demokratike*, 29 March 1992, p. 4.

91. The Social Democratic Party did not participate in the election. The party was founded on 23 March but legalized only on 23 April 1991. Given the fact that two of its key founders, former Minister of Education Skendër Gjinushi and leader of the youth organization Lisen Bashkurti, were closely identified with Alia's government and would have taken votes away from the APL, it is not surprising that the Communists delayed granting permission to the party until after the elections. See *Alternativa SD*, 12 July 1991, p. 1.

92. *Zëri i Popullit*, 21 March 1991, p. 1.

93. Louis Zanga, "Albania: The Multiparty Elections," *RFE/RL Report on Eastern Europe* 2, no. 17 (26 April 1991), pp. 1-6.

94. *Zëri i Popullit*, 16 March 1991, p. 1.

95. *Bashkimi*, 18 April 1991, p. 1. See also Commission on Security and Cooperation, U.S. Congress, *The Elections in Albania, March-April 1991* (Washington, D.C., April 1991); National Republican Institute for International Affairs, *The 1991 Elections in Albania* (Washington, D.C. 1991); National Democratic Institute for International Affairs, *Albania: 1991 Elections to the People's Assembly* (Washington, D.C., April 1991); and Senator Claiborne Pell, *Report to the Senate Foreign Relations Committee On Visit to Albania and Yugoslavia March 29 - April 6, 1991* (Washington, D.C., April 1991).

96. *Zëri i Popullit*, 2 April 1991, p. 1.

97. See Kristian Bukuroshi, Grigor Joti, and Genc Seferi, "An Analysis of the Results of the Pluralist Elections in Light of Some Statistics," *Zëri i Rinisë*, 20 April 1991, p. 4.

98. For a critical view of the role of foreign observers, see Janusz Bugajski, "Albania: the Domino That Didn't Quite Fall," *Christian Science Monitor*, 25 April 1991, p. 19; and Blaine Harden, "Visitors Too Quick to Approve Albanian Vote," *Washington Post*, 6 April 1991, p. A15.

99. Sali Berisha, "The Elections Are Over," *Rilindja Demokratike*, 10 April 1991, p. 1.

100. See editorial "The First Victory of Democracy," *Republika*, 4 April 1991, p. 1.

101. David Binder, "Albanian Troops Kill 3 Protesters," *New York Times*, 3 April 1991, p. A3; and Blaine Harden, "3 Die as Vote Protesters, Police Clash in Albania," *Washington Post*, 4 April 1991, pp. A19-A20.

102. AFL-CIO Department of Information, Press Release, 22 May 1991.

103. David Binder, "New Communist Government in Albania Resigns," *New York Times*, 5 June 1991, p. A15; and Blaine Harden, "Communists Quit in Albania After Extended Strike," *Washington Post*, 5 June 1991, A21.

104. "The Draft Constitution of the People's Socialist Republic of Albania," *Bashkimi*, 30 December 1990, pp. 3-6.

105. *Kushtetuta e Republikës Popullore Socialiste të Shqipërisë* [The Constitution of the People's Socialist Republic of Albania] (Tiranë, 1976).

106. "The Draft Constitution of the Republic of Albania," *Zëri i Rinisë*, 10 April 1991, pp. 1-3.

107. *Gazeta Zyrtare e Republikës së Shqipërisë*, no. 4 (July 1991), pp. 145-160. For background analysis, see Zanga, "A Transitional Constitutional Law," pp. 1-4.

108. *Zëri i Popullit*, 11 April 1991, p. 1.

109. Ibid., 12 April 1991, p. 1.

110. Ibid., 15 May 1991, p. 1

111. Ibid., 11 June 1991, pp. 1-2.

112. Ibid., 12 June 1991, pp. 1-2.

113. Ibid., 12 June 1991, pp. 1, 4.

114. Gjergji Zheji, "The Confusion of Conscience and the Habit of Dictation," *Rilindja Demokratike*, 5 February 1995, pp. 5-6.

115. *Zëri i Rinisë*, 12 June 1991, pp. 1-2. Interestingly, Agolli's speech was not published by *Zëri i Popullit*.

116. Quoted in Ian Traynor, "Hoxha Specter Rises with TV Show and Cold Truth," *Daily Telegraph* (London), 12 June 1991. See also Chuck Sudetic, "Albania's Communists in Upheaval," *New York Times*, 12 June 1991, p. A3. At the end of the Congress, in an ironic twist of events, Agolli was elected to the Party's presidency.

117. *Zëri i Popullit*, 3 July 1991, p. 1.

118. Dali Bilali, "What the Congress Left Unfinished, We Should Finish," *Zëri i Popullit*, 20 June 1991, p. 3.

119. Faik Kerpaçi, "Let Us Speak Openly with the People, Let Us Look Ahead," *Zëri i Popullit*, 7 July 1991, p. 1.

120. Quoted in *Zëri i Popullit*, 26 June 1991, p. 2.

121. See Louis Zanga, "Ramiz Alia under Attack," *RFE/RL Report on Eastern Europe* 2, no. 30 (26 July 1991), pp. 1-3.

122. Neshat Tozaj, "The Imperative of the Times," *Rilindja Demokratike*, 19 June 1991, p. 3. Alia denied Tozaj's allegations that he was responsible for the Shkodër incident. *Zëri i Popullit*, 28 June 1991, pp. 1-2. See also articles by Petro Dhimitri in *Republika*, 30 June and 11 July 1991.

123. See Arben Imami, "Open Letter to Mr. Ramiz Alia," *Rilindja Demokratike*, 6 July 1991, pp. 1, 6; and Alia's interview in *Zëri i Rinisë*, 30 November 1991, p. 2.

4

The Road to Democratic Victory

The Coalition Government

In the wake of the resignation of Prime Minister Fatos Nano's government, Albanian political parties reached an agreement on 4 June 1991, to form an interim coalition government and to hold new elections in May or June 1992. The immediate consequences of the agreement were the end of the general strike, the lowering of political tensions, and the improvement of Albania's prospects for foreign support. According to the agreement, ministers in the new government had to resign from their respective parties and were prohibited from running for office in the next elections.[1] The Communists' choice for prime minister was Ylli Bufi, a young and relatively unknown candidate member of the Party's Central Committee who had served as minister of food since 1988. He formed a government of experts that was dominated by noncommunists, although the Communist Party managed to retain control of the Ministry of Foreign Affairs and the Ministry of Public Order (formerly the Ministry of Internal Affairs). The Democratic Party, which only two months earlier had rejected Nano's offer of a coalition, agreed to participate in Bufi's government, receiving seven portfolios, including the Ministries of the Economy, Finance, and Defense. Gramoz Pashko became deputy prime minister and minister of the economy. His brother-in-law, Genc Ruli, became minister of finance. The Democrats also named Perikli Teta, a non-party-affiliated air force officer, minister of defense. Representatives of other opposition parties received less-critical portfolios.

The agreement between the Communists and the opposition parties, which signified the end of forty-seven years of one-party rule, symbolized a shared determination to prevent the country from sinking into total chaos. The decision presented both opportunities and risks for the opposition. It confirmed the fact than only six months after its creation, the Democratic Party had become a key political force. On the other hand, the Democrats now shared responsibility with the Communists for the nation's problems. Some felt that the opposition had "sold out," since Nano's government was about to collapse from the effects of the general strike, and these coalition partners were now "collaborating" with the Communists. The Democrats had taken over the two most critical posts in the government—the economic and finance ministries—at a time when the country was practically bankrupt. Moreover, the Communists were not interested in implementing radical economic reforms, because such reforms would undermine their dominant position in the economy.

Berisha and leaders of the other opposition parties used two arguments to justify their participation in a government with the Communists. First, these parties believed that their participation could forestall the country's descent into anarchy, which was damaging the prospects for a peaceful transition to democracy.[2] Berisha told a foreign journalist: "We are on the edge of total catastrophe. The country is disintegrating. We cannot wait anymore."[3] Pashko made a similar statement: "This country is just one step from catastrophe. This is a kind of *kamikaze* government. But someone has to take the responsibility."[4] In an appearance before a U.S. congressional committee in May 1991, Berisha appealed for immediate humanitarian assistance. He urged greater involvement by the United States in the reinvigoration of Albania's economy.[5] Secondly, the opposition argued that it joined the coalition government to forestall the imposition of a state of emergency by Alia or seizure of power by the military, although this was highly unlikely at this late stage.

In an address to the People's Assembly on 12 June, Prime Minister Bufi painted a grim picture of the situation in the country and appealed for foreign assistance. He said the general strike had crippled the country. Key sectors of the economy were paralyzed, anarchy reigned in the countryside, the balance of payments deficit had reached $400 million, and there was a dangerous breakdown of public order.[6]

International Reaction

Shortly after the People's Assembly approved Bufi's government, Albania was admitted as a full member to the Conference on Security and Cooperation in Europe and established ties with the European Community. Tiranë played host to a number of Western dignitaries, including U.S. Secretary of State James Baker. On the eve of Baker's visit, Berisha made a public plea for U.S. assistance: "Forty-seven years of Communist rule have made us the poorest country in Europe. We are desperate for humanitarian aid—food and medicine—as well as technological and economic assistance. Albania needs American business to invest in developing highways, textile industries and oil exploration. ... [W]ith the advice and friendship of the United States, I am certain that Albania will soon make its own contributions to the world."[7] Baker was given a massive and emotional welcome on 22 June 1991.[8] Several hundred thousand Albanians gathered in Tiranë's main square to hear the U.S. Secretary of State tell them that after a half-century interruption in relations, "America is returning to you." Baker said: "On behalf of President Bush and the American people, I come here today to say to you: Freedom works. At last, you are free to think your own thoughts. At last, you are free to speak your own mind. At last you are free to choose your own leaders. Albanians have chosen to join the company of free men and women everywhere. Welcome to the company of free men and women everywhere, the way our Creator intended us to be. You are with us and we are with you." Baker announced that the United States would give Albania approximately $6 million in humanitarian aid, but said that further U.S. assistance would be conditional on Albania's taking concrete steps toward democracy and a market economy. In an address to parliament, Baker, saying he was visiting Tiranë at Berisha's invitation, urged Albanians to put the vestiges of communism behind them. He said, "Let us see an end to all fear in Albania."Baker's visit was covered live by Albanian radio and television, and his speeches were published in the major newspapers. The elated Secretary of State told reporters: "I have been in politics now for 14 years, and I don't ever remember seeing something like that. This just happened and that makes it all the more extraordinary. That outpouring of genuine affection and support was because of the symbol of hope that America represents to people like this, who have had nothing to hope for so very long."[9] In a separate meeting with Berisha and other opposition representatives, the Secretary of State urged them to work closely together so that they could win in the next parliamentary elections.[10] Although Albanians had exaggerated expectations of what the United States could and would do for Albania, Baker's visit boosted the national morale and revived Albanians' optimism about their future.

Meanwhile, Italy, which had been the most affected by the flow of Albanian refugees, granted Tiranë more than $150 million in humanitarian and emergency economic aid. Greece and Turkey pledged $20 million each. The European Community also provided some humanitarian aid.

Reform Agendas

Bufi's government announced a program of reforms, that called for small-scale privatization, liberalization of prices, relaxation of foreign trade restrictions, and the development of a new financial system. Unfortunately, the program remained largely a dead letter and Albania made no headway toward reform. The coalition government was faced with numerous problems. Lawlessness all over the country had reached alarming proportions. The government's most pressing task was to obtain enough food and other consumer goods to prevent famine and keep the lid on popular dissatisfaction. Shortages of basic foodstuffs became critical, with starvation reported in some parts of the country.

The government also was faced with increasing demands for the return of or compensation for property seized by the Communists after 1945. Disagreements over whether to compensate former property owners and the nature of the compensation that ought to be provided further heightened tensions. The prohibitive cost and the impracticality of settling the many property claims forced political forces to postpone a decision. With regard to reprivatization of the land, uncertainty over ownership rights, and the government's failure to devise a plan to cope with claims on the land, caused chaos in the countryside. The peasants simply took matters into their own hands by seizing land and livestock. Albania, unlike any other former Communist country in Eastern Europe, witnessed a massive destruction of property during the initial stage of transition. Throughout the countryside, fixed assets that belonged to the state, such as schools, farm equipment centers, irrigation canals, and even hospitals, were destroyed. Berisha claimed that the secret police were behind the wave of vandalism, which continued into the early part of 1992. He said that through terror and destruction, the Communists were hoping to convince the population that Hoxha's dictatorship was better than democracy. In an interview with *Drita*, Berisha said he was convinced that Sigurimi had organized the exodus of some 20,000 Albanians to Italy in August 1991. He accused conservative Communist forces of trying

... to hamper the development of democratic processes, to debilitate the nation, and because they themselves are in their deaththroes, to bring the nation down with them. It is obvious to everyone that this scenario is brought into play whenever it suits this nation's eternal enemy—the Serbs. However, I wish to stress that all those who fled were, in general, innocent victims of the misery caused by the totalitarian socialist system. After the class struggle, the scenario of the exodus, which is taking away hundreds and thousands of children, young people, mothers, and fathers, is the most criminal act that the forces of the old regime have perpetrated against this nation and country.[11]

British journalist Catherine Field, who served as an adviser to the coalition government, echoed Berisha's statement: "This old guard, backed by a disgruntled secret police force, is on the ropes, but ready to fight back at a moment's notice. It was their endless foot dragging and the hidden but nonetheless threatening presence of the secret police which sent me scurrying home each day convinced that little had changed in Albania. Everyone is too scared to point the finger, but they believe that hard-line elements in the former Communist Party are orchestrating the country's instability and lawlessness. The thought sometimes made sleep difficult."[12]

The Democratic Party demanded full privatization of agriculture and the speedy and orderly breakup of cooperatives—ideas opposed by the Socialist Party. In July 1991, the People's Assembly passed a land law; however, it fell far short of what the opposition was demanding. The law stipulated that the government would distribute land free of charge to peasants, who would enjoy the right of ownership as long as they farmed the property. The sale of land was prohibited. In a move that exacerbated tensions in the countryside, the document did not recognize the rights of previous land owners. Article 8 of the law stated: "Neither former ownership nor the amount or boundaries of land owned before collectivization are recognized in the granting of land as the property of or for the use of physical or juridical persons."[13]

While Bufi spoke in general terms in favor of a market economy, he lacked sufficiently broad political support to introduce the radical reforms needed to invigorate the economy and attract foreign investments. The state remained in charge of the economy, and few inroads were made toward privatization. Enterprises were still managed the old way, by Communist-era holdovers whose professional experience made them ill suited for the transition to a market economy. Although the government signed agreements with several West European and American firms to engage in offshore oil exploration, foreign investment and the establishment of joint ventures to exploit Albania's many natural resources and to expand tourism did not materialize because of the lack of political stability. Western countries were willing to grant humanitarian assistance; however, they rejected Albanian requests for a large-scale infusion of credit because of the fear that massive aid would merely buttress the very system that needed reforming.

Downhill Decline

The emergence of a pluralistic political system had brought a sense of exhilaration to many Albanians; but as the overall situation in the country continued to deteriorate, the sense of euphoria evoked by the crumbling of the Communist order gave way to frustration, anger, fear, and a somber contemplation of the realities and challenges of building a new system. Within one year alone (July 1990-July 1991) an estimated 100,000 Albanians fled their country, almost all of them illegally, a hemorrhage that coincided with economic collapse. Albania was faced with a devastating brain drain. Hundreds and thousands of talented and educated people fled the country. The desperate attempt of some 20,000 Albanians to flee to Italy in August 1991, after Rome had said it would accept no more refugees and after it had returned thousands to Albania, was a dramatic indication of the widespread desperation and loss of hope for a better future. The wrenching dismantlement of the command system was leading to major social dislocations, with high political risks. According to a poll published in June 1991, the overwhelming majority of Albanian citizens believed the establishment of a genuine multiparty democracy and a market economy was essential to the country's economic development. But although there seemed to be wide agreement on the need for political reform, Albanians were divided over the pace of economic reform. A majority of those living in urban areas (52 percent) favored radical economic reforms, while rural Albanians were divided equally between those who favored radical reform (46 percent) and those who favored gradual changes (46 percent).[14]

Bufi's government enjoyed little authority and proved as ineffective as had Nano's. The coalition's consensus disintegrated very rapidly. Faced with mounting political tensions and economic difficulties, the government was unable either to initiate any meaningful reforms or to arrest the continued economic decline. The country literally came to a standstill. Members of the government proved weak, hesitant, and unprepared for leadership. None had extensive experience. Meanwhile, they had to govern in a populist political environment, faced with crushing pressures from labor unions and other dissatisfied sectors of the population. In many parts of the country, people took matters into their own hands, and the government became impotent in the face of general disorder. By the beginning of autumn, Albania had become totally dependent on foreign humanitarian assistance, primarily from Italy, the European Community, and the United States, to feed its population. In September 1991, Albania and Italy signed an agreement providing for Italian soldiers to supervise and distribute international humanitarian assistance. About one thousand Italian troops were stationed in Durrës and Vlorë.[15] But growing official corruption impaired foreign relief efforts, with humanitarian supplies being diverted to the black market or to repositories for use by bureaucrats and their underlings.

The coalition government lacked a strong figure that would inspire confidence in the administration. Although Bufi, by all accounts, was a decent person, he was an inefficient administrator. In retrospect, it appears that the Democratic Party had made a serious error in choosing Pashko as deputy prime minister and minister of the economy. An ambitious person who had embarrassed his party with irresponsible and contradictory statements during the election campaign, Pashko turned out to be ill suited to his high-level appointment. He had bragged openly that he, and not Bufi, was in charge of the government. But behind the scenes, Pashko was much more indecisive than he appeared in public, especially in his encounters with foreigners. The ineffectiveness of the coalition government encouraged an attitude of dependence on foreign humanitarian assistance. Albania's leaders could not bring themselves to bite the bullet and implement significant reforms.

The crumbling of the economy and growing social strife further destabilized the situation, with an increasing number of Albanians blaming the Democratic Party. By the end of summer 1991, there appeared to be significant disenchantment with the Democratic Party. Meanwhile, other forces attempted to take advantage of the perceptible decline in support for the largest opposition party.

In the early stages of political pluralism, the APL had prevented the creation of parties of the far right, labeling them "fascist" and "antinational." But parliament's approval in summer 1991 of a more liberal law on the organization of political parties led to an explosion of their numbers. By the end of the year, there were more than twenty parties, several of them rightist. King Zog's followers created the National Democratic Party. Its leaders questioned the Democratic Party's commitment to eradicate communism and said they would not open their ranks to former Communists. Advocating the return of the monarchy, the party called for a national referendum to decide whether King Zog's son, Leka, should return to the throne. Leka was two days old when his parents fled Albania, in the wake of the Italian invasion, in 1939. When his father died in Paris, in 1961, a group of loyalists proclaimed Leka king. After his expulsion from Spain in the 1970s for alleged arms trafficking, the pretender to the Albanian throne moved to South Africa. Founders of the National Democratic Party initially had the support of Legality followers in the West. Subsequently, however, Legality applied to the Albanian Ministry of Justice for recognition, and in early 1992, it was legalized. Nevertheless, there were no discernible differences in the programs of the two monarchist parties. But soon, Legality split into several factions, as exiled remnants of the party vied for control of party supporters in Albania.

Supporters of the National Front also formed their own party. In addition, this period saw the formation of at least three other parties that considered themselves rightist. With the exception of the National Democratic Party's demands for the return of the monarchy, the parties of the right had strikingly similar programs. They emphasized the need to instill in their fellow citizens notions of "Albanianism," claiming that under communism the Albanians had lost their true national identity. They insisted that Albanians had always been poor but proud of their ethnicity, while now they displayed little respect for their national symbols.[16] These parties recognized that Albania had become dependent on foreign aid, but they were resentful of the growing presence of foreigners, especially Italians, and emphasized the importance of the Albanians regaining their dignity. The mistreatment of Albanian refugees in Greece received wide publicity and led to anti-Greek sentiments. The disintegration of Yugoslavia and increased Serbian repression against Albanians in Kosova, and Greek support for Serbia's president Slobodan Milošević, raised the specter of a Serb-Greek encirclement of Albania. Some political parties used Kosova as a rallying point. While the Democratic Party insisted that Serbia recognize ethnic Albanians' right to self-determination and did not demand border changes, the parties of the right insisted on outright union of Kosova with Albania, contending that the injustices heaped upon the Albanian nation by its more powerful neighbors must be corrected.[17] These efforts of the rightist parties to capitalize on the increasing popular disenchantment with the Democratic Party met with limited success. The rightists attracted only a small membership, were unable to build a nationwide organization, and perhaps more importantly, failed to come up with a detailed program to arrest the deteriorating economic situation.

Cracks in the Democratic Party

Berisha expressed concern over the erosion of public support for the Democratic Party. In an interview with *Rilindja Demokratike* in July 1991, he launched a fierce attack on his party's critics and accused the Sigurimi of waging a campaign to discredit the Democrats. Berisha's interview reflected an effort to counteract growing public disaffection with the Democratic Party. Evidently perceiving a need to dispel any notion that there was an alternative to his party, Berisha said that the Democratic Party was the only force that could ensure the democratization of the country.[18] He also dismissed the chief editor of *Rilindja Demokratike*, Frrok Çupi. Among the many charges leveled against Çupi was the accusation that he had provided insufficient coverage of the increasingly influential association of former political prisoners.[19] Berisha also accused Çupi of being a Communist spy. In the flurry of mutual recriminations that followed his dismissal, Çupi accused Berisha of having followed the Hoxha regime's classical pattern of branding its opponents "enemies of the people."[20]

Concerned with the ineffectiveness of the coalition government, Berisha laid out a carefully crafted position that was evidently intended to attract support from the political right. He dismissed the claims of Socialist Party leaders that they had repudiated Communist ideals, accusing them of blocking the country's democratization. Berisha formed a united front with the Republican and Social Democratic Parties, the powerful Union of Independent Trade Unions, and the Society of Former Prisoners. On 22 August, the Democratic, Republican, and Social Democratic Parties issued a joint declaration pledging to coordinate their activities, with the aim of accelerating "the establishment of genuine democracy in Albania." The statement demanded the dissolution of the Sigurimi, sweeping reforms in the Ministry of Foreign Affairs, trial of former APL Politburo members, removal of all emblems and symbols of Communist rule, and compensation for former political prisoners. It also demanded greater opposition access to state radio and television, which had acted blatantly as a mouthpiece for the Communists, giving terse coverage of opposition activities.[21] The opposition parties' statement was followed by a similar action by the Independent Trade Unions.[22] In an article, Berisha claimed that democracy in Albania was seriously threatened "by an alliance of cryptocommunists, criminal elements from the ranks of the state security service, and ultranationalists." He urged all democratic forces to join the three opposition parties in what he termed "civil political action" until communism was uprooted from Albanian "soil and minds."[23] Through a series of joint activities, including massive rallies, the opposition forces stepped up demands for the eradication of communism, the arrest of former APL Politburo members, changes in the management of radio and television, and early parliamentary elections. Some fifty thousand people participated in a rally on 14 September in Tiranë's Skanderbeg Square, organized by the three opposition parties and the

Union of Independent Trade Unions. For the first time since 1945, protesters waved Albanian flags without the Communist red star.[24]

Berisha's new strategy attracted almost instant popular support, as the coalition government was increasingly viewed as a cover for the Communists to enrich themselves. Many believed that Gramoz Pashko, who had gotten out of touch with his party's leadership and rank and file, had behaved with undue deference in his relations with the Communists. Under the coalition government, some 30,000 small-scale units had been privatized. But the majority of these units were owned by members of the *nomenklatura*, who used their positions, contacts, skills, and experience to acquire state property when Bufi's government began the privatization process. While the Communists were gradually losing political power, they were reasserting their hold on the economy. There was widespread resentment that the *nomenklatura* was enriching itself under capitalism. Many blamed Pashko personally.[25] Moreover, members of the government, most significantly Pashko and Ruli, were accused of corruption. Many people came to resent the personal ostentation of coalition government officials, while ordinary citizens were making daily sacrifices. Pashko displayed an extraordinary lack of sensitivity to public opinion, sending his daughter to study abroad and hiring a public relations agent in London. Catherine Field, who worked as an adviser to the Bufi government, describes Pashko as "an ambitious political animal, who thrives on being a public figure. Power rather went to his head; he even got himself an agent in London, who used to handle pop singers."[26]

By the end of summer 1991, as it became clear that the Communists were using the coalition government to hinder the reform process and through personal contacts and corruption were taking control over the emerging private sector, opinion within the Democratic Party shifted considerably to the right on both political and economic matters. While in the beginning of the year the leftists, led by Pashko, controlled leading positions and influenced the tone of public debate within the Democratic Party, they were gradually shunned after the Democrats joined the coalition government. Strong anticommunist elements, who in contrast to Pashko's seemingly accommodating stance toward the Communists advocated a rapid eradication of communism, gained increased influence. Criticism increased against the leftists, who were seen as "Communist collaborators," particularly Pashko, whose father, as deputy general prosecutor in the late 1940s, was held personally responsible for the execution and imprisonment of many people. Moreover, the general assumption within his party's rank and file, fueled by Pashko's free-wheeling lifestyle, was that the deputy prime minister was simply out to further his own personal interests. Pashko was no longer an insider in the Democratic Party, and was not privy to many political matters. Long-simmering disputes between Berisha and Pashko over the pace and extent of the dismantling of the Communist system had become all too obvious to the membership and the general public.

Despite increasing pressure to quit the government, Pashko and other Democratic Party ministers, having tasted the sweet rewards of office, were reluctant to leave. They enlisted the support of influential top Democratic Party officials, including Azem Hajdari and Neritan Ceka, who favored continued participation in the coalition government. Moreover, concerned that the tide was turning against them, the leftists launched a desperate campaign to unseat Berisha as party leader. On the eve of the Democratic Party's first national convention, held at the end of September 1991, Pashko called a private meeting with Ceka, Ruli, Minister of Culture Preç Zogaj, and former chief editor Çupi of *Rilindja Demokratike*, to plot Berisha's replacement with Ceka. They reportedly agreed on a two-pronged strategy. First, they would insist that the Democratic Party chairman be elected by the party presidency, where they were confident they enjoyed the majority, and not by the party's national conference. In the event that convention delegates refused to accept this proposal, the leftists would then insist that former APL members not be considered for the party's top post. The approval of the latter suggestion would automatically exclude Berisha.[27]

Berisha became the object of an extraordinary personal attack. His foes spared no means to vilify him. He was charged with ruling the Democratic Party in an authoritarian manner and of being intolerant of criticism or opposition. The Socialists fueled the rift with extremely negative media coverage of Berisha. The leftists within the Democratic Party were portrayed as moderates, while Berisha was characterized as a reckless politician who would become a dictator if he ever came to power. Alia, as well as the new Socialist Party leadership, evidently believed that the leftist faction was more disposed than Berisha to reach an accommodation with the Socialists. Working behind the scenes, Alia wooed Berisha's opponents, particularly Pashko, Ceka, and Zogaj. In early September 1991, the President asked Ceka to accompany him on a tour of several European countries, where he formally signed the documents on Albania's accession to the CSCE.[28] Reportedly Alia also flirted with the idea that Ceka, who had never been a Communist, was the logical choice to succeed him as president at the end of his own mandate.[29] Ironically, Ceka had risen in the ranks of the Democratic Party leadership largely thanks to Berisha's support. He had not joined the student demonstrators in December 1990, nor was he a founding member of the party. He was brought into the party's leadership in February 1991 on Berisha's recommendation. His selection as leader of the Democratic Party's parliamentary group in April 1991 gave him increased visibility, thus enhancing his standing within and outside the party.

Convened in September 1991, the national convention of the Democratic Party became the scene of a fierce battle over the party line, as the split between Berisha's and Pashko's factions burst into open conflict. Pashko and his supporters launched a blistering attack on Berisha, criticizing what they termed his "street" tactics, and accusing the party leader of having usurped too much power in the leadership. They insisted that their party stay in the coalition government.

Although Pashko's group evidently enjoyed a majority in the party's presidium, having enlisted the support of Azem Hajdari, Arben Imami, and Eduard Selami, its efforts to gain a dominant voice in determining the party line failed. Pashko's demands that former Communists not be allowed to run for the top party post and that the presidency elect the chairman were rejected out of hand. Not surprisingly, Pashko, who had resigned from the APL four days after the creation of the Democratic Party, did not demand that former Communists be excluded from consideration for the post of prime minister. According to Pjetër Arbnori, Pashko wanted that post for himself.[30]

With the support of local party leaders and activists discontented with what they termed Pashko's neocommunist policies, Berisha successfully undercut his opponents and was reelected party chairman by an overwhelming majority. He received 449 votes, while his rivals Ceka and Hajdari got 77 and 9, respectively. Selami was reelected party secretary, while Ceka, Hajdari, and Imami were elected vice chairmen.[31] Although the public disputes at the convention were an embarrassment, the leftists' ability to sabotage Berisha's policies were limited because they had lost their bid to control the Democratic Party.

In the wake of his party's convention, Berisha, unhappy with the government's poor performance, gradually parted company with his ministers. In a statement issued on 29 October and directed at Berisha, Bufi's cabinet complained of lack of support by the political forces. The statement said: "Our country genuinely stands on the brink of economic, social, and political chaos."[32] Even when it had become obvious that participation in the coalition government was being used by the Socialists to discredit the opposition, Pashko and other Democratic Party ministers opposed calls to withdraw from the government.

But Berisha, capitalizing on his recent victory at the party convention, pushed ahead with dogged perseverance. Support for his policies and leadership expanded at all levels of the party. His opponents had been put on the defensive, and although conflict within the party leadership remained intense, Berisha had seized the high ground and had become unquestionably the dominant voice in laying down the political line. The Independent Trade Unions organized a series of strikes, while students in Tiranë and other cities rallied in support of opposition demands. Journalists at the state radio and television launched a strike demanding the resignation of the General Director Fatmir Kumbaro.[33] Some activists, however, went further than Berisha in their demands. At a student rally in Tiranë, Blendi Gonxhe, one of the leaders of the December 1990 student demonstrators, called for the removal of Hoxha's tomb from the martyrs' cemetery in Tiranë. In contrast to opposition leaders who were demanding that former APL Politburo members be tried on corruption charges, Gonxhe said that they should be tried on charges of genocide against certain strata of the population.[34] Berisha, however, opposed calls for political trials and a general settling of accounts with members of the Communist *nomenklatura.* In an interview with a foreign journalist, Berisha said:

I am firmly opposed to [political] trials. Do you know, every day under Hoxha a show trial was held somewhere in Albania, with false witnesses and so-called judges who had the written verdict in their pockets before they went into court. If we were to bring such people to trial, we would be forced to build more prisons and camps than there were in Hoxha's day. Instead, I am in favor of reconciliation. Every Communist regime rests on two pillars—fear and hate. But I want to replace fear with freedom and hatred with reconciliation; reconciliation is particularly important in a country like Albania, where the Communists tried to eradicate all religion. Only the very highest political leaders should be brought to trial, like Enver Hoxha's widow, Nexhmije, those who have grown fat at the expense of the people.[35]

Collapse of the Coalition Government

In November 1991, in a desperate effort to save his government, Bufi paid a private visit to the United States. His hopes of gaining the support of the U.S. government and the powerful Albanian American community were dashed, however, when the Secretary of State and other senior officials refused to receive him and most Albanian Americans ignored his visit.

On 26 November, a joint meeting of the Democratic Party's National Council and parliamentary group issued an ultimatum to Alia, threatening that the Democratic Party would withdraw from the coalition unless a series of demands were met by 3 December. The Democrats demanded that elections be held no later than 23 February 1992; that the persons responsible for the killing of Democratic Party activists in April 1991 in Shkodër be tried and sentenced; that changes be made at the state radio and television; and that former APL Politburo members and Mrs. Hoxha be arrested.[36] While Democratic Party ministers without exception opposed withdrawal from the government, on 27 November, the three Republican Party members of the cabinet—Teodor Kareco, secretary general of the Council of Ministers; Fatos Bitincka, minister of transportation, and Alfred Karamuço, chairman of the State Control Commission—sent an open letter to the president and the Council of Ministers sharply criticizing the government's work. Bufi termed their action unacceptable and dismissed them from the government on 1 December.[37]

Neritan Ceka and Genc Ruli were charged by the Democratic Party to negotiate with Alia. The president agreed to hold new elections, replace Kumbaro, and speed up the Shkodër trial. Kumbaro was replaced by Agron Çobani as general director of radio and television. Writer Skendër Buçpapaj was named deputy general director, while Bardhyl Pollo became director of domestic radio. Although still maintaining a hold over the state media, with the appointment of Democratic Party supporters Buçpapaj and Pollo, the Communists were clearly losing control over a very important institution.

As in previous crisis situations, Alia resisted until the last minute in accepting the main opposition demand—the arrest of Nexhmije Hoxha and former Politburo members.[38] Although Ceka claims that by 4 December Alia had agreed to all the demands,[39] a meeting of the Democratic parliamentary group concluded that the president had not fully met the demands, and approved the Democratic Party's withdrawal from the coalition government. At a news conference, Berisha accused the Communists of hindering Albania's democratization and seriously obstructing the implementation of reforms. He alleged that "alongside the legitimate state in Albania, there is a secret, covert, second state that governs the country according to the old laws." Conversely, in a move evidently intended to heal the wounds within the Democratic Party, Berisha expressed "unshaken appreciation" for the ministers who had served in the coalition government.[40]

Berisha had made a risky decision. For several days, he was at the center of a fierce and well-coordinated negative campaign. The Socialists accused him of placing his personal political interests above those of the nation, while Pashko, on a visit to London for negotiations with the European Bank for Reconstruction and Development, told the news agency Reuter that Berisha was leading Albania toward anarchy and chaos.[41] But more worrisome than Pashko's criticism was Ceka's defection. As Berisha was about to open the news conference on 4 December, the party's vice chairman unsuccessfully pleaded with him not to announce the Democrats' withdrawal from the government, insisting that Alia had pledged to accept all the demands of the Democratic Party.

Ceka chose a meeting that Alia called with him and Berisha in the President's office to announce his resignation from the Democratic Party. Claiming "a political trap," Berisha, who evidently was not aware that Ceka had been invited to the meeting, which was being televised live, walked out when the vice chairman of the Democratic Party began to read a statement denouncing his party's withdrawal from the government and calling on Berisha to resign. With Alia looking on, Ceka went on to read his statement, in which he said that the decision to withdraw from the government had not been approved by the party's National Council and therefore was not valid. He insisted that "Berisha's step represents a personal initiative, and there is no reason why the Democratic Party's ministers should withdraw from the government or for the government to resign. It has no doubt been the best government we have had since the war."[42] If Alia and Ceka had hoped that this action would undermine Berisha's position, they were grossly mistaken. Ceka's resignation was followed by an unprecedented outpouring of popular support for Berisha. At spontaneous rallies in Tiranë, Elbasan, and other cities, Ceka and Pashko were denounced as Communist lackeys. Meanwhile, the Democratic Party's Presidium and parliamentary group issued a statement fully backing Berisha.[43]

While the Republican Party supported Berisha's decision, the Social Democratic Party was critical. A statement issued on 6 December said the Social Democratic Party "considers the Democratic Party's step in withdrawing its ministers from the government, at a time when the nation's destiny is at a great historic crossroads and Albanian democracy is facing its most difficult test, to be overhasty."[44]

Berisha handled the crisis well, displaying formidable political skills. Compared to Berisha, his rivals Pashko, Ceka, Zogaj, and Hajdari were political lightweights. Not only did Berisha consolidate his own position, but the Democratic Party emerged with much more clearly defined objectives and experienced an immediate rebirth of grassroots support. With events rapidly moving in Berisha's favor, even senior party officials who had opposed withdrawing from the government joined his bandwagon. Upon his return from London, Pashko made a tactical retreat, telling a news conference that his interview with Reuter had been misinterpreted. He added, "I wish to stress that there are more things uniting Sali Berisha and myself than there are dividing us."[45] However, the disagreement over withdrawal from the government went beyond previous Berisha-Pashko differences, and in fact, heralded a qualitative change in their relations. A definite split between the two now appeared inevitable.

In their haste to blame Berisha, Socialist officials made irresponsible statements causing further insecurity. Prime Minister Bufi declared during a live television broadcast that Albania had food reserves for only six days. Although he corrected himself a day later,[46] the damage had been done. Bufi's statement caused nationwide panic, and riots broke out throughout the country, causing massive destruction. Security forces and civilians rampaged through the streets of many cities. Convoys with humanitarian assistance came under attack. In one incident, in the northern town of Fushë Arrës, thirty-five people died when a storage warehouse, which had been stormed by residents from the town and surrounding villages, caught fire, trapping numerous people inside.[47] Alia ordered the armed forces to guard and protect foodstores, warehouses, industrial and trade centers, and other public property.[48]

Meanwhile, the badly splintered Socialist Party refused to form a new government, thus acknowledging it could no longer govern the country. Nevertheless, the restyled Communists hoped the upcoming elections would confirm their party as an important, if not a dominant, political force. The democratic opposition, on the other hand, viewed the elections as a means to accelerate the end of Communist rule and enhance democratic development and good governance. Alia announced that new elections would be held on 22 March 1992 and asked the minister of food in the coalition government, Vilson Ahmeti, ostensibly a non-party member but with close ties to the Socialist Party, to form a caretaker government. The mandate of the new government was to attempt to restore law and order and prepare the country for new elections.

The 1992 Elections: The Democratic Victory

In the wake of the collapse of Bufi's government, Albania appeared to have descended into chaos. The authorities at both the national and local levels had literally lost the ability to carry out the basic functions of government. The police had become powerless, street crime was rampant, government warehouses were looted, and convoys carrying international humanitarian assistance were ambushed. Unemployment rose dramatically, as most factories were shut down, while poverty reached unprecedented levels. The countryside witnessed an unprecedented wave of devastating destruction of property. Throughout this period, President Alia watched from the sidelines, taking no concrete action to ameliorate the situation. The opposition blamed the Communists for the collapse of public order, insisting that the Socialist Party was deliberately letting the country slide into chaos to prove that Albania had done much better under communism than with political pluralism. The Socialists, on the other hand, blamed Democratic supporters.

The New Electoral Game

The Democratic and other opposition parties had criticized the majority-based electoral system used in the 31 March 1991 elections, which had given the Communists a number of seats greater than their share of total votes cast. Initially, the Democratic Party had insisted on a proportionally based system; but as popular support for the opposition grew, the Democrats switched their position, now expressing support for a majority-based system. The Socialist Party also changed its position. With their support dwindling, the Socialists correctly believed that the proportionally based system would better serve their interests. Other, smaller parties also insisted on a proportional system. Anxious to hold elections as early as possible, the Democratic Party compromised, and the result was a mixed system, approved by parliament on 4 February 1992.

In contrast to the previous law, which had divided the country into 250 election districts, the new law provided for 100 districts, which would have "an almost equal number of residents." The law stipulated that the final representation in parliament had to reflect the percentage of total votes that each party had won nationwide. The first 100 seats were to be decided on the basis of a majoritarian system in one-seat election districts, while the remainder would be filled based on a system of proportional representation nationally. In the single-seat election districts, the candidate with at least 50 percent of the votes cast in a first round, or with the most votes in a runoff, would be announced the winner. Parties fielding candidates in at least thirty-three election districts across at least nine administrative districts, and meeting the 4-percent threshold, were eligible for the supplemental pool of at least forty more seats. For the proportional seats, voters cast ballots for parties rather than for individual candidates. Each party participating in the elections compiled a list of its candidates. Party leaders were placed at the head of the list, thus automatically being ensured a seat in parliament if their parties gained at least 4 percent of the nationwide vote. A party that in the first round of votes obtained a higher percentage of seats than the percentage of popular votes would be penalized, while parties in the opposite situation would be favored by the distribution of supplementary seats. The law stipulated that parliament would have at least 140 seats, but the number of supplemental seats could be expanded to ensure strict observation of proportionality.[49]

While the law was praised for generally conforming to international standards, it came under criticism abroad for excluding ethnic-based parties from fielding candidates in the elections. The draft election law, prepared in January 1992 with the assistance of experts from the CSCE and the Council of Europe, contained an article allowing ethnic-based parties to participate; but as parliament was preparing to debate the law, the Albanian press published what was widely considered an inflammatory interview by Theodhori Bezhani, a leader of the ethnic Greek organization Omonia for the district of Gjirokastër. Bezhani was quoted as having said that Omonia would fight for the secession of "ethnic Greek areas" from Albania and for their unification with Greece. Many Albanians saw this as a serious threat to the territorial integrity of their weak state. Abdi Baleta, then a Democratic Party deputy and professor of law at Tiranë University, denounced Bezhani's statement and warned his compatriots of Greek territorial designs on southern Albania. Heated debates followed, with other deputies, both Democrats and Socialists, joining Baleta in criticizing Omonia. Some deputies demanded that the group be outlawed. The Democratic Party issued a statement calling on ethnic Greeks to distance themselves from Bezhani's stance.[50] Omonia critics also emphasized that the law on political parties approved by parliament in July 1991 specifically prohibited the creation of parties on an "ethnic, religious, or regional basis." After heated discussions, parliament changed the draft law. The final version of the election law prohibited ethnic parties from participating in the elections. Thus, Omonia, which in the 1991 elections had won five seats, was disqualified from fielding any candidates in the upcoming elections. This caused an uproar in the ethnic Greek community and in Greece, precipitating a serious deterioration in Tiranë-Athens relations. After significant international pressure, a compromise was reached. A new party was created, called the Union for Human Rights, which ostensibly was open to all Albanian citizens but in fact represented only the ethnic Greek community.

The situation in Albania had undergone dramatic changes since the first multiparty elections in 1991. Although procedurally correct, the 1991 elections were not perceived as having reflected the true will of the Albanian people. The incumbent Communists had shown a serious lack of commitment to the democratic process, only reluctantly agreeing to oversight by international election observers in the hope of securing international legitimacy. The opposition, on the other hand, was denied adequate access to the media and was prevented from campaigning freely throughout the country. But by March 1992, the Communists had become the underdog, as domestic and international pressures for reforms had dramatically intensified. Although the Socialist Party remained a formidable force, it suffered damaging setbacks. The opposition parties were undoubtedly in a much better position than the Socialists, having gained important political experience since the first multiparty elections.

Opposition parties also had succeeded in expanding ties with sister parties in other countries and with international institutions. The U.S. embassy, under the able leadership of Ambassador William Ryerson and his deputy Christopher Hill, openly promoted Albania's democratization process, exerting strong diplomatic pressure on the Communists. American assistance was critical in encouraging electoral reform, promoting meaningful elections, and leveling the playing field. Two American organizations, the National Democratic Institute (NDI) and the International Republican Institute (IRI), played an important role in providing Albanian political forces with preelection support, civic education, party training, and technical assistance. With grants from the United States Agency for International Development, these two institutes worked closely with the government and the opposition to prepare the country for free and fair elections.

The NDI concentrated on promoting and strengthening emerging democratic institutions and democratic culture. Its programs focused on strengthening parliament and developing an impartiality in the functioning of the political system. As part of its civic education effort, the NDI was instrumental in the formation of the Albanian Society for Free Elections and Democratic Culture, a neutral observer group above partisan politics. The group engaged in formal and nonformal civic education, and on election day, played an important role in monitoring and verifying election results through parallel vote tabulations. NDI Program Director Thomas O. Melia and Program Assistant Olga Milosavljevic led several preelection missions to Albania, holding discussions with party leaders, government officials, and journalists about international standards for free and fair elections.[51]

The International Republican Institute, under the leadership of former U.S. Congressman Jack Buechner and Program Officer for Albania Mary Catherine Andrews, worked very closely with opposition parties to develop a spirit of partisanship and to overcome the advantages the Communists had enjoyed in the 1991 elections. The IRI concentrated on working with the Albanians on the mechanics of organizing and financing political parties and operating effective election campaigns. It helped opposition leaders and activists with techniques for mobilizing grassroots support and in developing and disseminating messages of local and nationwide appeal. The IRI also provided the Democratic Party with material assistance, including vehicles, which made it possible for its candidates to travel to inaccessible areas, and office equipment for party headquarters in Tiranë and branches in other cities.[52]

Despite the grave situation,[53] the 1992 elections were far more orderly than those of the previous year and probably the only truly free elections in Albania's history. The opposition had drawn lessons from the 1991 elections, was much better organized, enjoyed greater resources, and had largely succeeded in taming the armed forces and the police. In contrast to the 1991 campaign, which witnessed police intimidation of opposition activists and supporters, in 1992, police forces were either neutral or sided with the opposition. Moreover, the element of fear, which had evidently played a major role in 1991, was gone.

Significantly, the media situation also had changed in favor of the opposition. Communist influence on the broadcast media had declined significantly after the December 1991 replacement of the management of state radio and television. Thereby the foundations had been laid for competing political forces to gain fair access to television during the election campaign. The Communists also had lost control over most local newspapers, whose coverage and political inclinations changed in favor of the opposition. Moreover, the electorate had undergone serious changes after the 1991 elections. The peasantry, initially suspicious and largely ignorant of the opposition's program, threw its overwhelming support behind the opposition. With the disintegration of the cooperative system and the peasants' resultant independence, the Communists could no longer rely on local officials to intimidate the peasantry. Other sectors of society, which had not been outspoken, took a decisive step. In a significant development on the eve of the elections, 182 intellectuals, including the nation's most prominent writers and scholars, issued a manifesto calling on voters to support the opposition. Insisting that the Socialist Party was no longer able to govern the country, the statement called on the Albanian people not to repeat the "mistake" of 31 March 1991 but to vote for the opposition.[54]

Opposition Platform and Strategy

The election platform of the Democratic Party called for the implementation of radical political and economic reforms and the restoration of law and order. It pledged "to fight for the fulfillment of the centuries-old hopes and dreams of our people: establishment of democracy based on human rights and fundamental free- doms, prosperity through economic freedom and social justice, and the integration of our nation with the new historic developments that have taken place in Europe." The party committed itself to drafting a contemporary democratic constitution and to carrying out radical reforms in the government bureaucracy: a separation of the state from the party and a genuine depoliticization of the army, security forces, and the state-controlled media, including radio and television and the Albanian Telegraphic Agency. Promising radical economic reforms aimed at creating a market economy, the Democratic Party pledged to work toward total privatization. It pledged to compensate former owners for the property confiscated by the

Communist regime and to verify that the property gained by new owners during the transition period had not been gained illegally. The Democratic Party promised to revise the land law, allow the sale of land to Albanian citizens, compensate former owners for the land the Communists had nationalized, and provide peasants with tractors, fertilizers, and seeds. In foreign policy, it promised a speedy integration of the country into the European mainstream.[55]

In short, the Democratic Party, which included in its ranks individuals with diverse interests but with a shared antipathy toward communism, mobilized popular support with a broadly inclusive political program that combined broad social interests. The rapid growth in the Democratic Party's membership and popularity reflected the widespread belief that it would represent the interests of the whole society. Berisha displayed unusual political ability to shape events, becoming unquestionably the driving force behind the movement to dislodge the Communists from power. Although he had no experience with politics before December 1990, Berisha proved a very dynamic and popular politician as well as an extremely effective campaigner, adroitly handling the issues. His tenacity and dynamism were critical in the Democratic Party's election victory.

Berisha took measures to heal the wounds caused by internal party divisiveness. He rejected calls by more radical elements within the party to purge the leftist faction, led by Gramoz Pashko, which had opposed the withdrawal from the coalition government. To the chagrin of the more anti-Communist wing of the party, Pashko and Genc Ruli, the former minister of finance, were included in the list of candidates for the upcoming elections. Evidently hoping to become prime minister, Pashko made a pragmatic retreat, declaring that Berisha had been correct in withdrawing his party from the coalition government. In an interview with a foreign magazine, Pashko said that the Communists had "abused our presence in the government, they used us as a political shield and left us with the responsibility of government but kept political power for themselves."[56] Ruli made similar statements, accusing the Communists of having used the coalition to prolong their rule. He also said that despite the fact that the opposition was in charge of several ministries, the bureaucracy had remained essentially Communist.[57] Berisha waged an unprecedented campaign, the likes of which Albania, or for that matter other former Communist Balkan countries, had never witnessed. In a manner reminiscent of U.S. presidential campaigns, Berisha traveled throughout the country, spreading his party's message of national reconciliation and a new beginning for Albania. In his public pronouncements he portrayed his party as the only political force that could get the country out of its predicament and attempted to allay fears that a Democratic Party victory would result in a widespread anti-Communist backlash. In an appeal that evidently struck a deep chord among many Communists and former Communists who feared reprisals, Berisha pledged there would be no revenge, maintaining that the Albanians were collectively responsible for the situation in which Hoxha's crimes had become possible. He told foreign journalists that "if we start to seek revenge,

Albania will never get to know democracy. ... If all those who are guilty were to be punished, then Albania would have to be turned into one gigantic concentration camp."[58]

Berisha led efforts to create an anti-Communist front with the Republican and Social Democratic parties, the powerful independent trade unions, and the influential organization representing former political prisoners. While the Democrats closely coordinated their activities with the trade unions and former political prisoners, which represented a significant voting bloc, their cooperation with the other two main opposition parties was less than genuine for political and ideological reasons.

By far the strongest of the three, the Democratic Party was not interested in forging a close alliance with the Republicans or the Social Democrats. The Republican Party, although the second opposition party to be established, had not been able to build a viable national organization because of internal leadership dissension, and thus was not considered a significant player. Its program did not differ much from that of the Democratic Party.[59] Some Republicans viewed the Democratic Party, and not the Socialist Party, as their main rival. In districts, where the Socialists were not considered serious contenders, the Republicans campaigned against the Democrats. The Social Democratic Party, the younger of the three opposition parties, was ideologically much closer to the Socialist than the Democratic party. Its leaders Skendër Gjinushi, former minister of education, and Lisen Bashkurti, former leader of the youth organization, had been considered reformist Communists before they broke away from the Party of Labor and formed their own party. Indeed, in the 1991 elections Gjinushi was an APL candidate. The Social Democrats strongly opposed shock therapy, which was a pillar of the Democratic Party's platform, insisting that the state must play a regulatory role. Although opposition leaders publicly spoke of a coalition, there was no close coordination of activities among the three parties. The Democratic Party rejected offers by its two junior partners to field joint candidates, but agreed not to challenge their leaders in their respective election districts.

The Socialist Party

The election campaign pitted a united Democratic Party, in a loose coalition with other opposition forces, against a largely demoralized and divided Socialist Party. Communist forces had been badly splintered. By the end of 1991, as it became evident that early elections would be held, the Socialist Party attempted to distance itself from the APL and improve its image by refining its methods. In a major speech at the party's first national conference in November 1991, Fatos Nano claimed that the Socialist Party was a totally new party and not an offspring of the APL. Nano added that his party did not support Marxist-Leninist ideology and had distanced itself completely "from the APL as a party-state, from its policy and its errors and those of Enver Hoxha."[60] The Socialist Party pledged to work toward a genuine democracy based on the rule of law and toward a market economy. But in contrast to the Democrats' radical economic program, the Socialists advocated gradual economic changes that would have preserved many social aspects of the old system.[61] The Socialist Party tried to persuade voters that it had truly severed its Communist connections and embraced a social philosophy rooted in democratic principles; but despite Nano's soothing words, the Socialists failed to demonstrate convincingly that they had undergone a democratic conversion.

In reality, the Socialists conducted a primarily negative campaign, with their newspaper *Zëri i Popullit* engaging in inflammatory tirades against Berisha and other prominent opposition leaders. Ironically, the Socialist propaganda machine attempted to discredit Berisha by emphasizing his past membership in the APL and ties with the former *nomenklatura*.[62] In a desperate effort to prove to the electorate that the Socialist Party enjoyed support abroad, the Socialist-controlled media, as they had done the year before, published messages of support from émigrés of dubious reputation.[63] But under increased domestic and international pressure, the Socialists were unable to conduct an impressive campaign, and appeared resigned to defeat. They also did not have the financial means they had enjoyed in the previous elections. Under popular pressure, Bufi had issued a decree in November 1991 confiscating most of the assets belonging to the APL, including buildings, offices, and vehicles.[64]

Throughout the campaign, the Socialists were on the defensive. Government corruption figured prominently in the campaign, with the opposition emphasizing the many privileges that the *nomenklatura* had enjoyed in Europe's poorest country. A Swiss doctor working in Albania, John McGough, claimed that in 1990 the Communists had secretly airlifted ten tons of gold to Switzerland.[65] Although Alia denied these charges,[66] the claim reinforced widespread perceptions that the Communists had plundered the nation's riches. The Socialists responded by attacking Democratic Party officials who had served in Bufi's government, particularly Pashko for his extravagant spending habits.[67]

The Kosovar Factor

Prominent ethnic Albanian politicians from Kosova, including Ibrahim Rugova and Adem Demaçi, interjected themselves in Albania's election campaign by openly supporting Berisha and his Democratic Party, which drew sharp criticism from the Socialists.[68] Bujar Bukoshi, Kosova's prime minister in exile, said: "Kosova and the whole Albanian nation have a great need for a strong and fully democratic Albania. For the sake of this stabilization, we hope and believe that the people will vote for the democratic opposition."[69]

However, there were some divisions within Kosovar ranks. In an ironic twist of events, Rexhep Qosja, who in December 1990 had been considered almost an idol by Berisha and other emerging opposition leaders, broke with the Democrats on the eve of the elections, over the issue of national reconciliation. Seeing their power slipping away and concerned about possible reprisals, Albania's Socialists had become the most ardent advocates of national reconciliation, citing as a model the reconciliation that had taken place among Albanians in Kosova in the wake of the intensification of the conflict with Serbia. In late 1991, a group of relatively unknown, ostensibly independent scholars, with Alia's support, made plans to convene a meeting of prominent personalities from a wide political spectrum from Albania, Kosova, and other Albanian-inhabited territories in the former Yugoslavia and the West. Organizers originally had scheduled the meeting for 28 November 1991, Albania's national holiday. But while the organizers attracted support in Kosova and abroad, with Qosja and Ismail Kadare agreeing to cochair the meeting, opposition forces in Albania, particularly former political prisoners, rejected the idea. In February 1992, a group of prominent Kosovars, including Qosja, linguist Idriz Ajeti, writer Ramiz Kelmendi, and trade union leader Hajrullah Gorani, went to Tiranë in hopes of reconciling differences between Alia and the opposition.[70] Alia evidently convinced the group to endorse plans to convene an all-Albanian meeting. Although national reconciliation was a major aspect of the Democratic Party's platform in both the 1991 and the 1992 elections, Qosja failed in his attempt to gain the opposition's endorsement of the proposed meeting.

Berisha insisted he could not participate in national reconciliation talks organized by the Communists, whose vicious class struggle had brought so much tragedy to the Albanian people. He argued that only former political prisoners could sponsor such a meeting. Moreover, he maintained that the prerequisite for national reconciliation was the final victory of democratic forces over Communism.[71] Qosja returned to Prishtinë empty-handed and Alia's plans for a national reconciliation convention collapsed. However, the incident resulted in what appears to be a permanent and nasty rift between Qosja and Berisha. Qosja's position reflected a poor understanding of the situation in Albania and lack of appreciation for the many Albanians unjustly persecuted by the Communists. It was also an indication of the gulf dividing Kosova's Albanians from the majority of their brethren in Albania. While in Kosova the enemy was Serbia, in Albania the enemy was within, and reconciliation seemed excruciatingly difficult in view of the Communists' reluctance to publicly express repentance.

Although the interjection of the Kosovars into Albania's elections and Qosja's rift with Berisha received widespread publicity, these events arguably did not influence the Albanian electorate. The issue of Kosova and other Albanian-inhabited territories did not figure prominently in the campaign, although almost all of the parties' programs contained references to ethnic Albanians' right to self-determination, including unification with Albania. Even in the northern parts of the country, which had a greater stake in the issue because of the danger of war in Kosova, the fate of Kosova did not seem to have great salience.

Western Power Players

What seems to have been of more critical importance was the position of Western powers, particularly the United States and Italy, which were seen as vying for influence in Albania. The Democrats attempted to convince the electorate that international support for Albania was conditioned on a Democratic victory at the polls. The United States publicly backed the Democratic Party. Within a year, Berisha had twice visited the United States for talks with administration officials and congressional leaders. U.S. Secretary of State James Baker had visited Albania in June 1991 at Berisha's personal invitation. U.S. Ambassador to Albania, William Ryerson publicly expressed support for the opposition and participated in Democratic Party-organized rallies, while the NDI and IRI provided significant assistance to the opposition.

Italy, on the other hand, was perceived as supporting the Socialists. According to Berisha, during the election campaign the Italian embassy in Tiranë was "turned into a divisional Communist Party headquarters."[72] To the great consternation of the Albanian opposition, Italian Prime Minister Bettino Craxi accepted honorary membership in the Albanian Socialist Party, thus giving the Communists, restyled as Socialists, a sense of legitimacy. Italy, which had provided more assistance than any other country to Albania, made no secret of its unhappiness with the Democratic Party's pro-American enthusiasm during the campaign. Soon after the election and the Democratic Party's victory, Italian Foreign Minister Giovanni de Michelis traveled to Durrës for a meeting with Berisha to "clarify certain controversies and misunderstandings." While de Michelis told Berisha that Italy was not jealous of other countries' presence in Albania, he reminded the future president that "U.S. Secretary of State James Baker [during his June 1991 visit to Tiranë] left 7 billion [*lira*] in aid, whereas Italy has granted some 400 billion."[73]

Final Tally

Altogether, eleven political parties participated in the elections, fielding 516 candidates. In addition, there were five independent candidates. Only five parties—the Democratic Party, the Socialist Party, the Social Democratic Party, the Republican Party, and the Agrarian Party—fielded candidates in at least thirty-three election districts, spread across at least nine administrative districts, making them eligible for supplementary seats if they achieved the 4-percent threshold. The others—the Union for Human Rights, the Christian Democratic Party, the

Ecological Party, the Popular Alliance, the Communist Party, and the Universal Party—ran candidates in a limited number of election districts and were not considered significant players.

The results surpassed even the opposition's most optimistic predictions, as the Democratic Party won a resounding victory. Its candidates won in ninety of the 100 election districts. The Socialist Party suffered a humiliating defeat, winning in only six election districts. The Union for Human Rights won in two districts, and the Social Democratic Party and the Republican Party in one each. The Republican Party did extremely poorly, failing even to get its leader, Sabri Godo, elected. Although in direct elections the Democrats won 90 percent of the seats, the distribution of supplemental seats favored the Socialist and Social Democratic parties, the only two other parties that achieved more than 4 percent of the nationwide vote. Thus, with 27.1 percent of the national vote, the Socialist Party received thirty-two supplemental seats, and the Social Democratic Party, with 5 percent of the vote, received an additional six seats. The Democrats received only two supplemental seats.[74] The final distribution of parliamentary seats was as follows: the Democratic Party, 92; the Socialist Party, 38; the Social Democratic Party, 7; the Union for Human Rights, 2; and the Republican Party, 1 (Table 4.1).

The opposition had been concerned about the possible violent reaction of Socialist supporters in case of a Democratic victory. Their fears, however, proved unfounded: The Socialists accepted defeat. In a statement to the Central Electoral Commission, the Socialist Party leadership said that "psychological terror" had been used against the Socialists, that the election law had been violated and the Socialist Party's supporters attacked in various parts of the country.[75] Nonetheless, an editorial in Zëri i Popullit pledged that the Socialist Party would play a constructive role in the opposition.[76]

TABLE 4.1 Albania's 1992 Parliamentary Elections

	Votes*	% of Votes	Seats	% of Seats
Democratic Party	1,046,193	62.08	92	65.71
Socialist Party	433,602	25.70	38	27.14
Social Democratic Party	73,820	4.30	7	5.00
Union for Human Rights	48,923	2.90	2	1.43
Republican Party	52,477	3.11	1	0.71
Other Parties	30,022	1.80	—	—
Total	1,685,037	99.89	140	99.99
Vote turnout				90.35 percent

*First round of voting, 22 March 1992.

Source: Fletorja Zyrtare e Republikës së Shqipërisë [The Official Gazette of the Republic of Albania], no. 2 (May 1992), p. 99.

At a news conference a day after the election, Berisha declared that Albania's long Communist nightmare was over. Quoting President John F. Kennedy's famous inaugural statement, Berisha called on Albanians to ask "not what your country can do for you, but what you can do for your country." He urged the people to unite around the Democratic Party and build a new Albania. He reassured the Communists that there would be no revenge, saying: "Albanians as a whole are at the same time the accomplices and fellow victims of the regime under which we lived. Our common responsibility and our common suffering must unite us with the ideals of democracy for the construction of a new Albania."[77]

The Transfer of Power

It had been widely assumed that Ramiz Alia would resign as president regardless of the outcome of the elections or the margin of an opposition victory. Pressure for his resignation had been building since summer 1991. Enver Hoxha's successor, who had overseen the gradual dismantling of the Communist monopoly on power, had lost all credibility. Despite his insistence that he fully backed the democratization of Albania's polity, until the end Alia clung to Communist ideals. Significantly, he could no longer even count on the backing of the Socialist Party. Eager to convince the populace that theirs was a new party, Socialist leaders did not invite Alia to join.

In a statement on national radio and television on 3 April 1992, only days after the final election results were announced, Alia said he was resigning "for the benefit of the homeland." He expressed hope that the new parliament would "entrust the country's leadership to a new personality who will be able to lead Albania following the majority's will."[78] Parliament accepted his resignation without any debate. Alia's unceremonious exit from Albanian politics signified the end of an era that had brought so much misery to the Albanian nation.

Now Berisha's politically risky decision to withdraw from the coalition government paid off. He was widely recognized as a tough politician and the best leader to succeed Alia and steer Albania through the turbulent times ahead. Moreover, his telegenic appeal and shrewd political instincts were instrumental in his party's election victory. During the campaign, he maintained a conspicuous silence on Alia's fate. His response to repeated questions by reporters as to whether he would succeed Alia was that his primary goal was to become "a free citizen in a free Albania." But he had become such a popular figure and indubitably the major force in shaping the anticommunist movement that there was no other serious contender for the nation's top post. On 9 April, parliament voted ninety-six in favor and thirty-five against to elect Berisha as the country's new President for a five-year term. The Socialists, who declined to put up their own candidate, voted against him. In his inaugural address, Berisha acknowledged the extremely difficult challenges of establishing a genuine democracy in Albania and reviving its economy. Echoing the theme of his election campaign, Berisha emphasized the importance of national reconciliation: "We have all been jointly responsible to varying degrees for the survival of the dictatorship, at least for the 99.9 percent vote we gave it out of fear. We were all also its victims, however. Let this mutual suffering and pain therefore unite us in joint responsibility to build a civilized society such as Spain and Portugal." The new President said that he would not move into the presidential palace but would continue to live in the same apartment. Addressing the Albanian people, he said, "I will remain among you, because that is where I feel stronger." He also pledged that Tiranë would support the Albanians in Kosova, expressing "unswerving faith that the Albanian cause is a just cause that can be fully solved within the framework of the Helsinki Final Act and the European Community's regional initiative."[79] In his first interview as President, Berisha repeated that Albania resembled "a wasteland," but expressed optimism about its future.[80]

Constructing the New Government

In an attempt to preserve party unity, the Democrats had not constructed a shadow government before the elections, although there were clear indications that they would win. They took over without a political team in place or detailed plans for the immediate future, and thus lost valuable time in assembling the new administration. While there appears to have been no disagreement regarding Berisha's election as president, there were fierce internal debates about other appointments. Azem Hajdari, Arben Imami, and Gramoz Pashko had actively lobbied respectively for the posts of Democratic Party chairman, speaker of parliament, and prime minister. In an attempt to appeal to the party's mainstream, the three had appeared at many rallies at Berisha's side. Teta and Zogaj hoped to be named to the posts they had held in the coalition government—respectively, minister of defense and minister of culture. However, the leftist faction could not muster enough support in the party's National Council, where decisions on appointments were made. Public opinion at the party's highest level had shifted significantly to the right in the wake of the collapse of the coalition government. Thus, Pashko and his supporters, with the notable exception of his brother-in-law Genc Ruli, were kept out of the new government.

On 10 April, Berisha appointed Aleksandër Meksi, a noted archaeologist, as prime minister. A founding member of the Democratic Party and a member of its Steering Committee, Meksi had worked for many years at the Institute for Cultural Monuments and the Institute of Archaeological Excavations.[81] Although he lacked experience in economics, he had distinguished himself in 1991 as deputy speaker of parliament, strongly pushing for an overhaul of the Communist legal system. The makeup of Meksi's cabinet suggested a strong commitment to economic reform. Bashkim Kopliku and Rexhep Uka were named deputy premiers and, respectively, ministers of public order and of agriculture and food. These appointments reflected Berisha's immediate priorities of restoring law and order and rehabilitating agriculture, considered crucial to the country's future. Kopliku, a graduate of the engineering faculty of Tiranë University, had developed the reputation of a tough administrator as chairman of the Durrës Executive Committee during 1991. Uka, an agronomist who had received his doctorate at the Athens Agricultural University, was the Democratic Party's leading spokesman on agricultural issues.

The highest economic post, that of minister of economy and finance, went to Genc Ruli. Berisha came under attack from some of his more radical supporters for giving such a key post to Ruli, who with the consolidation of the two ministries, wielded considerable power. Initially the self-protective Ruli had joined Pashko and other Democratic Party ministers in opposing Berisha's decision to quit the coalition government, but he subsequently repositioned himself on the winning side. Thus, many party members questioned Ruli's loyalty to the new government. Moreover, his record was tainted by persistent charges of corruption during his service in Bufi's government. The decision to give Ruli a key post was evidently driven by two important factors. First, as minister of finance in the coalition government, he had worked closely with the World Bank and the International Monetary Fund and could therefore provide continuity in Albania's important and growing relationship with the international financial institutions. Second, Ruli's appointment represented a sound political move to contain the rift with the leftist faction. In the final analysis, Ruli did not have a significant constituency within the party and could be dismissed at any time with limited political costs.

The biggest surprises in the new government were Alfred Serreqi and Safet Zhulali, the ministers of foreign affairs and defense, respectively. They were relatively obscure figures within the democratic movement. Neither had any prior experience in the sectors in which they were now taking charge. Serreqi, a medical doctor from Shkodër, had spent most of his professional life working as a doctor in the country's remote northeastern regions. In the coalition government he had held the post of deputy health minister. Serreqi's only experience in foreign policy was his short stint as chief of the Democratic Party's department of foreign affairs. If Serreqi appeared less than well qualified to take charge of Albania's diplomacy, there was nothing in Zhulali's background to prepare him for the defense minister's portfolio. He had taught mathematics at a high school in Dibër.

In line with the Democratic Party's preelection coalition with the other two main opposition parties, Fatos Bitincka of the Republican Party was appointed minister of transportation and communications (a position he had held in Bufi's cabinet), and Vullnet Ademi of the Social Democratic Party became general secretary of the Council of Ministers. Two former ministers without party affiliations retained their positions: Kudred Çela, minister of justice, and Abdyl

Xhaja, minister of industry, mining, and energy resources. Other cabinet members included Ylli Vejsiu, minister of education; Ilir Manushi, minister of construction; Tritan Shehu, minister of health and environmental protection; Dhimitër Anagnosti, minister of culture, youth and sports; Osman Shehu, minister of tourism, Dashamir Shehi, minister of labor, emigration, and social assistance; Maksim Konomi, chairman of the Committee on Science and Technology; and Blerim Çela, chairman of the State Control Commission.[82]

The post of speaker of parliament went to Pjetër Arbnori. His selection was controversial because it had been rumored that he had a past affiliation with the Sigurimi. Arrested in spring 1961 for having formed an underground Social Democratic Party, Arbnori was sentenced to death, but his sentence was later commuted to twenty-five years of imprisonment. While in prison, he was caught writing novels, which resulted in an additional prison sentence. He was released in August 1989.[83] Altogether, he had spent more than twenty-eight years in Communist prisons. Arbnori was accused by a fellow prisoner, Rev. Simon Jubani, of having collaborated with the Sigurimi while in prison.[84] Azem Hajdari, a persistent Arbnori critic, joined Rev. Jubani and Socialist Party leaders in accusing the speaker of parliament of being a Sigurimi agent.[85] Arbnori vehemently denied these allegations, in turn accusing his rivals of links with the former secret police.[86] Neither Rev. Jubani nor Hajdari was able to explain why Arbnori, if indeed he was a Sigurimi agent, was not granted an early release, as was the practice in such cases. In September 1995, *Rilindja Demokratike* published a letter, preserved in the national archives, that Arbnori had written to Chief Justice of the Supreme Court Shuaip Panariti in December 1964, in which Arbnori described in detail the horrible torture he was subjected to.[87]

To the chagrin of Hajdari and Imami, Berisha endorsed Eduard Selami, the thirty-two-year-old party secretary, to succeed him as Democratic Party chairman. A graduate of Tiranë University who had written his thesis on Enver Hoxha's "aesthetics,"[88] Selami had displayed impressive organizational skills. Although initially not a Berisha loyalist and ideologically much closer to the leftist than the mainstream faction, by the time elections were held on 22 March, Selami had emerged as Berisha's right-hand man, eclipsing other members of the leadership. In a meeting on 16 April, the Democratic Party's national conference overwhelmingly elected Selami as the new chairman: He received 411 votes out of 485. Hajdari and Imami, also candidates for the top post, were reelected deputy chairmen. Tomorr Dosti, the son of the nationalist wartime leader Hasan Dosti, and Arben Lika, a leader of the December 1990 student demonstrations, were elevated to the party's presidium.[89]

While Imami was not considered a serious contender for party chairman, the leftists had apparently pinned their hopes on Hajdari, who had been considered the party's number-two man. But Hajdari's star had been on the decline since the Democratic Party's first convention, in fall 1991, when he aligned himself with Berisha's rivals. While publicly he had continued to express unqualified support for Berisha, he tried behind the scenes to undermine the president's position. Hajdari evidently never forgave Berisha for having wrested the top party post away from him back in February 1991. As a leader of the student demonstrations that opened the way for Albania's multiparty system, Hajdari believed that he was entitled to inherit Berisha's mantle as party leader. Having suffered a humiliating defeat in competition with Selami, Hajdari demanded that he be given another influential position in the government. He unsuccessfully lobbied for the defense or public order ministry portfolios. Having just scored a stunning election victory, Berisha's supporters saw no reason to compromise with the leftist faction; but by refusing to placate its most powerful rivals, the mainstream faction of the Democratic Party had sown the seeds of an open split within its ranks.

Arguably, the Democrats were forced to recruit from a small pool of elites to build the new administration. The Democratic Party issued a statement saying that, "Undoubtedly there are weaknesses and the possibilities of selection have not ended. It was very difficult to find experienced people, especially in these fields, after everything was destroyed for fifty successive years, human beings above all, and when diplomacy, foreign trade, justice, etc., were the domain of Politburo members, their sons, bridegrooms, and friends."[90] Berisha publicly acknowledged that the cabinet was not an "ideal" one.[91] Characterized by the conspicuous absence of any women, it also was devoid of real economic leaders. Members of the cabinet were widely perceived as too indecisive to govern effectively in a political climate that would have taxed the skills of even the most experienced and adept. Most ministers were young, had meager if any experience, and appeared to lack the intellectual agility or political acumen that the country's fragile polity with its myriad problems demanded. Critics alleged that the Democratic Party was stacking the cabinet and the state bureaucracy with poorly qualified but politically supportive cronies. They charged that Berisha made appointment decisions with a small circle of inexperienced advisers, and expressed concern that he was not getting good enough advice.

During the election campaign, Berisha had sought to reach out to diverse groups and to incorporate their views in the Democratic Party's platform. But when it came to forming the government, no effort seems to have been made to select representatives of these diverse groups for the new cabinet. As a result of political compromises and lack of prior planning, new officials were appointed in a somewhat amateurish fashion.

The transfer of power from the Socialists to the Democrats was remarkably peaceful and smooth. Indeed, this was the first time in Albania's history that the change from one type of regime to another was accomplished without resort to violence. With this momentous event, Albania embarked on the difficult road of transition from a totalitarian, one-party hegemonic system to a pluralist democracy and a market economy.

Notes

1. *Zëri i Popullit,* 5 June 1991, p. 1.
2. *Rilindja Demokratike,* 5 and 15 June 1991.
3. *The Independent* (London), 12 June 1991.
4. *The Guardian,* 13 June 1991.
5. *Rilindja Demokratike,* 29 May 1991, pp. 1, 5.
6. *Zëri i Popullit,* 13 June 1991, pp. 1-3.
7. Sali Berisha, "The Last Domino," *The New York Times,* 20 June 1991.
8. See James A. Baker, III, with Thomas M. DeFrank, *The Politics of Diplomacy* (New York: G. P. Putnam's Sons, 1995), pp. 484-486.
9. *U.S. Department of State Dispatch* 2, no. 26, 1 July 1991, pp. 466-467.
10. Quoted in Thomas L. Friedman, "300,000 Albanians Pour into Street to Welcome Baker," *New York Times,* 23 June 1991, p. 1.
11. *Drita,* 11 August 1991, p. 1.
12. Catherine Field, "Appointment in Tirana," *Observer,* 1 March 1992.
13. *Zëri i Popullit,* 23 July 1991, pp. 1-2.
14. United States Information Agency, *Albanians Speak Out on Political Issues* (Washington, D.C.), Report M-99-91, 15 July 1991.
15. ANSA in English, 1015 GMT, 12 September 1991, in FBIS-WEU 91-177, 12 September 1991, p. 30.
16. When U.S. Secretary of State James Baker visited Tiranë in June 1991, he was met by hundreds of thousands of Albanians wielding American flags but very few waving Albanian ones. And many Albanians who sought refuge in Greece and Italy were said to be "ashamed" to admit their ethnic origin. See *Drita,* 2 June 1991, p. 3.
17. See the editorial "Albanianism: An Ideology the Fatherland Needs," *Atdheu* (organ of the monarchist National Democratic Party), 24 September 1991, p. 1.
18. *Rilindja Demokratike,* 24 July 1991, pp. 1, 6.
19. Ibid., 20 July 1991, p. 1.
20. See Çupi's interview in *Koha Jonë,* 9 August 1991, pp. 1-3.
21. Radio Tiranë Network in Albanian, 1800 GMT 22 August 1991, translated in FBIS-EEU 91-164, 23 August 1991, p. 2.
22. Radio Tiranë Network in Albanian, 1800 GMT, 26 August 1991, translated in FBIS-EEU 91-167, 28 August 1991, pp. 5-6.
23. Sali Berisha, "Civil Political Action and Democracy," *Rilindja Demokratike,* 4 September 1991, pp. 1-2.
24. Radio Tiranë Network in Albanian, 1800 GMT, 14 September 1991, translated in FBIS-EEU 91-179, 16 September 1991, 3-4. On the same day, the youth newspaper published an interview with Pashko in which he criticized Berisha's "populist" policies and said that early elections would harm the process of reforms. See *Zëri i Rinisë,* 14 September 1991, pp. 2, 4.
25. See article by Genc Myftiu in *Rilindja Demokratike,* 13 May 1992, p. 4.
26. See Catherine Field, "Appointment in Tirana," *Observer,* 1 March 1992.
27. Bujar Hoxha, "A Little History," *Rilindja Demokratike,* 11 August 1992, p. 1.
28. Neritan Ceka accepted Alia's offer to accompany him on his trip without prior consultation with the parliamentary group he headed or the party's leadership. See statement by the Democratic Party presidium and parliamentary group in Radio Tiranë

Network in Albanian, 1900 GMT, 9 December 1991, translated in FBIS-EEU 91-237, 10 December 1991, pp. 3-4.

29. Alia reportedly also toyed with the idea of being succeeded by writer Ismail Kadare. Since Kadare had declared on several occasions that he would not get involved in politics and refused to meet Alia during the President's visit to Paris, Ceka became the preferred choice. See Afrim Krasniqi, "What Is Going to Happen With Ramiz Alia?" *Tribuna Demokratike*, 17 April 1992, pp. 1-2.

30. *Rilindja Demokratike*, 11 August 1992, pp. 1, 4. See also Abdi Baleta, "The Revival of the 'Ceka Phenomenon': Why?" *Zëri i Rinisë*, 11 March 1992, pp. 3-4. Arjan Trebicka, "'Albania's New Democracy': Fiction or Reality?" *Balli i Kombit*, 22 April 1992, p. 4.

31. Radio Tiranë Network in Albanian, 1700 GMT, 29 September 1991, translated in FBIS-EEU 91-189, 30 September 1991, p. 5; and ATA in English, 0922 GMT, 30 September 1991, in FBIS-EEU 91-190, 1 October 1991, p. 5. For Communist reaction to Berisha's reelection, see Luan M. Rama, "The 'Democratic' Face of the Democratic Party," *Zëri i Popullit*, 1 October 1991, pp. 1-2.

32. Radio Tiranë Network in Albanian, 1900 GMT, 29 October 1991, translated in FBIS-EEU 91-210, 30 October 1991, p. 1.

33. Kumbaro, a member of the APL Central Committee, was appointed General Director of radio and television in the wake of the toppling of Hoxha's monument in Tiranë in February 1991. Responding to increased opposition demands for his resignation "for the sake of stability and peace in Albania," Kumbaro is alleged to have responded in early November: "I will leave Radio-Television only when Ramiz Alia goes." Radio Croatia in Albanian, 2045 GMT, 10 November 1991, translated in FBIS-EEU 91-218, 12 November 1991, p. 4.

34. Radio Tiranë Network in Albanian, 1430 GMT, 16 October 1991, translated in FBIS-EEU 91-201, 17 October 1991, p. 1.

35. *Svenska Dagbladet* (Stockholm), 13 December 1991, p. 6, translated in FBIS-EEU 91-245, 20 December 1991, p. 2.

36. ATA in English, 0950 GMT, 27 November 1991, in FBIS-EEU 91-229, 27 November 1991, p. 1.

37. Radio Tiranë Network in Albanian, 1900 GMT 1 December 1991, translated in FBIS-EEU 91-232, 3 December 1991, p. 3.

38. Mrs. Hoxha and former APL Politburo member Rita Marko were arrested on 4 December. Alia claimed that he did not give the order for Mrs. Hoxha's arrest and found out about it through "private channels." Alia, ... *Shpresa dhe zhgenjime*, pp. 89-90.

39. For Ceka's version of the events, see his 12 December 1991 letter to the leadership of the Democratic Party, published in *Koha Jonë*, 21 August 1994, p. 2; and interview in *Aleanca*, 20 December 1994, pp. 4 and 7.

40. Radio Tiranë Network in Albanian, 1430 GMT, 4 December 1991, translated in FBIS-EEU 91-234, 5 December 1991, pp. 1-3. The arrest of Mrs. Hoxha and former Politburo member Rita Marko was announced after Berisha's news conference. AFP in English, 1427 GMT, 5 December 1991, in FBIS-EEU 91-235, 6 December 1991, p. 5.

41. Pashko's interview with Reuter was given wide publicity by the Albanian media. See Radio Tiranë Network in Albanian, 1900 GMT, 5 December 1991, translated in FBIS-EEU 91-235, 6 December 1991, pp. 3-4.

42. Radio Tiranë Network in Albanian, 1900 GMT, 7 December 1991, translated in FBIS-EEU 91-236, 9 December 1991, pp. 3-4.

43. Radio Tiranë Network in Albanian, 1900 GMT, 9 December 1991, translated in FBIS-EEU 91-237, 10 December 1991, pp. 3-4.

44. Radio Tiranë Network in Albanian, 1900 GMT, 6 December 1991, translated in FBIS-EEU 91-236, 9 December 91, p. 2.

45. Radio Tiranë Network in Albanian, 1430 GMT, 9 December 1991, translated in FBIS-EEU 91-237, 10 December 1991, p. 2.

46. In a statement issued 6 December, Bufi said: "I am aware that the government crisis has aroused a great worry and uncertainty amongst people. I also know that the overview I presented on the economic state at the recent meeting of the government has aroused tension and somewhere even panic. Certainly the situation is difficult, but in no way hopeless and without [a] way out. If I said that we have, for instance, cereal reserves only for a week, this does not mean that we could not provide bread for the people. Wheat and other food articles [from international donors] continue to reach our country." ATA in English, 0912 GMT, 7 December 1991, in FBIS-EEU 91-236, 9 December 1991, p. 1.

47. Radio Tiranë Network in Albanian, 1700 GMT, 11 December 1991, translated in FBIS-EEU 91-239, 12 December 1991, pp. 2-3.

48. ATA in English, 1900 GMT, 7 December 1991, in FBIS-EEU 91-236, 9 December 1991, p. 6.

49. "Law on Elections for the People's Assembly of the Republic of Albania," *Fletorja Zyrtare e Republikës së Shqipërisë*, no. 1 (February 1992), pp. 36-48.

50. *Rilindja Demokratike*, 8 January 1992, p. 2. Bezhani continued to advocate Greek annexation of southern Albania. See his interview in *Helsingin Sanomat* (Helsinki), 25 March 1992, p. C1, translated in Joint Publications Research Service, *East Europe Report* (Washington, D.C.) 92-053, 30 April 1992, p. 1.

51. National Democratic Institute for International Affairs, *Briefing Report for the Albanian Elections, March 22 and 29, 1992* (Washington, D.C., 1992).

52. The International Republican Institute, *Trip Report: Albania Staff Mission, 9-16 December 1991* (Washington, D.C., 1991).

53. See Mary Battiata, "Albania's Post-Communist Anarchy," *Washington Post*, 21 March 1992, p. A18.

54. *Alternativa SD*, 13 March 1992, p. 3.

55. *Rilindja Demokratike*, 22 February 1992, pp. 1-4.

56. *East European Reporter*, March-April 1992, p. 55.

57. *Rilindja Demokratike*, 4 January 1992, pp. 1-2.

58. *Rzeczpospolita* (Warsaw), 25 February 1992, p. 6, translated in FBIS-EEU 92-045, 6 March 1992, pp. 2-3.

59. *Republika*, 1 March 1992, pp. 1-2.

60. *Zëri i Popullit*, 29 November 1991, pp. 1-4.

61. Ibid., 26 February 1992, pp. 1-3.

62. A Communist paper reproduced excerpts from an introduction to a medical textbook Berisha had published years ago, in which he had praised the APL. It was also disclosed that Berisha had given an autographed copy of the book to Hoxha's son Sokol. *24 Orë*, no. 7 (February 1992), p. 1. See also *Zëri i Popullit*, 20 March 1992, pp. 1, 3.

63. See letters by APL supporters in the Albanian American community Dedë Elezaj, Besije Qemal Vejseli, Meqo Shtino, and Vehap and Baudin Sela in *Zëri i Popullit*, 20 March 1992, p. 4.

64. Radio Tiranë Network in Albanian, 1430 GMT, 14 November 1991, translated in FBIS-EEU 91-221, 15 November 1991, p. 3.

65. See *Christian Science Monitor*, 19 March 1992.

66. *Zëri i Popullit*, 20 March 1992, p. 1.

67. Ibid., 20 March 1992, p. 2.

68. The Socialist Party issued a strong protest against a statement by Kosova's leader Ibrahim Rugova that an opposition victory was in the best interests of the Albanian nation. See *Zëri i Popullit*, 16 February 1992, p. 1.

69. Quoted in Radio Tiranë Network in Albanian, 1830 GMT, 17 February 1992, translated in FBIS-EEU 92-032, 18 February 1992, p. 3.

70. For Qosja's views on national reconciliation, see *Kuvendi '92 Mbarëkombëtar* (Tiranë), no. 2 (April 1992), pp. 1, 4.

71. *Rilindja Demokratike*, 12 February 1992, p. 1.

72. Quoted in *La Stampa* (Turin), 24 February 1994, p. 10, translated in FBIS-EEU 94-040-A, 1 March 1994, pp. 1-2. Italian Socialists, for their part, accused Berisha of being too pro-American. In July 1992, after President Berisha had visited Washington, he was criticized for being anti-Italian by deputy and member of the leadership of the Italian Socialist Party Francesco De Carli. The Italian official attacked Berisha's pro-American policy as a failure and reminded the Albanians: "It is a mistake to call on America to save Albania. Only Europe can save Albania." See *Zëri i Popullit*, 16 July 1992, pp. 1, 3.

73. Quoted in *La Repubblica*, 4 April 1992, p. 13, translated in FBIS-EEU 92-071, 13 April 1992, p. 36.

74. U.S. Commission on Security and Cooperation in Europe, *Albania's Second Multi-Party Elections, March 22 and 29, 1992* (Washington, D.C., April 1992), pp. 20-21.

75. *Zëri i Popullit*, 24 March 1992, pp. 3-4.

76. Editorial "Let Democracy Win," *Zëri i Popullit*, 24 March 1992, p. 1.

77. Radio Tiranë Network in Albanian, 1310 GMT, 23 March, 1992, translated in FBIS-EEU 92-057, 24 March 1992, pp. 4-5.

78. Radio Tiranë Network in Albanian, 1330 GMT, 3 April 1992, translated in FBIS-EEU 92-065, 3 April 1992, p. 2.

79. Radio Tiranë Network in Albanian, 1606 GMT, 9 April 1992, translated in FBIS-EEU 92-070, 10 April 1992, pp. 2-3.

80. Radio Tiranë Network in Albanian, 1432 GMT, 9 April 1992, translated in FBIS-EEU 92-070, 10 April 1992, pp. 3-4.

81. Radio Tiranë Network in Albanian, 2000 GMT, 10 April 1992, translated in FBIS-EEU 92-071, 13 April 1992, p. 2.

82. For profiles of cabinet members, see Radio Tiranë Network in Albanian, 1410 GMT, 15 April 1992, translated in FBIS-EEU 92-074, 16 April 1992, pp. 3-4. See also Remzi Lani, "Meksi's Cabinet or the 'Cabinet of Hope,'" *Zëri i Rinisë*, 15 April 1992, p. 1; and Louis Zanga, "Daunting Tasks for Albania's New Government," in *RFE/RL Research Report* 1, no. 21 (22 May 1992), pp. 11-17

83. *Rilindja Demokratike*, 8 April 1992, p. 1.

84. A former secret police officer, Luan Pobrati, claimed Arbnori's code name was *Koromania*. See *Zëri i Popullit*, 8 June 1993, p. 3.

85. Azem Hajdari, "A Free Man Has No One to Blame for His Misfortune," *Rilindja Demokratike*, 27 July 1993, pp. 1-2.

86. Pjetër Arbnori, "Only Those Who Challenged Death With Me Can Write My Biography," *Rilindja Demokratike*, 18 July 1993, pp. 1, 6.

87. *Rilindja Demokratike*, 23 September 1995, p. 1.

88. Eduard Selami, "Comrade Enver Hoxha's Thought on Aesthetics—An Important Contribution to the Enrichment of Our Aesthetics," *Nëntori* 37, no. 4 (April 1990), pp. 33-39.

89. Radio Tiranë Network in Albanian, 1730 GMT, 16 April 1992, translated in FBIS-EEU 92-075, 17 April 1992, p. 3.

90. Radio Tiranë Network in Albanian, 1330 GMT, 15 April 1992, translated in FBIS-EEU 92-075, 17 April 1992, pp. 2-3.

91. See Berisha's interview in *Rilindja Demokratike*, 22 April 1992, p. 1.

5

The Democratic Party in Power
(1992-1996)

Implementing the radical reforms necessary to establish a pluralistic democracy was difficult under the best of circumstances in Eastern Europe; but doing so in a destitute country such as Albania in 1992 seemed almost impossible. Of all the former Communist countries, Albania appeared least prepared for the painful transition from dictatorship to a pluralistic democracy and a market economy. The historical legacies of centralized, authoritarian rule and economic underdevelopment posed serious impediments to a rapid and smooth democratization of the Albanian polity. Atomized by close to fifty years of Communist misrule, Albania was in the midst of a serious political, economic, moral, and spiritual crisis during which large segments of the population had lost hope in their country's future.[1] Moreover, senior members of the incoming administration had virtually no previous political experience. But despite the overwhelming historical, political, and socioeconomic obstacles, the Democratic Party's impressive victory gave Albania its best chance in its eighty-year history as an independent state to attempt to achieve a functioning democracy, economic viability, and social and legal justice for its citizens.

A Daunting Agenda

The Democratic Party had made many campaign promises, triggering a wave of euphoria, and expectations were running very high for quick, visible changes. Many perceived democracy to mean individual benefits from the government—higher wages and more services. These expectations were bound to prove too high in a country emerging from four decades of Communist terror and social and economic devastation.

Having won a clear popular mandate for reform, the Democratic Party moved swiftly to fill the political vacuum that had been created during the previous year and a half of turmoil. The immediate priorities of the new government were to arrest the nation's further economic decline, restore law and order, begin the difficult task of institution building, and reintegrate the country into the international community after decades of isolation.

Dispelling hopes for a quick fix, President Berisha exploited his popularity and the Democratic Party's impressive election victory in building a broad political consensus to help implement economic transformation and recovery programs. He embarked upon an ambitious policy of opening up Albania and developing close ties with the West, particularly the United States. Insisting that his country had to start from scratch, Berisha focused on persuading Western democracies that Albania be treated as a special case because of the very repressive nature of its past Communist rule and long isolation from the outside world. Indeed, the international response to the Democratic Party's victory was very positive. Albania became the largest recipient of Western aid per capita in Eastern Europe. The United States, the European Community (now European Union), Italy, and other donors granted Albania substantial humanitarian and technical assistance. The World Bank and the International Monetary Fund announced major programs to help the country's economic recovery. Foreign experts from the United States and other countries were dispatched to Albania to provide much needed advice. Having secured foreign assistance, the government launched a midterm economic plan.

During the next two years, Albania succeeded in arresting the precipitous fall in production, reining in inflation, and reviving the agricultural sector. However, the implementation of painful reforms and determination to stick to tough IMF rules, discussed in greater detail in Chapter 6, caused considerable social dislocation and involved serious political risks. The opposition Socialist Party sought to capitalize on discontent caused by austerity measures by condemning the reforms for increasing economic inequality, concentrating wealth in a few hands, and creating a vast mass of poor people. But the president, apparently convinced that Albania could not afford half measures, left no doubt that his government was prepared "to sacrifice popularity by pressing ahead with reforms."[2]

Berisha viewed the establishment of the rule of law and the reform of the judicial system as urgent policy matters. The judicial system had been moribund for decades, abused by those in power to perpetuate their rule while dispensing justice to almost no one. In a speech in July 1992, Berisha said:

> Building a working state of justice is a basic condition for constructing a democratic society and integrating Albania into Europe. The destiny of Albania and the entire Albanian nation depends on the degree to which we are able to put a law-governed state into practice. An even more basic condition for this is respect for and defense of the law. This is the starting point of any democracy. A state that does not respect the law that expresses the will of the people will

only respect the will of one person or a group of persons, as in our case in the past, or else anarchy will prevail. Defense of and respect for democratic law is the starting point of every democracy, its fundamental necessity.[3]

The fall of communism had left the Albanian judicial system in a perilous state. Corruption had practically become institutionalized. Courts and law officials across the nation acted in cahoots with criminals. Judges, who in the old system had taken their orders directly from Communist officials, were left with little sense of jurisprudence and few notions of right and wrong. Poorly paid, understaffed, and overwhelmed by increasing case loads as crime continued to climb precipitously, they were highly susceptible to influence and bribes. Taking advantage of the political disarray, many Communist judges had developed the habit of giving justice to the highest bidder or to the most powerful. Honest judges, on the other hand, often feared dispensing justice to those to whom justice was due.

The judicial system had to be rebuilt practically from the ground up. The authorities stressed the need to lay foundations for the rule of law, to recruit honest people into the judicial system, and to improve facilities. The overwhelming majority of judges were purged. As Albania lacked qualified lawyers, judges, and prosecutors with untainted records, Communist-era holdovers were in many cases replaced by inexperienced youths. The Ministry of Justice organized a six-month crash course in law to train some four hundred judicial helpers. While the majority were later employed as paralegals or assistants, some were appointed as investigators, prosecutors, and even judges. The opposition accused the government of attempting to stack the judicial system with Democratic Party loyalists.

Arguing that increased corruption, lawlessness, gangsterism, and failure to punish those committing crimes could derail the country's democratic transition, the authorities gave the police emergency powers for a sweeping crackdown on crime. The government's swift action appears to have been welcomed by the majority of the population. However, critics charged that in many instances the police exceeded their authority, and accused the government of giving the green light for abuses that violated fundamental civil rights. Officials responded that without a semblance of law and order, Albania could not hope to implement radical reforms or attract foreign investments, and that human rights must be balanced by the need for public safety.

The authorities also announced that they would take determined action to root out corruption which had run rampant in the state bureaucracy under the coalition government. The majority of new entrepreneurs were linked to the Communist *nomenklatura*. Because of their former positions, networks of personal contacts, and experience with corruption, the former Communists and Sigurimi agents flourished under capitalism and controlled nearly all the new businesses. Berisha issued a presidential decree to deal with the corruption that he considered one of the most lingering legacies of Communist rule. It provided for inspecting wealth unlawfully acquired, particularly by former government officials, during the political turmoil that characterized Albania in 1991 and 1992. According to the president, the outcome of this battle against corruption would decide whether "we succeed in building a democratic state in accordance with our ideals or a republic racked by mafias, bandits, thieves, and criminals."[4]

Institutional Transformation

Having campaigned on the promise of establishing a genuine democracy based on the principles of separation of powers, an independent judiciary, and respect for human rights, the Democratic Party was expected to give a high priority to the adoption of a new constitution. Once in power, however, the Democrats were faced with an extraordinarily complex range of political, economic, and social issues. They failed to take advantage of the window of opportunity to secure speedy approval of the constitution. In retrospect, their procrastination in drafting a new constitution was a serious political mistake. In April 1992, the Democratic Party enjoyed unprecedented popular legitimacy. Moreover, there was a broad consensus among the anticommunist coalition for making a clean break with the past, while the Communists were debilitated by their humiliating defeat. Had Berisha focused on the issue, in all probability he could have pushed through parliament any version of a constitution, sparing Albania much subsequent political discord. Controlling 92 seats in the 140-member parliament, the Democrats would have had little difficulty in ensuring the support of their junior coalition partners, the Social Democrats and the Republicans, to obtain the two-thirds vote necessary to pass the constitution.

A special commission chaired by Prime Minister Aleksandër Meksi was given the task of drafting a new constitution. Meanwhile, parliament opted to amend and supplement the 1991 Law on the Main Constitutional Provisions. On the eve of Berisha's election as president in April 1992, the Democrats took advantage of the momentum of their electoral victory to push through parliament amendments enhancing the president's powers. In a reversal of the party's position a year earlier, when Ramiz Alia had been elected president, Democrats argued that the new president needed expanded powers to deal with the serious problems confronting the nation and to implement the political, social, and economic reforms promised by the Democratic Party in its electoral platform. The 1991 provisional constitution contained a number of critical deficiencies, the most important of which was the absence of separate chapters on human rights and the judiciary. These deficiencies were corrected with the addition, in April 1992, of a Chapter on the Organization of the Judiciary and the Constitutional Court, which provided for judicial independence,[5] and in March 1993, the Charter on Fundamental Human Rights and Freedoms, which contained guarantees of the freedoms of speech, religion, conscience, press, assembly, and association as well as assurances of the due process of law.[6] These changes set Albania apart from

East European countries that continued to operate based on their previous, Communist-era constitutions.

Although a lack of consensus among the country's main political forces prevented the adoption of a new constitution, the authorities were able to dismantle the underpinnings of the communist system. In one of its first actions, parliament approved the removal of communist symbols from the coat of arms and the flag.[7] The Communist Party, formed in summer 1991 by the most conservative wing of the APL, was banned. In early May 1992, the bodies of Hoxha and about a dozen other former top Communist officials, including Gramoz Pashko's father Josip Pashko, were removed from the national cemetery in Tiranë for reburial in a commoners' cemetery. Pashko reacted very strongly and the incident marked a point of no return in his conflict with Berisha and the mainstream faction of the Democratic Party. Reaction from the Communist camp was predictable: Berisha was accused of establishing a fascist dictatorship. Fatmir Zanaj, a member of the Socialist Party's presidency, was particularly aggressive in his criticism, accusing the president of employing "Communist methods." At a time when the Socialist Party leadership was officially attempting to distance itself from Hoxha and the APL, Zanaj publicly praised the former dictator and his closest collaborators. During a ceremony on the occasion of the reburial of Hysni Kapo, Hoxha's most trusted associate, Zanaj bluntly declared that the period that had ended with the March 1992 election would be known "as the epoch of the APL, the epoch of Enver Hoxha, Hysni Kapo, and other honorable people who fought and worked for the well-being of Albania."[8] In May 1992, parliament amended the Law on Labor Relations, allowing the authorities to transfer or dismiss employees of state-owned enterprises and institutions when deemed necessary to further the reform process. Purges were carried out in all the ministries. The security organs, including the once omnipotent secret police, the Sigurimi, renamed in 1991 the National Intelligence Service (SHIK), were reorganized and purged of procommunist sympathizers. Sigurimi men were widely believed to have been responsible for fomenting much of the criminal violence and the rampage that plagued the country before the Democratic Party's election victory. The head of SHIK, Irakli Koçollari, was replaced by Bashkim Gazidede, a Democratic Party activist from Dibër. Within months, reportedly 70 percent of the agency's employees were dismissed.[9] The Foreign Ministry bureaucracy, which reportedly had been staffed predominantly by the secret police, also underwent a sweeping purge. More than 50 percent of its personnel were dismissed and all ambassadors replaced.

The postcommunist government was faced with formidable challenges in reforming the military and restoring civilian control over the armed forces. At the time that the Democratic Party assumed power, an estimated 80 percent of military officers were members of the APL.[10] Thus, the Democrats saw the armed forces as the last stronghold of Communism and potentially a threat to the country's fledgling democracy. The appointment of Safet Zhulali, who had no military experience, as minister of defense caused significant discontent. Not only did senior military officers fear that the decommunization campaign would lead to the replacement of their top leadership, but they also resented having a civilian outsider appointed to such a sensitive post. Apparently with the encouragement of Socialist Party leaders, some senior officers openly refused to obey Zhulali, thereby also challenging President Berisha's authority as commander in chief. But both Berisha and Zhulali were determined to swiftly take control of the armed forces, insisting that radical reforms were necessary to create a professional depoliticized military, the purpose of which was to defend the country from outside aggression rather than to perpetuate the tenure of a corrupt, totalitarian party.[11] Despite considerable opposition within the senior ranks of the military, the armed forces were broadly restructured, the top leadership swiftly replaced, and young officers promoted into the top ranks. The authorities also banned the Union of Reserve Military Cadres, an organization that had been formed by disgruntled Communist military officers and that had organized public meetings denouncing the reforms under way in the armed forces. Military ranks, abolished during the cultural revolution, in the mid-1960s, were reinstituted, and Communist symbols were replaced by national symbols. The reforms created a smaller military, with a nonpolitical officer corps responsible to the democratically elected government and parliament. For the first time in Albania's history, a parliamentary commission was established to oversee the armed forces. Although Zhulali claimed that the military's combat readiness and discipline had improved considerably, the military continued to be plagued by poor morale, lack of discipline, and significant instances of draft avoidance. Zhulali devoted little attention to lobbying for increases in pay for servicemen and improvement of their living conditions. Perhaps even more troubling to the military leadership was the fact that many young Albanians displayed little sense of patriotism or willingness to defend their country. The Communist regime had manipulated the issue of national unity to such an extent that in the postcommunist period any interpretation of patriotism was considered by many, particularly the youth, as objectionable, anachronistic, or primitive.[12]

Although the new administration had taken bold measures, it missed the opportunity to take full advantage of its strong political position to rapidly push through its political, economic, and social agenda. No opposition party in Eastern Europe had come to power with such a convincing mandate as the Albanian Democratic Party. But decisionmakers, lacking experience and resources, were overwhelmed by myriad interrelated issues, all of which required immediate attention. As a result, tactical mistakes were made, that robbed the Democrats of their momentum. As mentioned above, they missed the opportunity to quickly draft a constitution and submit it for approval. Also, the government did not devote enough attention to neutralizing the antidemocratic and antireform influence of midlevel bureaucratic forces. Although they did conduct sweeping purges of the vital ministries of defense, public order, and foreign affairs, in most other ministries the replacement of top decisionmakers was not followed by sweeping changes at the midlevel and lower. As a result, remnants of the old Communist bureaucracy were able to undermine the government's program.

Democratic Party Split

As the first noncommunist party since 1945, the Democratic Party had developed into a broad, catch-all party—a coalition of many groups with diverse interests. But after the Democratic victory, splits intensified between the party's leadership and the leftist faction led by Gramoz Pashko. Disagreements emerged as to how far the government should go in its attempts to purge the administration of Communists and their supporters and to punish former top Communist leaders and Sigurimi criminals responsible for horrendous violations of human rights. Other complex policy issues involved the handling of secret police files, the growing economic power of the former *nomenklatura*, and compensation for those sections of society that had suffered most under the old regime. Pashko's faction opposed carrying out sweeping changes in the central bureaucracy or bringing the former *nomenklatura* to justice. But while there were disagreements over policy issues, personal animosities played a much more important role in widening the split, the root of which was the bitter enmity between Berisha and Pashko over the Democratic Party's withdrawal from the coalition government in 1991. The immediate source of current conflict was the omission of leading members of the leftist faction, including Pashko, Azem Hajdari, and Arben Imami, from the government. It is probable that had they been included in the cabinet, conflict would have been avoided or at least postponed.[13]

Ultimately, Pashko, Hajdari, Imami, and their supporters in the party leadership were forced to choose between seeking an official separation or remaining in a party in which they found themselves gradually marginalized. The conflict burst into the open in June 1992, when Hajdari suddenly left the country, announcing that he was going to the United States. This followed Hajdari's sharp criticism of the management of state television, which had refused to broadcast an interview in which he denounced the reforms under way in the armed forces. His statement claiming censorship at the state television received widespread coverage in the Socialist press.[14] Hajdari might have hoped that his actions would help him regain his glory as the leader of the December 1990 student demonstrations, but his sudden departure represented an act of desperation, which instead of gaining him support, in fact further diluted his popularity. Pashko reacted by making a startling statement in parliament that compared Hajdari's departure with Ismail Kadare's defection in 1990.[15] Pashko could not have chosen a more inopportune time for his remarks, as the lawmakers were in the midst of a debate on the deteriorating situation in Kosova. His statement caused an immediate and sharp reaction from his fellow Democratic deputies. On 25 June, he was expelled from the parliamentary group, but not from the party. Pashko suffered another insult when Hajdari issued a statement in the United States describing the comparison with Kadare's defection as "absurd." After a brief stay in New York, Hajdari returned to Albania, his hopes of enlisting the support of the Albanian American community having been dashed.

The rift within the Democratic Party intensified after the party's poor showing in the July 1992 local elections. In a serious political blunder, the Democrats moved slowly in holding local elections, thus losing a substantial degree of the support they had won in the March parliamentary elections. The timing of the local elections could hardly have been more inopportune. The government had begun implementing austerity measures, and only days before the elections, it had raised consumer prices in accordance with the IMF stabilization program. Concentrating on the serious hardship caused by the implementation of economic reforms, the Socialists waged an impressive campaign. Only four months after decisively winning the national elections, the Democratic Party lost more than 20 percent of its support. With a turnover of 70.5 percent, the Democratic Party won 43 percent of the general vote. The Socialist Party made an impressive comeback, winning 41 percent. Socialist candidates swept to victory in 23 of 42 mayoral races.[16]

Portending the first major split in the ranks of the Democratic Party, the leftists launched a blistering attack on Berisha. They also criticized the new government, focusing their attacks on Meksi's policies and the new cabinet's lack of qualifications. They cast doubt on whether ministers had enough practical experience to implement fundamental political and economic reforms. In mid-August 1992, an extraordinary conference of the Democratic Party's National Council expelled from the party Gramoz Pashko, Arben Imami, Preç Zogaj, and Arben Demeti, all members of the party's presidency. National Council members Ridvan Peshkëpia, Perikli Teta, and Edmond Trako also were expelled. Azem Hajdari escaped expulsion after he made a turnaround, denouncing the leftists and pledging loyalty to the Democratic Party.[17] Within months of the split, the leftist faction formed its own party—the Democratic Alliance. Neritan Ceka, the former deputy chairman of the Democratic Party, who had resigned in December 1991 because of disagreements with Berisha over withdrawal from the coalition government, was elected president of the new party.

The importance of the split arguably was exaggerated by Communist propaganda. The split did not have an immediate and significant impact on the Democratic Party, since Pashko and his supporters no longer enjoyed a strong constituency. With the exception of deputy Teodor Keko, no other prominent Democrat defected to their camp. Nevertheless, the loss of six deputies made the Democratic Party dependent on its two junior partners—the Social Democratic and Republican Parties—to secure the two thirds votes necessary to ratify a new constitution. But the Social Democrats and the Republicans were beginning to show signs of defiance. The Social Democratic Party, which was unenthusiastic about Berisha's shock therapy, maneuvered to capitalize on the Democratic Party's troubles, demanding greater representation in the government. The less influential Republican Party, with only one deputy in parliament, was gradually moving to the right, accusing the ruling party of not doing enough for those who had been most persecuted under communism.

Meanwhile, the Democratic Party's ascendant conservative wing, grouping former political prisoners and followers of the wartime National Front and Legality, called for a swift settling of accounts with the Communists, maintaining that only total decommunization would head off a future Communist threat. It saw Pashko and his supporters as too willing to compromise with the Communists, and insufficiently loyal to the Democratic Party's decommunization goals. The right wing insisted that there could never be national reconciliation without justice, spiritual cleansing, and public repentance by the former oppressors and executioners. It also urged the government to take immediate measures to prevent the Communists from converting their former political privileges into economic ones, and becoming the main beneficiaries of postcommunist transformation. Hysen Çobani, a former deputy chairman of the Republican Party, urged the Democratic government to act swiftly, warning that to prolong the decommunization process would be to play into the hands of the Communists. Çobani urged that "all those responsible for the economic and political genocide" carried out against the Albanian people during the long Communist rule should be brought to justice. He also said that secret police files should be opened immediately for all politicians.[18]

Indeed, former political prisoners and elements of the National Front and Legality had gained increased prominence with the Democratic Party. But the extent and nature of their influence on public policy were exaggerated by leftists. Berisha maintained a centrist position and displayed resilience and persistence in effectively juggling and balancing contending forces within the party. To the chagrin of his supporters to the right of the political spectrum, the president agreed only to "symbolic" trials against former Communist henchmen, insisting that democratic Albania must be capable of leniency and not permit hatred and revenge. Initially, he refused to order Ramiz Alia's arrest and to take strong action against other former high-level Communist officials, thereby fueling rumors that he had made a deal with his predecessor. There also were strong reactions, especially from former political prisoners, to Berisha's repeated statement that while all Albanians had suffered under communism they also bore "joint responsibility" for the survival of the dictatorship.[19] The former political prisoners insisted that reconciliation was best promoted not by letting bygones be bygones but by relentlessly examining past misdeeds and prosecuting those culpable for Communist transgressions. But despite increased pressure, the president apparently never contemplated launching a frontal assault against the former Communists and their power base. His policy was driven by his desire for national reconciliation, although the Communists' failure to express public remorse for their past actions made such reconciliation most unlikely.

Political Tribulations

Despite serious constraints, the Democratic Party government was able to lead, give direction, and determine the nature and pace of reforms. Within one year of assuming power, the government was credited with having restored stability and set the country on a promising political and economic course. In April 1993, Meksi reshuffled the cabinet, placing Bashkim Kopliku in charge of economic reforms. Agron Musaraj replaced Kopliku as minister of public order. Petrit Kalakula, chairman of the Democratic Party's powerful Tiranë branch and one of the most outspoken members of the party's right wing, became minister of agriculture, replacing Rexhep Uka, who was named minister for local government. The ministers of education and tourism, Ylli Vejsiu and Osman Shehu, lost their positions. Xhezair Teliti was named minister of education, and Edmond Spaho minister of tourism. Having survived an extremely difficult first year, it seemed that Albanians, while still grappling with the boundaries of their new found freedom, were settling down to a painful but relatively smooth transformation into a pluralistic democracy and a market economy.

Albania's political tradition has not been conducive to a democratic order or the development of a loyal opposition. Moreover, following sanctioning of political pluralism, changes in Albania had moved at a breathtaking pace. Not only were there no established fundamental rules of the political game, but Democrats and Socialists viewed each other as enemies rather than political opponents. In the first, short-lived multiparty parliament, the Democratic Party had not played the role of a loyal opposition, instead using its increased popularity to bring the Communists to their knees. Now, the Socialists were determined to pay back the Democrats in kind. The Socialist Party was unwilling to offer the new government even the minimal level of support normally expected after the inauguration of a new administration. Socialist leader Fatos Nano, who blamed the Democrats for the nationwide strike that had caused the downfall of his government in June 1991, after only two months in office, embarked on a personal vendetta against the new government.

The Socialist Challenge

Initially, the Socialist Party argued that the Democratic Party could not govern the country, and focused its propaganda efforts at convincing the Democrats to include the Socialists in the ruling coalition along with the Social Democratic and Republican Parties. But the Democrats, controlling almost two-thirds of parliament, were not disposed to compromise with the Communist successor party, let alone accept the idea of a coalition. After being rebuffed, the Socialists adopted a highly combative and disruptive posture. They used every opportunity to obstruct the transition process and to undermine Meksi, sounding alarms about his government's performance. The Socialist Party also mounted a campaign against the president and the Democratic Party, accusing them of revanchism. In this context, the Socialists claimed that rightist elements had usurped power within the Democratic Party and "a new dictatorship was knocking at Albania's door." All "democratic" forces were urged to create a "united front" against the "new dictatorship."[20] Encouraged by extremist Socialist leaders, many unemployed former secret police employees, who formed a militant core of the frustrated, discontented, and angry, openly attempted to whip up public unrest, thereby posing a tough challenge to the government.

In July 1993, the government arrested the Socialist Party Chairman Fatos Nano. Nano was accused of having misappropriated funds to the tune of $8 million during his short stint as prime minister in 1991. He was alleged to have approved the purchase of food from an Italian company at highly inflated prices and then to have falsified documents. Nano rejected the charges, accusing Berisha of attempting to liquidate his political opponents. He also took a strong anti-American posture, accusing U.S. diplomats in Tiranë of interference in Albania's internal affairs. The Socialist-controlled press had already begun a campaign against U.S. diplomats, particularly the very popular Ambassador William Ryerson, who had developed close relations with Berisha and other Democratic leaders.[21] Nano specifically accused Ryerson of plotting with the Democrats to move against him. In a manner reminiscent of the Communist era, he claimed Berisha had turned Albania into an American "banana republic."[22] Going beyond their usual practice of using harsh invective to attack Berisha and the Democratic Party, Socialist leaders called for the use of "all democratic means" to get the present government out of office.[23] In their zealous attempts to provoke massive protests, the Socialists organized rallies throughout the country; but their strategy backfired and they were unable to mobilize a large attendance at their rallies.[24]

The timing of Nano's arrest soon after his party had launched a campaign to force the ruling party to hold early elections led some observers to conclude that the arrest was politically motivated. Berisha rejected these charges, asserting that he viewed corruption as an evil that had to be uprooted if Albania's fledgling democracy were to have credibility. Nevertheless, Nano's arrest and trial further stiffened the Socialist Party's militant stand and turned the Socialist leader into a political martyr.

Following Nano's arrest, the authorities indicated that they would intensify the anticorruption drive. Former Prime Minister Vilson Ahmeti was tried and sentenced to two years in prison on charges of misusing his office. However, an appeals court overturned the ruling and ordered a new investigation, which resulted in the arrest of the director of the National Bank, Ilir Hoti, a holdover from the coalition government.[25] Ahmeti subsequently was acquitted, but Hoti received a ten-year sentence. Three other bank officials were sentenced to between four and seven years of imprisonment.[26] In November 1993, Minister of the Economy and Finance Genc Ruli was forced to resign after persistent opposition allegations that he was implicated in the illegal smuggling of cigarettes as well as in a financial scandal involving Frenchman Nicolas Arsidi. Arsidi had received $1.6 million from the Tiranë government to renegotiate Albania's foreign debt. Even while the press was reporting on his imminent arrest, Ruli continued to serve in parliament, allegations that he had amassed substantial wealth notwithstanding. The ruling party's failure to extend its highly publicized anti-corruption drive to include its own members seriously undermined the government's position.[27]

The Challenge From the Right

In the wake of the purge of Pashko's leftist faction, the right's clout grew significantly within the Democratic Party and society at large, posing an increasing challenge to the government, particularly on issues of land and property ownership and the reintegration into society of a large number of people who had been persecuted under communism. Right wing forces had taken advantage of Nano's arrest to urge the Democrats to fulfill their election promises to eradicate the Communist legacy. Indeed, the government had made significant efforts to deal with the plight of this substantial portion of its 1992 electorate. Former political prisoners and their families were given preferential treatment in employment, education, housing, and social services. But as the Democratic Party continued to stake out the middle ground on most issues, many of its supporters as well as the Republican Party, its junior partner in the coalition, shifted farther to the right. Meanwhile, the organization representing former landowners, the National Association Property With Justice, took an increasingly antigovernment position.

Some Democratic Party leaders expressed alarm at the growing strength of the right wing. The president's own pronouncements suggested that he, too, was concerned about the challenge from right extremists. The right wing received a severe blow in August 1993, when one of its most outspoken spokesmen, Minister of Agriculture Petrit Kalakula, was suspended as chairman of the Democratic Party's powerful Tiranë branch for having ostensibly made a profascist statement in parliament.[28] Berisha used the pretext of Kalakula's statement to send a clear signal to the right wing, and at the same time, to attempt to appease the Socialists, who were outraged by Nano's imprisonment. At a meeting of the Democratic Party's national council in mid-September 1993, Berisha made an unusually conciliatory speech aimed at placating the Socialists. Acknowledging that on certain issues, such as Albania's war of national liberation and war collaborators, the Democratic Party had deviated from its own program, Berisha said that corrective measures would be taken. He criticized public ceremonies that had been organized for the reburial of prominent anticommunist personalities from the World War II era, adding that the Democratic Party would never compromise or cooperate with "collaborators." He urged his party's parliamentary group not to misuse its majority status but to open a dialogue with the opposition and seek consensus on the drafting and approval of new legislation.[29] Echoing Berisha's statements, *Rilindja Demokratike* called for a purge of extremists from both parties, saying they were responsible for the tense political atmosphere.[30] But Berisha could not mollify the Socialists with Nano in prison.

Kalakula accused Berisha of being too soft on Communists and described the government in which he had served as neocommunist.[31] At a conference of the Democratic Party's Tiranë branch in November 1993, Kalakula, who had already resigned as minister of agriculture, was replaced as chairman of the party's Tiranë branch by Dylber Vrioni, a descendant of a landowning family. A month later, Kalakula, together with deputy Abdi Baleta, withdrew from the Democratic Party's parliamentary group. Baleta, who was not a member of the Democratic Party but was elected on its ticket, had already distanced himself from the group.[32] In the beginning of 1994, Kalakula and Baleta set up their own party, the Democratic Party of the Right, only to split among themselves less than a year later. Significantly, there were no other defections and the Democratic Party did not experience a major split. But Berisha's parting of ways with Kalakula and Baleta provoked a defection from the activist right—the very forces that until then had been among Berisha's most ardent supporters—while it encouraged, rather than appeased, the Socialists.

Although robbed of its two-thirds majority in parliament, the Democratic Party still commanded a comfortable majority, 84 out of 140 seats, and the government did not waver in its determination to continue with radical reforms. Berisha's vision continued to drive the agenda in parliament, which moved rapidly to create the legal framework for a market economy. After three years of a dramatic decline in production, in 1993 the economy grew by 11 percent. The Albanian currency remained stable and inflation was under control. And in a further sign of the growing stabilization, the Italian Pelicano Operation, which had been distributing international humanitarian assistance since fall 1991, completed its mission in November 1993.

Signs of Democratic Backtracking

While 1993 had been a relatively good year for the government, during 1994 the administration was plagued with a string of crises on the domestic and foreign fronts. High-profile embarrassments alienated the Democratic Party from a part of its electorate and some foreign supporters, and reinvigorated the Socialist opposition. Some of these situations could not have been headed off. However, in most cases, the Democratic Party undermined its own position through seriously flawed thinking, miscalculation, and inattention. Democratic Party and government leaders diminished some of their significant post-1992 gains by yielding to the pressures and temptations of the day and by failing to ensure a more accessible, participatory, and tolerant political environment.

By 1994, there were signs that the Democrats were backtracking from their commitment to democracy. Berisha showed a penchant for highly personalistic leadership, increasingly concentrating power in his own hands and adopting an uncompromising approach toward the opposition and dissidents within his own party. There were growing concerns about the government's adherence to due process, respect for democratic rights, increased harassment of the press, executive influence over the judiciary, and government accountability and transparency. Widespread wastage and corruption in the public sector cost millions of dollars and led to growing alienation. Some Albanians grew conspicuously wealthy while an ever larger majority felt left out of the uneven benefits conferred by their country's rapaciously free market economy. Corruption sapped the strength of democratic institutions struggling to demonstrate their legitimacy.

Government officials displayed growing impatience with public policy and engaged in practices and tactics that alienated public support. In the wake of the adoption of a controversial press law in 1993, several opposition journalists were arrested and tried on charges of having disclosed state secrets. Meanwhile, the government continued to maintain tight control over radio and television, prohibiting the establishment of independent broadcast media. The Democrats' failure to ensure open, genuinely independent broadcasting deprived Albania of alternative sources of information that would have enhanced the debate on collective norms and choices, and thus, the consolidation of the country's nascent democracy.

The government also engaged in actions and practices that were interpreted as violating human rights and intimidating critics. Security forces, particularly the secret police SHIK, intimidated government critics and opponents and engaged in actions which infringed citizens' civil and political rights. On several occasions, the police used excessive force and exceeded their mandate. During spring and summer 1994, the authorities were faced with increased pressures from former landowners and former political prisoners, some of whom adopted an increasingly aggressive stance against the government.[33] This was so, although it appears that faced with severely limited resources, the government was making genuine efforts to integrate former prisoners and their families into the new society.[34]

In May 1994, the Council of Ministers announced a decision to compensate former prisoners to the tune of 12,000 leks (about $1,200) in bonds for each year spent in prison or internal exile.[35] The Association of Former Political Prisoners and Formerly Persecuted Persons criticized the measure as falling far short of what the former prisoners were entitled to. The organization issued a list of ten demands, including the approval of a law guaranteeing the bonds' value in real leks.[36] When the government refused to meet the demands, former political prisoners went on a hungerstrike. A Tiranë court declared the hunger strike illegal and gave the strikers until 11 August to end their protest. Meanwhile, the Ministry of Public Order issued a statement alleging that out of 287 hunger strikers, 65 were former Sigurimi agents, and another 35 had been convicted for ordinary crimes and not for political reasons.[37] The strikers vociferously rebutted the government's allegations. After the strikers refused to obey a court order and disperse, on 12 August the police forcefully broke up the strike, drawing criticism from both the right and the left of the political spectrum. While arguably the strikers' demands could not be met, the government's use of force against people who had suffered years of imprisonment under the old regime raised serious concerns and caused some people to question the government's dedication to democratic ideals and the protection of human rights.

In addition, after months of gradual but steady improvement in Tiranë-Athens ties, on 10 April 1994, the authorities announced that two Albanian soldiers had been killed by Greek gunmen in the border town of Peshkëpia, causing an immediate uproar in Albania. A Greek nationalist organization, the Northern Epirus Liberation Front (MAVI), claimed responsibility. Against the backdrop of an escalating exchange of invective between Tiranë and Athens, Albania announced the arrests of five members of the Greek Albanian political organization Omonia on charges of espionage, fomenting separatism, and illegal weapons possession. A Tiranë court sentenced the five to between six and eight years. On appeal, the sentences were reduced. Subsequently, the Court of Cassation upheld the conviction but released the five on probation. The trial, which had been criticized for substantial procedural shortcomings, eroded trust between Tiranë and Athens and inflicted serious political damage on Berisha at home and abroad, also affecting Albania's relations with the United States and the European Union. Greece used the incident as a pretext to deport some 70,000 illegal Albanian refugees. The United States demonstrated its displeasure with Albania's action by putting on hold plans for an Albanian American Enterprise Fund. Albania's international image was tarnished by the Omonia trial. The politically savvy Berisha should have exercised more forethought about the potential consequences of the trial and should have anticipated the Greek reaction.

Designing a New Constitutional Order

Building new political institutions, guaranteeing human rights and associational autonomy, and establishing rules and procedures to promote the development and eventual consolidation of Albania's fragile democracy proved daunting tasks. The drafting of a postcommunist constitution had preoccupied Albanian leaders and legislators since the very first days of political pluralism; but disagreements among the country's main political forces prevented the adoption of a new constitution. A draft submitted by the Democratic Party was rejected in a referendum in November 1994. Nevertheless, the 1991 Law on the Main Constitutional Provisions was completely revamped and a new system was created, with checks and balances, safeguards for fundamental rights and freedoms, and judicial review. Albania's postcommunist institutional arrangements compared favorably with the constitutions adopted by other former communist countries in the initial phase of transition to democracy. But as a result of the failure to adopt a new constitution, the emerging order lacked a solid constitutional underpinning. The 1991 constitutional law and amendments approved in 1992 and 1993 did not have the legitimacy that a new, single charter—even without significant modifications from those documents—would have had if it were ceremoniously adopted by parliament or a constituent assembly or by popular referendum. Although the promulgation of a new constitution had become indispensable for the country's speedy democratization, Albania's two major political forces—the Democrats and the Socialists—refused to put aside their narrow political considerations and engage in serious bargaining and compromise. The Democratic Party failed to adopt an inclusive consensus-building approach in drafting and adopting a new constitution, which would have fostered respect for the basic concepts underpinning democracy and promoted national reconciliation and social harmony.

Lack of consensus prevented Albanians from resolving the broader question of what sort of a political system the country should have: presidential, parliamentary, or a blending of the two. Opinion was divided on the advantages and disadvantages of each system. While most political forces seemed to have settled on a parliamentary system, some Albanian analysts expressed fear that a weak presidency combined with a strong legislature based on the principle of proportional representation could unduly complicate decisionmaking in a political culture unaccustomed to accommodation and bargaining. However, few advocated a powerful presidency. Even Berisha insisted on a parliamentary system. Nevertheless, although the basic constitutional law provided for a parliamentary republic, in practice Albania developed a hybrid presidential-parliamentary system in which the president exercised broad decisionmaking powers, the prime minister displayed a deferential attitude toward the president, and executive oversight by the parliament was lacking.

The Executive

The basic constitutional law of Albania provides for "the separation of legislative, executive, and judicial powers" and safeguards on presidential powers. Following the constitutional arrangements in the newly emerging democracies in the region, the basic law states that "political pluralism is one of the basic conditions of democracy in the Albanian state." It provides assurances for the protection of the new, pluralist character of the state by stipulating a clear separation of political parties from state power and prohibiting party activities in the defense, internal affairs, and foreign affairs ministries; in diplomatic representations abroad; and among legal professionals and officers of the court.

While the basic law declares Albania "a parliamentary republic," the president is vested with broad powers. The president appoints the prime minister, and with the latter's proposal, other members of the cabinet. After consultation with the prime minister and the speaker of parliament, the president can dissolve the legislature when the latter's composition "does not allow the legislature to exercise its own functions and makes the governing of the country impossible." Significantly, the president cannot exercise this right during the last six months of his mandate. The president is designated Commander in Chief of the Armed Forces and Chairman of the Defense Council. The constitutional law also grants the president specific legislative powers. Subject to countersignature by the prime minister or another member of the cabinet, the president is empowered to issue decisions and decrees of individual character. With the same provision of a countersignature, the president may also sign, ratify, and denounce international treaties that have not been examined by parliament, and may appoint and discharge diplomatic representatives. Within fifteen days of the enactment of a law, the president can veto it—but only once—by resubmitting the legislation to parliament.

The delineation of presidential and legislative powers is accompanied by checks and balances to prevent the president from taking actions that infringe on citizens' civil and political rights. Presidential decrees require the countersignature of the prime minister or of a cabinet member and must be approved by the legislature. Parliament can override a presidential veto with a simple majority.

The president is empowered "in special instances" to call, attend, and chair meetings of the Council of Ministers and to set the agenda. The president also may propose to the legislature the holding of referendums; with the proposal of the prime minister, may appoint or discharge by decree ministers and "other individual members of government," submitting within ten days the decree for parliamentary approval; and may appoint the head and deputy head of the National Intelligence Service. The president can request from directors of executive government institutions information in writing related to their work.[38]

The prime minister is granted a leading role in the government. Acting together with the president, the prime minister can dismiss any minister without bringing down the government as a whole. The Council of Ministers inter alia is empowered to determine and direct the nation's domestic and foreign policy; to take actions to ensure, protect, and strengthen the rule of law and citizens' rights; to direct and control the activities of the ministries and other central institutions of the state administration; to draft the state budget and programs for the economic and social development of the country; and to sign international agreements and approve or renounce those that do not require ratification by parliament. Although the document grants the Council of Ministers a large degree of independence, it also gives parliament powers to supervise the functioning of the government. The composition of the Council of Ministers and its program must be approved by the legislature with a majority of votes and within five days of their submission. Parliament is required to consider a motion of no-confidence in the Council of Ministers or individual ministers within three days after its submission.

Motions of no-confidence can be requested "at any time," but must be supported by at least one-tenths of the deputies. In the event of a vote of no-confidence, the prime minister submits his or her resignation, and the president appoints a new prime minister. The government is required to provide oral explanations on the floor and written answers to deputies' requests for information. Parliamentary commissions are granted considerable powers of inquiry, including the right to call any government official to appear before them.

The Legislature

The 1991 Law on the Main Constitutional Provisions vests substantial powers in the parliament. The document provides that parliament elect the president for a five-year term by secret ballot and by a two-thirds majority of votes. If no candidate obtains a two-thirds majority in the first ballot, then in the second, final round, an absolute majority is sufficient for the president's election. Parliament is granted the right to initiate impeachment proceedings if the president betrays the country or violates the constitution. The president also can be removed from office if "his health condition prevents him from performing his duties." Parliament is also vested with the right to approve nominations for prime minister and members of the cabinet and to appoint members of the Court of Cassation as well as the Attorney General and his or her deputies. Parliament is granted other important powers, such as determining the basic orientation of domestic and foreign policy; approving the economic and social programs for the country's development, including the state budget; declaring partial and general mobilization, a state of emergency, or a state of war in the event of armed aggression; ratifying and denouncing treaties and agreements; granting amnesty; deciding on referenda; controlling the activity of the Council of Ministers, the Attorney General's office, state radio and television, and the Albanian Telegraphic Agency; and deciding on the creation or dissolution of ministries and other high organs. Legislative initiative can be exercised by the president, the Council of Ministers, individual deputies, and by petition with at least 20,000 registered voters' signatures.

The Judiciary

The 1991 provisional constitution did not regulate in detail the role of the judiciary, nor did it contain provisions for judicial review or for judicial invalidation of legislative enactments. An important step in Albania's efforts to establish the rule of law was the radical reorganization and strengthening of the judicial system. On 29 April 1992, parliament approved an amendment to the 1991 constitutional law, adding a chapter on "The Organization of the Judiciary and the Constitutional Court," creating a bi-partite system composed of the regular court system headed by a Court of Cassation (often also called a Supreme Court), and a separate Constitutional Court, with clear lines of jurisdiction between the two.[39]

The president is vested with the power to propose to the legislature candidates for chairman and deputy chairman of the Court of Cassation, while other members of the court are elected by parliament. Despite the proclaimed principles of full separation of powers and judicial independence, the regular court system is organizationally and logistically dependent on the Ministry of Justice. The judiciary also is denied the power and mechanism of self-governance. The Law on the Organization of the Judiciary and the Constitutional Court empowers the legislature to remove members of the Court of Cassation from the bench. Such control over the court by the parliament, whose laws could be at issue before the Court of Cassation, seem to violate the principle of the separation of powers. Equally troubling is the provision granting the High Council of Justice, headed by the president and consisting of the chairman of the Court of Cassation, the minister of justice, the general prosecutor, and nine lawyers, an administrative role. The council enjoys the sole authority to appoint, transfer, and take disciplinary action against judges and prosecutors.

The constitutional law does not grant the Court of Cassation the right to review the constitutionality of executive actions and statutes. Although recognized as "the highest judicial authority" of the land, the Court of Cassation nevertheless is required to refer all cases involving constitutional matters to the Constitutional Court. Thus, the regular court system is in fact deprived of the power to apply the constitution in the administration of justice, the most important function of the judiciary.

The nine-member Constitutional Court stands apart from the rest of the governmental apparatus and is responsible "only to the Constitution." The tribunal is vested with broad decisionmaking powers, including interpreting the constitution and constitutional laws; deciding on the compatibility of laws and bylaws with the constitution; reviewing the constitutionality of international treaties before their ratification; resolving disputes between different branches of government and between local government and central authorities; outlawing political parties and other political and social associations for unconstitutional activities; resolving constitutional issues dealing with the election of the president, the deputies, and the holding of a popular referendum; and examining criminal charges brought against the president. The court's jurisdiction is not limited to the resolution of specific disputes brought by parties with the appropriate standing. It can intervene on its own in constitutional disputes. In addition, the president, a parliamentary group, one-fifth of the deputies, the Council of Ministers, courts, local government organs, and private individuals can bring their complaints before the Constitutional Court. Cases also could come before the tribunal through referral from the regular courts.

The Albanian constitutional landscape changed significantly after 1992, when the Constitutional Court asserted its right to exercise judicial review. The Constitutional Court was called upon to decide important cases, and its role grew steadily. In May 1992, the Socialist Party challenged the nomination of two deputies to the High Council of Justice. The tribunal upheld the challenge, ruling that it was a violation of the principle of the separation of powers for the two deputies to keep their seats in the legislature and simultaneously serve in the High Council of Justice. The Constitutional Court invalidated a lustration law approved in February 1993 that permitted a commission established by the High Council of Justice to summarily revoke the licenses of lawyers who under the old regime had collaborated with the Sigurimi, had been employed as prison officials, or had served on Communist Party committees. In a landmark decision, in April 1994, the tribunal struck down two sections of the law on restitution that provided for an uneasy joint ownership of property by precommunist owners and new owners who had bought the property from the state in 1991 or later. The court also upheld the legality of the parliament's ban on the Albanian Communist Party (which had been imposed in 1991 by old guard Communists unhappy with the revamping of the APL), and denied the Socialist parliamentary group's challenge of Fatos Nano's imprisonment.

The Constitutional Court came under fire for its handling of the opposition's challenge to the 6 November 1994 constitutional referendum. In October 1994, the parliament approved by a majority vote the Law on Referendums submitted by Berisha. The Socialist and Social Democratic Parties immediately appealed to the Constitutional Court, challenging the constitutionality of the law. Only days before the scheduled referendum, three members of the court resigned, accusing Chief Justice Rustem Gjata of deliberately delaying hearings in the case. In January 1995, two months after the referendum had been held, the court issued a ruling upholding the law. But the delay had seriously undermined the court's authority. In a country that lacks a constitutional court tradition and has long been used to executive and legislative encroachments on the constitution, the Constitutional Court needs to be further strengthened and staffed with judges who are immune from political influence if it is to enforce constitutional principles.

Relations Between Branches of Government

Between 1992 and 1996, there was a remarkable degree of agreement between the presidency, the government, and the legislature on policy outputs and responses to sustain the reform impulse. Political struggles between the executive and the legislature in Albania were less pronounced and acrimonious than those in most other East European countries. But this was due more to the Democratic Party's ability to preserve its comfortable majority in parliament than to accommodation and compromise between the ruling party and the opposition. The fragmentation of the Democratic parliamentary group was surprisingly not as deep as many had predicted. The Democratic Party experienced only two splits, resulting in the defection of eight out of the original ninety-two deputies. The executive branch was in general successful in imposing discipline on parliamentary proceedings. Moreover, the president continued to keep a tight rein on his Democratic Party. Although there were cases when ruling party lawmakers assiduously ignored the government's entreaties, there was a remarkable consistency in the voting behavior of Democratic Party deputies, as they continued to toe the line on issues considered important by the president and the prime minister. This factor accounted for the fact that Albania experienced no paralyzing executive-legislative deadlock.

Albania's post-1992 political system was marked by a personalistic style of leadership. Berisha's strong leadership qualities and the pivotal role that he played in the dislodging of Communists from power helped make him the unquestionable linchpin of Albanian politics. He proved an activist president, shaping the nation's agenda during a period of momentous political, economic, and social changes. Despite serious constraints, he displayed a resiliency and tenacity that were hard to match. He provided effective leadership at a time when commitment to genuine reform seemed remarkably low, even among cabinet members. Whereas during this period Berisha continued to be viewed as an indispensable guarantor of Albania's transition to democracy, his control over the executive branch and confusion regarding institutional prerogatives also had a negative impact. The division of labor and responsibilities between different branches of government was not properly delineated. The president largely defined both domestic and foreign policies; overall, the most important policy initiatives came from his office. The prime minister and the cabinet were eclipsed by the president and his staff. Moreover, Berisha seemed to rely too much on a small circle of loyal advisers.[40] There were also allegations that the president often was unwilling to consider advice that conflicted with his views, settling into a self-protective style that suppressed internal debate and dissent. Critics claimed that there was no one among his closest advisers who could say "no" to him, and that no member of the cabinet would risk doing anything significant without his direct authorization. While such allegations were politically motivated, emanating as they did from rival politicians, former associates, and journalists, it is clear that Berisha's domination of the executive branch at times did distort the decision-making process, undermining good and effective administration and causing unnecessary delays in making decisions on major issues. However, at no time did his actual power vis-à-vis parliament exceed his constitutional powers.

Meksi turned out to be a weak prime minister. He maintained a low profile, which paved the way for others to become an important force in the cabinet, helping to shape policy as well as enunciate it. At times, his subordinates' opinions seemed to have a greater impact on policy formulation than those of the prime minister. Meksi's cabinet suffered from a seeming lack of direction and coherence. The prime minister failed to devise an effective mechanism to reconcile competing agendas and to develop, coordinate, and implement policy decisions smoothly.

Parliament came to play a significant role. During 1992-1996, substantial legislation was enacted into law. However, the frantic pace of approval often sacrificed the careful deliberation that many, complex issues demanded. The propensity to focus almost entirely on lawmaking also prevented the legislature from fully performing other vital functions, such as closer oversight of government agencies, public deliberations, and developing close contacts with electoral constituencies. Parliamentary leaders displayed a lack of appreciation for the wide range of functions that the legislature should perform in addition to lawmaking. While neither opposition nor Democratic Party deputies shied away from demanding information and answers to specific questions from state officials, including the prime minister and members of the cabinet, parliament was not broadly empowered and failed to establish an adequate committee structure to fully carry out its important oversight functions and ensure the accountability of the executive branch agencies.

The composition of parliament was overwhelmingly male and mostly middle-aged. Out of 140 members, only four were women; by 1994 their number had risen to eight as a result of replacements of deputies who were appointed to government positions or left parliament for other reasons. But perhaps the most salient feature of these new political elites was the high proportion of intellectuals and technical experts and the lack of political professionals or lawyers. Few had any parliamentary experience. Of the deputies elected in 1992, only fifty-two had served in the previous parliament. Although it was sometimes obstructionist, resembling more a contentious debating club than a lawmaking body, the legislature became the most important arena for deliberations about the country's politics. With the changing political situation, parliament rapidly shifted from the honeymoon period in 1992, when Democrats and their junior coalition partners voted as a bloc. While consensus on individual bills was not uncommon, lawmakers rarely demonstrated an ability to overcome significant party differences or to negotiate compromises on major issues. The ruling party, with its parliamentary majority, was generally lacking in its consensus-seeking efforts. Meanwhile, the opposition, particularly the Socialist Party, refused to share responsibility for parliament's actions.

Despite its undeniable accomplishments, the Albanian parliament failed to achieve a high degree of institutional credibility. With most lawmakers lacking in the skills of negotiation and compromise, parliament often failed to assert its interests on major political reform issues. A representative democracy cannot function properly in the absence of an interactive relationship between the electorate and its representatives. There was too little communication and feedback between Albanian elected officials and voters, and the influence of the broader public on the legislature was negligible. Parliament rarely held public hearings with experts outside the government. Moreover, lawmakers in general maintained very loose ties with their constituencies. Meetings between deputies and their electorates were intermittent and shallow. Few lawmakers took up work on behalf of their constituents.

The electoral system was partially responsible for the loose contacts between deputies and electorates. Few candidates, if any, had their own following within the election district. Indeed, political parties were permitted to field candidates even in districts where the candidates were not permanent residents. Having won largely because of their party, lawmakers were inclined to defer to party leaders. The 1992 electoral law also stipulated that deputies nominated to certain posts were to be replaced from their party's proportional list. Such practices undermined trust in the system. These two examples illustrate the point: When Berisha resigned his seat in parliament after his election as president, he was replaced by Perikli Teta, who was next in line on the Democratic Party's proportional list. In August 1992, Teta was expelled from the party together with five other deputies, after which he joined the newly created Democratic Alliance. Thus, 97.5 percent of the Kavajë electorate that had voted for Berisha were represented in parliament by a deputy for whom they had not voted and who was no longer even a member of the Democratic Party. In another case, the representative of the northeastern district of Tropojë, Besnik Mustafaj, was named ambassador to France immediately after the elections. His seat was taken by student leader Arben Lika, who had never lived in Tropojë and was unknown to Mustafaj's electorate. Before his arrest in 1994 and subsequent conviction on charges of corruption, Lika reportedly visited "his constituency" only once. Until September 1995, when Lika was replaced by Hysen Osmani, Tropojë voters in effect were unrepresented in parliament.

A key element in Albania's efforts to consolidate a democratic system has been the establishment of an independent judiciary. Changes were introduced in legal education that were aimed at imbuing students with a keen sense of ethics, justice, and a lawyer's obligation to society. Law schools in Tiranë and Shkodër began training in new fields such as contract law, commercial law, human rights, property law, ownership rights, and the like. In 1994, parliament approved a new law codifying the rights and duties of private attorneys and setting out the conditions necessary to become a qualified lawyer.[41] But overcoming the weight of half a century of Communist rule, during which the government displayed no regard for due process and considered the judiciary merely the voice of the ruling party, proved a daunting task. Although there was widespread recognition that Albania had made "tremendous strides in the respect shown for human rights and fundamental freedoms,"[42] there were still significant abuses of human rights, including instances of police brutality, procedural irregularities resulting in the denial of a fair trial, mistreatment of defendants, and occasional restrictions of the freedom of speech and press.[43] Officials attempted to minimize the significance of such reports by pegging the problem as the misdeeds of a few policemen, focusing attention on the problems facing the police, and underscoring the need for better education of police recruits.

The legal system also was plagued by many other problems. Many judges appointed since 1992 lacked the requisite training. Laws were published only in the official gazette and were not adequately disseminated, particularly outside the big cities. Judges complained that they lacked adequate resources and supporting staff. While these problems were recognized by the government, little was done to remedy the situation. The growth of professionalism was also retarded by the domination of the private legal community by former Communist judges, who for years had considered the judicial system an arm of the "dictatorship of the proletariat." Practically all the judges replaced after 1992 moved into private practice, forming a close-knit group. In an ironic twist of events, Kleanthi Koçi, who had served as Chairman of the Supreme Court during the last years of the Communist regime, was elected president of the national bar association formed in fall 1994.[44] The development of an Albanian legal profession with the attributes of a Western bar will have to await the emergence of a new generation of lawyers.

Constitutional laws guaranteed the independence of the judiciary; but in practice, the judiciary remained weak and subject to considerable executive pressure. The High Council of Justice, headed by the president, was accused of appointing, dismissing, and disciplining judges based on their political stand. According to an international human rights organization, the High Council of Justice had become "a principal instrument of the judiciary's subordination to the executive."[45]

The controversy surrounding former Chief Justice of the Court of Cassation Zef Brozi, who was dismissed by parliament in September 1995, seriously undermined the judiciary's integrity and diminished public confidence in the system. A Berisha confidant, Brozi had been appointed chief justice in 1993. At first, he was in the forefront of the Democratic Party's campaign to stamp out corruption within the judiciary and strengthen judicial independence, impartiality, and fairness; but eventually, his actions and behavior became a source of considerable controversy and raised serious questions about his judicial posture. In December 1994, General Prosecutor Alush Dragoshi accused Brozi of wrongfully releasing an alleged drug dealer and asked parliament to lift his immunity, as a prelude to filing charges against the chief justice. Brozi had ordered the release of a Greek citizen accused of drug possession after a panel of the Court of Cassation reversed the conviction by a lower court. He also had taken the unusual step of receiving in his office the family of the alleged drug dealer, which raised rumors that he had accepted a large bribe. Dragoshi's action coincided with a tense political situation in the wake of the 6 November 1994 referendum, which rejected the draft constitution submitted by Berisha. The Democratic Party faced serious internal problems as it contemplated its future strategy. In addition, the trial and sentencing of five ethnic Greeks on espionage charges had led to a serious deterioration in Albania's relations with Greece. The opposition, which in the past had denounced Brozi as a Berisha stooge, now took him under its wing in an effort to score propaganda points against the president.

Brozi denied any wrongdoing and suggested that the charges against him were politically motivated. Antigovernment analysts and newspapers claimed that the general prosecutor's action was connected with Brozi's stance on the November 1994 constitutional referendum. In an interview in late October 1994, the chairman of the Court of Cassation had criticized the rallies that were being held in connection with the referendum. He suggested that experts should explain the contents of the draft constitution, while political parties should be prohibited from campaigning in favor of or against it. Contrary to subsequent domestic and foreign press reports, Brozi, who was a member of the Constitutional Commission, did not criticize the draft constitution. In fact, he rejected criticism that the document granted too much power to the presidency. He also revealed that during commission deliberations, he had advocated the establishment of a presidential republic.[46]

Brozi appealed to the members of parliament to reject the general prosecutor's request, insisting that the independence of the judiciary was at stake. He also launched a media campaign, making acerbic comments in interviews with opposition newspapers. Brozi, however, overexposed himself, going beyond simply defending himself against the charges leveled by the general prosecutor and fellow jurists to comment on a variety of political issues unrelated to law and legal reform. Only a month before he was to rule on the appeal of five ethnic Greeks accused of espionage, Brozi said in an interview that it was the duty of all citizens as well as state and judicial organs to stop "those who might shamefully contribute to the deterioration of relations" between Albania and Greece. The chairman of the Court of Cassation said that Albania "needed" to improve relations with Greece "because of the fact that thousands of Albanians work there."[47] Many questioned whether the chairman of the Court of Cassation should have publicly concerned himself with the state of relations with a neighboring nation, clearly the prerogative of the foreign ministry.

It was in view of these events that on 1 February 1995, parliament, by a vote of 53 to 49, rejected the general prosecutor's request to lift Brozi's immunity. Brozi and the opposition were quick to hail the vote as a victory for the rule of law. However, the vote was more a strike at Berisha than a display of confidence in the chairman of the Court of Cassation. A week later, the Court of Cassation startled the nation by upholding a lower court's conviction of the five ethnic Greeks but releasing them on probation. While privately Berisha and the foreign policy establishment may have applauded the release because it immediately defused tensions with Athens, it is clear that the decision was influenced by politics.

Brozi's squabbles with executive branch officials continued unabated, with charges and countercharges from both sides. Brozi's public statements exceeded the scope of his judicial duties. Thus, although his statements drew close attention from the opposition press and perhaps enhanced his political stature, especially abroad, they further undermined the credibility of the system. Meanwhile, the

Ministry of Justice took steps to strengthen its administrative and financial control over the judiciary and unsuccessfully attempted to remove two justices, who had been nominated by the Democratic Party from the Court of Cassation. These steps reinforced charges of executive branch infringement of the separation of powers.

The conflict came to a head in July 1995, when Brozi reopened the case of Fatos Nano, the imprisoned Socialist Party leader. Under the Criminal Code then in force, Brozi requested that the plenum of the Court of Cassation review Nano's verdict. A hearing was scheduled for September 1995.[48] The government, however, claimed that the new Code of Criminal Procedure, which came into force on 1 August 1995, did not give the chief justice the authority to reopen the Nano case. The Constitutional Court, in a ruling on 19 September, blocked the Court of Cassation from reviewing Nano's case on the grounds that it conflicted with the new Code of Criminal Procedure.[49] Meanwhile, after an investigation, the Ministry of Justice accused Brozi of having violated the constitution by issuing orders suspending the execution of several rulings in civil cases. On 21 September, the Constitutional Court ruled in favor of a government petition declaring Brozi's actions unlawful and unconstitutional.[50] Only hours after the court's decision, parliament dismissed Brozi "because of his activities against the law and the constitution and his serious violations of human rights and freedoms."[51] The Brozi case poisoned the political atmosphere surrounding the Court of Cassation for a long time. The case also drew sharp criticism abroad, including an assertion by the U.S. State Department that the chief justice had been removed "under circumstances which do not appear to comport with democratic procedures."[52]

The Constitutional Conundrum

Establishing new institutions and a working legal system after decades of Communist dictatorship turned out to be much more difficult than dismantling the old order. The drafting of a new constitution stirred extensive political controversy. The commission appointed in April 1992, headed by Prime Minister Meksi, was expected to complete the drafting of a new constitution by the end of 1992. However, the timetable was derailed by disagreements on the institutional alternatives and the specific powers of each branch of government. The Socialists, joined by the Social Democratic Party and the Democratic Alliance, advocated reducing the president's powers, essentially confining the head of state to a merely ceremonial role. Berisha's supporters, on the other hand, argued that Albania needed strong executive leadership that could make timely decisions, especially in view of the country's political polarization, regional differences, religious diversity, and growing regional instability. Opposition criticism notwithstanding, Berisha's supporters did not advocate a powerful executive presidency modeled on that of France or of the United States but rather a system that would permit a stable combination of presidential and parliamentary government.

Politics played a major role in blocking agreement on a new constitution. Having failed in their efforts to use popular dissatisfaction with radical economic reforms against the government, the Socialists came to view the adoption of a new constitution as an instrument to provoke a parliamentary crisis and thereby force new elections. They actively sought to forge an alliance with other parliamentary parties in order to block the adoption of the constitution. The Social Democratic Party, the third largest party in parliament, had become increasingly disgruntled with what it considered its meager role in the government coalition. It sought to use the constitutional issues to extract a concession from the Democratic Party to greater Social Democratic participation in the cabinet—a demand the Democrats refused. However, six former Democratic Party deputies, who had formed the Democratic Alliance, sided with the Socialists.

Under increased domestic and foreign pressure—especially from the European Council, which had predicated Albania's membership on its adoption of a new constitution—in autumn 1994, Berisha tried to break the constitutional deadlock. Although the Law on the Main Constitutional Provisions clearly empowered parliament to adopt and amend the country's constitution, after a year of public diatribes, Berisha decided to circumvent the legislature and submit the draft constitution to a national referendum. In a televised speech, Berisha argued that it was impossible to reach consensus in the legislature and that the Socialists were attempting to use the occasion to create an "artificial parliamentary crisis."[53]

The draft constitution,[54] was in the mainstream of postcommunist constitutions that had appeared in other East European countries and generally adhered to international norms and standards, provided for the separation of powers and broad protection of human rights. The draft represented a hybrid of a presidential and a parliamentary system. There was nothing glaring about the allocation of powers to the president and the legislature that suggested that one side would dictate to the other. However, the draft contained weaker provisions for the judiciary, and gave the president more power in selecting judges for the Constitutional Court than did existing constitutional laws. In addition, the draft contained two articles that were widely interpreted as limitations on democracy and not in conformity with international norms and standards. Article 6 (3) prohibited the creation of political parties based on religion or ethnicity. Article 7 (4) stipulated that heads of the large religious communities "must be Albanian citizens born in Albania and permanently resident there for the past 20 years."[55] Had the draft constitution been approved, Archbishop Anastasios Yannoulatos, a citizen of Greece who was named temporary head of the Albanian Orthodox Church in 1992, would have been forced to step down.

The referendum, held on 6 November 1994, failed to break the constitutional deadlock: Albanian voters rejected Berisha's draft. With a turnout of 84.43 percent, 53.9 percent voted against and 41.7 percent in favor.[56] While acknowledging defeat, Berisha insisted that the referendum was nevertheless a victory for

Albanian democracy. He blamed the vote on discontent with the government's economic reform policies and the authorities' tolerant stand on corruption.[57]

Undoubtedly, economic discontent and voter anger at official corruption were the main reason for the referendum's defeat. The implementation of austerity measures, and their unintended consequences, such as the government's inability to pay sufficient attention to employment, education, primary health care services, nutrition, maternity and child care, and sanitation, were bound to affect the Democratic Party's popularity. Moreover, the failure to deal with corruption in the high echelons of government undermined the credibility of politicians and undercut the efficiency and effectiveness of public policy and programs, thus destroying the conditions necessary for fair competition and distorting the incentives needed for proper allocation of resources. Corruption not only had become a potent weapon of the antireform opposition, but even more importantly, it had soured many Albanians on the idea of democracy, serving as a deterrent to further political and economic development. There were signs of cynicism toward officials and growing anger at an emerging system that was increasingly perceived to reward most those who defied the law.

But there were other important factors that contributed to the rejection of the draft constitution. While in the past Berisha had worked successfully to sell his program, on the constitutional issues, he had shied away from building a broad consensus or seeking compromises, evidently believing that the public would support him. Only the Republican Party, which had been marginalized politically, and a faction of the Social Democratic Party led by deputy Teodor Laço, supported the draft constitution. All the other parties, from the extreme left to the extreme right, opposed it. Indeed, the debate over the substance of the draft constitution was overshadowed by the political campaign, as both sides came to see the referendum as a test of their public support. Evidently the majority of Albanians did not notice the subtleties of the judicial system and presidential powers that the opposition found so objectionable. Few appeared to have based their votes on the substance of the draft constitution.

Berisha's personal engagement apparently also turned off many voters. In campaign trips reminiscent of his March 1992 marathon, the president traveled all over the country, addressing rallies. This time, the "man of the people" was accompanied by a huge entourage of pompous bureaucrats who seemed far removed from the daily problems that ordinary Albanians faced. There was also a widespread belief that during the referendum campaign the president was too visible for too little reason, appearing almost nightly on national television.

Finally, the sharply contrasting voting patterns in the south and the north indicate that the conflict with Greece was also a significant factor. While the north backed the constitution, the south, which arguably was more vulnerable to Greek economic and political pressures, voted overwhelmingly against it; in some southern cities, up to 90 percent of the electorate cast negative votes. What accounted for the south's rejection of the draft was not concern with presidential powers or the independence of the judiciary, but ties with Greece and the fear that relations would further deteriorate if the constitution was approved and Archbishop Yannaoulatos forced to leave Albania. The Greek expulsion of some 70,000 refugees, many from the south, probably affected between 200,000 to 300,000 Albanian citizens, who depended on remittances from family members in Greece for their livelihood. Thus, by voting against the draft constitution, voters in the south clearly backed closer ties with Greece.

Political Consequences

The referendum altered Albania's political landscape, ushering in a period of greater partisan competition and setting the stage for months of political turmoil. Although in the final analysis the referendum was a sign of the maturing of voters long used to automatically approving their government's policies, the great experiment of Albania's democracy faced its deepest crisis to date. For the first time after the 1992 elections, the fragile gains of Albania's political and economic reforms seemed at risk.

The Socialist Party was quick to characterize the results as a repudiation of the Democratic Party's policies and a clear signal of voters' inclinations a year before general elections. The Socialists felt emboldened by the referendum results, which they interpreted as strengthening their position. They rejected Berisha's proposal that they form a commission to draft a new constitution, which would then be put to a referendum. The Socialists continued to insist that the constitution be ratified by the legislature. Buoyed by what they saw as the success of their hard-line position, the Socialists took a more inflexible line also on other issues, and renewed their demands for early elections. But while the result of the referendum represented a vote of no confidence in the Democratic Party, it was more a gesture of anger at the government than a genuine endorsement of the Socialist alternative.

The most spectacular fallout of the referendum was the split between Berisha and his closest confidant, party chairman Eduard Selami. The referendum caused a significant change in the alignment of forces, with a pro- and anti-Berisha cleavage. The president, who had staked a large amount of personal political capital on the approval of the draft constitution, emerged from the referendum with diminished support and a tarnished image. He came under pressure from Selami and some members of the Democratic Party parliamentary group to make sweeping changes in the cabinet. Long a critic of Meksi, whose job he apparently coveted, Selami launched an attack on the prime minister in an effort to dislodge him. Under the threat of resignation, Selami demanded that he replace Meksi as prime minister. In a move that could only be interpreted as aimed at humiliating Meksi, Selami subjected the entire cabinet to a secret vote of confidence by the parliamentary group. Meksi survived by a narrow margin, but seven members of the cabinet, including Deputy Prime Minister Bashkim Kopliku, Defense Minister Safet Zhulali, and Foreign Minister Alfred Serreqi, did not. Selami, supported by a number of deputies, maintained that the vote by the parliamentary group was binding. However, the president, who was unwilling to replace Meksi and some of the ministers that had fallen out of favor with Selami, insisted that the parliamentary group's action was only of a consultative nature.

On 4 December 1994, the president announced a major government reshuffle, replacing eight of the fifteen members of the cabinet, but retaining Zhulali and Serreqi. Kopliku, Minister of Local Government Rexhep Uka, Minister of Justice Kudret Çela, Minister of Finance Pirro Dishnica, Minister of Industry and Trade Selim Belortaja, Minister of Construction Ilir Manushi, Minister of Transport and Communication Fatos Bitincka, and Minister of Tourism Edmond Spaho were sacked. Minister of Culture Dhimitër Anagnosti had resigned amid press reports that he was about to be fired. The governor of Albania's central bank, Dylber Vrioni, was named deputy prime minister and minister of finance, while Albert Brojka became minister of industry, transportation, and trade. Hektor Frashëri was appointed minister of justice, and Teodor Laço, deputy chairman of the Social Democratic Party, minister of culture, youth, and sports.[58] Laço had broken ranks with his party's leadership by supporting the draft constitution and later formed a new party, the Social Democratic Union.

The new cabinet did not include any outspoken reformers and did not seem to have a clear governing philosophy, which raised concerns about its commitment to economic reform and democratic processes. Perhaps the most surprising change was the firing of Kopliku and the abolishment of his post, that of deputy premier responsible for economic reform. Although a year earlier Kopliku had emerged as a key figure in the government, he had failed to move to a high-profile role evidently because of his poor working relations with the prime minister.[59] Kopliku publicly criticized Meksi for his insufficient zeal in pursuing swift reforms. He insisted that the Democratic Party could not afford to slow the pace of reform, arguing instead for a speedy privatization and a purge of antireform elements from the bureaucracy.[60] The retention of Minister of Internal Affairs Agron Musaraj, a deeply unpopular figure whose performance had been widely criticized, was also a surprise. Critics charged that Musaraj was a reckless and ruthless politician who should not be entrusted with the nation's internal security.

In an attempt to regain the political initiative, Berisha called for a determined struggle against corruption; but his weakened position was reflected most dramatically in the parliament's refusal to lift the immunity of Chairman of the Court of Cassation Zef Brozi as a first step toward investigating and convicting him of a crime involving the release of an alleged Greek drug dealer whose case had been reversed, and of Democratic Party deputies Genc Ruli and Rexhep Uka, who were implicated in a corruption scandal. Both cases were part of the government's renewed anticorruption drive.

Meanwhile, Selami, having failed in his efforts to dislodge Meksi, began gradually to put some distance between himself and the president. Heretofore Selami had operated largely in Berisha's shadow, but the referendum had created opportunities for him to stake out a place of his own in Albanian politics. After a string of defeats, Berisha was in no position to risk a showdown with his own right-hand man, and he tried to placate Selami. The party chairman had not been closely identified with the referendum, so the vote was more a defeat for Berisha, and even more so for Meksi, the chairman of the drafting commission. The most glaringly hollow ploy in Selami's rebellion was his proposal, after the post-referendum government reshuffle, to combine the office of prime minister with that of the party chairman: The Democratic Party's 1992 election platform had called explicitly for the separation of the state from the party. In addition, it was widely known that Meksi was not interested in taking over the party chairmanship, nor was there popular support for combining the two positions. Thus, Selami's offer to resign his post rang false. At a meeting of the party's national council in late January 1995, Selami's proposal was rejected, and after a plea from other party leaders and an agreement that his idea would be discussed at the party's forthcoming national convention, he withdrew his resignation offer.[61]

Then, just when it appeared that the Democrats had closed ranks once again, Selami unexpectedly issued his strongest challenge to Berisha. In a speech at a party gathering in Shkodër, he suggested changes in the procedure for adopting a new constitution, saying that the constitution should be submitted to the parliament for approval, as the opposition had demanded.[62] This radical shift in Selami's stance seriously undercut Berisha's position. The Socialist Party, quick to take advantage of any sign of disagreement in the ranks of the Democratic Party, had a field day dissecting the latest misfortune plaguing the Democrats. Selami, who in the past had been a favorite target of Socialist propaganda, was now praised as a true democrat. But as Louis Zanga has pointed out, the opposition's support for Selami "was illusory since their only concern was how to discredit and weaken Berisha."[63]

The political landscape was jolted by the news of conflict between Berisha and Selami. A meeting of the Democratic Party presidency on 13 February took issue with Selami's statement. In a strongly worded speech, Berisha defended the government, and without mentioning Selami, denounced what he referred to as an antireform campaign organized by the "Iago of democracy."[64] After the meeting, Selami vowed an all-out fight to keep his post as chairman, while Berisha's supporters began preparing to dump him. On 5 March, an extraordinary party conference dismissed Selami: In an open vote, 607 out of 664 delegates voted against him.[65] Selami claimed that had the conference reached its decision by secret vote, a substantial number of delegates would have supported him; but it appears that he did not have a significant following either inside or outside the party. Although the former chairman and other Democratic Party senior leaders traded political sniping and public accusations, Selami did not leave the party, thus averting a damaging split. Nonetheless, because of Selami's prominence in Albanian politics and close ties to Berisha, his removal from his post had a substantial symbolic and political effect. It embarrassed the president, who personally had promoted him, and removed from the scene a bright, young, moderate politician who might have done much good in service of his country. The affair illustrated the escalating conflicts within the party as its leaders dealt with the results of the referendum and the complex mix of rank-and-file reactions and expectations.

The post-referendum political scene was characterized by increased polarization. Friction and intolerance increased significantly as the government and opposition parties intensified their campaign for the hearts and minds of the voters, resorting to militant rhetoric and political manipulation. The Socialist Party insisted that if it regained power, it would repeal a large part of the legislation enacted during the Democratic Party's government. This served only to intensify calls within the Democratic Party for stepping up the de-communization campaign.

One of the most hotly debated issues was the prosecution of the top leaders of the old regime. Albanians struggled with the legal and moral questions in contemplating who was culpable for Communist transgressions. After prolonged internal deliberations, in 1993 and 1994, Nexhmije Hoxha, Ramiz Alia, and nine former APL Politburo members and senior government officials were tried on charges of corruption and abuse of power. The proceedings were widely criticized as a mockery of justice.[66] Former political prisoners had urged that Alia and his associates be tried on charges of genocide.[67] However, unwilling to hold political trials at this stage, the government ended up charging the former Communist officials with what in the opinion of many Albanians were petty economic crimes. Moreover, the proceedings were handled so clumsily that the Communists won the propaganda war, as there was a widespread impression of irregularities and substantial legal errors. Virtually all of the old guard received only light sentences, which were further reduced on appeal and by amnesties; the rest were excused from serving because of ill health. Nexhmije Hoxha received the longest sentence—eleven years. With the exception of Mrs. Hoxha, all benefitted from the new penal code that went into effect in June 1995, after which they were released. Mrs. Hoxha was released in January 1997. Alia and his former associates made a concerted effort to capture the public eye, frequently granting interviews and publishing articles downplaying human rights transgressions under the old regime and heaping scorn on the Democratic government.

The right, outraged by the release of these former Communist leaders, criticized the government for not having done enough to make up for decades of dictatorship. They saw the government's leniency as inexplicable, a slap in the face of all former political prisoners, and they urged that the upper echelons of the *nomenklatura* not be permitted to elude prosecution for human rights violations. A group of more than thirty intellectuals in Tiranë formed an organization that called on the government to punish all those guilty of "genocide" against the Albanian people. In late 1995 and early 1996, dozens of former senior Communist officials, including Alia and former Politburo members, were tried and sentenced to long prison terms. They were charged with crimes against humanity under the new penal code, which allowed legal proceedings against crimes committed by the old regime. The government insisted that the objective of the *nomenklatura* trials was to determine responsibility for past abuses. However, there was some controversy, especially around the question of whether the trials would bolster reconciliation or build a thirst for vengeance. For those eager to forget the past, especially Sigurimi officials and former senior Communist officials, the trials were a chilling reminder of the depth of Albania's continuing anguish. Yet, the majority of Albanians, perhaps exhausted by the rapid shifts in politics, appeared indifferent to the fate of their former rulers.

The issue of how to handle Sigurimi files on collaborators and informants was a highly contentious matter, involving the reliability of the files and the social impact of opening them up.[68] Between December 1990 and March 1992, the Communists had had ample time to destroy or deliberately doctor secret police files. In June 1995, *Tribuna Demokratike*, the organ of the Democratic Party's Tiranë branch, reported that during his short stint as minister of internal affairs in April 1991, Gramoz Ruçi, a member of the top Socialist Party leadership, had ordered the burning of thousands of pages of top secret papers and documents, including lists of thousands of regime opponents to be "eliminated" in the event of war.[69] In addition to publishing several "death lists," the paper published an order signed by the former Minister of Internal Affairs Hekuran Isai, specifying the criteria to be used for drawing up the lists of regime opponents. Those on the lists were to be liquidated without trial.[70]

The ruling Democratic Party suggested that former Sigurimi officers possessed documents that they were using to blackmail people. The opposition, on the other hand, accused the government of manipulating the issue and using the files to discredit or blackmail its opponents. Opinions varied on how to deal with this complex question. Political forces on the right were unanimously in favor of opening all files. Others were more circumspect, demanding only disclosure only for politicians. Some insisted that the files be opened also for writers, artists, and journalists. Berisha maintained that probing too deeply into the Sigurimi would result in a national tragedy. While rejecting demands for the opening of all secret police file, the president agreed that files should be opened for all elected officials and politicians.[71] But in addition to Berisha's argument that opening the files would cause undue social problems, an additional contributing factor in his delaying action might have been the fact that there were a number of former Sigurimi agents and informers in the top echelons of the Democratic Party and among the parliamentary deputies. While refusing to disclose the names of former collaborators and informers in the ranks of the ruling party, government officials leaked the names of opposition politicians and journalists who had links with the secret police. Among the politicians named were Preç Zogaj, a top leader of the Democratic Alliance, and Skendër Gjinushi, chairman of the Social Democratic Party. Zogaj admitted that he had been recruited when he was seventeen years old, but added that he had never harmed anyone.[72] It was subsequently revealed that one of the individuals on whom Zogaj informed was Ismail Kadare.[73] Gjinushi, without denying the allegations that he was a Sigurimi informer, accused the president of manipulating the police files.[74]

As the May 1996 national elections approached, Albania remained divided by fiercely competing camps of Democrats and Socialists. The opposition forces were too disparate in outlook to identify and unite behind a plausible alternative capable of capturing the public imagination; they had no basis for an alliance, other than their distaste for Berisha. In addition, although the broader public had shown a lack of confidence in the government by rejecting the draft constitution, there was no evidence it was embracing the Socialist Party, the largest opposition force. The benefits of privatization and other economic changes were gradually but steadily filtering through to more and more people. Thousands of Albanians had taken to personal freedom and entrepreneurial opportunity with a fervor defying all forecasts. A thriving new class of entrepreneurs who saw their fate as linked with continued economic reforms, was rapidly emerging and staking its ground throughout the country. The government also continued to enjoy substantial international support, as Albania was seen as a stabilizing factor in the region. The decision by the Court of Cassation to release the five ethnic Greek defendants on probation led to an immediate and substantial diffusion in tensions with Greece. Following the Greek foreign minister's visit to Tiranë in March 1995 and the arrest in Greece of a group of seven armed men who had been planning terrorist actions in Albania, ties between Tiranë and Athens seemed to be back on track again. Albania's relations with its other neighbors, with the exception of Yugoslavia, remained warm, while its political, economic, and military cooperation with the United States and Western Europe continued to expand. In a clear signal of the recognition of the progress it had made in its difficult transition, in June 1995 Albania was granted full membership in the Council of Europe. A year after the referendum fiasco, the Democratic Party had made a remarkable political comeback.

The Democratic Party had taken the reins of power in 1992 at one of the most difficult periods in Albania's recent history. Given the scale and novelty of the challenges confronting Albania, the extent of disruption and social dislocation caused by painful reforms, and the weight of a turbulent historical legacy, postcommunist Albania witnessed significant institutional and legislative trans-formations aimed at establishing a new political order. But despite this progress, lack of solid democratic institutions and the failure to achieve a domestic political consensus on key national issues had tarnished the Democratic Party's rule. Basic institutions of democracy remained fragile, including parliamentary oversight of the executive, lack of an effective judicial system, conformity to the rule of law, and a weak and ineffective party system.

Notes

1. Robert Austin, "What Albania Adds to the Balkan Stew," *Orbis* 37, no. 2 (Spring 1993), pp. 259-279; and Marko Milivojevic, "Wounded Eagle: Albania's Fight for Survival," *European Security Study*, no. 15 (London: Institute for European Defense and Strategic Studies, 1992).

2. See Berisha's interview in *Financial Times*, 21 July 1994, p. 31.

3. Radio Tiranë Network in Albanian, 1330 GMT, 18 July 1992, translated in FBIS-EEU 92-139, 20 July 1992, p. 5.

4. Radio Tiranë Network in Albanian, 2010 GMT, 11 June 1992, translated in FBIS-EEU 92-114, 12 June 1992, p. 5.

5. Law no. 7561, dated 29 April 1992, in *Fletorja Zyrtare e Republikës së Shqipërisë*, no. 2 (May 1992), pp. 81-84.

6. Law no. 7692, dated 31 March 1993, in *Fletorja Zyrtare e Republikës së Shqipërisë*, no. 3 (March 1993), pp. 161-171.

7. Radio Tiranë Network in Albanian, 1600 GMT, 8 April 1992, translated in FBIS-EEU 92-070, 10 April 1992, p. 4.

8. *Zëri i Popullit*, 14 May 1992, p. 3.

9. Alban Kosova, "The Paralyzed National Intelligence Service," *Zëri i Popullit*, 4 July 1992, p. 3.

10. "The Truth About Reforms in the Military," *Luftetari*, 15 November 1992, p. 2.

11. See Zhulali's comments in *Zëri i Rinisë*, 25 April 1992, p. 1, and *Rilindja Demokratike*, 21 July 1992, p. 4.

12. An article in the military newspaper *Ushtria dhe Koha*, noting that "half of the Albanian state is occupied by its neighbors" and that Albanian citizens were being killed on the borders with Serbia, Macedonia, and Greece, posed the question: "Has not the time come for us to be more nationalistic?" (See Përparim Kapllani, "The Military: A Factor of Unity," *Ushtria dhe Koha*, 10 November 1993, p. 1.) An editorial in the same newspaper, in November 1994, complained of instances where orders were questioned or not carried out. The editorial said stern measures should be taken against all military men who question their superiors' orders ("The Order and Responsibility," *Ushtria dhe Koha*, 6 November 1994, p. 4).

13. Immediately after the government appointments were announced, in April 1992, both Pashko and Hajdari reiterated statements they had made at the beginning of the democratic process, to the effect that they were not interested in government posts. Pashko repeated a statement he had made in an interview with the Voice of America in December 1990: "I have waged the struggle for democracy in Albania because I love my children, and I want the day to come for them and all the children of Albania when I will turn to my students and teach them the truth, when I will speak and write the truth for them." Pashko said "I still stand by this ideal." (See *Rilindja Demokratike*, 25 April 1992, p. 3.) Hajdari, too, recalled a pledge he had made in December 1990 that he was not interested in "armchair posts." (See *Rilindja Demokratike*, 18 April 1992, p. 1.) Nonetheless, Pashko, whose abrasive political style had alienated many of his former colleagues, maintained that

he would continue his involvement in politics, and denied reports of a split with Berisha and the existence of "two currents within the Democratic Party." See Pashko's interview in *Rilindja Demokratike*, 29 April 1992, p. 3.

14. *Zëri i Popullit*, 24 June 1992, p. 1.

15. Pashko's statement was published in *Zëri i Popullit*, 24 June 1992, p. 1.

16. Radio Tirana Network in Albanian, 1000 GMT, 13 August 1992, translated in FBIS-EEU 92-157, 13 August 1992, pp. 3-4.

17. Radio Tiranë Network in Albanian, 1330 GMT, 14 August 1992, translated in FBIS-EEU 92-159, 17 August 1992, p. 6. Some Democratic Party leaders, particularly Selami, strongly urged the withdrawal of the parliamentary mandates of the deputies expelled from the party, since they had been elected on the Democratic Party ticket (Reese Erlich, "Albania's Troubled Democracy," *Christian Science Monitor*, 21 August 1992, p. 6.) Evidently convinced that the political costs of expelling the six deputies would be too high, Berisha blocked initiatives to withdraw their mandates. However, the names of Arben Demeti, Preç Zogaj, and Shahin Kadare were struck from the Democratic Party's supplemental list of deputies. Had the split within the Democratic Party occurred a month later, the three would have replaced deputies Bashkim Gazidede, Skendër Shkupi, and Besnik Mustafaj. Gazidede was named head of the SHIK, while Shkupi and Mustafaj ambassadors to Turkey and France, respectively. (Radio Tiranë Network in Albanian, 1730 GMT, 27 August 1992, translated in FBIS-EEU 92-168, 28 August 1992, p. 20.)

18. *Rilindja Demokratike*, 27 August 1993, p. 3.

19. See Berisha's interview in *Republika*, 18 June 1992, p. 3. An article by Zyhdi Morava was typical of the negative reaction from former political prisoners. Addressing Berisha, he wrote: "What have you done to us political prisoners, what have you done to us? The Christian thought that all of us are victims and jointly responsible [for the survival of the Communist dictatorship] has given important ammunition to Communist criminals. ... No, No! I and many of my former fellow political prisoners imprisoned by the Communist dictators will never accept that we are jointly responsible" (Zyhdi Morava, "What Have You Done to Us, Mr. President?" *E Verteta* (Tiranë), 4 May 1992, p. 6).

20. Kristaq Selami and Adnan Gjika, "In a United Front Against All Expressions of Dictatorship," *Zëri i Popullit*, 31 July 1992, pp. 2, 4.

21. Sejdi Musarai, "Current U.S. Policy and Albania," *Zëri i Popullit*, 18 July 1993, p. 2.

22. *Zëri i Popullit*, 28 July 1993, pp. 1, 3.

23. Ibid., 31 July 1993, pp. 1-3.

24. On 26 March 1994, Nano was sentenced to twelve years in prison. The Socialist Party leader appealed, but both an appeals court and the Court of Cassation confirmed the sentence.

25. *Rilindja Demokratike*, 5 November 1993, p. 1.

26. ATA in English, 1649 GMT, 27 December 1995, in FBIS-EEU 96-001-A, 2 January 1996, p. 3.

27. In a wholesale indictment of the new governing elite, the Chairman of the League of Writers and Artists, poet Bardhyl Londo, charged that politics had become the most "profitable" profession in Albania. He said politicians were enjoying the highest living standard in the country because of the massive wealth they had acquired illegally. (Bardhyl Londo, "A Human Democracy or a Politicized Democracy," *Rilindja Demokratike*, 5 December 1993, p. 1.)

28. During a heated exchange, Kalakula, responding to Socialist charges that he was "an extremist, revanchist, and a fascist," declared that he would rather be called a fascist than a communist. Socialist propaganda gave prominent coverage to Kalakula's statement, responding that this was proof that the "fascists" had usurped power within the Democratic Party (*Rilindja Demokratike*, 15 August 1993, p. 1.) In an interview, Kalakula attempted to clarify his statement and denied that he believed in fascism, adding that indeed his family had been persecuted during the fascist occupation of Albania (*Dita Informacion*, 8 August 1993, p. 6).

29. *Rilindja Demokratike*, 19 September 1993, p. 1.

30. Pëllumb Tare, "Extremes: Destabilizing Horses of Albanian Politics," *Rilindja Demokratike*, 3 December 1993, p. 3.

31. Kalakula's position was undermined by press revelations that he had married a woman from a prominent Communist family and had used his family connection to secure a good job, eventually serving as an adviser to the Tiranë Communist Party secretary and to the deputy prime minister on agricultural matters. The Democratic Party newspaper also published a handwritten letter by Kalakula, in which he denounced his own brother, who had been sentenced for antistate activities (*Rilindja Demokratike*, 14 December 1993, pp. 1-2; and Neshat Tozaj, "The Kalakula Incident and the Irony of Fate," *Koha Jonë*, 25 December 1993, p. 3). For Kalakula's reaction, see *Koha Jonë*, 6 January 1994, pp. 3-4.

32. A former member of the APL, Abdi Baleta served as ambassador to the United Nations during the late 1970s and the early 1980s, vociferously defending his country's isolationist policy. During his stint, Albania's U.N. mission increased its destructive activities among the Albanian American community, dividing it into pro- and anti-Hoxha elements. Following his return home, Baleta served as a judge and eventually was appointed professor of law at Tiranë University. In December 1990, he became a founding member of a human rights committee, which subsequently became known as the Albanian Helsinki Committee. Although he never joined the Democratic Party, initially because of his membership in the human rights committee and subsequently because he evidently wanted to keep his political options open, Baleta was elected to parliament in 1991 and 1992 on the Democratic ticket. His style and rhetoric earned him a solid reputation as an extreme nationalist and an anticommunist. He consistently argued that the revival of nationalism was vital to the nation's survival in the face of what he saw as growing Serbian-Greek encroachments on Albania (Abdi Baleta, "The Democratic Party is Erasing the National Issue From Its Political Program," *E Djathta*, 22 July 1994, p. 4).

33. In May 1994, a group of some sixty farmers in the northeastern town of Kukës went on a hunger strike when the government refused their demands for compensation for homes and property flooded by the Fierzë hydroelectric dam in the 1970s. When Minister of Public Order Agron Musaraj ordered the police to evict the hunger strikers from a government building, residents of Kukës and farmers from surrounding areas came to the strikers' defense. In the ensuing clashes, which reportedly lasted several hours, dozens of strikers and police officers were wounded. The strike ended after the government promised to compensate the farmers with land or in cash, to grant them long-term loans on favorable conditions to build home, and to help them resettle in other parts of the country (*Gazeta Shqiptare*, 14 May 1994, p. 1).

34. There were disagreements as to the exact number of former prisoners, but the Association of Former Political Prisoners and Formerly Persecuted Persons put the number at about 60,000. The organization claimed that some 700,000 people had their rights violated by the Communist regime (Radio Tiranë Network in Albanian, 1330 GMT, 27

May 1994, translated in FBIS-EEU 94-104, 31 May 1994, p. 2).

35. *Liria*, 18 May 1994, p. 1.

36. Ibid., 21 July 1994, p. 1.

37. Radio Tiranë Network in Albanian, 1330 GMT, 11 August 1994, translated in FBIS-EEU 94-156, 12 August 1994, p. 1.

38. Law no. 7558, dated 9 April 1992, in *Fletorja Zyrtare e Republikës së Shqipërisë*, no. 2 (May 1992), p. 63.

39. Law no. 7561, dated 29 April 1992, *Fletorja Zyrtare e Republikës së Shqipërisë*, no. 2 (May 1992), pp. 81-84.

40. Zija Çela, a prominent writer and an early Berisha supporter, charged that the president was surrounded by "mediocre advisers." See Çela's interview in *Rilindja Demokratike*, 12 September 1993, p. 5.

41. Law no. 7827, dated 31 May 1994, *Fletorja Zyrtare e Republikës së Shqipërisë*, no. 7, July 1994, pp. 346-357.

42. U.S. Commission on Security and Cooperation in Europe, *Human Rights and Democratization in Albania* (Washington, D.C., January 1994), p. 1.

43. Human Rights Watch/Helsinki, *Human Rights in Post-Communist Albania* (New York, 1996). See also U.S. State Department, *Country Reports on Human Rights Practices for 1995* (Washington, D.C., March 1996).

44. American Bar Association, Central and East European Law Initiative (CEELI), *CEELI Update* 4, no. 4 (Winter 1994), p. 3.

45. *Human Rights in Post-Communist Albania*, p. 15.

46. See Brozi's interview in *Gazeta Shqiptare*, 28 October 1994, p. 1.

47. See Brozi's interview in *Dita Informacion*, 8 January 1995, p. 5.

48. In the wake of Brozi's call for Nano's release, the Democratic Party-controlled press began a campaign to discredit the chief justice, going so far as to suggest that he was on the payroll of the opposition Socialist Party. *Rilindja Demokratike*, 18 July 1995, p. 1, and 19 July 1995, p. 1. The paper published Brozi's speech before parliament in July 1993, in which he strongly argued in favor of lifting Nano's immunity and declared that the Socialist leader was "guilty." At the time, Brozi was a member of parliament.

49. Radio Tiranë Network in Albanian, 1330 GMT, 19 September 1995, translated in FBIS-EEU 965-182, 20 September 1995, P. 4.

50. *Rilindja Demokratike*, 22 September 1995, p. 3.

51. *Gazeta Shqiptare*, 22 September 1995, p. 3.

52. See press release by the Office of the Spokesman, U.S. Department of State, "Judicial Independence in Albania," 6 October 1995.

53. Berisha said the Albanian people must have the right and the honor to approve "the first democratic constitution in our thousand-year history." Repeating an earlier statement, the president said that he favored the establishment of a parliamentary republic: "I personally have been and remain against a presidential republic ... because Albania has been a country of one-man rule for roughly five centuries, and what it now lacks is precisely the parliamentary tradition that countries with a developed democracy have had for centuries. A developed parliamentary tradition is as important for democracy as the air we breathe" (TVSH Television Network in Albanian, 1800 GMT, 3 October 1994, translated in FBIS-EEU 94-195, 7 October 1994, pp. 2-4).

54. *Rilindja Demokratike*, 6 October 1994, pp. 1-3.

55. In the wake of the conflict with Greece over the Omonia trial, there had been increased calls for the archbishop's expulsion. In a letter of protest to Berisha, the Albanian Orthodox Church said that Article 7 was in conflict with the secular character of the Albanian state and with the draft constitution's paragraphs that stipulated that religion was separate from the state. The Church said that Article 7 "restricts the freedom of religious communities to choose their leaders according to their objective needs and the existing possibilities." See *Zëri i Popullit*, 23 October 1994, p. 4.

56. TVSH Television Network in Albanian, 1900 GMT, 10 November 1994, translated in FBIS-EEU 94-219, 14 November 1994, pp. 1-2.

57. *Rilindja Demokratike*, 8 November 1994, pp. 1, 2, and 16 November 1994, p. 1.

58. TVSH Television Network in Albanian, 1900 GMT, 4 November 1994, translated in FBIS-EEU 94-234, 6 December 1994, p. 22.

59. In a news conference on 28 December 1994, Berisha explained the reasons why Kopliku was dismissed: "Mr. Kopliku has undoubtedly been one of the promoters of the reform, and has made an invaluable contribution in developing the reform. However, on the other hand, he has not developed a sense of teamwork, a sense that is extremely important for governing. He had several disputes with the chairman of the government and this is why Mr. Kopliku was not included in the new cabinet" (Radio Tiranë Network in Albanian, 1500 GMT, 28 December 1994, translated in FBIS-EEU 95-002, 4 January 1995, p. 6). Kopliku blamed Selami and Meksi for his dismissal. See Kopliku's speech at the Democratic Party's National Council meeting, *Rilindja Demokratike*, 2 February 1995, p. 3.

60. *Rilindja Demokratike*, 2 February 1995, p. 3.

61. Ibid., 31 January 1995, pp. 1-2.

62. Ibid., 11 February 1995, p. 1.

63. Louis Zanga, "Albania: Can the Democrats Win?" *Transition* 1, no. 12 (14 July 1995), p. 43.

64. *Rilindja Demokratike*, 14 February 1995, p. 1.

65. Ibid., 7 March 1995, pp. 1-2.

66. Before his sentencing, Alia told the court that he had a clear conscience. Ridiculing the proceedings, the former Communist leader said that when he looked back on his service to the nation, he had nothing to be ashamed of nor any reason to apologize for his actions. For a full text of Alia's statement, see *Zëri i Popullit*, 29 May 1994, pp. 1-2.

67. ATA in English, 1009 GMT, 6 September 1993, in FBIS-EEU 93-171, 7 September 1993, p. 4. Procommunist propaganda notwithstanding, the majority of former political prisoners did not call for an inquisition against Communist criminals. In an interview in May 1994, Rev. Zef Pllumi, who spent 25 years in prison, said: "I only ask that these people [Alia and other top Communist leaders] be morally punished, that they be pronounced responsible for the crimes they have committed against Albania, against humanity. That is all" (*Republika*, 29 May 1994, p. 3).

68. Reportedly one in four Albanians was a Sigurimi informer. According to an unidentified former top Sigurimi official, "Thousands of files were compiled, most of which are still preserved in the secret archives. They were of two kinds: the first group containing data collected by numerous informants, and the second group containing personal data on the informant himself. Generally, the data collected by informants were checked with a parallel spy network. There were never less than two persons working parallel for one file, and they did not know each other. In certain cases, verification was carried out by

operative techniques, mainly by recording telephone calls with tape recorders that were as small as a matchbox" (*Gazeta Shqiptare,* 29 June 1994, p. 1).

69. *Tribuna Demokratike,* 16 June 1995, pp. 4-5.

70. Ibid., 23 June 1995, p. 5.

71. *Rilindja Demokratike,* 9 July 1994, p. 4.

72. Preç Zogaj, "The Files Masquerade Does Not Recognize Only Secret Police Chiefs," *Aleanca,* 2 July 1994, p. 2.

73. For Kadare's reaction, see his interview in *Zëri i Rinisë* (Tiranë), 24 December 1994, p. 6.

74. *Alternativa SD,* 6 June 1995, pp. 1-2. See also "Gjinushi Spy In Residence During His Stay in France," *Rilindja Demokratike,* 30 January 1996, p. 3.

6

Economic and Social Transformation (1992-1996)

No country in Eastern Europe embarked on the path of reforms against such a catastrophic collapse of the economy as did Albania in 1992. Two years of widespread political unrest, following decades of Communist mismanagement and centralized planning, had led to widespread lawlessness and a virtual collapse of the economy. Albania's statistics painted a daunting picture. Between 1989 and 1992, Gross Domestic Product (GDP) fell by more than 50 percent. Industrial and agricultural production declined by as much as 60 percent and 30 percent respectively—by far the sharpest drop in production in any former Communist country. Albania had completely exhausted its foreign reserves and accumulated a hard-currency debt of more than half a billion dollars. Inflation toped 237 percent annually, while unemployment reached alarming proportions as virtually all factories, enterprises, and cooperatives shut down. The standards of government services were sinking: Health care was near collapse, and water, light, and sewage systems functioned erratically, if at all. Financially bankrupt, Albania became totally dependent on humanitarian assistance to keep its three million people alive at a subsistence level.[1] Building a market economy under such conditions and on the ruins of central planning would have been a daunting enterprise for any government, let alone a new, hastily assembled, and inexperienced leadership.

Through a macroeconomic stabilization program, determined leadership, and an unusually high degree of popular perseverance with painful but necessary reforms, within four years Albania achieved an impressive economic takeoff. It moved from the ruins of a totally state-owned economy to a market economy, with the private sector accounting for more than 65 percent of the GDP and about 70 percent of the national wealth in private hands. The vast majority of Albanians saw significant improvement in their everyday lives. But despite this progress, the economy continued to be plagued by serious structural problems. As the May 1996 parliamentary elections approached, the remarkable achievements of the early years of Democratic rule started to slip away and the momentum of reform and privatization was lost. Meanwhile, huge investments in mushrooming get-rich-quick schemes made the banks seemingly irrelevant and dried up capital for investments and production of goods and services of value to the economy. The collapse of pyramid schemes in early 1997 robbed thousands of citizens of their life savings, derailed the economic reform program, and plunged Albania into a political and economic crisis.

Macroeconomic Stabilization

Economic recovery was the centerpiece of President Sali Berisha's agenda. Having secured international financial backing and a standby agreement with the International Monetary Fund, in June 1992 the government announced a midterm economic plan to arrest the precipitous fall in production, rein in inflation, balance the budget, revive the agricultural sector, and obtain critical raw materials needed by vital sectors of industry to resume operation. At the same time, Albania began the difficult task of creating the legal structure and environment that would attract foreign capital and lay the foundations of a market-based economy. The government took swift measures to tackle perhaps the most explosive economic and social problem facing the country: It ended subsidies for agricultural and industrial goods and let prices rise, except for those on the most basic items, such as bread and milk, which were liberalized in 1993. Along with comprehensive steps to combat inflation, the lek—the Albanian currency—was made fully convertible. In a bold move only months after assuming power, Berisha also repealed a communist decree that provided that workers of enterprises closed for lack of raw materials would receive 80 percent of their wages. The measure, introduced by Ramiz Alia in summer 1990 to appease disgruntled workers, had ruined the economy, as most workers, guaranteed 80 percent of their wages, simply stopped working.

Predictably, the implementation of austerity measures caused considerable social dislocations. Many goods became so expensive that they were beyond the reach of most people. The urban population was especially hard hit. According to a study by the United Nations Development Program, between 1991 and 1993, real income in urban areas fell on average by 30 percent while during the same period, income in rural areas increased by 50 percent, as agriculture responded positively to price reform and privatization.[2] To cushion the effect on the public of the drastic rises in prices and unemployment, the government introduced social welfare measures, which included compensation for consumers unable to cope with the steep increases. The decision epitomized Berisha's strategy of balancing his desires to pursue radical economic reforms with the need to ensure the cooperation of powerful interest groups adversely affected by those reforms. The safety net ensured that those persons displaced by reforms had some form of government support until they were gainfully employed. The severity of the economic crisis was also mitigated by remittances from hundreds of thousands of refugees abroad. Conservatively estimated at more than $200 million a year, these remittances and the growth of private trading contributed to a significant increase in purchasing power.[3]

Berisha provided strong leadership during a very critical period, demonstrating an ability to build and sustain the coalitions necessary to ensure adequate political support for economic transition and to weather the social dislocations that such a transition was bound to cause. He recognized the vital importance of sustaining trade union support for reform. The pro-Democratic Union of Independent Trade Unions had played a critical role in the Democratic Party's electoral success. But once in power, the Democratic Party's interests diverged from those of the labor movement. The trade unions reacted negatively to the government's program, increasing pressure for a more gradual approach to reform.[4] Although the post-1992 election period was followed by a marked decrease in union activism because massive layoffs had reduced the unions' leverage, Berisha was careful to maintain open channels of communications with labor leaders and tried to address their concerns.[5] In return, the independent trade unions continued to support the government. Conversely, the government's relations with the pro-Socialist and less influential Confederation of Trade Unions of Albania remained tense. The confederation tried relentlessly to spread procommunist sentiments among the workers who had borne the brunt of the painful reforms, accusing the government of "plundering the people's wealth" through "unlawful" privatization and of neglecting employment, housing, health care, and education.[6]

The government was able to carry out its initial program without the widely predicted mass social unrest. However, the cabinet was divided between reformers who were willing to risk considerable social dissatisfaction for long-term economic gains and those who cautioned that more attention must be paid to meeting the immediate social and economic needs of the populace. While Prime Minister Aleksandër Meksi attempted to strike a balance between the two trends, Berisha, apparently guided more by his vision than by public opinion, continued to push for swift changes, urging the government not to succumb to the temptation of gradualism. In April 1993, in a move that seemed to reinforce Berisha's commitment to drastic reform the cabinet was reshuffled. In the shakeup, Deputy Prime Minister Bashkim Kopliku, who also held the position of minister of internal affairs, came out on top. He was put in charge of economic reform, retaining the position of deputy prime minister. Meanwhile, Rexhep Uka lost his posts of deputy prime minister and minister of agriculture and was named minister for local government. His demotion came as a surprise, since agricultural production had increased significantly. Minister of Tourism Osman Shehu also lost his position, evidently because of his slow progress in this vital sector for the country's economic revival.

Having successfully carried out major stabilization measures, in mid-1993, Albania embarked on the second and much more difficult phase of economic transformation. In July 1993, the International Monetary Fund, expressing public support for the government's determined efforts at stabilization and reform, approved Tiranë's request for a loan in the amount of about $60 million to extend structural reforms to cover the large public enterprises, the banking system, and the establishment of institutions critical to a market economy.[7]

Privatization

Albania carried out an ambitious mass privatization program. The principal objectives of the program were to broaden the country's economic and democratic base by strengthening the middle class and attracting foreign capital to support key industries. By 1996, agriculture, transportation, retail trade, and housing were almost totally privatized. The restructuring and privatization of large state-owned enterprises also had begun, and the government was actively seeking foreign partners for the privatization of sectors of strategic importance, including mines, electric power, and telecommunications. Officials claimed that 70 percent of the nation's wealth had been privatized.

Privatization, however, was controversial and caused considerable resentment. The law passed by the Communist-dominated parliament in 1991 was viewed by many as benefitting the old Communist *nomenklatura*. Before the March 1992 election, more than 20,000 shops and small businesses (by definition, those employing ten or fewer people) in the retail trade, services, handicrafts, and transportation were privatized. Most were sold at nominal fees or distributed free of charge. The majority of those who joined the ranks of Albania's fledgling businessmen in 1991 and 1992 were members of the former *nomenklatura*. They were the best trained to profit from the move to a market economy. Having dominated the economy as managers in the last days of Communist rule, former government officials used their old network of Party bosses, mid-level apparatchiks, and customs officials to acquire substantial wealth. The most profitable enterprises and shops were bought by former Communist officials, leading to widespread perceptions that although the so-called red mafia may have lost political power at the national level, it still held a tight grip over the economy.[8] Trade union officials complained that workers were in no position to take advantage of privatization because of the rapid and spontaneous nature of the process as well as their lack of capital and experience with a market economy. Privatization during this period was also carried out without consideration for former owners, who overwhelmingly supported the Democratic Party.

Berisha's government responded to concerns that the *nomenklatura* was enriching itself under capitalism by temporarily suspending the privatization process in April 1992. In an attempt to placate critics, particularly former landowners who demanded restitution, Berisha also issued a decree on verifying property gained during 1991. But actions taken immediately after the Democratic

Party's victory suggested disagreements within the government about what measures should be taken. Some, such as Blerim Çela, chairman of the State Control Commission, advocated a radical approach, which was also strongly supported by the powerful independent trade unions.[9] Çela suggested outright confiscation of all the property of former Communists before verification.[10] His proposal, however, was rejected as too radical, and the presidential decree on verification of property was not implemented. The authorities evidently were concerned about potential social unrest and adverse economic effects, were the decree fully implemented.

Despite the initial problems during 1992 and 1993, Albania saw the fastest pace of privatization of any of the postcommunist economies in the region. The rapid and almost total privatization of agriculture, which had began in mid-1991, as farmers took matters into their own hands, dismantled the cooperatives, and distributed the land and livestock among themselves, was termed one of the great success stories in Eastern Europe.[11] The government reorganized the land distribution process, and introduced a landtitling system. Most state farms were privatized, their fixed assets and working capital were sold, and the land was distributed to former statefarm employees.[12] By the end of 1996, more than 95 percent of the land had been privatized and 70 percent of it had been legally titled. In July 1995, the parliament passed laws regulating land ownership and its sale and purchase. Foreign investors were allowed to buy land, but had to invest three times the purchase price in the subsequent usage of the land.[13]

Albania also witnessed a rapid and sweeping privatization of small and medium-size enterprises (with fewer than 300 employees, or a book value of less than $500,000).[14] Wholesale and retail trade was almost totally in private hands; so were transportation, construction, and housing. In June 1993, the government adopted a decree "On the Measures for Accelerating the Privatization of Small and Medium Enterprises." A National Agency for Privatization was set up to oversee the process, although decisionmaking was decentralized. Boards composed of 22 or 23 members representing different political parties were established in all the districts and municipalities. The program combined voucher privatization with direct sales of stock to workers, management, and outside investors. According to official statistics, 41 percent of all objects privatized by the end of 1994 were sold to employees, 34 percent to domestic investors, and 25 percent to former owners.[15] In order to encourage participation at the local level, the government agreed that 28 percent of the revenues from privatization would go to the local government of the territory to which the enterprise belonged. Employees of the enterprise being privatized received 20 percent of the revenues.[16] At the end of 1995, there were more than 60,000 private enterprises. About 85 percent of these were small individual businesses, and the rest, joint enterprises. Close to 240,000 people were employed in private enterprises.[17]

Privatization and the Restitution Issue

A key problem that complicated privatization and inhibited foreign investment was the issue of land and property ownership, which remained one of the most lingering legacies of communism. The settlement of the claims of former owners, whose land and property had been confiscated without compensation, proved very difficult and time-consuming. During the 1992 election campaign, Democratic Party officials spoke of compensating former owners of agricultural land but did not promise full compensation or restitution. Immediately after assuming power, they were faced with thousands of claims by former owners who wanted their properties back. Former owners created an organization, the National Association Property With Justice, to lobby for their interests. The association, together with the organization representing former political prisoners, demanded full restitution of nationalized properties and land to their previous owners—an impossible task, given the demographic changes that had taken place during decades of communist rule.[18]

Berisha rejected these demands, arguing that accepting them would create enormous social problems. He insisted that the Democratic government could not accept blame for the actions of the Communist regime or engage in new injustices by attempting to displace thousands of citizens occupying properties that were not theirs before. Nevertheless, the government committed itself to compensating former owners to the extent permitted by the country's resources. In April 1993, parliament, over the Socialist Party's strong objection,[19] approved the Law on Restitution and Compensation, which provided compensation to former land-owners, but not full restitution. Former owners of 15 hectares or less were entitled to full compensation of their land; those entitled to parcels of between 15 and 1,000 hectares would receive compensation by vouchers based on a sliding scale. The law entitled former owners to reclaim unoccupied construction land. Reflecting the conflicting pressures on lawmakers from various interest groups, the law recognized co-ownership between former and new owners in cases when occupied land had been sold by the government to others after January 1991 for the purpose of building retail establishments. Former owners were entitled to rent payments for two years and joint ownership of the establishments thereafter.[20] However, the government made a tactical mistake by mixing up privatization with the restitution issue. It distributed to former owners and people persecuted by the Communist regime for political reasons vouchers with nominal values approximately equaling real leks, instead of relying on the market to determine the value of privatization vouchers.

The Law on Restitution and Compensation caused great confusion and antagonized both the new owners and the dispossessed. The former claimed that the law arbitrarily expropriated their property and violated their right to private property, while the latter termed it "a neocommunist law" designed to perpetuate Communist rule under the banner of democracy. In May 1993, Property With

Justice, which claimed to represent 150,000 families whose property had been confiscated by the Communists, organized a nationwide hunger strike. The strike immediately attracted the support of right-wing forces, with some extremists advocating violent confrontations to force parliament to change the law. When negotiations failed and the situation threatened to spiral out of control, the police used force to end the strike. Although the government showed resolve, the event shook the Albanian political scene and significantly eroded the anticommunist coalition that had ensured the Democratic Party's victory in 1992.

In a landmark decision, in April 1994, the Constitutional Court invalidated the two sections of the law on joint ownership. The court ruled that new owners had derived their right of ownership from the state and not from the former owners.[21] Yet the issue was far from settled, and it acted as a major obstacle to foreign investment. In August 1995, Berisha offered to compensate former owners with state-owned land on the coast.[22] He had hoped to reap significant political benefits from this move, but his proposal received a lukewarm response from former landowners while prompting very harsh criticism from the right and only cautious praise from the left.

The Privatization of Large State-Owned Enterprises

Not surprisingly, the Democratic government encountered tremendous problems in following through on the toughest part of its program—privatizing inefficient, state-owned enterprises, a legacy of Enver Hoxha's centrally planned economy. As in other East European countries, the privatization of large enterprises proved difficult and slow because of a lack of domestic capital, extremely high resource requirements of restructuring, and a lack of foreign investments.

The government was forced to continue to operate large, unprofitable enterprises because of the fear that shutting them down at a time when Albania had yet to attract substantial foreign investments would worsen the economic contraction and lead to a loss of confidence in the government's program. In 1993, some 32 key loss-making enterprises owned by the state were placed under the supervision of the newly created Enterprise Restructuring Agency. The agency's job was to restructure the firms and liquidate those that were unviable. In late 1994, it decided to close down at least ten large enterprises. Others were streamlined, in some cases their workforce being reduced by half.[23] But even the liquidation of a limited number of large enterprises, while a necessary aspect of the reform program, in the shortrun further deepened the industrial contraction. The emerging private sector was too small to absorb even a fraction of the army of unemployed that the liquidation or shutdown of unviable state enterprises caused. In early 1995, the government announced plans for a speedy privatization of large enterprises and utilities. All citizens of eighteen years of age and older were given privatization vouchers, which could be used to purchase shares in the commercial companies created with the privatization of state enterprises or in investment agencies.[24] Unlike some other East European countries, vouchers in Albania were transferable. The voucher distribution promised to expand owner-ship to the population at large; but lack of education and knowledge about vouchers led many to sell them at nominal prices. In a speech at an international conference on foreign investments held in Tiranë in June 1995, Berisha emphasized that Albania was determined to privatize its entire economy, including strategic sectors such as telecommunications, water and energy systems, mines, and banks.[25] Nonetheless, by the end of 1996, only a handful of large enterprises had been turned over to private ownership or transformed into shareholding companies.

Although privatization involved considerable political costs, particularly in swelling the ranks of the unemployed, the swift transfer of assets to private hands resulted in immediate and significant economic benefits for many other people. Still, despite official declarations to the contrary,[26] privatization in some cases was characterized by lack of openness and fairness. The program was often structured and implemented in a way that was obscure and confusing. There were allegations that politically influential Democratic Party members and well-connected special interests benefited disproportionately from privatization at the expense of the general public. While Socialist charges that the Democratic Party was rewarding primarily its supporters were not true, the government could have done better in ensuring fairer rule-making governing privatization and in safeguarding the interests of average citizens and consumers.

Foreign Aid

Once a pariah state, by the end of 1995, postcommunist Albania had become the darling of Western donors, receiving close to a billion dollars in foreign aid. Originally biased toward emergency food aid, the international community has targeted its assistance since 1994 at economic restructuring and sectoral development, economic infrastructure, job creation, development of human re-sources, and encouraging private investment. In addition to international financial institutions and organizations and the European Union, which since 1992 has granted Albania some $650 million in aid, principal bilateral donors have been the United States, Italy, Germany, and Japan. Between 1991 and 1996, the United States granted Tiranë $218 million in economic assistance, and in 1995, it established a $30 million Albanian American Enterprise Fund to promote private sector activity. Italy's grand total of aid was estimated at $420 million, Germany's at $210 million, and Japan's at $75 million.[27]

While donors complained that Albania was unable successfully to absorb foreign assistance, some Albanian economists expressed concern that the government was relying too heavily on foreign experts and not enough on domestic expertise. They claimed that a considerable part of international aid went to pay for the services of foreign consulting firms and contractors, most of whom had no prior experience in Albania. Albanian economists also criticized the International Monetary Fund and the World Bank, some warning that Albania was being used by the international financial institutions as "testing ground" for economic experimentation.[28]

The Albanian economy received a boost in July 1995, with the signing of an agreement with a consortium of forty-one Western banks to resolve the $500 million foreign debt it had inherited from the Communist government. According to this highly favorable agreement, Albania would pay off $100 million immediately, while the remaining $400 million would be cleared during a period of 30 years. In order to help Albania pay off the $100 million, the International Monetary Fund offered $11 million, the World Bank gave $25 million, and the Group of 24 some $43 million.[29] The deal was expected to help Albania obtain new commercial bank loans and attract foreign investments.

Economic Performance

In a speech at an extraordinary conference of the Democratic Party on 5 March 1995, Berisha asserted that his party "had carried out its historic contract" with the Albanian people, rescuing the "Somalia of Europe."[30] Indeed, despite serious difficulties, the results of the adjustment program were immediate and impressive. Albania achieved one of the highest growth rates in Eastern Europe, exceeding targets set by the International Monetary Fund.[31] By the end of 1993, consumption returned to and surpassed the pre-1990 level. The precipitous fall in production was arrested, and the GDP grew by 11 percent. Price liberalization had achieved its goals: Shortages were more or less eliminated—shops were well stocked, with better product quality and more variety than ever before, and output was stimulated. Private markets were thriving in many cities, and some industrial enterprises and factories, shut down for over a year because of lack of raw materials, resumed operation. Construction grew by 31.5 percent, and transportation by 13 percent. After a sharp two-year decline, agricultural production registered a 14.5 percent increase. Industrial output, however, declined by 10 percent, as many state-owned industrial enterprises remained closed or continued to operate far below full capacity. The continued contraction of industrial production caused a major change in the structure of output. While in 1990 industry and mining had accounted for 42 percent of the total GDP, in 1993, its share had fallen to 14 percent. Meanwhile, the share of agriculture increased from 36 percent to 56 percent.[32] Tight monetary policies and control of public expenditures resulted in the stabilization of the lek. The fiscal deficit, which in the first half of 1992 had skyrocketed to a staggering 50 percent of GDP, was reduced to 16 percent. The inflation rate plummeted to 31 percent, down from 237 percent in early 1992. No

East European country had achieved such a startling turnaround in inflation in its first year of reform.

During this period, progress also was made in establishing the legal and regulatory framework for a market economy. The parliament passed a series of laws, including a law instituting a two-tier banking system. In an attempt to increase exports and attract foreign capital, export licensing and controls were eliminated. In November 1993, parliament approved a new Foreign Investments Law, which created a legal framework for foreign investments and provided for compensation for expropriation. Foreign investors were not subject to capital controls, could acquire 100 percent ownership of commercial ventures, and were permitted to repatriate all their profits. In addition, they were granted four-year tax holidays, which could be extended for those who reinvested.[33]

The Albanian economy showed a strong performance in 1994 and 1995, registering GDP growth rates of 7.4 percent and 11 percent, respectively (Table 6.1). Industrial contraction continued in 1994 (deepening by 2 percent), but output picked up by a modest 2 percent in 1995. Agriculture, the driving force behind the country's economic recovery, increased by 6.8 percent in 1994 and 13 percent in 1995. The lek remained stable, inflation dropped to 6 percent, and the trade deficit decreased to 6.5 percent of the GDP in 1995. There was a significant pickup in retail trade, construction, and transportation, with a huge rise in motor vehicles. At the end of 1995, unemployment fell to 195,000, or 13 percent of the

TABLE 6.1 Selected Economic Indicators (Annual Percent Change)

	1991	1992	1993	1994	1995	1996
Real GDP growth	-27.1	-9.7	11.0	7.4	11.0	8.5
Industry	-29.0	0	-10.0	-2.0	2.0	1.0
Agriculture	-20.9	18.0	14.5	6.8	13.0	10.0
Construction	-30.4	5.0	31.5	15.0	15.0	n.a.
Transportation	-29.9	-20.0	13.0	18.0	19.0	n.a.
Inflation	104.0	237.0	31.0	16.0	6.0	16.0
Services	-13.9	5.0	11.0	7.4	14.0	n.a.
Exports fob $ m	82.0	82.0	120.0	141.0	187.0	270.0
Imports fob $ m	314.0	540.0	583.0	601.0	603.0	850.0

Sources: The Economist Intelligence Unit, *Country Report: Bulgaria, Albania*, fourth quarter 1995, p. 32, and fourth quarter 1996, p. 32; *Gazeta Shqiptare*, 20 February 1994, p. 3; International Monetary Fund, *Press Release* (Washington, D.C.), no. 94/65, 21 September 1994, p. 2; *Lajmi i Ditës*, 4 February 1995, p. 5; *Financial Times*, 19 February, 1997; *Albania*, 19 April 1997, p. 5.

able-bodied population. In 1996, the economy grew by 8.5 percent. However, the budget deficit rose to 10 percent of GDP as a result of increased government expenditures related to the parliamentary and local elections, combined with a drop in revenue collection. Inflation increased to 16 percent, compared to 6 percent in 1995.[34]

Continuing Problems

While Albania made significant progress, it still faced immense difficulties in achieving full economic recovery. Major problems included structural imbalances, unacceptably high unemployment, delays in overhauling the financial system, and inadequate transportation and communication infrastructure. Real GDP growth in 1996 was about 25 percent below the 1989 level. Unemployment no doubt remained the most explosive issue and the worst danger to Albania's fledgling democracy. In addition, the economy was characterized by serious growth imbalances. Agriculture, construction, and the service sector were the main driving forces behind economic growth. Despite the increase in agricultural production, it will take years before the agricultural sector can fully recover. The land that belonged to former cooperatives was divided into small private plots. The average size of a farm was only about 1.5 hectares, too small to support most farm families, which tend to be large. Most of the 400,000 newly created family farms lacked capital and agricultural inputs and had limited tools to work the land. In some parts of the country, especially the northeast, arable land is insufficient to support the growing population. Here, new jobs have to be created in order to prevent large-scale depopulation of the region.[35]

Moreover, Albania's economic recovery was also affected by the loss of traditional markets in Eastern Europe and the drastic decline of international prices for copper and other minerals, which in the past were major foreign currency earners for Albania. In addition, economic sanctions imposed by the United Nations against Yugoslavia between 1992 and 1995 had a devastating impact. Officials estimated that the sanctions against Yugoslavia cost Albania between $300 million and $400 million annually.[36]

The prospects for Albania's technologically obsolete industry remain bleak. Privatization of unprofitable large enterprises will be extremely difficult, and given the country's resources and priorities, the cost of a technological overhaul is prohibitive in the mid term. With industry's poor performance and the relatively poor quality of goods being produced, the Albanian market was swamped by imported consumer goods. The gap between imports and exports reached alarming proportions in 1995—20 percent of GDP. In 1996, exports amounted to $270 million, compared to $187 in 1995. During the same period, however, imports grew from $603 million to $850 million.[37] Before 1990, Albania was the world's third largest chromium producer. In the early 1990s, Albania experienced a drastic decline in chromium output as most mines were closed down. The sharp drop in world chromium prices deterred potential foreign investors who could have helped overhaul Albania's chromium mining and processing industry. Huge capital will be needed to upgrade Albania's antiquated technology.

Oil output fell from a record 2.25 million tons in the early 1970s to about 500,000 tons a year in 1996. In an effort to accelerate the pace of oil and gas exploration, in late 1995, Albania offered further concessions to international oil companies for onshore and offshore exploration. Since 1992, international oil companies have invested some $150 million in offshore drilling. Officials were optimistic that with the introduction of modern exploration and production technologies the prospects of the oil and gas sectors would significantly improve. But while output increased, it remained below the level of the late 1980s.

Poor infrastructure, the uncertainty of land tenure arrangements, an undeveloped banking sector, bureaucratic barriers, and instability in the region discouraged foreign investors. By 1996, Albania had attracted less than half a billion dollars. Italy accounted for 53 percent of all foreign investments in Albania; Greece held second place, with 27 percent.[38] Although the Albanian investment law was described as one of the most liberal in the region, hopes for massive foreign investments did not materialize. Even in tourism, one of the most attractive targets, investments remained modest. Albania appealed for international assistance to improve its infrastructure, which was simply inadequate to sustain the country's rapidly growing economic activity. The World Bank, the European Bank for Reconstruction and Development, the European Union, and individual Western donors offered to finance numerous infrastructure projects. In June 1995, Albania secured a pledge from the Group of 24 for $1.3 billion for infrastructure investments. The three-year public investment plan is directed toward modernizing Albania's energy, agriculture, and telecommunications sectors; improving water supplies; upgrading the transport system; and rehabilitating health and education services.[39] In October 1995, the European Union granted Albania $275.6 million for 1996 to 1999 under its PHARE aid program. About $80 million are to be used for direct investment in production and infrastructure, and $93.6 to improve roads and ports linking Albania with Greece and Italy. The rest of the grant will be used primarily to promote human and natural resources.[40] However, Albania estimates that several billion dollars would be required to fully modernize its roads, airports, and port facilities.

While Albania received international assistance to modernize its tax administration, improve the government's ability to sustain and improve revenue collection, and support the development of a private banking system,[41] it encountered serious difficulties in establishing a modern financial system. The economy remained highly dependent on external financial factors. These included continued foreign assistance, foreign investment, and remittances from Albanian refugees in Greece. Foreign aid was likely to decrease, and foreign investments had never been substantial. Remittances from refugees, which in 1995 reportedly amounted to 25 percent of the GDP,[42] were likely to decrease gradually. However, the situation of Albanian workers in Greece was dependent on the overall political relations between Tiranë and Athens. Any deterioration in bilateral ties, as during 1994 when Athens deported more than 70,000 Albanians to protest the trial of five ethnic Greeks on espionage charges, would be reflected immediately in the economy. Large-scale expulsions of Albanian workers from Greece, or less likely from other Western countries, would have an immediate, devastating impact on the Albanian economy.

The lack of capable administrators at the top levels of the government bureaucracy was also a serious drawback. The Communists had destroyed the small class of private entrepreneurs that existed when they took power, and prevented the emergence of a managerial class. Thus, with the collapse of central planning in 1991, Albania lacked qualified decisionmakers who could supervise the transition to a market economy. Although young, democratically oriented technocrats were placed in senior positions and a flock of new civil servants joined the bureaucracy, competence was scarce. In addition, the bureaucracy was rife with procommunist apparatchiks, many of whom positioned themselves in opposition to market reforms.

At times, the decisionmaking process seemed seriously flawed, with unacceptable delays in reaching important decisions. With few exceptions, top economic decisionmakers seemed to lack a genuine commitment to implementing the reform program. Berisha, the moving force behind the reform program, appeared to have surrounded himself with advisers whose economic expertise was questionable at best. In his handling of major economic issues and crises, he sometimes appeared ham-handed and inconsistent, which raised questions regarding the quality of information and advice the president was receiving. Top decisionmakers also showed a degree of confusion regarding the role of the state in the new economic system. Having just emerged from a system in which the state made all the decisions, some officials went to the other extreme, arguing that the government should play no role in a market economy. The result was a runaway economy regulated more by rapacious groups than by the government.

Corruption and Crime

Although Albania's macroeconomic stabilization program was successful, the relatively slow improvements in employment, housing, education, and wages injected a large dose of skepticism into Albanians who were anxious to see the market economy bear immediate and tangible results. Albanians had yet to see major improvements in roads, sewers, telephones, and other modern amenities. At the same time, the government began to be overwhelmed by waves of alleged wrongdoing and impropriety. From civil servants who demanded small bribes to big businessmen who payed off cabinet ministers for major favors, corruption became a growth industry. Many officials and politicians who were role models in 1992 fell victim to greed and the mania for quick profits, siphoning off funds marked for economic development. This was most dramatically illustrated by the massive smuggling of oil and other strategic items from Albania to Yugoslavia in violation of United Nations sanctions from 1992 to 1995. While the government denied involvement, it was clear that without the connivance of highly placed officials, the smuggling could not have continued so successfully for such a long period.

Corruption had been present under communism, too, but it was more circumscribed and more secretive. Too many high-level postcommunist officials, who saw public office as an opportunity to enrich themselves, amassed great wealth from illegal sources. The post-1992 elite seemed to be enjoying privileges similar to those of their Communist predecessors. Lack of public accountability for political and economic transactions threatened to discredit both the political and the business establishments, as many ordinary citizens came to believe that everything was for sale. The government claimed that the struggle against corruption was at the top of its agenda; yet government anticorruption efforts were halfhearted at best.[43] With few exceptions, government officials escaped criminal prosecution for their nefarious activities. A decree issued in December 1995 requiring political office bearers and senior public servants to disclose their assets did little to increase the public's trust in government.

Crime was another serious menace to Albania's democratic and economic development. In February 1996, a car bomb exploded outside a supermarket in the center of Tiranë, killing four people and wounding thirty others.[44] In summer 1996, several senior security officials were assassinated, creating a climate of fear and insecurity throughout the country. In October 1996, Minister of Internal Affairs Halit Shamata announced that a terrorist group calling itself "Revenge for Justice" had been uncovered. Shamata said the organization was responsible for the carbombing of a supermarket in Tiranë in February and for the killing of the General Director of Albanian prisons, Bujar Kaloshi, in July 1996. The group, which was blamed also for other political assassinations, bank robberies, and kidnaping, was headed by Leart Shyti, son of senior Sigurimi official and former Deputy Minister of Internal Affairs Hajredin Shyti, who had been convicted of the 2 April 1991 killings of Democratic Party activists in Shkodër.[45]

With an increase in street crimes such as robberies, mugging, rapes, prostitution, and smuggling, organized crime's tentacles spread deep into society. Many police and government officials were said to be on the payroll of criminal organizations. In addition to protection and enforcement rackets, extortion, money laundering, and drug trafficking, the forces of organized crime succeeded in penetrating and taking over legitimate private businesses through alliances with corrupt government officials. Many small businesses, such as cafes and stores, were reportedly owned by criminal groups involved in drug trafficking, money laundering, and smuggling.[46] Albania also witnessed the revival of blood feuds, caused primarily by disputes over property and old quarrels. Between 1992 and 1994, the number of blood feuds-related murders increased fourfold. In 1992, about 40 percent of those committing these crimes were between the ages 18 and 25. About 95 percent had only eight years or less of formal education.[47]

The Rise of Pyramid Schemes

As in other East European countries and Russia, the fall of communism and the demise of the centrally planned economy in Albania led to the rise of a number of pyramid schemes that eventually robbed thousands of citizens of their life savings. But in contrast to bogus investment plans in other East European countries, Albania's pyramid schemes operated for a significantly longer period and involved a substantially greater number of inhabitants. Moreover, they were tolerated, and to an extent, promoted by the government, which saw them as free enterprise.

Get-rich-quick schemes sprang up in 1991. Taking advantage of the political turmoil and power vacuum that characterized the first phase of transition from Communism to pluralism, dubious businessmen set up several fraudulent pyramid schemes, primarily in Tiranë. Initially these schemes made little headway because the economy had practically collapsed and the population lived in extreme poverty. But as Albania embarked on the road to recovery, fraudulent companies, promising impossibly high returns, increasingly gained ground.

Several factors contributed to the rise of get-rich-quick schemes. Having emerged from close to half a century of a rigidly centralized economic system that had outlawed all private property, Albanians at all levels displayed a remarkably poor understanding of how a market economy works and an unusual lack of knowledge about investing and financial institutions. Second, the government delayed reforming the banking system; no private banks were permitted to be established. On the other hand, there was little trust in state banks. Lack of an efficient banking system led many Albanians to invest their savings in the pyramids. Third, the investment schemes operated with at least tacit government approval and enjoyed support across the political spectrum, including among officials of the Socialist Party, the country's largest opposition force. Another factor that may have contributed to the longevity of pyramid schemes in Albania was the possibility of money laundering. The Italian mafia and other foreign crime rings, working closely with domestic groups, may have used the pyramid schemes to launder profits from drug and arms trafficking and refugee smuggling. According to some sources, organized crime groups may have pumped hundreds of millions of dollars into the unregulated schemes.[48]

Between 1991 and 1996, there were at least nine companies that were suspected of operating as pyramid schemes, the most important being Vefa Holding, Gjalica, Xhaferri, Populli, Kamberi, and Sudja. Some of these companies strongly denied involvement in pyramid schemes, maintaining that they were corporate holdings. Founded in 1991 by Vehbi Alimuçaj, Vefa Holding became Albania's largest company. It acquired numerous holdings all over the country, including supermarkets, food processing plants, tourist centers, a ferry line, and a mine. Gjallica, headquartered in Vlorë and operating mainly in the south and in the northeastern city of Kukës, was involved in tourist development, hotels, and gas stations. Other companies, such as Kamberi, Cenaj, and Silva, also claimed to have legitimate businesses. Xhaferri and Populli, on the other hand, portrayed themselves as charitable organizations.

The government claimed that it had no role to play in regulating such companies, insisting that it was a matter of citizens lending and borrowing among themselves. Not only did the government fail to warn citizens of the dangers of investing in unregulated pyramid companies, but it provided its own stamp of approval by maintaining close links with some of the companies. The collapse of pyramid schemes in early 1997, discussed in Chapter 9, wiped out the savings of more than half a million Albanians, eroded the significant economic progress made since 1992, and seriously undermined Albania's political stability.

Social Developments

Albania's postcommunist leadership was confronted with daunting challenges in managing the human dimension of the transition from a centrally planned economy that had guaranteed cradle-to-grave welfare benefits to a market economy with low wages in the public sector but prices comparable to those on the world market. As a 1995 United Nations report underscores, Albanians remained "the poorest Europeans," both in terms of basic statistics related to production levels, such as GNP and per capita income, and in terms of access to adequate health services, education, and public services.[49] In 1996, Albania's per capita income was roughly $800, and wages in the public sector averaged $80 dollars a month.

Safety Net

The breathtaking pace of political and economic reforms that Albania witnessed after 1992 led to far-reaching social transformations. The postcommunist government, operating in an environment of scarce resources, went to great lengths to address the plight of the population and to mitigate the impact of the transition for the thousands of Albanians in poverty or near poverty. Even Berisha's most outspoken critics have acknowledged the significant improvements achieved between 1992 and 1996. Nevertheless, many Albanians continued to face considerable social and economic deprivation, and much remained to be done to ensure a satisfactory quality of life for the population at large.

The high costs of social security for the groups most affected by austerity measures seriously strained the government's resources. But foreign aid and substantial foreign exchange transfers by workers abroad helped mitigate the situation. Remittances from refugees abroad in cash, clothing, medicines, and household appliances were estimated at close to one billion dollars a year.

In 1996, Albania's working-age population was estimated at about 1.7 million, but only 1.54 million were actively employed. The postcommunist period witnessed a remarkable change in the structure of employment, with a dramatic shift of labor from industry to services and agriculture. At the end of 1996, an estimated 750,000 people worked in the private agricultural sector, 269,000 in the state sector, and about 129,000 in the private nonfarming sector.[50] The private sector accounted for more than 70 percent of the labor force, 65 percent of them in agriculture. In 1989, some 62 percent of the labor force had worked in the state sector, and 38 percent in the cooperative sector.

In early 1997, officials claimed that some 162,000, or about 10.7 percent of the workforce, were registered as unemployed, down from 394,000, or 27 percent, in 1992. Some 38,000 received unemployment insurance.[51] Another 20,000 unemployed received benefits from state-owned enterprises. More than 100,000 families were receiving economic assistance from the state. In addition, the rapidly growing number of retired people presented a serious problem to the government. The number of retired people entirely dependent on the state for income had increased from 371,652 in 1991 to 474,000 in 1995.[52]

The government also had to deal with the situation of thousands of former political prisoners and their families. It adopted an affirmative action policy, insisting that former political prisoners and their families deserved special treatment to help them overcome the lingering effects of Communist persecution. Former political prisoners were granted approximately $1,200 for each year spent in prison. In addition, they were given preference in privatization and in hiring for government jobs, education, and housing.[53] In the main urban centers, such as Tiranë, Vlorë, Durrës, and Shkodër, apartment blocks were constructed specifically to house former political prisoners. These measures became a source of intense controversy. The disadvantaged group of former prisoners complained that the government was doing too little, while others, particularly from the left of the political spectrum, cried reverse discrimination, arguing that the use of preferences contradicted the constitution's guarantee of equal protection under the law.

Regional Disparities

The economic changes since 1992 had a regional impact, further widening regional disparities that had manifested themselves in the communist period. The central and southern parts of the country fared much better than the mountainous regions. The majority of new businesses were concentrated in the country's main population centers, while in the northeastern and north-central regions, private sector activities remained limited. Some 25 percent of Albania's 60,000 private enterprises in 1994 were based in Tiranë; 38 percent operated in the districts of Durrës, Elbasan, Fier, Korçë, Shkodër, and Vlorë; the remaining 37 percent were scattered throughout the rest of the country.[54] Moreover, most Albanian workers in Greece, Italy, and other Western countries were from the eastern coastal, eastern central, and southern border regions. Emigration to the West from the remote, northern areas was negligible.[55] Thus, Albania's mountainous, mineral-rich regions were much more vulnerable to economic crisis than were the lowlands, and the resulting regional income disparities sharply increased. With crumbling mining and metallurgic plants, and given the relative scarcity of farmland for productive agriculture, the north-central and northwestern districts experienced massive unemployment. In some regions, the unemployment rate was greater than 50 percent. Employment prospects remained grim, as private firms in these regions were being created very slowly and foreign investments were lacking.

Lack of economic opportunities caused large-scale migrations from the countryside. Since the early 1990s, an estimated 65,000 rural families have moved into urban areas.[56] The influx from the countryside, especially in Tiranë, Shkodër, and Durrës, increased pressure on urban infrastructures, including transportation, communications, sanitation, and housing. Newcomers also were blamed for increased social disorder in the cities. The pressures of migration are unlikely to lessen in the near future. If Albania fails to generate new jobs by expanding the private sector more rapidly, developing tourism, and reviving the mining industry, it risks a massive depopulation of its northeastern regions.

As a result of continued economic problems and competition for scarce resources, tensions between the north and the south have increased. Some northerners, insisting that the Communist regime had pursued a policy of "internal colonialism" against the north,[57] demanded greater allocation of resources for the development of the north. Southerners, on the other side, criticized Berisha for his tacit approval of the migration of thousands of northerners, who took over land in areas surrounding Tiranë and in the coastal regions.

The Communist imposition of a national standard language, based primarily on the southern dialect, also came under attack in the north. But efforts by a group of linguists in Shkodër to revisit the issue of a standard language met with lukewarm support even among northern intellectuals. While some experts continued to denounce the way the standard language was imposed by the Hoxha regime, there appeared to be widespread agreement that the Albanians could not go back on this issue.[58]

Although political leaders in general avoided inflammatory rhetoric on the north-south issue, some Socialists and a part of the left-oriented press attempted to fan the tensions, evidently hoping to exploit the resentment of some southerners against Berisha, a northerner. Soon after Berisha assumed the office of president, the Socialists launched a campaign against him, accusing the president of appointing too many northerners in high positions. In a highly polemical article, the former speaker of parliament, Socialist Party Deputy Kastriot Islami, suggested that the campaign of purging Communists from the state bureaucracy was being directed primarily against southerners.[59] The Democrats vehemently criticized Islami, accusing him of fanning regional differences.[60] A north-south political division of Albania was discernable, with more support for the Democratic Party in the north and a pro-Socialist belt in the south; but at this time political differences between urban and rural areas appeared to be stronger than those separating north and south.

The possibility of Kosova's eventual union with Albania also seems to have created apprehension in some parts of the country. The addition of Albanians from Kosova would significantly tip the balance in favor of the north. Some expressed concern that because of the woeful state of Albania's economy, the Kosovars could easily "take over" Albania. Berisha's decision in 1992 to grant dual citizenship to all Albanians abroad, including those in the former Yugoslavia, was criticized by some as making indigenous Albanians second-class citizens in their own country.

Nevertheless, mainstream Albanian political forces acted with discretion in preventing the simmering Geg-Tosk resentment from erupting into the open. Although the history of relations between Gegs and Tosks is not fraught with conflict, any attempt by demagogues or extreme forces to exploit the issue in furthering their political agendas could have serious repercussions for Albania's national unity.

Religious Revival

After decades of savage Communist attempts to stamp out religion, Albania has witnessed a remarkable religious revival. Old churches and mosques were renovated, and new ones constructed. Although lacking even basic religious awareness as a result of atheist propaganda, many young Albanians turned to religion for spiritual peace at a time of economic hardship and social upheaval. However, the process was accompanied by latent tensions in certain parts of the country, misguided attempts by some forces to use religion to further their political interests, and a heated debate about the historical role of religion in multi-confessional Albania.

For centuries, Albania served as a battleground for the Roman Catholic Church, the Orthodox Church, and Islam. The great religious schism of 1054 resulted in the split of Albania into a Catholic north and an Orthodox south. Islam was introduced following Albania's conquest by Turks in the fourteenth century. By the end of the seventeenth century, the majority of the population had converted to Islam. At the end of World War II, some 70 percent of Albania's population was Muslim; 20 percent, Orthodox; and 10 percent, Roman Catholic.[61] Muslims are spread all over the country; the Catholics inhabit the northern districts, and across the border, areas in Montenegro and Kosova; and the Orthodox live mainly in the southern districts of Gjirokastër, Korçë, Berat, and Vlorë. Unlike neighboring Serbia and Greece, where a single, powerful church historically has helped foster national unity, Albania's three main religions at times tended to divide the country, each claiming to represent the germ of true Albanian identity. Nevertheless, Albanians traditionally have displayed a high degree of religious tolerance.

Enver Hoxha pursued a fierce campaign against religion, confiscating religious properties and imprisoning or executing many clerics. In 1967, the Communist regime proclaimed Albania the world's first atheist state, closed all houses of worship, and outlawed public religious practices. With freedom of religion denied by Hoxha's regime, Albanians in the West and Kosova kept their religious beliefs alive. In Boston, the Albanian Orthodox Church in America, founded by the Harvard-educated archbishop and former Albanian Prime Minister Bishop Fan S. Noli, served as both a religious and a national institution, bringing together the Albanian community. Under the leadership of Rev. Arthur E. Liolin, the Albanian Orthodox Archdiocese in America became an important link in the life of Albanian Orthodoxy. During the 1960s and the 1970s, Albanians built churches, mosques, and *tekkes* in New York, New Jersey, Connecticut, Illinois, and Michigan. Through their many publications and gatherings, Albanian American religious institutions attempted to draw attention to the violations of religious rights by the Communist regime. The Albanian Catholic Information Center in San Francisco, led by the late Gjon Sinishta, spearheaded Albanian American efforts to publicize the lack of religious rights in Albania. With its annual *Albanian Catholic Bulletin*, the center documented the atrocities perpetrated against believers, especially the clergy, in Albania.[62] The first Albanian Catholic Church in the United States was established in the late 1970s in the Bronx, New York, headed by Monsg. Zef Oroshi, a distinguished clergyman who had translated the New Testament into Albanian.[63] His successor, Rev. Zef Mirdita, returned to Albania in April 1993 and was consecrated by Pope John Paul II as the Archbishop of Tiranë and Durrës.[64] The Albanian Catholic community in Michigan, led by Rev. Prenk Ndrevashaj and Rev. Anton Kqira, was also very active.

The most important Albanian Islamic centers in the United States are to be found in New York and Michigan. Under the leadership of Sali Myftiu and Imam

Isa Hoxha, the Albanian Muslim community in the late 1960s built a mosque in New York City. The center put out an annual publication, entitled *Përpjekja Jonë* (Our Effort).The spiritual leader of Albanian Muslims in Michigan is Imam Vehbi Ismaili, a noted theologian whose works have been translated into several languages. Michigan is also the seat of the Albanian Bektashi Tekke, established by the late Baba Rexhep.

Albanians in other countries, although less effective and not as well organized as Albanian Americans, also played an important role. Albanians in Italy were influential in convincing the Vatican and the Italian government to maintain the spotlight on Hoxha's horrendous violations of human rights. Foreign radio broadcasts in Albanian, particularly by the Voice of America and Radio Vatican, kept the faith alive among many listeners in Albania, reminding them that the outside world was sympathetic to their plight. In addition, Radio Vatican continued to broadcast basic religious instruction at a time when the clergy in Albania was prohibited from performing religious rites.

Under Ramiz Alia, the antireligious campaign continued but was significantly less intense than during his predecessor's era. In August 1989, in the most significant indication of a possible change in the regime's stance toward religion, Mother Teresa, the Albanian-born nun and winner of the Nobel Prize, was permitted to visit Tiranë. In May 1990, the government lifted a ban on religious propaganda, but believers were unable publicly to resume practice of their religions until 4 November 1990. On that day, thousands of Catholics and Muslims gathered in Shkodër to hear Rev. Simon Jubani give the first public mass since 1967. A recording of the 4 November 1990 mass was smuggled and excerpts, including Rev. Jubani's dramatic speech, were broadcast to Albania by the Voice of America's Albanian Service.[65]

The communist repression of religion had a devastating impact on institutionalized religion. Most clerics were executed or perished in prisons or labor camps, and many churches and mosques were destroyed. With the demise of communism, Albanian Muslims abroad and Islamic countries took immediate steps to help resurrect Islam in Albania. Albanian Catholic communities abroad and in Kosova as well as the Vatican, made similar efforts to help the Catholic Church. In November 1994, Pope John Paul II named the first Albanian cardinal. The 84-year-old Cardinal Mikel Koliqi had spent 21 years in Communist prisons and 23 years in internal exile.[66] The Albanian Orthodox Church, however, was in a more precarious position as assistance was forthcoming only from Greece, and the latter's political motives were suspect. Disagreements over the status of the church had traditionally been a point of contention between Albanians and Greeks. Viewing church affiliation as a determinant of nationality, Athens traditionally had tended to consider all Albanian Orthodox believers ethnic Greeks—a position interpreted by the Albanians as evidence of Greek irredentist claims to the southern parts of their country.

The Albanian Orthodox Church declared its independence in 1922 and was recognized by the Ecumenical Patriarchate in 1937.[67] The church statutes called for the primate to be "of Albanian nationality and citizenship." The demise of communism found the Albanian Orthodox Church leaderless—there were no Albanians in or outside the country with the level of theological education necessary for church leadership. During a meeting between Foreign Minister Muhamet Kapllani and his Greek counterpart in July 1991, in Korfu, Albania accepted Greece's proposal that a representative of the Greek Patriarchate go to Albania to assist in the revival of the Albanian Orthodox Church.[68] In June 1992, the Ecumenical Patriarchate of Constantinople, the ancient seat of Orthodox Christian authority in Istanbul, Turkey, appointed Metropolitan Anastasios Yannoulatos, a Greek national, leader of the Albanian Orthodox Church.[69] Although the appointment was considered temporary, intended to last only until an Albanian national was found eligible to become the church's primate, the enthronement of Metropolitan Yannoulatos was marked by controversy. Ever since, Albanian and Greek clerics have been fighting an ecclesiastical war over who will lead Albania's Orthodox Church. Clerics in Elbasan and Berat refused to recognize Metropolitan Yannoulatos as church leader. Many Albanians viewed the appointment as a ploy by the Greeks to control the Albanian Orthodox Church. A group of Albanian Orthodox intellectuals and youths protested the appointment, insisting that it violated the statutes of the Albanian church.[70] The appointment also was protested by the Albanian Orthodox community in the United States.[71] In the view of many Albanians, the Orthodox Church had lost its independence and had fallen under Greek influence. Some critics charged that Metropolitan Yannoulatos was using his position to further Greek national interests rather than those of the Albanian church. The fight for Albania's Orthodoxy posed complications not only for the Albanian Church but also for Tiranë-Athens relations. By approving Metropolitan Anastasios Yannoulatos's appointment, the Albanian government seemed to have given Greece a powerful advantage.

In the aftermath of the fall of communism, Albania was invaded by foreign missionaries who considered the country ripe for conversion to what many Albanians viewed as alien creeds. While foreign missionaries operated freely, there were some complaints that they were taking advantage of Albania's vulnerabilities and stirring up religious intolerance.[72] However, Albania generally was praised as a example of harmony among different religions. The principle of the separation of church and state was firmly established and there was no evidence to suggest that religious affiliation played a role in official appointments, employment, or educational opportunities, although Albanian media occasionally reported some religious tensions. Many Catholics complained that under Hoxha's rule they suffered double oppression: from Communists and from Muslims. Non-Muslims criticized the construction of mosques with assistance from the Islamic world and Albania's membership in 1992 in the Organization of Islamic Countries, arguing that this could open the door to Islamic fundamentalism.

Some Albanian intellectuals engaged in polemics about the role of religion, arguing, oddly, in a vein similar to that pursued by Hoxha in justifying the outlawing of religion, that multiconfesionalism had undermined Albania's national union. Kiço Blushi claimed that Albanians were never able to present a unified position on the national question because of their religious differences.[73] In a spirited critique of Blushi's argument, Abdi Baleta argued that Albanians had survived foreign attempts at assimilation thanks to their multiconfesionalism.[74] Although there was no evidence that increasing links with the Muslim world were giving rise to Islamic fundamentalism,[75] some, among them surprisingly, the prominent exiled writer Ismail Kadare,[76] expressed concern that the fact that the majority of Albanians were Muslims was likely to complicate Albania's efforts to achieve full integration in the European community of nations, implying that conversions to Christianity would aid those efforts. In what was widely seen as an irresponsible action that could undermine the nation's religious harmony, the newspaper of the leftist Democratic Alliance published an article in August 1995 calling on Muslim Albanians to convert to Christianity.[77]

While most observers generally continued to use the pre-World War II figures with regard to the current religious composition of the Albanian population, some took exception, arguing that as a result of the Communist regime's antireligious policies a large percentage of Albanians were now atheist. Neshat Tozaj called for a new census to determine the population's true religious composition.[78] In a long-winded and polemical response, Baleta said that with his "anti-Islamic" stand, Tozaj, as well as Kadare, Blushi, and the Albanian Ambassador to France Besnik Mustafaj, who publicly criticized Albania's membership in the Organization of Islamic Countries, were inciting discord among religious communities and between Albania's north and south. After a historical review of the tolerance that Albania's Muslims and Christians displayed toward each other, Baleta accused Tozaj, former Communists, and the leftist press of having fallen under the influence of Serbia and Greece, which for political reasons were spreading the fear of Islamic fundamentalism in Albania. He suggested that Europe could learn a lot from Albania, which he characterized as a model of religious harmony and tolerance.[79] A similar stand was taken by Hysen Çobani, who expressed concern about the politicization of religion and denounced those who were advocating the conversion of Muslims.[80] Others accused former Communists and leftist forces of using religion for political motives, with potentially pernicious consequences.[81]

Albania's Muslims have a long secular tradition, and while religion remained a potential source of conflict, there was no evidence of Islamic fundamentalism. Indeed, as Pope John Paul II remarked during his April 1993 visit, Albania remained a model of religious coexistence.[82]

Health Care and Education

The postcommunist civil unrest and economic difficulties, combined with Albania's long isolation, lack of contact with foreign experts, and slow introduction of new technologies, had a devastating impact on the nation's public health services. In 1991-1992, the seriously debilitated physical infrastructure of hospitals and clinics, the collapse of the domestic pharmaceutical industry, and the widespread lack of basic medicines and medical supplies brought the health system to the brink of collapse. In many parts of the country, particularly rural areas, people did not even have access to the most rudimentary preventive health services.[83] Infectious diseases like cholera, dysentery, diphtheria, and measles, which had largely been conquered in the past, made a comeback as a result of poor hygiene, poverty, and a crumbling infrastructure of public sanitation. Liver disease, hepatitis, and intestinal illnesses such as dysentery spread, largely because of water pollution and poor maintenance of water purification systems. Severe shortages of drugs and essential medical supplies restricted the capacity of hospitals and clinics to care for newborn infants and older people with chronic diseases.

Western aid was tailored to provide essential medical supplies, including enough vaccines to inoculate against infectious childhood diseases. The World Bank granted Albania a $12.4 million credit in 1994 to assist in building an institutional capacity for planning and management of health services, mainly by rehabilitating and streamlining the existing network of public health facilities.[84] By 1995, with international assistance, health services had been restructured, and many hospitals either renovated or closed down. With the privatization of pharmacies, the availability of drugs also improved significantly. Nevertheless, most Albanians continued to lack adequate health care services.

The Communist regime had devoted considerable attention to the cultural and educational development of the country. In 1945, about 80 percent of the population was reportedly illiterate; by the end of the 1980s, the authorities claimed illiteracy had practically been eliminated. The rapid expansion of educational and occupational opportunities, especially for previously unprivileged sectors of the society, raised the cultural level of the population. The Communist government built an impressive network of professional and vocational schools. By the mid-1980s, more than 740,000 Albanians, out of a total population of three million, attended school at all levels, with a teaching staff of more than 40,000. The University of Tiranë, established in 1957, had an enrollment of 12,500 students. However, as was the case with the economy, education was rigidly centralized, with the emphasis on vocational education and the training of technicians and skilled workers.

The Communists conducted a well-coordinated process of political socialization designed to instill Marxist-Leninist attitudes in the populace. To this end, Albanians were subjected to a relentless propaganda campaign, at times with violent overtones. Albania's "new socialist man" was expected to acquire appropriate communist traits, morality, and atheistic ideas, as well as to be free of any remnants of past, "bourgeois" culture. By the end of the 1960s, military training had become a part of the entire school system, and students, together with their teachers, were required to engage in manual work. Education and social advancement were strictly controlled, and those individuals who did not have a "good" biography could not pursue studies beyond high school or climb the social ladder. The effects of the government's merciless persecution of "class enemies" will be felt for years if not decades to come.

One of the victims of the political upheaval that accompanied the demise of Communism was the cultural and educational development of the country. To make matters worse, most of the schools in the countryside were literally destroyed during 1991-1992. Enrollment at all levels declined significantly as large numbers of Albanian youths fled the country or were forced to work to help their families. According to the United Nations Development Program, secondary school enrollment declined in 1992 to 45 percent of the relevant group, and in 1993-1994, to 34.7 percent. Similar losses were also registered at the primary level. The quality of higher education declined, as institutions of higher learning were beset by financial problems and loss of personal incomes. Thousands of teachers emigrated abroad or switched to other jobs. Between 1991 and 1995, at the University of Tiranë alone, 297 professors and instructors left the system.[85]

As part of its program, the Democratic government took measures to depoliticize the educational system, developing a new, nonideological curriculum. The university system was reorganized, and in addition to the University of Tiranë, new universities were established in Shkodër, Elbasan, Vlorë, Gjirokastër, and Korçë. However, Albania's domestic economic and political problems limited the government's ability to address the country's educational crisis. From 1992 to 1994, funds allocated for education amounted to less than 4 percent of the country's GDP. Clearly, without outside assistance, Albania will not be able to make a large contribution to solving its educational problems in the nearterm.

Not surprisingly, the government turned to foreign donors for assistance in rehabilitating school facilities. In August 1994, the Soros Foundation granted Albania $9 million to assist in the rejuvenation of primary and secondary education. The project focused on bringing the level of Albanian education up to Western standards. Experts estimate that as much as $200 million is needed for the full rehabilitation of the country's educational system.[86] Intellectuals were among the groups most adversely affected by the transition. Although they may not have had a passionate attachment to communism, the intellectuals were coopted as its strongest public supporters, and as a result enjoyed a privileged social position. The democratization process and the transition to a market economy left many intellectuals behind. Many lost their status and self-identity, as few could become entrepreneurs. Politically, they split into camps and factions, making their influence on public policy insignificant. Feeling abandoned by the state, some intellectuals became increasingly cynical about the current situation and the future of the country. This was met with a sharp response from progovernment forces. Writer Lazër Stani, who in 1995 became chief editor of *Rilindja Demokratike*, challenged intellectuals not to stay on the sidelines but to make their contribution to building a new society. He strongly denounced leftist intellectuals who used every opportunity to belittle the country's post-1992 achievements, accusing them of being "servants" of the old regime. Stani added that such people had no moral right to preach democracy now to the rest of the nation.[87] Lutfi Dervishi, a young journalist, denounced what he called the intellectuals' misguided "rebellion" against the postcommunist government: "What is this delayed 'rebellion' of some intellectuals? There was a time when we desperately needed rebels and dissidents against the [Communist] regime and none were to be found. Now, when this government needs support from all corners, particularly from the intellectuals, they become antigovernment, original. Now that they should be speaking out, because they are truly free, they keep silent, and when they open their mouths, they say: 'Don't bother us! We are intellectuals.'"[88] Nonetheless, the prominent poet Bardhyl Londo, a supporter of Berisha's government, urged the authorities to pay greater attention to the intellectuals and to create an environment in which the latter could play a greater role in supporting the further democratization of Albanian society.[89]

Changing Gender Roles

Before World War II, women in Albania had the status of second-class citizens and were subjected to social and economic discrimination.[90] Hoxha's regime placed great emphasis on improving the status of women.[91] Overtly discriminatory practices were eliminated, and the rights of working women were promoted through special legislation, which guaranteed them the right to a job, social security, health care, and education. In 1990, women accounted for 47 percent of the work force, 30 percent of Communist Party members, 30.6 percent of elected party officials, 30 percent of members of parliament, 40.7 percent of members of people's councils, and 30 percent of judges.[92] Although the equality of the sexes was enshrined as official doctrine, a gap remained between the regime's official position of ensuring equality and the actual status of women. Female representation among the government and managerial elites remained low. Working women bore more than an equal burden of stress and complained that they continued to have more than an equal share of work that had to be done at home. Moreover, despite the significant increase in women's educational qualifications, the regime was not successful in completely eliminating gender-related differences in employment and education. Most women held unskilled manual jobs. Notwithstanding the fact that women had joined the cabinet and even the party Politburo thanks to a quota system, their influence on decisionmaking was minimal.

Perhaps no segment of the Albanian population was more adversely affected by the postcommunist transition than women. Since 1990, the gap between women and men has widened. More than half of the officially registered unemployed in 1996 were women, and the salaries of those who were working, usually in professions such as medicine and teaching, were very low, in some instances below the subsistence level. Moreover, women's representation in the cabinet, parliament, local government, nongovernmental organizations, and political parties and groups was extremely low. Before the 1996 elections, there were only eight women in parliament, seven of them representing the ruling Democratic Party and the other the Socialist Party. Suzana Panariti, who in August 1995 replaced Albert Brojka as minister of industry, transportation, and trade, had the distinction of being the only woman in the cabinet. Of the twelve members of the Court of Cassation, two were women; and the nine-member Constitutional Court had only one woman. With so few females in the political and social limelight, many women feared they would remain voiceless.

Nevertheless, Albanian politicians and media were beginning to show greater awareness of the problems associated with the increase in gender inequality after the demise of communism. Several women's organizations, under the aegis of various broader political and social entities, intensified their efforts to raise the profile of women's issues. Nonetheless, Albania lacked a genuine feminist movement with a clearly defined program aimed at the political empowerment of women.[93] Various political parties, following the lead of the Democrats, launched a concerted campaign to increase women's representation within their ranks. Still, more attention needed to be devoted to women's legal status, health, and access to financial services and credit.

Toward a Civil Society

In contrast to former communist countries in Eastern Europe that experienced the emergence of special interest groups as early as the 1970s, Albania saw no autonomous group activity until the end of the communist monopoly on political power, in December 1990. The intermediary realm between state and society was nonexistent previously, as the ruling Communist Party controlled every aspect of life. This legacy of the old regime, combined with the fact that even before the Communist takeover Albania lacked civic traditions and independent social movements and associations, posed formidable barriers to the construction of a free and lively civil society, which is considered an important element in the consolidation of democracy.

Nevertheless, significant political changes and economic transformation—particularly privatization and the gradual emergence of a prosperous middle class capable of materially supporting independent political organization—prompted the growth of intermediary, civil-societal organizations and groups. Postcommunist Albania witnessed the rise of myriad professional associations, societies, cultural organizations, clubs, women's organizations, unions, business organizations, environmental groups, and other voluntary groups openly competing in the public realm.[94] They defined their purpose as civic action to advance public interest by applying pressure on state institutions, influencing policy processes, stimulating political participation, and enhancing governmental accountability, transparency, and openness.

The Society for Democratic Culture (SDC), sponsored by the U.S. National Democratic Institute for International Affairs, emerged as one of the most important indigenous civic groups in Albania. Through a wide program of nonpartisan activities, the Society attempted to promote tolerance, openness, and understanding in Albanian society. Perhaps best known for its role in voter education and mobilization and in election monitoring, the group promoted broad-based citizen participation in the country's political and economic life. The Society for Democratic Culture attempted to promote public dialogue at the grass roots by sponsoring community meetings on various subjects. In addition, jointly with the National Democratic Institute, the SDC worked with parliament to enhance communication between lawmakers and constituent groups.[95]

Another important organization was the Helsinki Committee, which monitored respect for human rights. Cooperating closely with international human rights organizations, the Helsinki Committee exposed instances of police brutality and other government abuses. It also advocated judicial and legal reforms, and improved prison conditions. However, the effectiveness of the human rights organization was undermined by the fact that it was dominated by prominent personalities from the communist period, such as historian Arben Puto, and thus came to be viewed primarily as working in opposition to the Democratic government. The author of numerous works, Puto had close ties with the APL leadership—two of his sisters were married to members of the Politburo. As one of the regime's most favored scholars, Puto was permitted to travel and conduct research abroad. He also was picked by Hoxha to serve on the commission that drafted Albania's last communist constitution, which sanctioned the one-party rule, abolished religion, and prohibited the establishment of any autonomous association or organization. He was a leading advocate of the 1974 constitution, defending its "class character" and its provision enshrining the "dictatorship of the proletariat." In a speech to a national conference, Puto argued that the constitution reflected the will and interests of the Albanian masses: "The idea of the workers' class hegemony in a socialist state is in no way in opposition to people's sovereignty, because the working class is the only social class in a position to represent the fundamental interests of the wider working masses."[96]

Former political prisoners and right-wing forces sharply criticized Puto, insisting that because of his activities under the old regime, he had no moral authority to lead the country's only human rights organization. Although in late 1992 he was forced to resign under pressure as chairman of the Helsinki Committee, Puto continued to play a leading role. In addition to being criticized as "one of the most zealous activists and propagators of the Albanian Communist Party" and serving the interests of the former *nomenklatura,*[97] Puto faced allegations that he had used the Helsinki Committee for private gain. Internal committee disagreements resulted in the resignation of several prominent anticommunist activists, including Jusuf Vrioni and Maks Velo. Velo accused Puto of harming the reputation of the human rights organization by defending "crimes committed by the Communists and their authors" and benefitting materially from his work with the Helsinki Committee.[98] Pirro Vila, a former political prisoner, accused Puto of having supplied Hoxha with documents from British archives, which the dictator used as "evidence" to eliminate his opponents. The writer insisted that Puto was "unworthy of leading this noble and honored forum, because you were always a loyal servant of the Enverist dictatorship that trampled down honest people."[99] Puto was forced to resign as committee chairman in 1992, but continued to play a leading role on the committee. Despite the controversy surrounding him, the Helsinki Committee performed a valuable function and its reporting of human rights violations seemed in line with those of foreign human rights organizations.

A wide range of other civic groups engaged in the broad sphere of social interaction aimed at influencing public policy. However, their identities were mostly one-dimensional rather than crosscutting, which limited their impact on government policy. With the exception of trade unions, few nongovernmental associations were strong enough to exert effective pressures on state institutions. Indeed, even the trade unions were not terribly successful in giving voice to the interests of ordinary working people. The radical economic transformation had driven major industries out of business, thereby marginalizing the trade union movement both politically and economically.

Perhaps the biggest obstacle to the emergence of viable civic organizations and groups was the lack of genuine autonomy from the state or political parties. Very few youth and gender organizations, cultural and intellectual associations, think tanks, and artistic networks could claim to be free from political control or influence. Although Albania's emerging constitutional order provided opportunities for a free public debate and for competing interests to express themselves freely, at times, the state displayed contempt toward grassroots organizations and movements. In most cases, it attempt to restrict their autonomy and freedom of action. Lack of capable leadership and organizational capacity also hindered the forging of a civil society. Many intellectuals who were perhaps best equipped to organize and lead civic actions shied away, engaging instead in political party work. Few prominent intellectuals committed themselves to what they saw as the mundane task of building civil-societal organizations.

As a result, a huge chasm continued to separate the public sphere from the private, and a robust civil society remained a distant goal. Nevertheless, voluntary civic organizations and groups were beginning to play an increasing role in exposing state abuses and corruption, nurturing a mature civic spirit, and fostering increased governmental responsiveness and accountability.

The Role of the Media

Following the introduction of political pluralism in December 1990, the media situation in Albania changed rapidly and dramatically. Within a short period, Albania developed an extensive, lively, and outspoken press that spanned a broad political spectrum. However, the Communist legacy was still evident in the media's low level of professionalism and in the absence of genuinely independent newspapers.

Six years after recognizing freedom of speech and press Albanians had yet to attain the standards of Western journalism or adopt a code of media ethics. The emergence of a truly independent press was hindered by the overall political situation, financial difficulties, and lack of qualified journalists. Although there were more than two hundred registered newspapers, almost all of them were closely affiliated with or financed by different political parties and groups. Journalists continued to see their role more as advocates of a particular point of view than as objective reporters. Most articles reflected a free mix of fact, comment, and opinion, without regard to standards of fairness or balanced reporting. There were profound differences between accounts of events and the actual situation. In general, there was less actual news coverage than reaction to current news in the form of editorials and commentaries. Progovernment newspapers expressed unequivocal support for the government, rarely criticizing official policies and actions. They viewed any criticism of government as criticism of democracy itself. The opposition papers, on the other hand, were generally too cynical and negative in their coverage, devoting little attention to complex issues, overplaying government failures, and giving short shrift to positive news. Indeed, some opposition and so-called independent newspapers focused almost exclusively on the misdeeds and failings of the Democratic Party and government figures, at times even engaging in deliberate disinformation.[100]

The most important newspapers were those that belonged to the main political parties and several so-called independent papers. *Rilindja Demokratike,* the organ of the Democratic Party, consistently supported the government's political and economic policies. It published reports on a range of subjects, from political, economic, and social issues to history, environmental news, the arts, and culture. While its editorial policy unequivocally supported the government, *Rilindja Demokratike* tried to temper this support by expressing concern over the social costs of reforms, corruption among officials, and other issues. Nevertheless,

Rilindja Demokratike was unable to set the tone of the Albanian press, and its circulation dropped drastically. *Zëri i Popullit*, the official daily of the Socialist Party, retained its traditional orientation. In addition to its antigovernment diatribes, the paper devoted considerable attention to workers' interests and social and economic issues. *Alternativa SD* and *Aleanca*, organs of the Social Democratic Party and the Democratic Alliance, respectively, were popularly viewed as left of center. They ceased publication in 1996. *Republika, Balli i Kombit, E Djathta,* and *Atdheu,* published by the Republican Party, National Front, the Democratic Party of the Right, and the monarchist Legality, respectively, were strongly in favor of broad decommunization. In addition to anticommunism, these papers bore strong overtones of nationalism.

Among nonparty newspapers, *Gazeta Shqiptare, Koha Jonë, Albania,* and *Dita Informacion* were the most important. A joint venture printed in Italian and Albanian, *Gazeta Shqiptare* was perhaps the only independent paper in the country, providing reliable reporting, without any polemics or apparent political bias, of political, economic, financial, and business news.

The former Communist Party paper in Lezhë, *Koha Jonë was* declared independent in 1991. It soon gained prominence as a result of its tabloid journalism, extreme opposition to the ruling Democratic Party, and several highly publicized governmental actions against its reporters. One of *Koha Jonë's* most prominent reporters was Frrok Çupi, who was fired in 1991 as the first editor of *Rilindja Demokratike* for allegedly being a Sigurimi agent. He used the paper to wage a relentless personal vendetta against the Democrats, particularly Berisha. Writing under his own name as well as pseudonyms, Çupi published numerous aggressive and highly provocative articles in *Koha Jonë* as well as in the Socialist papers *Zëri i Popullit* and *24 Orë.*

Although ostensibly independent, *Koha Jonë* openly promoted the positions of the Socialist and Democratic Alliance parties on both domestic and foreign policies, focusing almost exclusively on the misdeeds and failings of government officials. Before the 1996 parliamentary elections, the paper took a particularly negative stand on Albania's rapidly expanding relationship with the United States, especially in the military field,[101] accusing Berisha of developing excessively close relations with Washington at the expense of ties with Europe. At times, it also engaged in deliberate disinformation and misrepresentation of U.S. policy toward Albania and belittled U.S. assistance.[102] *Koha Jonë* not only violated the norms of reportorial balance but also showed a lack of insight into the nature of information and the public responsibilities of the press. The most glaring examples of the paper's deliberately false reporting appeared in September 1995, during Berisha's visit to the United States and his meeting with President Bill Clinton. *Koha Jonë* correspondent Ben Blushi went to great lengths to put a negative spin on what both U.S. and Albanian officials described as a very successful visit. Indeed, the paper went so far as to add a sentence of its own to the official White House statement issued after the Clinton-Berisha talks.[103] This and several subsequent incidents of blatantly inaccurate reporting prompted the U.S. Ambassador Joseph E. Lake to publicly complain about *Koha Jonë* coverage.[104] Subsequently, as the Socialist Party softened its anti-American rhetoric in preparation for the elections, *Koha Jonë*'s criticism of the United States also subsided. And in the wake of the United States criticism of Berisha following the 1996 elections, *Koha Jonë* became Albania's most pro-American paper.

Koha Jonë came under attack from the government and right-wing forces for its "antinational" stand. There were persistent allegations, vehemently denied by the paper, that it received financial assistance from Athens and Belgrade. During periods of high tension between Tiranë and Athens, *Koha Jonë* provided unusually favorable coverage of Greece, regularly publishing the Greek government's statements on bilateral ties. On foreign policy issues, the paper's position was indistinguishable from Greek criticism of Tiranë's policies. At the same time, the paper was critical of Albania's ties with Turkey and Macedonia, while it urged the ethnic Albanians in Kosova to give up their aspirations of secession from Serbia. Sharply criticizing Tiranë's support for Kosova's independence and questioning the legitimacy of Kosovar Albanian leader Ibrahim Rugova, *Koha Jonë* accused the government of having sacrificed the interests of the ethnic Albanians in Macedonia for better relations with Skopje. The paper also took a strong anti-Muslim stand, echoing Greek and Serbian statements that Albania could become an island of Islamic fundamentalism. Notwithstanding its highly partisan, sensational, and notoriously unreliable reporting, *Koha Jonë* became the country's most widely read daily. The paper expanded its coverage of national and local news as well as economic reportage and analysis.

Albania, which began publication in 1995, became best known for its opposition to the Socialist and other leftist parties and its coverage of national news, particularly political infighting, party alliances, coalitions, and feuds. Its editorial policy and overall coverage, however, bespoke a strong sense of affiliation with the government, including the secret police, and the Democratic Party. Regarded as less important than *Albania,* the leftist *Dita Informacion* provided good coverage of regional, particularly southern issues, including those of the ethnic Greek minority.

The replacement of the Communist regime did not produce quick advances in broadcasting policy. Radio and television remained under state control. Efforts to establish independent radio and television stations were hindered by political resistance to a liberalized broadcasting system. The opposition accused the ruling Democratic Party of using state radio and television to advance its own interests and deny other parties equal access. Television coverage of the November 1994 referendum was sharply criticized as too partisan. In summer 1995, Bardhyl Pollo, until then director of Radio Tiranë, replaced Skendër Buçpapaj as general director of radio and television. By sacking Buçpapaj, who had become a favorite target of the opposition, the Democrats raised hopes that they would move radio and television away from the front lines of the political struggle. Although government officials expressed public support for plans to make television public and to permit private radio and television stations, the Democratic Party opposed efforts to break its control over the state media.

The relationship between the government and the media was largely adversarial. Journalists lashed out against what they considered malicious and short-sighted efforts by the authorities to restrict freedom of the press, regulate national press policies, and limit the media's access to the government. Officials, for their part, complained that the press was too sensationalist and negative, and that some journalists confused freedom of the press with license to abuse their power. Many came to see the press itself as part of the problem. Bardhyl Londo, a respected writer, chastised the press for its irresponsible and biased reporting. In an article in September 1993, Londo took strong issue with the opposition and so-called independent newspapers' characterization of the postcommunist government as a dictatorial regime.[105] Some observers expressed concern that the press could undermine the democratization process by not giving proper and fair treatment to authority and by concentrating such a weight of attention on the alleged failings of officials and state institutions. There was widespread agreement that lack of media respect for the presidency, parliament, and the judiciary was contributing to a loss of faith in these institutions, which in the long run could represent a threat to democracy and the country's political stability. In a letter published in 1993, Ismail Kadare, who had come under severe criticism in some Albanian newspapers, declared: "This is not freedom of the press, but freedom to ruin the Albanian nation. During such troubling times, when our nation is threatened by dangerous, corroding waves, when it needs encouragement, equilibrium, and trust more than ever, such an antiwave can have fatal consequences. Discouragement, and the creation of the idea that all the values of this nation are questionable and unstable, are daily leading to the erosion of Albanianism and at times even to the denial of the motherland."[106]

In a highly questionable effort to regulate media behavior, in October 1993 parliament passed a press law, that left room for government abuse and contained heavy punitive measures against rebellious media. Both domestic and foreign observers criticized the law as being too restrictive and warned that it could limit the voice of journalists who opposed government policies. The law held editors and publishers responsible for the content of their publications and provided large fines for publishing anything the government considered secret or sensitive. While there was general agreement that the press, overwhelmingly leftist controlled, had gone too far, it was clear that the situation could not be improved through legal measures. Officials had failed to realize that the law was not likely to determine media behavior and that professionalism was not something that could be ensured through government restrictions.

In January 1994, two *Koha Jonë* journalists were arrested. The paper had published an article by its reporter Martin Leka on a classified order signed by Defense Minister Safet Zhulali instructing off-duty officers, noncommissioned officers, and civilians employed by the army to leave their sidearms in barracks. In a tendentious article and under a huge headline, the paper accused Zhulali of disarming the army.[107] Leka; ministry employee Romeo Lici, who was charged with passing the classified document to the journalist; and the paper's chief editor, Aleksandër Frangaj, were arrested and charged under the penal code for revealing state secrets. Lici and Leka were sentenced to 4 years and 18 months, respectively, while Frangaj was released. An appeals court, however, found Frangaj guilty and passed a sentence of five months. The authorities also took action against two other journalists from the opposition papers. Shyqyri Meka, an editor with *Zëri i Popullit*, and Ilirian Zhupa, chief editor of the newspaper *Populli Po*, were convicted of libel. The convictions of the journalists were widely perceived as directed at intimidating government critics. *Koha Jonë* had become even more egregious than *Zëri i Popullit* in its inflammatory tirades against the government. Ironically, it was government action against *Koha Jonë*.

Berisha showed sensitivity to mounting domestic criticism and international censure of the jailing of the journalists. In an apparent effort to mute the domestic and international outcry, he pardoned the four journalists on World Press Freedom Day, 3 May 1994. The president urged the journalists "to use free speech to tell the truth and to affirm it, to consolidate the values of democracy, to respect the people and their dignity, and to build a society based on law and free initiative."[108] The presidential pardon, however, did little to improve the government's adversarial relationship with the opposition press. Officials displayed striking ineptitude by taking opposition journalists to court on charges of slander or revelation of state secrets. These cases attracted considerable attention and had a damaging effect on Albania's image abroad. In December 1995, Blendi Fevziu, chief editor of the Democratic Alliance's newspaper *Aleanca*, was found guilty of slandering a senior government official and fined $2,000. The case against Fevziu, one of the more serious opposition journalists, was denounced by international human rights and journalistic organizations. Only days after his conviction, Fevziu was pardoned by Berisha.

In the period before and immediately after the 26 May 1996 elections, there were several highly publicized incidents of government actions against journalists from *Koha Jonë* and other opposition papers. In the wake of a bomb explosion in Tiranë in February 1996, *Koha Jonë* offices were raided and its reporters harassed and beaten. Reporter Ylli Polovina, who had written an article in November 1995 saying that the attempted assassination of Macedonia's President Kiro Gligorov by car bomb could be a prelude to similar actions in Albania, was arrested on charges of inciting terrorism. He was found guilty, fined about $300, and then released from custody. Only days after the parliamentary elections, Bardhok Lala, a reporter with *Dita Informacion*, was allegedly kidnaped and brutally beaten by the secret police.

Attacks on opposition journalists raised serious questions about the government's commitment to protect freedom of the press. The fact that no charges were ever brought against pro-Democratic Party journalists—such as *Rilindja Demokratike* and *Albania* reporters who published highly slanderous and unsubstantiated articles against opposition leaders—exposed the government to charges of targeting only opposition journalists and applying the law selectively.

In addition to difficulties with the government, Albanian media faced other significant problems. Journalists in general had become extensions of political parties, as the first commitment of newspapers seemed to be to the political parties or groups that sponsored them. Economic factors continued to drive the media environment. The old distribution system had collapsed and a new one had yet to emerge. There were practically no domestic subscriptions, and papers were not regularly distributed in the countryside. By the end of 1996, the combined daily circulation of the country's five largest papers was under 60,000 copies. *Koha Jonë* led with a circulation of about 25,000, followed by *Albania* with 12,000; *Zëri i Popullit*, 10,500; *Gazeta Shqiptare*, 7,400; and *Rilindja Demokratike*, 5,000.[109] All the papers, especially nonparty ones, remained highly vulnerable to market forces. Widespread newsprint shortages resulted in skyrocketing prices. In 1994, the government imposed a 15-percent advertisement tax and a new tariff of 30 percent on newsprint. Albanian newspapers called for an exemption of print media from customs duties on newsprint and printing equipment, payment of profits tax and value-added tax, and for media discounts on postal, telegraph, and telephone costs. In August 1994, nine newspapers suspended publication for four days to protest what they claimed were unjust and excessive government taxes and tariffs.[110]

Economic and financial difficulties continued to present a serious danger to the development of a free and independent press. In summer 1996, *Koha Jonë* was forced to close down for several days because of high expenses and debts. The paper resumed publication only after it received a $135,000 loan from the Prague-based Media Development Loan Fund, supported mainly by George Soros. The financial rescue of *Koha Jonë* was strongly criticized by other newspaper publishers, who insisted that it set a dangerous precedent and presented a threat to free competition. Sixteen newspapers issued a joint statement criticizing the Soros Foundation for providing assistance only to *Koha Jonë*. The papers also appealed to the government to ease the tax burden and help with the distribution network.[111]

Despite its difficult circumstances, the press as a whole had managed to exercise heretofore unheard-of license both in reporting and in editorial comment. The absence of a balanced presentation of facts and views, the emotional and partisan tone of reporting, and the high degree of manipulation and disinformation seriously eroded the media's credibility. Journalistic organizations did little work to promote fundamental principles of fair and accurate reporting. Precisely because of its lack of credibility and because it could therefore be ignored without political consequences, the press in postcommunist Albania had limited influence on political events and did not appear to serve as an effective check on corruption or the abuse of power. The adoption and implementation of ethical rules would help restore the media to a position where it is essential to democracy. Officials must also recognize that the media should not be controlled or regulated by the government, but should be regulated by their own professional association. In the medium term, journalists must be trained in the new tradition, and new communications institutions must be developed. This should lead to the gradual replacement of the old guard by the younger generation.

Notes

1. Louis Zanga, "Albania Reduced to Total Dependence on Foreign Aid," *RFE/RL Research Report* 1, no. 8, 21 February 1992, pp. 46-48. See also Mary Catherine Andrews and Gulhan Ovalioglu, *Albania and the World Bank: Building the Future* (Washington, D.C.: The World Bank, 1994); and International Monetary Fund, "Albania," *IMF Economic Reviews*, no. 5 (July 1994); and Robert Cohen, "Economic Transformation in Albania," in Joint Economic Committee, U.S. Congress, *East-Central European Economies in Transition* (Washington, D.C.: U.S. Government Printing Office, 1994), pp. 579-598.

2. United Nations Development Program, *Human Development Report: Albania 1995* (Tiranë, 1995), p. 18.

3. According to the Economist Intelligence Unit, in 1993 Albanians consumed more and had a better quality of life than at any time in their recent history. The Economist Intelligence Unit, *Country Report: Romania, Bulgaria, Albania* (London), 2nd quarter 1994, p. 63.

4. The National Council of Independent Trade Unions issued a statement in July 1992 reemphasizing its support for reforms but demanding a cushioning of its effects. The statement stressed that trade unions "will not allow the government to apply a drastic reform and shift the whole burden of its grave consequences onto the shoulders of the working people, especially on the city workers, who are at present the most affected" (Radio Tiranë Network in Albanian, 1730 GMT, 28 July 1992, translated in FBIS-EEU 92-146, 29 July 1992, p. 3).

5. *Sindikalisti*, no. 149, November 1993, pp. 1-2. In September 1994, the government and the pro-Democratic Party trade unions signed an agreement concerning the indexing of inflation for most consumer goods. The agreement, signed by Meksi and the President of the Union of Independent Trade Unions Valer Xheka, called for regular, biannual meetings between government and union leaders to discuss issues of mutual concern (Radio Tiranë in English, 1900 GMT, 29 September 1994, in FBIS-EEU 94-191, 3 October 1994, p. 2).

6. *Zëri i Popullit*, 10 March 1995, p. 2.

7. International Monetary Fund, Press Release, no. 93/28, 14 July 1993.

8. As a World Bank study noted: "Privatization in 1991 and early 1992 lacked transparency and fairness as a result of the confiscatory practices and preferential positions of the former *nomenklatura*. Some beneficiaries of privatization have earned large profits by Albanian standards, causing considerable resentment"(Andrews and Ovalioglu, *Albania and the World Bank: Building the Future*, p. 68).

9. Vilson Qendro, a trade union official, urged the government to tackle the issue of corruption among the former *nomenklatura*. He argued that Communist managers "using business trips abroad and disregarding the purpose of these trips, forged connections for

their own private interests and are now putting themselves forward as co-owners, purchasing one factory or another." He added, "Communist business executives now sell automobiles in the town squares." Qendro said that in all its meetings with the president and the new government, the Union of Independent Albanian Trade Unions had demanded: "the renewal of the entire administrative structure. ... No economic reform can be carried out or have any effect with the old administration in power. The renewal of the administration will help, especially psychologically, to restore confidence among the people. There can be no reform with Communists or pseudodemocrats at the top" (Vilson Qendro, "Transition and Corruption," *Sindikalisti*, 6 May 1992, p. 2).

10. See interview with Blerim Çela in *Rilindja Demokratike*, 15 July 1992, p. 2.

11. See Jane Martinson, "One of the Biggest Success Stories," *Financial Times*, 2 October 1995.

12. Andrews and Ovalioglu, *Albania and the World Bank: Building the Future*, p. 37, and *IMF Economic Reviews*, no. 5 (1994), p. 8.

13. European Bank for Reconstruction and Development, *Transition Report 1995: Investment and Enterprise Development* (London: HMSO Publication Center, 1995), p. 33.

14. See Kutlay Ebiri, "Development of the Private Sector in Albania," *Tirana Monthly Review* (World Bank Albania Resident Mission, Tiranë), September 1993, p. 2.

15. *Rilindja Demokratike*, 7 January 1995, p. 4.

16. *Human Development Report: Albania 1995*, pp. 12-13.

17. B. Permeti, "How Much of Albania Is in Private Hands?" *Republika*, 21 November 1995, p. 3.

18. In a petition to Berisha, the Property With Justice organization demanded the return of "all kinds of property that the Communist dictatorship regime forcibly and arbitrarily nationalized, to the legal owners and heirs." It also called for the annulment of "all laws, decrees, and resolutions of the Council of Ministers and the District Executive Committees issued between 1 December 1944 and 1 January 1992, which nationalized, confiscated, and otherwise affected the sacred rights of private property" (*Republika*, 28 May 1992, pp. 1-2).

19. *Zëri i Popullit*, 15 April 1993, p. 1.

20. *Rilindja Demokratike*, 21 April 1993, p. 2.

21. *Gazeta Shqiptare*, 14 April 1994, p. 1.

22. *Rilindja Demokratike*, 4 August 1995, p. 1.

23. *Gazeta Shqiptare*, 20 October 1994, p. 3.

24. *Lajmi i Ditës*, 28 March 1995, pp. 1-2.

25. ATA in English, 1202 GMT, 29 June 1995, in FBIS-EEU 95-130-A, 7 July 1995, pp. 2-3; ATA in English, 1830 GMT, 4 August 1995, in FBIS-EEU 95-158-A, 16 August 1995, pp. 2-3. See also "Albania Moves As Fast as It Can to Privatization," *Wall Street Journal*, 14 November 1995, p. A13.

26. Bashkim Kopliku, "Privatization Has Been and Is Being Carried Out With Professionalism, Justice, and Transparency," *Rilindja Demokratike*, 18 November 1995, p. 3.

27. See Prime Minister Meksi's speech at the Democratic Party convention, *Rilindja Demokratike*, 5 April 1996, p. 6.

28. See interview with economist Aristotel Pano in *Rilindja Demokratike*, 1 December 1993, pp. 2, 4.

29. ATA in English, 1744 GMT, 27 July 1995, in FBIS-EEU 95-155-S, 11 August 1995, p. 3.

30. *Rilindja Demokratike*, 7 March 1995, pp. 1-2. See also *Kontrata e Partisë Demokratike me Shqipërinë* [The Democratic Party's Contract with Albania] (Tiranë, 1995).

31. See special survey on Albania in *Financial Times*, 2 October 1995, and Marianne Sullivan, "Albania Rides the Wave of Capitalism," *Transition* 2, no. 20 (4 October 1996), pp. 15-17.

32. *Gazeta Shqiptare*, 20 February 1994, p. 3; and *IMF Economic Reviews*, no. 5 (1994), p. 5.

33. *Rilindja Demokratike*, 7 November 1993, p. 2. See also Pirro Dishnica, "The Introduction of Foreign Capital—An Important Aspect of Reviving the Economy," *Rilindja Demokratike*, 20 January 1994, pp. 1-3.

34. *Rilindja Demokratike*, 31 December 1996, p. 1.

35. Adrian Civici, "Agrarian Policy Should Be Based on Clear Ideas About the Future Development of Agriculture," *Rilindja Demokratike*, 14 October 1993, p. 2.

36. See Berisha's news conference in ATA in English, 1424 GMT, 9 December 1995, in FBIS-EEU 95-241-A, 15 December 1995, pp. 2-6.

37. Economist Intelligence Unit, *Country Report: Bulgaria, Albania*, fourth quarter 1996, p. 32.

38. United Nations Development Program, *Albanian Human Development Report 1996* (Tiranë, 1996), p. 12.

39. *Omri Daily Digest*, no. 107, part II, 2 June 1995; and *Financial Times*, 2 October 1995, p. 30.

40. *OMRI Daily Digest*, no. 210, part II, 27 October 1995.

41. *World Bank News*, 11 August 1994, p. 4.

42. *Republika*, 23 November 1995, p. 3.

43. In an interview in December 1994, Blerim Çela, chairman of the State Control Commission, acknowledged that the anticorruption drive had met with stiff opposition at all levels of the government bureaucracy. He lamented the fact that his commission did not have the power to take disciplinary measures against officials involved with corruption *(Lajmi i Ditës*, 13 December 1994, p. 1). In the wake of the November 1994 referendum, Berisha characterized corruption as "a serious problem" and promised an active campaign to root it out: "Many voted no [in the referendum] because they have seen a minister or mayor arrange things to his own advantage or have seen a Democratic Party branch chairman work to build up his own power. They have seen privileges and manifestations of corruption, toward which the people are very sensitive. The cases of corruption should be identified, detected, and condemned, and the Democratic Party should have no hesitation in this"(TVSH Television Network in Albanian, 1900 GMT, 15 November 1994, translated in FBIS-EEU 94-222, 17 November 1994, p. 3). Former Deputy Prime Minister Rexhep Uka and former Minister of Finance Genc Ruli were publicly accused of illegal activities, but parliament refused to lift their immunities.

44. *New York Times*, 27 February 1996, p. A5.

45. *Rilindja Demokratike*, 17 October 1996, p. 2; *Gazeta Shqiptare*, 17 October 1996, p. 9.

46. Gus Xhudo, "Men of Purpose: The Growth of Albanian Criminal Activity," *Transnational Organized Crime* 2, no. 1, Spring 1996, pp. 1-20.

47. *Rilindja Demokratike*, 14 February 1995, p. 2.

48. OMRI Daily Digest, no. 32, part II, 14 February 1997.

49. *Human Development Report: Albania 1995*, p. 16.

50. See interview with Minister of Labor and Social Affairs, Elmaz Sherifi in *Zëri i Popullit*, 5 April 1997, p. 5. See also the Institute of Statistics, *Tregu shqiptar i punës në tranzicion* [The Albanian Labor Market in Transition] (Tiranë, 1995), p. 4.

51. *Zëri i Popullit*, 5 April 1997, p. 5.

52. *Albania*, 5 November 1995, p. 2.

53. See article by Bashkim Kopliku in *Rilindja Demokratike*, 1 October 1995, p. 5, and Prime Minister Meksi's speech at the Democratic Party convention, *Rilindja Demokratike*, 5 April 1996, p. 6.

54. *Republika*, 21 November 1995, p. 3.

55. *Rilindja Demokratike*, 16 December 1995, p. 4.

56. ATA in English, 1115 GMT, 6 October 1995, in FBIS-EEU 95-195-A, 10 October 1995, pp. 4-5.

57. Alfons Zeneli,"The North Under the South's Iron Heel,"*Koha Jonë*, 11 October 1991, p.3; and interview with deputy Abdi Baleta in *Zëri i Rinisë*, 9 September 1992, p. 4.

58. Bahri Beci, "The Albanian Standard Language and Its Dialectic Foundations," *Albania*, 3 November 1995, p. 5.

59. *Zëri i Popullit*, 31 May 1992, p. 2.

60. An article in the Democratic Party's newspaper noted that a "balance" existed between Gegs and Tosks in Prime Minister Aleksandër Meksi's government and posed a rhetorical question: "Why should Albania's president necessarily be from the south and not the north?" *Rilindja Demokratike*, 6 June 1992, p. 1.

61. Stavro Skendi, ed., *Albania* (New York: Frederick A. Praeger, 1956), p. 57. The majority of Albanian Muslims are Sunni. However, there are also many *Bektashis*, a liberal sect and an offshoot of Shia Islam. Albania also witnessed the development of crypto-Christianity, i.e., Christians who publicly professed Islam but privately practiced Christianity. See Skendi's *Balkan Cultural Studies* (Boulder: East European Monographs, distributed by Columbia University Press, 1980), pp. 151-162, and 233-251. See also H. T. Norris, *Islam in the Balkans: Religion and Society between Europe and the Arab World* (Columbia: University of South Carolina Press, 1993).

62. Gjon Sinishta, *The Fulfilled Promise: A Documentary Account of Religious Persecution in Albania* (Santa Clara, CA: H & F Composing Service/Printing, 1976).

63. Msgr. Dr. Joseph J. Oroshi, transl., *Shkrimi Shëjt: Katër Ungjijt dhe Punët e Apostujvet* [The New Testament: The Four Gospels and the Acts of the Apostles] (Bronx, NY: Albanian Roman Catholic Center, 1978).

64. "New Bishop to Aid Albanian Reawakening," *New York Times*, 14 February 1993, p. 10; and "Pope Helps Albanians Celebrate Their 'Resurrection,'" *The Sun* (Baltimore), 26 April 1993, p. 3A.

65. See the Directorate of Radio Tiranë's International Service, *Buletini i radiove të huaja në gjuhën shqipe* [The Bulletin of Albanian-Language Foreign Radios], no. 625, 3 December 1990. The Rev. Simon Jubani was freed from prison in April 1989 after serving twenty-six years for religious activity. Former speaker of parliament Pjetër Arbnori, who has been accused by Rev. Jubani of being a secret police informer while in prison, claimed the ceremony was held with the Albanian government's acquiescence. He said that Communist Prime Minister Adil Çarçani visited Shkodër in early November 1990, and at a party meeting, indicated that authorities would now tolerate religious activities. On Çarçani's instructions, the Shkodër police chief reportedly summoned Rev. Jubani and told

him that he could hold a public mass. In any case, the mass was a milestone in Albania's public life. See Pjetër Arbnori, "Only Those Who Challenged Death With Me Can Write My Biography," *Rilindja Demokratike*, 18 July 1993, pp. 1, 6.

66. *Lajmi i Ditës*, 1 November 1994, p. 1.

67. On the history of the Albanian Orthodox Church, see *Fiftieth Anniversary Book of the Albanian Orthodox Church in America 1908-1958*, compiled by Metropolitan Fan S. Noli (Boston: The Albanian Orthodox Church in America, 1960).

68. ATA in English, 0959 GMT, 2 July 1991 in FBIS-EEU 91-128, 3 July 1991, p. 3.

69. Teodor Papapavli, "The Revival of the Albanian Orthodox Church," *Alternativa SD*, 12 May 1992, pp. 2-3.

70. Many apparently feared that through this decision the Greek government was taking advantage of Albania's vulnerability, to establish a state within a state. See Petro Dhimitri, "A Historic Mistake of the Albanian Orthodox Church," *Rilindja Demokratike*, 4 August 1992, pp. 1, 4.

71. Albanian Orthodox Archdiocese in America, *News Release* (Boston), 3 August 1992, pp. 1-2.

72. On foreign missionaries, see Henry Kamm, "'Hallelujah' Is Heard in the Arch-Atheist's Temple," *New York Times*, 10 June 1993, p. A4; and Isuf Hajrizi, "Many Albanians Troubled by Invasion of Foreign Clerics," *Illyria* (New York), 4-6 October 1993, pp. 1, 3.

73. See articles by Kiço Blushi, "Who Sows National Discord," *Tirana*, no. 486 (September 1992), pp. 2-3, and "Who Benefits from National Discord," *Zëri i Rinisë*, 11 November 1992, pp. 3-4.

74. Abdi Baleta, "Albanians Do Not Quarrel; Others Incite Them," *Patrioti*, no. 12 (October 1922), pp. 1-3.

75. Frances Trix, "The Resurfacing of Islam in Albania," *East European Quarterly* 28, no. 4 (January 1995), p. 533.

76. Kadare has warned of what he considers the danger of Albania's "Asianization." See his interview in *Dita Informacion*, 2 May 1993, p. 5.

77. Pirro Prifti, "Albania Between Three Religions," *Aleanca*, 25 August 1995, p. 10. In a second installment published in March 1996, the author argued that despite economic and social changes, Albania could never advance on a par with other European countries unless it adopted a single religion (Pirro Prifti, "New Historical Facts for Religious Unification," *Aleanca*, 22 March 1996, p. 8).

78. Neshat Tozaj, "'Albania, an Islamic Ammunition Arsenal?...'" *Zëri i Popullit*, 10 January 1995, p. 3. Tozaj said the title of the article was from a French magazine.

79. Abdi Baleta, "Albania, Neither an Islamic Island nor an Islamic Ammunition Arsenal, but a Garden of Religious Harmony," *E Djathta*, 17, 20, 24, 27 January 1995, and 3 and 7 February 1995.

80. Hysen Çobani, "Muslim Faith, Like Orthodox and Catholic Faiths, Is a Component Part of the National Conscience," *Rilindja Demokratike*, 15 January 1995, p. 4.

81. Mero Baze, "Who Is Encouraging Religious Movements in Albania?" *Tribuna Demokratike*, 11 April 1995, pp. 1, 3; and Bilall Shaini, "Religion in the National Prism," *Republika*, 22 February 1996, p. 5.

82. AFP in English, 1155 GMT, 25 April 1993, translated in FBIS-EEU 93-078, 26 April 1993, p. 3.

83. A senior French medical official, who visited Tiranë in the beginning of 1991, compared Albania's appalling health conditions to the Middle Ages (AFP in English , 1758 GMT, 18 March 1991, in FBIS-EEU 91-054, 20 March 1991, p. 6).

84. World Bank, IDA News Release No. 95/16ECA, 8 November 1994.

85. *Human Development Report: Albania 1995*, pp. 38-41.

86. Michael Vachon, "Repairing Albania's Schools," *Open Society News* (Summer 1995), pp. 3-7.

87. Lazër Stani, "In Search of a Lost Glory,"*Rilindja Demokratike*, 21 May 1995, p. 3.

88. Lutfi Dervishi, "The Criteria for (Self-)Designation As an Intellectual," *Republika*, 30 September 1993, p. 1.

89. See Londo's interview in *Rilindja Demokratike*, 17 December 1995, p. 4.

90. See Ian Whitaker, "'A Sack for Carrying Things': The Traditional Role of Women in Northern Albanian Society," *Anthropological Quarterly* 54, no. 3 (July 1981), pp. 146-156.

91. See John Kolsti, "From Courtyard to Cabinet: The Political Emergence of Albanian Women," in Sharon L. Wolchik and Alfred G. Meyer, eds., *Women, State and Party in Eastern Europe* (Durham: Duke University Press, 1985), pp. 138-151; Hafizullah Emadi, "Development Strategies and Women in Albania," *East European Quarterly* 27, no. 1 (March 1993), pp. 79-96; and Fatos Tarifa, "Disappearing from Politics: Social Change and Women in Albania," in Marilyn Rueschemeyer, ed., *Women in the Politics of Postcommunist Eastern Europe* (Armonk, NY: M. E. Sharpe, 1994), pp. 133-138.

92. Thimi Nika, "Our Concept of Democratic Rights and Freedoms Is Realistic," *Rruga e Partisë* 37, no. 2 (February 1990), p. 61.

93. Elsa Ballauri, "The Albanian Feminist Movement: Does It Exist?" *Aleanca*, 23 June 1995, p. 17. See also Afërdita Zëri, "Women and Time," *Krahu i Shqiponjës* (Tiranë), no. 41 (October 1995), p. 3.

94. By 1994, in addition to some 30 political parties, there were 80 associations, and about 25 trade unions. See *Lajmi i Ditës*, 3 March 1994, p. 2.

95. National Democratic Institute for International Affairs, *Civic Education and Parliamentary Dialogue in Albania 1991-1994* (Washington, D.C., 1995), pp. 1-2.

96. Arben Puto, "Sovereignty and Its Political and Class Aspects in the New Draft Constitution," in *Konferenca Shkencore për Problemet e Kushtetutës* [Scientific Conference on the Problems of the Constitution], 2, (Tiranë: 8 Nëntori, 1976), p. 95.

97. ATA in English, 0928 GMT, 20 August 1992, in FBIS-EEU 92-163, 21 August 1992, p. 2.

98. Maks Velo, "Puto Shields Crime," *Rilindja Demokratike*, 21 January 1996, p. 3. See also a letter to Helsinki Committee signed by eleven former student colleagues of Puto, "Let Christine Von Kohl [director of the International Helsinki Federation] Know Who Arben Puto Is," *Rilindja Demokratike*, 21 January 1996, p. 3.

99. Pirro Vila, "Enough, Mr. Puto," *Liria*, 19 June 1992, p. 6.

100. One of the more celebrated cases of deliberate disinformation involved reporter Gavrosh Levonja. In August 1996, the progovernment paper *Albania* published an article on an alleged meeting between Democratic Alliance leaders Neritan Ceka and Gramoz Pashko with representatives of the Greek American lobby in Boston. The item was widely disseminated by the state news agency ATA as proof that the two opposition leaders were collaborating with Albania's "enemies." Subsequently, Levonja admitted that he had written the article with a Boston dateline and had faxed it to *Albania* only moments before

the paper was scheduled to go to press. Assuming that the article had come from Boston, as the fax number on it indicated, *Albania*'s editorial staff decided to run the piece without checking its veracity or source. Levonja said that he wanted to embarrass *Albania's* manager Ylli Rakipi, an outspoken critic of the Democratic Alliance and a close Berisha supporter. While *Albania* was duped, Levonja's image as a serious journalist was badly tarnished. Nevertheless, his action was not condemned by his colleagues or by journalistic organizations, and he continued to write for *Koha Jonë* and other papers. (See Gavrosh Levonja, "This Is the Chief Editor's Style," *Koha Jonë*, 18 August 1996, p. 5.) Albanian newspapers often distort, slant, and quote out of context statements by foreign governments and officials. In March 1996, the Socialist Party newspaper *Zëri i Popullit* republished the U.S. State Department's 1995 report on human rights in Albania. The paper's version, however, contained serious translation errors and distortions of and omissions from the original. The U.S. Embassy in Tiranë issued a statement emphasizing that the *Zëri i Popullit* version "does not accurately reflect the version of the report as approved and published by the Government of the United States of America." United States Information Service, *News Release* (Tiranë), 15 March 1996.

101. In July 1995, in the wake of the stationing of two U.S. spy planes at the Gjader airbase, from which they conducted reconnaissance missions over Bosnia, *Koha Jonë* published a series of articles alleging incidents between American and Albanian soldiers at the base. These reports were denied by both U.S. and Albanian officials. See *Koha Jonë*, 13 July 1995, p. 2, and 18 July 1995, p. 3. For a reaction to the paper's reporting on Albanian-U.S. relations, see Mentor Shehu, *"Koha Jonë* in the Language of Communist Tradition Against 'American Imperialism,'" *Rilindja Demokratike*, 15 July 1995, p. 2.

102. A typical example of *Koha Jonë* reporting on U.S.-Albanian relations was an article in May 1995 by reporter Emin Barçi. Barçi wrote that Berisha's promise that the United States "would help our country has turned out to be something relative and hard to grasp for the majority of Albanians. Tangible U.S. aid given to the Berisha administration is no more than three million dollars a year." See Emin Barçi, "Berisha Seeks Clinton on the Threshold of the Elections," *Koha Jonë*, 30 May 1995, p. 3. The U.S. Embassy in Tiranë issued a statement saying that U.S. nonmilitary assistance to Albania since 1992 amounted to more than $130 million. Noting that it had provided the paper with information on the exact amount of U.S. assistance, the embassy expressed concern that *Koha Jonë* chose to report a distorted amount. The U.S. Embassy's statement was published in *Rilindja Demokratike*, 1 June 1995, p. 1.

103. *Tribuna Demokratike*, 15 September 1995, p. 3.

104. See letter by Ambassador Joseph E. Lake in *Koha Jonë*, 9 November 1995, p. 2.

105. Bardhyl Londo, "Concentrating Only on the Negative Leads to Destruction," *Rilindja Demokratike*, 5 September 1993, p. 3.

106. See Kadare's letter to the Italian-Albanian newspaper *Katundi Ynë*, republished in *Republika*, 21 November 1993, pp. 1-2.

107. Martin Leka, "Safet Zhulali Orders the Mass Disarmament of the Albanian Army," *Koha Jonë*, 21 January 1994, pp. 1-2.

108. *Rilindja Demokratike*, 4 March 1994, p. 1.

109. *Koha Jonë*, 8 November 1996, p. 19.

110. *Aleanca*, 30 July 1994, p. 2.

111. The joint statement was signed by the country's leading newspapers. See *Rilindja Demokratike*, 26 July 1996, p. 1.

7

Foreign Policy and
the National Question

Traditionally at the margins of European politics, Sali Berisha's Albania pursued three broad foreign policy objectives: increasing interaction with Western powers to strengthen its security and prevent the Yugoslav war of secession from spreading to Albanian-inhabited territories; seeking international economic assistance for the implementation of radical reforms; and negotiating a modus vivendi with neighboring countries that simultaneously would protect the rights of ethnic Albanians there.

Security Concerns and Military Reforms

In the wake of the end of the Cold War and despite regime change, small, weak Albania faced a security threat from its neighbors who, in the past have claimed large, compact, Albanian-inhabited territories and who continue to harbor ambivalent attitudes on the existence of Albania as an independent state. The violent dismemberment of the former Yugoslavia dramatically changed the political landscape of the Balkans, creating new challenges for Tiranë's foreign policy. Buffeted by pressures from its more powerful neighbors to the north and the south, Albania found itself in the eye of the Balkan storm. As a front-line state and with a vulnerable geopolitical position, Albania faced the ever present danger of direct military confrontation with Serbia over Kosova, home to two million ethnic Albanians.[1]

Lacking a military capability sufficient to deter Serbian aggression, Albania sought protection in broader security alliances, forging close links with the United States, Turkey, and other NATO members.[2] In December 1992, Albania became the first former Warsaw Pact country to request membership in NATO.[3] In February 1994, Berisha traveled to Brussels to personally sign Albania's agreement to participate in NATO's Partnership for Peace program. This was followed, in January 1995, by an individual cooperation accord with NATO under the Partnership for Peace program. Although the program did not represent a security commitment, Berisha declared that in the event of a war with Yugoslavia, "we will be counting on NATO and the United States."[4] He insisted that strengthening ties and eventually integrating with Western military structures were Albania's best security options.

At the same time, however, Berisha emphasized the importance of modernizing the Albanian military.[5] The armed forces were restructured, shifting from a division to a corps structure, and hundreds of officers, from all branches of the military, were sent for training in the United States, Turkey, Germany, and other NATO member nations. Albanians adopted a new military doctrine, drafted with the assistance of Western military advisers. This doctrine emphasized the military's defense functions and considered the use of military force as only one facet of Albania's national security strategy. It emphasized that Albania did not consider any state its military foe, had no territorial claims against other countries, and rejected border changes by force.[6] The new military doctrine, entitled "The Policy of Security and Defense of the Republic of Albania," was formally presented in August 1995. Nevertheless, Albanian leaders recognized the reality that their armed forces were not in a position to effectively deter any potential adversary, let alone repel direct aggression. Moreover, efforts also were made to modernize the army, but the acquisition of new, modern weapons was beyond Albania's financial capabilities.

Albania came to play an important role in NATO's strategy of preventing the expansion of the Yugoslav conflict, placing its air and port facilities at NATO's disposal.[7] Albania's naval forces cooperated very closely with the U.S. Sixth Fleet and other NATO forces.[8] Louis Bouvard, chairman of the North Atlantic Assembly, the forum of NATO and former Warsaw Pact member nations, described Albania as a "true partner" of NATO.[9] At the meeting of NATO's defense ministers and ministers of fourteen Partnership for Peace countries in June 1995, Albanian Defense Minister Safet Zhulali repeated Albania's invitation to make its facilities available to NATO for peacekeeping missions in the former Yugoslavia.[10] In this context, Albanian leaders continued to remind their Western partners that their country's ultimate aim remained full NATO membership.[11]

Realizing that their country was not on the short list for full NATO membership, Albanians expanded bilateral military ties with the United States, Turkey, and Germany to address their immediate security concerns. Albania signed military cooperation agreements with Turkey, Germany, Italy, and France. These agreements provided for the training of Albanian officers, exchange programs, joint maneuvers, and aid for the Albanian army. Bilateral agreements on military cooperation also were concluded with Bulgaria, Croatia, and Macedonia. In March-April 1996, Albania hosted a meeting of regional defense ministers aimed at boosting security cooperation in the Balkans. The ministerial meeting was attended by defense ministers from Bulgaria, Macedonia, Turkey, and Italy, as well as by U.S. Secretary of Defense William Perry.[12] In a welcoming speech, Berisha called for "a new vision of Balkan security and understanding."[13] And in July 1996, large scale military exercises code-named "Peaceful Eagle '96," were held in Albania. According to a U.S. Information Agency survey, the Albanian public was solidly behind participation in the Partnership for Peace program and more eager to join NATO than most other East Europeans. An overwhelming majority of 84 percent expressed support for full membership in the Western military alliance, and 70 percent favored stationing NATO troops in Albania. [14]

Relations With the United States

From the beginning of Berisha's administration, there was a discernable tilt in Albania's foreign policy toward the United States, which had strongly supported Albania's democratization. In the early 1990s, there was probably no country in Europe in which there was as much good will toward the United States as in Albania. This was reflected during Secretary of State James A. Baker's visit in June 1991. During 1991 and 1992, American Ambassador William Ryerson and Deputy Chief of Mission Christopher Hill played a key role in encouraging Albania's democratization process, exerting considerable pressure on the Communists to make sure the transition was smooth and peaceful.

Once in office, the Democrats were eager to forge strong ties with the United States. One of Berisha's first trips abroad as president was a visit to the White House in June 1992 for discussions with President George Bush. Berisha's goal was to enlist the help of the United States in implementing radical political and economic reforms and in preventing the spread of war to Kosova. Berisha emphasized that Albania was a friend and a strategic ally that could serve important U.S. interests in the troubled Balkans. Indeed, the two countries developed extensive political and military ties. Albania came to play a key role in the overall U.S. strategy aimed at containing the Yugoslav conflict and cultivating a peaceful and stable Balkan region.[15] Between 1992 and 1996, the United States committed over $200 million to addressing Albania's humanitarian needs and in assisting its political and economic transformation.

Berisha's pro-American stance was attacked by Socialist Party spokesmen, who charged that Berisha was overly optimistic in his pursuit of a close relationship with the United States, making his country a pawn in America's Balkan interests. Official Socialist statements revealed continuing suspicions about the intentions of the United States toward Albania and urged greater reliance on Italy, which during the election campaign in 1992 had solidly supported the former Communists. A recurrent theme in leftist foreign policy analysis was that Italy, and not the United States, was Albania's "natural ally." The Communist media responded to Berisha's 1992 visit to Washington with increasingly sharp attacks on the United States. A series of articles in the Socialist daily *Zëri i Popullit* contained a litany of complaints about the onerously small sums of U.S. aid, which recalled the Socialist reaction to Baker's 1991 visit: "Six million dollars for three million Albanians." Berisha was accused of emphasizing Tiranë's relationship with Washington at the expense of Albania's national interest in closer ties with Europe.[16] The Socialists were particularly opposed to expanding Albanian-U.S. military ties, and they warned of wide-ranging negative consequences for Albanian security interests.

Criticism of Albania's pursuit of close ties with the United States, however, had little impact on Berisha's conduct of foreign policy. Tiranë-Washington relations grew closer under President Bill Clinton's administration. In October 1993, Albania and the United States signed a memorandum of military understanding. U.S. military advisers were attached to the Albanian General Staff, while numerous Albanian officers were trained in the United States.

Meanwhile, senior U.S. defense officials emphasized Albania's critically important role for stability in the Balkans.[17] During a visit to Albania in July 1994, Secretary of Defense William Perry praised Albania for its constructive role in preventing the spread of war from Bosnia to Kosova. Perry expressed strong U.S. support for Albania's independence and reform efforts.[18] U.S. and Albanian forces held a series of joint military exercises in Albania. In July 1995, the United States deployed two Predator spy planes in Gjader, near Lezhë, to conduct reconnaissance missions over Bosnia, gathering infrared and other intelligence on military activity there for U.N. peacekeepers. About one-hundred American military men and civilians were stationed in Albania to operate the unmanned planes by remote control.[19]

This excellent bilateral relationship, however, was adversely affected in 1994 by the Albanian-Greek dispute. Athens and the Greek American lobby exerted considerable pressure on the White House to convince Berisha to release five ethnic Greeks, members of the Omonia organization, who had been arrested and tried on espionage charges. Berisha defied intense American pressure to release the five. Although Washington dispatched envoys to both capitals and President Clinton publicly urged Greece to open a direct and unconditional dialogue with Albania to resolve bilateral differences,[20] there was a widespread perception in Tiranë that U.S. policy in this instance was too heavily influenced by the Greek American community and that Washington favored Athens over Tiranë. Albanian officials noted the irony that the United States, which had undertaken a major effort to promote the rule of law in Albania, now was urging Berisha to short-circuit the judicial process and release the ethnic Greeks.

Lacking as strong a constituency in the United States as Athens and unable to offer an acceptable explanation of the Omonia case, Tiranë soon saw the effects of its intransigence. Washington linked a planned visit by Berisha to the satisfactory resolution of the Omonia case, and put plans for a $30 million Albanian-

American Enterprise Fund on hold. With growing strains in Albanian-Greek relations, the White House also came under pressure to replace Ambassador William Ryerson, who was criticized for being identified too closely with Berisha and for allegedly not having done enough to improve the situation of Albania's ethnic Greek community. In October 1994, before the end of his three-year appointment, Ryerson, who was described by Baker as "an exceptional Foreign Service officer,"[21] was replaced by Joseph Lake, a career foreign service officer who had served as ambassador to Mongolia and who had no previous experience in Albanian politics. On his departure, Ambassador Ryerson received Albania's highest honor, the Order of the Flag. In a farewell ceremony, Berisha stated: "Direct United States support and the direct interest taken by President Bush in the victory of democracy in Albania were extremely important and won the deepest gratitude of Albania and the Albanians, a gratitude that they will feel forever. It was and will remain a historic contribution to the close friendship between our two countries."[22] Conversely, Ryerson's replacement was welcomed by the Socialists. A senior party official accused Ryerson of having contributed to the "destabilization of the last ruling communist party in Albania," and of bringing the Communists "to their knees."[23]

Following the Albanian Court of Cassation's decision to release the Omonia defendants on probation in early 1995, Tiranë-Washington relations seemed back on track and in September Berisha was invited to the White House for discussions on regional issues, economic and military cooperation, and Albania's progress on the road to democracy. U.S. spokesmen described the Berisha-Clinton meeting as "very positive." According to a White House statement, Clinton expressed appreciation for "Albania's responsible role in regions of the former Yugoslavia with large ethnic Albanian populations" and assured Berisha "that the United States strongly supported autonomy for the people of Kosovo and would continue to work toward that end."[24] The Albanian leader welcomed his visit to the United States as an opportunity to reaffirm both Tiranë's strong ties with Washington and Albania's important role in regional affairs. During his trip, Berisha also visited the Pentagon and offered the United States the use of bases in Albania.[25] Socialist Party leader Servet Pëllumbi was quick to criticize Berisha's offer of bases, describing the president's offer as "irresponsible."[26] Government officials responded by accusing the Socialists of failing to make distinctions between narrow internal squabbles and higher national interests.

Berisha voiced great satisfaction with the results of the visit,[27] while the progovernment press hailed the president's visit as a boost to Albania's inter-national standing. Opposition media commentary was decidedly mixed, with some commentators portraying the visit as a plus for Albania and Berisha and others criticizing it as insignificant. Some papers, such as *Koha Jonë* and *Aleanca*, which had sent their own correspondents to Washington, gave an unusually negative spin to the visit and a sinister interpretation of Berisha's talks with Clinton and other U.S. officials. Right-wing politicians particularly criticized Berisha for allegedly being too accommodating toward the United States and not sufficiently assertive in advancing Albanian interests vis-à-vis Kosova and Macedonia.

On the eve of the May 1996 parliamentary elections, the United States urged the Albanian government to ensure that the balloting would be free and fair. Following these elections, as noted in the next chapter, bilateral ties experienced considerable strain when the United States described the electoral process as flawed. European countries, usually less concerned with human rights as a factor in foreign policy, did not sustain their criticism of the elections, leaving Washington, which in the past had strongly backed Berisha, as his most vocal foreign critic.

Relations With Western Europe and Other Regions

Notwithstanding Albanian efforts to build a special relationship with the United States, Tiranë also aggressively pursued European integration and reached out to Italy, Germany, France, the United Kingdom, and other Western countries. Between 1992 and 1996, the European Union committed some $650 million in humanitarian and economic assistance to Albania. Albania's closest bilateral ties in this period were those with Italy and Germany. Italy became Albania's leading West European donor, granting its impoverished neighbor $420 million dollars.

Confronted with waves of Albanian refugees in 1991-1992, Rome had been forced to take a more active approach in its relations with Albania. The Italians launched a program of humanitarian assistance for Albania, and with Tiranë's agreement, stationed a military contingent of about 900 soldiers in Durrës, code-named Pelicano, to distribute international humanitarian aid. The substantial assistance that Italy provided during 1991 and 1992 was critical for Albania. However, harsh Italian treatment of Albanian refugees and the behavior of Italian soldiers in Albania increased anti-Italian feelings and concerns about Rome's growing influence in Albania. Many feared that Albania would become trapped, as it had in the 1920s and 1930s, in a client-patron relationship with Italy, with far-reaching consequences for the country's independence. Moreover, during the election campaign in 1992, the Italians responded to their suspicions of the Democratic Party's close links with the United States by publicly supporting the Socialists. While Berisha considered ongoing Italian financial support critical for Albania's economic recovery, he was anxious to phase out military cooperation in the form of the Pelicano operation as soon as possible. Many Albanians, recalling the Italian annexation of their country in 1939, were suspicious of Rome's long-term intentions, and considered the stationing of Italian soldiers in Albania an infringement on their country's sovereignty. The Italian side, on the other hand, complained about what it saw as Albanians' lack of appreciation for the assistance they had received.

Cooperation with Italy began to lag after the Albanian government's rejection of Rome's request to extend the Pelicano operation. During a meeting in Tiranë in December 1993 with visiting Italian Defense Minister Fabio Fabbri, Berisha said that Albania was ready to expand its military cooperation with Italy, but that it would preserve "its own identity and sovereignty."[28] Subsequently, following government changes in Rome, bilateral relations improved. Italy became Albania's largest trading partner and held first place also in the total amount of foreign investments.[29] Berisha's visit to Rome in October 1995 represented a significant move to mend fences. On this occasion, several accords were signed, including a friendship treaty and agreements on economic and military cooperation. Then, in April 1996, Italian President Oscar Luigi Scalfaro visited Tiranë and promised continued Italian support for Albania's economic recovery. Nonetheless, the continuous, illegal flow of Albanian refugees continued to present problems for both sides. While Albania urged Italy to sign an agreement regulating the immigration of Albanian seasonal workers, Rome pressed its neighbor to take more effective measures to stop, or at least substantially decrease, illegal immigration.

Another West European country that provided substantial aid to Albania was Germany. Bonn provided assistance for the reconstruction of water and power supplies; the promotion of small and medium-sized businesses; and the development of agriculture, transport, and light industry. The Germans also were helping to rebuild the Rinas airport, Albania's only international airport. Despite the deepening relationship with Bonn, Albanian officials expressed disappointment that Germany was not more forthcoming with political and economic assistance. Albanian expectations were high in this regard because Albanians had always viewed Germany as more favorably inclined toward their national question than any other European power. Moreover, notwithstanding its June 1995 admission into the Council of Europe,[30] Albania's long-term objectives remained full integration into the European Union and membership in NATO.

Albania also expressed interest in developing relations with Russia, with the aim of expanding economic cooperation and in the hope of tempering Moscow's support for Belgrade on the Kosova issue. The two countries exchanged high-level delegations several times, and Prime Minister Meksi visited Moscow in April 1995. Meksi and his Russian counterpart Viktor Chernomyrdin signed a series of agreements on economic, scientific, and technical cooperation, and initialed a treaty on friendship and cooperation.[31] However, relations were not likely to expand significantly, for political and economic reasons. Russia consistently supported the Serbs and was vocally adamant against Kosova's separation from Serbia. Indeed, with its own internal problems, Russia saw little advantage in expanding economic ties with distant Albania.

Tiranë's relations with its former East European allies were cordial, but interaction remained limited, as all of Eastern Europe was more interested in forging closer ties with members of the European Union. Nonetheless, Albania attempted to develop good ties with Bulgaria, Croatia, and Slovenia. In 1993,

Berisha and his Bulgarian counterpart, Zhelyu Zhelev, signed a treaty of friendship and cooperation. Tiranë, suspicious of the establishment of an axis between Serbia, Greece, and Bulgaria, was anxious to be on good terms with Sofia. During his visit to Bulgaria in April 1994, Berisha praised Zhelev for rejecting an invitation from Greek Prime Minister Constantine Mitsotakis for a secret meeting with Greece and Serbia in 1991. According to Berisha, "the creation of a Greek-Serbian-Bulgarian axis was planned at the meeting, which intended to review Macedonia's fate and could have brought about the division of Macedonia among the three Balkan neighbors."[32]

Albania also signed a series of agreements on economic cooperation with Slovenia and Croatia; but despite its excellent political relations with the two former Yugoslav republics, the latter's follow-through on the economic agreements was weak. However, in the longer run, prospects are good for Slovene and Croatian companies to invest in Albania's tourism, construction industry, agriculture, and food production and processing.

Following the Democrats' rise to power, Albania sought to cultivate a special relationship with Turkey. The two countries signed a treaty of friendship and cooperation and a defense cooperation pact. Hundreds of Albanian officers were trained in Turkish military schools. Turkey expressed support for the construction of an international highway linking the port of Durrës with Istanbul through Skopje and Sofia. In October 1995, during a meeting at the United Nations on the occasion of the world organization's fiftieth anniversary, President Demirel met with his counterparts from Albania, Bulgaria, and Macedonia, and reached an agreement with them on the four-year project. The World Bank, the European Bank for Reconstruction and Development, and the United States had reportedly agreed to finance the billion-dollar project.[33]

In late 1992, Albania became a member of the Organization of Islamic Countries, evidently hoping to become the beneficiary of economic assistance also from this group. In 1993, the Islamic Development Bank pledged to set up a fund of $100 million to encourage investments in Albania. Although Albania's decision to join the Organization of Islamic Countries was clearly prompted by economic and not religious motives,[34] Berisha came under sharp criticism from the opposition for this move.

The Socialist Party claimed that Tiranë's close identification with the Islamic world would lead Europe to reassess its policy toward Albania. Predictably, the Socialists ignored that the roots of Berisha's policy went back to the previous administration, when the parliament had approved Albania's observer status in the organization, in 1991. The Democratic Alliance also joined in the criticism. Raising the specter of the danger of Islamic fundamentalism in Albania, leaders of the Democratic Alliance warned that membership in the Islamic Conference threatened Albania's very survival by setting it apart from the rest of Europe. Berisha countered this criticism by stressing the advantages of potential economic assistance from the Islamic nations and expressing confidence that Albania's membership in the Islamic Conference would not adversely affect its ties with the West.[35]

It is fair to say that those who criticized Berisha on this issue did so with ulterior political motives and not out of any genuine concern about the danger of Islamic fundamentalism in Albania. A U.S. Information Agency poll in March 1996 confirmed that the majority of Albanians tend to identify with the West. An absolute majority of 88 percent said they were more part of the European community of nations, while only 8 percent felt they were more part of the "Muslim community."[36] Critics were unable to answer the question of how Albania's integration into Europe could have proceeded any faster, had it not joined the Organization of Islamic Countries. Realistically, there was little potential for the emergence of fundamentalist Islamic organizations or groups advocating a return to the traditional ways, creeds, and practice of Muslims. Albania's Muslims have never strictly applied the rulings of the Koran. Still, given Western sensitivities to Islamic fundamentalism, the opposition hoped to score propaganda points and raise doubts in Western Europe and the United States about the direction of Berisha's foreign policy.

Relations With Neighbors

Traditionally, one of Albania's most important foreign policy objective has been preventing an Athens-Belgrade alliance directed against Tiranë, and failing that, finding a Great Power ally to keep potential Greek-Yugoslav designs on its territory in check. The disintegration of Yugoslavia caused a realignment among the Balkan countries, threatening once again to revive old territorial conflicts. Albania's Balkan policy conundrum involved balancing competing and equally compelling interests. But whereas Berisha's foreign policy had in general been quite successful and his country was back on the international political map, Albania's efforts to open a new chapter in relations with its contiguous neighbors had mixed results. Ties with Yugoslavia, Macedonia, and Greece continued to be characterized by enduring bilateral conflicts of interests, driven to a great extent by minority issues. Meanwhile, given the salience of the unresolved status of ethnic Albanians in the former Yugoslavia, Tiranë's neighbors were suspicious of Albania's long-term territorial ambitions.

Yugoslavia

Albania's relations with Yugoslavia remained frozen, as Tiranë watched with alarm increasing Serbian repression of the Albanians in Kosova. Tiranë became an outspoken critic of Serbia and one of the most vehement proponents of Western military action against Belgrade. As mentioned earlier, Albania sought greater interaction with the West to counter the perceived military threat from Serbia, therefore offering its air and sea facilities to NATO for peacekeeping missions in the former Yugoslavia. Belgrade, for its part, responded to what it saw as Tiranë's hostile stance by maintaining large numbers of troops on their common border. Between 1992 and 1996, dozens of Albanian citizens were killed in border incidents. The Albanian government strongly supported the imposition of U.N. sanctions against Yugoslavia. It provided important assistance for sanctions enforcement, permitting a NATO naval interdiction force to operate in its waters and hosting a sanctions assistance mission along its border with Yugoslavia. Nevertheless, the imposition of sanctions on rump Yugoslavia had an adverse economic impact on Albania. The northern part of Albania, economically the most depressed region, was hard hit. During 1994-1995, there was massive embargo-busting, primarily in the Shkodër area. Thus, while Tiranë publicly opposed the suspension of the international trade embargo against Serbia and urged the international community to link the issue with progress on Kosova, Albanian officials privately welcomed the lifting of sanctions in late 1995.

While maintaining a hostile posture toward Belgrade, Tiranë also sought to take advantage of tensions between the two partners in the rump Yugoslavia. In the most dramatic demonstration of Albania's new approach to foreign policy, Berisha offered an olive branch to Montenegro. With growing friction between Podgorica and Belgrade, Montenegrins had expressed a slightly more moderate position on Kosova. Taking advantage of the policy nuances of the two Yugoslav republics, Berisha suggested that Montenegro be treated more favorably than Serbia. In September 1993, Montenegro's President Miomir Bulatović, visited Tiranë. Although the new course was unpopular domestically as well as in Kosova, Berisha apparently hoped to drive a wedge between Serbia and Montenegro. With the suspension of U.N. sanctions against rump Yugoslavia, trade between Albania and Montenegro increased. In December 1995, Albanian Minister of Energy and Mineral Resources Abdyl Xhaja visited Podgorica. He signed a series of agreements on economic cooperation in the electric power industry, the oil industry, trade, and geological research.[37] Contacts grew between Albanians on both sides of the border after Montenegro eased restrictions on visas for Albanian citizens. But despite Tiranë's detente with Podgorica, the issue of Kosova remained the key to any long-term reduction in tensions with Yugoslavia.

Macedonia

For Tiranë, Macedonia, home to a large ethnic Albanian community, is a source of deep angst, a foreboding that destabilization of the fledgling country could lead to Serbian intervention, and consequently, Serbian-Greek encirclement of Albania. Berisha strongly supported Macedonia, insisting that an independent state separating unfriendly Serbia and Greece was in Albania's vital national interests. Emphasizing the auspicious convergence of political and economic interests between the two countries, in an attempt to counterbalance the close alliance between Serbia and Greece, Berisha sought to forge close ties with

Macedonia. In April 1993, Albania became one of the first countries to recognize Macedonia,[38] drawing strong criticism at home and a sharp response from Athens. The decision was in line with Berisha's policy of discouraging separatist tendencies among ethnic Albanians in the hope of strengthening Macedonia's stability. In response, the opposition claimed that Berisha had recognized Macedonia unconditionally, thus losing any leverage over Skopje with regard to the position of ethnic Albanians. Berisha's response was simple: "An independent Macedonia is better than a Macedonia under Milošević."[39]

Berisha exerted a moderate influence on ethnic Albanians, urging them to participate in Macedonia's political life and to work for the stability of the new state. At the same time, Albania strongly supported Macedonia during its economic isolation as a result of the Greek embargo. While walking a fine line in its pronouncements on the Macedonia-Greece conflict and avoiding harsh criticism of the Greek embargo, Albania offered Macedonia its port and transport facilities. In contrast to Berisha's support for Macedonia, the opposition Socialist Party and the Democratic Alliance took a stand closer to Greek views on Macedonia. Socialist Party Deputy Chairman Servet Pëllumbi, in a speech at the party's second national conference in February 1994, criticized the government for what he termed its "tolerant and often irresponsible" policy toward Macedonia. He said the government had "both been in a hurry [to strengthen ties with Macedonia] when there was no need, and has kept silent when it should not have done so."[40]

Differences over the status and treatment of the ethnic Albanian minority in Macedonia continued to plague efforts by Albanian and Macedonian leaders to forge a healthy relationship. A series of incidents in 1993—the killing of an Albanian officer by Macedonian border guards, the arrest of a group of prominent ethnic Albanians accused of planning to create underground paramilitary units and of smuggling arms from Albania, and Tiranë's support for a radical faction of the largest ethnic Albanian party in Macedonia—caused serious strains in bilateral relations.

As a result, Albanian officials sharpened their rhetoric concerning President Kiro Gligorov's failure to deliver on promises to improve the status of ethnic Albanians. In an unprecedented move that raised serious questions about Tiranë's posture toward Skopje, Albania publicly called for the replacement of the leaders of the Party for Democratic Prosperity (PDP), thereby intensifying the struggle for power within the party.[41] The PDP leadership, headed by Nevzat Halili, had come under increased criticism for its participation in the Macedonian coalition government and for not being forceful enough in advancing Albanian interests. Tiranë's endorsement of the faction led by Arbër Xhaferi and Menduh Thaçi, which advocated a more militant policy calling for the withdrawal of the PDP from the government, seemed to run counter to Albania's earlier policy of urging ethnic Albanians to pursue their interests through political dialogue with Skopje and within Macedonia's institutional framework.

Skopje sharply criticized the hardening of Albania's position, accusing Tiranë of interference in its internal affairs. The deterioration of Tiranë-Skopje ties, which coincided with a general deterioration in relations among the southern Balkan countries, caused concern in Washington. The United States urged Albania to mend fences with Macedonia. Berisha responded by reining in the more radical PDP faction and taking measures to patch up differences and boost relations with Macedonia. In a meeting with Xhaferi and Thaçi in Tiranë, in March 1994, Berisha urged them to rely on dialogue and democratic means to promote Albanian interests, insisting that an independent and stable Macedonia was in the interest of peace and stability in the Balkans.[42] In a May 1994 meeting with Gligorov in Pogradec, the President offered Albania's facilities to Macedonia and praised Skopje's plans to open an Albanian Pedagogical School and to hold a new census. In his effort to discredit his critics' claims about his meeting with Gligorov and more broadly about Albanian-Macedonian relations, Berisha expressed strong support for Macedonia's independence, insisting that this was in the vital interest of Albania.[43] The official media, with typical rhetorical flourish, praised the meeting as a demonstration of Albania's constructive role in regional affairs.

However, although Berisha's summit meeting with Gligorov and his undiminished support for Macedonia's stability were praised internationally, they gained him little domestic political capital. The upbeat assessment of government officials contrasted with commentary by the opposition and the antigovernment media, which criticized the meeting as having accomplished little and accused Berisha of having sacrificed the interests of Albanians across the border. Opposition leaders questioned the feasibility of Albania's seeking a closer relationship with Macedonia, remained sensitive to questions of reciprocity, and expressed concern that Skopje was gaining unilateral advantages.

Macedonian leaders, for their part, were clearly buoyed by the meeting and appeared willing to work toward improving bilateral ties. But statements by senior officials suggested that Skopje resisted making significant changes in its stance toward ethnic Albanians in order to advance relations with Tiranë. Macedonian officials apparently believed that crises in Albania's relations with Serbia and Greece limited Tiranë's options. Then, too, with the strengthening of its international position—by admission into the Council of Europe and the Organization for Security and Cooperation in Europe (OSCE), and the defusion of tensions with Greece—Macedonia became less interested in pursuing a close relationship with Albania.

The Albanian government faced considerable pressure from across the political spectrum to take strong action in February 1995, when Macedonian authorities used the police in an attempt to prevent the opening of an Albanian-language university in Tetovë. Tiranë denounced the violence and warned that the incident could force Albania to "reconsider" its policy toward Macedonia.[44] The Tetovë incident sharpened the dilemma the Albanian government faced in formulating policy toward Macedonia.[45] Although official Tiranë viewed the controversy surrounding the Tetovë University as unwelcome, its reaction was restrained. But in contrast to the government's overall temperate position and desire to avoid aggravating its already frayed relationship with Skopje by creating the impression of interference in its internal affairs, Albania's parties across the political spectrum denounced the Macedonian move and criticized Berisha for being too patient with Skopje's failure to be more accommodating toward the ethnic Albanian population.

By the end of 1996, the goodwill evident between Albania and Macedonia during the first years of Berisha's administration had largely dissipated. Both sides were restrained by their domestic political situation from taking any bold moves to attempt a breakthrough in relations.

Greece

Ties with Greece represent an important aspect of Albania's overall foreign policy. Since the early 1990s, however, several issues have served as a bone of contention, significantly constraining the expansion of bilateral relations. First, Athens has complained about the treatment of ethnic Greeks in Albania, charging violations of their human and religious rights. It also has alleged that Tiranë was pursuing a systematic policy of forcing ethnic Greeks to leave the country. Although ethnic Greeks, estimated at about 70,000 by Albania and at more than 200,000 by Greece, continued to have some legitimate grievances, particularly regarding Greek-language education, there was no credible evidence that the Albanian government systematically repressed the Greek minority. Many Greeks had indeed fled Albania,[46] but they had done so mainly for economic reasons, joining some 300,000 Albanian citizens who had left the country in search of jobs and a better life in Greece. While in Greece there was a strong current of opinion which linked the rise of crime to the Albanian element, Tiranë complained that Athens was using the issue of illegal Albanian refugees, whose annual remittances of more than $200 million played a critical role in Albania's economic recovery, as a bargaining chip to extract concessions from Albania on domestic and foreign policy issues. Moreover, conflicting national interests continued to cloud relations. Greece was distressed by Albania's decision to recognize Macedonia, and by its deepening political and military relationships with Turkey and the United States. Albania, always wary of the creation of an Athens-Belgrade alliance directed against Tiranë, considered Greece's close relationship with Serbia worrisome.

After an initial improvement in relations in the wake of the Democratic victory in Albania, the festering uneasiness, fueled by deep mutual suspicions, erupted in mid-1993, when Albanian authorities deported a Greek clergyman, Archimandrite Khirsostomos, who had been caught disseminating maps that included substantial portions of Albania within Greek borders. This incident led to a rapid deterioration of relations between the two countries. Within days, Athens retaliated by returning some 30,000 Albanian refugees. Moreover, Greek Prime Minister Constantine Mitsotakis issued a list of five demands, which included Archimandrite Khirsostomos's return to Albania; the opening of minority schools at all levels; the free development of political, educational, cultural, and social organizations by the Greek minority; and return of Greek property confiscated by the Hoxha regime. The Greek leader dramatically raised the stakes by drawing a parallel between the position of ethnic Greeks in Albania and Albanians in Kosova. Mitsotakis insisted that whatever status Tiranë demanded for Kosova also be granted to the ethnic Greeks in southern Albania.[47] Berisha responded that Mitsotakis's demands were unacceptable.[48]

There were striking differences, however, between the government and the opposition on the posture toward Greece. The Socialist Party and the Democratic Alliance charged that Berisha's foreign policy was slavishly pro-American, and that this had damaged ties with Greece. In June 1993, at the conclusion of a visit to Greece by Socialist leader Fatos Nano, the Socialist Party and Andreas Papandreou's PASOK had signed a joint statement, which stressed that Albania could hope to obtain her objective of full integration into Europe only with Greek help. The statement expressed strong opposition to foreign military involvement in the Balkans. Paradoxically, there was no mention of Kosova.[49]

Athens's goal appeared to be not only to weaken Berisha's position by extracting concessions of special status for the Greek minority but also to raise the specter of Greek intervention in the south, should Albanians push for Kosova's unification with Albania.[50] Greece vehemently opposed Kosova's separation from Serbia, claiming that this would radically upset the status quo in the Balkans. Not surprisingly, Greece's newly threatening stance resulted in an upsurge of domestic support for Berisha and in calls to halt the alleged Hellenization of southern Albania. There was anger among Albanians over the refugee deportations, and more generally, over the parallel Athens had drawn between the small ethnic Greek community in Albania and the roughly two million Albanians in Kosova.

Albania figured prominently in the 1993 Greek election campaign, with both Mitsotakis and Andreas Papandreou, leader of the Pan-Hellenic Socialist Movement (PASOK), publicly criticizing Berisha. Soon after PASOK's victory, however, Greek Foreign Minister Karolos Papoulias visited Tiranë, and an agreement was reached on the creation of a mixed commission to deal with contentious issues.[51] But while Papoulias spoke of a new chapter in relations, progress was slow. Indeed, Albania and Greece experienced some of the worst tensions in their relationship in decades, in the wake of an armed attack on the Albanian military post of Peshkëpia in April 1994. A Greek organization calling itself the Northern Epirus Liberation Front (MAVI) immediately claimed responsibility.[52] Nonetheless, Berisha, in comments that underscored his strong displeasure with the Greek government and marked a sharp escalation in Tiranë's anti-Greek rhetoric, lashed out against Athens in blunt terms, accusing Greece of state terrorism. He said the Greek government bore "full responsibility" for the attack and suggested that Greece and Serbia were coordinating their actions with the aim of destabilizing the entire region. The Albanian president accused Greece of "expansionist goals."[53] While the Greek government denied Albanian charges and denounced the attack on the military post,[54] Athens refused to take any significant steps to curb the Greek extremists.[55]

Soon after the Peshkëpia incident, Albanian authorities arrested five members of the ethnic Greek organization Omonia on charges of espionage and illegal weapons possession. The Omonia trial drew international criticism for procedural shortcomings.[56] As both sides engaged in charges and countercharges, Tiranë-Athens relations sank to their lowest point since the restoration of diplomatic ties in 1971.

Feeding into a continuing undercurrent of hostility toward Albania among Greek nationalists, the arrest of Omonia members provided grist for more virulent anti-Albanian forces in Greece.[57] The authorities began a massive deportation campaign of Albanian refugees. Within a short time, more than 70,000 Albanians were deported, putting significant social and economic strains on Albania. The Greek media, which seemed to drive Athens's policy, reverted to the kind of virulent anti-Albanian rhetoric that had been characteristic of Greek commentary in the past but had become less frequent after Berisha came to office in 1992. Among the shriller pronouncements in the progovernment media, Greek officials warned of impending armed conflict. Concomitantly with pressure on Berisha, Athens embarked on an aggressive campaign to discredit the Albanian government internationally and to portray the former Communists and the leftist Democratic Alliance as liberal and pro-Western. In addition, the powerful Greek lobby in the United States took up the cause of Albania's ethnic Greeks. As mentioned above, the White House, under strong Greek pressure, put on hold plans for a $30 million Albanian-American Enterprise Fund. Athens also was able temporarily to block European Union plans to grant Albania some $40 million in aid.

The Albanian opposition attempted to gain political capital from the dramatic setback in Tiranë-Athens relations by blaming the imbroglio on Berisha and implying that the Albanian government was either incompetent or deliberately fomenting the crisis. Leftist press coverage ran true to form, with *Zëri i Popullit, Koha Jonë,* and *Aleanca* giving broad, judgmental coverage vilifying Berisha for indifference to the damage caused to bilateral ties. Right-wing forces, on the other hand, called on the government not to give in to what they perceived as Greek interference in Albania's internal affairs.[58] The right feared an erosion of national sovereignty, pointing to the Greek grip on the economy, the use of the Greek currency in the south, and the widespread Albanian practice of adopting Greek names when applying for visas to go to Greece. There also were increased calls for the expulsion of Archbishop Anastasios Yannoulatos, who in 1992 had been appointed head of the Albanian Orthodox Church by the Ecumenical Patriarchate of Constantinople.

The political fallout from the incident in Peshkëpia and from the Omonia trial continued to bedevil bilateral relations for months. Inept presentation and poor public relations also adversely affected Albania's image abroad, and more importantly, cast a dark cloud over Tiranë's special relationship with Washington. The release of the Omonia defendants in early 1995 resolved a peculiar situation in which Albanian-Greek relations had become hostage to the fate of five ethnic Greeks. It also cleared the way for Papoulias's visit to Tiranë after months of mutual recriminations and tit-for-tat diplomatic hostilities. Albanian officials hailed the visit as a success, particularly on economic and refugee issues. A statement issued by Berisha's office put an unusually optimistic spin on Papoulias's visit, suggesting greater flexibility by Athens on bilateral relations and portraying the Greek foreign minister as being accommodating toward Tiranë's views on refugees and other bilateral issues. Similarly upbeat in its assessment, *Rilindja Demokratike* observed that bilateral ties had fully regained their health and warmth, which was also important for the entire region.[59]

Although Papoulias's visit produced little progress toward a Greek reconciliation with Albania, it did pave the way for further negotiations and behind-the-scenes maneuvering to resolve contentious issues.[60] In June 1995, the Albanian parliament passed a law on private education, allowing the establishment of private religious and foreign-language high schools. Albania's shift on the issue of education, which had been a major irritant in bilateral relations, signaled that Tiranë was willing to address some of Athens's key concerns as a step toward improved relations. The decision suggested that the leadership was taking a more flexible position in order to pave the way for a proposed meeting between Berisha and Greek president Konstandinos Stefanopoulos.

Despite continued mutual suspicion, by the beginning of 1996, the two countries seemed well on the way to reconciling their differences. Leadership changes in Athens had a positive impact on Tiranë-Athens relations as the new Prime Minister, Costas Simitis, adopted a less emotional approach to Albania and appeared to make concrete efforts to nurture a healthy relationship with the northern neighbor. On Athens's part, the change also represented an acknowledgment that its previous pressure tactics had merely increased Albania's concerns about Greek intentions. Albania, for its part, while still wary of Athens's intentions, was mindful of Greece's importance and economic relationship, and clearly welcomed efforts to improve ties. With rising tensions in Kosova and increasing difficulties with Macedonia, Albania desperately needed to calm the tensions on its southern border and put an end to the seemingly endless series of crises with Greece. Moreover, both countries had strong incentives to maintain good ties. Their growing political and economic relations provided benefits to both. Albania counted on a strong flow of remittances from Albanian refugees to help support its program of economic revival. Greece, already Albania's second biggest trading partner after Italy, hoped to develop a larger stake in the Albanian market.

President Konstandinos Stefanopoulos paid a groundbreaking visit to Tiranë in March 1996. The two countries signed a friendship treaty, which for the Albanians had come to be regarded as a key security issue. Albania pledged to respect the rights of the ethnic Greek community, open new Greek-language schools, and take measures to guard its border against illegal crossings.[61] The visit added momentum to bilateral relations, as both Albania and Greece committed to an expansion of their political, economic, and military cooperation. Soon after Stephanopoulos's visit, Albanian foreign and defense ministers paid separate visits to Athens and signed agreements on seasonal workers and on boosting military ties. In July 1996, Greek troops participated in military exercises organized in Albania within the framework of NATO's Partnership for Peace program. Athens even pledged to support Albania's full membership in NATO and its association with the European Union.

While the steady normalization of Albanian-Greek ties since early 1995 was one of the most positive recent developments in the southern Balkans, the domestic dynamics in both countries put a break on major improvements in their relations. Leaders of both countries were unable to dispel completely the terrible mistrust that exists between the two sides. Many Greeks continued to harbor a mistrust of Albanian motives and the treatment of ethnic Greeks. Although only some Albanians on the extreme right feared that the Greeks would go so far as to occupy southern parts of their country, Greece was widely seen as exploiting Albania's political and military weakness and economic dependence. It remains to be seen whether the crises in recent years were a passing storm in Albanian-Greek relations or whether the relationship is in danger of succumbing to the powerful nationalist impulses sweeping the Balkans. Decisionmakers on both sides have begun to display a greater understanding of the underpinnings of one another's policies. Yet Albanian and Greek leaders must strive to avoid confrontational rhetoric and to develop a strategy of handling disagreements and incidents—which are sure to arise in the future, as they have in the past—and avoid the tendency to escalate every incident into a crisis.

The Albanian National Question

Ever since Albania gained its independence in 1912, the issue of Kosova and other predominantly Albanian-inhabited territories that were forcefully incorporated into Yugoslavia have presented Tiranë's policymakers with a unique national and foreign policy predicament. Successive Albanian governments have publicly accepted the notion of the inviolability of borders and have trod carefully so as not to encourage irredentism among ethnic Albanians, fearing that opening the border issue would have serious repercussions. But despite official statements that it accepted existing borders, Albania essentially remained a revisionist state. It was never content with its borders, although circumstances forced it to acquiesce to the status quo. Most Albanians never viewed Kosova and other Albanian-inhabited territories as legitimate parts of Serbia and the former Yugoslavia, and most continue to believe that the borders should be reviewed.

Contrary to the hopes of many Albanians, the end of the Cold War, the demise of communism, and the dismemberment of the former Yugoslavia were not followed by the resolution of their national question. Kosova's Albanians, unarmed and severely battered by years of Serbian military crackdown, were inadequately prepared to take advantage of the opportunities created by those historic developments. Concomitantly, the disintegration of Yugoslavia coincided with a time of great turmoil and political upheaval in Albania, which had just embarked on the difficult transition from more than four decades of Communist dictatorship. Moreover, how to adjust to the as yet undefined domestic and regional environment was the key question that would have taxed even the most farsighted and penetrating of leaders, let alone those who were just entering politics and were forced to operate under very serious constraints.

Paradoxically, from the point of view of most Albanians, the national question became more complex in the wake of the collapse of the Yugoslav federation. Albanians in Kosova were now separated from their kin in Macedonia by a new, international border. In its efforts to promote the rights of ethnic Albanians, Tiranë had to harmonize its national interests vis-à-vis Belgrade and Skopje and engage in delicate balancing to avoid an alliance between Serbs and Macedonians, who dislike Albanians much more than they do each other. In short, the dramatic change in the geopolitical landscape of the Balkans further complicated Albanians' attempts to meet their national challenges in a comprehensive and cooperative manner.

The Albanians in Kosova

A formerly autonomous province and a constituent unit of Yugoslavia where ethnic Albanians account for 92 percent of the population and ethnic Serbs for 8 percent, Kosova has long been a bone of contention between Serbs and Albanians, both of whom claim the region on historical and ethnic grounds. In medieval times, Kosova was part of the Serbian state. However, the Albanian national movement in the 1870s had its origins in Kosova, and it was there that the Albanians waged the major struggle that led to the proclamation of Albania's independence from Turkey in 1912. Relations between Albanians and Serbs have fluctuated from uneasy coexistence to outright hostility as Serbia continued to hold a tight grip over Kosova. It was only after the dismissal in 1966 of Aleksander Ranković, Yugoslavia's vice president and secret police chief, and large-scale Albanian demonstrations in autumn 1968, that Belgrade granted Albanians autonomy. Yugoslavia's 1974 constitution recognized Kosova, jointly with Vojvodina, Serbia's other province, as a constituent federal unit. However, the new constitutional arrangements fell far short of what the Albanians had demanded: republic status for Kosova, with the theoretical right to secede. Since the early 1960s, the Serbs had been confronted with a weakening demographic base in Kosova. By the mid-1970s, the proportion of Serbs was no longer sufficient to man all the strategic positions in the political, economic, and administrative fields. Meanwhile, as the proportion of Albanians staffing the province's top and medium levels of the party and state bureaucracy increased, many Serbs complained that Kosova's wide powers of self-rule were undermining Serbia's statehood and threatening Serb presence in the province. Tensions between the two ethnic groups were further exacerbated by economic problems, as Kosova had remained the country's most backward region.

In March-April 1981, Belgrade used the army to crush massive ethnic Albanian protests demanding that Kosova be proclaimed a republic. Serbia's leaders took advantage of the unrest to circumscribe Kosova's autonomy and roll back gains that the Albanians had enjoyed after the promulgation of the 1974 constitution. The conflict assumed a new dimension with Slobodan Milošević's rise to power in Serbia in 1986. Relying on nationalism to consolidate his power, Milošević purged the moderate elements within the Serbian leadership, accusing them of being soft on Albanian nationalism, and initiated an inflammatory media coverage, accusing ethnic Albanians of carrying out "genocide" against Kosova's Serbs.[62] During 1988-1989, Milošević launched a campaign to bring Kosova under Serbia's total control by pushing through constitutional changes. In contravention of Yugoslavia's constitution, in 1989, Serbia suspended Kosova's autonomy and imposed martial law in the province. In July 1990, Albanian members of the provincial parliament declared Kosova an independent unit within the Yugoslav federation. In response, Milošević suspended the local parliament and government, fully integrating Kosova into the republic of Serbia.[63] Belgrade authorities also shut down the Albanian-language television and radio stations and the daily *Rilindja,* and launched a policy of political, economic, and cultural marginalization of ethnic Albanians. Albanians in leading government and administrative positions were replaced by Serbs. More than 120,000 Albanian workers were fired; many also were evicted from their apartments. The police force was cleansed of all Albanians. And when Albanians refused to accept Serbian programs, the Albanian-language university and all other educational institutions, including elementary schools, were closed down. Serbia pursued a policy of unprecedented repression, depriving the ethnic Albanians of their security and basic human rights. Belgrade also imposed discriminatory legal and administrative measures. Police brutality, violence, arbitrary searches, seizures and arrests, and torture and ill-treatment of detainees became daily routine, leading to massive migrations of Albanians.[64]

Throughout the post-World War II period, ethnic Albanians had not advocated union with Albania, although they had pushed for greater political autonomy. Before the suspension of Kosova's autonomy and the subsequent independence of Slovenia and Croatia, Kosovar Albanians had not considered secession a practical option. While various political groups and organizations had emerged as early as the 1950s and 1960s, there was no strong Albanian irredentist movement. Meanwhile, Albania's claims to Kosova had remained dormant. Under Enver Hoxha's rule, Albania offered no more than perfunctory support to ethnic Albanian demands that the status of Kosova be elevated to that of a republic, apparently in the hope of seeing the entire issue fizzle. Hoxha's successor, Ramiz Alia, was even less supportive of the Kosovar Albanians, going so far as to accept that Kosova's status was an internal Yugoslav issue.

The abolishment of Kosova's autonomy led to the discrediting and eventual disintegration of the local, predominantly Albanian, League of Communists, which had been loyal to Belgrade, and in the eyes of most Albanians, had not fought hard enough to preserve the province's autonomy. But more importantly, Serbia's crackdown led to the emergence of a new political elite and to a qualitative change in the nature of Albanian demands, from a republic within Yugoslavia to outright secession. In December 1989, a group of intellectuals led by literary critic Ibrahim Rugova created the Democratic League of Kosova, the first non-communist party to be formed in Kosova since World War II. Although other political parties also were formed, the Democratic League rapidly expanded its membership, becoming the dominant political force in the region. Rugova argued that Kosova, as a constituent federal unit of former Yugoslavia with re- cognized borders, was entitled to independent statehood. In a 1991 referendum, the Kosovar Albanians voted overwhelmingly for independence and appealed for recognition to the European Community. Although Kosova was a former federal unit, the European Community (now European Union) adopted the position that it was not entitled to independent statehood since it was a "province" rather than a "republic."[65] In May 1992, the ethnic Albanians organized multiparty elections, and Rugova was elected president. Serbia declared the elections illegal and thwarted Rugova's plans to convene the parliament.

Kosovar Albanians, nevertheless, proceeded to establish parallel institutions, creating a state within a state. Relying on nonviolent methods, a novel approach in a region known for its history of violent resolutions of ethnic conflicts, Albanians attempted to resist what amounted to Serbian colonial rule and efforts to change the ethnic structure of the region's population by forcing Albanians to flee and encouraging Serbs to settle there. Although the Serbs continued to maintain a heavy army presence in the region, the only authority the Albanians recognized was that of Rugova, who refused to follow the Balkans' well-worn path of violence. The close-knit family structure and national solidarity made it possible for the Albanians to stave off Serbia's economic pressures. A private educational system was setup. Instruction in the Albanian language was carried out in private houses, mosques, churches, restaurants, garages, barns, and other temporary locations. A solidarity fund, financed locally and by the diaspora in Western Europe and the United States, provided assistance to the neediest, especially to the families of Albanians imprisoned on political charges. Teachers and doctors working at private clinics received token financial assistance from the solidarity fund. Successful Albanian entrepreneurs at home and abroad adopted needy families, providing them with year-round material assistance.

At the end of 1996, the situation in Kosova could be described as neither peace nor war. While both Serbs and Albanians publicly expressed readiness to open talks, beyond this point there was a huge perceptual gap between Belgrade and Prishtinë about the underpinnings of Serbian-Albanian coexistence. Neither side seemed willing to give up its maximalist demands, which would have opened the way for serious negotiations. Belgrade had pursued two central goals: Ensuring Kosova's integration into Serbia, and breaking the will of the Albanians by brute force. It had succeeded in neither; but Milošević had not yet given up. There was no shift in the official position, no recognition that Serbia might be better off to let Kosova go than to be forever in conflict with the Albanian majority there. The costs to Serbia of keeping Kosova under its control were high, but still acceptable. Although some Serbs were evidently not willing to pay the price of keeping Kosova within Serbia, as they had come to believe that only the direst of actions—war—could succeed in deterring the Albanians from the path of independence, there were no signs of significant changes in Serbia's political mood on the Albanian issue. Many Serbs were willing to acknowledge that the suspension of Kosova's autonomy was a terribly misguided move; but few were able to liberate themselves from the Kosova syndrome. Moreover, there had been no significant pressure—either from the Albanians or from the international community—that would force Milošević's government to change its behavior.

Similarly, ethnic Albanians showed no inclination to back away from their one central, strategic goal: self-determination. They continued to display remarkable staying power in the face of severe repression, refusing to accept the legitimacy of Serbia's rule and pursuing their demands for independence with passionate intensity. Rugova, however, saw independence from Serbia not as an objective that could be achieved overnight but rather as a long-term process. While he continued to stick to his position that Kosova's separation from Serbia was nonnegotiable,[66] he indicated that ethnic Albanians would defer unification with Albania indefinitely. Cognizant of the difficulty of any Serbian leader's accepting Kosova's independence, Rugova supported a gradual dissociation. As an interim arrangement, he proposed the establishment of an independent Kosovar state, which would remain neutral and maintain close ties with Serbia and Albania. He indicated willingness to accept an initial agreement on less controversial issues, while postponing the thorny issue of the status of Kosova to an unspecified later date.

The West was supportive of Rugova's nonviolent approach in confronting the acute political and economic injustices that the Albanians in Kosova lived under. Two successive U.S. administrations warned Milošević that in the event of a Serb-inspired conflict in Kosova, Washington would be prepared to "employ military force against the Serbs in Kosova and in Serbia proper."[67] The Clinton administration reportedly had "seriously considered" dispatching American forces to Kosova in May 1993, when troops were sent to neighboring Macedonia.[68] The late NATO Secretary-General Manfred Woerner publicly declared that the extension of fighting to Kosova "had to be stopped at all costs."[69] Concomitantly, Western officials exerted pressure on Rugova not to take any action, including convening the parliament elected in 1992, which Serbia might interpret as provocation. But while Western powers and the Albanians shared the common objective of preventing the outbreak of war in Kosova, beyond that point their interests did not coincide. The United States and the European Union did not recognize Kosova's independence, insisting only on the restoration of the autonomy that the province had enjoyed in Yugoslavia earlier. Moreover, Western powers had resigned themselves to what in their view was an ongoing, low-intensity ethnic conflict. Violence in Kosova was considered relatively minuscule by comparison with events such as those in Bosnia, parts of the former Soviet Union, and other trouble spots.

On the issue of independence, Kosova's Albanians did not even enjoy Tiranë's full support. Although a Kosova settlement remained a vital national security issue, Albania's options were severely limited, and its overriding concern remained the prevention of armed conflict. Albania's armed forces were grossly inadequate for the country's defense much less to conduct a Kosovar war of liberation against Yugoslavia's superior military. While insisting that Tiranë was doing everything within its power to prevent the outbreak of an armed conflict with the vastly more powerful Yugoslavia, Berisha repeatedly stated that Albania would not stand idly by if Serbia attempted to resolve the Kosova issue by military force. The president maintained that for Albania and the Albanians, the first priority had been and remained the prevention of conflict. But he added that "in the event of a conflict in Kosova or in other territories inhabited by the Albanians, the Albanian nation will react and resist with all means at its disposal."[70]

Meanwhile, although Albania had endorsed Rugova's plan for a neutral state, Tiranë had done this in a lukewarm manner. Talk of confederation between Albania and Kosova, let alone unification, was considered premature or unrealistic. Berisha called for direct talks between Prishtinë and Belgrade, with a third party, preferably the United States, serving as mediator. Responding to increased criticism that Albania was not doing much for Kosova, Berisha pointed out that in international fora and at bilateral meetings, Tiranë had demanded the restoration of all institutions abolished by Serbia in 1990 and "full respect for the human and national rights of Albanians in Kosova." Berisha added that Albania believed that "violent border changes were unacceptable and the worst option for the Albanians." He called for a status of Kosova that would satisfy both Albanians and Serbs.[71] Indeed, Berisha went so far as to state that Albania could not speak for Kosova and that the issue could be solved only through a dialogue between Rugova and the Serbian leadership.[72]

However, the stalemate with Serbia, continued repression, and the exclusion of Kosova from Balkan peace talks heightened the perception among many ethnic Albanians that the Rugova leadership was incapable of defending their interests. Rugova had been the embodiment of the Kosovar struggle, and until recently, his leadership had not come under serious scrutiny. Other Albanian political parties and groups were willing to cut Rugova a bit of slack, mainly because of the extraordinary circumstances under which he had to operate. But if Rugova was perceived as the right person in 1990, six years later serious questions were being raised about his leadership. The Albanian nonviolent movement had lost momentum, the masses had largely been demobilized, and since 1992 there had been no organized resistance to Serbia's increasingly repressive measures. The huge gap between Rugova's pronouncements that ethnic Albanians would not accept anything less than independence and their practical inability to force Belgrade to consider separation became more glaring. Under Rugova's leadership, the Albanians clearly defined separation as their goal, yet they had not been willing to fight for it. This was not only a reflection of lack of capacity and will, and resignation in the face of overwhelming odds, but also of failed leadership. Obviously, lack of significant resistance had undermined the Albanians' position in the eyes of Belgrade and their Western supporters. Moreover, the failure to convene the parliament, set up a functioning administrative machinery, and make local Albanian institutions the empowering authority, along with the postpone-ment of elections scheduled for May 1996, seriously undermined Rugova's position. So did the establishment of a government in exile (Bonn), with Bujar Bukoshi serving as prime minister, rather than in Prishtinë.

Rugova's critics maintained that the situation of the ethnic Albanians had become much worse than it was in 1990, when Serbia suspended Kosova's auton-omy. Some advocated active forms of resistance, arguing that continued Serbian repression was likely to lead to a situation in which the Albanians would be unable to mount any resistance. In a statement issued in November 1995, the Forum of Albanian Intellectuals of Kosova, led by Rexhep Qosja, termed Rugova's policy a total failure and warned that the Albanian issue was being sacrificed for "regional peace and stability."[73] There were increased demands that the Albanians reexamine their aims and objectives and the means of achieving them. Some prominent personalities, including Qosja, human-rights activist Adem Demaçi, and journalist Veton Surroi, cast aspersions on Rugova's ability to effectively lead the Albanian movement. There were also increasing differences between Rugova and Prime Minister Bukoshi. While Rugova continued to express optimism and to claim international support for Kosova's independence, Bukoshi offered a more realistic assessment, noting that the ethnic Albanian issue had not figured in any international peace plan for the former Yugoslavia and that no state had recognized Kosova's independence. Bukoshi decried the loss of willingness to take direct action that had marked Kosovar Albanian protests in the late 1980s and the beginning of the 1990s. He warned of dire consequences unless the national movement was reinvigorated and the masses remobilized.[74]

While some of the criticism against Rugova was misplaced and politically motivated, he did seem to have lost the initiative and he had become a symbol of the status quo. Rugova's leadership was slipping into a quagmire of broken promises and frustrated expectations. He continued to insist that good behavior and peaceful resistance eventually would be recognized and rewarded. However, Rugova's claims of international support for the Albanian cause had run up against the creeping realization that the international community was treating Kosova simply as a minority issue and appeared willing to forgive Serbian oppression of ethnic Albanians in order to secure Belgrade's cooperation in achieving a semblance of peace in Bosnia.

The exclusion of Kosova from the peace talks on former Yugoslavia was seen as an egregious omission and an enormous affront to Albanians in both Kosova and Albania. The end result of the Dayton agreement—the de facto division of Bosnia, the very outcome that the United States and the European Union had originally pledged to avoid—raised serious concerns in Kosova. Dayton shattered what had become a widespread belief, nurtured by Rugova, that the solution to Kosova's problem lay on the horizon.[75] It was questionable whether Kosovar Albanian leaders at this juncture could oppose a humiliating solution imposed under duress by the Serbian occupation and in the absence of international support. This could involve some sort of a semi-autonomous status, or even worse, partitioning and ethnic cleansing. Albanians wondered whether Washington's warnings to Milošević reflected what the United States was prepared to do in Kosova. Western declarations that Kosova was part of Serbia hardened Belgrade's position, deepening the frustration and humiliation of Albanians on both sides of the border. By supporting the Serbian position and tolerating massive violations of Kosovar Albanian human, civil, national, and political rights, the international community demonstrated its total obliviousness to Albanian rights and sensitivities. A mood of foreboding seemed to have settled over Albanians in Kosova. The result further diminished Rugova's stature among his former supporters and led to a progressive radicalization of the Kosovar Albanian masses. There were increasing calls for more drastic actions against Serbia, while a heretofore unknown organization, calling itself the Kosova Liberation Army, took responsibility for a series of synchronized violent attacks, directed primarily at the police.

The Dayton agreement had serious implications for Kosova. While on the one hand it seemed to close the door on secession, in essence the agreement legitimized partitioning and ethnic cleansing. It was precisely in the post-Dayton period that prominent Serbs began publicly to speak of the desirability of partitioning Kosova. In June 1996, Aleksandar Despić, head of the Serbian Academy of Arts and Sciences, warned that given the high birth rates among Albanians, by the middle of the twenty-first century, Serbia would become a bilingual state, with the number of ethnic Albanians being the same as that of

Serbs. He warned that this would pose a serious threat to the fate of the Serbian nation in their own state. Despić went on to suggest talks with Albanians on partitioning the region.[76] The problem with this solution is that partitioning of Kosova, where the Serbs are scattered and account for only about 8 percent of the total population, is likely to lead to war and massive sufferings. It is also likely that the Serbs would want to retain the largest, mineral-rich parts of Kosova, which would involve the forcible resettlement, or ethnic cleansing, of more than a million Albanians. The Kosovar Albanians were quick to respond that partitioning was unacceptable.[77] Meanwhile, talk of partitioning caused fear among Kosova's Serbs and Montenegrins that Milošević would sell them out, as he had the Croatian Serbs in Krajina.

The fate of Bosnia accentuated Albanian anxieties that the outside world, which had displayed a lack of political will to force Serbia to the negotiating table with the Kosovar Albanians, might remain indifferent in the event of war. The exclusion of Kosova from Balkan peace talks had reinforced the belief among ethnic Albanians that the international community did not care about their plight and that it rewarded those who had used violence rather than peaceful means to achieve their national objectives. Disappointed with lack of support from the international community, prominent personalities in both Kosova and Albania accused the outside world of having betrayed Kosova. But the fact was that Kosovar Albanians had not revolted because they were unable to do so, due to the level of Serbian repression and the Albanians' lack of organization—and not as a favor to the international community.

Except for condemnations of human rights violations, the international community had done little to pressure Serbia. Moreover, in the post-Dayton period, the attitude of the international community was becoming more accommodating toward Serbia, whose support was considered essential for the success of the Bosnia peace agreements. Serbia was gradually and unmistakably being readmitted into the international community, which from Prishtinë's point of view meant that the community of nations had absolved Belgrade of responsibility for its brutal repression of Albanians since the early 1980s. European powers were reluctant to link the issue of Serbia's reintegration into the international community with the solution of the Kosova conflict. Although the human rights situation in Kosova had not improved, soon after the Dayton accords, the European powers recognized Yugoslavia.[78] The United States, on the other hand, was more supportive of the Albanian cause. Washington refused to send an ambassador to Belgrade, and blocked Yugoslavia's membership in the United Nations, the World Bank, the International Monetary Fund and the Organization for Security and Cooperation in Europe. In July 1996, the United States opened an information office in Prishtinë. The U.S. Information Service center was viewed by most Albanians as an embassy, although the office had no formal diplomatic role.

During a meeting with Milošević in Belgrade in February 1996, Secretary of State Warren Christopher said that Yugoslavia "will never achieve full acceptance into the international community, will never achieve full approbation by the United States until it reconciles the status of Kosovo."[79] In a meeting in Washington in December 1996, Rugova was assured by Christopher that an "outer wall" of sanctions against Serbia would remain in place until significant progress had been made in Kosova. According to a State Department statement, Christopher "reaffirmed strong U.S. support for the restoration of full human and political rights" to the people of Kosova.[80] However, both the United States and the European Union continued to regard Kosova as part of Serbia, insisting only on the restoration of Kosova's previous autonomy.

In September 1996, Rugova and Milošević signed an agreement that would allow Albanian students to return to Kosova's schools and university. The agreement, brokered by the Sant'Egidio Community, a Rome-based Roman Catholic peace group, was hailed as a major breakthrough and fueled hopes of tangible benefits. But as the year went on and authorities in Belgrade refused to implement the agreement, there was deep disappointment and frustration among ethnic Albanians.

Rugova faced the toughest challenge to his leadership in the aftermath of the outbreak of prodemocracy demonstrations in Belgrade in November 1996. His reaction was that there was no difference between Milošević and Serb opposition leaders and that the Belgrade protests were an internal Serbian affair. Critics seized the opportunity to denounce Rugova's passive stand and to call for peaceful protests and demonstrations. The Albanian government expressed public support for the Serbian opposition coalition, and in an unusual move, urged Kosova's Albanians to stage their own peaceful demonstrations. Human rights activist Adem Demaçi, who in December 1996 became chairman of the Parliamentary Party of Kosova, arguing that Rugova's policies had failed and that there was a need for more aggressive action against Milošević, sent a public message of support to Belgrade protesters. While neither Demaçi nor other Rugova critics had any illusions about the Serb opposition's stand on Kosova, they strongly believed that Albanians had a better chance of achieving their political objectives if Milošević was forced out of office and Serbia moved toward democracy. Rugova strongly opposed demonstrations, urging his followers to desist from actions that could cause Kosova to descend into violence. But his failure to regain the initiative, combined with the continued deterioration of the general situation — deepening social and moral crisis, breakdown of schools, family, and economy, and growing emigration—weakened his influence. Rugova's leadership is threatened, as an increasing number of ethnic Albanians no longer accept that there is no alternative to pacifist resistance. There is a serious danger that Kosovar Albanian moderates will be marginalized as radicals win greater support. Unless there is progress soon, peaceful resistance could lose out to frustration, leading to violence, and thereby ending hopes for a nonviolent resolution of the conflict.

The Albanians in Macedonia

The simmering feud between Albanians and Macedonians represents a significant threat to Macedonia's stability and long-term survival as an independent entity.[81] The ethnic Albanians, who are overwhelmingly Muslim, have had a long, troubled relationship with the Orthodox Macedonians. Under the old, Communist regime, they were fiercely repressed and had few chances for political and cultural expression. In the 1970s, they made significant strides in asserting their rights, but the unrest in Kosova in 1981 had immediate and serious reverberations in Macedonia. In the mid-1980s, Albanians in Macedonia found themselves in a more menacing position than those in Kosova, as Skopje embarked on a severely repressive policy, purging Albanian officials and teachers, shutting down Albanian-language schools, imprisoning many Albanians for alleged nationalistic activity (including attendance at Albanian weddings), banning "offending" Albanian names, and destroying the traditional walls around Albanian homes.

There was a close coordination between Belgrade and Skopje in their attempts to roll back Albanian gains and root out Albanian nationalism. Just as Serbia forced through constitutional changes limiting Kosova's autonomy, in 1989 the Macedonians amended their constitution, too, defining Macedonia as a "national state of the Macedonian people." The 1974 constitution had defined the republic as "a state of the Macedonian people and the Albanian and Turkish minorities." The 1989 amendments were seen by Albanians as eroding the political and cultural rights guaranteed them by the 1974 document.[82] Albanians maintained that the changes, which were reaffirmed in Macedonia's new constitution, adopted in 1991, relegated them to the status of second-class citizens.

Ethnic Albanians were ill prepared for and ambivalent about Macedonia's independence. They had closely identified their fate with that of the Albanians of Kosova, endorsing demands for a separate republic that would have included all Albanians in the Yugoslav federation. Macedonia's independence and the continued inclusion of Kosova within Yugoslavia meant that links between Albanians in Kosova and Albanians in Macedonia were severed, in many cases separating close relatives on different sides of the border. Some Albanians apparently preferred that as long as Kosova remained part of Yugoslavia, Macedonia continue to as well. Others maintained that not only would the recognition of Macedonia's independence serve to negate Albania's eventual claims to that country's Albanian-inhabited areas, but it would also delegitimize ethnic Albanian claims for full cultural and political rights. However, the silent majority of Macedonia's Albanian population accepted the new state, hopeful that their status would improve.

As Macedonia embarked on the road to independence, ethnic Albanians formed their own political parties. The first and most important was the Party for Democratic Prosperity, formed in August 1990. Nevzat Halili, an English-language teacher from Tetovë, was elected party chairman. Similar to the Democratic League in Kosova, the PDP was more a mass movement than a political party in the strict definition of the term. It rapidly gained membership, becoming the primary political force among Albanians in Macedonia. This period also witnessed the founding of other, less influential political parties, along with several human rights and social organizations. The political parties and groups succinctly articulated ethnic Albanian grievances and pressed the government of the newly created state for greater political and cultural autonomy. The Albanians objected to the fact that constitutionally they were considered a national minority, and they demanded equal national status with the Macedonians. Other demands included holding a new, internationally supervised census; the recognition of Albanian as an official language; Albanian-language education at all levels, including the university; free use of Albanian national symbols; proportional representation in government, economic, and cultural administration; and unimpeded development of the Albanian-language media.[83]

Relations between Albanians and the new Macedonia were afflicted by twists and turns. The Albanians boycotted the independence referendum in protest at Skopje's failure to recognize ethnic Albanians as a constituent nation. However, unlike their brethren in Kosova who boycotted elections in Serbia and Yugoslavia, Albanians in Macedonia participated in that country's 1991 elections, winning 23 seats in the 120-seat parliament. Albanian parties also joined the coalition government, holding four ministerial posts and the deputy premiership. But as progress was slow in coming, a referendum was held in January 1992. The overwhelming majority of Albanians voted for autonomy within Macedonia.[84] Three months later, Albanians declared an autonomous republic, Ilirida.[85] These efforts, however, failed, largely because ethnic Albanians lacked a unified leadership and because Tiranë, concerned that ethnic unrest in Macedonia would lead to Serbian intervention, refused to endorse plans for a separate Albanian republic within Macedonia.

Soon, cracks emerged within the PDP regarding the best strategy and tactics to be employed in negotiations with Skopje. During 1993, a faction led by Menduh Thaçi, which advocated a more militant approach, increasingly gained ascendancy. Thaçi's group argued that the party's participation in the coalition government had rendered Albanians politically ineffective. The announcement in November 1993 that Macedonian authorities had uncovered an Albanian plot, implicating Tiranë and the PDP, further fueled tensions within the largest ethnic Albanian party. The police arrested a group of seven Albanians, including Husein Haskaj, deputy defense minister, and Mithat Emini, former secretary general of the PDP, for allegedly having attempted to create underground paramilitary units and smuggling weapons from Albania during 1991.[86] Ethnic Albanian politicians did not deny that plans existed for a parliamentary organization, but claimed these plans were made with President Gligorov's approval, as both Albanians and

Macedonians at the time were taking precautions against potential confrontation with the Yugoslav army.

In February 1994, the Party for Democratic Prosperity suffered a major split. Arbër Xhaferi, a respected intellectual educated in Prishtinë, was elected leader of Thaçi's faction. The other, more powerful faction, supported by ethnic Albanian deputies and members of the cabinet, elected Xheladin Murati, deputy chairman of the Macedonian parliament, as its chairman.[87] However, within months Murati resigned, and he was replaced by Abdurahman Aliti. With both factions claiming to be the true heir to the PDP, the Macedonian government recognized Aliti's faction and resorted to all sorts of measures to put pressure on Xhaferi's supporters. Finally, Xhaferi's faction was registered as the Party for Democratic Prosperity of Albanians in Macedonia.[88] The split within the PDP seriously weakened the unity of the Albanian side, hindering efforts to counter Skopje's strong but measured reaction to Albanian moves to assert greater autonomy. But with encouragement from Albania and the international community, ethnic Albanians sought to achieve their objectives by working within the system. In the 1994 election, ethnic Albanians won 19 seats in parliament. The Party for Democratic Prosperity secured 10 seats; the Party for Democratic Prosperity of Albanians, 4; the People's Democratic Party, 2; and independents, 3. The PDP agreed to join the government, arguing that thereby it could better advocate Albanian interests.[89]

While Skopje refused to initiate constitutional changes to reflect an improved status for ethnic Albanians, it did agree to hold a new census. The size of the Albanian community had become a highly contentious issue, with Albanians claiming to represent between 30 percent and 40 percent of the country's total population. Hoping that a new count would help ease interethnic tensions, in 1994 the international community organized and financed a new census. Ethnic Albanians were said to number about 442,000, or about 23 percent of the total population. But instead of easing tensions, the new census exacerbated them, at least in the short-run. Albanians had used the size of their community as the most important element in their drive for greater rights. When international monitors defended the results as adequately accurate, the Macedonian government insisted that the census proved that Albanians, representing less than a quarter of the total population, could only claim minority status. Predictably, ethnic Albanians disputed the census results, claiming the results had been manipulated. A law on citizenship, adopted in October 1992, stipulated a fifteen-year residency requirement for eligibility. The Ministry of Internal Affairs was empowered to rule "at its discretion" on requests for citizenship and to invalidate previously issued certificates of citizenship.[90] This left hundreds of thousands of Albanians uncounted. Macedonian authorities claimed the law was intended to deny citizenship to Albanians leaving Kosova. However, local Albanians responded that more than 200,000 Albanians from Macedonia, who during the 1970s and the 1980s had moved to other parts of Yugoslavia in search of jobs and had since returned to Macedonia, had been denied citizenship.

Ethnic Albanians continued to express disappointment with the government's slow progress in addressing their grievances, claiming discrimination in all fields.[91] In 1994, Macedonians accounted for 80.6 percent of those employed in the state sector, while Albanians accounted for only 10.4 percent.[92] In the same year, Albanians made up only 5.2 percent of students attending Macedonian universities, while Macedonians accounted for 90 percent.[93] By 1997, the Albanian proportion had increased to only 7.3 percent.[94] The Albanians were also heavily under represented in government institutions. In October 1995, PDP Chairman Abdurrahman Aliti disclosed figures indicating that not much headway had been made in ensuring greater Albanian representation in government agencies. He said that in the Ministry of the Interior, the Albanians made up only 4.19 percent, compared to 91 percent for the Macedonians. In the Defense Ministry, the picture was even bleaker: The Albanians accounted for 3 percent, and the Macedonians, for 85 percent. The state administration continued to be dominated over-whelmingly by the Macedonians: 90 percent; the Albanians accounted for only 4.39 percent.[95]

Education had become a particularly contentious issue, with ethnic Albanians saying that failure to institutionalize Albanian as an official language infringed upon their rights. Despite repeated promises, the opening of an Albanian-language Pedagogical Academy in Skopje was postponed. In 1994, Albanians took matters into their own hands, announcing plans to set up an Albanian-language university in Tetovë. Founders stressed that instruction at the university would be based on Macedonia's educational system.[96] Fadil Sulejmani, a native of Tetovë who had received his doctorate at Belgrade University and had taught at the University of Prishtinë, was elected rector of the university.[97]

Almost without exception, Macedonians in and outside the government opposed the opening of the university, arguing that as a minority, Albanians did not have the right to higher education in their mother tongue.[98] There was wide-spread concern that Tetovë University could become a hotbed of Albanian nationalism, now that Prishtinë could no longer play the role of an Albanian Piedmont for the Albanians in Macedonia. Some Macedonians interpreted moves to open an Albanian-language university as an initial step toward secession from Macedonia and urged the government to reassert its authority over Tetovë.

On 16 February 1995, the authorities attempted to prevent the opening of the university. The next day, clashes broke out between ethnic Albanians and the police in Reçica e Vogël (Mala Recica), near Tetovë. A thirty-three-year-old Albanian was killed, and twenty-eight people were wounded. Sulejmani, the rector of the university, and several other activists, including Nevzat Halili, a former leader of the PDP who in 1994 had formed his own political party, were arrested and charged with inciting Albanians to rebel.[99] The violent incident, however, was followed by mutual deescalation. Both sides appeared eager to avoid a crisis, and they backed off from the collision course on which they had embarked. Sulejmani and other activists who had been sentenced were released on bail pending appeals to higher courts. Although Skopje still considered the university illegal, the authorities avoided an all-out crackdown that might alienate many Albanians.[100] The Albanians, for their part, avoided provocative actions, although they continued to press Skopje to legalize the university. The Albanian political parties all made public pronouncements of support for Tetovë University—some more earnest than other. While Xhaferi's party threw its full support behind Sulejmani, the Party for Democratic Prosperity's endorsement was lukewarm, at best.

The Macedonian government showed no signs of reassessing its position on granting Albanians constituent status or on legalizing Tetovë University. As a result, the gulf between the two communities widened. By 1996, having secured membership in the Council of Europe and the OSCE and an end to the Greek embargo, and having taken moves toward a rapprochement with Belgrade, the government's position on the Albanian issue seemed to have hardened. Meanwhile, with the Skopje-Athens reconciliation, Tiranë's leverage with Macedonia declined significantly. Given Macedonia's intransigence, the issue continued to sour the already uneasy relationship between the two neighbors, and the Albanian government came under greater pressure to take at least symbolic action.

In a wide-ranging interview with *Nova Makedonija*, in February 1995, Abdurrahman Aliti, the PDP leader, acknowledged the widely held view in the Albanian community that his party's efforts to gain greater rights for Albanians by working through established political institutions had not yielded satisfactory results. He said, "The most the Albanian ministers can do is either dissociate or distance themselves from the government's positions, and that amounts to zero."[101] But while Aliti continued to insist that the PDP would continue to work within the system,[102] the Party for Democratic Prosperity of Albanians and the People's Democratic Party, which advocated a tougher stance, gained increased ascendancy at the expense of the mainstream PDP.[103] In mid-1996, these two parties formed a coalition, withdrew their deputies from parliament, and called for civil disobedience.[104] The Party for Democratic Prosperity of Albanians and the People's Democratic Party also warned that if the government continued to refuse to address Albanian grievances, then Albanians should consider establishing alternative political institutions. With heightened interethnic tensions, the PDP faced the danger of being outflanked by the other two parties, which were increasingly taking the initiative in organizing actions in support of Albanian rights.[105] In June 1997, the Party for Democratic Prosperity of Albanians and the People's Democratic Party merged, forming the Democratic Party of Albanians.

Although it could not be denied that the position of the Albanians in Macedonia had improved, particularly compared to a decade earlier, they were far from equal to Slav Macedonians. As Human Rights Watch/Helsinki noted in a 1996 report, "Ethnic Albanians have been denied many of the basic rights guaranteed them in both Macedonian and international law."[106] With a great deal of paranoia on both sides, and with the Tetovë University events having brought out the worst fears of both, communication between the two communities dropped to a dangerously low level. The country was gradually but indisputably moving toward segregation rather than integration.[107] With anti-Albanian attitudes permeating all levels of Macedonian society, government officials resorted to an increasingly confrontational and uncooperative stance.

Macedonia faces seemingly irreconcilable differences between its two ethnic groups. Albanians, with their long experience of domination and discrimination by Macedonians, are unlikely to see themselves as equal citizens of Macedonia if Skopje continues to refuse to raise their constitutional status to that of constituent nation. Indeed, their commitment to the state of Macedonia remains highly questionable. Unless Skopje develops a formula to reconcile Albanians' demands for greater rights with Macedonians' desire for a unified state, ethnic Albanian assertiveness could endanger not only Macedonia's state-building process but its very survival as an independent country. If Macedonians refuse a pact with Albanians, Macedonia is likely to face a situation in which the Albanians dramatically increase their demands—including that of political autonomy—and the Macedonians harden their position. The future of Macedonia will be determined largely by the extent to which Macedonians and Albanians can transform their current tension-ridden relationship into a durable equilibrium.

With the end of the war in Bosnia, the dangerous interplay between Albanian, Serb, and Macedonian national aspirations and historical and cultural claims is emerging as one of the most significant problems awaiting resolution in the Balkans. Albanians are seemingly set on a collision course with their Slav neighbors in both Yugoslavia and Macedonia. Peaceful resolution of the conflict in Kosova seems remote, as the two ethnic groups remain wedded to their uncompromising positions, with the Serbs insisting on Kosova remaining within Serbia, and Kosovar Albanians demanding independence. An outbreak of hostilities in Kosova could lead to a massive refugee influx, overwhelming Macedonia and destroying its delicate ethnic balance; but in addition to the potential threat originating from Kosova, Macedonia must deal with its own growing ethnic discord. Although tensions there have not yet reached a critical level, the gulf between ethnic Albanians and Macedonians has widened, prompting longtime Balkan observer Misha Glenny to suggest that the former Yugoslav republic "is heading down the same path as Bosnia."[108] An implosion in either Kosova or Macedonia could rapidly spiral out of control, possibly igniting a wider Balkan war involving Albania, Bulgaria, Greece, Serbia, and Turkey.

Albanian decisionmakers in Tiranë, Prishtinë, and Tetovë face highly controversial and potentially explosive challenges. The status of ethnic Albanians in Yugoslavia remains Tiranë's most important and difficult national challenge; but impoverished Albania is preoccupied with completing its own painful transition. Thus, internal and external factors have forced it to put the national issue on the back burner. While most other countries in the region have been swept by a dangerous wave of nationalism, Albania has pursued a policy of constructive engagement with its neighbors, becoming a strong advocate of Balkan cooperation. In a region prone to crisis, miscalculation, and tragedy, Albania emerged as a responsible player and a key factor for the stability of the region. Given the overwhelming Yugoslav military superiority, Albania was keenly aware that an outbreak of armed hostilities in Kosova would have disastrous consequences for Albanians on both sides of the border. However, despite the increased coordination and consultations between Tiranë and Prishtinë, Kosovar Albanians' deference to Tiranë cannot be taken for granted.

Kosova's Albanians recognize that Serbia's preponderant power will prevent them from achieving their ultimate goal of unification with Albania in the immediate future. However, they do not see unification as an objective that can be achieved overnight, but rather as a long-term process. Thus, at the same time as Kosovar leaders continue to stick to their position that separation from Serbia is nonnegotiable, they have indicated that they will accept an interim arrangement. Rugova advocates the establishment of a neutral Kosovar state as an interim arrangement, while other ethnic Albanian leaders, such as Adem Demaçi,[109] speak of a confederation, with Kosova enjoying an equal status with Serbia and Montenegro.

Albanians in general recognize the hard political and military realities in the region and further afield, but, many refuse to accept them as permanent. There should be no doubt that for most Albanians, both inside and outside the state of Albania, the ultimate goal remains a unitary state of all Albanians. Before Albania's implosion in 1997, trends in Kosova and Macedonia suggested that the idea of unification was gaining increased support and a unified Albania was no longer viewed as an unrealizable dream. Given the bitter history of Albanians' struggle for autonomy in former Yugoslavia; the decades of severe repression, humiliation, and frustration; and the imposition of an apartheid system in Kosova, the continued coexistence of Albanians and Serbs within the republic of Serbia seems almost unimaginable. Indeed, if Slavs, with a commonly shared history and language, could not live together, it is unrealistic to expect Serbs and Albanians, deeply imprinted with mutual fear and distrust, to do so. In contrast to the pre-1990 period, Belgrade is now unlikely to find legitimate ethnic Albanian leaders willing to abandon Albanian national aspirations. Younger generations of Kosovar Albanians are growing up with minimal or no contact with the Serbs; indeed, few even speak Serbian.

The gulf between Albanians and Serbs is probably unbridgeable. Surveys conducted in Kosova highlight the potential for an explosion of ethnic tensions, as Albanians and Serbs hold diametrically opposed stands on the province's status. A poll conducted in September 1995 revealed that Albanians and Serbs disagreed on nearly everything. While Albanians appeared split between establishing a separate Kosovar state (57 percent) and uniting with Albania (43 percent), not a single Albanian respondent expressed support for Kosova remaining within Yugoslavia, even if it regained autonomy.[110] According to a survey commissioned by the U.S. Information Agency in February-March 1996, nearly all Albanians (94 percent) believed that achieving independence from Serbia for Kosova was "a cause worth dying for," while virtually all Serbs in the region opposed Kosova's independence (99 percent) or unification with Albania (99 percent). An astounding majority of both Albanians (81 percent) and Serbs (77 percent) rejected the option of autonomous status within Serbia. Ninety-three percent of Albanians supported secession from Yugoslavia; 72 percent favored unification with Albania.[111]

In the postcommunist era, Albania and the ethnic Albanians have undergone profound psychological transformations. Before the 1990s, Albanians in Kosova and in Albania had very limited contacts with, and had been poorly informed about, each other. Their initial contacts after the demise of communism in Albania were not altogether positive. Many regarded themselves as far apart and having competing interests, and support for Kosova in Albania was not widespread.[112] A close review of the media in the early 1990s—both progovernment and opposition—revealed a significant gap between the desire to see an end to Serbian occupation of Kosova and the willingness to go to war over Kosova. A 1993 U.S. Information Agency poll found limited sentiment in Albania for aiding the Kosovars militarily. More than half of those polled (55 percent) said they would not come to Kosova's aid militarily, even in the event of an attack by Serbia. Although a large majority (78 percent) believed that Kosova should not remain part of Yugoslavia, public opinion in Albania seemed divided about whether Kosova should be unified with Albania. Some 47 percent expressed support for a separate Kosovar state, while 38 percent said they favored eventual unification and 6 percent, immediate unification of Kosova and Albania.[113]

However, as Albania evolved from the harshly authoritarian state of the past into a pluralistic democracy and interaction increased between ethnic Albanians and their mother country, public opinion in Albania was gradually, but unmistakenly, shifting in favor of Kosovar Albanians. Although in 1993 less than half of the respondents to a USIA survey in Albania favored military intervention on behalf of Kosovar Albanians, in 1996, some 61 percent believed Albania should come to Kosova's defense in case of a Serb military attack. The overwhelming majority (85 percent) had a favorable opinion of Kosova, and 94 percent of those who advocated defending Kosova believed that the province should not remain part of Serbia.[114] Contrary to conventional wisdom, the differences between Albanians in Kosova and those in Albania are no more pronounced than among those in different regions of Albania itself.

The salience of the Albanian national question is likely to increase. Given current demographic trends and in the absence of a devastating war or some natural calamity, within a decade the Albanians will become the third largest nation in the Balkans, right after the Serbs and the Greeks. With dwindling chances that ethnic Albanians in Yugoslavia and Macedonia can achieve their human and national rights in those countries, and with the rising tide of nationalism in the region, it is likely that the Albanian diaspora will eventually push for unification with Albania. A violent confrontation between Albanians and their neighbors would most likely consume the region in brutal and prolonged violence, causing massive casualties and destruction of property, and creating hundreds of thousands of refugees.

The Albanian question portends much greater consequences for regional peace and stability even than the fate of Bosnia. But the international community does not seem to have understood the broader regional and international implications of trends in Kosova and Macedonia. The Albanian question has received scant attention, and thus, preventive international diplomacy, intervention, and enforcement have been lacking. With the exception of rhetorical statements directed at Serbia, Western countries have failed to take concrete steps to mediate the Albanian-Serb conflict. They continue to propose autonomy for ethnic Albanians, treating the problem of Kosova as though it were simply a matter of individual human rights instead of national rights. Autonomy would be unacceptable to the majority of Albanians, and as Robert Austin has stated, its long-term sustainability would be in doubt.[115]

In view of Yugoslav wars of secession and the de facto partitioning of Bosnia, borders in the region can no longer be considered sacrosanct. The international community, which has significant leverage with all parties, must redouble its efforts to prevent the outbreak of violence and find a lasting solution. Western powers should exert strong pressure on Serbia to accept a peaceful divorce with Kosova. The Serbs must be convinced that they have lost Kosova; they might keep it through force, but not inevitably. Border changes reached by mutual agreement would foster regional economic and political cooperation. To refuse to consider border changes is to risk implosions and even war, as Kosova remains a dangerous potential source of conflict and instability for Serbia and the region at large. The international community should also pressure Macedonia to negotiate a new relationship with ethnic Albanians. Slavic Macedonians cannot continue to be the backbone of Macedonia's political system without formidable challenge from Albanians. A more durable solution must be found.

If stability and peace in the Balkans are to be assured, the Albanian question must be addressed with a view toward the long term. Without greater international involvement, it is difficult to imagine the Albanians and the Slavs peacefully resolving their disputes, or the Albanians evading the nationalist forces that have engulfed some of their neighbors. Developments in the Albanian-inhabited Balkan lands, if not managed appropriately by the international community, have the potential to disrupt the entire region, with dangerous ramifications for European peace and stability.

Notes

1. A nationwide poll conducted by the U.S. Information Agency in March 1996 indicated that the majority of Albanians were quite concerned about an external threat to their country's security. Some 61 percent of respondents said they were very concerned and 15 percent somewhat concerned that another country might attack Albania. U.S. Information Agency, Office of Research and Media Reaction, "On Security Matters, Albanian Public Looks to the West," *Opinion Analysis*, M-73-96, 2 April 1996, p. 2.

2. Adem Çopani, "The New Dimensions of Albania's Security Posture," *NATO Review*, no. 2 (March 1996), pp. 24-28; and Marianne Sullivan, "Seeking the Security of Military Might," *Transition* 1, no. 15 (25 August 1995), pp. 8-10.

3. According to Berisha's military adviser Adem Çopani, Albania viewed its expanding relationship with the Western alliance as "a strong security anchor that would help Albania develop its potential with the least instability and disorder and free from threat and intimidation. In its desire to draw closer to the West and overcome a sense of isolation and insecurity, Albania aims initially to integrate itself with the Atlantic security system, in a further step towards eventually gaining full membership in NATO." Adem Çopani, "The Democratic Process and Albanian Security Policy," *NATO Review*, no. 40 (October 1992), p. 23. See also Adem Çopani and Constantine P. Danopoulos, "The Role of the Military in the Democratization of Marxist-Leninist Regimes: Albania as a Case Study," *Mediterranean Quarterly* 6, no. 2 (Spring 1995), pp. 117-134.

4. See Berisha's interview in *Slobodna Dalmacija* (Split), 7 May 1994, pp. 6-7, translated in FBIS-EEU 94-096, 18 May 1994, p. 5.

5. *Ushtria dhe Koha*, 14 June 1995, pp. 1-2.

6. The Council of Defense, *Politika e Sigurimit dhe e Mbrojtjes e Republikës së Shqipërisë* [The Security and Defense Policy of the Republic of Albania] (Tiranë: The Military Publishing House, 1995). See also interview with General Sheme Kosova in *Mbrojtja*, no. 10 (October 1995), pp. 4-7; Ali Koçeku, "On the New Military Doctrine," *Mbrojtja*, no. 6 (June 1995), pp. 6-8; and Ali Koçeku and Zija Lagji, "On the Vision and Contents of the New Albanian Military Doctrine," *Ushtria dhe Koha*, 31 May 1995, p. 1.

7. Yugoslavia sharply protested Albania's decision to allow the stationing of U.S. spy planes and readiness to place its airports, sea ports, and other facilities at the disposal of NATO forces for possible military intervention in the region. In a démarche in February 1994, the Yugoslav government said such moves on the part of the Albanian Government were "aggravating tensions in the region and presented a threat to the security of the Federal Republic of Yugoslavia." Tanjug Domestic Service in Serbo-Croatian, 1753 GMT, 18 February 1994, translated in FBIS-EEU 94-036, 23 February 1994, p. 43. There were numerous incidents on the border, almost always involving Yugoslav soldiers shooting and killing Albanian citizens. In addition, Yugoslav military aircraft repeatedly violated Albanian airspace.

8. On the restructuring of Albanian naval forces, see Muharrem Kuçana and Çapajev File, "Opinions: On the Need for the Renovation and Further Structural Strengthening of Our Naval Forces," *Mbrojtja*, no. 6 (June 1995), pp. 3-5.

9. Rome Ansamail Database in English, 1440 GMT 11 March 1994 in FBIS-WEU 94-049-A, 14 March 1994, pp. 2-3. General George Joulwan, the supreme commander of the Allied Forces in Europe, visited Albania in April 1994 and indicated that "the alliance is open for cooperation with Albania." TVSH Television Network in Albanian, 1800 GMT, 7 April 1994, translated in FBIS-EEU 94-069, 11 April 1994, p. 2.

10. *Ushtria dhe Koha*, 10 June 1995, p. 1.

11. In a conference organized by the Albanian North Atlantic Association, Berisha said: "Integration into NATO is a matter of vital interest for Albania. In it, we see not only an international guarantee of the country's security, but also a guarantee for the new Albanian democracy." TVSH Television Network in Albanian, 1900 GMT, 17 November 1995, translated in FBIS-EEU 95-224, 21 November 1995, pp. 2-3.

12. Greece refused to participate in the Tiranë defense ministerial meeting, criticizing Albania's decision not to invite Serbia and Romania and objecting to U.S. participation. Athens Elliniki Radhiofonia Radio Network in Greek, 1600 GMT, 22 March 1996, translated in FBIS-EEU 96-058, 25 March 1996, p. 1.

13. *Rilindja Demokratike*, 2 April 1996, pp. 1-2.

14. U.S. Information Agency, Office of Research and Media Reaction, "On Security Matters, Albanian Public Looks to the West," *Opinion Analysis*, M-73-96, 2 April 1996, p. 1. See also Genc Pollo's speech at the Albanian Atlantic Society, *Ushtria dhe Koha*, 14 June 1995, p. 4.

15. See John Pomfret and David B. Ottaway, "U.S., Albania Form 'the Weirdest Relationship,'" *Washington Post*, 20 November 1995, pp. A1, and A18.

16. In a series of lengthy articles in *Zëri i Popullit*, Hamdi Dega, who had been dismissed from the Albanian Telegraphic Agency in summer 1992 because of his close ties with the Communist *nomenklatura*, attacked Berisha's pro-American policy and described the reception given to Secretary of State Baker in Tiranë in June 1991 as "shameful." Dega said Berisha was needlessly alienating Europe, particularly Italy, and added that Rome had given Albania "ten times more assistance than the supergiant" America. *Zëri i Popullit*, 6 August 1992, pp. 2-3. Dega's other articles were published in *Zëri i Popullit* on 22, 29, and 30 July, and 5 August 1992. See also Ylli Polovina, "The Irritation of Europe," *24 Orë*, 22 August 1993, pp. 4-5.

17. During his visit to Tiranë in January 1995, U.S. Assistant Secretary of Defense Joseph Nye said that Albania had become one of the main pillars of stability in the Balkans. According to Nye, "The responsible position that Albania has taken toward its neighbors is a major contribution to stability in the Balkan region." *Reuter*, 31 January 1995.

18. *Rilindja Demokratike*, 21 July 1994, p. 1, and John F. Harris, "Once Reclusive Albania Warmly Welcomes U.S. Defense Chief," *Washington Post*, 22 July 1994, p. A20. See also Safet Zhulali, "The Importance of William Perry's Visit to our Country," *Rilindja Demokratike*, 29 July 1994, pp. 1-2. The army newspaper referred to Perry as "the best friend of the Albanians." See editorial: "Welcome Dr. Perry!" *Ushtria dhe Koha*, 23 July 1994, p. 1.

19. John Pomfret, "U.S. Builds Arc of Alliances to Contain Serbia's Power," *Washington Post*, 19 December 1995, pp. A1, A28.

20. See President Clinton's interview in *I Kathimerini*, 8 January 1995, translated in FBIS-WEU 95-005, 9 January 1995, p. 52.

21. James A. Baker, III, with Thomas M. DeFrank, *The Politics of Diplomacy* (New York: G. P. Putnam's Sons, 1995), p. 486.

22. *Lajmi i Ditës*, 6 October 1994, pp. 1, 2.

23. Fatmir Zanaj, "Is U.S. Policy Toward Albania Going to Change Now That Mr. Ryerson Is Leaving Our Country?" *Kombi*, 26 April 1994, p. 3.

24. The White House, Office of the Press Secretary, "President Clinton Meets with Albanian President Berisha," 12 September 1995.

25. Christina Nifong, "Poor but Strategic Albania Tries Hard to Be a U.S. Ally," *Christian Science Monitor*, 18 September 1995, p. 7.

26. *Zëri i Popullit*, 15 September 1995, p. 2.

27. *Rilindja Demokratike*, 16 September 1995, p. 1.

28. TVSH Television Network in Albanian, 1900 GMT, 3 December 1993, translated in FBIS-EEU 93-232, 6 December 1993, p. 2.

29. *Albania*, 12 October 1995, p. 2.

30. *Rilindja Demokratike*, 30 June 1995, p. 1.

31. Moscow ITAR-TASS in English, 1140 GMT, 11 April 1995, translated in FBIS-SOV-95-071, 13 April 1995, p. 5.

32. Skopje MIC in English, 13 May 1994, in FBIS-EEU 94-095, 17 May 1994, p. 4.

33. *Albania*, 24 October 1995, p. 2.

34. Robert Austin, "What Albania Adds to the Balkan Stew," *Orbis* 37, no. 2 (Spring 1993), p. 276.

35. *Rilindja Demokratike*, 6 December 1992, p. 1. See also Louis Zanga, "Albania Moves Closer to the Islamic World," *RFE/RL Research Report* 2, no. 7 (12 February 1993), pp. 28-31.

36. U.S. Information Agency, Office of Research and Media Reaction, "On Security Matters, Albanian Public Looks to the West," *Opinion Analysis*, M-73-96, 2 April 1996, p. 2. Peter F. Sugar, a seasoned observer of Balkan history, has written: "Almost all Muslims living in Albania, Kosovo, Bosnia, Macedonia, and European Turkey are either Hanafi or Hanbali Sunnis and have nothing to do with any fundamentalism. Yet the fear of Muslim fundamentalism is spreading. I do not know who is responsible for the rumors making the rounds in Yugoslavia, Greece, and even Bulgaria. The danger is that constant repetition of this 'danger' might convince a growing number of people that it really exists." Peter F. Sugar, "Nationalism and Religion in the Balkans Since the 19th Century," *The Donald W. Treadgold Papers In Russian, East European and Central Asian Studies* (Henry M. Jackson School of International Studies, The University of Washington), no. 8 (July 1996), p. 37.

37. Tanjug in English, 2218 GMT, 5 December 1995, in FBIS-EEU 95-234, 6 December 1995, pp. 58-59.

38. Radio Tiranë Network in Albanian, 1330 GMT, 26 April 1993, translated in FBIS-EEU 93-079, 27 April 1993, p. 7.

39. ATA in English, 1821 GMT, 15 April 1993 in FBIS-EEU 93-072, 16 April 1993, p. 1.

40. *Zëri i Popullit*, 8 February 1994, p. 4.

41. *Rilindja Demokratike*, 2 December 1993, p. 1.

42. TVSH Television Network in Albanian, 1900 GMT, 3 March 1994, translated in FBIS-EEU 94-043, 4 March 1994, p. 2. In a subsequent meeting with the OSCE head of mission in Macedonia, Ambassador Norman Anderson, Berisha implicitly expressed support for the main faction of the PDP, praising them for their participation in the government coalition. Commenting on Berisha's new stand, a Macedonian analysis said, "Now Tiranë is moving Thaçi toward direct cooperation with the government, urging him to take actions within the institutional framework, which is totally opposite to the recent statements of the faction's leader." See B. Geroski, "Did Tirana 'Turn its Back' on Thaci," *Vecer*, 27 April 1994, p. 3.

43. ATA in English, 1808 GMT, 22 May 1994 in FBIS-EEU 94-101-A, 25 May 1994, p. 1. On the eve of elections in Macedonia, Berisha urged the ethnic Albanians to participate fully: "Their registration and participation in the elections are especially important for them, for the consolidation of their rights and for the stability of Macedonia. Withdrawal from the election process and from a free vote does not serve the freedom and rights of Albanians there or even the stability of Macedonia, which is very important for Albanians. I hope that the Albanians will have wisdom and vote for their best candidates. In politics, self-condemnation is the same as sentencing; therefore, it is not a very good idea to accept it." *Rilindja Demokratike*, 11 October 1994, pp. 1-2.

44. *Gazeta Shqiptare*, 22 February 1995, p. 1.

45. In July 1996, Albania's parliament passed a resolution expressing support for the Tetovë University and denouncing the jailing of Fadil Sulejmani and other university activists. ATA in English, 1845 GMT, 31 July 1996, in FBIS-EEU 96-150, 2 August 1996, pp. 5-6. The Albanian parliament's action drew a sharp response from Skopje. *Nova Makedonija*, 7 August 1996, p. 1, translated in FBIS-EEU 96-155, 9 August 1996, p. 40.

46. Frederick Kempe, "The Greeks—Frontier Fever: Greek-Albanian Border Holds Latest Tensions in Balkan Powderkeg," *Wall Street Journal/Europe*, 4 March 1993, p. 1. See also Nicholas Gage, "The Forgotten Minority in the Balkans: The Greeks of Northern Epirus," *Mediterranean Quarterly* 4, no. 3 (Summer 1993), pp. 10-29.

47. Athens Elliniki Radhiofonia Radio Network in Greek, 1105 GMT, 14 July 1993, translated in FBIS-EEU 93-134, 15 July 1993, pp. 54-57.

48. Radio Tiranë Network in Albanian, 1730 GMT, 15 July 1993, translated in FBIS-EEU 93-135, 16 July 1993, p. 1.

49. *Zëri i Popullit*, 17 June 1993, p. 1. An editorial in *Zëri i Popullit*, accused the Berisha government of not having a clear appreciation of Greece's critical role in regional and European affairs. *Zëri i Popullit*, 18 June 1993, pp. 1, 4.

50. In mid-1992, Greece had offered to mediate in the Albanian-Serb conflict, but both Prishtinë and Tiranë rejected the offer, questioning Athens's ability to serve as an honest broker. ATA in English, 1202 GMT, 20 August 1992, in FBIS-EEU 92-163, 21 August 1992, p. 2.

51. ATA in English, 0911 GMT, 16 November 1993, in FBIS-EEU 93-219, 16 November 1993, p. 2.

52. *Elevtherotipia*, 11 April 1994, p. 3, translated in FBIS-EEU 94-070, 12 April 1994, pp. 55-56. In October 1994, MAVI released a four-page leaflet giving a detailed description of the attack at Peshkëpi. The organization said it had declared war on Albania so that the issue of ethnic Greeks in Albania would return to the "forefront among the other [Greek] national issues." (See *Elevtherotipia*, 7 October 1994, p. 4, translated in FBIS-EEU 94-197, 12 October 1994, pp. 52-53.) In March 1995, only days after Foreign Minister Karolos Papoulias made a fence-mending visit to Tiranë, Greek authorities announced that they had arrested seven men with assault rifles and paramilitary gear near the border with Albania. The seven, suspected members of MAVI, were apparently planning a cross-border raid into Albania. Greek police confirmed that the fourteen Kalashnikov assault rifles it confiscated from the seven men had been stolen from an Albanian military post near Peshkëpia.

53. ATA in English, 0821 GMT, 12 April 1994, in FBIS-EEU 94-070-A, 12 April 1994, pp. 1-2.

54. Athens Elliniki Radhiofonia Radio Network in Greek, 0400 GMT, 11 April 1994, translated in FBIS-WEU 94-069, 11 April 1994, p. 35.

55. Journalist Ylli Rakipi charged: "Efforts to Hellenize Albania have become Greek state policy. Hundreds of anti-Albanian bulletins, books, maps, and calendars are being published. Dozens of mass protest rallies are being staged to call for the liberation of Northern Epirus." (Ylli Rakipi, "We Should Tell Greece Everything We Think," *Republika*, 24 April 1994, p. 1.) In an effort to gain international support, Albania appealed to the European Union and the U.N. Security Council. In a letter to the Security Council president, Foreign Minister Alfred Serreqi asked that Greece be ranked among the countries that sponsored state terrorism (See ATA in English, 0814 GMT, 14 April 1994, in FBIS-EEU 94-072-A, 14 April 1994, p. 1). While the United States and West European countries urged restraint on both sides, Turkey expressed understanding for Albania's plight. A spokesman of the Turkish Foreign Ministry was quoted as saying that "countries that plan to pressure their neighbors through the actions of terrorist groups should realize that they cannot be left out of the negative developments that stem from such provocations." See Ankara TRT Television Network in Turkish, 1700 GMT, 15 April 1994, translated in FBIS-WEU 94-074, 18 April 1994, p. 57.

56. Minnesota Advocates for Human Rights, *The Albanian Trial of Five Ethnic Greeks for Espionage*, Trial Observation Report (Minneapolis, MN), September 1994; Peggy L. Hicks, "Albanian Legal Reform Faces Continuing Challenges," *Mediterranean Quarterly* 6, no. 2 (Spring 1995), pp. 75-91; and "Albania: The Greek Minority," *Human Rights Watch/Helsinki* 7, no. 4 (February 1995), pp. 10-13.

57. Greek politicians and commentators engaged in scathing criticism of Berisha, depicting the president as an extremist nationalist and an Islamic fundamentalist, comparing him to Enver Hoxha, and expressing support for the opposition. Columnist Stavros Liyeros accused Berisha of trying to give Albania a "Muslim orientation." He wrote: "It is no accident that the Socialist Party and the liberal Democratic Alliance, which react to the cultivation of tension in Greek-Albanian relations, have a European orientation and look forward to a pluralistic—politically and religiously—Albania. Berisha's policy so far has managed essentially to divide the Albanian people and forfeit the neighboring country's national unity" (Stavros Liyeros, "The Ankara-Tiranë Relations," *I Kathimerini*, 16 September 1994, p. 1, translated in FBIS-WEU 94-182, 20 September 1994, p. 53). Former Greek President Khristos Sartzetakis demanded that Albania grant autonomy to Greek-inhabited areas. Sartzetakis also was reported as saying that Greece should "claim the return of this territory" (*Elevtherotipia*, 13 September 1994, translated in FBIS-WEU 94-194, 6 October 1994, p. 40). Meanwhile, Miltiadhis Evert, chairman of the opposition New Democracy, urged that Greece take drastic measures against Albania, including the expulsion of all Albanian refugees and the freezing of all Albanian assets in Greece (Athens Elliniki Radhiofonia Radio Network in Greek, 1700 GMT, 7 September 1994, translated in FBIS-WEU 94-174, 8 September 1994, p. 66). Evert's comments drew a sharp response from the former Greek Foreign Minister Mikhail Papakonstandinou (See *I Kakathimerini*, 18 September 1994, translated in FBIS-WEU 94-190, 30 September 1994, p. 57). Earlier, Papakonstandinou had called for "a calm, objective dialogue" with Tiranë, adding: "The only point of tension [between Athens and Tiranë] is the Albanian treatment of the minority. Thus, we must find a way to talk with them. ... Greece must make a brave diplomatic initiative for a political solution. There is no other way out. We must realize this" (See Athens Elliniki Radhiofonia Radio Network in Greek, 1700 GMT, 7 September 1994, translated in FBIS-WEU 94-174, 8 September 1994, p. 65). Former Ambassador Nikos Makridhis counseled restraint toward Albania and called for a reassessment of Greek policy. He suggested that the term "Northern Epirus," which the Albanians connoted with

Greek territorial claims, not be used; that a special international commission be established to review the Peshkëpia incident; and that the Athens government curb Greek extremist groups and organizations (*Elevtherotipia*, 19 July 1994, translated in FBIS-WEU 94-145, 28 July 1994, pp. 41-42).

58. In June 1994, *Republika* published a letter that Omonia leader Sotir Qiriazati had sent to former Prime Minister Mitsotakis on 8 April 1994, requesting support for ethnic Greek efforts to create a "government" in the Greek-inhabited areas of southern Albania. Qiriazati wrote that international conditions were ripe for "the internationalization" of "the North Epirus problem" (*Republika*, 29 May 1994, pp. 1-2). On 19 June 1995, *Republika* published the text of a second letter that Qirjazati sent Mitsotakis on 30 May 1994, demanding support for autonomy for Albania's ethnic Greeks.

59. Editorial "A Victory for Wisdom and Reason—The Aftermath of Mr. Papoulias's Visit to Tiranë," *Rilindja Demokratike*, 15 March 1995, p. 1.

60. Marianne Sullivan, "Mending Relations With Greece," *Transition* 1, no. 15 (25 August 1995), pp. 11-16; and Kerin Hope, "Greece Builds Neighborly Ties," *Financial Times*, 22 September 1995, p. 4.

61. *Rilindja Demokratike*, 22 March 1996, p. 1.

62. Vesna Pesic, *Serbian Nationalism and the Origins of the Yugoslav Crisis* (Washington, D.C.: United States Institute of Peace, 1996), pp. 15-17.

63. Elez Biberaj, "Kosova: The Balkan Powder Keg," *Conflict Studies*, no. 258 (February 1993), pp. 5-8. See also Laura Silber and Allan Little, *Yugoslavia: Death of a Nation* (New York: TV Books/Penguin USA, 1995), pp. 37-47, and 58-73; and Mark Thompson, *A Paper House: The Ending of Yugoslavia* (New York: Pantheon Books, 1992), pp. 125-147.

64. The systematic violation of ethnic Albanians' human and political rights has been thoroughly documented by international human rights organizations. See "Yugoslavia (Serbia and Montenegro) Persecution Persists: Human Rights Violations in Kosovo," *Human Rights Watch/Helsinki* 8, no. 18 (D) (December 1996); Helsinki Watch, *Yugoslavia: Human Rights Abuses in Kosovo, 1990-1992* (New York, October 1992); Human Rights Watch/Helsinki, *Open Wounds: Human Rights Abuses in Kosovo* (New York, 1993); The Committee on International Human Rights of the Association of the Bar of the City of New York, *The Kosovo Crisis and Human Rights in Yugoslavia* (New York, February 1991); and International Helsinki Federation for Human Rights, *From Autonomy to Colonization: Human Rights in Kosovo 1989-1993* (Vienna, 1993).

65. Susan L. Woodward, *Balkan Tragedy: Chaos and Dissolution After the Cold War* (Washington, D.C.: Brookings Institution, 1995), p. 214.

66. David Owen, *Balkan Odyssey* (New York: Harcourt Brace & Company, 1995), p. 76.

67. President George Bush issued the first warning in December 1992. See David Binder, "Bush Warns Serbs Not to Widen War," *New York Times*, 28 December 1992, p. A6, and John M. Goshko, "Bush Threatens 'Military Force' If Serbs Attack Ethnic Albanians," *Washington Post*, 29 December 1992, p. A10. President Clinton's administration repeated the warning on several occasions.

68. Ted Galen Carpenter and Amos Perlmutter, "Strategy Creep in the Balkans," *National Interest*, no. 44 (Summer 1996), p. 56.

69. DPP in German, 0733 GMT, 11 December 1992, translated in FBIS-WEU 92-239, 11 December 1992, p. 1.

70. *Rilindja Demokratike*, 7 December 1993, p. 3. In an interview in August 1996, Berisha said: "Albania is doing everything to prevent a conflict. However, Albania will not tolerate a division and accept ethnic cleansing because the Albanians have lived there [in Kosova] since time immemorial" (*Die Presse*, 16 August 1996, p. 8, translated in FBIS-EEU 96-163, 21 August 1996, p. 1). See also Llazar Semini, "Albania Warns Serbia on Kosovo," *Washington Post*, 16 August 1995, p. A26.

71. *Rilindja Demokratike*, 18 October 1995, p. 2, and 27 December 1995, p. 3.

72. In a news conference in March 1995, Berisha said that Kosova "has its own leaders who have the people's mandate and who represent the interests and legitimate rights of the Albanian people of Kosova" (*Rilindja Demokratike*, 23 March 1995, p. 3).

73. *Bota Sot* (Zurich), 27 November 1995, p. 2.

74. See Bukoshi's interviews in *Koha* (Prishtinë), 10 January 1996, pp. 7-9, and in *Slobodna Dalmacija* (Split), 5 March 1997, p. 7, translated in FBIS-EEU 97-046, 12 March 1997.

75. See Ismije Beshiri, "Kosovar Independence Lacks International Backing," *Transition* 2, no. 6 (22 March 1996), pp. 52-54.

76. "What Did the Serbian Academicians Say?" *Flaka e Vëllazërimit* (Skopje), 8 June 1996, p. 12, translated in FBIS-EEU 96-114, 12 June 1996, PP. 69-70; and Banja Luka *Glas Srpski*, 22-23 June 1996, p. 2, translated in FBIS-EEU 96-129, 3 July 1996, pp. 51-52. Despić's proposal was endorsed by a Serbian American scholar (see Alex N. Dragnitch, "Divide and Conquer in Kosovo," *Washington Post*, 29 July 1996, p. A19). See also Ekavi Athanassopoulou, "Hoping for the Best, Planning for the Worst: Conflict in Kosovo," *World Today* 52, nos. 8-9 (August-September 1996), p. 29; and Cord Meyer, "Pressures to Resolve the Crisis in Kosovo," *Washington Times*, 9 August 1996, p. A19.

77. Shkelzen Maliqi, "Jettisoned to Keep SS Serbia Afloat?" *WarReport*, no. 43 (July 1996), p. 14. The idea of partitioning Kosova had been taboo in both Albania and Kosova. But in 1995, political scientist Arben Popoci warned that a partition could be forced upon the Albanians (Arben Popoci, "Between Agreement and Coercion," *Republika*, 1 June 1995, p. 4).

78. The International Helsinki Federation for Human Rights denounced the EU decision, insisting that the human rights situation in Kosova had not improved. In a statement in April 1996, the organization said that ethnic Albanians were being subjected to "ethnically-based apartheid." Paris AFP in English, 1555 GMT, 12 April 1996, in FBIS-EEU 96-073, 15 April 1996, p. 59.

79. *OMRI Daily Digest*, no. 25, part II, 5 February 1996.

80. U.S. Department of State, Office of the Spokesman, *Statement on Meeting Between Dr. Ibrahim Rugova and Secretary of State Christopher*, 13 December 1996.

81. See Robert W. Mickey and Adam Smith Albion, "Success in the Balkans? A Case Study of Ethnic Relations in the Republic of Macedonia," in Ian M. Cuthbertson and Jane Leibowitz, eds., *Minorities: The New Europe's Old Issue* (New York: Institute for EastWest Studies, 1993), pp. 53-98; and Thomas Buck, "Fear and Loathing in Macedonia: Ethnic Nationalism and the Albanian Problem," *International Affairs Review* 5, no. 1 (Winter 1996), pp. 1-23.

82. Milaim Fejziu, "The Political and Legal Position of the Albanians in the Current Constitution of the Republic of Macedonia," in the Democratic Forum for the Protection of Human Rights and Liberties in Macedonia, *Dëshmi për diskriminimin e rëndë të shqiptarëve në Maqedoni* [Evidence for the Harsh Discrimination of Albanians in Macedonia] (Tiranë: Eurorilindja, 1995), pp. 77-81.

83. See Hugh Poulton, *Who Are the Macedonians?* (Bloomington and Indianapolis: Indiana University Press, 1995), pp. 182-191. See also the review of Poulton's book by Misha Glenny in *New York Review of Books* XLII, no. 18 (16 November 1995), pp. 24-28; Robert Austin, "Albanian-Macedonian Relations: Confrontation or Cooperation?" *RFE/RL Research Report* 2, no. 42 (22 October 1993), pp. 21-25; and Mirjana Najcevska, "Reforming Inter-ethnic Relations," *WarReport*, no. 35 (July-August 1995), pp. 40-41.

84. Tanjug Domestic Service in Serbo-Croatian, 0940 GMT, 15 January 1992, translated in FBIS-EEU 922-011, 16 January 1992, pp. 59-60.

85. Tanjug in English, 0906 GMT, 16 April 1992 in FBIS-EEU 92-074, 16 April 1992, pp. 41-42.

86. Skopje MIC in English, 10 November 1993, in FBIS-EEU 93-217, 12 November 1993, p. 62. See also *Vecer* (Skopje), 5-6 February 1994, pp. 6-7, translated in FBIS-EEU 94-025, 7 February 1994, p. 43-44.

87. *Rilindja*, 16 February 1994, p. 3.

88. TVSH Television Network in Albanian, 1635 GMT, 22 April 1995, translated in FBIS-EEU 95-078, 24 April 1995, p. 36.

89. See Teuta Arifi, "Political Pluralism for Albanians," *WarReport*, no. 35 (July-August 1995), p. 42.

90. Tanjug Domestic Service in Serbo-Croatian, 1220 GMT, 10 November 1992, translated in FBIS-EEU 92-219, 12 November 1992, p. 42.

91. According to the Chairman of the Gostivar-based Democratic Forum for the Defense of Human Rights and Freedoms, Milaim Fejziu, "Albanians in Macedonia are subject to unprecedented discrimination in all spheres of life, especially in education, in the media, and in the institutions of the system." See Fejziu's interview in *Flaka e Vëllazërimit*, 17 December 1993, pp. 12-13.

92. *Flaka e Vëllazërimit*, 2 March 1994, p. 6.

93. International Research and Exchanges Board Roundtable Report, *Macedonia: Ethnic and International Issues* (Washington, D.C., 27 April 1995), p. 13.

94. Skopje MIC in English, 19 February 1997 in FBIS-EEU 97-035, 24 February 1997.

95. *Flaka e Vëllazërimit*, 27 October 1995, p. 3. See also Predrag Dimitrovski, "Radical Song Echoes Over Border," *Vecer* (Skopje), 25-26 May 1996, pp. 4-5, translated in FBIS-EEU 96-104, 29 May 1996, pp. 44-45.

96. *Flaka e Vëllazërimit*, 19 December 1994, p. 2. Interestingly, the founding meeting was held at the headquarters of Xhaferi's party. See *Rilindja*, 18 December 1994, pp. 1, 3. The Albanian Foreign Ministry welcomed the decision, saying that the university would meet the Albanians' "legitimate need" for higher education and would "fulfill the commitment of the Macedonian president and government for the integration of the Albanians with the Macedonian state" (Radio Tiranë in English, 1900 GMT, 19 December 1994, in FBIS-EEU 94-244, 20 December 1994, p. 1).

97. *Nova Makedonija*, 2 December 1994, p. 4, translated in FBIS-EEU 94-234, 6 December 1994, p. 67.

98. Extremists accused the government of making "too many" concessions to the Albanians. Some went so far as to deny Macedonia's multinational status. Ljubisa Georgievski, leader of the radical nationalist Internal Macedonian Revolutionary Organization-Democratic Party of Macedonian National Unity, bluntly asserted: "Multi-nationalization means federalization and breaking up the Macedonian unity. Today, when all of Europe is making national states, our national elite is proposing multi-nationality."

One state belonging to two peoples means war. ... This multi-national concept is leading us to war" (Skopje MIC in English, 16 September 1994 in FBIS-EEU 94-182, 20 September 1994, p. 44. Emphasis added.). See also David Binder, "Balkan College for Albanians Fights to Stay Alive," *New York Times,* 14 February 1996, p. B12.

99. In a related development, which was meant to send a message to local activists, Macedonian authorities expelled some thirty prominent Kosovar Albanians, most of them members of the former Kosova parliament, which had declared the region a republic in September 1990. Iljaz Ramajli, chairman of the former Kosova parliament, was expelled to Albania, while others were handed over to Serbia. As part of an agreement between Rugova and Gligorov, the deputies had been given refuge in Macedonia. However, now Skopje was upset with the role of Rugova's supporters in setting up Tetovë University.

100. Tetovë University was financed by the Albanians in Macedonia and in the diaspora. In 1996, the university had six faculties, with about 1,300 students and a teaching staff of 150. *Kosova Daily Report* in English, 26 March 1996, in FBIS-EEU 96-062, 29 March 1996, p. 57.

101. *Nova Makedonija,* 10 February 1995, p. 4, translated in FBIS-EEU 95-029, 13 February 1995, pp. 33-34.

102. See Aliti's interview in *Nova Makedonija,* 4 May 1996, p. 14, translated in FBIS-EEU 96-095, 15 May 1996, pp. 53-55.

103. Iso Rusi, "Macedonia: Independent Parties, Fraternal Links," *WarReport,* no. 41 (May 1996), p. 31.

104. See interview with Menduh Thaçi in *Fokus,* 8 December 1995, pp. 4-10, translated in FBIS-EEU 95-243, 19 December 1995, pp. 39-43. See also Duncan M. Perry, "On the Road to Stability—Or Destruction?" *Transition* 1, no. 15 (25 August 1995), pp. 40-48.

105. In July 1996, the Party for Democratic Prosperity of Albanians and the People's Democratic Party organized rallies throughout western Macedonia and Skopje to protest the jailing of Fadil Sulejmani and four other university activists. Originally, Sulejmani had been sentenced to two and a half years, but a Skopje district court in June 1996 reduced his sentence to one year. In July 1996 he was jailed to finish the remainder of his sentence.

106. Human Rights Watch/Helsinki, *A Threat to "Stability": Human Rights Violations in Macedonia* (New York, 1996), p. 27.

107. According to Kim Mehmeti, Macedonia was undergoing "a stealthy 'Yugo-slavisation,' the silent introduction of a nationality-based apartheid at every level except those that can be 'paraded' for international consumption. ... The more secure its outer borders become, the less care is taken of internal law and order. This is encouraging national segregation, criminality, and general insecurity" (Kim Mehmeti, "Disappearing Democracy," *WarReport,* no. 41 (May 1996), p. 31).

108. Misha Glenny, "Heading Off War in the Southern Balkans," *Foreign Affairs* 74, no. 3 (May-June 1995), p. 99.

109. See Demaçi's interview in *Bota Sot,* 14 December 1996, pp. 6-7.

110. Julie Mertus, "A Wall of Silence Divides Serbian and Albanian Opinion on Kosovo," *Transition* 2, no. 6 (22 March 1996), pp. 48-51.

111. U.S. Information Agency, Office of Research and Media Reaction, "Ethnic Albanians Willing to Die for Kosovo's Independence," *Opinion Analysis,* M-58-96, March 19, 1996, p. 1.

112. Fatos T. Lubonja, "We Albanians and Kosovars, We Kosovars and Albanians," *Koha Jonë,* 4 June 1995, p. 8.

113. U.S. Information Agency, Office of Research, "Albanians Seek Security as Balkan Conflict Continues," *Opinion Research Memorandum,* M-253-93, 17 November 1993, p. 2.

114. Asked whether the Albanians in Kosova and the Albanians in Albania were different, somewhat similar, akin, or one and the same nationality, 19 percent of respondents said they were different, 26 percent somewhat similar, 33 percent akin, and 19 percent one and the same. U.S. Information Agency, Office of Research and Media Reaction, "Albanian Public Prepared to Defend Kosovo," *Opinion Analysis,* M-69-96, 1 April 1996, p. 1.

115. Austin, "What Albania Adds to the Balkan Stew," p. 279.

8

The Party System and
the 1996 Elections

In the academic debate about transition and democratization, it is generally accepted that democracy can be established and endure only if there is a strong multiparty system and those in power are held accountable through regular and competitive elections. Political parties play a critical role in promoting and organizing political participation, articulating interests, and formulating program and policy alternatives. Regular and competitive elections channel political action into peaceful contests among elites. In a genuine democracy, elections are the only legitimate means through which power changes hands. Without responsive political parties through which multiple voices can articulate their ideas, and elections held at regular intervals, new political interests cannot be organized and incorporated into the formal political system. Rules restricting electoral competition and the politicization of the electoral system are likely to lead people to seek redress for their grievances outside the system. Thus a strong party system and free and fair elections are hallmarks of a stable democracy.

Volatile Party System

Albania, like much of postcommunist Eastern Europe, has seen a volatile party system come into being. By 1996, the number of registered political parties had risen to more than thirty. But with the exception of the Democratic and Socialist Parties, few looked like real national parties. Most did not develop deep-rooted group loyalties and much popular support. They had no clear social bases and minimal institutionalization, lacked easily identifiable ideology, and took paradoxical stands on many issues. The Democratic Party described itself as a center-right party; but on some issues, particularly social and economic ones, it consistently took a leftist position. Other parties, too, maintained stands that contradicted their proclaimed ideologies. Most parties were still loose agglomerations

TABLE 8.1 National Membership of Major Albanian Parties (1996)

Democratic Alliance	15,000
Democratic Party	130,000
Legality	6,200
National Front	12,300
Republican Party	19,500
Social Democratic Party	23,000
Social Democratic Union	10,000
Socialist Party	110,000
Union for Human Rights Party	10,000

Sources: Rilindja Demokratike, 5 April 1996; *Zëri i Popullit,* 24 March 1996; ATA in English 1127 GMT, 24 January 1996, in FBIS-EEU 96-018-A, 26 January 1996, pp. 4-5; and International Republican Institute, *IRI Observation Report on the Albanian Parliamentary Elections of May 26, 1996* (Washington, D.C., 1996), Appendix III.

of disparate groups rather than genuine parties linked to articulate constituencies. Many overlapped ideologically and in their social appeal, making it difficult to describe their ideological stand in terms of the traditional left-right continuum.

Albania has yet to see the emergence of viable parties that articulate the competing interests and preferences of individuals. Like other fledgling democracies in the region, Albania has witnessed instead a tendency toward increasing party fragmentation. Most parties experienced several splits, driven mainly by personal rivalries and intrigues rather than political principles. Interestingly, Albania was spared the emergence of extreme leftist as well as extreme rightist parties with significant popular backing. The country's most significant parties fell into a relatively narrow political spectrum. While they disagreed over the process and pace of change, all advocated a multiparty system, integration with the West, and a market economy.

Despite significant institutional and political changes since the demise of the Communist party-state, the Albanian political scene continued to be dominated by two main actors—the Democratic Party and the Socialist Party. Most other parties had small memberships (see Table 8.1), and if they are to survive, they must differentiate themselves and broaden their appeal to a skeptical electorate.

The Democratic Party

Formed in December 1990, the Democratic Party developed into a broad catch-all party. It was the only party with a clear political and economic program that was designed to appeal to multiple interests and divergent groups. Unlike his predecessor Ramiz Alia, who during his one-year tenure (April 1991-April 1992) as president of "democratic" Albania cut his links with the Socialist Party (reportedly at the latter's insistence) and sought to portray himself as a national leader above politics, President Berisha closely linked his own fortunes with those of the Democratic Party. He evidently believed that he could not exercise decisive leadership and implement fundamental reforms without the strong backing of his party. He retained his membership in the party presidency, maintaining very close contacts with other party leaders as well as with the rank and file. His opponents had hoped that once in office, he would abandon his partisanship and become the president of "all the people," but Berisha left no doubt about his partisan political option, zealously promoting the Democratic Party's program. Indeed, he made no attempt to differentiate between his role as head of state, and therefore a symbol of the nation, and his party's program.

As the first noncommunist party since 1945, the Democratic Party resembled less a traditional party than an umbrella organization including various individuals. Thus, it was not surprising that after its victory, the party's unity cracked under pressure of competing personalities and political tendencies. In August 1992, Gramoz Pashko, Arben Imami, and several other senior members of the leadership were expelled. Later that year, they formed the Democratic Alliance. In 1993, Petrit Kalakula was dismissed as chairman of the party's Tiranë branch for advocating extreme, rightist policies. But despite these splits and the fact that it never became an ideologically cohesive force, the Democratic Party was remarkably successful in retaining its absolute majority in parliament. Between 1992 and 1996, only eight deputies elected on the Democratic ticket defected to other parties. These defections had a minimal impact on legislation outcomes.

Although the Democratic Party retained a wide base of support that cut across all segments of the society, the perils and pitfalls of governing the country during a crisis took a toll on its vitality and affected its popularity. If the Democratic Party in 1992 enjoyed a public mandate unassailable by the divided opposition, it soon found itself in the unenviable position of being under attack by both the right and the left. After assuming power, the Democrats began to distance themselves from former political prisoners, followers of right-wing nationalist parties, and trade unions. In addition, the Democratic Party, which controlled almost all government posts, increasingly came to be seen as a party tolerant of high-level corruption. Although their control was limited to some extent by the overall economic and social situation, party bosses in Tiranë and at the district level held a tight grip over the distribution of public sector jobs to party stalwarts; helped supporters secure government benefits and services; helped new entrepreneurs obtain contracts, licenses, and credits; and so on. By failing to take decisive action against its own people suspected of corruption and nepotism, the Democratic Party risked confirming the impression of being a fundamentally corrupt party. Some government officials, including ministers and other senior officials, proved as infected by amorality as their Communist predecessors had been, flaunting their booty, nepotism, and bullying disregard for the rule of law. On too many occasions, government actions showed that official brutishness remained a deep-rooted reflex. With the memory of the Communist mismanagement beginning to fade, debate about the government's performance and the corruption and incompetence of the senior members of the cabinet intensified. Persistent allegations of corruption, incompetence, and nepotism were politically damaging to the Democratic Party and created a perception of scandal, which reduced public confidence in the government.[1] By the end of 1994, the ruling party seemed to have lost support to the Socialists and other left-wing parties as well as to its right-wing opponents, and was facing a pincer threat to its dominance of Albanian politics.

The defeat of the November 1994 constitutional referendum, which had been closely watched by all as a bellwether of the 1996 national elections, shattered the Democratic Party's complacency, sending its leaders into weeks of soul-searching. In a speech at the meeting of the party's National Council on 15 November 1994, Berisha blamed the Democratic Party—"its presidency, its branches, its sections, and others"—for losing the referendum and stressed that the referendum, should serve as a signal of "alarm" for all party structures.[2] In the wake of the referendum, Democratic Party leaders appeared divided, or at best, timid and confused, as they sought some new strategy. As a result of the initial confused reaction, contradictory statements, and conflicting signals about the future course of action, both government and Democratic Party officials appeared to have lost political stature. The referendum's defeat also intensified internal polarizing conflicts, causing a bitter struggle over the ideological direction the party should take to regain competitive strength. Party Chairman Eduard Selami, who had overseen the party's shift to the left after Kalakula's ouster in August 1993, advocated measures to placate the opposition. He suggested that the Democrats accept opposition demands that parliament take up the drafting of a new constitution, a position strongly opposed by the president.

In the wake of Selami's ouster as party chairman in March 1995, Berisha turned his immediate attention to the reinvigoration of the party. He argued that the Democratic Party had to regain political equilibrium and prove its ability and effectiveness, or face the prospect of losing power in 1996. He began the difficult tasks of reconstituting the old anticommunist coalition with centrist and rightist forces and of forging new alliances with various political groups. The president, however, was unwilling to yield to the blandishments of right-wing forces on the thorny property issue, insisting that priority had to be given to broader national interests and problems.

With elections only a year away, and a resurgent opposition aided by an anti-incumbent fever, the Democratic Party faced a race against time. It also faced a formidable task in rallying support among the disaffected Albanian public, most of which did not embrace the Socialist Party but which had lost confidence in the government following three and a half years of painful reforms. In spring and summer 1995, the Democratic Party launched an aggressive campaign to regain the initiative. There was a massive purge of corrupt and inefficient party officials at lower levels; however, the anticorruption drive did not extend to senior government officials and lawmakers, despite persistent reports of widespread corruption among their ranks. Powerful forces within the government and parliament strongly opposed such moves. Moreover, Berisha did not appear eager to address corruption at the top, apparently out of fear that high-profile cases would undermine his party's electoral chances.

The extent of the renovation of the Democratic Party became evident at its national convention in April 1996. Berisha disclosed that more than 60 percent of all party organs had been renovated.[3] Some 65 percent of the party's National Council members were new. Several prominent members of the council were dropped, including Genc Ruli, Rexhep Uka, and Mitro Çela.[4] Tritan Shehu was elected as party chairman, replacing Selami. A close friend of Berisha, Shehu was also a medical school graduate. Before becoming secretary-general of the party in December 1993, Shehu had served as health minister.[5] The Rector of Tiranë Agricultural University, Besnik Gjongecaj, became the new general-secretary of the party. Albert Brojka and Ferdinand Xhaferri retained their posts as foreign relations secretary and organizational secretary, respectively.[6]

While the elections in 1992 had been a referendum on communism, the 1996 vote was largely viewed as a referendum on Berisha's four years in power and on faith in his policies. Although the humiliation of defeat in the constitutional referendum had shattered their confidence, by spring 1996, the Democrats had recovered, regaining the upper hand in Albanian politics. The economy was one of the best-performing former Communist economies. The rule of law was slowly beginning to take hold and the controversy surrounding the replacement of the Chief Justice of the Court of Cassation, Zef Brozi,[7] which had done considerable damage to Berisha's international image, had been largely forgotten. There was also good news on the foreign policy front. Albania had developed very close ties with the United States and Western Europe, and had been admitted into the Council of Europe. Relations with Greece and Italy had improved significantly.

In the months leading up to the elections, polls indicated substantial support for the ruling party and for Berisha personally. A survey by the European Commission's Eurobarometer, conducted in November 1995, showed that Albania was the most optimistic of the nineteen Central and Eastern European states surveyed regarding their development of democracy and of a market economy:

According to the four classic indicators of the Central and Eastern Eurobarometer (country direction, support for market economy, democracy satisfaction, and human rights), Albanians seem to be the most optimistic of those interviewed for this survey. The level of our indicators has risen spectacularly. Albanians are happier now than at any time in the last five years with the direction in which their country is going, the creation of a market economy, and the way in which human rights are respected in their country. For the first time since 1991, the majority of citizens in Albania are also satisfied with the way democracy has developed in their country.[8]

Some 79 percent of Albanians believed the country was moving in the right direction, placing Albania at the top of the list of countries surveyed. Croatia came in second, with 66 percent, followed by Estonia (57 percent), the Czech Republic (55 percent), and Macedonia (48 percent). Support for a market economy was also most evident in Albania, with 76 percent of people interviewed considering the market economy "right" for their country. Some 76 percent of Albanians said their economic situation was better than the year before, and 73 percent believed the country's economic situation would improve during the coming year. The survey also showed that Albania had the highest number of people satisfied with the development of democracy: an absolute majority of 59 percent (compared to 41 percent dissatisfied). Only in two other countries did people satisfied with their democracy outnumber those who were dissatisfied: Croatia (52 percent) and Poland (50 percent). The proportion of people in Albania satisfied with the level of respect there for human rights was the highest of all the countries surveyed: 75 percent.[9]

A survey commissioned by the U.S. International Republican Institute showed 61 percent of Albanians interviewed were satisfied with the progress of economic reforms. The poll showed a strong approval rating for Berisha: 74 percent said they had a favorable impression of the president. A majority of 41 percent said they would vote for the Democratic Party, and only 19 percent for the Socialist Party.[10] Only three months before the 1996 national elections, the high level of public satisfaction with the state of affairs was also confirmed by a survey commissioned by the U.S. Information Agency. An overwhelming majority of Albanians, 86 percent, said the economy was better than ever, and 76 percent expressed support for the free market economy. The poll indicated that 67 percent of Albanians were satisfied with the progress of economic reform thus far, and the same proportion believed their financial situation would improve over the next twelve months.[11] The USIA survey also showed the Democratic Party leading the Socialist Party by an approximate margin of two to one. Some 75 percent of those interviewed voiced a favorable opinion of Berisha.[12]

The Socialist Party

Albania's second largest political force, the Socialist Party, adopted its current name and western European social-democratic labels at the 10th Congress of the Albanian Party of Labor, in June 1991. While its leaders maintained that the Socialist Party was a new organization, unburdened by the Communist past, the Socialist Party preserved the APL's strong internal structure, nationwide network, and organizational resources, and remained the best-organized party.[13] Moreover, the party refused to express remorse, to apologize for Communist crimes, or to rehabilitate the huge number of party members who had fallen victim to Hoxha's many purges. Its criticism of Hoxha was halfhearted and its claims of renovation disingenuous.

After its humiliating defeat in 1992, the Socialist Party displayed little commitment to democratic values and practices. It pursued a very disruptive policy, in an attempt to force the Democratic Party to hold early elections. Focusing on the egalitarian and anticapitalist sentiment of workers who suddenly found themselves in a free-market society, the Socialists took every opportunity to undermine the Democratic government, hoping to make gains by tapping into public dissatisfaction over the rate of privatization, unemployment, and corruption. While working to sanitize their image and nominally endorsing the transition to democracy, the Socialists attempted to block the process of transition at every step of the way.

Despite significant turnover in the Socialist Party's membership since 1991, the mantle of leadership did not pass to a younger, different generation. There was not a great deal in the Socialist Party leaders' background to separate them from the APL. The party leadership itself was heavily dominated by conservative Communists, led by its Chairman Fatos Nano, who was imprisoned in mid-1993 on charges of misappropriation of foreign assistance. Nano had been closely linked to the most conservative faction of the APL, his father having served as a close Hoxha adviser and as director of state television. For years, Nano worked in the Institute of Marxist-Leninist Studies headed by Nexhmije Hoxha. In 1990, as an up-and-coming member of the APL, Nano developed a reputation as an economic reformer. Nevertheless, he opposed political pluralism and desperately attempted to perpetuate the APL's rule. Writing in the literary newspaper *Drita* in October 1990, only two months before Ramiz Alia was forced to permit the creation of opposition parties, Nano rejected the notions of political pluralism and a free-market economy, emphasizing that Albania had to develop its own political and economic model, within the existing socialist system.[14] In February 1991, as the Communist party-state lay on its deathbed, Alia named Nano prime minister, replacing Adil Çarçani. At the time, Nano was the antithesis of the old guard—refined, educated, and genteel.

Nano's closest allies in the leadership were Deputy Chairmen Servet Pëllumbi and Namik Dokle and Secretary-General Gramoz Ruçi. All three were closely linked to the old regime and had questionable democratic credentials. Pëllumbi, a renowned Marxist theoretician, was alleged to have spied on his own students, some of whom were sentenced for antistate activities. Like Nano, Pëllumbi had forcefully argued against permitting the establishment of opposition parties. Writing in the APL's authoritative theoretical journal *Rruga e Partisë* in May 1990, he attacked Western pressures on Albania to sanction political pluralism as "political terrorism" against Marxism-Leninism. He insisted that the introduction of a multiparty system was contrary to Albania's traditions and to "the ideological homogeneity that characterizes our socialist society."[15] In the old regime, Dokle had served in senior positions as a trade union official and chief editor of *Zëri i Popullit*. But of the three, Ruçi appeared the closest to Nano. A ruthless and a widely feared Communist *apparatchik*, Ruçi had served as a district APL first secretary in Tepelenë. When Nano became prime minister, he appointed Ruçi to the sensitive position of minister of internal affairs. It is widely believed that Nano orchestrated the violence against the Democratic opposition through Ruçi, following the downing of Hoxha's monument in Tiranë and the killing of Democratic Party activists in Shkodër in 1991.

The party continued to be dominated by militant elements of Hoxha's old party. This group swiftly recovered from the initial shock of losing power, and its leading representatives became increasingly outspoken, publicly defending the past and even Hoxha. Pragmatic Communists, who joined the party in the late 1970s and during the 1980s, represented the second dominant group. They were unwilling to denounce the past and were inclined to stress the positive rather than the negative accomplishments of the Hoxha-Alia regime. The third and smallest group was represented by the younger generation, which advocated that the party dump its past ideological baggage. Grouped around the party youth organization, the Eurosocialist Youth Forum, this group criticized the inclusion of Marx in the party's program, and called for a new party identity.[16] However, it did not enjoy significant support among the party's rank and file.

Disagreements between the young Socialists and the party leadership came to a head in July 1995, during the second congress of the Eurosocialist Youth Forum. In a speech to the congress, Servet Pëllumbi called for changes in the youth organization "to make a greater commitment to the Socialist Party's alternative for the forthcoming elections."[17] Pandeli Majko was replaced as chairman of the youth organization by Ilir Meta.[18] However, the reformist wing of the party was further marginalized in October 1995, when a vote of confidence demanded by Nano resulted in the dismissal of Bashkim Zeneli and four other members of the top leadership. Zeneli had emerged as a leading advocate of the democratization of the party.[19]

While the Socialists were shaken by Nano's imprisonment, his successors managed a smoothly unified party, squelching factional disputes for the party's greater good. Pëllumbi turned out to be a shrewd politician who managed to straddle the divisions between the stand-patters and the younger reformists in his party. In contrast to Nano's confrontational approach, the soft-spoken Pëllumbi worked hard to improve his party's image. He tried to present the Socialist Party as a credible alternative to the Democratic Party in the face of social and economic difficulties. As part of efforts to improve their image, the Socialists also kept their distance from former president Alia.

In late 1994 and the beginning of 1995, as the Democratic Party faced its severest crisis since assuming power, the Socialists attempted to seize the initiative from Berisha. They adopted a more combative stance and mounted a counter-attack, asserting that Berisha's unchallenged moment in the spotlight had come to an end. In preparation for the 1996 elections and in a bid to establish credibility as a moderate force, the Socialist Party toned down its anti-Western, particularly anti-American, rhetoric. The Socialists maintained that they would not depart from the basic goals of Albania's democratization, creating a market economy and seeking integration with Western Europe. However, their commitment to democratic values and practices remained questionable, and their acceptance of market forces was qualified. They rejected Berisha's policy of shock therapy and massive privatization, advocating instead gradual economic reforms and a continued state role in regulating the economy. The Socialists called for a social market economy, with a commitment to cushioning the social impact of economic reform, which would require considerable government intervention and a fairer distribution system.

Despite its liabilities as successor to the Communist Party, the Socialist Party approached the 1996 elections with great optimism. Party ideologues insisted that significant segments of the population, that blamed the Democratic Party for ending their Communist social benefits were likely to identify with the Socialist Party. The Socialists also hoped to benefit from the fact that the Social Democratic Party and the Democratic Alliance had moved increasingly to the left, which served to discourage Socialist defections to these parties. However, the Socialists failed to take into account that despite the shock of painful reforms, the majority of Albanians had benefitted from the reforms implemented by the Democratic government. Moreover, the Socialist Party had not reformed itself sufficiently to be accepted by the Albanian public and the outside world.

The Social Democratic Party

The third-largest bloc in the 1992-1996 parliament, holding seven seats, the Social Democratic Party has its roots in the reformist wing of the APL. Some of its leaders had a distinctly Communist background; they were quick-change artists who had faithfully served Alia's regime. Party Chairman Skendër Gjinushi served as minister of education in Adil Çarçani's government. As Communist rule teetered under the sagging economy and anticommunist demonstrations, Gjinushi represented the Communist government in negotiations with demonstrating students in December 1990 and hunger strikers in February 1991. He then joined with other Communist reformers, including the leader of the Communist youth organization, Lisen Bashkurti, to form the Social Democratic Party.[20] Other party leaders, including historian Paskal Milo, also had close links with the Communist government.

With an electoral support of some five percent in 1992, the Social Democratic Party came in third, a more impressive performance than expected. Dissatisfaction with the Communist regime had improved the Social Democratic Party's odds, as many voters with a leftist orientation opted for this party rather than vote for the Socialist Party. Although ostensibly allied with the Democratic Party and a participant in the governing coalition from 1992 until the end of 1994, the Social Democratic Party was highly critical of the government. In parliament, the Social Democrats allied themselves with the Socialists on many issues, particularly economic reforms. In June 1993, they boycotted parliamentary sessions because of the delay in adopting a new constitution. The gulf between the two former allies widened farther after the Social Democratic Party sided with the Socialist Party in opposing the draft constitution referendum in 1994. Gjinushi formally ended his party's coalition with the Democrats in December 1994, after Berisha named Teodor Laço, until then deputy chairman of the Social Democratic Party, minister of culture. Laço, who had supported the draft constitution, accused Gjinushi of having turned the Social Democratic Party into an appendix of the Socialist Party. A faction led by Laço, and including writer Bardhyl Londo and Deputy Foreign Minister Arian Starova, formed the Social Democratic Union.[21] Laço said the new party would be "a genuine social democratic party, one not influenced by the old Communist mentalities and practices."[22]

The Democratic Alliance Party

Formed in late 1992 by what its critics call the Communist wing of the Democratic Party, the Democratic Alliance Party stood out as the fourth most important political force in the 1992-1996 parliament, with six deputies. The party leadership was composed of former senior Democratic Party officials with nationwide name recognition. Party President Neritan Ceka and Secretary-General Arben Imami had served as deputy chairmen of the Democratic Party. Other members of the leadership included Gramoz Pashko, Preç Zogaj, Teodor Keko, and Perikli Teta. Self-described as a center-left party and without a large-scale popular following, the Democratic Alliance claimed to represent the urban, middle-class, and intellectual strata.

The Democratic Alliance was an outspoken critic of the government and frequently voted with the Socialists. In parliament, Alliance deputies engaged in headline-grabbing disruptions, attempting to advance their personal and party agendas. Arben Imami and Ridvan Peshkëpia on numerous occasions were expelled from parliament for improper conduct.

The Democratic Alliance took a particularly critical stand on foreign policy issues. It was the only party that advocated accommodation with Serbia, even at the expense of Kosovar Albanians' interests.[23] In a politically questionable action, in October 1993, Ceka visited Belgrade, where he had discussions with senior Yugoslav officials. The visit was denounced by the government and the pro-government papers, as well as by Albanian political forces in Kosova, as tantamount to national betrayal.[24] In August 1995, Ceka urged the government to accept Serbian refugees who had left the Croatian region of Krajina.[25] The Democratic Alliance also attempted to forge close ties with Greece. In March 1993, a Greek parliamentary delegation became the first foreign delegation to hold official talks with the Democratic Alliance. A statement issued at the end of discussions in Tiranë blamed the Albanian government for the problems in Albanian-Greek relations, adding that Albanian refugees in Greece were suffering because of the "Albanian state's challenge of the Greek state."[26] The party's pro-Greek stand became even more evident in summer 1993, during tensions with Athens, when it issued a strongly worded statement, practically placing all the blame on Tiranë.[27] The progovernment media alleged that the Democratic Alliance and its leaders had received financial assistance from Greece.[28] One observer noted that the Democratic Alliance had never taken a position on any issue—domestic or foreign—that conflicted with Greece's Albania policy.[29] Alliance leaders also took an unusually anti-Islamic stand.[30]

The Democratic Alliance closely coordinated its activities and policies with the Socialist Party; but collaboration with the Socialists left the Democratic Alliance vulnerable to attacks from the right and center-right. The party's move to the left also caused a rift between the dominant leadership, led by Ceka, and the respected lawyer and former political prisoner Spartak Ngjela. In November 1993, Ngjela failed to garner enough support in the party's General Assembly to replace Ceka as party president.[31] In August 1994, Ngjela resigned in protest of the Democratic Alliance's close association with the Socialist Party. Ngjela disclosed that the Socialist Party had asked its supporters in many areas to support and join the Democratic Alliance. He quoted Socialist Party Secretary-General Gramoz Ruçi as saying, "We have ordered specific Socialist Party cells in the districts to join the ranks of the Democratic Alliance."[32] Gramoz Pashko, who had been kept on the sidelines because of his father's close association with Hoxha and corruption allegations while he served in the coalition government in 1991, was believed to share Ngjela's views, but did not join him. Nevertheless, in September 1994, he sharply criticized the party's leadership. In an interview, Pashko said: "The Democratic Alliance does not know how to attract the electorate. ... We too often lack clear political thinking. Our opposition is often defective, or worse, personal, like that of the Socialist Party. The Democratic Alliance's leaders in their statements and articles do not know how to establish their position in the political spectrum and are turning the Democratic Alliance simply into a party of protest or an umbrella rather than a convincing alternative."[33]

The Democratic Alliance continued to be plagued by internal fissures over relations with the Socialists. While the majority in the leadership worked closely with the Socialists against the Democrats, some saw any cooperation with former Communists as a compromise of principles. Others in the leadership took up the middle ground between the two positions, choosing to emphasize the permissible forms of contact and cooperation with the Socialist Party but generally embracing the idea of a coalition with the Social Democratic Party. As the 1996 national elections approached, the Democratic Alliance attempted to expand its organizational structure and base of support. Hoping to become the kingmakers of Albanian politics, leaders of the Democratic Alliance expressed willingness to enter into a coalition with any force against the Democratic Party.

The Republican Party

The second opposition party to be formed after the APL was forced to sanction political pluralism, the Republican Party initially operated largely in the shadow of the Democratic Party. Fractious and unpredictable, in the 1992 elections, it failed not only to meet the 4-percent threshold but also to get its chairman, Sabri Godo, elected to parliament. It won only one seat in parliament. The party's poor performance was attributed to the lack of a clear program, acrimonious intraparty struggles, and leadership problems. Nevertheless, as a result of its pre-1992 election coalition with the Democrats and the Social Democrats, the Republican Party received two portfolios in Prime Minister Aleksandër Meksi's first cabinet.

More than any other Albanian political force, the Republican Party was faced with an identity crisis. In an attempt to create a social base, it moved steadily to the right, adopting an increasingly demagogic posture on many issues, including the thorny question of restitution for former property owners. Godo apparently believed that the only way to revive his party's fortunes was to move to the right and adopt a tougher stance on property issues. By 1994, the Republican Party's profile had changed to essentially that of a single-issue party. It embarked on a campaign designed to return the property confiscated by the Communists to its rightful, original owners. It gradually distanced itself from the ruling party, claiming that the Democrats had monopolized administrative leadership and political life, thus marginalizing other partners in the coalition. Although it supported Berisha's draft constitution,[34] in the wake of the defeat of the referendum, the Republican Party withdrew from the coalition.[35]

The Right

Composed of a group of loosely defined parties with limited grassroots reach and vying to outbid each other in their anticommunist positions, the Right remained superficially divided. Right-wing parties claimed that the Democratic Party's reluctance to return property to its original owners and expose the criminal nature of communism was preparing the ground for the return to power of the Socialist Party.

In addition to the Republican Party, the most important right-wing parties were the two historical parties National Front and the monarchist Legality. Their main base of support was the small class of former landowners and former political prisoners. The two parties demanded the restoration of property rights and a thorough decommunization. They also had a strong nationalistic component, advocating the unification of Kosova and other Albanian-inhabited territories in the former Yugoslavia with Albania. They had accused neighboring countries of attempting to undermine Albania's economic and social structure by orchestrating economic chaos, political unrest, and social upheaval. They consistently expounded on the need for a nationalist-democratic fusion to counter Serbian-Greek pressures and designs. But the dilemma the two parties faced was that there was no significant bloc of voters attracted to their agenda. They were unable to build a nationwide organization or to expand their base of support.

The Democratic Party of the Right, formed in 1994 by former Democratic Party deputies Petrit Kalakula and Abdi Baleta, did not develop into a significant force. Its program called for the abrogation of major legislation, particularly laws on land and privatization, to "honor the legitimate rights of former owners in towns and countryside by total and unconditional restitution of their property, arbitrarily grabbed by the Communist state."[36] In spring 1995, the party began to unravel in acrimony, at what was intended to be the start of a campaign to strengthen the right in preparation for the 1996 elections. Personal resentment erupted between Kalakula and Baleta, and the latter was expelled from the party in May 1995.[37] The dramatic party rift again highlighted a growing tendency toward fragmentation of political parties. Party members accused the untested Kalakula and Baleta of needlessly dividing the party on a matter of personal ego rather than substance. Baleta went on to form the Party of National Restoration, which advocated the unification with Albania of Kosova and other Albanian-inhabited regions in former Yugoslavia.

As disenchantment grew with the Democratic Party on a number of issues, particularly property restitution, calls increased for the creation of a right-wing alliance to counterbalance what was termed "the unproclaimed alliance of left-wing forces which, under various labels and slogans, are aiming to reestablish the socialist form of government."[38] In February 1995, six right-wing political organizations announced the formation of the Albanian Right League. A fourteen-point resolution was signed by the Republican Party, National Front, Legality, Association of Former Victims of Political Persecution, Democratic Unity Party, and the Association of Former Victims of Economic and Political Persecution. The Albanian Right League pledged to fight for the restitution of property to its legitimate former owners and called for trials of Communist crimes during the war and down to the present day. They accused Berisha of not doing enough to prosecute former APL officials and to expose the criminal nature of communism. A coordinating committee with a rotating leadership was established.[39] However, on the eve of the 1996 elections, the Right League collapsed as a result of personal animosities and bickering among the leaders of its various parties. While a coalition or merger of these forces could have had a significant effect on the political arena, individually none of the right-wing parties represented a serious political force.

Other Parties

Among other parties, the most important was the Union for the Protection of Human Rights, which represented the ethnic Greek community in Albania. While its stronghold was in the south, in the ethnic Greek-inhabited areas, it expanded its activities, opening branches in many areas of the country where there were no ethnic Greeks. The party used its strong ties with Greece in an attempt to expand its influence.

The 1996 Elections

Albania's first multiparty elections in March 1991 were held based on an electoral law adopted in November 1990, before the Communist regime was forced to sanction political pluralism. The law provided for single-member, winner-take-all districts. It favored the Albanian Party of Labor, which easily won a majority of 169 seats out of 240 seats in the new parliament. The Democratic Party won 75 seats; the ethnic Greek minority organization Omonia, 5; and the Communist-dominated Committee of Veterans, 1. The opposition had unsuccessfully advocated the adoption of a proportional system, insisting that such a system would better express the will of the electorate than a majoritarian system. By the time of the March 1992 elections, the political situation in the country had changed dramatically, and the two major parties reversed their positions. The Socialist Party sought to change the electoral system because it recognized that the old arrangement now offered more advantages to its main rival. Supporters of the majoritarian system, primarily representatives of the Democratic Party whose election prospects had increased significantly since March 1991, argued that such a system was more likely to provide for decisive governance, while the proportional system would lead to polarization, party fragmentation, and governmental paralysis. But opponents claimed that a majoritarian system would consolidate a two-party dominant system and thus marginalize smaller parties. A proportional system, they argued, would maximize representativeness and foster conciliation and compromise, so necessary for Albania's fledgling democracy.

Leaders of the major political parties engaged in long and strenuous discussions on the virtues and perils of different electoral systems. Finally, in February 1992, parliament adopted a new law, changing Albania's electoral system from a majoritarian to a mixed one with a 4-percent threshold. The inclusion of a threshold reflected the desire of party elites to attempt to ensure only a moderate number of parties in the new parliament. Although in the March 1992 elections the Democratic Party won a decisive majority, 90 of the 100 seats in direct elections, the electoral system helped the Socialist and Social Democratic parties, the only two other parties that made the 4-percent threshold. In single-member districts with plurality elections, the Socialists won in six districts and the Social Democrats in one. But the electoral system awarded the two parties a greater number of proportional seats than their share of national vote justified. Thus, having won 27.1 percent and 5 percent, respectively, of the national vote, the Socialist Party received an additional 32 seats, and the Social Democratic Party, 6. The Democrats, who won 62 percent of the overall vote, received only 2 additional seats from the proportional list.

The New Electoral Framework

In preparation for the 1996 elections, there were increasing calls for changes in the electoral system. With the exception of the Democratic Party, all other parliamentary parties continued to prefer some type of proportional system over a majoritarian one. However, with increased polarization between the ruling and opposition parties, the Democrats expressed concern that a proportional system would lead to a fractured parliament and a weak coalition government, at a time when the country needed strong and decisive government. After heated debates, in January 1996, the Democratic Party-controlled parliament, over the strenuous objections of most other parties, approved changes in the 1992 election law. According to the Democrats, the new electoral rules were fashioned to give Albania a more responsive political system and rule by a stable, clear-cut majority.

However, in reality, the new law was likely to enhance the position of the larger parties and in the long run lead the country in the direction of an adversarial two-party system. The number of single-member districts was increased from 100 to 115, while the number of proportional seats was decreased from 40 to 25. While the 1992 electoral system had ensured that the final election results would reflect the overall percentage of votes received by all parties that passed the 4-percent threshold, the new law changed the representative form of parliament, shifting away from a proportional system to a majoritarian one. The distribution of proportional seats was designed to favor parties that won the largest number of seats among the 115 single-member districts. The reduction and change in the distribution of proportional seats was viewed as consigning many smaller parties, competing for the same group of voters, to oblivion. The changes also discouraged smaller parties from participating in the election as a bloc. Each party in a potential alliance had to win 4 percent of the total vote to be eligible for supplementary seats. The new law also made changes concerning the composition and selection of the electoral commissions and providing equal access to state radio and television. It gave the president, rather than parliament, the responsibility for determining the boundaries of electoral districts.[40]

The new election law failed to address disputes between regional and national party officials that went to the heart of who would control the electoral process. Regional officials were eager to assert their power over the elections and the candidates. But the law favored party oligarchs at the center who continued to dominate the selection of nominees and who could use the proportional slates to get their allies elected. Under this system, in which party bosses at the national level had discretion as to who would run on the party list, local authorities had little impact on the selection of candidates. Moreover, contacts with the electorate remained loose as the old practice of nominating candidates who were not residents in the electoral district continued. And the role of party conventions remained limited, as the outcome of the preconvention struggle was decisive and usually determined the convention selection process. Clearly, there was a need to democratize the nominating process by empowering local organizations to choose their party's nominees.

The approval of the new law drew a barrage of criticism from the Socialist and other parties, including allegations that the Democratic Party had used its incumbency to change the political playing field. Indeed the new election law and legislation passed in late 1995 had stacked the rules in the Democratic Party's favor. In September 1995, parliament enacted the "Law on Genocide and Crimes Against Humanity Committed in Albania During Communist Rule for Political, Ideological, and Religious Motives," barring former Communists and Sigurimi collaborators from seeking public office until 2002. Under the law, members of the former APL Politburo and Central Committee, ministers, deputies, district party secretaries, presidents of the Supreme Court and general prosecutors, and former Sigurimi agents and informers were prohibited from holding posts in parliament, the government, the judiciary or the state-run media.[41] The lustration law barred leading opposition politicians from the Socialist, Social Democratic, and Democratic Alliance Parties from participating in the forthcoming parliamentary elections. Opposition parties denounced the law, arguing that it was designed to rid the ruling party of opponents before the elections. International human rights organizations also criticized the law for banning people from holding public office for having held a particular position in the old regime rather than for having committed a specific crime.

On 30 November, parliament passed the "Law on Verification of the Moral Character of Officials and Other Persons Connected with the Protection of the Democratic State," regulating the opening of Sigurimi files and setting up a state screening commission for those seeking public office.[42] Six of the seven members of the verification commission were appointed by the government; the other was named by parliament.[43] Opposition parties strongly criticized the verification law, claiming that the screening commission would target opposition candidates. Among senior opposition figures disqualified were Socialists Servet Pëllumbi and Kastriot Islami, Social Democratic leader Skendër Gjinushi, and Democratic Alliance senior officials Preç Zogaj, Perikli Teta, and Ridvan Peshkëpia.

Party Platform and Strategy

The preelection political scene was characterized by increased polarization, friction, and intolerance. Both Democratic Party and opposition officials resorted to inflammatory rhetoric and vicious personal attacks, poisoning the country's public discourse. Tensions increased significantly as the elections approached and political parties launched their campaign for the hearts and minds of voters. The campaign was marred by personal attacks as Democratic and opposition supporters resorted to acts of physical intimidation. There were also Socialist charges of police interference, and harassment and intimidation of the party's candidates and supporters.

Although officially the campaign period did not begin until early April 1996, Albanian political parties had begun preparations for the elections soon after the constitutional referendum in 1994. The campaign focused almost exclusively on domestic issues, with the economy being the most important underlying theme. Foreign policy issues were far down on the list. The issue of Kosova was almost nonexistent in the campaign. Right-wing forces harped on feelings of humiliation by the Serbs, but even among these forces, the issue was at most a subdued theme. Voters apparently conceived of their political preferences in terms of parties rather than issues. This became particularly evident in single-member districts, where party affiliation, rather than the candidates' qualifications, remained the critical factor.

The Democratic Party fielded candidates in all 115 electoral districts. Less than a third of incumbent Democratic deputies were renominated as candidates; 78 percent of candidates were new.[44] With its confidence restored and its organizational supremacy, the Democratic Party ran a vigorous campaign, redefining itself as a center party and staking out a middle-of-the-road position. The Democrats cast the race as a choice between stability and continued growth, on the one hand, and a return to the past and great uncertainty.[45] Concerts featuring prominent musicians were staged across the country under the slogan "With Us, Everyone Wins."

With the opposition's focus on economic and social dislocations and government policy failures, Berisha and other party officials conceded there had been mistakes during four years of Democratic Party rule, but claimed that a Socialist victory would derail market reforms and spark instability. Berisha appealed to the core constituencies of the 1992 Democratic Party-led coalition—workers, intellectuals, youths, unions, former political prisoners, and reformed Communists. The glue that held the 1992 coalition together was the shared sense of unity in bringing down communism. By 1996, in the face of dramatic changes and as the memory of Hoxha's regime receded, the electorate had broken into increasingly complex units, in which economic factors, more than the struggle against communism, shaped partisan allegiance. Realizing that it could not rely heavily on the same themes that had worked in the 1992 election, the Democratic

Party decided on a strategy of stressing the positive elements of its four-year rule and of advertising Socialist leaders' political links to the communist past. The Democrats highlighted the most extreme ideas in the Socialist Party's program, calling attention to the split between conservative and reformist wings of the Socialist Party, and suggesting that Socialist officials lacked experience to run the country in the new circumstances of a market economy. The Democrats also devised strategies to appeal to new voters and to the large number of voters who professed to be independent.

Ignoring opposition criticism that he had become far too deeply enmeshed in the day-to-day running of the Democratic Party, Berisha became his party's principal voice in the campaign. Reminiscent of 1992, Berisha, the consummate campaigner, crisscrossed the country, attempting to convince voters that they were choosing between stability and steady growth versus another revolution and uncertainty. Taking credit for the democratization of the country and revival of the economy, Berisha attempted to convince the electorate of the virtues of reform and the dangers of radically altering the status quo. In his pronouncements, the president pulled no punches in blasting former Communists, referring to the Socialist, Social Democratic, and Democratic Alliance Parties as the "Red Front" and appealing to voters to remember the Communist past. Having clearly positioned his party in the political center, with characteristic optimism, Berisha offered a clear vision for the future. This contrasted sharply with the Socialists' stolid, often sour performance on the campaign trail. Leaders of the Socialist, Social Democratic, and Democratic Alliance Parties all seemed to give the same speech, describing Albania as teetering on the brink of economic and social disaster and political upheaval.

In response to the Socialist Party's growing alliance with the Social Democratic Party and the Democratic Alliance, which had formed a Center Pole coalition, Berisha took measures to assuage right political forces. Although his efforts did not produce spectacular results, the right, fearing a Socialist victory, gradually lined up behind the Democratic Party. Thus, Berisha succeeded in turning the contest into a two-party race, to the frustration of other parties.

As election day approached, the Democratic Party hoped to benefit from the electorate's fear that a Socialist Party victory could well undermine the fragile new market economy and bring about a destabilizing impasse and a period of turmoil. The Socialist Party had few if any people with hands-on market economic experience. Most Socialist experts still clung to an old world view, with little understanding of how a market economy works. While few voters expected the Socialists to reverse Albania's democratic, free-market reforms, most evidently agreed that further reforms would be impossible if former Communists came to power, because their inexperience and ideological commitments would lead Albania back to an inefficient and rigidly administered economy.

The Democratic Party continued to enjoy strong Western support. Despite the Socialists' concerted efforts to convince the West that their victory would not mean a return to the totalitarian past, Western officials expressed their preference for the Democratic Party over the Socialist Party by heaping praise on the Democrats' economic and political reforms. Although following the removal of Chief Justice Zef Brozi in September 1995, the United States had been holding Berisha somewhat at arms lengths, Secretary of Defense William Perry and Undersecretary of State for Global Affairs Timothy Wirth visited Albania in March and April 1996, respectively. Less than a month before the elections, Foreign Minister Alfred Serreqi was invited to Washington for a meeting with Secretary of State Warren Christopher.[46] In a statement after the meeting, the State Department stressed that, "As a good friend and supporter of democratic Albania, the United States has a strong interest in Albania's ongoing process of consolidating democracy and the rule of law." The statement added that Serreqi had assured Christopher that the May 26 elections would be free and fair and that the Secretary welcomed these assurances.[47] The United States stopped short of an outright endorsement of the Democratic Party, but it left little doubt that it preferred to have the Democrats remain in power. Still, Washington made clear that it wanted to see honest, free, and fair elections. In an interview with the Voice of America's Albanian Service only a week before the elections, Undersecretary of State for Global Affairs Timothy Wirth praised Albania's political and economic achievements under Democratic Party rule. He also praised the controversial law barring certain former Communists and Sigurimi collaborators from seeking public office. Wirth said that the appeal mechanism had been fair and proved the independence of the judiciary. But the senior U.S. official urged the Albanian government to ensure a level playing field for all contenders through fair access to the state-controlled radio and television, and poll monitoring. He warned that if the elections were not free and fair, America's enthusiasm for assisting Albania would be dampened.[48]

Meanwhile, some visiting Western dignitaries made no effort to hide their fears that a Socialist victory would lead to chaos and political conflicts in Albania. During preelection visits to Tiranë, European conservatives such as Alois Mock of the European Democratic Union, Klaus Welle of the European Christian Democrats, and Pierre Lellouche, an adviser to the French President Jacques Chirac, expressed public support for the Democrats. Leni Fischer, the president of the Council of the European Parliament, praised the controversial law barring certain former Communists and Sigurimi collaborators from seeking public office. Michel Pericard, the parliamentary head of President Chirac's Rally for the Republic Party in the French senate, caused an uproar in opposition ranks when he took part in Democratic Party rallies.

The Socialist Party's strategy was to blame Berisha and the Democrats for current problems, depict the president as inclined toward authoritarianism, and accuse the government administration of being corrupt and incapable. The Socialists pointed out the chinks in the government's performance and the Democratic Party's program, particularly in unemployment, corruption, crime, housing, education, and health care. They focused their propaganda on charges that the ruling party had left the country without a constitution. Under the motto "Together with us, for a genuine democracy!" the Socialist Party pledged to secure a law-governed state and the independence of the judiciary. The Socialist platform advocated a greater role for the state in the economy, more subsidies, and a bigger budget for social security. The Socialist Party painted its economic program in generalities and vague platitudes to avoid offending non-Socialist voters, and made populist pledges of increased employment, education, and health care without saying how they would achieve them. While the Democrats emphasized issues clearly relevant to the lives of ordinary Albanians, the Socialists did not offer a coherent program and engaged in political pandering, speaking in sweeping terms of a total revolution. Socialist attempts to tell increasingly optimistic Albanians that the country was in the midst of a serious political, economic, and social crisis were not credible. In addition, the Socialists caused widespread fear by insisting that if they regained power they would repeal much of the legislation enacted during the Democratic Party's government and carry out widespread purges of the government bureaucracy.[49]

Having prepared for the next elections since their 1992 defeat, the Socialists acted as if their victory was a foregone conclusion. This complacency was influenced by the Socialists' gains in the July 1992 local elections and by the defeat of the 1994 constitutional referendum. The Socialists also expected to benefit from a number of other favorable conditions, including the party's institutional strength, a stable constituency, residual loyalties, and disunity in the anticommunist front. The Socialist Party made little effort to expand its support beyond its traditional constituency, such as by attempting to win the support of trade unions or even the many former Communist Party members who had been victims of the great purges in the 1970s and the 1980s. Moreover, the battle did not, as the Socialists had expected, focus exclusively on the hardships of reform and government political blunders, but also on the fear of the Communists' return to power. The campaign appeared to have added little to the Socialist Party's core constituency of retirees and down-and-out blue-collar workers.

Despite its attempts to redefine itself as a social democratic party and tone down its anti-Western rhetoric, the Socialist Party also encountered difficulty in convincing the outside world that it had become a bona fide reformist force and was not a proto-Communist party. A delegation led by Servet Pëllumbi and consisting of deputy chairman Ilir Meta, party spokesman Kastriot Islami, and member of parliament Anastas Angjeli paid a highly publicized visit to Washington for talks with U.S. officials, including Richard Schifter,[50] a top aide to President Clinton widely viewed as having close ties to the Greek American lobby and disliking Berisha. While U.S. contacts with the opposition were part of a policy of maintaining contact with a broad spectrum of Albanian society, the Socialists attempted to portray the visit as indicative of U.S. support for their party. Initially, they planted a story in *Koha Jonë* that they had been officially invited by the State Department, which prompted the U.S. side to issue a statement denying the report.[51] Indeed, the Socialists' attempts to counter U.S. support for the Democrats by expanding their own contacts with Washington were unsuccessful. U.S. and West European officials remained suspicious of the Socialists. While few feared that a Socialist victory would signal a return to Hoxha's dictatorship, they believed it probably would lead to a retreat from democratization and a slowdown of privatization.

On the eve of the elections, it was evident that the Socialists had failed to broaden their domestic and international appeal. All polls showed them trailing far behind the Democrats.

The Social Democratic Party and the Democratic Alliance had formed a left-center bloc, called the Center Pole. They agreed to divide the majority of the electoral districts between them and to run only one candidate in each district. In their programs, they called for consolidation of the rule of law, adoption of a new constitution, and establishment of a social market economy.[52] The left-center coalition ran a campaign that ranged from vacuous to incoherent, making Berisha the only issue. Center Pole leaders were widely regarded as colorless personalities with an uninspiring style. Lack of real political direction led to the Center Pole's self-absorption and to its never-ending rows about Berisha rather than about popular issues. Skendër Gjinushi, Paskal Milo, Neritan Ceka, Arben Imami, and Gramoz Pashko engaged in blistering attacks on the president and in constant arguments over who was the true heir to the December 1990 revolution. Pashko went so far as to declare that the May 26 elections were a vote on Berisha solely and not on Albanian political parties and their programs. In an interview, Pashko said, "26 May is the day to overthrow Berisha and his clan."[53] The excesses and utter self-aggrandizement of Pashko and other Center Pole leaders made them barely tolerable to many of their party supporters, let alone to the electorate at large. Even their closest associates acknowledged that their campaign rhetoric was too harsh, too angry, and lacking in vision.[54]

The Center Pole encountered insurmountable difficulties in expanding its support. This was largely a reflection of its cataclysmic campaign rhetoric, in which Center Pole leaders described Albania as gripped by decay and teetering on the brink of apocalypse. That view was lost on the majority of Albanians, who were enjoying the fruits of the social and economic changes since 1992.

Other players in the 1996 parliamentary elections were the right-wing Republican Party, National Front, Legality, and the ethnic Greek Party for the Protection of Human Rights. However, the much rumored coalition of right-wing forces failed to materialize. The Republican Party promised to impose law and order and to return property to its rightful owners. Its striking motto was "Our nation's future begins with our families." The Republican Party pledged to help former political prisoners.[55] The other parties had similar programs, which could be summarized under the broad themes of multiparty democracy and market economy. None had the political and financial resources to wage unified campaigns.

Role of the Media

The media played an important role in the campaign, but reporting was generally biased. Flexing the powerful muscles of incumbency, the Democrats strictly controlled state radio and television coverage, which echoed their campaign themes. Most of the coverage, including news, was slanted in favor of the ruling party. Moreover, during the campaign, the airwaves were saturated with anticommunist films and documentaries, including meetings of the APL Politburo. Nevertheless, political parties, particularly the Democratic and Socialist Parties, made innovative uses of television. For the first time in Albania's history, paid television commercials were used to reach voters.

The press in general displayed a tendency to focus on personalities rather than on issues, and failed to debate the differences responsibly. Berisha and his party were faced with increasingly hostile, negative coverage from the opposition and independent press. Most prominent newspapers campaigned openly against the Democrats. The so-called independent papers provided far from disinterested reportage and commentary. They promoted opposition candidates and policies, generally supporting the Socialists. *Koha Jonë,* the most widely read newspaper in the country, eagerly supported the Socialist Party and the Center Pole. Its election coverage consisted almost exclusively of anti-Democratic Party material. A controversial and aggressively partisan paper, *Koha Jonë* was harshly and persistently critical of the Democratic Party and feverishly anti-Berisha. It published inflammatory articles lampooning the president and his closest associates. *Koha Jonë*'s image was further sullied when its director Nikollë Lesi and editor in chief Aleksandër Frangaj announced their candidacies for the Social Democratic and Democratic Alliance Parties, respectively. Other so-called independent papers played a similar role. The progovernment *Albania*, on the other hand, openly promoted Democratic Party candidates.

The preelection period also saw the appearance of new papers, the most important of which was *Drejt*, published by writer Kiço Blushi, who had served on Ramiz Alia's presidential council in 1991. *Drejt* campaigned openly against the Democratic Party, publishing inflammatory, feverishly anti-Berisha articles by prominent left-leaning ideologues. It was widely believed that the paper, which ceased publication after the elections, was financed by the Socialist Party.

The Election Results

Altogether, 1,180 candidates representing 24 political parties took part in the election. In the first round, on 26 May 1996, the Democratic Party won 95 out of 115 direct seats; the Socialist Party, 5; and the Union for Human Rights Party, 2 seats.[56] In the second round, on 2 June, the Democratic Party won 6 seats; the Republican Party, 3; and the National Front, 1. On 16 June, balloting was repeated in seventeen electoral districts, in which the Central Electoral Commission said there were irregularities. The Democrats won in all seventeen districts. The second round and the partial rerun, however, were boycotted by the Socialists, the Democratic Alliance, and the Social Democratic Party. The Democratic Party received 55.53 percent of total votes cast in the first round, compared to 62 percent in the 1992 election. The Socialists finished with 20.37 percent, down from 25.7 percent in 1992. The Republican Party won 5.74 percent of the vote, enough to replace the Social Democratic Party as the country's third-largest political force. Two other parties passed the 4-percent threshold: the National Front (4.97 percent) and the Union for Human Rights Party (4.04 percent). The final tally showed that the Democratic Party had scored a bigger landslide victory than in the

TABLE 8.2 Albania's 1996 Parliamentary Elections

	Votes*	% of Votes	Seats	% of Seats
Democratic Party	914,218	55.50	122	87.00
Socialist Party	335,40	20.40	10	7.00
Republican Party	94,567	5.70	3	2.00
National Front	81,822	5.00	2	1.50
Union for Human Rights	66,529	4.00	3	2.00
Legaliteti	34,019	2.10	—	—
Social Democratic Union	32,430	2.00	—	—
Democratic Alliance	25,679	1.50	—	—
Social Democratic Party	25,019	1.50	—	—
Christian Democratic Party	21,068	1.30	—	—
Democratic Union Party	11,789	0.70	—	—
National Unity Party	3,939	0.20	—	—
Total	1,344,619	99.90	140	99.5
Voter turnout				89.00 percent

*First round of voting, 26 May 1996
Sources: Rilindja Demokratike, 22 June 1996, p. 2, and 3 July 1996, p. 2; and International Republican Institute, *IRI Observation Report on the Albanian Parliamentary Elections of May 26, 1996* (Washington, D.C., 1996), p. 32.

1992 elections, winning 122 seats, or 87 percent, of the total 140 seats in the new parliament. This gave it the two-thirds needed to make constitutional changes. The Socialist Party came in second, with 10 seats, down from 32 seats in 1992. The National Front and the Union for the Protection of Human Rights won 3 seats each, and the Republican Party, 2. The Social Democratic Party and the Democratic Alliance were soundly defeated, failing to make the 4 percent necessary to gain entry into the parliament. The Social Democratic Union, led by Teodor Laço, appeared to have benefitted little from the Democratic Party's heavy-handed efforts to boost it, winning only 2 percent of the general vote (Table 8.2).[57]

The Opposition Boycott

Only hours before the polls were scheduled to close on 26 May, the Socialist Party pulled out of the voting, claiming large-scale election irregularities. The Socialists declared that they would not accept the results or recognize the new parliament. The Social Democratic Party, the Democratic Alliance, and several other minor parties joined the Socialists. Although the Socialists' decision came as a surprise to most foreign observers, it was very likely premeditated. The decision was made by a small circle of Socialist leaders, including Servet Pëllumbi, Kastriot Islami, and Gramoz Ruçi, all of whom had been banned from running for public office under the lustration law. They evidently hoped that the Socialist withdrawal would lead to the cancellation of the elections, the annulment of the lustration law, and the holding of new elections.[58] Before election day, the Socialists had made repeated allegations that the Democratic Party would manipulate the results. Socialist warnings were designed to enlist outside support, especially since all polls showed the Democratic Party leading the Socialists by more than 20 percent. The Socialists withdrew from the balloting after 80 percent of the voters had already cast ballots, and after exit polls had suggested a victory for the Democratic Party.

An exit poll on election day, commissioned by the International Republican Institute predicted that the Democrats would win 56 percent of the vote, compared to 22 percent for the Socialists. IRI's exit poll predicted that the Democratic Alliance would win 5 percent; the Republican Party, 4 percent; the Social Democratic Party, 3 percent; and the Union for Human Rights Party 2 percent; and that the remainder would be split among a number of smaller parties. The survey found that support for the Democratic Party

> ... was spread relatively evenly throughout the country, as well as among various demographic groups. The PD was stronger in the north than in the south; stronger in cities than in villages; stronger among higher income and higher educated persons; stronger among younger people; and equally strong among men and women. However, even in their weakest regions and demographic sub-groups, the Democratic Party enjoyed a significant margin of support over the

Socialist Party, the strongest opposition party. Concerning the fairness of the campaign, the vast majority (70 percent) of the respondents found the campaign to have been conducted in a fair manner.

An overwhelming majority of 85 percent of voters said they believed that their country was going in the right direction, 67 percent said they were satisfied with the progress of economic reform, and 62 percent expressed approval of Berisha.[59]

Socialist representatives left their posts at electoral commissions at the same time throughout the country. Given Albania's poor infrastructure, it is only remotely possible that the Socialists could have spread the word within such a short period of time to all polling stations around the country. In addition, on election day itself, there were no major incidents or widespread irregularities that would have warranted such a decision. While logistical problems did hamper balloting in some places, the voting was largely peaceful, as Albanians generally avoided violence and calm prevailed around the country. By pulling out at the last minute and ordering their representatives in electoral commissions to leave before the vote count had commenced, the Socialist Party and its allies contributed to the subsequent irregularities in ballot counting. But despite the opposition's irresponsible action, the government could not absolve itself of the responsibility to ensure a normal process and prevent election irregularities.

Berisha responded by rejecting charges of vote fraud and accusing the Socialists of creating problems to mask their humiliating defeat. He also acknowledged the need for domestic reconciliation and urged the Albanians to heal the wounds of a bitter campaign. Rhetoric aside, there was an exultant mood among the Democrats and their supporters. Although he denounced the boycott, Berisha could not hide his joy that the Socialists had committed "political suicide."[60] Clearly, for the Democrats, the Socialist Party remained an unreformed party and a dangerous threat to the country's fledgling democracy. Its possible elimination from the political scene, especially if it came as a result of the Socialist leaders' own political blunder, was seen as a positive development that in the long run would contribute to the full consolidation of democracy in Albania.

Political Fallout

The elections were followed by a series of political missteps on the part of the government. On 28 May, opposition leaders, defying a police ban, attempted to stage a rally in the central city square in Tiranë. In clear view of dozens of international observers and foreign reporters, riot police broke up the crowd, beating demonstrators, including several opposition leaders, such as Pëllumbi, Gjinushi, Imami and Pashko.[61] The authorities argued that they had to take action to prevent a possible bloody confrontation between supporters of the Democratic Party and those of the opposition; but their argument was dismissed by most observers.

Undoubtedly, the opposition intended to provoke the authorities and to gain international publicity. Instead of exercising restraint given the charged political atmosphere, the government fell into the Socialists' trap. Predictably, the police handled the incident clumsily, and their use of unnecessary and excessive force against opposition leaders rightly caused an international outcry.

The incident also led to a hardening of the attitude of international observers, most of whom initially had not supported Socialist Party claims of systematic voter fraud and intimidation. OSCE's Office for Democratic Institutions and Human Rights (ODIHR) issued a critical report, saying that the administration of the election seriously departed from the electoral law and that "in many instances the implementation of the law failed to meet its own criteria." It added that decisions of the polling station commissions were not made by majority vote, but by the arbitrary decisions of the government-appointed commission chairman and secretary. The report accused the authorities of failing to ensure that political campaigning was conducted in a fair and free atmosphere. It said there were serious irregularities in the counting process and an unusually huge number of invalid ballots.[62] The delegation of the OSCE Parliamentary Assembly blamed both the government and the opposition for the irregularities. Yet it did not question the lawfulness of the newly elected parliament, recommending only that Albanian parties consider holding new elections "after a reasonable but limited period of time."[63] The U.S. National Democratic Institute for International Affairs said, "Widespread electoral irregularities, together with the violent reaction against protesters on 28 May, compromised the integrity of the election process."[64] Meanwhile the International Republican Institute said in a statement, "While not widespread, observed voting irregularities raise serious questions about the conduct and integrity of a number of Albania's 1996 parliamentary contests."[65] Conversely, some observer groups rejected claims of systematic voter fraud and intimidation. The British Helsinki Human Rights Group expressed the view that the elections were basically free and fair.[66] A member of the group, Jonathan Sunley, wrote that "compared with the elections ... in Armenia, Georgia, Belarus and Russia, all of which were issued a clean bill of health, the infringements and irregularities in Albania were minor."[67]

In the wake of the elections, the government came under increased international pressure, including pressure from the United States. On 1 June, the State Department issued a statement saying that Albania's parliamentary elections had been marred by numerous irregularities and represented "a significant step backward" from the 1992 elections. The State Department urged the government and all political parties "to seek assistance from the international community in investigating irregularities and identifying districts in which elections should be repeated." The statement urged Albanians to consider recommendations of observer delegations "to improve the electoral process to ensure that the irregularities which occurred in this election do not recur." The State Department also blamed the Albanian opposition, saying that its pullout from the election had made it "impossible to gauge the true dimension of problems subsequently observed during the vote count, and contributed to a lack of integrity in the counting process."[68]

While there was widespread agreement that the irregularities were insufficient to change the results and that there was no evidence of a centrally directed plan to rig the elections, Albanian leaders did not receive high marks for their handling of the postelection crisis and international reaction. Despite the harsh criticism, none of the observer groups disputed that the Democratic Party had won a clear majority or questioned the lawfulness of the new parliament; most accepted that the elections reflected the voters' wishes. Instead of engaging in damage control and working with friendly countries and international institutions, which were willing to assist the government in rectifying the irregularities observed on 26 May, Tiranë adopted an uncompromising position. It charged that some observers, particularly those with the OSCE, held a pronounced political bias in favor of the Socialist Party. Berisha complained that ODIHR's report had been biased. The Albanian president seemed particularly outraged by the fact that the monitoring group had not deemed it necessary to even mention the withdrawal of the opposition parties from balloting and the withdrawal of their representatives from electoral commissions before the vote count had even begun.[69]

Some observers maintained that there was some truth to the Albanian government's claims. Anthony Daniels, member of the British Helsinki Human Rights Group, argued that the OSCE had given its stamp of approval to elections in several former Communist countries that were characterized by more wide-spread irregularities than those that characterized Albania's balloting. Daniels also asserted that the OSCE "was determined from the very outset to condemn the government of Sali Berisha for election fraud." He alleged that many OSCE observers "were sympathizers with the former regime."[70] Nevertheless, the Albanian government's strategy of attacking the integrity of foreign observers backfired. More importantly, the government ignored requests by the United States, the European Union, and the OSCE to postpone the 16 June repeat of elections in 17 districts until an international mechanism had been set up to investigate irregularities and to make recommendations for corrective action. Berisha also declined to receive a high-level U.S. delegation, led by Undersecretary of State for Global Affairs Timothy Wirth and Rep. Eliot L. Engel, a strong supporter of Albanian issues in the U.S. Congress, for discussions on the disputed parliamentary vote.[71]

The political cost of Tiranë's defensive stand soon became evident. Although at first the United States had called on Albania merely to correct the irregularities of 26 May and to repeat elections in some districts, in July Washington called for new elections. In testimony before the House of Representatives Subcommittee on Human Rights and International Operations, Senior Deputy Assistant Secretary of State Rudolf V. Perina said the Albanian government had not taken adequate steps to redress shortcomings in the parliamentary election. The senior State

Department official urged the Albanian government to open a political dialogue with the opposition as a first step to holding free and fair local elections, adopting a new constitution, and holding new parliamentary elections at the earliest opportunity. Perina announced that the United States had initiated a thorough review of its relationship with Albania, including assistance programs.[72] Meanwhile, some members of Congress, led by Rep. Tom Lantos, urged the administration to suspend economic assistance to Albania until new elections were held.

During summer 1996, U.S.-Albanian relations experienced considerable strain. Once Berisha's strongest ally, Washington became his harshest critic. The United States was in the forefront of international efforts in urging Albania to address problems surrounding the parliamentary elections. However, the Europeans, particularly the Italians and the Greeks, took a milder line on Albania's disputed elections and were not willing to go as far as Washington in putting pressure on Tiranë. For Italy and Greece, the overriding objective remained Albania's stability and prosperity. The Italians, recalling the 1991 landing of thousands of Albanian "boat people" on their coast, were careful not to undermine Berisha's government. They feared that instability in Albania could trigger a new influx of refugees, requiring huge relief programs and threatening Italy's social stability. Although Italy also urged Albania to repeat the elections, Rome did not initiate a review of its assistance to Albania. Greece, on the other hand, maintained a conspicuous silence on postelection developments in Albania, continuing to expand ties in all fields. The European Union's concern about election irregularities was largely supplanted by worry about the stability of Albania itself.

The New Government

President Berisha attempted to assure the domestic and international public that Albania's democratization process was on track and that the ruling party would use the next four years to deepen institutional reforms and ensure the country's political stability. The Democrats moved swiftly, convening the new parliament on 2 July 1996.[73] Berisha unexpectedly asked Aleksandër Meksi to form the new government. The president seems to have made his decision for transparently political reasons. Before the elections it had been widely reported that Berisha would not reappoint Meksi for another term. The president had become impatient with Meksi's inefficiency. Moreover, the prime minister faced a barrage of charges of corruption and nepotism. Opposition newspapers were full of allegations that he had used his position to amass enormous wealth for himself, his family, and friends. Although Berisha, widely perceived even by his critics as incorruptible, may have preferred to see Meksi out of the political picture, the controversy surrounding the elections limited his options. He evidently feared that the failure to reappoint Meksi, who after all was credited for Albania's post-1992 economic achievements, would cause a rift within the Democratic Party, precisely at this critical time when he needed the party to stand firmly united behind him. If circumstances dictated that Meksi be reappointed, Berisha also seemed determined to curtail the prime minister's powers and influence. None of the ministers closely associated with Meksi were retained. Party Chairman and Berisha confidant Tritan Shehu was appointed deputy prime minister and minister of foreign affairs. In a highly unusual move, which indicated that the party chairman had been given wide powers and was likely to exercise real power over the cabinet, Shehu accompanied Meksi at meetings with other political parties regarding the formation of the new government. Coverage in the state controlled radio and television and in the progovernment newspapers left the distinct impression that the prime minister and his deputy were equal partners.

The new cabinet consisted of sixteen ministers and nine secretaries. Only five ministers retained their posts: Minister of Defense Safet Zhulali, Minister of Mining and Energy Abdyl Xhaja, Minister of Culture Teodor Laço, Minister of Health Maksim Cikuli, and Minister of Industry, Transportation, and Trade, Suzana Panariti. The unpopular Minister of Internal Affairs Agron Musaraj was dumped. So were Deputy Prime Minister Dashamir Shehi, who had harbored ambitions to replace Meksi and had been regarded as a front-runner for the position, and Minister of Foreign Affairs Alfred Serreqi. Dylber Vrioni was downgraded from the post of Deputy Prime Minister and Minister of Finance to Minister of Privatization. Halit Shamata, who had served as chairman of the Commission for Laws and Constitutional Issues from 1992 to 1996, became Minister of Internal Affairs. Kristofor Peçi, a former member of the Court of Cassation, became minister of justice. Party Secretary-General Besnik Gjongecaj was named minister of higher education and scientific research, a newly created post. In addition to Suzana Panariti, another woman gained a ministerial post: Arlinda Keci was named minister of labor and social issues.[74]

Contrary to expectations, the Democratic Party's election victory did not produce new policy breakthroughs. Despite Meksi's pledge to proceed with swift economic and political reforms,[75] the prime minister, from the very beginning of his second term, betrayed a lack of will to lead. With mostly a dormant domestic agenda and eclipsed by his deputy Tritan Shehu, Meksi never seemed able to seize the moment and summon the strength to deal with truly tough challenges, including the rapid expansion of get-rich-quick schemes.

The Opposition in Disarray

Postelection developments caused disarray in the leftist opposition parties. Socialist, Social Democratic, and Democratic Alliance leaders could not but face the fact that the elections basically reflected the popular will and that their defeat had more to do with their political incompetence than election irregularities. Socialist leaders appeared divided and confused about the strategy and tactics to be pursued in the new political environment. Party deputy chairmen Servet Pëllumbi, Luan Hajdaraga, and Namik Dokle and their supporters attempted to keep the pressure on the Democrats, emphasizing the importance of preserving party unity. Others, fearing that the parliamentary elections could mark the Socialists' last hurrah as a formidable political force, publicly attacked the leadership. There were increasing calls for the party to examine its responsibility for the defeat. An editorial in *Zëri i Popullit* acknowledged that the party had not succeeded in convincing the electorate to vote for it and that it had misread the November 1994 referendum defeat as indicating support for the Socialists.[76]

In the wake of Nano's imprisonment in 1993 the Socialists had cultivated a public image of a united leadership; but soon after the election defeat, a fierce power struggle broke out, inspired largely by the imprisoned party chairman. Having lost confidence in Pëllumbi and others who managed the party in his absence, Nano saw the election defeat as an opportune moment for sweeping leadership changes. Although Nano was careful to portray his efforts as aimed at purging the old guard and reforming the party's policies—demanding that all references to Marxism be deleted from the Socialist Party program and sacking his closest associate, the highly unpopular former Minister of Internal Affairs Gramoz Ruçi[77]—the struggle had more to do with clashes over power and personalities than over ideology. The officials that Nano recommended for top posts, such as Rexhep Meidani and Kastriot Islami, could not be identified as reformers. In 1991, Meidani had served on Alia's presidential council and was chairman of the Central Electoral Commission. Islami, described by his close associates as cunning and ruthless, was unpopular within and outside the party. A former minister and a renowned conservative, Islami had played a destructive role as speaker of Albania's first multiparty parliament in 1991-1992. The pro-Nano group also coopted Pandeli Majko, the former chairman of the Eurosocialist Youth Forum, who had been replaced in that post in October 1995.

After weeks of vicious, public, personal attacks between Nano supporters and opponents, the Socialist Party held a tumultuous congress in late August 1996. In a move that undermined his efforts to portray the struggle with his opponents as a clash between reformers and conservatives, Nano chose Sabit Brokaj, a member of the old guard, to read his report to the congress. The imprisoned leader lashed out at his deputies, Pëllumbi, Dokle, Hajdaraga, and Ilir Meta, and called for their resignation. He attacked the party leadership for lack of political initiative and poor leadership.[78] Pëllumbi resigned, arguing that his views differed profoundly from those of Nano. After heated debates, Nano was reelected as chairman. With Nano's recommendation, Rexhep Meidani was elected secretary-general, and would serve as acting leader while the party chairman remained in prison. He won by only three votes over his main rival, youth organization leader Ilir Meta. Namik Dokle, the only one of the four former party deputy chairmen to be elected to a senior post, became party organizational secretary. Pandeli Majko was elected secretary for public relations, and Maqo Lakrori, a former minister of education, secretary for foreign relations.[79] The congress also dropped all references to Marx from its program and officially condemned Hoxha's dictatorship.[80] But these changes were too little, too late. The congress was seen as a victory for the conservative wing of the party. Indeed, five years after the party had changed its name, key members of the new leadership still were closely identified with Alia, the country's last Communist president.

In an interview following the congress, Servet Pëllumbi accused Nano of displaying authoritarian tendencies and said the Socialist Party was in danger.[81] Meanwhile, Ilir Meta argued that the party had failed to renovate itself, focusing only on achieving symbolic distance from Enver Hoxha. Meta said Nano had transformed the party into an authoritarian organization. He added that without internal democracy, the Socialist Party would have a difficult time convincing the electorate that it was interested in building a democratic society.[82]

In retrospect, the Socialists made a serious political blunder in engaging in a public power struggle and holding their congress before the October 1996 local elections. Party infighting overshadowed changes in the party's program and deflected attention away from the Democrats and the problems connected with the parliamentary elections. Moreover, the power struggle further demoralized the Socialist Party's rank and file. The election of people from the old regime to positions of leadership damaged the party's image domestically and internationally. In short, the Socialist Party emerged from the congress in a considerably weaker position.

In the case of the other two main leftist opposition forces, the Social Democratic and Democratic Alliance parties, comprising the Center Pole, the general elections confirmed that they lacked an electoral base. Although claiming to occupy a position in the political center, the two parties had shifted too far to the left, holding positions essentially identical with those of the Socialists on political and economic issues. This, plus their lack of charismatic leaders, adversely affected their electoral fortunes. Faced with the threat of being swept off Albania's political map, the Social Democratic and Democratic Alliance parties could not develop a coherent strategy. The Center Pole's position was further undermined after the elections, when the Socialists ignored them and unilaterally decided to enter into direct talks with the Democrats. Disagreements between the Socialists and the Center Pole became increasingly evident.

While Skendër Gjinushi continued to hold a tight grip over his Social Democratic Party, Neritan Ceka and his deputy Arben Imami came under increased attack from the party rank and file. Disagreements with the leadership intensified in September 1996, when the Democratic Alliance became the only party to boycott roundtable discussions with Berisha. Ignored by the Democrats from its very inception, the Democratic Alliance, together with thirteen other parties, was invited to send a representative to discussions with the president aimed at reaching consensus on the local elections. Instead of taking advantage of the meeting to put forth its own views on the important issues under discussion, the Democratic Alliance's representative Gjergj Zefi left the meeting before the talks began. This stand was more a reaction to the Democratic Alliance leaders' enmity toward Berisha and their expulsion four years earlier from the Democratic Party rather than the result of any clear policy objective. Even some party officials, such as Blendi Fevziu and Preç Zogaj, also strong critics of Berisha, denounced the walkout as a politically immature action. Fevziu warned that the Democratic Alliance risked marginalizing itself.[83] Criticizing the leadership's unbridled anti-Berisha rhetoric, Zogaj insisted that the Democratic Alliance's obsession with its personal struggle against the president had prevented it from developing an electorate. He said that the Democratic Alliance had to move beyond the point of harsh rhetorical criticism and establish its base of support.[84]

Albania's third multiparty elections were viewed as a litmus test of its commitment to democratic governance and speedy reform and as an indication of whether the Albanians had appropriated the values of pluralistic democracy. The beneficiary of substantial U.S. and West European political, economic, and military assistance between 1992 and 1996, Albania had been considered a star performer among the postcommunist states. Although Western observers, even before the elections, had expressed concern regarding erosion of democratic freedoms, executive influence over the judiciary, the ruling party's increased intolerance of dissent, and state control of radio and television, Albania was widely praised for the great strides it had made in just four years. But the 1996 developments suggested that the ruling Democratic Party had failed to sustain the democratic momentum of recent years by incorporating and refining democratic procedures, ensuring an environment that would facilitate free and fair competition for political power and encourage inclusive participation in the political process. Its domestic and international credibility was badly tarnished as anxiety increased about the movement toward a de facto one-party system. The controversial elections delegitimized the electoral process and obscured the otherwise remarkable success that Albania had achieved since 1992. The Democratic Party, a genuinely popular party enjoying strong international support, had missed the opportunity to move the country decisively toward democracy.

Notes

1. See Louis Zanga, "Albania: Corruption Takes Its Toll on the Berisha Government," *Transition* 1, no. 7 (12 May 1995), pp. 12-14.

2. *Rilindja Demokratike,* 16 November 1996, p. 1.

3. Ibid., 5 April 1996, p. 1.

4. Ibid., 7 April 1996, p. 1.

5. Ibid., 6 April 1996, p. 1.

6. Ibid., 23 April 1996, p. 1.

7. In an unusual move, on the eve of the elections, Zef Brozi published a long article urging Albanians to vote against the Democratic Party. Zef Brozi, "Vote Against the DP [Democratic Party]," *Koha Jonë,* 21 May 1996, p. 9.

8. The European Commission, *Central and Eastern Eurobarometer* (Brussels) no. 6, (March 1996), p. 24.

9. Ibid., pp. 27-36.

10. International Republican Institute, *Albania, December 1995: National Survey* (Washington, D.C.), January 1996.

11. U.S. Information Agency, Office of Research and Media Reaction, *Albanian Public Broadly Positive on Economy* (Washington, D.C.), M-74-96, 2 April 1996.

12. U.S. Information Agency, Office of Research and Media Reaction, *Democratic Party Heavily Favored in Albania* (Washington, D.C.), M-68-96, 29 March 1996.

13. The Socialist Party was also believed to have stashed funds abroad. Exiled writer Ismail Kadare claimed that the APL Politburo had made a decision in the mid-1960s to deposit huge amounts of money abroad, to finance the Communist Party in the event it was overthrown. Kadare had close relations with Hoxha's regime and was in a position to possess such knowledge. *Gazeta Shqiptare,* 22 June 1993, p. 1; and *Dita Informacion,* 2 May 1993, p. 5.

14. Fatos Nano, "Democratic Processes Increase the Role of the Intelligentsia," *Drita,* 7 October 1990, pp. 2-3, and 16.

15. Servet Pëllumbi, "'Political Pluralism in Theory and Practice," *Rruga e Partisë* 37, no. 5 (May 1990), pp. 87-96.

16. See *Dita Informacion,* 23 March 1995, pp. 4-5.

17. *Gazeta Shqiptare,* 9 July 1995, p. 5.

18. Ibid.

19. Other members of leadership who were dismissed were Maqo Lakrori, Fatmir Kumbaro, Xhevat Lloshi, and Luan Shahollari. See *Zëri i Popullit,* 18 October 1995, p. 3, and *Gazeta Shqiptare,* 20 October 1995, p. 3.

20. Lisen Bashkurti became secretary-general of the party. In summer 1992, he was appointed ambassador to Hungary. Later, he broke with Gjinushi and continued to hold senior posts in the foreign ministry.

21. See Laço's interview in *Rilindja Demokratike,* 7 January 1995, pp. 1-2.

22. *Lajmi i Ditës,* 22 December 1994, p. 1.

23. See interview with Arben Imami in *Koha Jonë,* 5 January 1994, p. 5.

24. *Rilindja,* 23 October 1993, pp. 1, 3.

25. *Gazeta Shqiptare,* 15 August 1995, p. 3.

26. *Aleanca,* 12 March 1993, p. 2.

27. Ibid., 6 July 1993, p. 1.

28. Afrim Krasniqi, "Greek Anti-Albanianism and Tiranë's Reaction," *Rilindja Demokratike,* 1 July 1993, p. 4.

29. Hysamedin Feraj, "People Defy Politics," *Republika,* 26 February 1995, p. 3.

30. Dritan Sukthi, "The Democratic Alliance's Anti-Islamism Is Anti-Albanianism," *Balli i Kombit,* 22 January 1994, p. 2.

31. *Aleanca,* 28 November 1993, pp. 4-5.

32. *Dita Informacion,* 7 August 1994, p. 5.

33. *Aleanca,* 27 September 1994, p. 2.

34. See resolution of the Republican Party's second congress in *Republika*, 23 October 1994, pp. 1-2.

35. Ibid., 8 December 1994, p. 1.

36. For the program of the Democratic Party of the Right, see *E Djathta*, 10 and 17 June 1994.

37. Ibid., 24 May 1995, p. 2.

38. "Resolution of the National Council of the Albanian Republican Party," *Republika*, 14 April 1994, p. 1.

39. Ibid., 9 February 1995, p. 1.

40. For an English translation of the 1996 election law, see International Republican Institute, *IRI Observation Report on the Albanian Parliamentary Elections of May 26, 1996* (Washington, D.C., 1996), Appendix V.

41. *Gazeta Shqiptare*, 21 September 1995, p. 1; *New York Times*, 24 September 1995, p. 3; and Kevin Done, "Albania Plans Law to Purge Ex-Communists," *Financial Times*, 25 October 1995, p. 4.

42. *Fletorja Zyrtare*, no. 26, December 1995, pp. 1139-1143. According to the law, files for all other citizens will remain closed for 30 years.

43. National Democratic Institute for International Affairs, *Report on the Pre-Election Environment in Albania* (Washington, D.C.), 9 April 1996, p. 4.

44. *Rilindja Demokratike*, 25 April 1996, p. 1.

45. See the Democratic Party's platform in ibid., 14 May 1996, pp. 2-7.

46. Ibid., 10 May 1996, p. 1.

47. U.S. State Department, "Secretary's Meeting with Albanian FM Serreqi," Press Guidance, 9 May 1996.

48. Wirth's interview was republished in *Rilindja Demokratike*, 21 May 1996, p. 3.

49. *Zëri i Popullit*, 2 May 1996, pp. 2-10.

50. Kastriot Islami, "Successful Visit of the SP to the USA," *Zëri i Popullit*, 1 May 1996, pp. 6, 13.

51. U.S. Department of State, "Visit of Albanian Socialist Party Leaders," Press Guidance, 22 April 1996.

52. The electoral platforms of the Social Democratic and Democratic Alliance Parties were published in the supplement to *Poli i Qendrës*, 7 May 1996.

53. See Gramoz Pashko's interview in *Koha Jonë*, 12 May 1996, p. 9.

54. Blendi Fevziu, "Democratic Alliance: The Big Loser," *Koha Jonë*, 26 October 1996, p. 5.

55. *Republika*, 9 May 1996, p. 2.

56. *Rilindja Demokratike*, 30 May 1996, p. 1.

57. Ibid., 22 June 1996, p. 2, and 3 July 1996, p. 2.

58. See Hamdi Jupe, "For a New Unity in the Socialist Party," *Zëri i Popullit*, 21 November 1996, p. 4.

59. See International Republican Institute, *IRI Observation Report on the Albanian Parliamentary Elections of May 26, 1996* (Washington, D.C., 1996), p. 30.

60. ATA in English, 2139 GMT, 27 May 1996 in FBIS-EEU 96-104, 29 May 1996, p. 2; and *Washington Times*, 27 May 1996, p. A1.

61. Jane Perlez, "Riot Police Beat and Arrest Albania Election Protesters," *New York Times*, 29 May 1996, p. A6; and Steve Pagani, "Police Beat Politicians, Block Protest In Albania," *Washington Times*, 29 May 1996, p. A11.

62. Organization for Security and Cooperation in Europe, Office for Democratic Institutions and Human Rights, *Observation of the Parliamentary Elections Held in the Republic of Albania May 26 and June 2, 1996* (Warsaw), 12 June 1996.

63. Organization for Security and Cooperation in Europe, Parliamentary Assembly, *Report on the Parliamentary Elections in Albania, 26 May 1996* (Vienna), June 1996, p. 8.

64. National Democratic Institute for International Affairs, "Comment on the May 26, 1996, Albanian Elections," 31 May 1996.

65. International Republican Institute, "Albania Parliamentary Election Observation, Mission Preliminary Statement," 28 May 1996.

66. The British Helsinki Human Rights Group, *Albania 1996: Democracy or Dictatorship?* (Oxford, 1996).

67. Jonathan Sunley, "Albanian Election Wasn't Stolen," *Wall Street Journal Europe*, 7 June 1996.

68. U.S. Department of State, Office of the Spokesman, *Albanian Parliamentary Elections*, 1 June 1996.

69. *Rilindja Demokratike*, 6 September 1996, p. 1.

70. Anthony Daniels, "Eye of the Beholder," *National Review*, 1 July 1996, p. 43. Daniels reveals that one observer had been an active member of the Danish-Albanian Friendship Society in the 1970s and had run tours to Albania for sympathizers of Hoxha's regime, and that the Socialist Party had been asked to arrange cars and interpreters for the Norwegian delegation, which contained the largest number of observers and was coordinated by the OSCE. See also James Phillips, "Setting the Record Straight on the Albanian Elections," *Executive Memorandum* (Heritage Foundation, Washington, D.C.), No. 453, 14 June 1996; and Bob Hand, *The Albanian Parliamentary Elections of 1996* (Commission on Security and Cooperation in Europe, June 1996), p. 5.

71. In a news conference, President Berisha denied that he had refused to meet with Wirth. He said he had merely requested a different date for the meeting. See *Rilindja Demokratike*, 22 August 1996, p. 3.

72. Testimony of Rudolf V. Perina, Senior Deputy Assistant Secretary of State, before the House International Relations Committee, Human Rights and International Operations Subcommittee, 25 July 1996.

73. The composition of the new parliament was remarkable for the absence of lawyers: There were 41 teachers, 24 engineers, 19 economists, 16 doctors, 12 agricultural workers, 3 journalists, 2 artists, and 7 representing other professions. *Gazeta Shqiptare*, 13 July 1996, p. 3.

74. *Rilindja Demokratike*, 12 July 1996, p. 1

75. See Meksi's program, submitted to parliament, in ibid., 23 July 1996, pp. 3, 5-7.

76. Editorial "Reforming the Socialist Party for the Sake of Political Success," *Zëri i Popullit*, 6 July 1996, p. 1.

77. Ruçi resigned from all party posts. Ibid., 9 July 1996, p. 3.

78. Ibid., 25 August 1996, pp. 9-17.

79. Ibid., 31 August 1996, p. 1.

80. Ibid., 10 November 1996, pp. 7-10.

81. Ibid., 27 August 1996, p. 2; and *Gazeta Shqiptare*, 7 September 1996, p. 3.

82. *Albania*, 31 August 1996, p. 3.

83. Blendi Fevziu, "The Democratic Alliance Party Between Emotions and Politics," *Koha Jonë*, 6 September 1996, pp. 3, 24.

84. Preç Zogaj, "What Future for the Democratic Alliance?" *Poli i Qendrës*, 18 September 1996, p. 4. A representative of the party's moderate faction, Zogaj was attacked as being in cohorts with Berisha. *Koha Jonë* published a photograph of Zogaj and Berisha, taken at a cocktail party. In an editorial, the paper accused Zogaj of plotting with the president against his party's leadership ("The Democratic Alliance Party Secretly Cooperates With Berisha?" *Koha Jonë*, 13 September 1996, p. 1). Zogaj responded angrily to the picture and editorial, accusing *Koha Jonë* of having erased from the picture Aleksandër Frangaj, co-owner of the paper. See Preç Zogaj, "Here Is 'the Secret Agreement,'" *Poli i Qendrës*, 14 September 1996, pp. 1, 2.

9

Albania in Turmoil

The flawed May 1996 parliamentary elections greatly damaged Albania's democratic image and obstructed the process of political consolidation under Berisha's leadership. The contentious balloting suggested that Albania's post-communist political elites had not crafted mutually acceptable rules concerning elections and procedural democracy in general. Both the ruling Democratic Party and the opposition, particularly the Socialist Party, bore responsibility for election irregularities. Their leaders demonstrated a lack of will to move beyond narrow, partisan interests, by ignoring democratic norms and procedures, and thereby delegitimizing the country's rudimentary democratic institutions. Living up to their reputation as a disloyal opposition, the Socialists boycotted the electoral system, refusing to pursue their complaints through established legal channels and doing everything within their power to undermine the government. The Democrats, on the other hand, steadfastly denied charges of having manipulated the elections and refused to correct visible election irregularities. Steeped in the old, Communist political culture, government and opposition leaders alike displayed a poor understanding of the rules of representative democracy, still viewing politics as a zero-sum game, in which the winner takes all and the loser loses entirely.

This political stalemate and the drift away from democratic processes significantly increased the political, economic, and social strains on Albania's fragile democracy. The election controversy wasted the Democrats' domestic and international legitimacy, distracted the government from taking significant policy initiatives or tackling pressing economic and social issues, and eroded the efficacy and effectiveness of the state. These factors, in turn, alienated the public from still shaky democratic institutions and combined disastrously with failed pyramid schemes to set in motion a political avalanche of demands that by March 1997 would lead to the breakdown of the Democratic government along with almost complete disintegration of Albania's political and social fabric.

Post-1996 Election Developments

In the wake of the May 1996 elections, the Democratic Party found itself maneuvering through a new political landscape. The Socialist Party refused to accept its ten seats in the new parliament, although one Socialist deputy, Sali Rexhepi, broke ranks with his party and took his seat. Together with the Social Democratic and Democratic Alliance Parties, the Socialists embarked on a campaign of vilification and delegitimization of the government at the same time as Albania's performance on democracy and human rights came under close international scrutiny.[1]

Consequently, the Democrats faced significant international pressure to reach out to the now marginalized opposition and ensure their participation in the October 1996 local elections. In order to bring about some degree of reconciliation within the Albanian body politic, they opened a dialogue with the Socialists. Then, after complaints from other political parties that they had been excluded, the Democratic Party broadened the political dialogue. The U.S. International Republican Institute played a major role in breaking the post-26 May deadlock by mediating discussions between Albanian political parties. Peter Dickinson, the IRI's resident representative in Tiranë, brought together the representatives of all the major parties for a series of discussions on improving campaign practices and election laws. After some initial hesitation, the authorities moved to implement most of the IRI's and other foreign observers' recommendations for legal and procedural changes in the electoral law. First, Berisha issued a decree establishing a permanent Central Electoral Commission in August 1996. Then, in a major breakthrough, on 4 September, the president held roundtable discussions with representatives of thirteen political parties, and in a surprise move, accepted most of the opposition's demands regarding the procedures for the local elections. The agreement improved the balance of party representation on electoral commissions, with the post of vice chairman going to the Socialist Party; provided that the lustration law be applied only in mayoral cases; increased time on radio and television for opposition parties; and changed the law on public meetings so that political parties were no longer required to obtain permission for indoor meetings, as well as to clarify and to simplify the procedures for obtaining permission for outdoor meetings. The new measures also approved sanctions against election officials who abrogated their official election-related responsibilities.[2]

Local Elections

Albania's local elections, held on 20 October 1996, were seen as a major test for the Democratic Party and the opposition, especially the Socialist Party.[3] Both hoped to use the results to reinforce their political position: the Democrats, to reconfirm their 26 May victory; the Socialists, to prove that the government had "stolen" the parliamentary election. Leaving nothing to chance, the Democrats mobilized all their resources in an aggressive campaign. The Socialists, handicapped by internal feuding and lacking an alternative program, waged a miserable and inept campaign.

The Democratic Party won a landslide victory, sweeping 58 of 64 city halls, or 90 percent. The Socialist Party won only 4, or 6.25 percent. The remaining 2 mayoralties went to an independent candidate, and in Shkodër, to a candidate representing a coalition between local branches of the National Front and Legality. The Democrats also swept 86 percent of the communes, winning in 267 of 310. The Socialists won in 15 communes, or 4.5 percent, down from 59.8 percent in 1992. The Human Rights party won in 9 communes, the Republican Party in 6, the National Front in 4, the Social Democratic Union in 4, the Christian Democratic Party in 1, and independent candidates in 5 communes. Overall, the Democrats gained 52.5 percent of the party vote against the Socialists' 31.3 percent. The Republican Party followed with 3.5 percent, the Center Pole with 3.1 percent, the National Front with 2.4 percent, and the Human Rights Party with 2.3 percent.[4] In a surprise development, the Democratic Party lost the race for mayor in Shkodër, which had been its most important stronghold. The Democratic Party's Artur Luka was a relatively weak candidate, with a questionable past. From 1988 to 1991, Luka had been employed as an accountant in the Ministry of Internal Affairs. The National Front and Legality, which fielded a joint candidate, were able to exploit Luka's past association with the Ministry of Internal Affairs and the government's "neglect" of Shkodër.

The results of the local elections, which more or less confirmed the overall voting in the parliamentary balloting, were a serious blow to the opposition, particularly the Socialist Party and the Center Pole. Foreign observers confirmed that despite some administrative and logistical problems, the local elections were generally free and fair and reflected a true majority view.[5] The Council of Europe expressed satisfaction with the conduct of the election, although it added that there were some instances of irregularities that it hoped would be investigated by the Central Electoral Commission. The United States, too, expressed satisfaction. With the international monitors certifying that the elections were free and fair, the opposition parties could not blame Berisha for their defeat.[6]

In the wake of local elections, the Socialist Party faced perhaps its gravest crisis. Although the former Communists still retained significant support, they were fragmented and dispirited, and seemed to have exhausted their electoral base. Indeed, the Socialist Party had become largely a party of older people, those on fixed income, and those who had been unable or unwilling to participate in the new, more competitive market society where they were not guaranteed either salaries or jobs—in other words, those who had suffered from the collapse of Communism. Their defeat fueled the simmering debate within the party over its leadership's policies. One analyst described Socialist leaders as "shocked, paralyzed, and speechless."[7] The faction that had lost out in the struggle for power at the August 1996 congress called for the resignation of Rexhep Meidani, Kastriot Islami, Pandeli Majko, and other party leaders. There were even some calls for Nano's replacement. Ilir Meta, leader of the Eurosocialist Youth Forum, said that Nano and members of the party presidency were responsible for the humiliating defeat. The youth leader warned that unless there were radical changes in its leadership, the Socialist Party was in danger of being replaced by right-wing forces as the country's second-largest political force.[8] Secretary-general of the Eurosocialist Youth Forum, Monika Kryemadhi, perhaps best expressed the sentiment of the reformers: "We young people do not wish to compromise and link our name to this class of overthrown politicians who were in power in 1990 and who closed the universities and opposed the establishment of political pluralism."[9]

For the Democratic Alliance and Social Democratic Parties, 1996 turned out to be a politically disastrous year. They were unable to organize sufficiently to sustain an effective nationwide campaign. The results of the local elections were particularly humiliating for the Democratic Alliance, confirming that the party remained essentially a narrow group of notables and their intellectual followers centered in Tiranë. Party President Neritan Ceka failed to garner even five percent of the vote in his race to become mayor of Tiranë. By the end of the year, the Democratic Alliance appeared to be disintegrating, while the Social Democratic Party was drifting toward political irrelevance. Having long deluded their supporters by overestimating their electoral chances, leaders of these two parties blamed the Socialists for having agreed to participate in the elections.

The Union for Human Rights, the geographically concentrated ethnic Greek minority party, suffered a major erosion among its supporters. There were also signs of heightened tensions within the Republican Party. While Republican leader Sabri Godo expressed satisfaction with the results, other members of the leadership were critical and suggested that Godo was personally responsible for the fact that their party failed to win a single city hall. Meanwhile, the right, savoring the victory of the National Front and Legality candidate for mayor in the largest northern city of Shkodër, claimed it had become a force in Albanian politics. However, in reality, the right-wing forces remained too badly split to be able to repeat their Shkodër victory in other parts of the country.

The Politics of Democratic Breakdown

With the successful conduct of local elections, Albania passed an important test. But this was not sufficient to restore full confidence in Albania's fragile democracy. Rather, the political process remained stalemated while Albania's polarized and fragmented political elites engaged in endless squabbling. The Democratic Party interpreted the results of the local elections as confirmation that the 26 May elections were free and fair.[10] Commanding the absolute majority of positions in parliament and having scored a stunning victory in the local elections, the Democrats now controlled all levers of power. Albania had become de facto a single-party state. Instead of taking advantage of its new victory to engage the opposition, the Democrats refused to initiate serious negotiations in order to narrow the huge chasm of mistrust between them and their opponents. Perhaps the biggest mistake of the ruling party was its hesitation to begin drafting a new constitution. In a shift from its previous stand, the Democratic Party insisted that only parliament or a commission appointed by the legislature could draft the constitution, while the opposition called for the establishment of an all-party commission outside parliament. The Democrats hoped to use the issue of the constitution to force the Socialists to take their seats in parliament. Predictably, the Socialists refused, arguing that their participation would legitimize the May 1996 election results. Even if the Socialists had agreed to return to parliament and accept the Democrats' suggestion, other opposition parties still would have been excluded from the actual drafting process.

This transparent lack of willingness to engage in an inclusive process of drafting the constitution did little to improve the government's image or arrest the deterioration in Albanian relations with the United States. In a statement issued on 31 October, the State Department had said that the local elections "were sufficiently democratic to be accepted as an expression of the people's will." The statement went on to urge Albania to build on these elections by establishing an open and inclusive process for developing a constitution and then holding new parliamentary elections.[11]

Throughout the second half of 1996, the United States attempted to fine tune a government that prior to the parliamentary elections appeared to have made considerable progress down the road toward democracy. Washington put pressure on Berisha in the form of a thorough review of its cooperation with Tiranë that tied U.S. assistance programs to specific actions by the Albanian government. Senior U.S. officials issued repeated public condemnations of Berisha's government. But instead of facilitating domestic political compromise, the U.S. criticism and conditionality largely made Berisha and the Democrats vulnerable to a backlash from the former Communists and other forces whose democratic credentials were even more questionable. The predictable, though unintended consequence of U.S. pressure was to undermine the authority and credibility of the Democratic government. Although Berisha was substantially responsible for Albania's drift away from the United States, Washington's persistent criticism in effect allied the Clinton administration with the Socialists at a time when the United States had no vested interest in improving the political fortunes of the repackaged APL Socialist Party.

The State Department's blunt approach backed the Albanian president, once one of the closest American allies in the post-Cold War Balkans, into a corner. Gradually, Berisha began to place greater emphasis on his country's relations with West European countries, which after the October 1996 local elections, had muted their criticism of Albania's democratic backsliding.

The loss of international legitimacy along with the growing marginalization of the opposition seriously undermined the Albanian government's stability. By November 1996, the government had lost its political initiative and its base of support had narrowed considerably. The Democratic Party's legitimacy now rested largely on the government's economic performance. However, in a climate in which the controversy surrounding parliamentary elections had sapped the government's moral authority and political clout, the reform program dangled in a state of suspended animation. Major economic problems were put on the back burner, while tax revenues plummeted, the budget deficit and inflation grew, and foreign investors stayed away. After several years of low inflation, the rate of inflation jumped to close to 20 percent in 1996, compared to about 6 percent in 1995. The budget deficit in 1996 was around $260 million—some 11 percent of gross domestic product—while the central bank had foreign exchange reserves of just $270 million.

These economic problems were further compounded by the rapid expansion of get-rich-quick investment schemes. Led by insecure officials who sought easy compromises, the government avoided hard choices and abandoned efforts at economic reform. This inadequate response was a direct result of the weakness of the political foundation on which the government stood.

Although there were palpable signs of mounting popular discontent with government corruption, mismanagement of the economy, and the Democrats' monopolization of political power, Albania did not seem to be in a revolutionary situation. The European Commission's annual survey of public opinion in Central and East European countries, showed that in November 1996 Albanians remained very satisfied with the development of democracy and human rights in their country and strongly supported the development of a market economy. A great majority of Albanians (75 percent) believed the country was moving in the right direction, and only 13 percent said the country was moving in the wrong direction. Some 75 percent of Albanians questioned said they were satisfied with the way democracy was developing in their country; only 24 percent expressed dissatis-faction. Albanians also expressed high optimism about economic development and their household finances. Some 75 percent of those interviewed said their financial situation was better than a year earlier, and only 6 percent held the opposite view.[12] But within weeks of the poll, the collapse of multiple pyramid schemes would cause a radical change in public attitudes toward the government.

The Pyramid Schemes Crisis

While pyramid companies had been active since the early 1990s, their operations expanded dramatically in summer and fall 1996.[13] Thousands of unwary investors put their savings in get-rich-quick schemes, which promised impossibly high returns, some of them offering interest rates of up to 50 percent a month. Earlier depositors made huge profits from the deposits of those who followed them. This encouraged some to sell all their property and belongings in order to reinvest in the pyramids that promised three-digit annual returns. Many impoverished Albanians sold everything they had, including homes, farms, livestock, and belongings, in the expectation of doubling their cash in a matter of weeks. By fall 1996, several hundred thousand Albanians had become dependent on interest from their deposits in pyramid schemes for their livelihood or to supplement their meager wages. According to conservative estimates, Albanians invested close to half a billion dollars in the funds.[14]

It may well be that many Albanians, poorly educated and with little experience of the free market, were simply taken in by the claims of investment opportunity. The suspicious investment companies launched a well coordinated publicity campaign to convince Albanians that they were not pyramid schemes. In an article in November 1996, a spokesman for Vefa Holdings, reputedly the largest pyramid scheme, claimed the company had invested "several hundred million dollars" in various projects, including "mines, supermarkets, tourism, processing industries, production lines in light industry and the food industry, stock raising complexes, catering, sea and land transportation, and other cultural and sports activities." The spokesman strongly denied that Vefa was a pyramid business.[15] Many Albanian investors explained the high returns with reference to the possibility of money laundering, as the Italian mafia and other international crime groups were suspected of having used these investment companies to launder their profits from drug and arms trafficking and refugee smuggling. There were also allegations, fiercely denied by the ruling Democratic Party, that senior government officials, including former Minister of Internal Affairs Agron Musaraj and Minister of Defense Safet Zhulali, were involved with trafficking in drugs and illegal arms, and with selling oil to Serbia in violation of U.N. sanctions.[16]

Given that several major schemes operated in Albania, one might have anticipated great heterogeneity in people's attitudes toward them. In fact, the pyramid schemes fiasco reflected an incredible failure of leadership on all sides, although the authorities were most responsible. Government and opposition leaders, the press, and popular opinion were all, without serious exception, supportive of the schemes. No meaningful warnings were issued by the government, opposition, media, or international financial institutions until it was too late. The Democrats, preoccupied with the political fallout of the May elections and preparing for local elections, had not been willing to take the political risk of shutting down the schemes. Moreover, there were reports that some of the companies had contributed to the election campaign of the ruling party as well as to that of the opposition.

Indeed, some officials defended these companies as something normal for a developing capitalist economy, adding that they were operating within the law. Senior officials continued to give tacit endorsement to the investment funds. In an interview in November 1996 with the progovernment paper *Albania*, Blerim Çela, chairman of the State Control Commission, said he did not believe that these firms faced bankruptcy. He said there was nothing illegal about them, adding "I think that these firms are involved in a good business, because they help people."[17] Arben Kallamata, a foreign ministry official and a former Nieman scholar, denounced the correspondent of an Albanian American newspaper who had written about the looming crisis, as "a hack journalist from the Bronx." He also dismissed the media's coverage of pyramid schemes as mere propaganda.[18] As late as November 1996, Prime Minister Meksi attended an anniversary celebration for Vefa Holding, the biggest investment company. Meanwhile, opposition parties did not publicly condemn the existence of the pyramid schemes, nor did they call for government intervention. Indeed, during the election campaign, the Socialists, who had close ties with at least two pyramid schemes, Xhaferri and Populli, pledged not to take action against the pyramid schemes, if they came to power. There were also press reports that leading opposition politicians as well as senior government officials had invested in the get-rich-quick schemes.

Despite subsequent claims, before September 1996, the International Monetary Fund and the World Bank also failed to publicly alert Albanians to the looming crisis. The international financial institutions continued to praise Albania's economic progress, and none of their publications mentioned the pyramid schemes.[19]

The Albanian state television and independent newspapers provided widespread, positive coverage of the pyramid schemes, ran their ads, and prominently featured the schemes' directors. The media not only failed to warn people, they encouraged them to invest. Advertisements by pyramid enterprises provided a good source of income to the television and newspapers. In addition, many progovernment and opposition journalists were reportedly on the payroll of pyramid schemers. In an article published in early October 1996, Ben Blushi, then chief editor of *Koha Jonë*, deplored IMF calls to close down the pyramid schemes, urging the international financial institution instead to exert pressure on the Albanian government "to license moneylending companies and turn them into private banks." Blushi took the government to task for "unconditionally" bowing to the IMF.[20] The progovernment newspaper *Albania* published a long commentary by a lawyer who argued that "moneylending" was legal.[21] The organ of the Republican Party, *Republika*, was blatant in its support of pyramid schemes. In mid-November 1996, *Republika* published a survey of what it described as a group of "world finance specialists." The paper assured investors that they need not fear that they would lose their investments: "The majority [of specialists questioned] conclude that moneylending will operate normally in the near future, and that there is no immediate danger of any bankruptcy. Should the Albanians therefore continue to play with moneylending? The belief of the sixteen specialists employed in moneylending is 'Yes!' In that there is no forecast of the collapse of even one of the moneylending firms, an opportunity to enrich yourself in this way must not be passed up."[22]

In November, an IMF delegation urged Prime Minister Meksi to impose strict controls on the pyramid schemes, and refused to sign a new agreement with Albania. The Albanian parliament appointed a commission to investigate the operation of pyramid schemes, which by this time had amassed incredibly large amounts of money. But this measure came too late. Pyramid schemes were already beginning to crumble, and huge amounts of money evidently had already been transferred abroad. In November 1996, the Sudja company, which had operated mainly in Tiranë, stopped making payments, while Sandër Grunasi, the director of a small Grunasi fund, fled the country with $13 million.[23] In mid-January 1997, Sudja declared bankruptcy and its owner was arrested.[24] This was followed by the collapse of the Xhaferri and Populli foundations. The government seized $255 million held in state banks by Xhaferri and Populli.[25] On 24 January, the authorities arrested the directors of the two funds, Rrapush Xhaferri and Bashkim Driza, as well as some fifty similar operators throughout the country.[26] Rrapush Xhaferri admitted that his company, which began operations in 1993, was a pyramid scheme.[27] After weeks of rumbles of discontent, in mid- and late January, protests broke out in Tiranë and several cities in the south. Protesters in Vlorë, Lushnje, and Berat set fire to government buildings, including city halls, courts, police stations, land registry offices, and Democratic Party offices. Despite police actions, the protests continued to gain momentum.

Government Reaction

Although the government had ample warnings that the sudden dismantling of the pyramid schemes would have dangerous repercussions, it had not devised a clear strategy for mitigating these effects, which threatened the livelihood of tens of thousands of people. International financial institutions also did not have any helpful suggestions for a soft landing. Faced with the dilemma of how to compensate depositors without destroying the economy, the government agreed to only partial repayments. It also pledged to help the most severely affected people by offering them public jobs as well as by providing credits to new businesses. Lacking resources and afraid of triggering hyperinflation, the government refused cash handouts. In early February 1997, the authorities began repaying investors in Xhaferri and Populli from the two firms' deposits, which had been frozen in the state banks. Investors in Xhaferri and Populli funds began receiving partial compensation of 50 percent to 60 percent of their losses. They were given the choice of cash or savings deposits. Most investors, however, refused the partial compensation, hoping to get full compensation later.

The government did not realize how vulnerable it was to economic setbacks. The collapse in early February 1997 of the Vlorë-based Gjallica company, which reportedly had attracted about $300 million in deposits although its assets amounted to only a fraction of that amount,[28] caused immediate and widespread unrest. For days security forces battled angry protesters in Vlorë, finally abandoning the city altogether. Unrest rapidly spread to other southern cities. While many investors knew that the pyramid schemes had no sound economic basis and that eventually they would crumble, they now blamed the government.

The outbreak of protests gave the fractured and demoralized opposition new determination. Although the opposition had not criticized the schemes earlier, it moved to capitalize on the widespread despair in the wake of the collapse of the pyramid schemes. Opposition leaders traveled to Vlorë in order to encourage the protesters, making inflammatory speeches against the government. Now the Socialist Party, which had consistently pursued an obstructionist policy, saw the unrest as a long-awaited opportunity to force the government to make political concessions, and perhaps even to dislodge the Democrats from their position of power. Having experienced significant internal fragmentation and having been denied access to state power, the Socialists welcomed and indeed incited the outbreak of unrest. Senior Socialist Party official Sabit Brokaj and former Minister of Internal Affairs Gramoz Ruçi, who had emigrated to Greece in summer 1996, began to organize disaffected former military and Sigurimi officers in Vlorë, Berat, Tepelenë, Gjirokastër, and Sarandë. Meanwhile in Tiranë, opposition parties, led by the Socialists, created a loose coalition called the Forum for Democracy, on 30 January 1997. The Forum, which brought together such incongruous bedfellows as the Socialists and the Association of Former Victims of Political Persecution and the Democratic Party of the Right, organized demonstrations demanding Meksi's resignation, the establishment of a technical government, and early parliamentary elections. Without giving much thought to the possible impact of their actions, opposition leaders launched a shameless campaign of extraparliamentary agitation, encouraging an assault on and the toppling of elected authorities.[29]

Concomitantly, opposition newspapers fueled the unrest by engaging in psychological terror. Zëri i Popullit and the ostensibly independent Koha Jonë, whose chief editor Ben Blushi had published a commentary in December 1996 deploring what he called the Albanians' lack of a "spirit of protest,"[30] fanned the flames of violence through inflammatory rhetoric and tacit approval of attacks on the police and state institutions.[31] These newspapers, with their inaccurate and exaggerated antigovernment reports, caused widespread panic. They published highly inflammatory articles, claiming that Berisha had hired mercenaries from the north as well as Albanians from Yugoslavia to put down protesters in the south.[32] The latter allegation was also picked up by leading opposition politicians. Former political prisoner Kurt Kola, leader of the Forum for Democracy, claimed that Slav-speaking mercenaries were operating in Vlorë.[33] Meanwhile, former Chief Justice of the Court of Cassation Zef Brozi issued a statement in the United States appealing to the international community to stop all support for Berisha's "totalitarian regime." He attacked the Democratic Party for having "stolen" the people's votes in the 1996 elections and for "stealing the people's money." Brozi blatantly called for overthrow of the government, saying that "Albanians should not allow themselves to be governed by an illegitimate Parliament and Government."[34]

As the economic crisis intensified, so did the opposition's challenge to Berisha. The gulf between the two sides was so wide that Albania's polarized political elites could not cooperate in devising policies that might have staved off the subsequent turmoil. The government resorted increasingly to undemocratic means to suppress opposition political activity, denying the Forum permission to hold demonstrations in Tiranë's central square. There were frequent clashes between opposition supporters and security forces that harassed opposition politicians, government critics, and journalists alike. Meanwhile, the rapidly spreading unrest caused a rift within the ruling party. Fourteen prominent members of the Democratic Party, including former Deputy Prime Ministers Dashamir Shehi and Bashkim Kopliku, former Foreign Minister Alfred Serreqi, and former Finance Minister Genc Ruli, issued a statement demanding Meksi's resignation. The group also demanded "the final removal of President Berisha from the party presidium and the elimination of the direct or oblique power he exercises over the Democratic Party." Their demands were rejected as a capitulation to the Socialists. In turn, Berisha's supporters blamed the group, which consisted almost entirely of former senior government officials, for the crisis.[35]

Armed Revolt

The collapse of the pyramid schemes sparked an armed revolt that swept away the government's authority over most parts of the country, deepened Albania's pain, and isolated the country from current democratic currents. While Albanians throughout the country had invested in the pyramid schemes, the unrest was centered in the wealthier southern regions, particularly in Vlorë. The more prosperous south had profited more than the north by the changes instituted after the fall of communism. While the north remained isolated and suffered from the U.N. sanctions imposed on Yugoslavia, Vlorë, Sarandë, and Gjirokastër profited from the rapid expansion of economic ties with the outside world. Tens of thousands of Albanians from these regions had found refuge in Greece and Italy. Remittances from refugees probably amounted to several hundred million dollars annually. These regions, particularly Vlorë, also prospered by smuggling oil, arms, and immigrants. Thus having profited more from the post-1992 changes and being beneficiaries of huge remittances from abroad, southerners arguably had lost more money than people in the north when the get-rich-quick schemes collapsed.

However, there were also other important factors that spurred protests in the south. The fierce rivalry between the Democratic Party and the Socialist Party reflected the old, regional divisions within Albanian society. Berisha's support was weakest in the south, which remained a Socialist stronghold. There were widespread perceptions that with Berisha as president, the south had lost out in the political power struggle. The post-1992 reforms had resulted in the purge of several thousand former senior military and secret police officers, most of whom were from Vlorë and other southern cities. The opposition openly fueled the north-south divide, accusing the president of giving northerners senior positions at the expense of southerners. But with the exception of the police forces, which contained a higher percentage of people from the north, the higher echelons of the government and indeed the Democratic Party itself continued to be dominated by southerners. Nevertheless, the failed pyramid schemes added to the political grievances that had been building since the May 1996 elections. Disgruntled Communists, retired army generals, and former Sigurimi members played an important role in organizing the antigovernment protests. Another factor was the involvement of criminal gangs, particularly in Vlorë, which in addition to having served in Hoxha's times as a recruiting ground for Sigurimi had developed an unsavory reputation as a center of illegal activities, with close ties to international crime groups, particularly those based in Italy.

The government's inability to mitigate the effects of the collapse of pyramid schemes on the average investor and the incapacity of state institutions to control social unrest demonstrated Berisha's increased weakness. The president had been viewed by both supporters and detractors as a strong and determined leader. But in his handling of the crisis, he wavered and appeared indecisive. The end of his five-year term was approaching, and he evidently was attempting to avoid a showdown before his reelection, which under the constitution could not be postponed to a date later than 9 March. Moreover, Berisha came under intense pressure from the United States and some West European countries to show restraint.[36] This pressure impacted negatively on the decisionmaking process in Tiranë, which sent the wrong message to the opposition and protesters. Thus, Berisha publicly rejected Meksi's request in early February 1997 that a state of emergency be proclaimed in Vlorë. In retrospect, a forceful stand at this point might have quelled the protests.

At the same time, Berisha continued to display an unusual lack of appreciation for the magnitude of the crisis and the widespread anger that had built up against his party's mismanagement of the crisis. Even in the face of growing unrest and the government's inability to use its repressive capabilities effectively, the president refused to make a pragmatic retreat, drop Meksi as prime minister, and compromise with the opposition in the hope of stabilizing the situation. Standing behind the inept prime minister, Berisha made an absolute error of political strategy that later would force him to negotiate with the Socialists in a way he had eschewed in the past. The president's inability to formulate an adequate political response to the crisis only intensified the unrest and political discontent.

In an attempt to contain the unrest and drum up support, in early February 1997, Berisha embarked on a trip around the country, addressing selected audiences. In a town meeting in Tiranë, Berisha took responsibility for not having warned citizens against investing in fraudulent schemes and pledged that the government would help the people most affected, particularly those who had lost their homes. He promised welfare assistance to families without incomes, and favorable credits to people engaged in private enterprise.[37]

The president's message, however, had no impact. With unrest spreading and parliament scheduled to reelect him to a second five-year term on 3 March, Berisha on 1 March announced Meksi's resignation and said a new, Democratic Party-led government would be established.[38] But Meksi's resignation was too little, and came too late. The situation in the south deteriorated with the brutal massacre of several members of the secret police in Vlorë. In a nationwide televised address, Berisha promised to crush the "terrorist rebellion," which he said had been organized by former Communists and former secret police in co-operation with foreign intelligence services.[39] On 2 March, the Albanian parliament declared a state of emergency, imposing a dusk-till-dawn curfew. Army and security forces were given the power to fire without warning at any armed resisters; public gatherings were restricted; and censorship was imposed on the media.[40] Bashkim Gazidede, chief of the secret police, was put in charge of enforcing the state of emergency. Army Chief of Staff, General Sheme Kosova, was dismissed. He was replaced by Berisha's personal military adviser, Major General Adem Çopani. On 3 March, parliament reelected Berisha to a second five-year term.[41]

The declaration of the state of emergency touched off a wave of international criticism. U.S. State Department spokesman Nicholas Burns expressed concern that the state of emergency was being used "to stifle legitimate free expression." Burns also criticized parliament's reelection of Berisha amid the crisis, adding that "this step is likely to increase polarization rather than facilitate a solution."[42] West European countries also expressed concern that the state of emergency and restrictions on civil liberties could be used by Berisha to muzzle the opposition and move toward authoritarian rule. The international community placed tremendous pressure on Berisha to compromise, thus undercutting his efforts to restore law and order.

The state of emergency came too late to quell the revolt. Armed gangs in the south advanced in stunning fashion from city to city, effectively dislodging locally elected authorities. Thousands raided army barracks abandoned by police forces, army commanders, and ordinary soldiers, and took huge stocks of heavy weapons and ammunition. With the situation getting out of hand, on 6 March, Berisha reached an agreement with the opposition parties. The rebels were given forty-eight hours to hand over their arms and ammunition, military operations were suspended for forty-eight hours, and all rebels were pardoned. In addition, the parties were to start consultations on the appointment of a new prime minister and a special commission to be established to investigate the pyramid schemes.[43] However, the rebels took advantage of the cease-fire to reinforce their positions. Former Communists, Sigurimi, military leaders, and organized crime groups that had lost money with the collapse of pyramid schemes joined forces, with the aim of setting up an organized movement. Rebel committees were set up in key cities, including Vlorë, Tepelenë, Sarandë, and Gjirokastër. Disgruntled military officers emerged as key figures: Generals Skendër Sera and Luftar Petroshati in Vlorë; former General Agim Gozhita in Gjirokastër, and retired Army Colonel Xhevat Koçiu in Sarandë.[44] None of these men could be considered agents of democratic change: All had very close links with the Socialist Party, and in all probability, were acting on orders from the Socialist leadership. The rebels refused to lay down their arms, demanding Berisha's resignation. Although the Socialists publicly stated that they had no control of the rebels, they also made no effort to distance themselves from them. Meanwhile, Democratic Alliance leaders Arben Imami and Ridvan Peshkëpia joined the rebels in the hope of leading the political wing of the anti-Berisha movement. Peshkëpia insisted that "only extreme solutions could results in any change in the governing of this country."[45]

Albania's fragile democracy unraveled rapidly under the pressure of armed revolt. Government authority evaporated throughout the south, and the armed forces disintegrated. Officials subsequently estimated that the damage the army suffered during the revolt amounted to several billion leks. The logistic network was totally ruined, while the coastal and air observation systems and the electronic surveillance network were seriously damaged. Most of the navy's vessels and military helicopters had fled to Italy.[46]

Several factors contributed to the disintegration of the national army. The military was ill suited to policing activities and reluctant to fire against civilians. Moreover, Defense Minister Safet Zhulali and the top military echelons displayed a catastrophic failure of leadership. As a result of post-1992 reforms, deep cuts had been made in military manpower and spending. As many as two-thirds of the officers may have been purged after 1992. This had deprived the armed forces of experienced career officers and had led to widespread demoralization. Many recently promoted senior officers were incompetent. While old, Communist values and traditions were abandoned, the troops were given no new values to defend and had no clear sense of purpose. The armed forces were plagued by dangerously low morale because of miserable accommodations and poor pay. In addition, many soldiers and their families had lost money in the pyramid schemes. Berisha bore a share of the blame for the military's pitiable state: Despite Zhulali's incompetence and growing evidence of the defense minister's involvement in illegal activities, including arms sales to other countries, the president had continued to express confidence in Zhulali.

As the rebel forces that controlled nearly half of the country moved from victory to victory and threatened to make Tiranë their next goal, the state began to crumble from within. In an effort to stave off complete disintegration, the

Democratic Party relinquished control of the government and accepted a humiliating agreement with the opposition. On 9 March, Berisha reached an agreement with ten political parties, which provided for the creation of a national reconciliation government, general amnesty for rebels, the surrender of arms within one week, and parliamentary elections in June 1997.[47] The agreement marked an unexpected turnabout from Berisha's strong opposition to a coalition with the Socialist Party. Only days earlier, the president had rejected the idea, saying that a coalition with the Socialists would be a deathblow to Albanian democracy. In an interview published by *Der Spiegel* on 3 March, Berisha had declared that he would "never" agree to a coalition with the Socialists.[48]

The Socialist Party's Bashkim Fino, who had served as mayor of Gjirokastër from 1992 to 1996, became prime minister. In appointing Fino, who apparently was popular in Gjirokastër and also had contact with some rebel leaders, the president hoped to calm the revolt. The Democrats retained the Ministry of Internal Affairs, while the Socialists took control of the defense and finance portfolios. Spartak Ngjela, a lawyer who had spent seventeen years in prison, was proposed by the Legality Party as minister of justice. Deputy Foreign Minister Arjan Starova, a representative of the Social Democratic Union, became minister of foreign affairs. In addition to the Democrats and the Socialists, seven other parties were represented in the broad-based government of national unity. The Democratic Alliance, whose leader Neritan Ceka had openly campaigned for the post of prime minister, declined to take part in the government, ostensibly because Berisha refused to give the opposition the post of internal affairs.

The rebels welcomed Fino's appointment but sent Berisha an ultimatum, demanding that he resign by 20 March. Otherwise, they threatened to march on Tiranë and place the president under house arrest.[49] With rebels in the south insisting on Berisha's resignation, on 11 March, unrest spread to the north, and pro-Berisha supporters began to break into weapons depots in Bajram Curri, vowing to defend the president if need be. A similar pattern developed in Kukës, Shkodër and Tiranë. A shady group calling itself the Committee for National Salvation threatened to mobilize Berisha's supporters. In a statement, the group warned Fino against negotiating with the rebels, adding that it was "determined to protect under any circumstances all the democratic institutions of the country, property, and the freedom of citizens from a possible military attack."[50] Berisha dismissed the rebels' ultimatum, while Fino publicly stated that he opposed the president's forced resignation because it would create a power vacuum.

By mid-March, the government could exercise limited sovereign authority only over territory outside Tiranë and Durrës. As Albania continued sliding into anarchy, the U.S. Ambassador to Tiranë, Marisa Lino, ordered the evacuation of American citizens. Throughout Albania, army warehouses were raided, shops looted, and banks and government offices torched. Close to one million automatic weapons fell into civilian hands. Disorder reigned in most parts of the country, and armed bandits openly preyed upon a helpless citizenry. Guards deserted the prisons, allowing inmates to escape. Armed, violent, convicted criminals roamed throughout the country, terrorizing the population. Albania became the only country in the world where all the prisoners had walked out of the jails. Fatos Nano, the chairman of the Socialist Party who had been imprisoned in 1993 on corruption charges, and Ramiz Alia, Albania's last Communist leader, were released from prison. Subsequently, Berisha pardoned Nano. Albania's terrifying slide into anarchy was perhaps best characterized by the new Minister of Justice Spartak Ngjela, who said: "All structures of the state have failed. In this moment, we are a natural state, if you know your Hobbes."[51]

Multinational Protection Force

Albania's sensitive geostrategic position makes this tiny Balkan state a long-term strategic headache for the international community. Franz Vranitzky, the former Austrian chancellor, was named the personal representative to Albania of the chairman-in-office of the OSCE. Vranitzky's mission was to facilitate a dialogue among Albania's political forces. Berisha appealed to the West European Union for intervention to end the violent chaos and restore peace and state authority. The Europeans, however, rejected Berisha's calls for direct military intervention.

Italy was the European nation most immediately affected by the turmoil in Albania. By mid-March, some 15,000 Albanians had fled to Italy, forcing the Italian government to declare a national state of emergency.[52] Virtually overnight, Albania climbed to the top of Italy's national security agenda, and Rome took the lead in establishing a Multinational Protection Force create a secure environment for the safe delivery of international assistance to Albania. On 28 March, the U.N. Security Council approved Resolution 1101, authorizing the creation of the protection force under Italy's leadership.[53] The deployment of the force of six thousand began on 15 April. Troops from Italy, France, Greece, Turkey, Spain, Romania, and several other European countries secured the major points of entry into Albanian territory by sea and by air, and assured freedom of movement along major thoroughfares connecting essential distribution centers. The United States refused to take part in the multinational force.

Although the deployment of the multinational force had a calming effect, its mission fell far short of the help that Albania desperately needed to restore law and order: The force had been given the mandate to provide protection to humanitarian relief efforts, when all agreed that Albania in fact was not faced with a humanitarian crisis. Italy and other participating countries lacked the political will to launch an operation to disarm armed gangs, restore law and order, and help create the necessary conditions for free and fair elections. Given its limited mandate, the multinational force made little impression on ordinary Albanians, many of whom wondered why the international community was spending several million dollars a day on a force that stood by idly while criminal, armed gangs continued to terrorize the civilian population.

Berisha Under Siege

The revolt severely damaged Berisha's already shaky credibility and left him politically crippled. His leadership credentials were disputed as never before. Critics argued that Berisha had lost his way, that he was leading the country adrift. Meanwhile, the Albanian president was insulated from all but a handful of close advisers, and did not appear in public for an extended period of time. Prominent members of his own party who had begun to see the president as a political liability broke ranks to save their own skins.

At the most critical moment, Berisha could not count on international support. Post-Dayton developments in the Balkans had reduced the immediacy of Albania's strategic value. Moreover, Berisha, who had been unwilling to heed foreign advice, particularly from the United States, had come to be seen as an authoritarian leader. Indeed, his former Western allies made no secret of their desire to get him out of power. This international pressure on Berisha to resign further eroded his standing, and prolonged the unrest by encouraging his opponents. International contacts with rebel leaders undermined peace efforts. Instead of being marginalized, known criminals and former *nomenklatura* officials were legitimized by meetings with Italian, Greek, and OSCE officials. With Berisha being at his most vulnerable, *The Financial Times* published a report saying that the United States had lost confidence in Berisha's ability to handle his country's crisis and had called for his removal. The new U.S. position was reportedly expressed at a meeting of NATO ambassadors in Brussels.[54] With this action, the United States essentially had allied itself with the armed rebels. In a television interview, Undersecretary of State for Political Affairs Peter Tarnoff said that rebel leaders who had met, on an Italian ship off shore with the OSCE envoy Franz Vranitzky "are able to represent the hopes and aspirations of the people in the south."[55] Shortly thereafter, Italy's Foreign Affairs Under Secretary Piero Fassino publicly asserted that Rome wished to see Berisha resign.

The international community did not seem to have given much thought to alternatives to the Democratic Party as it deliberately isolated and undermined Berisha. Indeed, the president's forced resignation might well have left a power vacuum, thereby further destabilizing the situation and possibly leading to civil war and uncontrolled rebellion throughout the country. Berisha's supporters were likely to react violently, thus leading to virtually certain disintegration of the national reconciliation government. Moreover, foreign pressure on Berisha to resign went counter to the international community's public stand that the Albanians should be able to address their grievances within the existing democratic framework. After all, Berisha was the duly elected president.

Tiranë did not publicly react to U.S. calls for Berisha's ouster, but the Albanian Foreign Ministry did object to Fassino's comments, accusing Rome of "unacceptable interference" in Albania's internal affairs.[56] Berisha responded angrily: "It is impossible for an Italian to tell the Albanians who should be their president or tell a president chosen in free elections what to do. ... It is more than an interference in another country's internal affairs."[57]

The president and other senior Democratic Party officials accepted partial responsibility for the chaos, but at the same time, attempted to shift the blame elsewhere. In a report to parliament, the chief of the secret police, Bashkim Gazidede, said the revolt was the result of a conspiracy organized by foreign intelligence services and the Greek lobby in the United States.[58] Gazidede failed to provide credible evidence to back his allegations, and his statement was widely seen as a major public relations blunder. Realistically, these charges further damaged Albania and deprived the Berisha government of any goodwill it still enjoyed in Washington.

In the wake of the turmoil, Berisha faced his most serious challenge from within the Democratic Party. A group of disgruntled former senior government and party officials, led by former Deputy Prime Minister Dashamir Shehi, launched a blistering attack against the president. However, the group could not muster significant support within the party. In the wake of their defeat at the National Council meeting in April, the group split from the Democratic Party and formed the Movement for Democracy Party. Although the Democratic Party emerged from the crisis largely intact structurally, it faced a difficult task in reconsolidating its power and status. As its real power slipped away, the Democratic Party desperately attempted to cling to the trappings of power.

Meanwhile, the Socialist, Democratic Alliance, and Social Democratic Parties, which had encouraged the populace to rebel against Berisha, made every effort to take advantage of the situation. Although the Socialists headed the national reconciliation government, they took no steps toward implementing one of the most important measures stipulated by the 9 March agreement—disarming the rebels. Immediately after being pardoned by Berisha, Fatos Nano had pledged to turn into a "peacekeeping, peacemaking missionary," to convince rebels in the south to lay down their weapons.[59] Yet, the Socialists remained steadfast in their support of rebels—despite the latter's outright stand against the constitutional order and denial of the state's representative institutions.[60] The Social Democratic and Democratic Alliance Parties also continued to support the rebels. Judged by the public pronouncements of some of their leaders, including Skendër Gjinushi, Paskal Milo, Neritan Ceka, and Arben Imami, the two parties had indeed transformed themselves into antiestablishment parties advocating the violent overthrow of the government. Not surprisingly, Socialist leaders and their allies did not have strong motivation to use their influence in the south to convince the rebels to lay down their arms. The duplicitous stand of the Socialist Party became evident when the Socialists, jointly with the Republican, Social Democratic, and

Democratic Alliance Parties, signed a statement with eight other political parties and eighteen salvation committees in Vlorë, calling for Berisha's resignation.[61]

Impact of the Revolt

The revolt seriously shook the public's confidence in Albania's political, economic, and social system and derailed the country's transition to democracy. State institutions collapsed, and the state's ability to regulate daily life vanished. The political elites, who failed to put aside their differences and cooperate in halting the disintegration of the Albanian polity, were badly discredited. Steeped in the Communist traditions of intolerance and high-stakes class struggle, they displayed little respect for democratic procedures or debates, and viewed politics as an exclusively combative contest. The instincts of the old elites, their ingrained Communist socialization, habits, and views, had survived largely intact. Even at the most critical periods, few chose to concentrate on the dangers facing their country, engaging instead in political posturing and obscure ideological squabbles. All of the political parties' commitment to democracy was shown to be questionable. The crisis also showed that the post-1992 system did not provide ordinary Albanians much of a forum in which to articulate their views. Not enough effort had been made to explore citizens' concerns, let alone to heed them.

The collapse of the pyramid schemes not only provoked a devastating social outburst, but it destroyed much of the socioeconomic and political progress Albania had made, and endangered the country's future and territorial integrity. The destruction of property was estimated at several hundred million dollars. After several years of impressive growth, the unrest brought the economy to a standstill, triggered inflation, weakened the national currency, increased unemployment, and undermined any immediate prospects for foreign investment. The lek, which had been one of the most stable currencies in Eastern Europe, depreciated by as much as 50 percent between January and June 1997. Officials estimated that during 1997, the economy would contract by 8 percent. This economic crisis caused a profound erosion of the government's revenues base. The budget deficit was estimated to have jumped to between 16 and 17 percent of gross domestic product, and inflation to have soared as high as 55 percent.

The revolt also seriously undermined Albania's regional position. From an island of stability in the troubled Balkans, Albania was transformed overnight to a potential geopolitical flashpoint. Albania's implosion led Greece to reassess its ties with Macedonia. In a major policy shift, Greece shed its confrontational tactics of the early 1990s and moved to improve relations with Macedonia. Greek Foreign Minister Theodoros Pangalos traveled to Skopje and Belgrade to discuss common strategies for dealing with the Albanian imbroglio. The crisis in Albania also seriously undermined the negotiating position of ethnic Albanians in Kosova. Belgrade was now less likely to engage in negotiations with the Albanians, while the latter were coming under increased international pressure to give up their demands for secession. On 1 October, Serbian police brutally suppressed Albanian student demonstrations in Prishtinë and several other Kosovar cities. Students were demanding the implementation of the 1996 Milošević-Rugova agreement on the reopening of Albanian-language school facilities and institutions. A Serbian government statement declared in no uncertain terms that "Serbia will never allow the existence of a separate Albanian state of Kosovo with a separate education system and university."[62] Meanwhile, dozens of Albanians were arrested and tried on charges of membership in the Kosova Liberation Army, which was accused by the Serbs of carrying out attacks on police stations and other security targets.

The implosion of Albania also appeared to have emboldened extreme nationalist forces in Macedonia. Skopje hardened its position, adopting a more confrontational approach in addressing ethnic Albanian grievances. As state authority collapsed and anarchy spread throughout Albania, the Macedonian Foreign Minister, Ljubomir Frckovski, was quoted as saying: "We expect a more direct dialogue with the Albanians [in Macedonia], now that Tiranë is no longer in a position to intercede on behalf of the Albanian cause in the Balkans. ... For now, our government is not doing anything, but the minute we notice any kind of action by the Albanians, we will react in order to radically prevent them."[63] Macedonian students held protests in March against proposed Albanian-language programs at the Skopje University's pedagogic faculty, chanting "Albanians to the gas chambers." Tensions reached a boiling point in early July, when Macedonia's parliament passed a law stipulating that the flags of ethnic minorities could be hoisted from public buildings only on certain state holidays and next to the Macedonian flag: Officials in the predominantly Albanian-inhabited cities had hoisted the Albanian flag from public buildings since the beginning of the year. On 9 July, just a day after the passage of the law, special Macedonian police forces took down Albanian flags flying outside the town hall in Gostivar, sparking massive protests by ethnic Albanians. At least three Albanians were killed and dozens wounded during violent clashes with police. Hundreds more were arrested, including Gostivar's mayor, Rufi Osmani.[64] The incident led to a dangerous exacerbation of interethnic tensions and seriously undermined the position of the Party for Democratic Prosperity, a partner in the governing coalition of Prime Minister Branko Crvenkovski. Minister of Internal Affairs Tomislav Cokrevski acknowledged that he had asked the prime minister not to inform the five Albanian members of the cabinet in advance of the police intervention.[65] While the police action was welcomed by the majority of Macedonians, the developments in Gostivar could not but drive a deeper wedge between the two communities.

The 1997 Elections: Albania's Second Chance?

The national reconciliation government was tasked with restoring law and order and creating proper conditions to permit the people to express their will in the 29 June parliamentary elections. This vote was widely seen as Albania's last chance to restore stability, patch its political system back together, and rebuild confidence in democracy. But despite the grave problems confronting their country, Albanian politicians found it excruciatingly difficult to cooperate with one another. They constantly jockeyed for political advantages, placing their narrow interests above those of the nation. They came close to abdicating their responsibility for preparing and conducting the elections that were intended to be a first step in the solution of their country's political and economic crisis.

Political cohabitation between Berisha and Fino, who came from two fiercely competing parties with differing political philosophies, became a source of constant conflict. Plagued by serious disagreements between the Democrats and the Socialists, the government did not have effective capacity nor did it enjoy sufficient political support to carry out basic government functions and begin to deal with the country's dire social and economic plight. Despite full international support, Fino's government was too weak to assert its authority and stop the drift toward violence. Little headway was made in reconstituting the military and police forces. With the exception of Tiranë, Durrës, and a few other cities, there was no obvious state authority exercising control; most of the country was controlled by criminal groups. In some areas, national salvation committees were created in the vacuum of central and local authority; but salvation committees proved unable to conduct the everyday administration of local power, and exercised only a semblance of control. The continuous political strife took a very heavy toll. There were widespread human rights abuses: Between March and July 1997, close to two thousand people were killed and some ten thousand wounded. Albanians' basic rights to security, food, shelter, education, and health services were largely unfulfilled.

Albania's political leaders seemed to have learned few if any lessons from the crisis. Preparations for the elections were dogged by disputes between parties over electoral procedures, with the Democrats and Socialists widely seen as mutually obstructionist. Election gamesmanship continued until voting day. After weeks of haggling and deal making, Franz Vranitzky, the OSCE special envoy, brokered a compromise on procedures for the elections. On 9 May, ten political parties signed a six-point political contract that called for a mixed system of proportional and majority representation in the new parliament; the dissolution of national salvation committees before the announcement of the date of the elections; and the appointment of an international election coordinator.[66] While the Socialists and other political parties favored the adoption of a proportional electoral system, the Democrats defended the majority system, insisting that the country needed a stable, majority parliament. In retrospect, the Democrats had grossly miscalculated voter sentiment and the opposition's organization. They would have fared much better under a proportional system. Nevertheless, the new electoral law provided for 115 winner-take-all seats. The number of seats allotted according to each party's share of the overall vote was increased to 40 (as compared to 25 in the 1996 law), thus raising the total number of seats in parliament to 155.[67] Berisha delegated the authority to appoint the members of the Central Electoral Commission to Fino. The commission in turn was empowered to name members of the district commissions. The Democratic Party-controlled parliament also passed a proposal to hold a referendum on retaining a republican state or establishing a constitutional monarchy.

The 9 May agreement also called for the revision of the controversial lustration law so that only former Communist Party Politburo members and Sigurimi collaborators would be barred from seeking electoral office.[68] Thus, Fatos Nano and many other leading opposition figures, including Social Democratic Party leader Skendër Gjinushi, were permitted to run for office.

As a result of the deep mistrust dividing Albania's political forces, many politicians preferred to let the OSCE conduct and supervise the elections. The international community, however, refused, agreeing only to provide technical assistance and monitors, sending more than 500 observers, plus technical experts and other advisers. The international organization prepared the ballot papers and the ballot boxes to minimize the possibility of fraud, and helped Albanians compile new voter lists, since many lists had been destroyed during the March uprising. Catherine Lalumiere, former secretary-general of the Council of Europe, was appointed special election coordinator, as were Sir Russell Johnston of the Council of Europe and Javier Ruperez of the OSCE Parliamentary Assembly. This trio had the task of determining whether the elections were free and fair. Although the United States had refused to send troops to Albania, Washington provided full moral and political support to the OSCE mission.

With the arrival of international troops, Albania had settled into an uneasy stalemate. However, Prime Minister Fino's government proved largely ineffective, and on the eve of the elections, Albania lacked even a modicum of order. Despite chaotic conditions in the country, the international community refused to revise the mandate of the Italian-led multinational forces to assist Albanians in restoring the constitutional order, disarming and dissolving armed gangs, and creating a safe and secure environment for free and fair elections. In view of the absence of proper conditions, the wisdom of holding early elections was questionable.[69]

On 9 June, Brian Pridham, chief of the OSCE's monitoring operation in Tiranë, resigned, accusing the OSCE of having decided in advance to validate the elections. In a preelection assessment report, the highly respected U.S. National Democratic Institute declared that Albania lacked even "the minimum conditions for legitimate elections." The NDI asserted that unless dramatic improvements in electoral conditions were achieved, "a postponement will not only be advisable but will be required to avert a potential electoral failure."[70] Nonetheless, key international actors insisted that the elections be held on 29 June at all costs, expressing concern that a delay would only lead to further unrest. From the very beginning, OSCE officials attempted to lower expectations, acknowledging that the Albanian elections would not meet generally accepted international standards and insisting that they were expecting only reasonably acceptable elections.

The international community also exerted pressure on Albanian political parties to make a preelection commitment to accept the results of the balloting. On 23 June, under the auspices of the Roman Catholic organization Sant'Egidio, the Democratic, Socialist, and Social Democratic Parties met in Rome and signed what was termed as "A Pact for Albania's Future." The signatories pledged to respect the results of the elections, if the international community accepted them, and to cooperate in the postelection period, giving the opposition a greater say in the governing of the country, including control over important parliamentary commissions and the state audit commission.[71] The leaders of the Republican Party and the National Front also attended the meeting, but they refused to sign the pact because of their objection to the formula for the distribution of the forty seats to be contested by proportional representation.

The Campaign

Thus, with the state of emergency still nominally in force and most parts of the country eluding the control of the authorities, Albanians headed toward the 29 June elections. Throughout the campaign, there was a clear political polarization, with the Democrats, eager to maintain their power, on the one side, and the Socialists, determined to regain power, on the other. These two larger parties sought partners among the smaller parties in a competition for control of the country's parliament. The Democratic Party created an alliance with small, right-parties, including the monarchist Legality, the Christian Democratic Party, the Social Democratic Union, and the Democratic Union Party; but these parties enjoyed limited popular support and were therefore inconsequential. The Democrats would have fared much better if they had been successful in including in their coalition a broader range of right-wing parties. However, many right-wing forces refused to cooperate with the Democrats, believing that they stood a better chance, alone, of attracting the votes of those disenchanted with the ruling party and concerned about the former Communists regaining power. Thus, the Republican Party, the National Front, the Christian Democratic Union Party, the newly created Movement for Democracy, the Conservative Party, and the Right Democratic Party set up the United Albanian Right preelectoral alliance. This right-wing bloc portrayed itself as an alternative force to the country's two major parties, opposing what it termed the Socialist Party's communism and the Democratic Party's neocommunism. The Socialist Party, in turn, signed an electoral pact with the Social Democratic and Democratic Alliance Parties, agreeing to field joint candidates in about half of the country's electoral districts and to form a coalition government if they won the elections.[72]

The resulting campaign was one of the most violent and least democratic in postcommunist East Central Europe. A politically poisonous atmosphere gripped the entire country, and the extreme polarization increased the process of national disintegration, threatening the unity and integrity of the country. A surge in political violence, mainly directed against the Democratic Party, added to the climate of fear. The capital was hit by a wave of bombings: On 4 June, Berisha escaped an assassination attempt while on the campaign trail in a village near Durrës. More than twenty people were wounded in a blast at a Tiranë cafe owned by Lush Përpali, a leading member of the Socialist Party and deputy minister of internal affairs. Only days before the elections, Berisha was caught in a gun battle during a rally in Lushnje, during which at least eight people were wounded. The Democratic Party's Secretary for Foreign Affairs, Leonard Demi, was taken hostage and beaten by pro-Socialist armed gangs in Sarandë. During the campaign, the north-south schism became wider, with the Democrats waging their campaign mainly in the north, and the Socialists, in the south. The Democrats were forcibly prevented from campaigning in most electoral districts in the rebel-controlled south, while the Socialists encountered considerable problems north of Tiranë.

Far from demonstrating any progress in unifying the country and returning it to a semblance of normality, the violent and unruly campaign fortified competing and seemingly irreconcilable visions of the nation. The campaign was devoid of debate or new issues: Berisha waged a determined campaign for political survival, blaming the Socialists for the armed uprising and the subsequent anarchy and warning that the revolt jeopardized Albania's experiment in democracy and market economy. Berisha pledged that if returned to power, the Democratic Party would restore law and order within months. The Democrats also announced an emergency program for the country's economic revival and the reestablishment of political stability.[73] However, Berisha's inability to attract large crowds, and his increased problems while campaigning even in former Democratic strongholds, indicated that his party's invincibility had crumbled. The party's mishandling of the pyramid schemes crisis, combined with perceptions of widespread corruption at the highest levels of government and increased foreign criticism of government policies, had substantially eroded the Democrats' political base.

The Socialist Party and its allies likewise stuck to a single, essential message: Berisha personally was responsible for the mess.[74] Projecting a moderate image and preaching the virtues of democratic tolerance, Fatos Nano, who had been pardoned by Berisha in March after almost four years of imprisonment on corruption charges, maintained that a Socialist victory would herald a more relaxed social atmosphere and greater political pluralism. Nano pledged to create a broad-based government and to transform Albania into a truly parliamentary system. Perhaps more importantly, he promised to reimburse investors for their losses in pyramid schemes. In a speech at a rally in Vlorë on 9 June, the Socialist Party leader said his party was "committed to using every opportunity and to ensuring special resources to refund and compensate the money lost in the firms that have been declared bankrupt."[75] Nano's statement was seen as highly irresponsible. Even Fino disavowed Nano's promise. He told an Italian newspaper: "No Albanian politician should in any way attempt to turn such a sensitive issue to his own electoral advantage by telling the people lies. I believe that no one is in a position to refund that money."[76]

If there had been any doubts about the Socialists' ties with armed rebels in the south, they were dispelled during the election campaign. While campaigning in Vlorë, Gjirokastër, and Sarandë, Nano, Gjinushi and other leftist leaders were surrounded and protected both by leaders of the national salvation committees and by criminal groups, including gangster Myrteza Çaushi, popularly known as Zani. Moreover, several prominent rebels appeared on the election lists of the three leftist parties or ran as independent candidates. Albert Shyti, the leader of the salvation committee in Vlorë, who had publicly threatened to kill Berisha, ran as a candidate of the Social Democratic Party.[77] Despite having signed several agreements that called for the disbanding of rebel committees, Nano refused to urge the armed gangs to disband, using them as a lever to extract concessions from the Democrats. Indeed, Nano was quoted as telling the Italian ambassador to Tiranë, "We'll keep them in case of emergency."[78] The Socialists used the armed gangs to incite violence and prevent Democratic Party candidates from campaigning in the south.

The absence of a powerful third alternative worked in favor of the Socialists. The Social Democratic Party and the Democratic Alliance allied themselves closely with the Socialists, in effect becoming appendages of the latter party. As in 1996, the right was unable to offer a viable alternative. The Movement for Democracy also did not have enough time to develop into a real party, nor were its leaders viewed as credible. After all, founders of the Movement for Democracy had served in senior government and party positions, and bore direct responsibility for the crisis that had engulfed the country. Thus, in the end, it was again a race between the Socialists and the Democrats.[79]

The Results

On 29 June, in an atmosphere of high tension, Albanians defied the threat of violence and turned out in large numbers to cast their ballots in a contest that many regarded as a plebiscite on Berisha's stewardship. The elections were marred by shootings, with gunmen menacing voters, burning ballots, and pressuring polling officials. In the predominant majority of districts in the south, Democratic Party representatives could not take their seats in the local polling commissions. Despite these problems, however, the voting proceeded without large-scale violence. Voter turnout was reported at 72.96 percent: 1,308,023 out of 2,031,342 registered voters cast their ballots in the first round.

The results of the elections provided evidence of an angry electorate, deeply disappointed with the Democratic Party's stewardship. The Socialist Party scored a decisive victory, capturing 79 of the 115 seats contested under a straight majority vote, or 52.71 percent of the vote. The Socialists also won another 22 seats of the 40 allocated under a proportional system. Altogether, the Socialist Party won 101 seats. The Social Democratic and Democratic Alliance Parties benefitted from their close association with the Socialist Party, winning 9 seats, or 2.49 percent of the vote, and 2 seats, or 2.73 percent, respectively. The Agrarian and National Unity Parties, two other small groupings allied with the Socialists, won 1 seat each. The Union for Human Rights, which represented the ethnic Greek minority, won 4 seats.

The Socialists' victory was not confined to their traditional power base in the south. They demonstrated a truly national reach, making significant inroads in Tiranë, Shkodër, Kavajë, Elbasan, and other traditional Democratic strongholds. The Socialists had capitalized on the widespread disenchantment and economic hardship created by the collapse of the pyramid schemes. Many voted for the Socialists more out of anger with the Democrats than in support of the Socialists' plans, although many appear to have believed Nano's campaign promise to reimburse those who had lost savings in the failed get-rich-quick schemes.

In a stinging rebuke, Berisha's Democratic Party was reduced to 27 seats in parliament; and 3 of those 27 seats were ceded to the three small parties that had concluded a preelection alliance with the Democrats and were included in the Democratic Party's proportional list (Table 9.1). In the previous legislature, the Democratic Party had held 122 of 140 seats. The Democrats were completely wiped out in the south, and suffered a dramatic drop in support in central and north Albania. Leading Democrats, including former Prime Minister Aleksandër Meksi, party Chairman Tritan Shehu, party Deputy Chairman Ali Spahia, former Interior Minister Halit Shamata, Secretary General Genc Pollo, and Berisha's top adviser Fatos Beja, were defeated in direct electoral contests. The Democrats did not win a single constituency in Tiranë; they also lost in Kavajë, their traditional stronghold. Albanians surveyed with amazement the near obliteration of the Democratic Party.

Election results indicated that Albania remained essentially a two-party system. Between the two of them, the Democratic and Socialist parties garnered more than two-thirds of the general vote. Only the Social Democratic Party did relatively well, gaining 9 seats, but this was thanks to its preelection coalition with the Socialists.

Surprisingly, support for the restoration of the monarchy was higher than expected, particularly in the northern regions of the country. Leka Zogu, the claimant to the Albanian throne, who returned to Albania in April 1997, had campaigned hard, traveling throughout the country and conveying a message of "peace, unity, and brotherhood." Official results indicated that 66.74 percent of voters opted for a republic, while 33.26 percent chose the monarchy.[80] However, Leka Zogu said that data compiled by his supporters showed that more than 50 percent of Albanian voters had voted for the restoration of the monarchy. He alleged that the Socialists had manipulated the results.

TABLE 9.1 Albania's 1997 Parliamentary Elections

	Votes*	% of votes	Seats	% of seats
Socialist Party	690,003	52.71	101	65.1
Democratic Party	336,167	25.82	24**	15.5
Social Democratic Party	32,537	2.49	9	5.8
Union for Human Rights	37,191	2.71	4	2.5
National Front	30,693	2.34	3	1.9
Legality	42,567	3.28	2	1.3
Democratic Alliance	35,598	2.73	2	1.3
Republican Party	31,573	2.41	1	0.6
Social Democratic Union	10,457	0.80	1	0.6
Christian Democratic Party	12,728	0.98	1	0.6
Democratic Union Party	10,997	0.84	1	0.6
National Unity Party	3,784	0.29	1	0.6
Agrarian Party	10,421	0.80	1	0.6
Right Democratic Party	9,837	0.76	—	—
Movement for Democracy	3,802	0.29	—	—
Christian Democratic Union	3,734	0.29	—	—
Conservative Party	3,400	0.26	—	—
National Covenant Party	1,865	0.14	—	—
Democratic Progress Party	669	0.05	—	—
United Right Coalition	—	—	1	0.6
Independents	—	—	3	1.9
Total	1,308,023	100.00	155	99.5
Voter turnout			72.96 percent	

*First round of voting, 29 June 1997.

** The Democratic Party won 27 seats but ceded three of its proportional seats to the leaders of the Social Democratic Union and the Christian Democratic and Democratic Union Parties.

Sources: Central Electoral Commission, *Buletin: Rezultatet e Zgjedhjeve Parlamentare, Qershor 1997* [Bulletin: The Results of the June 1997 Parliamentary Elections] (Tiranë, 1997), pp. 62-63, and 69.

Under OSCE auspices, more than 800 international monitors, including 112 parliamentarians, observed the elections, with the multinational protection force providing logistical and security support. Their ability to do so effectively was questionable given the security situation and the large security details that followed them everywhere they went. Moreover, despite the large number of foreign monitors, OSCE teams were able to observe voting at only a fraction of the more than four thousand polling stations throughout the country. Most observers saw the elections as less than fair.[81] Clearly, the Democratic Party was prevented from fairly contesting seats throughout large parts of the country. Nevertheless, the OSCE was eager to give its stamp of approval and glossed over serious irregularities, ignoring the total lack of the rule of law and the inherently undemocratic conditions under which the balloting was held. A day after the elections, Catherine Lalumiere, the special coordinator for the international election observers, said that "the elections can be considered as adequate and acceptable." While acknowledging that there were some serious problems with the counting process in a few electoral districts, Lalumiere said that "voters were generally able to cast their ballots without fear or intimidation."[82] In its final report, the OSCE wrote: "These elections can be deemed as acceptable given the prevailing circumstances. They should constitute the foundation for a strong, democratic system that the Albanians want and deserve."[83] Given the anti-Berisha slant in Western capitals, however, it is questionable that the OSCE would have considered the June 1997 elections "acceptable" had the Democrats won. The international community's isolation of the pro-Western Democrats and its embrace of the Socialists was a major contributing factor to the Socialist Party's stunning victory.

The United States, Italy, and other West European countries praised the elections. However, in many respects, the much-criticized 1996 balloting was cleaner than the June 1997 elections. As a *Daily Telegraph* editorial put it, the elections were forced on Berisha "by the gun, and the scale of the Socialist victory was achieved by the same intimidatory means."[84] Given the circumstances under which the elections were held, the balloting indeed did not reflect the political will of the Albanian electorate. By validating such deeply flawed elections, the international community compromised its own standards of free and fair elections and sent the wrong message, thereby legitimizing the Socialist-inspired insurrection.

A day after the elections, and before the final results were announced, Berisha conceded victory. In a nationally televised address, the president said that although the elections had taken place "in a very abnormal" situation, he would respect the results. He urged his supporters to respect the people's verdict and work for the consolidation of democracy in Albania.[85] The president resigned on 23 July. In a statement to parliament, Berisha accused the Socialists of having exploited the pyramid schemes crisis to organize a "Communist, armed rebellion," and added: "I hope that the times to come will grant all Albanians the opportunity to reassess again with cool heads the five years of democracy and the five months of the rebellion."[86]

Meanwhile, in early August, less than two months after the elections, the last soldiers of the Italian-led multinational force withdrew from Albania. The U.N. Security Council praised the mission as a success.[87] But although Western officials were quick to praise Rome for having organized and led the force, the reality was that the mission had done little to address Albania's real needs, while it raised serious concerns about European peacekeeping or peace making operations that lack NATO or U.S. leadership. As an American analyst put it:

> The lessons for European peacekeeping are sobering. Italy—starkly faced with a serious influx of Albanian refugees—barely mustered the political cohesion to implement even this limited mission. The Italians and others proved willing to "declare victory" and go home, despite the shortcomings and failures of the mission and the international intervention as a whole to address the fundamental breakdown of authority in the country. As during the war in Bosnia, Europe has again failed to fulfill even its own minimalist, risk-averse mission in response to violence that threatens the region's security. Absent U.S. leadership, Europe has failed another test of its own resolve and ability to face tough post-Cold War challenges.[88]

The Socialist Comeback

Despite the country's political polarization, the transition from the Democrats to the Socialists was orderly. Nano became prime minister, while Rexhep Meidani, a physicist who had joined the Socialist Party in 1996, replaced Berisha as president. The Socialists emphasized that real power would be concentrated in the hands of the prime minister and that the post of president would be symbolic. Nano formed a coalition government, which in addition to members of his party, included representatives from the Social Democratic, Democratic Alliance, Agrarian, and Human Rights Parties. The Socialists reserved for themselves thirteen of the twenty-two cabinet posts. Interim Prime Minister Bashkim Fino became deputy prime minister. Kastriot Islami, a close Nano ally who had served briefly as minister of education in 1991, was appointed minister of state "to the prime minister." Sabit Brokaj, considered one of the most hard-line members of the Socialist leadership, who played a major role in organizing the rebellion in Vlorë, received the defense portfolio. Ylli Bufi, who had served as minister of food in Adil Çarçani's government and as prime minister of the coalition government in 1991, was placed in charge of the ministry of public economy and privatization. Arben Malaj, minister of finance in Fino's government, retained his post. The Social Democratic Party's Paskal Milo and Gaqo Apostoli were appointed ministers of foreign affairs and public works and transportation, respectively. The Democratic Alliance also received two ministerial portfolios: Neritan Ceka was appointed minister of internal affairs, and Arben Imami, minister of institutional reforms. The leader of the Agrarian Party, Lufter Xhuveli, became minister of agriculture. The health ministry went to Leonard Solis of the Human Rights Party. Thimio Kondi, a former member of the Constitutional Court, became minister of justice.[89] Skendër Gjinushi, the chairman of the Social Democratic Party, took over as speaker of parliament.

The selection of cabinet members did cause some rumblings within the Socialist Party. Nano refused to submit the names of his cabinet members for prior approval to the party's highest body. In turn, members of the party's General Steering Committee accused the prime minister of dictatorial tendencies. Perhaps the biggest criticism of the new cabinet was that it contained too many ministers from the last Communist government and few reformers. It was questionable whether old guard members of the cabinet, including Nano, were up to the tasks facing the country. With one or two exceptions, the cabinet suffered from a lack of talented, non-Marxist trained economists. The reformist wing of the party complained that no reformers were included in the cabinet.[90] This could lead to problems for Nano in the future and may foreshadow a split within the party. In autumn 1996, there were indications that the reformist wing, under Ilir Meta's leadership, were planning to establish a separate party. These plans were thwarted by the subsequent revolt. Nevertheless, Nano was likely to face increased challenges from a younger generation that appeared poised in the wings.

Another criticism was that Nano had given influential positions to leaders of parties allied with the Socialists, although those parties enjoyed very limited popular support. It was obvious that some of the ministers were selected purely for political reasons and not because they were necessarily the best qualified candidates. Neritan Ceka was a dubious choice for minister of internal affairs, a traditionally powerful post that controls the police and local government. There was nothing in Ceka's background that would qualify him for the job. Moreover, he was known for outrageous claims and statements directed at his opponents. But perhaps the most problematic selection was that of Arben Imami, a political radical who in March 1997 had joined rebels in the south.[91] Ironically, a man who under normal conditions would have been put on trial for leading an armed revolt against the country's constitutional order was put in charge of introducing sweeping institutional reforms and drafting a new constitution. The prime minister apparently wanted to be seen as sharing responsibility for governing the country with other forces. But perhaps more importantly, he hoped to assure the international community that he had assembled an inclusive governing group to lead the country to political and economic recovery—a condition for sustained international assistance.

The turmoil that followed the collapse of pyramid schemes indicated significant regional division. However, Nano's government was the most regionally biased government since Hoxha's regime in the 1950s and 1960s. Seventeen of the twenty-two ministers and state secretaries in the new cabinet, plus the president and the speaker of parliament, were from the south. Nano's failure to reach out to the north, where the former Communists are deeply distrusted, raised doubts as to whether he was up to the tasks of healing his country's divisions.

The Socialist government confronted three immediate tasks: restoring law and order, initiating a process of national reconciliation, and reviving the flagging economy and putting the country's finances back into basic order. Soon after the government was formed, special police forces were sent from Tiranë to the primary urban centers in the south, including Vlorë. By the end of November 1997, Albania seemed to have achieved a degree of order and stability, but the security situation remained tenuous. The government had not yet succeeded in fully regaining physical control throughout Albania and maintaining its administrative presence in all parts of the country. The campaign to collect weapons from civilians had yielded discouraging results. Moreover, in certain areas of the country, the government appeared to have agreed to share power with pro-Socialist criminals who had played a major disruptive role during the election campaign.[92] This could open the way to political influence for criminals, drug traffickers and mafia groups. Italians were particularly concerned that Albania was becoming a hub for powerful mafia networks engaged in smuggling drugs, weapons, and illegal immigrants.

The full normalization of the security situation will depend on how rapidly the Albanians rebuild their police and armed forces. Many of the new police recruits appear to have little or no professional training in fundamental human rights practices and in correct behavior with the public. However, the West European Union has agreed to send dozens of experts to help train and equip Albania's police forces. Although NATO, in the framework of its Partnership for Peace program, appeared to be in the best position to help Albania rebuild its army, the Western alliance, its rhetoric notwithstanding, was moving too slowly, leaving Greece and Italy to fill the vacuum. But Athens and Rome, both of whom signed military cooperation agreements with Tiranë, had ulterior motives and were already engaged in a struggle for influence in Albania, with Greece being favored by Nano and his Foreign Minister, Milo. Nano was widely believed to be under strong Greek influence, one factor being that his family moved to Greece while he was in prison. His foreign policy tilt toward Greece caused a strong reaction among Albanians, with some expressing concern about the "Hellenization" of southern Albania.[93] Although Italy had organized and led the multinational force, Albania chose to sign its first military cooperation agreement with Greece. The agreement stipulated that Greek officers would help in the reorganization of the Albanian army.[94] After the withdrawal of the multinational forces, a residual Greek force remained in Albania to help rebuild the army. Greek Prime Minister Costas Simitis became the first foreign head of state to visit Tiranë after the formation of the new government. Simitis promised that Greece would support Albania's political and economic reform efforts.[95] Nano's preferential treatment of Greece seems to have caused considerable consternation in Rome. While it remains to be seen how developments will unfold, given the history of Tiranë's troubled relations with its two neighbors, it seems a bad idea to have Greece or Italy oversee Albania's political reconstruction, let alone rebuild the Albanian military. Albania's long-term national interests, as well as stability in the region, would have been better served if these tasks were performed by more neutral parties.

Tiranë also faced daunting external security challenges. As Janusz Bugajski noted, the situation in Kosova was approaching boiling point. Growing sectors of Kosova's population had become disenchanted with Ibrahim Rugova's pacifist policies, Belgrade had shown no sign of seeking a compromise with Prishtinë, and Kosovar Albanians were losing faith in the international community's efforts to bring Slobodan Milošević to the negotiating table.[96] Nano's government not only failed to take any steps to develop contingency plans to deal with a possible conflict on its borders but chose this inauspicious time to hold senior-level bilateral talks with Belgrade without any conditions on progress on the Kosova issue. In a move that reflected the strong Greek influence over Albania's foreign policy and Athens' attempts to rehabilitate Milošević, Nano met the Serbian leader at a Balkan summit meeting in Crete. The two leaders reportedly agreed that Serbia would grant ethnic Albanians basic human rights but not autonomy, and that Tiranë and Belgrade would exchange ambassadors.[97] Ironically, Nano chose to engage the Yugoslavs, accept that the issue of Kosova was Serbia's internal affair, and upgrade relations with Belgrade at the cost of support for Prishtinë and a time when the United States and the international community were still treating Yugoslavia as a rogue state and were calling for a special status for Kosova. As Patrick Moore noted, the Nano-Milošević meeting may have served only to exacerbate the situation in Kosova.[98] Soon after the Nano-Milošević meeting, violence in Kosova increased sharply with several Albanians and Serbs being killed. This spate of violence coincided with the a trial of seventeen ethnic Albanians accused of membership in the Kosova Liberation Army. Albania's new policy toward Serbia was peculiarly divisive and a source of mutual recrimination between the government and the opposition, particularly the Democrats.[99] It also met with universal opposition in Kosova.[100]

In addition to the security issue, the Socialists also faced a serious challenge in reviving the flagging economy. Albanians had wasted a tremendous opportunity and now had to start from the beginning. During the campaign, Nano had been vague about his economic policies, with the exception of his promise to make job creation a primary goal. Following the elections, however, he espoused the conservative, pro-market economic policies that were championed by the Democratic Party. He pledged to proceed with the privatization of large and medium-sized enterprises, fully liberalize the economy, establish private banks, and heed the IMF's advice on Albania's microeconomic reconstruction.[101] Previously sharp critics of Berisha's strategy of total privatization, the Socialists announced that they would favor the privatization of strategic sectors, including oil, power, mineral industries, water resources, and tourism. Nano also backtracked from his scandalous campaign pledge to give investors the money they had lost in pyramid schemes.[102]

In collaboration with the IMF and the World Bank, the government launched a short-term program to initiate macroeconomic stabilization. The IMF announced a $12 million package of post-conflict emergency assistance, a type of assistance previously provided only to Bosnia and Rwanda. In an attempt to stabilize the soaring Albanian budget deficit, the authorities agreed to increase the value-added tax from 12.5 percent to 20 percent. On 22 October, a donors' conference, held in Brussels, reaffirmed the international community's commitment to help Albania, but conditioned aid on the strengthening of democratic institutions, the restoration of security, the closing down of the remaining pyramid schemes, and the adoption of sound economic policies. The conference pledged some $100 million to cover balance-of-payment and budgetary needs for the six-month period from October 1997 to March 1998. An additional $500 million was pledged for the next three years for investments and technical assistance.[103]

Although the Brussels conference gave the government a much-needed boost, Albania still faced serious economic difficulties. The voters who handed the Socialist Party a landslide victory expected Nano to respond swiftly to the persistent economic hardships stemming particularly from high inflation and growing unemployment. An estimated one million Albanians were living in poverty, with unemployment encompassing as much as 30 percent of the labor force. However, Nano had yet to take bold steps toward realizing his pledges for social and economic reform. Indeed, the process of change was slow and incremental and there appeared to be a total disconnect between the authorities and the populace. Nano's government was increasingly seen as unable to deliver on its promises, thus setting the stage for disappointment. There was a deep gap between words and deeds, as the government, seemingly afflicted by semi-paralysis, appeared unable to provide real leadership. Public dissatisfaction was likely to increase as the deleterious social effects of economic reforms were felt.

With the June 1997 elections and the peaceful transfer of power, Albania had weathered a serious trauma. The Albanians had a second chance to repair their democracy and build a viable, legitimate pluralist polity. But the elections can offer the hope of peace and stability only if they are followed by a genuine political opening and national reconciliation.

Notes

1. See Miranda Vickers and James Pettifer, *From Anarchy to a Balkan Identity* (New York: New York University Press, 1997), pp. 266-290.

2. *Rilindja Demokratike*, 5 September 1996, p. 1.

3. The elections were closely watched by the international community to ensure that the balloting was free and fair. On the eve of the elections, the OSCE's Office for Democratic Institutions and Human Rights withdrew when the Albanian authorities agreed to accredit only fifteen of its thirty-seven monitors. In a sign of solidarity with ODIHR, the OSCE's Parliamentary Assembly also withdrew its monitors. But the elections were monitored by several hundred observers from the Council of Europe, the United States, Italy, and other countries and organizations.

4. ATA in English, 2025 GMT, 30 October 1996, in FBIS-EEU 96-213, 30 October 1996; and *OMRI Daily Digest*, no. 210, part II, 30 October 1996, and no. 123, part II, 4 November 1996.

5. National Democratic Institute for International Affairs, *Preliminary Statement of the International Observer Delegation to the Albanian Local Elections* (Washington, D.C.), 22 October 1996. See also Bob Hand, "Albania's Local Elections Held Amidst Controversy," *CSCE Digest* 19, no. 11 (November 1996), p. 5.

6. Blendi Fevziu, "The Opposition Lost Everything It Had," *Koha Jonë*, 22 October 1996, p. 2.

7. Vladimir Prela, "Much Ado About Nothing," *Koha Jonë*, 3 November 1996, p. 1.

8. See Meta's interview in *Gazeta Shqiptare*, 30 October 1996, p. 3. A commentary in the Socialist Party newspaper asserted that the party had lost contact with the electorate and its rank and file. It added that the Socialists' electoral chances also were hurt by the fact that they had not clearly dissociated themselves from their Communist past. See Spiro Leshnica, "Why the Socialist Party Lost [the Elections]?" *Zëri i Popullit*, 2 November 1996, p. 6.

9. B. Z., "Eurosocialist Youth Forum in Conflict With the Party," *Dita Informacion*, 26 November 1996, p. 2.

10. "A Natural Victory," *Rilindja Demokratike*, 23 October 1996, p. 1.

11. U.S. Department of State, Office of the Spokesman, *Albania: Local Elections*, 31 October 1996. The U.S. position was reaffirmed immediately after President Bill Clinton's reelection in November 1996. Undersecretary of State for Global Affairs Timothy Wirth emphasized: "One of our foremost objectives with Albania is to promote democratic development, including an inclusive constitutional process and parliamentary elections organized under the new constitutional framework. We have no intention of abandoning this effort" (See Under Secretary of State for Global Affairs Timothy Wirth's letter to the editor in *New York Times*, 9 November 1996, p. 22).

12. The European Commission, *Central and Eastern Eurobarometer* (Brussels), no. 7 (1997), pp. 11-18.

13. Elez Biberaj, Peter R. Mueser, Robin Remington, and Mircea T. Maniu, "Land Mines on the Road to Market Economies in Romania and Albania: Pyramid Schemes and Individual Investment in the 1990s," *Occasional Papers*, no. 9707 (May 1997), St. Louis: University of Missouri, Center for International Studies.

14. Former Prime Minister Meksi put the figure at "no more than $500 million to $600 million." See interview with Meksi in *Klan* (Tiranë) 1, no. 11, 15 June 1997, p. 21.

15. Arben Iliazi, "Vefa's Business and the Pyramids of the Press," *Albania*, 2 November 1996, p. 3.

16. *The Independent*, 14 February 1997.

17. See Blerim Çela's interview, "I Do Not Believe the Money-Borrowing Firms Will Go Bankrupt," *Albania*, 21 November 1996, p. 3.

18. Arben Kallamata, "Foul Political Speculation Over Moneylending," *Albania*, 14 November 1996, p. 3.

19. *Gazeta Shqiptare* reporter Andrea Stefani has suggested that the IMF and the World Bank, which had representatives in Albania and followed developments there closely, must share at least some blame for not publicly warning of the impending danger. Stefani wrote: "Prestigious financial institutions with long experience and strong forecasting ability were present during this ongoing march of Albanians to their catastrophe and did not warn of it. Why? In the best of cases, because they were blind to it. If this were the case, does it not constitute a scandal in itself? The IMF experts made their concern over the pyramid investment schemes public by the end of [1996], when it was too late. By that time, their words were not alarm bells but the death knell. This goes to show that the tragedy that had already begun cannot carry the exclusive label 'Made in Albania.'" Andrea Stefani, "Pyramids and the Collapse of Albanian Economy: Did IMF Betray Us?" *Gazeta Shqiptare*, 29 April 1997, p. 1. Stefani was very critical also of the role of Albanian banks, accusing them of "an alliance with the pyramid schemes." See Andrea Stefani, "'96: When the Banks Became Pyramids," *Klan* 1, no. 10 (8 June 1997), pp. 28-29.

20. Ben Blushi, "The Government Trifles With Moneylending," *Koha Jonë*, 8 October 1996, p. 7.

21. Zylfo Veledi, "Interest and Dormant Albanian Capital," *Albania*, 30 October 1996, p. 3.

22. A. Kola, "Should the Albanians Continue to Play With Moneylending?" *Republika*, 16 November 1996, p. 4. Only days after *Gazeta Shqiptare* warned of the imminent collapse of Sudja pyramid schemes, *Republika* assured Sudja depositors that their payments were "guaranteed" for "at least the next three years." A. Kola, "This Is How You Should Invest In Return for Interest," *Republika*, 17 November 1996, p. 6.

23. Sandër Grunasi left Albania on 6 November 1996, reportedly using an official passport. See *Zëri i Popullit*, 23 January 1997, p. 9.

24. *Albania*, 24 January 1997, p. 3.

25. Tiranë TVSH Television Network in Albanian, 1900 GMT, 16 January 1997, in FBIS-EEU 97-012, 16 January 1997.

26. ATA in English, 2158 GMT, 24 January 1997, in FBIS-EEU 97-017, 24 January 1997.

27. See Rrapush Xhaferri's interview in *Albania*, 23 January 1997, p. 3. Bashkim Driza had worked for Xhaferri but in July 1996, he set up his own company, Populli. Ironically, Driza is head of the People's Party, a left-wing party with close links to the Socialist Party.

28. Kevin Done and Kerin Hope, "Violence as Fourth Albanian Fund Collapses," *Financial Times*, 6 February 1997, p. 2.

29. See comments by opposition leaders Skendër Gjinushi, Neritan Ceka, and Kastriot Islami, *Koha Jonë*, 6 February 1997, p. 3.

30. In a commentary on the occasion of the sixth anniversary of the student demonstrations that forced the Communists to permit the establishment of opposition parties, Ben Blushi wrote: "Where are we Albanians, who lit a fire in the winter of 1990 for want of some electrical wiring? Where are we Albanians, when not far away from us, in Serbia, student protests are uprooting the system? ... [It] appears that the Albanians have lost one thing that they possessed six years ago, the spirit of protest." Blushi sharply criticized the opposition for its failure to organize protests against Berisha, adding that the opposition "has been turned into a branch of the state." Ben Blushi, "8 December 1990, Day of Protest Against the Regime," *Koha Jonë*, 8 December 1996, p. 1.

31. G.L., "Milošević Surrenders, Berisha Not Yet," *Koha Jonë*, 6 February 1997, p. 1.

32. *Koha Jonë*, 9 February 1997, p. 2.

33. *Zëri i Popullit*, 14 February 1997, p. 4.

34. Zef Brozi, "Statement Regarding Albania Crisis," Fairfax, VA, 30 January 1997. In a subsequent article, Brozi termed Berisha's regime "the most barbaric and bloody" dictatorship ever experienced by the Albanians. He said people were justified in taking up arms against the government, calling the insurrection "a democratic revolution." Zef Brozi, "Albania at the Crossroads, but Not Without Hope," *Koha Jonë*, 11 June 1997, p. 8.

35. *Rilindja Demokratike*, 21 February 1997, p. 1.

36. For a critical view of the American position on the Albanian crisis, see Daniel McAdams, "U.S. Role in Albania Red Revival?" *Washington Times*, 17 March 1997, p. A15. See also James Phillips, "Albania's Democracy Hijacked By Socialists," *Washington Times*, 27 March 1997, p. A15, Jonathan Sunley, "Small War in Albania," *Salisbury Review*, Autumn 1997, pp. 33-39; and Mark Almond, "Behind Albania's Chaos," *Wall Street Journal*, 14 March 1997.

37. ATA in English, 0036 GMT, 16 February 1997, in FBIS-EEU 97-032, 19 February 1997.

38. *Rilindja Demokratike*, 2 March 1997, p. 1.

39. Ibid., 4 March 1997, p. 3.

40. The text of the law on the state of emergency was published in *Fletorja Zyrtare e Republikës së Shqipërisë*, no. 2, March 1997, pp. 44-45. Unknown arsonists, widely believed to be associated with the secret police, burned *Koha Jonë*'s office in Tiranë. This prompted the New York-based Committee to Protect Journalists to name Berisha among the world's ten "enemies of the press." ("CPJ Names 10 Enemies of the Press on World Press Freedom Day, May 3," Committee to Protect Journalists, New York, 3 May 1997.)

41. *Rilindja Demokratike*, 4 March 1997, p. 1.

42. U.S. Department of State, *Daily Press Briefing Index*, 3 March 1997.

43. Radio Tiranë in English, 1715 GMT, 6 March 1997, in FBIS-EEU 97-065, 6 March 1997.

44. Paradoxically, Koçiu was managing director of Vefa in Sarandë. Lara Santoro, "Civilian Revolt in Albania: Rage Gives Rise to Militias," *Christian Science Monitor*, 10 March 1997, p. 6.

45. See interview with Ridvan Peshkëpia in *Flaka e Vëllazërimit*, 22 March 1997, p. 7.

46. See Defense Minister Shaqir Vukaj's testimony before the Albanian parliament on 23 April 1997, in *Zëri i Popullit*, 25 April 1997, p. 2.

47. *Rilindja Demokratike*, 11 March 1997, p. 1.

48. *Der Spiegel* (Hamburg), 3 March 1997, pp. 166-169, translated in FBIS-EEU 97-055, 3 March 1997.

49. Gjolek Malaj, a rebel commander from the town of Memaliaj, warned that if Berisha did not resign, the rebels were "prepared to send people to bombard him." He told reporters that fifty men were already on their way to Tiranë to arrest the president. Reuter, 11:30 EST, 20 March 1997.

50. ATA in English, 1229 GMT, 13 March 1997, in FBIS-EEU 97-072, 15 March 1997.

51. Quoted in Jane Perlez, "Albania Arming a New Police Force," *New York Times,* 16 March 1997, p. 12.

52. Charles Trueheart, "Italy Declares Emergency to Handle Albanian Influx," *Washington Post,* 20 March 1997, p. A23.

53. John M. Goshko, "U.N. Approves Italy-Led Force for Albania," *Washington Post,* 29 March 1997, A14; and Paul Lewis, "U.N. Backs Sending Troops to Restore Order in Albania," *New York Times,* 29 March 1997, p. 4. See also Bob Hand, "Albanian Turmoil Causes the International Community to Respond," *CSCE Digest* 20, no. 5 (May 1997), pp. 44, 58.

54. "U.S. Says Berisha Should Quit," *Financial Times,* 15-16 March 1997. See also Steven Lee Myers, "U.S. Long Shot in Albania Fails to Pay Off," *New York Times,* 20 March 1997, p. A6.

55. "Albania in Anarchy," *Newshour with Jim Lehrer,* 14 March 1997.

56. ATA in English, 1831 GMT, 8 April 1997, in FBIS-EEU 97-098, 8 April 1997.

57. *Die Presse* (Vienna), 10 April 1997, p. 3, translated in FBIS-EEU 97-100, 11 April 1997.

58. ATA in English, 2009 GMT, 26 March 1997, FBIS-EEU 97-085, 28 March 1997.

59. Lara Santoro, "Albania's Chaos Begins to Form Political Order," *Christian Science Monitor,* 18 March 1997, p. 5.

60. The more conservative members of the Socialist Party openly called for the violent overthrow of President Berisha. Writer Dritëro Agolli went so far as to accuse the Socialist and other opposition parties of having "betrayed the [anti-Berisha] democratic revolution." Agolli argued that rebel committees should not give up their arms until Berisha was forced out of power. See Agolli's interview in *Koha Jonë,* 23 May 1997, p. 13.

61. Rome RAI Radio Uno Network in Italian, 0700 GMT, 29 March 1997, translated in FBIS-EEU 97-088, 1 April 1997.

62. Tanjug in English, 1451 GMT, 1 October 1997 in FBIS-EEU 97-274, 2 October 1997.

63. Skopje MIC in English, 18 March 1997 in FBIS-EEU 97-077, 19 March 1997.

64. Guy Dinmore, "Macedonia's Volatile Ethnic Mixture Approaches the Boil," *Financial Times,* 22 July 1997, p. 3.

65. Editorial "Coalition of (Dis)Trust?" *Dnevnik* (Skopje), 21 July 1997, p. 6, translated in FBIS-EEU 97-203, 23 July 1997. See also Fabian Schmidt, "Western Macedonia's Vicious Circle of Violence," *RFE/RL Newsline* 1, no. 73, part II, 15 July 1997; and Aleksandar Damovski, "The EU's White Gloves for the Macedonian 'Sides,'" *Dnevnik,* translated in FBIS-EEU 97-210, 30 July 1997. As a Macedonian journalist noted, the government had given the Albanians a stern warning, but without taking into account the possible long-term repercussions of its actions: "Those events were a significant message, directed to every Albanian, for them to feel humiliated and psychologically abused, so that all of them, regardless of whether they were loyal or not, will understand

that in this "democratic and civil" oriented Macedonia, there is only one ruler—the Macedonians. ... The Albanians understood this message very well this time. ... It was very clear for all to see: The recordings broadcast on TV were repeated so often that only the blind could not see how the police of "all citizens" is trampling on people lying on the sidewalks, older men, who raised their hands to show that they were not armed ..., and every Albanian during these moments had to feel on his body the heavy boot of the police. Such unimaginable brutality ... was in fact "psychological torture" intended to instill fear in every Albanian." Skopje MIC in English, 17 July 1997 in FBIS-EEU 97-199, 21 July 1997.

66. *Rilindja Demokratike,* 10 May 1997, p. 1.

67. *Fletorja Zyrtare e Republikës së Shqipërisë,* no. 6, May 1997, pp. 105-117.

68. Ibid., pp. 118-119.

69. Daniel McAdams, "Admitting Defeat in the Albanian Elections," *Strategy and Policy* (Washington, D.C.: Balkan Institute), 26 June 1997, p. 1.

70. National Democratic Institute for International Affairs, *Statement of the National Democratic Institute for International Affairs (NDI) Pre-Election Delegation to the 1997 Albanian Parliamentary Elections,* Tiranë, 15 June 1997.

71. *Zëri i Popullit,* 24 June 1997, p. 1.

72. "Pact for the Government of Albania and the Reconstruction of Democratic Institutions," *Zëri i Popullit,* 28 June 1997, p. 2.

73. "The Democratic Party's Program to Stabilize Public Order, Overcome the Crisis, and Revive the Country Economically (Emergency Phase)—How We Will Extract Albania From Chaos," *Rilindja Demokratike,* 8 June 1997, p. 2.

74. See the Socialist Party's electoral platform in *Zëri i Popullit,* 27 June 1997, pp. 8-9.

75. *Zëri i Popullit,* 10 June 1997, p. 3.

76. *La Repubblica* (Rome), 13 June 1997, p. 15.

77. In an interview, Shyti declared that regardless of the election results, the president must go. "Dead or alive, we will topple Sali Berisha from his throne on 30 June, if a free ballot does not do this." *Albania,* 8 June 1997, p. 5.

78. *Washington Times,* 29 June 1997, p. A6.

79. For an in-depth analysis of the 1997 elections sees Shinasi A. Rama, "Failed Transition: Elite Fragmentation and the Parliamentary Elections of June 29, 1997," *International Journal of Albanian Studies* 1, no. 1 (Fall 1997), pp. 82-125. See also Misha Glenny, "Albania: Heart of Darkness," *New York Review of Books* XLIV, no.13, 14 August 1997, pp. 32-36; and Richard W. Carlson, "Observing the Albanian Powder Keg," *American Spectator,* November 1997, pp. 43-47.

80. Radio Tiranë Network in Albanian, 1330 GMT, 14 July 1997, translated in FBIS-EEU 97-195, 16 July 1997.

81. Jonathan Sunley, "Albania's Elections Taint the Victor," *Wall Street Journal Europe,* 2 July 1997, p. 8.

82. *International Herald Tribune,* 1 July 1997, p. 5.

83. Organization for Security and Cooperation in Europe, *Final Report: Parliamentary Elections in Albania, 29 June-6 July 1997* (Warsaw), July 1997, p. 1. See also U.S. Commission on Security and Cooperation in Europe, *Albania's Parliamentary Elections of 1997* (Washington, D.C.), July 1997.

84. "Free, But Not Fair," *Daily Telegraph,* 2 July 1997.

85. *Rilindja Demokratike,* 1 July 1997, p. 1.

86. Radio Tiranë Network in Albanian, 1330 GMT, 23 July 1997, translated in FBIS-EEU 97-204, 24 July 1997.

87. United Nations Daily Highlights, 14 August 1997.

88. "Operation Alba's Disappointing Legacy," *Military Watch* (Washington, D.C.: Balkan Institute) 2, no. 16, 7 August 1997, p. 1.

89. *Zëri i Popullit,* 26 July 1997, p. 3.

90. Adrian Cani, "The Socialist Party Divides Power, Pinpoints New Leaders," *Gazeta Shqiptare,* 24 July 1997, p. 2.

91. See interview with Arben Imami in *Koha Jonë,* 16 April 1997, p. 4.

92. The Memaliaj rebel leader Gjolek Malaj was given permission by the Nano government to establish a "private police force." Malaj told the press that he had turned down an offer to take a senior position in Ceka's Ministry of Internal Affairs. See *Koha Jonë,* 12 October 1997, p. 19.

93. See Hysamedin Ferraj, "Brokaj Will Defend Greece From Albania," *Albania,* 10 August 1997, p. 4; and Koço Mandri, "Political Business Offer," *Republika,* 5 August 1997, p. 2; and editorial "Pangalos' Anti-Italian Inventory," *Albania,* 6 August 1997, p. 1.

94. Neritan Alibali, "The Italians Leave Albania," *Republika,* 8 August 1997, p. 3.

95. *Zëri i Popullit,* 16 October 1997, pp. 1-5.

96. Janusz Bugajski, "The Kosovo Crisis and U.S. Policy," testimony before the House Albanian Issues Caucus and the Human Rights Caucus, 6 November 1997.

97. *RFE/RL Newsline,* 1, no. 153, part II, 5 November 1997, and Belgrade BETA in Serbo-Croatian, 1525 GMT, 4 November 1997, translated in FBIS-EEU 97-308, 6 November 1997.

98. Patrick Moore, "The Balkan Arc of Instability," *RFE/RL Newsline,* 1, no. 154, part II, 6 November 1997. See also "Kosovo On the Brink," *Economist,* 1-7 November 1997, p. 51.

99. Besnik Mustafaj, "Did the Crete Sun Melt Away the Serb-Albanian Ice at All?" *Albania,* 13 November 1997, p. 4.

100. *Kosova Daily Report in English,* no. 1,271, 6 November 1997, in FBIS-EEU 97-310, 7 November 1997; Blerim Shala, "Nano's Attitude and Kosova's Woes," *Zëri,* 15 November 1997, p. 25; and Fehmi Agani, "European Attitudes and Legitimate Demands," *Zëri,* 15 November 1997, pp. 6-7.

101. See Nano's platform of the new government, submitted to parliament on 28 July, in *Zëri i Popullit,* 29 July 1997, pp. 3-9.

102. "Let Us Look to the Future, Not at the Cash Desks of Pyramid Schemes," *Zëri i Popullit,* 3 October 1997, p. 3.

103. European Commission and World Bank, *Albania Donors Conference, Chairmen's Conclusions,* Brussels, 22 October 1997, p. 3.

Conclusion

Albania has experienced serious difficulties and zigzags in its transition from a Communist party-state with a highly centralized economy to a multiparty system and a market economy. In the initial period of its five-year rule, the Democratic Party restored the nation's stability, instituted far-reaching political, economic, and social reforms which were remarkable for both their pace and their scope, and brought a degree of prosperity. However, the new elites had no tradition of democratic problem solving, and a limited understanding of their rights and responsibilities. In a country steeped in authoritarianism, they lacked a willingness to compromise, and relied on command rather than bargaining. The concept of accountability remained largely alien. In the end, the Democrats were unable to provide transparent and accountable governance.

The international community had been so eager to declare Albania a success that it was willing to overlook clear warning signs that the democratic experiment was going awry. But the flawed 1996 elections caused the United States and other Western countries to reassess their policies toward Albania. President Berisha's unwillingness to compromise cost him his international support, which in turn eroded his domestic support. That and the debacle surrounding the collapse of pyramid schemes provoked a backlash, with much of the public anger aimed personally at the president. Berisha, who had played a pivotal role in overseeing Albania's democratization, saw all the gains he had achieved unravel in a matter of weeks, as his country slid into almost total anarchy. By March 1997, he had lost the public relations battle at home and abroad. Berisha had come to be widely perceived as an authoritarian leader, while the Socialists, who had done everything possible to create problems and obstruct government progress, were seen as innocent victims. There was no question that the Socialist Party was behind the armed revolt, but the Socialists were absolved from responsibility and criticism was directed almost exclusively at the president.

For many Albanians, the Socialists and their political pedigree remain a reason for concern. A genetic mutation of the Hoxha-Alia Party of Labor, the Socialist Party had played a destructive role during the Democratic Party's rule, and it regained power through a disguised coup. There are lingering doubts about whether the Socialist Party had indeed reformed. Fatos Nano represents perhaps one of the most remarkable political comebacks in Albanian history, but his democratic credentials and leadership abilities are questionable. A protégé of Nexhmije Hoxha, the late dictator's widow, under whom he worked in the Institute of Marxist-Leninist Studies, Nano had steadfastly opposed political pluralism and the establishment of a market economy, until the very end of one-party Communist rule. When Berisha and other democratic-minded intellectuals created the first opposition political parties at the end of 1990 and the beginning of 1991, Nano was elevated to the top of the rapidly crumbling Communist regime. His short stint as prime minister in 1991 was not terribly impressive. As chairman, he has led the Socialist Party with an iron hand, surrounding himself with hard-liners, leaving little room for free debate, and sidetracking reformers. It was only in August 1996 that Nano agreed to remove the name of Karl Marx from the Party's program. Although in his public pronouncements he has been careful not to even mention Hoxha, Alia, and other former Communist leaders, Nano, as well as his closest associates, exhibit basically a dictatorial way of thinking.

Nano's mandate is deeply flawed, since the results of the balloting are most likely not a true indication of Socialist Party support. The elections were more a defeat for Berisha than a victory for the Socialists. Although election results were accepted by the Democrats, the balloting did not automatically restore the system's legitimacy. Indeed, with all their obvious limitations, the June 1997 elections can only be seen as a starting point for the restoration of law and order and for the creation of conditions for a more genuine election in a year or two.

While at this writing it is too early to predict how the political system will adjust to the radical changes in power, the Democrats' humiliating defeat fore-shadowed a profound shake-up in the national political scene. With rhetoric oscillating between fiery bluster and declarations of willingness to compromise, there were indications that the Socialists and the Democrats were failing to assume joint responsibility for resolving their country's problems. In the euphoric days before the elections, both sides had pledged to work for national reconciliation. But soon after the Socialists' victory, the ideal seemed a distant dream, as the governing coalition and the new opposition undermined the process by failing to find common ground and advance the process of reconciliation.

Since their return to power, the Socialists and their allies have used their two-thirds majority in parliament to amend the constitutional law and to ram major legislation through with little or no debate. With only a token of opposition, there has been little opportunity to engage in parliamentary opposition as a means of holding Nano's government accountable and transparent. Indeed, the parliament has come to serve essentially as a rubber stamp to approve decisions already made by the Socialist leadership. With his heavy-handed treatment of Democratic deputies and his partisan attitude, the Speaker of parliament Skendër Gjinushi, was largely responsible for the climate of confrontation and the lack of debate that characterized parliamentary sessions. In October 1997, the parliament set up a commission to probe the events of the early months of that year. However, the commission was not based on the quest for truth or legitimate justice but on politics. The governing coalition seemed intent on indicting and perhaps dealing a deathblow to the Democratic Party rather than finding the truth.

Postelection politics rapidly devolved into a deadly, winner-take-all struggle for the spoils.[1] Despite many virtuous promises that there would be no revanchism, Nano lost no time in purging the public administration and packing it with Socialist Party militants. Paskal Milo, Neritan Ceka, and Sabit Brokaj launched sweeping purges aimed at cleansing their ministries of allegedly incompetent Democratic appointees. Almost all the ambassadors were replaced, including the Ambassador to the United States, Lublin Dilja. In September 1997, some twenty generals, including Chief of Staff, Adem Çopani, Deputy Chief of Staff, General Armand Vinçani, and commanders of the marine and antiaircraft forces, were dismissed. Former Communist security and military officers, who had been dismissed after 1992, were appointed to leading positions. Many of those who were purged to make way for them had been trained in the United States and Western Europe and were unequivocally pro-Western. Other ministries also were subjected to sweeping purges.

The selection of former Constitutional Court justice Thimio Kondi as minister of justice had raised hopes for the depoliticization of the judiciary. But only weeks after the new government assumed power, it became clear that the judiciary would remain under strong political pressure. Kondi ordered that all court proceedings immediately be suspended and judges take their annual holiday. However, Chief Justice of the Court of Cassation Avni Shehu and Chairman of the Tiranë District Court Qazim Gjonaj defiantly rejected Kondi's order as a flagrant violation of the judiciary's independence. They insisted that judges and assistant judges were not part of the administrative staff and therefore not under the minister's subordination.[2] In August, the parliament amended the procedure for electing members to the much-criticized High Council of Justice and moved to increase their number from nine to thirteen. The new law, which allowed the executive and legislative branches to appoint most of the members of the High Council of Justice, was sharply criticized as endangering the independence of the judiciary. The council ordered the dismissal of dozens of judges, including the Chairman of the Appeals Court, Prel Martini, who had sentenced Nano, and Gjonaj, who had publicly criticized Kondi's measures.[3] None were given a chance to appeal the decision of the High Council of Justice. The court system was packed with Socialist Party militants and recruits from the old guard. In November, the parliament approved a constitutional amendment paving the way for the replacement of members of the Constitutional Court on a rotational basis. The move came after the tribunal ruled that a recently approved law regulating pyramid schemes was unconstitutional since it violated the right to private ownership of businesses. The parliament also amended the constitutional law to permit the authorities to audit and administer private companies that in the opinion of the government endanger the country's economic interests.[4]

Meanwhile, at the request of the newly named prosecutors, Albanian courts dismissed charges of genocide and crimes against humanity against more than thirty Communist-era top officials, including former President Ramiz Alia and former Ministers of Internal Affairs Hekuran Isai and Simon Stefani. The prosecutors had argued that the former officials could not be sentenced for crimes against humanity, since Albanian laws of the time did not refer to such crimes.

In a clear violation of the principle of university autonomy, all university rectors were replaced, as was the top leadership of the Academy of Sciences. Enver Hoxha's nephew, Luan Omari, who was one of the drafters of Albania's 1976 constitution, was named a member of the new team tasked with reorganizing the Academy of Sciences.

Nano's government also moved swiftly to assert control over the state-controlled media. In a highly questionable and hasty move, parliament approved a measure increasing the membership of the managing board of Albanian Radio and Television from eleven to twenty-one. The entire top management was fired and replaced by trusted people. Although according to the law only parliament can dismiss the General Director of the Albanian Radio and Television, the board fired Bardhyl Pollo and replaced him with Albert Minga, a television producer. *Koha Jonë* reporter Martin Leka was appointed director of Radio Tiranë. Eduard Mazi became director of television. Frrok Çupi, a *Koha Jonë* political commentator best known for his ceaseless vendetta against Berisha and his articles inciting rebellion in the south, was appointed director of the Albanian Telegraphic Agency.

Although it was natural for the incoming administration to replace top executives of central administration, the widespread purges of the government bureaucracy and the state-controlled media were obviously politically motivated. Less than four months after assuming power, the Socialists had thoroughly cleansed the public administration of Democratic supporters. Most of the new appointees in senior posts were sons and daughters of the old Communist *nomenklatura*, and many had close family or personal ties with the powerful clan of Hysni Kapo, Hoxha's closest associate. In addition, the Socialists restricted the authority of the predominantly Democratic Party-controlled local governments. More than 400 local officials were summarily dismissed and replaced with Socialist supporters. Such retribution could not but undermine national reconciliation.

Meanwhile, the Democrats, shattered by their loss of power, had problems finding their place in the new Albania, and refused to play the role of a constructive opposition. After boycotting the first sessions of parliament to protest election irregularities, the Democrats, led by Berisha, entered the parliament on 13 August. However, following the shooting in parliament of Democratic Party Deputy Azem Hajdari by a Socialist legislator, the Democrats again boycotted the parliament and staged demonstrations calling for the government's resignation and early elections. The Democratic Party's positions on many issues, including the drafting and approval of a new constitution, closely paralleled those of the Socialist Party in 1996, when the Socialists claimed that the parliament was illegitimate and insisted on roundtable discussions on the adoption of the country's new basic law. But only by playing a constructive role and participating in the parliament could the Democrats hope to provide a check on the power of a possibly abusive and authoritarian Nano government.

The Socialists, who continued to view Berisha as the chief obstacle to their plans, demonstrated a great aptitude for political mischief. In an attempt to sow confusion and mutual suspicion among the Democrats, the Socialists launched a coordinated campaign to weaken Berisha and openly promoted others, including former party leader Eduard Selami, for the top post in the largest opposition party.[6] In addition to cajoling Berisha's opponents, the Socialists resorted to all sorts of means to put pressure on the former president to resign as party leader and retire from politics. Ostensibly acting at the request of a former Democratic Party deputy and a Berisha opponent, Minister of Justice Kondi asked the Commission on the Scrutiny of Figures to verify whether the former president had collaborated with the Sigurimi.[7] Commission chairman Nafiz Bezhani, a respected lawyer and former justice of the Court of Cassation, rejected Kondi's request.[8] Senior government officials went so far as to threaten to press legal charges against the former president. But despite this campaign, Berisha was reelected as chairman at the party's convention in late October. Genc Pollo, who since 1992 had served as chief adviser to Berisha, became deputy chairman, while Ridvan Bode, the former finance minister, was elected secretary-general of the party.[9] Nevertheless, Berisha's position remained precarious. He needed a strategy to rehabilitate himself personally and politically; to rebuild relations with former allies; to mend fences with foreign governments, particularly the United States; and to base his dealings with his Socialist rivals on cooperation rather than confrontation.

Many questions remain about how Albania will be run under Socialist Party rule and whether the post-Berisha leadership can meet the challenges confronting the country. If Nano permits himself to be driven by revenge, attempts to settle the score with Berisha, and marginalizes the Democratic Party, this will have fatal consequences for the country. To succeed, the Socialists need to build a consensus with the Democrats. How the Socialists use their new power and how they handle the opposition will become a yardstick of Albania's credibility as a democratizing state—as will the Democrats' ability to play the role of a constructive opposition.

During 1992-1997, Albanians were unable to achieve the substantive features of democracy due to the failure of the country's major political actors to respect democratic norms and procedures, the absence of a strong party system, and serious economic constraints. The tumultuous events of 1997 reflected that there was no deep-rooted attachment to democracy or democratic values among the elites and the populace at large. Albanians in general did not appear to understand that preserving the legitimacy of the state, even if there was a desire to vote out the current government, is an essential component of democracy. Yet, despite the severity of the crisis, Albania survived the political and economic convulsion and returned to the task of completing the difficult political transition that began with the victory of the Democratic Party in 1992.

With a peaceful alternation in political leadership through elections—the linchpin of any democratic system—Albania passed a significant test. Although it has met most of the institutional, formal prerequisites for democracy, Albania still remains a partially developed democracy, or a protodemocracy. It would be presumptuous to assert that the Albanians will be able to consolidate a working democracy in the near future. Rather, the 1997 elections should be seen as a first step toward Larry Diamond's minimalist definition of electoral democracy.[10] A new government has been elected. But since this was largely a vote against perceived failings of Berisha's government, it remains to be seen if the Socialist policies will be acceptable and, indeed, whether or not laws can be made and enforced.

The most important, immediate task is the need to extend the government's authority throughout the country. As Juan J. Linz and Alfred Stepan have emphasized: "Free and authoritative elections cannot be held, winners cannot exercise the monopoly of legitimate force, and citizens cannot effectively have their rights protected by a rule of law unless a state exists. ... No state, no democracy."[11] At the time of this writing, Albania lacks properly functioning military, police, and judicial systems, and the allegiance of the population to the state remains questionable. Should Albania again revert to a state of anarchy and be unable to execute its sovereign responsibility in the enforcement of its own laws, then its future as an independent state will be seriously in doubt. Indeed, Albania could slip into the category of failed states. A clash between Italian, Greek, Yugoslav, and other regional interests could increase the danger of a second partitioning of the country. Thus, the establishment of a minimally competent state, and maintenance of public law and order are of supreme importance.

There seems to be consensus between the major players on what kind of Albania should be created: a country at peace with itself and its neighbors, a freely elected government focused on meeting the population's basic needs, a free market economy based on fiscal discipline and reduced corruption, and enhanced respect for human rights. But achieving these objectives will require a long, difficult period and a high level of cooperation within the Albanian body politic. In the past, the country's main political actors have engaged in seemingly endless squabbling and refused to cooperate to halt the country's downward spiral. Failure to reach an agreement on the rules of the political game and then to abide by them could again unleash deep enmity and violence, derailing any hope for Albanian democracy and spreading instability deeper into the troubled Balkan region.

If Albania is to regain its stability, it needs to give people a way to vent their feelings by legitimate means: through political institutions, responsive political parties, a fair electoral process, a free media, and a vibrant civil society. Albanians must correct the institutional deficiencies of the post-1992 political system and decide on which institutional arrangements are best suited to promote the consolidation of democracy in their country. Clearly, Albanians need to develop the concept of executive accountability to the legislature. This will involve strengthening parliament, making it an arena for national decisionmaking and conflict resolution. The new constitution must clearly delineate the powers of the executive and the legislature, ensure independence of the judiciary, and provide security from arbitrary power and adequate safeguards for civil liberties.

Political parties, currently underdeveloped and fragmented, need strengthening, if they are to participate meaningfully in the political process. Parties so far remain largely vehicles of individual leaders. Almost without exception, dissidents have failed in their attempts to challenge their established party leaderships, having been marginalized or forced to form separate parties. Although political participation has been concentrated almost exclusively within parties, citizen identification with parties remains relatively weak, as these groups have failed to develop clear policy positions and defend them against shifting political allegiances among the leadership. While there are no reliable polls about public attitudes toward parties, the available evidence suggests that many Albanians are skeptical of the parties and their activities. They are turned off by internecine warfare and by what they perceive as unnecessary partisan conflicts. But despite their low level of political institutionalization, political parties remain the most important political actors. However, several rounds of elections will probably be necessary before a stable system of relatively disciplined, responsible parties can emerge.

Whether Albania can return to consolidate its fragile democracy depends to a large degree on whether the rule of law becomes a permanent feature of the country's political landscape. Both among the public and among officials, there does not seem to be a good understanding of what the rule of law means. In a country where historically there have been very few national institutions actively promoting human rights and little public awareness of rights, there is a need to educate government officials in law and freedoms practiced by developed democracies, and about institutions and methods used to protect human rights. If Albania is to become a working democracy, it must develop a culture of rights and duties, in which law and order are realities of daily life and not matters left to police officials and judges. It must inculcate civic values that will make democratic ideals part of the Albanian moral fiber. While Albania has many good laws on the books, they are seldom fully implemented. What Albanians seem to urgently need is a comprehensive training program for law-enforcement officials, to help build a credible justice system, which would ensure the promotion of the rule of law and international human rights standards. There is also a need to raise the level of awareness of the Albanian public about their rights under the law. Although the institutional features of a democratic government are largely in place, the development of a civic culture lags far behind. As A. E. Dick Howard has noted: "Ultimately, for rights to be respected there must be a mature civic spirit—an attitude in the minds of ordinary citizens. A nation of people who do not understand the basic precepts of free government are unlikely to keep it alive and vibrant."[12] New attitudes and values are precisely what Albanians need to develop.

The key to a democratic future for Albania is the empowerment of its emerging civil society and the establishment of a domestic institutional capability among individuals and associations committed to democratic development. While there are numerous nongovernmental organizations, Albania needs to strengthen its indigenous civic associations and organizations. An improved enabling environment for nongovernmental organizations would foster a vibrant and engaged civil society that would be in a good position to demand accountability and responsiveness from the government and state institutions.

The development of democracy depends largely on an open, spirited debate. Therefore, free media are crucial to the process of democratic transformation and consolidation. In order to play the role of partner in the democratic process, the media must become independent and well funded, to provide news from a recognizably independent standpoint. The government must become more transparent and ensure full freedom of the press. It is vitally important for the consolidation of Albania's democracy that the media and the government share the responsibility of serving democracy. This requires that the press provide objective and balanced reporting, and the government permit free, diverse, and independent broadcasting and guarantee meaningful and equitable access to the state media for all political forces. The improvement of communication between the government and the press will in turn help the whole Albanian society grow politically, economically, socially, culturally, and spiritually.

There is wide agreement that the consolidation of democracy is closely associated with the establishment of democratic institutions, the functioning of a multiparty system, and genuinely competitive elections. But regardless of the results achieved in the political realm, it is difficult to envisage a functioning democracy in Albania without substantial economic recovery. Albania's implosion in early 1997 testifies to the fragility of emerging democracies and the importance of economic performance to their survival. Most Albanians still await economic empowerment. Government failure to bring about significant economic improvements, alleviate extreme poverty, and solve daily pressing problems with basic public services could lead to dangerous disenchantment and cynicism about the benefits of democracy. Democracy will be solidified and deepened only if basic economic problems are addressed. Arguably, Albania has good prospects for economic and social recovery. It has a relatively well-educated working force and ample hydroelectric and oil resources, and it is relatively rich in mineral resources. Its beautiful and pristine Adriatic coast offers excellent prospects for the tourist industry. With international assistance, Albania's recovery could be manageable, though arduous. But the key to economic recovery is perseverance in continuing with the reform program and restoration of political stability.

Rampant government corruption remains a major source of discontent. Little headway has been made in creating a civil service based on merit, and the political class is widely perceived as self-serving and corrupt. There are no recognized standards of ethical conduct for government employees, and corruption, nepotism, and the use of official position for private gain are widespread. Reports of cabinet officials, members of parliament, judges, and bureaucrats amassing large wealth and improperly using their positions to help family and friends cannot but undermine the willingness of ordinary Albanians to endure the pain of economic reform. Obviously, new structures of state oversight, increased wages for civil servants, and more open and accountable business procedures are needed to root out corruption in private contracts. Unless swift measures are taken to establish effective legal and political constraints, to seriously address the issue of corruption, and to establish and uphold standards of accountability, integrity, and honesty in civil service, graft and patronage could come to be considered normal business practices in Albania. Failure to root out corruption will have dire political, economic, and social implications. High-level corruption can lead to the squandering of the country's resources as well as to popular loss of confidence in its political leadership and institutions.

The emergence of a new generation of leaders who are better prepared to cope with the complex problems of democratic governance is essential for the successful democratization of Albania. Early opposition to Communist rule in Albania, unlike most other East European countries, was spearheaded by individuals who either were members of the Communist Party or had close links with the establishment. This was not surprising, given the Albanian Communist regime's brutal treatment of its opponents, decimation of the precommunist political elite, and lack of any independent organizations. The democratization process had contributed to a significant transformation of the country's political elite. Despite the high turnover, however, current elites share a significant resemblance to their Communist predecessors. Political party leaders, deputies, cabinet members, directors of central institutions, leaders of civil society groups and associations, and editors and reporters of major newspapers largely come from the intelligentsia—the broad stratum of intellectuals and technical experts that provided vital support to the old Communist system and moved up the social ladder thanks to the considerable privileges they enjoyed under communism. In the past, most had embraced the Communist Party's values unquestioningly, and they reinvented themselves as democrats by discarding the Communist ideology only after the old regime lost the capacity to maintain its hold on power. Few among the elites in charge of public policy or in a position to influence it can claim persecution or dissident status under the old regime. Communism bred a culture of intolerance and prevented the development of such political skills as coalition building, negotiation, and compromise. These traits can be seen as readily among those in the Socialist government as in the opposition. Thus, as long as current leaders continue to dominate, the Albanian polity will likely remain intensely politicized. Clearly, there is a need for new generations of elites, uncontaminated by Communist-style thinking, and hopefully, committed to a more reasoned style of politics. There is also a need to strengthen groups that encourage a heightened sense of civility and a more broad-based participation in the country's life.

As Albania stands poised at the threshold of the twenty-first century, it faces an array of daunting challenges. The process of full consolidation of democracy will probably require generations. While Albania's democratization will depend primarily on the choices that the Albanians make and the strategies they pursue, continued moral, political, and material support from outside also will remain crucial. Indeed, without sustained international assistance to promote tolerance, democracy, and the rule of law, and financial support to stabilize the economy, Albania might again plunge back into anarchy. The United States, which has been the most influential promoter of Albanian democracy, together with its allies, has the chance again to encourage Albania's democratic forces to take risks necessary for democratic consolidation and the establishment of a functioning market economy. Albania remains a country of critical geostrategic importance, due to its location and the possibility of violent ethnic conflict in Kosova and Macedonia. The international community has a stake in Albania's stability and prosperity. Continued turbulence in Albania is likely to fuel regional instability and generate chronic refugee flows, sending fresh waves of unwelcome immigrants to Italy and Greece. Conversely, a stable, democratic Albania will contribute to regional peace and stability.

Notes

1. The British Helsinki Human Rights Group, *Albania 1997: Politics and Purges* (Oxford), November 1997.

2. See comments by Avni Shehu and Qazim Gjonaj in *Rilindja Demokratike*, 1 August 1997, p. 3. See also interviews with Gjonaj in *Rilindja Demokratike*, 3 August 1997, p. 3, and *Albania*, 11 September 1997, p. 4.

3. *Rilindja Demokratike*, 4 October 1997, p. 4.

4. *RFE/RL Newsline* 1, no. 164, part II, 20 November 1997.

5. See Sh. Daka, "Selami or Berisha?" *Zëri i Popullit*, 30 August 1997, p. 4.

6. *Zëri i Popullit*, 16 October 1997, p. 6.

7. ATA in English, 1704 GMT, 16 October 1997 in FBIS-EEU 97-290, 20 October 1997.

8. *Rilindja Demokratike*, 28 October 1997, p. 1.

9. Larry Diamond, "Is the Third Wave Over?" *Journal of Democracy* 7, no. 4 (October 1996), p. 7.

10. Juan J. Linz and Alfred Stepan, "Toward Consolidated Democracies," *Journal of Democracy* 7, no. 2 (April 1996), p. 14.

11. A. E. Dick Howard, *Constitution Making in Eastern Europe* (Washington, D.C.: Woodrow Wilson Center Press, distributed by Johns Hopkins University Press), p. 19.

Selected Bibliography

American Bar Association. Central and East European Law Initiative (CEELI). *Analysis of the Code of Judicial Ethics for the Republic of Albania.* Washington, D.C., 1994.

Andrews, Mary Catherine, and Gulhan Ovalioglu. *Albania and the World Bank: Building the Future.* Washington, D.C.: The World Bank, 1994.

Angjeli, Anastas. "Problems of Albanian Democracy." *Mediterranean Quarterly* 6, no. 4 (Fall 1995), pp. 35-47.

Åslund, Anders, and Örjan Sjöberg. "Privatization and Transition to a Market Economy in Albania." *Communist Economies and Economic Transformation* 4, no. 1 (1992), pp. 135-150.

Athanassopoulou, Ekavi. "Hoping for the Best, Planning for the Worst: Conflict in Kosovo." *The World Today* 52, nos. 8-9 (August-September 1996), pp. 226-229.

Austin, Robert. "Albanian-Macedonian Relations: Confrontation or Cooperation?" *RFE/RL Research Report* 2, no. 42 (22 October 1993), pp. 21-25.

————. "What Albania Adds to the Balkan Stew." *Orbis* 37, no. 2 (Spring 1993), pp. 259-279.

Austin, Robert, Kjell Engelbrekt and Duncan M. Perry. "Albania's Greek Minority." *RFE/RL Research Report* 3, no. 11 (18 March 1994), pp. 19-24.

Beshiri, Ismije. "Kosovar Independence Lacks International Backing." *Transition* 2, no. 6 (22 March 1996), pp. 52-54.

Biberaj, Elez. *Albania and China: A Study of an Unequal Alliance.* Boulder: Westview, 1986.

————. *Albania: A Socialist Maverick.* Boulder: Westview, 1990.

————. "Kosova: The Balkan Powder Keg."*Conflict Studies*, no. 258, February 1993, 26 pp.

Bërxholli, Arqile, Sejfi Protopapa and Kristaq Prifti. "The Greek Minority in the Albanian Republic: A Demographic Study." *Nationalities Papers* 22, no. 2, 1994, pp. 427-34.

Beshiri, Ismije. "Kosovar Independence Lacks International Backing." *Transition* 2, no. 6 (22 March 1996), pp. 52-54.

Blejer, Mario I., Mauro Mecagni, Ratna Sahay, Richard Hides, Barry Johnston, Piroska Nagy and Pepper, Roy. *Albania: From Isolation Toward Reform.* Washington, D.C.: International Monetary Fund, 1992.

Brandt, Hartmut. *Albania's Development Problems Between Land Reform and Large-Scale Privatization.* Berlin: German Development Institute, 1994.

Brewer, Bob, ed. *My Albania: Ground Zero.* New York: Lion of Tepelena Press, Inc., 1992.

Brown, J. F. *Hopes and Shadows: Eastern Europe After Communism.* Durham, NC: Duke University Press, 1994.

Buck, Thomas. "Fear and Loathing in Macedonia: Ethnic Nationalism and the Albanian Problem." *International Affairs Review* 5, no. 1, (Winter 1996), pp. 1-23.

Carnegie Endowment for International Peace. *Unfinished Peace: Report of the International Commission on the Balkans.* Washington, D.C., 1996.

Central Electoral Commission. *Buletin: Rezultatet e Zgjedhjeve Parlamentare, Qershor 1997* [Bulletin: The Results of the June 1997 Parliamentary Elections]. Tiranë, 1997.

Cohen, Robert. "Economic Transformation in Albania." Pp. 579-598 in U.S. Congress, Joint Economic Committee, *East-Central European Economies in Transition.* Washington, D.C.: U.S. Government Printing Office, 1994.

Çopani, Adem. "The New Dimensions of Albania's Security Posture." *NATO Review*, no. 2, March 1996, pp. 24-28.

Çopani, Adem, and Danopoulos, Constantine P. "The Role of the Military in the Democratization of Marxist-Leninist Regimes: Albania as a Case Study." *Mediterranean Quarterly* 6, no. 2, Spring 1995, pp. 117-134.

Costa, Nicholas J. *Albania: A European Enigma.* Boulder and New York: East European Monographs, distributed by Columbia University Press, 1995.

Council on Foreign Relations, Center for Preventive Action. *Toward Comprehensive Peace in Southeast Europe: Conflict Prevention in the South Balkans.* New York: The Twentieth Century Fund Press, 1996.

Cviic, Christopher. *Remaking the Balkans.* New York: Council on Foreign Relations Press for the Royal Institute of International Affairs, 1991.

Danopoulos, Constantine P., and Adem Chopani [Çopani]. "Departyizing and Democratizing Civil-Military Relations in Albania." In John P. Lowell, and David E. Albright, eds. *To Sheath the Sword: Civil-Military Relations in the Quest for Democracy.* Westport, CT: Greenwood Press, 1997.

Elsie, Robert. "The Albanian Media in Kosovo and the Spectre of Ethnic Cleansing." *Südost-Europa* 44, nos. 9-10 (1995), pp. 614-619.

———. *History of Albanian Literature.* 2 vols. Boulder: East European Monographs, distributed by Columbia University Press, 1995.

Emadi, Hafizullah. "Development Strategies and Women in Albania." *East European Quarterly* 27, no. 1 (March 1993), pp. 79-96.

Fischer, Bernd Jürgen. *King Zog and the Struggle for Stability in Albania.* Boulder: East European Monographs, distributed by Columbia University Press, 1984.

———. "Albanian Nationalism in the Twentieth Century." Pp. 21-54 in Peter F. Sugar, ed., *Eastern European Nationalism in the Twentieth Century.* Washington, D.C.: American University Press, 1995.

Gage, Nicholas. "The Forgotten Minority in the Balkans: The Greeks of Northern Epirus." *Mediterranean Quarterly* 4, no. 3 (Summer 1993), pp. 10-29

Gashi, Alush, ed. *The Denial of Human and National Rights of Albanians in Kosova.* New York: Illyria Publishing Co., 1991.

Gessen, Masha. "The Parallel University: A Journey Through Kosovo's Secret Classrooms." *Lingua Franca* 5, no. 1 (November-December 1994), pp. 30-40.

Hall, Derek. *Albania and the Albanians.* London: Pinter Reference, 1994.

Harxhi, Edith. *An Invitation to Albania: An Overview of Albania's Resources and Economy.* Tiranë: Besa, 1995.

Hicks, Peggy L. "Albanian Legal Reform Faces Continuing Challenges." *Mediterranean Quarterly* 6, no. 2 (Spring 1995), pp. 75-91.

Hudhri, Ferid. *Albania and Albanians in World Art.* Athens: Christos Giovanis A.E.B.E., 1990.

Human Rights Watch/Helsinki. *Human Rights in Post-Communist Albania.* New York, 1996.

————. *Open Wounds: Human Rights Abuses in Kosovo.* New York, 1993.

Hutchings, Raymond. *Historical Dictionary of Albania.* Lanham, MD, and London: Scarecrow Press, 1996.

Imholz, Kathleen. "Can Albania Break the Chain? The 1993-94 Trials of Former High Communist Officials." *East European Constitutional Review* 4, no. 3 (Summer 1995), 54-60.

International Helsinki Federation for Human Rights. *From Autonomy to Colonization: Human Rights in Kosovo, 1989-1993.* Vienna, 1993.

International Republican Institute. *IRI Observation Report on the Albanian Parliamentary Elections of May 26, 1996.* Washington, D.C., August 1996.

Jacques, Edwin E. *The Albanians: An Ethnic History from Prehistoric Times to the Present.* London: McFarland & Company, 1995.

Logoreci, Anton. *The Albanians: Europe's Forgotten Survivors.* London: Victor Gollancz, 1977.

Lombardi, Ben. "Kosovo: Introduction to Yet Another Balkan Problem." *European Security* 5, no. 2 (Summer 1996), pp. 256-278.

Marmullaku, Ramadan. *Albania and the Albanians.* Hamden, CT: Archon Books, 1975.

Marović, Miodrag. *Balkanski Džoker: Albanija i Albanci* [The Balkan Wild Card: Albania and the Albanians]. Bar, Montenegro: Kulturni Centar, 1995.

Mead, Alice. *Journey to Kosova.* Cumberland, ME: Loose Cannon Press, 1995.

Mertus, Julie. "A Wall of Silence Divides Serbian and Albanian Opinion on Kosovo." *Transition* 2, no. 6 (22 March 1996), pp. 48-51.

Mickey, Robert W., and Adam Smith Albion. "Success in the Balkans? A Case Study of Ethnic Relations in the Republic of Macedonia." Pp. 53-98 in Ian M. Cuthbertson, and Jane Leibowitz, eds. *Minorities: The New Europe's Old Issue.* New York: Institute for EastWest Studies, 1993.

Mihaljov, Mihajlo. "Kosovo: A New Situation." *Uncaptive Minds* 9, nos. 1-2 (Winter 1996-Spring 1997), pp. 95-98.

Milivojevic, Marko. "Wounded Eagle: Albania's Fight for Survival." *European Security Study,* no. 15. 48 pp. London: Institute for European Defense and Strategic Studies, 1992.

Minnesota Advocates for Human Rights. *Press Restrictions in Albania.* Minneapolis, MN, December 1995.

————. *Trimming the Cat's Claws: The Politics of Impunity in Albania.* Minneapolis, MN, March 1992.

Minnesota Lawyers International Human Rights Committee. *Human Rights in the People's Socialist Republic of Albania.* Minneapolis, 1990.

National Agency for Privatization. *Country Privatization Report.* Tiranë, 1995.

National Democratic Institute for International Affairs. *Albania: 1991 Elections to the People's Assembly.* Washington, D.C., 1991.

————. *Albanian Local Elections, October 20-27, 1996, Final Report.* Washington, D.C., 1996.

————. *Civic Education and Parliamentary Dialogue in Albania, 1991-1994.* Washington, D.C., 1995.

National Republican Institute for International Affairs. *The 1991 Elections in Albania.* Washington, D.C., 1991.

Neza, Agim, and Miranda Hanka. *Travellers' Guide to Albania.* Aylesbury, Eng.: ACO UK, 1993.

Norris, H. T. *Islam in the Balkans.* Columbia: University of South Carolina Press, 1993.

O'Donnell, James. "Albania's *Sigurimi*: The Ultimate Agents of Social Control." *Problems of Post-Communism* 42, no. 6, November-December 1995, pp. 18-22.

Organization for Security and Cooperation in Europe, Office for Democratic Institutions and Human Rights. *Observation of the Parliamentary Elections Held in the Republic of Albania, May, 26 and June 2, 1996.* Warsaw, 12 June 1996.

Pano, Nicholas C. "Albania." Pp. 17-64 in Joseph Held, ed., *The Columbia History of Eastern Europe in the Twentieth Century.* New York: Columbia University Press, 1992.

————. *The People's Republic of Albania.* Baltimore: Johns Hopkins University Press, 1998.

————. "The Process of Democratization in Albania."Pp. 285-353 in Karen Dawisha and Bruce Parrott, eds., *Politics, Power, and the Struggle for Democracy in South-East Europe.* Cambridge: Cambridge University Press, 1997.

Pettifer, James. *Blue Guide: Albania.* 2nd ed. New York: W. W. Norton, 1996.

Pipa, Arshi. *Albanian Stalinism: Ideo—Political Aspects.* Boulder: East European Monographs, distributed by Columbia University Press, 1990.

————. *The Politics of Language in Socialist Albania.* Boulder: East European Monographs, distributed by Columbia University Press, 1989.

Prifti, Peter R. *Socialist Albania Since 1944: Domestic and Foreign Developments.* Cambridge, MA.: MIT Press, 1978.

Puebla Institute. *Albania: Religion in a Fortress State.* Washington, D.C., 1989.

Pula, Gazmend. "Modalities of Self-Determination: The Case of Kosova as a Structural Issue for Lasting Stability in the Balkans." *Südosteuropa* 45, nos. 4-5 (1996), pp. 380-410.

Rama, Shinasi A. "Transition, Elite Fragmentation and the Parliamentary Elections of June 29, 1997 in Albania." *International Journal of Albanian Studies* 1, no. 1 (Fall 1997), pp. 82-125.

Ramet, Sabrina P. "The Albanians of Kosovo: The Potential for Destabilization." *The Brown Journal of World Affairs* 3, no. 1 (Winter-Spring 1996), pp. 353-372.

Rosenberg, Tina. "Albania: The Habits of the Heart." *World Policy Journal* 11, no. 4 (Winter 1994-1995), pp. 85-94.

Rugg, Dean S. "Communist Legacies in the Albanian Landscape." *Geographical Review* 84, no. 1 (January 1994), pp. 59-73.

————. "Albania as a Gateway." Pp. 135-148 in Derek Hall and Darrick Danta, eds., *Reconstructing the Balkans: A Geography of the New Southeast Europe.* New York: John Wiley & Sons, 1996.

Sandström, Per, and Sjöberg, Örjan. "Albanian Economic Performance: Stagnation in the 1980s." *Soviet Studies* 43, no. 5 (1991), pp. 931-947.

Schmidt, Fabian. "Albania: The Opposition's Changing Face." *Transition* 1, no. 11, 30 June 1995, pp. 44-48.

364

———. "Albania's Tradition of Pragmatism." *Transition* 2, no. 7 (5 April 1996), pp. 33-35, and 63.

———. "Bolstering an Image of Democracy." *Transition* 2, no. 24 (29 November 1996), pp. 43-45.

———. "An Old System Blends Into the Present." *Transition* 2, no. 18 (6 September 1996), pp. 50-53.

———. "Teaching the Wrong Lesson in Kosovo." *Transition* 2, no. 14 (12 July 1996), pp. 37-39.

Schnytzer, Adi. *Stalinist Economic Strategy in Practice: The Case of Albania.* New York: Oxford University Press, 1982.

Sjöberg, Örjan. *Rural Change and Development in Albania.* Boulder: Westview, 1991.

Sjöberg, Örjan, and Michael L. Wyzan. *Economic Change in the Balkan States: Albania, Bulgaria, Romania and Yugoslavia.* London: Pinter, 1991.

Sullivan, Marianne. "Albania Rides the Wave of Capitalism." *Transition* 2, no. 20 (4 October 1996), pp. 15-17.

———. "Albanians Still Struggle for Information." *Transition* 1, no. 18 (6 October 1995), pp. 39-41.

———. "Mending Relations With Greece." *Transition* 1, no. 15 (25 August 1995), pp. 11-16.

———. "Seeking the Security of Military Might." *Transition* 1, no. 15 (25 August 1995), pp. 8-10, and 72.

———. "Socialists on the Campaign Trail." *Transition* 2, no. 11 (31 May 1996), pp. 38-39, and 64.

Sunley, Jonathan. "Small War in Albania." *Salisbury Review,* Autumn 1997, pp. 33-39

Tarifa, Fatos. "Disappearing from Politics: Social Change and Women in Albania." Pp. 133-151 in Marilyn Rueschemeyer, ed., *Women in the Politics of Postcommunist Eastern Europe.* New York: M. E. Sharpe, 1994.

Transnational Foundation for Peace and Future Research. *Conflict Mitigation for Kosovo.* Lund, Sweden, 1996.

———. *Preventing War in Kosovo.* Lund, Sweden, 1992.

Trix, Frances. "Bektashi Tekke and the Sunni Mosque of Albanian Muslims in Albania." Pp. 359-380 in Yvonne Yazbeck Haddad and Jane Idleman Smith, eds. *Muslim Communities in North America.* Albany: State University of New York Press, 1994.

———. "The Resurfacing of Islam in Albania." *East European Quarterly* 28, no. 4 (January 1995), pp. 533-549.

United Nations Development Program. *Albanian Human Development Report, 1996.* Tiranë, 1996.

———. *Human Development Report: Albania, 1995.* Tiranë, 1995.

U.S. Commission on Security and Cooperation in Europe. *Albania's Parliamentary Elections of 1997.* Washington, D.C., July 1997.

———. "Challenges to Democracy in Albania." *Hearing Before the Commission on Security and Cooperation in Europe.* 104th Congress, Second Session, 14 March 1996.

———. "Democratic Developments in Albania." *Hearing Before the Commission on Security and Cooperation in Europe.* Washington, D.C., 102th Congress, First Session, 22 May 1991.

———. *Human Rights and Democratization in Albania.* Washington, D.C., January 1994.

Veremis, Thanos. "Kosovo: The Powder Keg on Hold." *Balkan Forum* 4, no. 2 (June 1996), pp. 27-44.

Vickers, Miranda. *The Albanians: A Modern History.* London: I. B. Tauris, 1995.

————. "The Status of Kosovo in Socialist Yugoslavia." *Bradford Studies on South Eastern Europe* no. 1 (1994), 64 pp.

Vickers, Miranda and James Pettifer. *Albania: From Anarchy to a Balkan Identity.* New York: New York University Press, 1997.

Ward, Philip. *Albania: A Travel Guide.* Cambridge: Oleander Press, 1983.

Winnifrith, Tom, ed. *Perspectives on Albania.* New York: St. Martin's Press, 1992.

The World Bank and the European Community. *An Agricultural Strategy for Albania.* Washington, D.C.: World Bank, 1992.

Xhudo, Gazmen. *Diplomacy and Crisis Management in the Balkans: A U.S. Foreign Policy Perspective.* New York: St. Martin's Press, 1996.

————. "Men of Purpose: The Growth of Albanian Criminal Activity." *Transnational Organized Crime* 2, no. 1 (Spring 1996), pp. 1-20.

Zanga, Louis. "Albania: Can the Democrats Win?" *Transition,* 1, no. 12 (14 July 1995), pp. 41-43.

————. "Albania: Corruption Takes Its Toll on the Berisha Government." *Transition* 1, no. 7 (12 May 1995), pp. 12-14.

————. "Albania: Signs of Progress, but Much Still to Be Done." *RFE/RL Research Report* 3, no. 1 (7 January 1994), pp. 103-105.

————. "A Transitional Constitutional Law." *RFE/RL Report on Eastern Europe* 2, no. 22 (31 May 1991), pp. 1-4.

Zickel, Raymond, and Iwaskiw, Walter R. Eds. *Albania: A Country Study.* Washington, D.C.: Federal Research Division, Library of Congress, 1994.

Index